MAP
of the
LANDMARKS
in
ANCIENT DOVER
H. E. HAYES

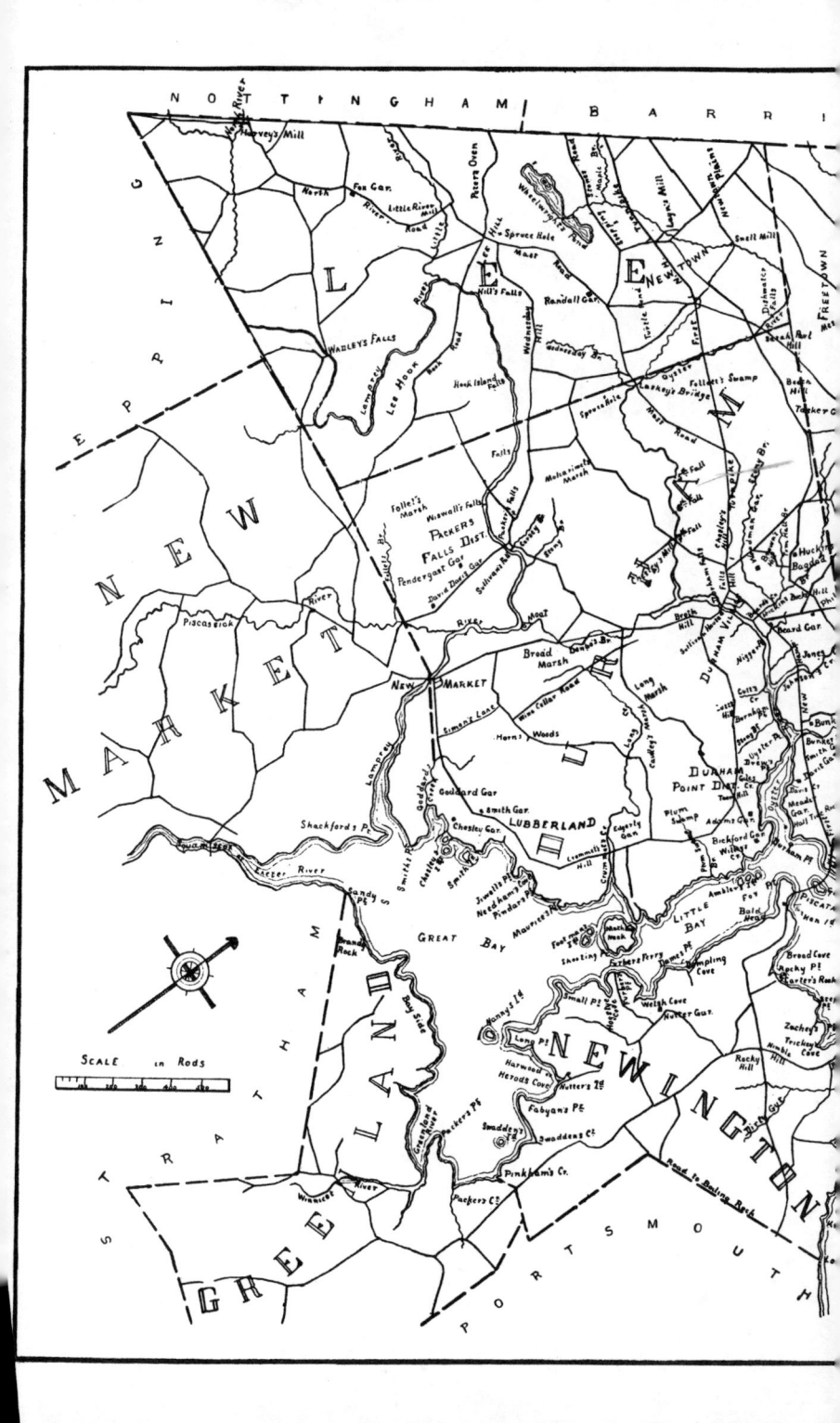

NOTTINGHAM
BARRINGTON
EPPING
NEW MARKET
LEE
DURHAM
NEWINGTON
GREENLAND
STRATHAM
PORTSMOUTH
Harvey's Mill
Fox Gar.
North River
Little River Mill
Little River Road
Peters Oven
Wheelwright's Pond
Spruce Hole
Mast Road
Hill's Falls
Randall Gar.
NEW TOWN
Snell Mill
Wadley's Falls
Lamprey River
Lee Hook
Hook Road
Hook Island Falls
Wednesday Hill
Wednesday Br.
Spruce Hole
Oyster River
Laskey's Bridge
Follet's Swamp
Follet's Marsh
Wiswall's Falls
PACKERS FALLS DIST.
Pendergast Gar.
David Davis Gar.
Sullivan's Falls
Stony Br.
Piscassick River
Moat
Broad Marsh
Durham Village
Beard Gar.
NEW MARKET
Simon's Lane
Wine Cellar Road
Horns Woods
Long Marsh
DURHAM POINT DIST.
Goddard Gar.
Smith Gar.
Chesley Gar.
LUBBERLAND
Edgerly Gar.
Plum Swamp
Adams Gar.
Bickford Gar.
Shackford's Pt.
Squamscott or Exeter River
Sandy Pt.
Smith's Pt.
Jewell's Pt.
Needham's Cove
Pindar's Pt.
Maurice's Pt.
Crummett's Hill
LITTLE BAY
Ambler's Id.
Fox Pt.
Bald Head
GREAT BAY
Brandy Rock
Footman's Id.
Mathes Neck
Shooting Pt.
Furbers Ferry
Dames Pt.
Dumpling Cove
Broad Cove
Rocky Pt.
Carter's Rock
Small Pt.
Welsh Cove
Nutter Gar.
Hanny's Id.
Long Pt.
Bay Side
Harwood or Herods Cove
Nutter's Id.
Fabyan's Pt.
Zachey's Pt.
Trickey's Cove
Nimble Hill
Rocky Hill
Swadden's Id.
Swaddens Cr.
Packers Pt.
Greenland River
Pinkham's Cr.
Packers Cr.
Winnicot River
Road to Boiling Rock
SCALE in Rods

LANDMARKS

IN

ANCIENT DOVER,

NEW HAMPSHIRE.

BY

MARY P. THOMPSON.

COMPLETE EDITION.

Copyright 1991

Heritage Books, Inc.

Copyright 1892 by Mary P. Thompson

Facsimile Reprint
Published 1991 By
Heritage Books, Inc.
1540-E Pointer Ridge Place
Bowie, Maryland 20716
(301) 390-7709

ISBN 1-55613-499-1

A Complete Catalog Listing Hundreds of Titles on
History, Genealogy, & Americana
Free on Request

PREFACE.

The township of Dover, New Hampshire, originally comprised not only the present city of that name, but the townships of Durham, Lee, Madbury, Rollinsford and Somersworth, the greater part of Newington, a portion of Newmarket, and nearly, if not quite, the whole shore of Greenland along the south side of the Great Bay.

A complete list of the old localities and landmarks of this extensive region has necessarily required a great amount of research. The list given in the present work is based on the early town records, especially those of Dover proper; on the county records at Exeter prior to 1773; on the New Hampshire Provincial and State Papers; and on local and family traditions. All the grants and conveyances of land referred to in this work have been personally examined by the writer, unless otherwise intimated. The orthography and phraseology of these records have been retained as far as possible, even when no direct quotations have been made.

The present edition of the "Landmarks in Ancient Dover" entirely supersedes the first one. The numerous errors in that edition have, as far as discovered, been carefully corrected in this, and several hundred new localities have been added.

Among the most important corrections are those relating to *Herod's Cove*, *Pinkham's* and *Swadden's Creeks*, and the ancient bounds of the Bloody Point settlement once known as *Kenney's Creek* and *Hogsty Cove*. Numerous places along the Greenland shore of the Great Bay are herein proved to have been a part of Ancient Dover. And whereas the first edition of this work was only supplementary to what others had written, the present edition is a complete register of all the noteworthy localities within the limits of Ancient Dover, not only of early times, but also those of more recent date, as well as many places in Barrington, Nottingham, and Rochester, mentioned in connection with the public highways or with the inhabitants of Dover.

A few of the places mentioned in this work have not been positively identified, in spite of much research; but the neighborhood has in all cases been indicated, and some points given which, it is hoped, will lead to their identification. The writer will feel greatly obliged for any information bearing thereon, and for the correction of any errors discovered in the work.

DURHAM, N. H., May 26, 1892.

LANDMARKS IN ANCIENT DOVER.

ABBOTT'S BROOK. This brook is in the north-eastern part of Somersworth, and connects Cole's pond with the Salmon Falls river. About midway in its course it is joined by a brook from Rochester. "Abbott's brook" is mentioned in the Atlas of Hitchcock's Geology of N. H. The name is derived from Moses Abbott, who formerly resided on the south side of this brook.

ABBOTT'S ISLANDS. Richard Dame, on his map of Newington in 1805, gives this name to some small islands at the mouth of Laighton's cove. No islands are there, however, except at extremely high tide, when High point, and perhaps one or two other projections, are sometimes severed from the mainland. The origin of the name does not appear.

ADAMS' POINT. This point of land, originally called *Mathews' Neck*, is on the Durham shore, at the Narrows, between Great and Little bays. The present name was derived from Elder John Adams, a descendant of the Rev. Joseph Adams of Newington, who was the uncle of John Adams, the second president of the United States. Elder Adams acquired this neck of land by a mortgage from Timothy Dame of Newington, May 1, 1830, which was never redeemed. The deed describes it as a farm of eighty acres, "commonly called *Mathews' Neck*," bounded north by the land of Joseph Kent's heirs, and on the other sides by Great and Little bays, and the coves and creeks that run into said bays." (See *Mathews' Neck*.)

ADDER'S SWAMP. This swamp is in Durham, at the upper side of Cutt's hill, opposite the Burnham house, on the south side of the road to Durham Point. It belongs to the heirs of the late Col. Joseph Burnham.

ALLEY POINT. This name is given on Whitehouse's map of 1834 to a point on the eastern shore of the Cochecho, above the Narrows. The name was derived from Samuel Alley, whose land here is mentioned Dec. 30, 1734, when Edward Ellis conveyed to John MacElroy 30 acres of land, "beginning at ye lower end of a brook called *Stony brook*, and running up to ye road y^t leads from Jabez Garland's, and so by ye road to ye parting fence between Samuel Alley's land and said lot, and from s^d Alley's land to Wm. Thompson's, thence as s^d Thompson's fence runs to Cochecho salt river, and along s^d river to ye lower end of ye s^d *Stony brook*." Samuel Alley and wife Elizabeth conveyed to Job Clement, March 28, 1758, fifty acres of land where they then dwelt, bounded N. by said Clement's land, E. by Amos Howard's, W. by Garland's and Paul

Harford's to Cochecho river, running down said river till it comes to Howard's land, near *Champion's rocks.*

AMBLER'S ISLANDS. These islands, three in number, are so called on Smith's map of Durham.[1] They lie off Durham Point, near the mouth of Oyster river. The largest, about an acre in extent, is now called *Mathes island*, from a recent owner. The next in size is *Sassafras island*, and the smallest is *Hen island*. They are all now owned by Mr. Jeremiah Langley. This group derived its name from Elder John Ambler, who once owned land on the neighboring shore, now belonging in part to Mr. Langley. He was chosen deacon of the Oyster River church, Oct. 19, 1718, and ordained " elder," Nov. 16, 1721.

ANTHONY'S BROOK. The name of this brook was derived from Anthony Emery, who, May 2, 1642, bought of Stephen Tedder six acres of land on the Newichawannock, confirmed to him by the town of Dover the 7th, 6 mo., 1648, together with an additional grant which extended to " *a brook* that lyeth on the southeast against the Newichwannick." This brook is referred to March 19, 1693–4, when three score acres of land were granted to John Hall, Jr., on Salmon Falls river, " on ye north side of y^e *brooke*, above *Antonies.*" Three score acres were also laid out to Robert Euans, Jr., Ap. 7, 1696, on the north side of *Antony's brook.* John Wingate, Nov. 5, 1702, conveyed to Paul Wentworth three score acres adjacent to Salmon Falls, beginning at a pitch-pine tree on the north side of *Antonies brook*, and thence running S. E. three score rods by the Salmon Falls river. Richard Rookes, schoolmaster, Aug. 9, 1731, conveyed to Thomas Wallingford, innholder, 60 acres of swamp and upland in the parish of " Summersworth," granted to John Hall, Jr., March 19, 1693–4, " beginning at a bass tree by ye upper pier, at ye upper Boom at ye river," thence running 60 rods south to *Antony's brook*, so called. This brook, which has lost its ancient name, and is now insignificant in size, passes through Sill swamp, comes to Salmon Falls village back of the railroad station, and empties into the Salmon Falls river.

ASH SWAMP. Mentioned March 19, 1693–4, when 20 acres of land " between *Tole End* and *Ash swamp*" were granted to John Haise. Israel Hodgdon's land at *Ash swamp*, originally granted to William Thompson, above *Nock's marsh*, is mentioned Feb. 22, 1720, as beginning at the river (Bellamy), leaving a highway four rods wide between Nock's old bound and Thompson's fifty acres. This swamp is called *Cochecho log swamp*, March 17, 1658–9, when William Thompson's fifty acre grant was laid out to him beyond it, with Thomas Nock's land on the southeast, and Bellamies Bank freshet on the south-west. Moses Wingate, Sept. 12, 1752, bought of Nathaniel Hanson twenty acres in " *Cochecho swamp* or *Ash Swamp*," which land Hanson had by inheritance.

Edward Evans' grant of 30 acres of swamp land " near *bellemies bank*

---

[1] Smith's map of Durham, often referred to in these Landmarks, was drawn by D. Smith in April, 1805. It is the oldest map of the town that has come to light.

pond, between the two rivers," June 23, 1701, was laid out in *Ash swamp*, beginning at "an asp tree on the south side of *barbadus* [Barbadoes] *way*."

Robert Evans of Mendon, Mass., sold Joseph Meder of Dover, June 5, 1711, sixty acres of land granted his father, Robert Evans, Sr., in *Cochecho swamp*, on the south side of the way that goeth to a place commonly called *Barbadoes*. This land was conveyed to John Hanson in 1713. *Nock's marsh*, on the western side of Dover, is a part of the old *Cochecho* or *Ash swamp*.

Another *Ash swamp*, between the Cochecho and Salmon Falls rivers, is mentioned March 23, 1702, when Paul Wentworth had a grant of 80 acres there.

An *Ash swamp* in the present town of Lee is spoken of July 19, 1721, when ten acres were laid out to Joseph Jones "at a place called the *Ash swamp*, above *Whelrit's pond*," on the south side of John Thompson and Moses Davis's land. This was part of a grant to Anthony Nutter in 1694. James and Sarah Clark of Biddeford (Me.), Nov. 9, 1741, conveyed to Jonathan Thompson 60 acres in the town of Durham, "at a place commonly called y^e *Ash swamp*,"— half of a six-score acre grant which said Clark bought of Moses Davis, Jr., formerly of Oyster River, deceased. This tract began at a pitch-pine tree on the south side of the highway that leads by *Peter's Oven*.

John Gray[1] sold Samuel James Stevens, March 2, 1747–8, a tract of land in Durham, on the north side of *Ash Swamp*. This land was sold Aug. 22, 1750, to Jonathan Thompson, Jr., whose descendants still own it. It is on the upper side of Little river, between Lee Hill and Nottingham.

A large swamp in South Newmarket is still known as *Ash Swamp*.

ASH SWAMP BROOK. Mentioned Dec. 31, 1750, when Miles and Abigail Randall of Durham conveyed to Simon Randall 80 acres of land at "a place commonly called y^e *Ash swamp brook*," part of 100 acres which their father, Nathaniel Randall, deceased, bought of Joseph Smith, "bounded on the south side of ye mast road." A bridge over *Ash brook* is mentioned in the Durham records of 1753 and 1754, and *Ash Swamp-bridge* is mentioned several times between 1755 and 1763. This brook is the outlet of Ash swamp. It crosses the road from Lee Hill to Nottingham, near Mr. John Thompson's, and empties into Little river.

ATKINSON'S HILL. This hill is in the south-western part of the Back River district, not far from the old Pascataqua bridge. It is partly in Dover and partly in Madbury, and is so named from the Hon. Wm. King Atkinson, who acquired land here at the close of the last century. It is often mentioned in the Madbury records as "*Laighton's Hill*," a name derived from the Laighton family that owned land in this vicinity for nearly 200 years, descendants of Thomas Layton of the Dover Combination of 1640. (See *Royall's Cove*.)

---

[1] John and George Gray are mentioned as trained soldiers on the south side of Oyster river, in 1732.

The Atkinson house, now owned by Mrs. Simpson, is in Madbury. The Laighton house, owned by Mr. Prescott, is in Dover. The road from Dover to the old Pascataqua bridge crosses Atkinson hill between these two houses.

This height affords an admirable view of the neighboring waters extending from the mouth of Oyster river and the opening into Little bay, to a great distance down the Pascataqua. The river directly in front is nearly a mile in width, and dotted by islands, two of which once formed links in the Pascataqua bridge; and beyond the broad expanse are the beautifully varied shores of Newington. Daniel Webster, who often crossed Atkinson hill on his way to and from Portsmouth when it was court time at Dover, declared this view unsurpassed by any other in New England. (See *Laighton's Hill*.)

BACK COVE. This cove is at the mouth of Minnow brook, at the lower end of Dover Neck, on the west side. It is mentioned June 25, 1704, when Richard Pinkham, Sr., and wife Elizabeth, conveyed to Ralph Hall 3½ acres of land adjacent to y^e *Back Cove* on Dover Neck, butting on Back river at the west, and bounded N. by John Dam's land, E. by low street, and S. by a lane running down to the *Back cove*, which land formerly belonged to their grandfather, Thomas Layton. Ensign Joseph Beard, Oct. 7, 1713, confirmed to Ralph Hall the right to one acre of land on Dover Neck, bounded N. by land conveyed by Joseph Beard, Sr., to Captain Thomas Tibbets, E. by land sold said Tibbets by Richard Pinkham, S. by a lane that led from high street to the *back cove*, and W. by the lane formerly called the Dirty lane.

BACK RIVER. The early settlers gave this name to the river at the west side of Dover Neck, as far as the head of tide water, above which it was called *Bellamy's Bank river* or *freshet*[1] to its source in Barrington. It is mentioned as early as Sept. 20, 1647, when Joseph Miller conveyed to John Goddard 20 acres on the west side of *Back river*. The name is still retained.

Back River, as a district, is also frequently mentioned in the public records of the last 200 years. It comprises the whole territory between Back river itself, and the Durham line from Cedar point to Johnson's creek bridge.

BACK RIVER GARRISONS. There seem to have been at least five garrisons in the Back River district.

I. DAM'S GARRISON, otherwise DAME'S. John Cross is mentioned as serving at "*Will Dam's garrison*" from Jan. 7 till Feb. 6, 1695; John Bickford from May 12 till June 8, 1695; John Tucker and John Miller

---

[1] The name of "*freshet*" was given by the early settlers to the fresh portion of a stream, to distinguish it from the tidal part towards the mouth, which is salt. "*Oyster river freshet*," and "*Bellamy Bank freshet*," are often mentioned in the old records, meaning that part of those streams above the head of tide water. An English critic, objecting to Dr. Jeremy Belknap's use of this term as unknown to him, Belknap replied, "Our forefathers brought the word from England," and he cited Milton's *Paradise Regained* as good authority for its use:

"All fish from sea or shore,
　Freshet or purling brook, or shell, or fin."

(See Belknap's *History of New Hampshire* (1792) Vol. III, *Preface*.)

from Nov. 4 till Dec. 5, 1695, and Ephraim Jackson from Dec. 5 till Jan. 7, 1696. (*N. H. Prov. Pap.*, 17 : 648.)

The precise situation of this garrison is not known, but it was in the Back River district, apparently on the lot granted John Dam in 1642, which was "Number eleven," next above the lot of John Upgrove, otherwise Newgrove.

Forty acres of land, granted to John Dam in 1656, were laid out to his son John Sept. 16, 1702, beginning at a white oak on the line between this land and that of Joseph Tibbets. A highway is mentioned between Dam's land and that of James Newt, which led to a landing-place at the head of James Newt's creek. This creek is above Hopehood's point. (See *Nute's Creek*.)

Wm. Dam, Sr., of Dover, in consideration of the love, good-will, and affection he bore to his loving son William, conveyed to him, June 7, 1712, one half of the *new house* he was then building, and half of the land on which it stood, with one third of his orchard, and also three acres of land bounded S. by the land of New Groue and James Newt, E. by the river, being all his land on that side of the creek. And Wm. Dam, Jr., that same day, bound himself to be at one third part of the charge of moving the house in which he then dwelt at the west end (24 ft. long and 30 ft. wide), up to the *Logg house*, and set it there. Wm. Dam conveyed to Jacob Allen, Ap. 7, 1724, " one half of *a dwelling Logg House*, set in Dover, on the westerly side of ye back river, which was formerly y^e *dwelling house of Wm. Dam, Sr.*, together with the land on which it stands, and part of ye upper orchard containing two rows of apple trees next said Jacob's part of ye orchard ; also 4¼ acres lying in y^e *spruce pasture*."

James Nute of Dover conveyed to James Tuttle, Feb. 3, 1770, 28 acres of land on the west side of Back river, at the N. E. corner of said Tuttle's other land bought of Tristram Pinkham, and running along by said river to the heirs of Wm. Dam, deceased, then westerly by said Dam's land and thatch-bed till it came to the west side of the creek, to high-water mark, and running across a point of land till it came to said James Tuttle's other land.

II. DREW'S GARRISON. The Back River garrison of this name is still in a good state of preservation, and is a picturesque feature of the road known as *Spruce Lane*. It is now owned by Mrs. Rounds, and contains an interesting collection of furniture and domestic utensils of colonial times. It was probably built by John Drew, who owned land at Back River between the lots of Robert Huckins and Thomas Whitehouse, June 6, 1698, when he acquired the Huckins lot, called " No. 16 " in the numbering of the Back River grants. The Pomfrett lot, No. 17, was sold him Feb. 5, 1701-2, by Pomfrett Whitehouse, grandson of Wm. Pomfrett. Richard and Sarah Paine of Boston conveyed to him June 5, 1705, 20 acres, " with ye marsh and flatts belonging thereto, being ye 18th of ye twenty acre lots on the west side of Back river, and abutting on Back river." Israel Hodgdon conveyed to John Drew, Sr., March 1, 1705-6, three fourths of an acre of salt marsh on the north side of the *Little freshit* or *brook* that goes out of the *deep gutt*, so called, that is in ye 18th lot of ye twenty acre lotts on the west side of Back river, joining John Drew's other thatch-bed.

"*Drew Garrison*" is so called June 21, 1779. (See *Spruce Lane*.)

III. FIELD'S GARRISON. This garrison stood on the present "Paul Meserve farm," so called, near the Back River school-house, but on the opposite side of the road. It was built by Zacharias Field, who was taxed at Oyster River in 1664, and owned land at Back River as early as 1670. The Rev. John Pike relates that, July 8, 1707, John Bunker and Ichabod Rawlins were going with a cart from *Lieut. Zach Field's garrison* to James Bunker's for a loom, when they were slain by the Indians.

The highway that led to *Field's garrison*, and thence to Capt. Gerrish's gristmill, as ye way goes to Cochecho, is mentioned March 6, 1710–11. (*N. H. Prov. Pap.*, 17 : 710.)

IV. MESERVE'S GARRISON. This is called the "*Harvey Garrison*" in Sanford & Evert's county atlas. It was still standing a few years since in a ruinous condition near the house of Mr. Gerrish P. Drew, but having been partly blown down, it had to be completely demolished. It is said to have been built by Clement Meserve, whose land adjoining the Field land is mentioned in the middle of the last century.

V. TORR GARRISON. The first garrison of this name was perhaps built by John Knight, whose "plantation already improved" on the west side of Back river is mentioned Ap. 11, 1694. Leah Knight, his widow, married Benedictus Torr, who seems to have been in possession of the Knight land, Feb. 22, 1709–10, when John Gerrish of Dover, and wife Elizabeth, conveyed to Benedictus Torr, and Leah, his wife, 36¼ acres in Dover township, lying to the westward of the *mast bridge*, on the west side of the Bake (Back) river, beginning at the south-west corner of the lot formerly sold by Major Richard Waldron to John Knight, deceased, but at this time in the tenure of said Benedictus Torr and Leah, his wife, thence running on a S. S. W. point three score and five rods to a Plase (place) called by the name of *Tom Drew's oven*. One bound of this land was a pine tree on the south side of the *mast path*. (See *Mast Bridge*.)

The first Torr garrison is said to have been burned by the Indians, but another was soon after erected by Benedictus Torr, which stood nearly opposite the present residence of Mr. Simon Torr. When taken down some years ago, a part of the timbers were used in the construction of the farm buildings.

BAGDAD. This name has been given for the last three score years or more to a corner east of Brown's hill in Durham—not for anything oriental in the scenery or in the style of architecture of the buildings, or any magnificence of sentiment among the residents. On the contrary, at the time this corner received its name, it was notable for its squalor and poverty and lowness of morals; and the name was, perhaps, given by some rural philosopher, who found it as good a place to moralize in as Mirza did on the high hills of Bagdad, where he went to muse and moralize on the condition and fate of humanity. And here, as on Mirza's hills, there is a "long hollow valley" beneath, in the depth of which courses Huckins brook, along the upper side of Buck's hill.

Some say, however, that the name of Bagdad was given by the boys of this corner, who had been reading the "Arabian Nights," and the name so tickled the popular fancy, by the very force of contrast, as to be at once universally accepted.

BALD GADE, otherwise BOLD GADE, mentioned in a Tibbets deed of the middle of last century. It was apparently in Somersworth, but the name has not been retained.

BALD HEAD. This is a small bluff on the Newington shore of Little Bay, just above Fox Pt., which has a bald, sandy aspect, facing the water, but otherwise is covered with verdure.

BALLARD'S BROOK. This name is often given to that part of Stony brook where it is crossed by the road from Durham village to Madbury. The bridge across it is also called *Ballard's bridge.* (See *Stony Brook.*)

BANTOM'S POINT, otherwise BAMPTON'S. This point, according to Whitehouse's map of Dover, is on the west side of the river Cochecho, below the Narrows. Matthew James of Somersworth, Dec. 29, 1741, conveyed to his son John 12 acres and 128 rods of land, compassing one acre in John Bamton's possession, beginning at his fence and running down to a landing-place on Cochecho river. It joined Samuel Tibbets' land. John James sold this land to Jonathan Watson, who, Dec. 2, 1746, conveyed to Ambrose Bampton 12 acres 128 rods, towards the upper end of Dover Neck, compassing one acre already in said Bampton's possession, and running down to a *landing place* on the Cochecho river. "Ambrous Bantom" belonged to Capt. Thomas Millet's Company in 1740. (See *Clark's Ferry.*)

BARBADOES. This name was given about two hundred years ago to a district on the present borders of Dover and Madbury that comprised BARBADOES MARSH, BARBADOES PLAIN, BARBADOES POND, BARBADOES SPRING, and BARBADOES WOODS. A road led to this district, sometimes called *Barbadoes way,* which is mentioned May 30, 1702. (See *Broad Turn.*) Robert Evans of Mendon (Mass.), June 5, 1711, conveyed to Joseph Meader of Dover, 60 acres of land granted his father Robert Evans, Sr., laid out in Cochecho Swamp, on "the south side of *the way* that goeth to a place commonly called *Barbadoes.*" Joseph Meader conveyed this tract to John Hanson in 1713. Benjamin Evans, April 10, 1739, conveyed to Hercules Mooney, schoolmaster[1], eleven acres in "ye place commonly called *Barbadoes*" on the north side of the way from Littleworth to Barrington, beginning at Robert Hanson's bound. Thirty acres were granted to Joseph Evans in *Purbadies* (Barbadoes) woods, Ap. 6, 1702. John Wingate, in his will of 1714, gives his son Edmund thirty acres in *Barbadoes woods,* which, according to a deed from Si-

---

[1] This was Col. Hercules Mooney, a native of Ireland, who not only taught school many years in Durham, Newington, and Somersworth, but served with distinction in the Seven Years' War and at the Revolutionary period. His first wife was Elizabeth, daughter of the above Benjamin Evans.

mon and Joanna Wingate to their brother Moses in 1736, were on the south side of the road that led from *Barbadoes spring*. Thomas Hanson of Dover, in his will of Sept. 18, 1728, gives his son Timothy sixty acres in *Barbadoes woods*. March 23, 1752, Henry Bickford of Dover sold Daniel Hayes twenty-eight acres in *Barbadoes woods* in two lots. One was next the Wingate land, on the south side of "*Barbadoes highway*." One side of this lot extended to Bellamy river. It is now owned by Mr. George O. Hayes.

Pomfrett Whitehouse, Feb. 9, 1732-3, conveyed to Nathaniel Hanson 32 acres in *Barbadoes woods*, granted his father, Pomfrett Whitehouse, in 1702, and laid out to him in 1721. Fifteen acres were laid out to Nathaniel Hanson on *Barbadoes plain*, Ap. 13, 1737.

Barbadoes Pond is spoken of as early as 1693, and again March 28, 1722, when Israel Hodgdon had eight acres laid out in *Barbadus woods*, on the east side of *Barbadus pond*, west of Richard Scammon's land.

Barbadoes pond brook is mentioned March 27, 1739, when Joseph Hanson's thirty-acre grant was laid out on both sides of this brook, at the westerly corner of Peter Hayes' land.

Ten acres of swamp and upland were laid out to John Tuttle, S^r., June 23, 1701, in the woods above *burbadus spring*. Only one spring appears to have been mentioned in early times, but at a later day all the springs of this vicinity were comprised under the name of "*Barbadoes springs*." They are now sometimes called *Kelley's springs*. They are south-east of the pond, and are of importance as the source from which the Dover aqueduct gets part of its supply of water. (See *Kelley's Springs*.)

The name of Barbadoes is no doubt a reminiscence of the days when wood and lumber from this region were sent to the West Indies in exchange for supplies of sugar, molasses, and other commodities. There was constant trade in early times with the island of Barbadoes especially.[1] Robert Nanny, a signer of the Dover Combination, had an estate there. Thomas Beard of Dover was living there July 24, 1668. One of the early Hansons of Dover went there, and, according to tradition, there found a wife. Complaint was made Oct. 4, 1683, of the pine boards sent from N. H. to *Barbadoes* and elsewhere. (*N. H. Prov. Pap.*, 1 : 468.) "Richard Gerrish, Command^r of ye ship Benjamin," built on the Pascataqua, and "now bound for *Barbadoes*," is mentioned in Aug., 1698. (*Ibid.*, 17 : 678.)

Among the custom-house returns at Portsmouth of the "entries inward" in the short space of one week in 1692 are the following: Sept. 17, 1692, the bark *Mary*, of Kittery, from *Barbadoes*, with rum and limestone ballasts ; and the *Friends Endeavor*, of Portsmouth, from *Barbadoes*, Nicholas Follet, commander, with sugar, molasses, and salt ; Sept. 19, the

---

[1] The island of Barbadoes is said to have derived its name from the long beard-like streamers of moss which hang from the branches of the trees, giving them a strange, venerable aspect,—
"Like harpers hoar, with beards that rest on their bosoms."

brigantine *Friendship*, of Portsmouth, from *Barbadoes*, Samuel Rines, com^r, with salt, English goods, etc.; and Sept. 22, the bark *Friends Increase*, of Portsmouth, from *Barbadoes*, John Cutt, com^r.

Robert Cutt of Portsmouth for a time lived at Barbadoes, and there married his first wife. The Vaughans of Portsmouth also traded there, and there died Cutt, son of Wm. Vaughan, and grandson of Richard Cutt. Michael Hicks, as stated in his will of 1688, was born at Barbadoes. Antipas Boyes, the son-in-law of Valentine Hill of Oyster River,[1] traded with Barbadoes; and there, about 1706, died his son, Antipas, Jr., whose estate fell to his cousin, Nathaniel Hill of Oyster River, son of Valentine. As late as Ap. 11, 1752, mention is made of Nathaniel Thompson's shipping goods from Barbadoes on the sloop *Nancy* (his brother, James Thompson, captain), consigned to Benjamin Mathes and Jonathan Thompson, Jr., of Piscataqua. These four men all belonged in Durham.

So constant was our intercourse with Barbadoes in early times that even official letters to and from England were sometimes despatched by way of that island. (*N. H. Prov. Pap.*, 17: 601.)

But in these days the island of Barbadoes, with which we once held such close commercial relations, is chiefly known to us through Captain Cuttle's famous nautical song:

"For the Port of Barbadoes, boys!
   Cheerily!
Leaving old England behind us, boys!
   Cheerily!"

BARNES'S ISLAND. This is a little island near the eastern shore of Oyster river, not far above the mouth. It now belongs to Mr. J. S. Chesley. It is referred to July 5, 1643, when Valentine Hill had a grant of land extending " from a creek over against Thomas Stevenson's, at Oyster river, that hath *an island in the mouth of it*, to the head of that creek in Royall's cove," etc. The present name was given it early this century by the boatmen on the river, who left one of their mates, nick-named " Capt. Barnes," on this island, and he was forced to swim ashore. It is sometimes called *Bodge's island*.

BARRINGTON OAK. This name is given to the present boundary tree at the Barrington terminus of the line between Lee and Madbury. It is a white oak, which stands where the roads from these three towns meet, at the side of the highway adjacent to the old Pinkham land, now belonging to Mr. Laban Emerson. Barrington oak seems to have sprung up since the line between Barrington and Madbury was perambulated Dec. 28, 1801. According to the Madbury records, the dividing line at that time ran to the western corner of Madbury, about one rod north-west of an *apple-tree* in Mr. Richard Pinkham's orchard.

BARTLETT'S FALLS. This name is given on the state map of Lee,[2] in 1803, to a dam just below the Little river saw-mill, in Lee, where Josiah Bartlett of Haverhill, Mass., acquired a grist-mill privilege May 3,

---

[1] Antipas Boyes (or Boyce) and Hannah Hill were married in Boston by Gov. John Endicott, Jan. 24, 1659.

[2] The so called " state maps," mentioned in this work, belong to the valuable collection of maps in the state-house at Concord, N. H.

1774. (See *Thompson's Falls*.) Another Josiah Bartlett, in his will of 1858, gives his son Alfred his mill and mill privilege on "Little river stream." This was lower down.

BARTLETT'S HILL. This name is sometimes given to the hill at the upper side of Little river mill, where the cellar of the Bartlett house can still be traced. It is otherwise called *Thompson's Hill*. On the top was once a whip-saw pit, owned by a Follet.

BARTLETT'S SPRING. Mentioned in the report of the Great Falls committee for the supply of water, Dec. 2, 1890. It is on land now owned by Mr. Bartlett, on the way from Great Falls to Rochester, below Tate's brook.

BAY HILL. Mentioned Nov. 28, 1679, when Lieut. Walter Neale confirmed unto George Huntress the right to a tract of land in Greenland, upon ye hill called *Bay Hill*, on the west side of John ffilbrook's land, beginning at a white oak on the top of said hill. This hill is at the west of Mr. J. C. Weeks' farm, a quarter of a mile from the Great Bay shore, on the highway to Greenland village.

BAY SIDE. This name, in a restricted sense, is given to that part of the Great Bay shore in Greenland, above the mouth of Winnicot river. It is also given to the neighboring railway station. A "school at *Bay side*" is mentioned in 1787, at which time the master was Clement Weeks, a graduate of Harvard College.

BEAN'S POINT. See *Stephen's Point*.

BEARD'S CREEK. This is the first inlet on the north side of Oyster river below Durham Falls. The name is derived from Wm. Beard, who was living at Oyster River, June 16, 1640, when he conveyed to Francis Mathews his house and land, "situate, lying, and being in Oyster river, next adjoining ye land of Darbey field."

This creek is mentioned in 1660, when John Woodman had a grant of twenty acres "at the head of *William Beard's creek*." (See *Stony Brook*.) And again in 1663, when Benjamin Mathes conveyed land to John Woodman on "the west side of *Wm. Beard's creek*."

There was a public *landing-place* at the head of Beard's creek as early as 1689, in which year a road was laid out from it extending to Newtown. The town of Durham conveyed this landing-place to Jonathan Woodman in 1779. (See *Brown's Hill*.) This creek is often called "*Woodman's creek*" in the Durham records, being partly bordered by the land attached to Woodman's garrison. (See *Beard's Garrison*.)

The bridge on the turnpike road across Beard's creek, near the mouth, is called in the town records by various names, according to the owner of the adjacent land, such as *Steele's bridge*, *Kingman's bridge*, and now *Coe's bridge*.

BEAUTY HILL. This hill is in Barrington, north-east of Bodge's pond. Said to have been so named from the number of rustic belles in that vicinity at one period.

BEAVER DAMS. The most noted beaver dam in ancient Dover was at Bellamy Hook, a little above the mouth of the Mallego. It is mentioned in 1659, when Thomas Wiggin's grant of 200 acres was laid out on a branch of Bellamy river, " neare y^e *Great Beaver Dam*."

Thomas Edgerly, Jr., March 19, 1693-4, had a grant of five acres of fresh marsh "on the north side of ye marsh Will Tasker and Jn°. Derry hath cleared above y^e *great beaver dam*," which was confirmed to him Ap. 2, 1694. Twenty acres of fresh marsh were granted John Derry and William Tasker, July 14, 1703, above the *great beaver dam* on Bellamy's bank river, where the s^d Derry and Tasker hath cleared, beginning at a tree near the *beaver dam* on the south side of said river.

John Davis, Sr., conveyed to Samuel Chesley, Ap. 26, 1719, five acres of fresh marsh "above *Great Beaver Damm*," originally granted to Thomas Edgerly, March 19, 1693-4. Samuel Chesley conveyed this marsh, that same day, to Eli and John Demerit, Samuel Davis, and others, evidently for the benefit of the mill built not long after at Bellamy Hook. (See *Demerit's Mill*.)

This was no doubt called "*Great*" Beaver Dam in order to distinguish it from a smaller beaver dam a little further up the Bellamy, just above Ricker's bridge, and immediately below the so called *Deep Hole*, which is a hollow in the channel of the river, noted as a favorable place for catching perch, pickerel, and shiners.

There are traces of several beaver dams in Durham, the most perfect of which is near the head of Beard's creek, beneath the tongue of land where the Woodmans are buried.

There was also a beaver dam in the south-western part of Lee, near North river. (See *Beaver Brook* and *Pond*.)

Mention is made of a beaver dam in Somersworth, Oct. 21, 1734, when 20 acres of land were laid out to Ebenezer Wentworth "where he then dwelt, above the *beaver dam*, near the lower end of *Peter's Marsh*, so called, by the brook." And, March 23, 1736, 20 acres were laid out to Samuel Walton, "beginning at a black ash in a maple swamp, near east from the *beaver dam* that is on the brook that cometh through *Peter's marsh*." This large beaver dam was near Mr. Thomas Ranlet's, where that part of Peter's Marsh brook, now called "Tate's brook," is crossed by the road from Great Falls.

The remains of another beaver dam are still to be seen in Rollinsford, on the east side of Fresh creek, above the road to Eliot.

The great number of beavers in N. H. in early times, especially in the vicinity of the Newichawannock, is evident from the amount killed in the course of a few months in the year 1633, as shown by the accounts of Ambrose Gibbons. (*N. H. Prov. Pap.*, 1 : 71-2 and 2 : 558.) It is not surprising that these interesting animals were speedily exterminated.

BEAVER BROOK, BEAVER POND, and BEAVER POND MEADOW. Beaver pond' is mentioned March 5, 1729-30, when ten acres of swamp, granted to James Thomas in 1701, "up above Little river, at a place called *Beaver Pound*," were laid out to Ebenezer Smith. And three score acres of upland and meadow, granted to Roger Rose, were laid out to John Smith May 13, 1726, beginning at a white ash tree on the south side of "a meadow called the *bever Pond medow;*" thence running N. W. by N. 60 rods, to a maple; then S. W. by W. 22 rods, "where the two brooks meet in the medow," etc.

Beaver pond, formed by the overflow of the beaver dam below, is no longer to be seen, but the meadow where it stood is in the south-western part of Lee, between the site of Fox garrison and North river. This meadow seems to have been acquired last century by Ephraim Davis and John Sias. It now belongs to Mr. Kenerson and Mr. B. F. Lang. It was drained by Beaver brook, which was the outlet of the pond. The beaver dam was on this brook, about ten rods from the old Sias house. A spring, about 30 rods from the house, is still called the *Sias spring*.

Two brooks are mentioned above. One of them is now dry most of the year, and has no name. The other is *Beaver brook*, which flows from the meadow to the boundary line of Lee and Nottingham, where it receives *Davis's brook*, that rises back of Mr. Obadiah Davis's house. It then runs half a mile northerly—contrary to the direction of the other brooks in this vicinity—crosses the Kelsey meadow in Nottingham and empties into *Pea Porridge brook*, which, a hundred rods beyond, empties into Little river.

BECK'S POINT and SLIP. Beck's Slip was a landing-place at *Beck's point*, on Fore river. This point is mentioned July 2, 1718, when Wm. Parker, of Portsmouth, conveyed to Nicholas Harford a dwelling-house and four acres of land on Dover Neck, beginning at a landing-place commonly called *Beck's point*, and extending west by the highway side to ye high street, then south by ye street to Samuel Haines' land, thence east by Haines' land down to ye fore river.

A road was laid out March 16, 1721-22, from high street to *Beck's slip*, no doubt to facilitate access to *Harford's ferry*, which Nicholas Harford in 1717 had been licensed to run from this slip to Kittery—that is, to the opposite shore; for Kittery then extended up the Newichawannock, and included the present town of Eliot and the Berwicks.

Thomas Cushing of Boston, and Mercy, his wife, Aug. 23, 1736, conveyed to Capt. John Gage five acres of land, with buildings, etc., bought of Nicholas Harford, on the east side of Dover Neck, lying between the land of Joseph Roberts and ye highway that leads down to ye landing-place commonly called *Beck's slip*, bounded westerly by the main road over Dover Neck down to Hilton's Point, northerly by Roberts' land, south by the highway from said main road to said landing-place, and easterly by Fore river, running from the river to the main road, including a strip four rods wide running along the river from said highway to the wharf on the river side, built by said Harford; with the privilege of *the Ferry from said landing-place over to Kittery Shore.*

Beck's Point was so named from Henry Beck of the Dover Combination of 1640. He seems to have settled in Portsmouth. "Henry Beck of Sagamore Creek in ye town of Portsmouth, planter" and Ann, his wife, are mentioned in the county records at Exeter, Sept. 1, 1668.[1]

---

[1] Henry Beck was the ancestor of Theodore Romeyn Beck, the author of Beck's Botany and several works on medical jurisprudence.

The landing-place at Beck's slip and Harford's ferry, afterwards Morrill's ferry, is now owned by Mr. Geo. W. Ford.

BEECH HILL. This hill is on the confines of Durham, Lee, and Madbury. It is mentioned the 4th, 9 mo., 1652, when Philip Chesley had a grant of 100 acres, one half of which was laid out in 1661 "att a place called the *Indian graves*, on the west side of *beach hill*." Twelve score acres of land were granted Capt. John Woodman and his sons, John and Jonathan, March 19, 1693-4, "on ye south side of *beach Hill* and so down to the swamp." (Follet's Swamp.) Part of this land is now owned by Mr. Moses Gilman Woodman, a direct descendant of Capt. John Woodman.

When Lee was separated from Durham, Jan. 17, 1766, the line of division began at Paul Chesley's house at *Beech hill*. When the bounds were perambulated in 1798, the line began at the place "where the house of Paul Chesley stood."

The name of Beech Hill is still retained, though the beech trees from which it was no doubt derived have all disappeared.

BELLAMY BANK RIVER or FRESHET, otherwise BELLAMY RIVER. This river rises at Chesley's lower pond, now Swayne's, in Barrington (See *Chesley's Ponds*), and flows into Madbury, where it is joined by the Mallego at Bellamy Hook. Below the Barbadoes region it receives Church's brook, after which it passes through the Bellamy district in Dover. At the head of tide water it takes the name of "*Back river*," and flows along the west side of Dover Neck, and finally empties into the Pascataqua river.

Dr. Ham of Dover ascribes the name of Bellamy to William Bellew, who, in 1644, owned a house and twenty acres of land on the north side of this stream, which he sold to Christopher Lawson. His name is otherwise written Ballew. "William Ballew" is the witness of a deed from Thomas Larkham to Wm. Walderne, Sept. 13, 1642. (*N. H. Prov. Pap.*, 1 : 163.) "William Ballew" is also one of the petitioners concerning Wm. Walderne's estate, Oct. 27, 1647. (*Ibid.*, 1 : 188–9.) "Will Bellew" is a witness to a deed from "Darby ffield" to John Bickford July 17, 1645. He is apparently the "Mr. Belley" who had a grant of six acres in Cochecho marsh in 1648. As his name does not appear in the Dover rate-list of that year, this grant was no doubt made in view of his former rights, and belonged to his assignee.

The derivation of the name of Bellamy river from Wm. Ballew is doubtful. He was a petty land-owner for a brief period, and has left no proof of his importance but the "Mr." prefixed to his name in one or two instances. Besides, Wm. Ballew's land seems not to have been on the fresh part of the stream to which the name of Bellamy has always been confined, but lower down, on the part called "Back river."

"The fifth of September, Anno Domi, 1644, William Bellew soulde [sold] his house situate in Dover, with ye appurtenances, unto Christopher Lawson, with twenty acres of land *on ye back river*, and thirty pounds in goods, for thirty thousand of pine staves to be paid the first of August, 1646, etc. (*County Records*, Exeter.)

The supposition that Belleman's Bank is a contraction of "Bellewman's Bank" is therefore hardly admissible. Besides, Belleman's Bank was certainly not the original name of this stream. The earliest form of the name was undoubtedly Bellamies Bank, greatly varied as to orthography. It is so called as early as 1648, the very year Wm. Ballew had a grant of six acres in Cochecho marsh. "Belleman's Bank" is mentioned in 1658. It is evidently a corruption, and one that is ignoble to the ear. It is, however, frequently found in the old records. It is called "*Bellamy's Bank*" Oct. 17, 1683, by Major Richard Waldron, who was at Dover in the time of Wm. Ballew, and may be considered indisputable authority as to the name. The word "Bank" was perhaps added to the name of the plantation here in imitation of "Strawberry Bank" at the mouth of the Pascataqua.

A different origin of the name is suggested by the term of "*ye old planting-ground*"[1] in the following deed: Thomas Beard of Dover, Aug. 6, 1654, conveyed to Richard Waldron a quarter part of the saw-mill (on Bellamy river), with all the iron works, ropes, wheels, and all implements and housings, with all the logs and the grant of timber by the town, and likewise *ye old planting-ground*, commonly called *Bellemies Bank*, with 20 acres more, granted by the town of Dover. (See *Bellamy Falls*.)

There were, however, people of the name of Bellamy in New England as early as 1644, when mention is made of John Bellamy of New Haven, merchant, who two years later was lost at sea, on his way to London. Mathew Bellamy of New Haven is mentioned in 1658, and again in 1675, when he had a grant of land at Saybrook, Conn.

Bellamy Bank, as a locality, is mentioned May 31, 1675, when the commons above Little John's creek were set apart "on ye west side of ye way y^t goes to *Belamyes bank*."

The disuse of the word "Bank" is ascribed to Wm. Hale after he acquired the falls next above Sawyer's mills. The name of *Bellamy* is now given to the district around these falls, as well as to the falls themselves.

BELLAMY FALLS and MILLS. The first falls in the Bellamy river are at the outlet of Swayne's pond in Barrington, where a reservoir dam was erected for the benefit of Sawyer's mills in 1863–4, and enlarged in 1881. The land here was conveyed by Elijah Austin to Isaac Wendell Oct. 28, 1823, for the Great Falls Manufacturing Company, which se-

---

[1] "Old planting-ground" was an expression generally applied to the land planted by the Indians. "*Runacwitt's old planting-ground*" in Kittery is mentioned in the York records. The "*Squammagonake old planting-ground*" is mentioned in 1686, in a deed from Hoope Whood and other Indian sagamores to Peter Coffin. "*Mahermit's planting-ground*" in the Packer's Falls district, Durham, is mentioned Oct. 9, 1735. (See *Pendergast Garrison*.) Andrew Wiggin of Quamscot conveyed to Joshua Bracket, Sept. 1, 1719, a tract of land "bounded att a clump of trees standing in a piece of *old planting-ground* nearly forty rods below Sandy Point, beginning at a stake in a piece of the *old Indian ground* 15 rods from high-water mark, about 40 rods below Sandy Point." Other instances might be given of the Indian corn-grounds, which were generally near the falls or some other important point on the rivers.

cured all the water powers on the Bellamy in 1823-24, now controlled by the proprietors of Sawyer's mills.

Just below the reservoir dam are *Hall's mills*, consisting of a saw-mill on the lower side, run by water power, and a steam mill on the other side for axe handles, etc. About a mile below are *Mr. Israel Pierce's saw-mill* and *grist-mill*, which formerly belonged to Jonathan Young. These mills are in Barrington. The uppermost mill within the limits of ancient Dover stood at *Bellamy Hook*, in Madbury, where a dam was built by Ely Demerit in 1719. This mill is now gone. (See *Demerit's Mill*.)

A short distance below the Hook once stood a mill for a brief period, built by Samuel Davis.

At the next falls were the *Gerrish mills*, also in Madbury. The river here flows between two steep hills. On the south side, below the bridge, was a grist-mill, and on the opposite bank a saw-mill. (See *Gerrish's Mill*.)

Between Gerrish's mill and the present Boston & Maine railway bridge was a saw-mill on the Hayes land, built a century ago at least. It was burned down Nov. 10, 1853, at which time it belonged to Mr. Oliver Hayes.

Further down was another saw-mill, long since removed. The water privilege here was owned by the Hayes family in 1825, when the old mill-site is stated to be half a mile above Col. Samuel Dudley's factory, which was at the chief falls in the Bellamy district.

About fifty rods above Dudley's falls once stood a "day" saw-mill, owned by the neighboring farmers, but the fall is no longer perceptible, having been overflowed by the raising of the dam below after the Dudley privilege was acquired by Mr. Richardson. This mill appears to have stood on the Hanson land, perhaps part of the tract mentioned Sept. 22, 1755, when Paul and Mary Gerrish, of the parish of Madbury, conveyed to Solomon Hanson a tract of 40 acres, 96 rods, in Dover, on the north side of Bellemin's Bank river, being part of ye land commonly called *Beard's hundred acres*, beginning at *a considerable fall* in said river.[1] It extended from Ensign Joseph Beard's land to the river, and the conveyance included " the sole privilege of s^d fall " on the north side of the river.

The chief falls in the Bellamy district have been called by various names, according to the different owners of this water privilege. A complete account of their mills would occupy too much space for this work. Among them may be mentioned *Dudley's, Watson's, Richardson's,* and *Hale's mills*. A saw-mill and grist-mill stood here Aug. 11, 1826, when the bridge between them, called *Dudley's bridge*, was swept away. This bridge was so named from Col. Samuel Dudley, who once had a mill on the south side for woollen cloths, carding, and machinery. He afterwards sold this factory to Daniel

---

[1] Thomas Beard's 100-acre grant adjoined the 100 acres southward of Capt. Waldron's log swamp, conveyed by Henry Nock, Feb. 18, 1718-19, to John Hanson and Thomas Hanson, Jr. (See *Nock's Marsh*.)

Watson, who converted it into a grist-mill. At a later day it was used for other purposes, and was finally acquired by Mr. Augustus Richardson toward the middle of this century. A grist-mill now stands here, owned by the proprietors of Sawyer's mills.

The mill privilege on the opposite side of the river was leased for fourteen years to Nathaniel Watson, Jan. 15, 1830, by Stephen, Abijah, Martha, and Anna Hanson. *Watson's mill* is mentioned Ap. 3, 1839, when Stephen and Abijah Hanson conveyed to Augustus Richardson a tract of six acres, beginning at the division of the roads to Lee, Dover, and the Bellamy district; also another parcel of land, known as *Watson's mill privilege* on said river, which tract was a square, measuring nine rods each way, beginning in the centre of said river, four rods below the dam, and thence running up the centre nine rods, and turning to the right, at right angles, and running nine rods, and so on, till the square was completed, being all the land owned by the said Hanson, on the north side of the river, or between the river and the Lee road; the saw-mill standing on the tract last described being excepted from the sale. This was of course the mill leased to Watson.

The Great Falls Manufacturing Co. acquired control of the water power in the Bellamy district by various purchases in 1823–24. In a deed from Jesse Varney (who had obtained a part of the old Dudley privilege) to Isaac Wendell, agent of the above Company, Ap. 2, 1823, mention is made of the *cotton factory* at Bellamy. This was the *Hanson factory*, built by Zaccheus Hanson, father of the above Stephen and Abijah, at a dam just below Dudley's falls, where the present saw-mill stands. It was bought and removed by Alfred I. Sawyer in 1832. The saw-mill here was erected some years later by Mr. Augustus Richardson, who acquired the whole water privilege at Bellamy by various deeds between 1839 and 1850. He also had a grist-mill, and established other works.

Richardson's mills and privilege were acquired by Wm. Hale by different conveyances. The final one seems to have been in 1867. A few years later he conveyed them to the proprietors of Sawyer's mills. There are still two dams here. At the upper one, the old Dudley privilege, is a grist-mill on the south side of the river. At the lower dam, where the cotton factory once stood, is a saw-mill on the north side. The highway passes between these two mills.

The remaining falls in the Bellamy are below Libbey's bridge, now Sawyer's bridge. They are three in number. A grist-mill stood at the upper falls, near the bridge, before 1711, when the road from Lamprey river to Salmon Falls is mentioned as running past Field's garrison to "*Capt. Gerrish's grist-mill* as ye way now goes to Cochecho." (*N. H. Prov. Pap.*, 17 : 710.) It is again spoken of in 1735, as will be seen below. At the beginning of this century it was owned by Benjamin Libbey. *Libbey's mill* and *bridge* are often mentioned in the Dover records. Enoch Libbey conveyed to Andrew Pierce, March 22, 1822, "a certain mill privilege and *grist-mill* owned and occupied by my late father Benjamin Libbey; also the whole right I have of erecting a dam on the southerly side of said river, on said privilege, and below the same," with the understanding that any overflow or damage done by erecting a dam below said privilege should be paid for. This purchase was made for the Great Falls Man. Co. The privilege here was leased to Alfred I. Sawyer in 1824. He gave notice July 27, 1824, that on the 1st of September following, he should "carry on the business of cloth-dressing at the place formerly known as *Libbey's mills*." He also ran the grist-mill, and a few years later established a flannel mill. He bought the rights of the Great Falls Man. Co. in 1845. After his death in 1849 the business was continued by his brothers. In 1858 they purchased the *Moses mill* at the lower falls, so named from C. C. P. Moses, who bought this privilege from the Great Falls Man. Co. in 1845, and built on the site of the Osborne foundry a paper-mill, which he converted into a flannel mill in 1855. From these two woollen mills have sprung up, through the able management of the Messrs. Sawyer, the present extensive manufactories of fine cloths and suitings. Their company was incorporated in 1873. There are three dams at Sawyer's mills. The lowest has a fall of 20 ft. and 80 horse power. This is at the head of tide water, to which point barges and small schooners can ascend Back river. The other two dams have a fall of 12 ft. and 50 horse power.

The earliest saw-mill on the Bellamy is supposed to have stood at the head of tide water. The falls here were granted to John Dam, Thomas Layton, and Wm. Pomfrett the 23d, 8 mo., 1649, but were afterwards acquired by Thomas Beard, Wm. Follet, Thomas Layton, and Philip Lewis. Thomas Layton conveyed his quarter part of the saw-mill here to Richard Waldron, Ap. 8, 1653. Thomas Beard and wife Mary, conveyed to Waldron his portion Dec. 6, 1654, together with "*ye old planting ground* commonly called *Bellemies Bank;*" Philip Lewis conveyed his quarter June 4, 1657; and Wm. Follet of Oyster River his part, Ap. 27, 1675. The entire mill and water privilege here, having been thus acquired by Major Waldron, he gave half of it as a marriage portion to his daughter Elizabeth, wife of John Gerrish, which gift he ratified by an indenture of Oct. 17, 1683, confirming unto John Gerrish of *Bellamy's Bank* one half of said mills, together with a moiety of all housings, lands, tenements, meadows, marshes, pastures, gardens, woods, swamps, water courses, mills, dams, head weirs, ponds, fishing, fowling ways, profits, privileges, rights, commonages, hereditaments, emoluments, and appurtenances, to him, his heirs, and assigns forever.

John Gerrish afterwards acquired the whole privilege. Here stood the Gerrish mills of early times, near which was no doubt the Gerrish garrison. These mills and the privilege were inherited by his sons, Col. Timothy Gerrish of Kittery, and Col. Paul Gerrish of Dover, who, Oct. 28, 1735, made a division of the land and water privilege left them undivided by their honored father, John Gerrish, Esq. A line was drawn, beginning at a certain rock about four rods from the southerly end of the bridge over Belleman's Bank river, on yᵉ westerly side of the road yᵗ leads over said bridge to Durham, thence running W. S. W. 64 rods to another marked rock, then S. S. W. 148 rods to a beech tree. It was agreed that all the land on the easterly side of the above line should belong to said Timothy, and that on the westerly side to said Paul. It was moreover agreed that "the privilege of yᵉ falls where the *gristmill* now stands upon Belleman's Bank river shall remain in partnership within yᵉ compass of sᵈ Timothy's land down to the flowing of the tide, and yᵗ yᵉ *Great Falls* in yᵉ sᵈ river, above yᵉ sᵈ *gristmill Pond*, lying within yᵉ compass of sᵈ Paul Gerrish's land shall remain to said Paul's own use."

Andrew Gerrish, Dec. 1, 1753, conveyed to Mr. Jonathan Cushing, clerk, ten acres on the east side of Back river, a little below the lowermost falls, where he then had a *sawmill* standing, beginning at the river, by the highway that leads across said river below the aforesaid *sawmill*, thence running down the river 55 rods to Capt. John Winget's land, then E. S. E. by said Winget's land to the road that leads from Dover Neck to Cochecho, etc.

BELLAMY BANK POND. This name is given to Barbadoes pond June 23, 1701, in a grant of land to Edward Evans. (See *Ash Swamp*.)

BELLAMY HOOK. This Hook is in Madbury. It is a deep bend in the Bellamy river at the mouth of the Mallego. (See *Demerit's Mill*.)

BENNET'S CROSSING. This crossing is on the Boston and Maine R. R., between the Durham and Newmarket stations. It is so called from John and Eleazar Bennet, owners of the adjacent land, and descendants of Abraham Bennick of Lubberland. (See *Goddard's Garrison*.)

BETEL'S POINT, otherwise BEETLE'S. This name is given to Ragg's Pt., on the Newington shore of the Long Reach, March 15, 1731-2, when James Rawlins and "Rebeck," his mother, and Deborah, his wife, conveyed to Josiah Downing a tract of land by yᵉ main river at a certain Point commonly called or known by yᵉ name of *Beetle's Point* or *Ragg's Point*, between yᵉ land of Capt. John Downing and yᵉ land of Samuel Rawlings, being the whole breadth of James Rawlins' land fronting on the salt water, running up from yᵉ water side into the land of said James, and carrying the whole breadth upward until three acres be accomplished. When this land was conveyed to Jonathan Battishall by Josiah Downing, June 25, 1737, the line began "at the main river at *Betel's Point* or *Ragg's Point*."

Joshua Downing conveyed to Nathaniel Mendum of Portsmouth, June 12, 1744, a tract of 50 acres in Newington, bounded easterly by the Pascataqua river, southerly by yᵉ lands of Jonᵃ Battishall and Samˡ Rowlings, decᵈ, westerly by yᵉ road yᵗ leads to Bloody Point, and northerly by the land of Richard Downing.

Capt. Thoˢ Tibbetts of Dover (aged 88 years) testified about 1750 that ever since his remembrance the Point of land where Jonathan Battishal's dwelling-house then stood in Newington was commonly called and known by the name of *Jeffry Ragg's Point*. (N. H. *Town Papers*, XII: 715.)

Betel's point was on the shore of the Rollins land, just below Patterson's lane. The name is apparently a contraction of Battishall. (See *Ragg's Point*.)

BICKFORD'S POINT. Mention is made of " the poynt whearon John Bickford now dweleth," the 7th, 4 mo., 1675. The road from Oyster river falls to *Bickford's Poynt* is mentioned in a grant to Nicholas ffollett, laid out Ap. 11, 1694. This road is spoken of in a deed from John Downing to Benjamin Mathes, Sept. 7, 1738, as " ye highway y^t leads from ye falls to ye ferry called *Bickford's Ferry*." The Durham records, Aug. 15, 1754, mention " the highway from *Bickford's point* to Durham falls."

Bickford's Point was on the shore of Little Bay, near the mouth of Oyster river, where the Bickford garrison once stood. It is now owned by Jeremiah Langley, Esq.

BIG RIVER. The people of South Lee sometimes give this name to the neighboring part of Lamprey river, no doubt to distinguish it from Little river, which in some old deeds is called " Lamprey little river."

BIRCH POINT. A point of this name, on the shore of Goddard's creek, is mentioned June 15, 1734, when Abraham Bennick of Durham conveyed to Joseph Chesley and Eleazar Bennick " twenty acres in that part of Durham called *Lubberland*, adjacent to the *Lubberland Marshes*, beginning at a red oak by ye side of ye marsh over against *Burch Point*, near where ye fence now stands, and runs N. N. E. over ye old *Shop Hill*, strait over a large flat rock marked J. E. until it comes to ye path used to go from Lubberland to ye lower falls, which is near four rods over said rock, from thence to run strait to *ye old garrison seller* [no doubt the cellar of the Goddard garrison] near E. S. E.—thence strait to a great rock marked J. E. which stands by ye path w^h goes to *ye landing place*, thence to Perkins his salt marsh," and thence to the first bound. This Birch Point is mentioned twice in a deed of Ap. 19, 1745, from Nathaniel Doe to Ralph Cross. (See *Doe's Neck*.)

Another BIRCH POINT is on the Newington shore of the Pascataqua river, below Bloody Point. (See *Pine Point*.)

BLACK HALL. Mentioned in the Durham records, July 2, 1740, when a highway was laid out, beginning at a pitch-pine tree standing near the *mast way* on the south side of the *spruce swamp* (on Lee Hill), and then running along the old way till it comes to the way that goes to *Blackhall*, then along that way to the head of the town. Blackhall is near the head of Marston's mill-pond, in Nottingham, and perhaps was so named in contradistinction to Whitehall in Rochester, to which a road led at the other side of ancient Dover.

BLACKSNAKE HILL. This hill is in Durham, on the north side of " Oyster River freshet," between the Mast road and the B. & M. railroad. It is a part of the farm of the late Benjamin Thompson.

BLACKWATER BROOK and MARSH. Blackwater brook rises in the southern part of Rochester, flows through the north-western part of Somersworth into Dover, and empties into the river Cochecho above Hussey's falls. There have been two saw-mills on this brook in the course of the present century. The first one was owned and operated by Isaac Twombly, and the other by his son Allen, but neither of them is now standing.

Blackwater bridge, otherwise called *Mast bridge* because on the Mast road to Whitehall, is mentioned June 23, 1701, in a grant of 30 acres to Tristram Heard. That same day Paul Wentworth had a grant of 15 acres of marsh " on the west side of *black water* marsh." A petition was made to the town of Dover, May 3, 1739, for a road to be laid out " from Scatterwitt, so called, through *Black water woods* near Long hill to the Rochester line." Blackwater, as a locality, is often mentioned in the early records, and this name is still given to one of the school districts in Dover.

BLIND WILL'S NECK. This is a point of land in the south-west part of Rochester, near the Dover line, formed by the junction of the Cochecho and Isinglass rivers. It was here that a friendly Indian sagamore named Blind Will was killed in March, 1677, having been sent with a scouting-party by Major Waldron to watch the movements of some hostile Indians, who fell suddenly upon the party and killed the greater part. This neck is mentioned March 17, 1736, when Samuel Tibbets conveyed to his son Ichabod a part of his second division in Rochester, " at a place called *Blind Will's Neck,* lying on yᵉ S. W. of a marsh commonly called *Long marsh.*" And again Dec. 3, 1745, when Jonathan Young of Dover conveyed to his son Jonathan a tract of land " at *Blind Will's Neck,* at or near two marshes called *Long marsh* and *Great Marsh.*" Humphrey Hanson conveyed to his brother Ephraim, Oct. 8, 1765, "three acres at *Blind Will's Neck,* so called, in Rochester, on yᵉ very S. E. point of said Neck, nearly opposite the mouth of Blackwater brook, joining partly to the Isinglass portion of the river, and partly to the Squommonogonnock branch," being the land he purchased of John Smith Ap. 27, 1739.

BLOODSUCKER'S POND. (See *Parsonage Pond.*)

BLOODY CORNER. This name has long been given by the popular voice to the corner at the intersection of Washington, Green, and Orange streets, in Great Falls village.

BLOODY POINT. This name was given as early as 1633 to a neck of land between the Long Reach and the western branch of the Pascataqua river, which for eighty years formed part of ancient Dover. The lower bound of this neck originally extended from Canney or Kenney's creek, on the shore of the Long Reach, to Hogsty Cove at the mouth of the Great Bay. Nearly a year after Bloody Point was made a separate parish, its name was changed to *Newington* by Gov. Joseph Dudley. This was done May 12, 1714. (*N. H. Prov. Pap.*, 3 : 562.)

The story generally related to account for the name of Bloody Point seems ridiculously inadequate to an appellation of such tragical import. But the real history, too long to be given here, is not of a mere bloodless encounter between Neale and Wiggin in 1632, but of a far more serious contest about rival patents, that involved the title to all the lands along the Pascataqua. Capt. Wiggin, from the first, was devoted to the interests of Massachusetts Bay, which sought control over New Hampshire. Capt. Neale, who was Mason's attorney, was strongly opposed to the pretensions of Massachusetts. Their conflict, therefore, was not wholly personal, but represented the strife of contending parties. The Bloody Point region was a kind of debatable ground—a border land between Strawberry Bank and Hilton's Point, along whose pleasant shores the members of both factions were disposed to lay out lands for themselves; and their alarm, their sanguinary mood, and their resolution to defend their claims, are all embodied in the name they gave this point as a perpetual defiance to those who would dispossess them—a name far better suited to their temper of mind than to the actual encounter between Walter Neale and Thomas Wiggin.

The Indian massacre, to which some writers ascribe the name of Bloody Point, from a popular tradition in Newington, if it ever took place at all, must have occurred too long after this name had been given it to be worthy of any consideration.

The early settlers at Bloody Point gave this name, in a restricted sense, to the projection directly opposite Hilton's Point, now the Newington terminus of the bridge across the Pascataqua from Dover Point. A little to the west is the old landing-place of Knight's ferry. This ferry is often called *Bloody Point ferry* in the early records. It is mentioned in the Diary of John Adams, afterwards President of the United States, who gives an account of a visit to his uncle, the Rev. Joseph Adams of Newington, June 30, 1770. He says that after "a cheerful and agreeable dinner," he "then set off for York over *Bloody Point ferry*, and arrived at Woodbridge's half an hour after sunset."

In connection with Bloody Point and Dover (once called Northam) it might be mentioned that a place near the village of Northam, Eng., has for centuries been known by the name of the *Bloody Corner*, from a fight with the Danes which occurred there in the reign of King Alfred.

BLOODY POINT PLAINS. Mentioned Dec. 19, 1685. (See *Pitch Pine Plains*.)

BOILING ROCK. This ancient bound is in the Pascataqua river, off the Eliot shore, above the Narrows. It is mentioned May 26, 1656, when the division of the Squamscot Patent was made—the first division of which comprised "all the land from Bloody Point unto the *boyling Rock* for breadth." President Cutt, in his will of 1680, speaks of his thirteen acres at *Boyling Rock*, bought of Jaffrey Currier.

BOOM. The Rev. John Pike, in his journal, speaks of Mr. Waldron's "coming over the *Boom*" April 28, 1704. This boom was a floating bridge on the Cochecho river, "by Col. Waldron's, above the falls." It was made of three or four pieces of hewn timber laid side by side, wide enough for horses and cattle to pass over in file; but teams were obliged to ford the river below the falls. (See *N. H. Town Pap.*, XI: 540.) The falls here referred to are in Dover city.

There was a boom across Lamprey river in early times, as well as on the

Cochecho. Dec. 15, 1712, the town of Dover voted to give twenty-five pounds " for building a *boom* over Lampereel river." A tract of twenty-five acres adjoining this part of the river then belonged to Philip Chesley, who sold it to Joseph Duda, reserving for himself four rods for a highway from *ye country boom* over Lamper river on the north side, down to the mill, and one fourth of an acre adjoining said mill, for landing logs. Before this boom was built, there was a ferry across the river. In 1671 Philip Crommet was licensed to keep a ferry across Lamprey river, at the rate of two pence for each person, and six pence for man and horse.

There seem to have been two booms, at least, on the Newichawannock. " The *upper boom* " there, is mentioned Aug. 9, 1731, as 60 rods north of Anthony's brook. Robert and Judith Cole, Sept. 28, 1731, conveyed to Thomas Wallingford 8 acres of land, beginning at the pier of the *upper Boom*, about half a mile above ye upper Salmon Falls mills, and thence extending up the river.

BRANDY ROCK. Mentioned in 1709, when a number of the inhabitants " living within the bounds of Quamscott patent " (the part now called Stratham), but " never yet been joined to any town," petitioned the Governor and Council for the charter of a township, " beginning at a rock called *Brandy Rock*, near Sandy Point, and to run up to the River by the mouth of a creek called Wheelwright's creek," etc. (*N. H. Prov. Pap.*, 3 : 405–6.)

Brandy Rock is one of the bounds between Greenland and Stratham. It is a few rods above the Stratham railway-station, at the side of the road leading from the station to the main road to Exeter.

BRANSON'S CREEK. Mentioned the 10th, 8 mo., 1653, when Wm. Drew had a grant of 60 acres of upland on the north side of *Branson's creek,* joining his marsh next Thomas Willie's land. He afterwards assigned this land to his son, Francis Drew.

Charles Adams had a neck of land granted him in 1656, on the south side of *Branson's creek,* bounded from the western branch upon a south line to the Great Bay. This land was conveyed to Joseph Kent Feb. 15, 1711–12, by Henry Nock and his wife Sarah, daughter of Charles Adams. Jonas Bine had an " out lot " in 1654, on the S. W. side of *Branson's Creek,* next Charles Adams' lot, and joining George Webb's,[1] right over against a place called the *hay stack.* He sold this land to John Bickford and John Hill in 1668. It is called "*Brand's Krick,*" Oct. 9, 1691, when Francis Drew conveyed to Thomas Drew all his right to 60 acres belonging to the estate of his father, Wm. Drew, late of Dover, deceased.

The name of this creek was derived from Geo. Branson, whose name is on the Dover rate-list of 1648. He died before July 2, 1657, on which day certain jurymen were appointed, under oath, to inquire into the cause of his death. John Alte, who seems to have been the foreman, testified

---

[1] George Smythe, administrator of the estate of Geo. Web, deceased, conveyed to Oliver Kente in 1651, " a messuage or tenement in *Oyster River plantation,* formerly in the possession of sd Geo. Web, but then in the tenure of sd Oliver Kent, containing by estimation one acre and a half."

"that Branson went well out of his house, and he (Alte) went after him, and found Branson lying on the ground, crying that the bull had killed him, with one wound up towards his shoulders, and another against the small of his back, with his members all brook." (*County Records*, Exeter.)

John Alt and Richard York were appointed administrators of Branson's estate July 2, 1657. Branson's creek is on the Durham shore of the Great Bay, and is now known as *Crummit's creek*. (See *Long Creek*.)

BREAKNECK HILL. This hill is south of Cole's pond in Somersworth, on the road from Rocky Hills to Great Falls, after it crosses Tate's brook. It is a mass of round cobblestones dangerous for teams, and was so named, it is said, because an ox once fell, in descending it with a load, and broke his neck.

BRISTOL. This name was given to the settlement at Hilton's Point as early as 1633, and is mentioned on an old map of 1634. It was derived from the town of Bristol, England, whence came the first pioneers of New Hampshire. The explorers of the Pascataqua under Martin Pring in June, 1603, were sent over by the enterprising merchants of Bristol. The Hilton Point settlement of 1623 was also under their patronage. And they formed the greater part of the Plymouth Company, from whom Edward Hilton obtained his patent of 1630, one of the promoters of which was Sir Ferdinando Gorges, who had a house at Bristol. "The Bristol men's plantation in Piscataqua" is mentioned March 25, 1633, in a letter from Edward Howes of London to Gov. John Winthrop of Massachusetts.

The situation of Dover Point and Neck is not unlike that of Bristol, Eng., which stands on the ridge of a peninsula between the Avon and the Frome, and connected with the rest of Gloucestershire by a neck of land.

BROAD COVE. This cove is on the Newington shore, between Fox Point and Stephen's Point, now Bean's. "*Broad Cove* below foxe poynt" is mentioned in 1659, when a grant of land to Henry Langstar was laid out. (See *Dumpling Cove*.) And again Oct. 27, 1701, when the town voted there should be "a highway from Mr. Harrison's to *broad cove freshett*, and so to the highway from bloody poynt Road to *Stephen's poynt*, or *broad Cove*, where it should be thought most fitt." (See *Stephen's Point*.) John Crockett conveyed to John Downing, July 6, 1719, house and land, on the road from Newingington meeting-house to *Broad Cove*, yᵉ house standing on the left-hand side of the road as you go to the water side at *Broad Cove;* with another tract on the right-hand side of the road, joining said Downing's land at the north, and that of John and Richard Carter at the east or northeast, being part of the estate of his father, Joshua Crockett, deceased.[1]

Another BROAD COVE is on the Lubberland shore of Great Bay, adjacent to the Smith lands. (See *Red Rock*.) It is mentioned Dec. 9, 1679, when John Alt's grant of 80 acres in the Great Bay was laid out, beginning

---

[1] Joshua Crockett's wife was Sarah, daughter of Thomas Trickey.

at Richard Yorke's marked tree in the *Broad cove*, and running thence by the water side 40 rods towards *Needom's Point*. In the grant of this land to " John Olt," the 10th, 8 mo., 1653, this cove is spoken of as "the *Great cove* above Needom's Point." Mention is made of it July 17, 1705, when Roger Rose of Portsmouth conveyed to John Smith land and houses at Lubberland, in the town of Dover, bought of John York, beginning at a great white oak 2 or 3 poles above *York's marsh*, in the creek commonly called Goddard's creek, then N. by E. 60 rods to the middle of a valley or gutter, thence to the N. E. bound tree marked R. Y. and then S. E. to a tree in the *Broad Cove*. This cove is again mentioned Ap. 19, 1757, when Eleanor (Stevenson) McCalvey, widow, conveyed to Joseph Footman all her rights to land between that of Footman and Pinder, extending along a channel to a great rock near the head of *Broad Cove*. (See *Needham's Cove* and *Point*.)

There is a third *Broad Cove* on the Rollinsford shore of the Newichawannock river, mentioned March 27, 1701-2, when Jonas Hambleton conveyed to Nicholas Waldron 20 acres of land at a place called *broad cove*, granted Thomas Young, bounded northerly by the lot of Joseph Jenkins; easterly, at the lower end, by the Newichawannock river, where it measured 24 rods; southerly by the lot of Jeremiah Tibbets, and westerly, at the upper end, by the lot of Thomas Roberts. John Haggins, of Berwick, admin^r of the estate of Daniel Haggins, conveyed to John Tibbets, June 24, 1805, 8 acres of thatch ground at a place called *Broad cove*, beginning at Samuel Hussey's fence at high water mark, and running E. 2 deg. S. 32 rods, at low water mark in the Newichawannock river. The name has not been retained.

BROAD COVE CREEK or FRESHET. Mentioned in 1659 as "*the freshett that goeth into Broad Cove*." (See *Dumpling Cove*.) Geo. Walton conveyed to Eleazar Coleman, Feb. 27, 1718-19, 50 acres of land in Newington, at a place called *Broad Cove*, bounded westerly by land of said Coleman, southerly by Wm. Shackford's, and northerly upon *ye creek in broad cove*, being all that parcel of land formerly Capt. Henry Langstar's, except ten acres sold to Samuel and John Shackford. This brook is generally called *Carter's brook*, but often takes the name of the adjoining proprietor. (See *Carter's Brook*.)

BROAD MARSH. This marsh is in Durham, between Long marsh and the Moat. It is mentioned May 17, 1705, when Sarah Nutter, "widdo of Anthony Nutter, late of Dover, deceased," and their sons, John, Hateuil, and Harry, sold Roger Roase (Rose) of Portsmouth, 128 acres between Lampereel river falls and Oyster river falls, laid out to said Anthony Dec. 1, 1662. This land began at the north-east end of an island, evidently the Moat island, and included " all the *Broad Marsh* at ye end of y^e *Long marsh*," except two acres at the head of it laid out to Thomas ffuttman. The whole tract included fifty acres of upland granted Hateuil Nutter, father of Anthony, in 1643, and sixty acres adjoining, afterwards given Anthony, on the south-east side of his marsh, extending to a "hollow near the lower end of the moat," and up that hollow to the head of another marsh, no doubt Moharimet's.

A *Broad marsh* on the Greenland shore is mentioned Ap. 9, 1729. (See *Wigwam Point.*)

BROAD TURN. Mentioned March 19, 1693-4, when Mark Giles had a grant of 20 acres " as near the *Broad turn* as may be." This grant was laid out May 30, 1702, on the south side of *Barbadoes way*, above the *broad turn*. The right of a highway four rods wide was reserved, to go through this land "from the *broad turne* into the *ash swamp*." Ralph Twómbley had a grant of 30 acres "near the *broad turn* in Cochecha swamp," March 19, 1693-4. It was laid out to Wm. Twombley, "successor of Ralph Twombley, Jr., deceased," Nov. 4, 1702, on the N. E. side of the way from the *Broad turn* to Barbados. The bounds of the ancient cartway, five rods wide, that led from *Tolend falls* into the Cochecho swamp, were renewed March 4, 1703-4, running on a W. by S. point, as the way then went, till it met with the other way that led "from *broad turne* into said swamp." John Haise conveyed to Ichabod Haise, Aug. 15, 1721, twenty acres of land " in Dover, near Cochechoh, at a place called by yᵉ name of *broad turn* or *Littleworth*, bounded 40 rods by the highway, and 80 rods by Wm. Twombley's land on the N. E. and S. W."

BROOKIN'S MARSH. Mentioned Nov. 28, 1804, when Valentine Mathes conveyed to John Bunker two acres of upland, salt marsh, and thatch-bed, situate and lying in Durham, adjoining Jones's creek, and commonly called *Brookin's Marsh*, bounded north by Jacob Joy's land, west by the creek aforesaid, and southerly and easterly by said Bunker's land. This small marsh was so named from Wm. Brooking, who is mentioned Oct. 16, 1684, when Thomasine Mathews, relict of ffrancis Mathews of Oyster River, out of love and affection to Will Brooking, yᵉ son of Godferie Brooking, deceased, her well beloved grandchild, conveyed to him three acres of upland and a parcel of marsh adjoining the north-east side of Johnson's creek, with half an acre on the S. W. side of said creek.

Godfrey Brooking was drowned at the Isles of Shoals Dec. 10, 1681, leaving a wife and four small children. Wm. ffollet of Oyster River calls Hannah Brooking, apparently the widow of Godfrey, his "daughter-in-law." (*N. H. Prov. Pap.*, 17: 610.)

Wm. Brakin is mentioned among the men sent over by Capt. John Mason in 1631.

BROTH HILL. This is a well known height at the south end of Durham village, commanding a beautiful view of the Oyster river valley and the hilly, winding village beyond, in its most picturesque aspect. The hamlet on this hill is quite distinct from the village proper, and is the centre of one of the old school-districts, generally called the " Broth-Hill district." There is a story that this name was given in derision of the favorite dish of the workmen once employed in the Durham ship-yards, for whom several cottages had been built on this height. But it was no doubt derived from the Coolbroth or Colbath family that once lived here

—a name since happily illustrated by Vice-President Henry Wilson, whose name originally was Colbath.

The Rev. Curtis Coe of Durham gives another variation of this name in his record of the burial of "Downing *Colbroath*," Dec. 14, 1785.

BROWN'S BROOK. This name is sometimes given to the easterly portion of Peter's Marsh brook, between the part called Tate's brook and the Salmon Falls river into which it empties.

BROWN'S HILL. This hill is in Durham, north of Woodman's garrison, on the old road to Dover. The Durham records mention it May 3, 1779, when the town appointed "Ebenezer Thompson, Esq., and John Smith, 3d, to agree with Mr. Jonathan Woodman for a strip of land in his pasture to make the road more convenient over *Brown's Hill* (so called) . . and to convey to s⁴ Woodman in exchange therefor all the right that the town has to the landing-place at the head of *Woodman's Creek*" (Beard's Creek).

BUCK'S HILL. This name is given to a hill in Durham, a little east of Huckins brook, on the way from Bagdad to the Back River district.

BUMFAGGIN. Forty-two acres of land in Barrington, "at a place called *Bumfaggin*," are mentioned June 18, 1811, in the inventory of the estate of John Layn of Newtown, Lee. *Bumfaggin woods* are in the western part of Barrington, below Stonehouse Pond. *Bumfaggin road* leads through these woods into Nottingham. The name is said to be associated with the noted Leathers tribe.

BUMFORD'S PLAINS. So called from Robert Bumford of Barrington, who, Feb. 23, 1760, conveyed to his son Robert 50 acres "in the two Mile Streak, so called, being all that lot of land where I now dwell, which I bought of George Jaffrey, Esq., deceased." In the time of Hatevil Bumford, the first half of this century, *Bumford's plains* were used as a training field for the county militia. "*Barrington Training*" day drew an immense crowd to these plains every year, or to the other training-ground near the old meeting-house in Barrington.

BUNKER'S CREEK. This is the first inlet on the easterly side of Oyster river below Johnson's creek. The name is derived from James Bunker, who was at Oyster River as early as 1653, and built a garrison near this creek. Bunker's creek is often mentioned in the county and town records of the last two hundred years. Wm. Hill conveyed to Henry Hill, Nov. 11, 1734, one third of the farm in Durham where said Henry then lived, adjoining a creek commonly called *Bunker's creek*, on the north side, beginning at a red oak at the head of this creek, then running north to Henry Rines's land, and along this land to the land Joseph Jenkins bought of Wm. Clay. A grist-mill on Bunker's creek is mentioned May 8, 1768, when Eliphalet Hill conveyed to Clement Meserve one fourth of this mill which he bought of Jonathan Bunker.

Bunker's bridge is on the first N. H. turnpike road, across this creek. There was a double stone dam at this bridge the first half of this century, with a tide-mill adjoining, but they are both now gone. The brook that empties into Bunker's creek is sometimes called the *Dirty Slough*.

Bunker's Lane is mentioned March 17, 1857, when Daniel Smith conveyed to James M. Bunker 107 acres in Durham, bounded westerly by *Bunker's lane*, so called, and the *Mill Pond*. This lane is the old road across Follet's Rocky hill.

BUNKER'S NECK. Mentioned June 23, 1701, when a strip of land was granted Nathaniel Lumas (Lamos) and Richard Clay " between Stories hundred acres and *bunker's neck*, to be equally divided, bounded on stories hundred acres on the north-east and *bunker's neck* on the south-west."

Richard and Mary Clay, Ap. 6, 1702, conveyed to Samuel Perkins " four or five acres of land between *James Bunker's Neck* and Follett's hundred acre lott, with other lands adjacent thereto."

Bunker's Neck is in Durham, on the upper side of Oyster river, between Johnson's creek and Bunker's creek. William Follet and James Bunker, the 10th, 8 mo., 1653, had a grant of all that neck of land between Thomas Johnson's creek and Oyster point, " from yᵉ head of Johnson's creek where yᵉ salt marsh ends, to yᵉ head of yᵉ other creek where Jonas Bine's marsh is, except William Storey and Mr. Mathews's grants, and likewise yᵉ cartways for the transporting of timber."

BURGETT PARK. This is a place of popular entertainment at the lower side of Willand's Pond, adjoining the electric railway from Dover to Great Falls. So called from Mr. H. W. Burgett, the proprietor, who, Oct. 1, 1890, acquired 20 acres of land for this purpose from the heirs of Rufus Ham, eastward of Mr. Benjⁿ Hussey's, and on the same side of the highway.

BURNT GROUND. Mentioned March 19, 1693-4, when Joseph Meader had a grant of 30 acres of " land and swamp " on the S. W. side of the path to the *burnt ground bridge*, in Follet's swamp. This is apparently the bridge across Oyster river, below Dishwater mill. Philip Chesley's grant of 30 acres was laid out Jan. 23, 1701, above Thomas Wille's, upon the *burnt ground*. It was on the north side of the road from Oyster River to Newtown. The name is indicative of an extensive fire in the forest in early times.

BUZZELL'S HILL. This hill is on the cross road from Madbury to the First N. H. turnpike-road, between the Samuel Demeritt house and that of Mr. I. Blake Hill; the former of which is in Lee, and the latter in Durham. The boundary line between these two towns crosses the brow of this hill, and the road crosses Oyster river at its foot, on the Lee side. It is familiarly called *Buzzy Hill*.

CALDWELL'S BROOK. This brook rises in Barrington, one branch at *Creek pond*, and the other in *Great swamp*, back of the Two-Mile school-house. These branches unite, and form what is otherwise called *Maple brook*, which empties into Oyster river above Wheelwright's pond. Wm. Caldwell acquired land in Newtown the middle of the last century, at or near Bunker's corner. (See *Maple Brook*.)

CALVES-PEN ISLAND. Mentioned Ap. 1, 1662, when " a tract of land and marsh on the north side of Winnicot river in yᵉ Great Bay " was divided between Philip Lewis on one side, and Thomas Nock and Henry Tibbets on the other; said Lewis binding himself to lay no claim to "the marsh y^t lyeth within ye bounds of the *calves-pen marsh,*" except what had already been laid out to him on the N. W. side of the island, commonly called and known by ye name of y^e *calves-pen island,* situate within ye Great bay aforesaid." Philip Lewis's land fell to his daughter Hannah, wife of John Johnson, who also acquired the marsh of Henry Nock of Oyster river, which was half of the marsh that previously belonged to his grandfather Tibbets on the north side of Winnicot river. John Johnson and Hannah conveyed the above land and marsh to Nathaniel Huggins May 25, 1696.

Calves-Pen island is no longer to be traced. It was probably an island at high tide, that has disappeared with the draining of the marshes.

CAMPIN'S ROCKS. This name is given to a well-known ledge that projects from the right bank of the Cochecho, at the Narrows. It is mentioned in a grant to Joseph Sanders in 1660,[1] and again Oct. 25, 1669, when he sold John Heard 30 acres "on Dover Neck, near Cochecho, right up from *Campin's Rocks,*" joining Tobias Hanson's land. Jabez Garland and wife Dorcas, July 7, 1694, conveyed to Timothy Hanson 30 acres of land "upon Dover Neck, near *Campon's Rocks,*" laid out to Joseph Sanders, and sold by him to John Heard, and given by John Heard, deceased, to his daughter Dorcas, wife of said Jabez. This tract was adjacent to the lands of Timothy, Thomas, and Tobias Hanson. Richard Scammon conveyed to Joseph Estes, March 23, 1738-9, 4 acres and 32 rods of land on "ye southerly side of ye road from Cochecho down to *ye landing at Campain's Rocks,*" adjoining the land that was James Hanson's. The name of these Rocks is otherwise written. They are called *Camping rocks* in a grant to the Rev. Mr. Sever in 1711, and *Champion's rocks* in a deed from Samuel Alley to Job Clement, March 28, 1758. Campin is no doubt a corruption of Campion or Champion. A Robert Champion of Dover is mentioned in 1657, when a jury of twelve men, "sworn to inquire into his death," declared that he had been drowned by accident. (*County Records,* Exeter.) This may be a key to the popular tradition that Campin's rocks were so called from a man who, pursued hither by the Indians, was forced to jump into the river in order to escape. A Clement Campion is mentioned as early as 1644, when he brought a suit against Wm. Payne for carrying pine staves and masts into the Bay, for which Payne was fined 20 shillings and costs. (*County Records,* Exeter.) He seems to have lived in Portsmouth. "Master" Clement Campione's house is spoken of, Jan. 12, 1652, as opposite Furson's island, now Noble's, which is on the right side of the Pascataqua river, a little below Cutt's cove. It stood no doubt on *Campion's Neck,* mentioned July 10, 1655, which comprised the land from the North burying-ground to Raine's shipyard in Portsmouth.

---

[1] Joseph Sanders was killed by the Indians June 28, 1689.

CAMPRON RIVER. This name is given to Lamprey river the 27th, 10 mo., 1647, in a grant of the mill privilege thereon to Ambrose Gibbons and others. "*Camperon*" is mentioned in a law-suit of 1713. This was probably an error of the recorder. The name of *Lamprone* is repeatedly given to this river in the town records of Exeter. (See Bell's *Hist. of Exeter*, p. 437.)

CAMSOE, otherwise CAMSIE and CAMPSEY. Mentioned in David Kincaid's will of June 13, 1719, in which he gives his " loving wife Anne," 40 acres of land he bought of Moses Davis, Sr., "now called by ye name of *Campse*." Ann Kincaid conveyed to Robert Thompson, Aug. 14, 1723, 40 acres of land at Oyster river, given her in the last will and testament of David Kincaid,[1] deceased, commonly called by the name of *Camsoe*. It is also mentioned in the Durham records, Jan. 29, 1733-4, when a road was laid out on the north side of the mast path, "beginning at a place called *Camsey*, at the S. W. corner of Mr. Robert Tomson's fence," and extending to Willey's way in Newtown, and by that way to the head of the town.

This land lies along the banks of Oyster river, on the north side of the mast road, on the confines of Lee and Durham. It no longer bears the name of Camsoe; but a spring thereon, remarkable for the purity of its water, is still known as "*Camsie spring*." A popular tradition attributes this name to an Indian who is said to have frequented this spring in early times. The name, however, does not appear till after the land was purchased by David Kincaid. A similar name is found in Scotland, whence the Kincaids are said to have sprung. Scott, in his "Legend of Montrose," sings of the fishermen, who,

"On St. Bridget's morn,
Drew nets on Campsie side."

Claverhouse's black book in "Old Mortality" mentions "a conventicle among the *Campsie hills*." Alexander Smith also speaks of the Campsie hills, and quotes the old song:

"The Campsie Duke's a-riding, a-riding, a-riding."

And the Earl of Huntingdon, in the "Fortunes of Nigel," longs to "hear the Tay once more flinging himself over the *Campsie Linn*."

CANAAN. This name is given to a district in Barrington, above the Two-Mile Streak. It is mentioned on Holland's map of 1784.

CANNEY'S BRIDGE. Mentioned in the Madbury records of 1794, when Moses Canney furnished plank for the repair of this bridge. It is on the Mallego river, in the upper part of Madbury.

CANNEY'S BROOK. This brook rises in the swampy lands in the upper part of Dover Neck, and is fed by *Canney's spring*, an abundant, never-failing source of excellent water on the old Canney land, in the rear of Mr. S. R. Horne's house. The brook crosses the so-called "Middle

---

[1] This was the "David Kinked," who, according to the Rev. John Pike's journal, was attacked Sept. 8, 1708, by three Indians at his house "some considerable distance from Woodman's garrison," but "thro Mercy" he and his lad made their escape. He died in February, 1722-3, but his son lived to go to the siege at Louisbourg. *Kincaid's Brook* is mentioned in the Durham records of 1765. The name is usually pronounced *Kink-et*, and is sometimes found so written.

road" a little below the house, and further down is joined by *Varney's brook* on the land of Mr. Wm. P. Tuttle. At the head of tide water it becomes *Little John's creek.*

It is related of Thomas Canney, a sea captain of the last century, that, drinking one day at his ancestral spring, he fell in, and came near being drowned. "A pretty story it would have been for the newspapers," he exclaimed when rescued, "that Capt. Canney, after sailing all around the world, only came home to get drowned in Tom Canney's spring!" This Capt. Canney, an esteemed member of the Society of Friends, died May 16, 1805, aged 95.

CANNEY'S CREEK or COVE, otherwise KENNEY'S.[1] This is an inlet from the Pascataqua river, on the eastern shore of Newington, and one of the bounds of ancient Dover. It derived its name from Thomas Canney, or Canning, of the Dover Combination of 1640, who, as early as 1652, had a grant of land on the upper side of this creek, which was afterwards acquired by James Rawlins. It is mentioned in 1657, when the lower bounds of Dover were defined as running "from *Kenney's creek* to Hogsty Cove, with all the marsh from that place round about the bay up to Cotterill's Delight, with four hundred acres of upland adjoining." The lower boundary of Dover, as recorded in 1701, ran from the middle of Quamphegan falls down the river to Hilton's Point; thence to *Kenney's creek*, and thence in a direct line to Hogsty Cove, and from this cove to the mouth of Lamprey river.

A tract of 240 acres was laid out to Capt. Bryan Pendleton next to James Rawlins, Dec. 5, 1661, beginning at *Kenney's Cove*, and running down by the river 80 rods to pyne cove, etc. (See *Pine Cove*.) James Rawlins, Aug. 25, 1662, mortgaged to Bryan Pendleton 100 acres of land " lying in the long reach, from *Canney's cove* upward nyntie od pole by ye water side, and so up into the woods, together with the land in tillage, with ye corn upon it, and his then dwelling house, with two cows." This mortgage seems to have been redeemed, for James Rawlins sold the Canney land to Matthew Nelson Sept. 12, 1679. Nelson sold it to George Huntress. "George Huntris," in his will of June 8, 1715, gives his sons, Samuel and John, his farm where they then dwelt, lying by the side of the Long Reach, part of which he bought of Matthew Nelson, part of John Pickering, and part of Wm. Vaughan, the whole containing 150 acres, part of which lay "in the township of Portsmouth, and part in Newington, which was Dover."[2]

---

[1] Canney's Creek is called *King's creek* in the Mass. records May 22, 1656. (See *N. H. Prov. Pap.*, I : 222.) The latter name may have been given it by the settlers at Strawbery Bank, from Richard King, who, as early as 1649, owned *Clampering island*, now *Leach's*, further down the river.

[2] The Pickering land, above mentioned, was, in part, a tract of 35 acres conveyed to John Pickering, Jr., by Benjamin Rawlins Sept. 13, 1689, bounded by ye land formerly bought by Matthew Nelson, beginning at ye river side, by ye edge of ye bank, and running along Nelson's land 129 rods, then north 43 rods, with the same breadth down straight to the river, and so to the first bound, keeping said breadth of river at the other end : and, in part, a grant of six acres from the town of Dover to John Pickering Ap. 16, 1694, and laid out to Geo. Huntress, Sr., June 16, 1699. For the Vaughan land, see *the Gore*.

Samuel and Jonathan Huntress, Ap. 3, 1758, made a division of their farm of 71 acres, held in common, bounded north by the land of Saml Rawlins' heirs, east by the Pascataqua river, south by the land of Samuel Brown of Salem, and westerly by the road leading to Portsmouth. With the record of this division, in the County Registry, is a plan of said farm, including Kenney's creek or cove. Jonathan's portion extended to the mouth of this cove. Samuel's part was above, " with the right of a road two roads wide to a watering place near *Kenny's cove.*" Samuel Huntress died shortly after this division was made, and was buried near the " Upper Huntress," on land now owned by Miss Mary Huntress. His gravestone bears the following inscription: " Here lies the body of Samuel Huntress, died April 28, in the y^r 1758, aged 71 y^s.."

The above-mentioned Huntress land, as shown, extended south to the land of Samuel Browne of Salem. And Jonathan Huntress, in the conveyances of his portion to Gideon Walker at a later day, describes it as bounded south by Wm. Browne of Salem. The Brown land was the old Vaughan land, originally granted to Brian Pendleton, extending from Kenney's creek to Pine cove. It was acquired by Wm. King of Salem, son of Mary (Vaughan) King, who conveyed it to Samuel Brown Ap. 20, 1738. The deed describes it as bounded north by the Huntress land. This land, amounting to 400 acres, extended into the pitch-pine plains of Newington. It was conveyed by Wm. Browne of Salem to James Stoodly Feb. 21, 1770. Wm. Stoodly, son of James, sold this land to Nathaniel Folsom, March 26, 1790, and confirmed the sale by another deed of Aug. 7, 1792, after which it became known as the *Folsom farm.* Over 54 acres of this farm were afterwards acquired by the Frink brothers, who sold this tract to Winthrop Pickering May 12, 1856. The deed describes it as bounded north by the land of Amos Dow (previously Walker's or the Huntress land) and extending south along the river to land formerly owned by Samuel Hill, deceased. Winthrop Pickering conveyed this land to Stephen Paul, Ap. 29, 1862. Whence it is evident that the Kenney or Canney's creek of early times, which in part separated the Huntress land from the Pendleton land—afterwards Browne's, then Stoodly's, and then Folsom's land—was the one now known as *Paul's creek.* It has been obstructed and greatly disfigured by the railway, but its former dimensions can still be traced.

CANNEY'S ISLAND, otherwise KENNEY'S. This island is mentioned Ap. 23, 1743, when John and Prudence Johnson of Durham conveyed to Samuel Weeks two acres of salt marsh in Greenland, bounded on the S. E. side by *Wille's creek,* on the S. W. side by *Kenes creek,* and on the N. W. by an island called *Kenies Island.* Samuel Weeks, in his will of Sept. 15, 1745, gives his son Matthias " the island lying by the Great Bay called *Kenney's island.*" This island is about half a mile above Winnicot river, and is now owned by Mr. J. Clement Weeks. It is a finely wooded upland of 20 acres on the shore of Great Bay, between Canney's creek and Willey's creek, which at high tide surround it with water. It is now merely called "*the island*" without any prefix. Notwithstanding its old name, this island originally formed part of a grant to Thomas Willey, which was adjacent to that of Thomas Canney. Leonard Weeks conveyed to his son Samuel, Ap. 23, 1706, "all the mash [marsh] and *Island of upland*" which he bought of Thomas Willey. (See *Willey's Spring*.)

CANNEY'S MARSH and CREEK, otherwise KENNEY'S. Canney's marsh is on the Greenland shore of the Great Bay, adjacent to *Canney's creek*, and now forms part of the Weeks land. It is so named from Thomas Canney of Dover, who, before 1651, had a grant of nine acres of marsh on the S. W. side of the Great Bay, "bounded on the south running into ye marsh of *George Webb's creek*, and ye whole marsh in tire till you come out of ye Great Bay at ye north end upon a cove, a neck of land all on ye S. E. side between Geo. Webbes and that. More, two small spots lying by the water side, near to the above marsh, bounded upon ye south west side of ye Great Bay." Thomas and Grace Kenney of Dover, May 4, 1696, conveyed to Leonard Weeks of Greenland "three acres of meadow on the Great Bay, given by Ould Thomas Kenny to his son Thomas, deceased, as appears by a deed to his son Joseph." Leonard Weeks conveyed to his son Joseph, Ap. 3, 1706, one acre and a half of salt marsh, lying westward of *Canney's creek*, so called. And, Ap. 23, 1706, he conveyed to his son Samuel Weeks "*the marsh* I bought *that was Cannyes*, that lyeth next to Wm. ffurber's marsh, excepting the *cove* and flatts belonging to it, which I have given to my son Jonathan Weeks, and one acre and a half of salt marsh and flatts that I have given to my son Joseph, lying by the westward side of *Cannies Crike.*" This creek is again mentioned Ap. 23, 1743, when John and Prudence Johnson conveyed to Samuel Weeks two acres of salt marsh bounded "on the southwest side on *Kenes creek.*"

CANNEY'S POINT, otherwise KENNEY'S. Mentioned in Wm. Week's will of June 13, 1777, in which he gives his son Joshua a piece of land in Greenland, on *Kenney's Point*, adjoining the river or Bay, and on the S. E. side of a piece of salt marsh he bought of John Allen.

CAPTAIN'S HILL. This is a little hill on the old road formerly called Low street, in the lower part of Dover Neck. It is said to have derived its name from Capt. Thomas Wiggin, but no authority is given for this statement.

CARD'S COVE. This name is now given to Pomeroy's cove, from Capt. Thomas Card, who lived on the north side. He died about twenty years ago at the advanced age of 100 years and 22 days. Card's cove is on the east side of Dover neck, nearly half a mile above Dover Point. It is crossed at the west end by the Portsmouth & Dover railway.

CARTER'S BROOK. This brook is often mentioned in the early records as "the freshett that goeth into Broad Cove," and "the creek in Broad Cove." (See *Broad Cove Freshet*.) It is mentioned June 13, 1839, when Cyrus Frink conveyed to Wallis Lane a tract of land in Newington, beginning at Rocky Point, at

Landmarks in Ancient Dover. 39

Carter's brook, so called, thence running west to a stake in the marsh 3 rods N. W. of the site of the *old mill* formerly owned by John Coleman, and along said creek to a marked rock, then S. to a rock beside the road from Pascataqua bridge to Portsmouth, thence E. by said road to *Carter's Lane*, then N. to the first bound. This land was conveyed March 17, 1842, to Mr. F. W. de Rochemont, who sold it to Mrs. Mary Orr of Boston, March 21, 1847. Hence the name of *Orr's brook* and *De Rochemont's brook*, by which it is sometimes called.

CARTER'S LANE. This is an old road in Newington, leading to Rocky Pt., laid out early in the last century. Geo. Walton conveyed to Samuel and John Shackford, Feb. 27, 1718-19, ten acres of land (part of fifty acres bought of Henry Langster) "running down between the freshet and *the lane* that goes to Rocky Poynt." Carter's Lane is now the western boundary of Mr. Valentine M. Coleman's farm. It is one's ideal of a rural lane, being left almost entirely to nature—the pathway grassy from present disuse, shady with overhanging trees, and bordered with a tangle of rose-bushes, vines, and shrubs, and its lower extremity washed by the ebb and flow of the tide around the great flat ledge called *Carter's Rocks*.

CARTER'S MARSH. This marsh is mentioned in 1658. (See *Robert's Creek*.) It is on the Greenland shore, where Richard Cater or Carter had a grant, afterwards conveyed to Thomas Packer. (See *Hall's Marsh*.)

CARTER'S ROCKS. These rocks are on the Newington shore of Broad Cove, a little below *Carter's brook*. At high tide they are separated from the shore, but at other times form a projection from the main land that is commonly called *Rocky Point*. Here was once a landing-place, to which led the old road now called *Carter's Lane*. The name is derived from one of the oldest families in Newington. Richard Carter was living near Pine Pt. before 1648. Among his descendants were John and Richard Carter, who owned land in the vicinity of Broad Cove in 1719. (See *Broad Cove*.)

There is a ledge off Penhale Point, on the Cornish coast of England, called *Carter's Rock*, from people of that name living on the neighboring shore.

CART-WAY. This name was given as early as 1648 to the road that led from Cochecho Falls to the Great Cochecho marsh, north of the "Great hill." It is now the Garrison Hill road. Several other cart-ways in early times are mentioned, one of which led from Tolend falls into Cochecho Log Swamp, and another across Bunker's Neck, "for transporting timber," mentioned as early as 1653.

CAULLEY'S MARSH. This marsh is in the Durham Point district, and still retains its ancient name. Matthew Giles's land at *Colles marsh* is mentioned in 1658. Thirty acres were granted "Mr. Thomas Edgerlie, Sen[r].," March 19, 1693-4, "between *Collies marsh* and the *hornes*." John Ambler, Jan. 31, 1725-6, conveyed to "Zebulon Trickey of Kitery, Co. York, province of Mass. Bay," seven or eight acres "on y[e] high way y[t] goes from *team hill* to *Collyes marsh*."

Col. James Davis, in his will of Oct. 18, 1748, gives his son Daniel 17 acres granted him in the common land in Durham, adjoining *Caulley's marsh*. And the land of Francis Footman " at a place called *Caulley's marsh* " is mentioned in the county records of 1752. A portion of Caulley's marsh that formed part of the estate of Robert Mathes, is now owned by Mr. John Meader.

No Caulleys appear in the early rate-lists of Dover. The name may be a corruption of Crawley. Thomas Crawley was brought before the Dover authorities July 14, 1657, for three offences, viz :—for living idly in his calling, for stirring up strife between neighbors, and for drinking with Matthew —— [perhaps Matthew Giles] 14 pints of wine at one time at the house of John Webster. For the last offence he was fined, and for the two others admonished and required to pay the fees. This did not subdue him, however. A suit was brought against him June 26, 1660, by Thomas Canney for slandering his daughter Phebe, then under age, after which Thomas Crawley disappears from the Dover records.

CEDAR POINT. This point is so called the 5th, 5 mo., 1652, in the grant of Goat Island to Wm. Pomfrett. It is now owned by Mrs. Alley. It is on the upper shore of the Pascataqua, below the mouth of Oyster river, and at the southwest side of Royall's cove. It is a bound of the three townships of Dover, Durham, and Madbury. When the bounds between Dover and Madbury were perambulated Jan. 19, 1793, the line began " at *Cedar point*, so called, by the river," then ran north 40 deg., or thereabouts, to the southwest corner of Joseph Jenkins' house, thence north 34½ deg. W. to a beech tree on Stephen Hanson's land, on the north side of the road to Barrington, thence on the same point about 6 ft. from the corner of Dr. Ezra Green's pasture, and thence north 34½ deg. W. to the Barrington line.

When the line between Durham and Madbury was perambulated Jan. 9, 1802, it began at " a long rock on *Cedar Pt.*, so called, on the west side of the back river," marked M. on the north, and D. on the south ; thence ran about north 55°, 30' west, to a red oak on the north side of the creek, on land lately belonging to the heirs of Thomas Wallingford, deceased, thence on the same course to the middle of *Johnson's creek bridge*, thence N. by E. to, and across, Beech hill, and thence to the north-east corner of the town of Lee.

CEDAR SWAMP. This swamp, which is partly in Greenland, and partly in Portsmouth, did not form part of ancient Dover, but is mentioned in connection with its inhabitants. Nathaniel Huggins of Greenland, Jan. 2, 1723–4, conveyed to his son Nathaniel two acres of fresh marsh lying by yᵉ side of Samˡ Neal's meadow, joining to yᵉ *Cedar swamp*. Thomas Pickering of Newington, in his will of Ap. 4, 1782, gives his son William " my *cedar swamp* in Portsmouth, bought of John Holmes."

CHAMPERNOWNE'S CREEK. Mentioned April 15, 1664, when Samuel Haines had 80 acres of his " divident land " laid out to him adjoining Francis Drake's, " neere *Capt. Champernoune's creek*," thence running west 72 rods to the cartway at the fence between "Gudman Haynes and Walter Neale." (*Portsmouth Records.*) This creek rises in the Great Swamp, flows through Greenland, and empties into the Great Bay east of Packer's Point, but the name is no longer in use. It is now called *Packer's creek*, from Thomas Packer who acquired part of the Champernowne lands, and sometimes *Peirce's creek*, from Col. J. W. Peirce, who bought part of the Packer estate.

CHANNELL'S ISLANDS. (See *Chesley's Islands.*)

CHARLES'S POINT. Mentioned, apparently about 1654, when Jonas Binn or Bine had the grant of an island of two acres, or thereabouts, next Charles Adams' lot, at ye entrance into Little Bay, over against a point called by the name of *Charles's point*. The only islands at the entrance into Little Bay are Ambler's islands, the largest of which does not contain more than one acre. Goat island, below, has about three acres, but was already granted to Wm. Pomfrett in 1652. Charles's Point is supposed to have been named from said Charles Adams, but the land where his garrison stood was within the mouth of Oyster river, not at the point, which was owned by Jonas Binn or Bine. (See *Jonas Point.*) The only other land owned by Charles Adams near the river was at Branson's creek, near the mouth of the Great Bay.

CHERRY HILL. This name is given to the homestead of the late Lorenzo Stackpole in Rollinsford, from the profusion of wild cherry trees in the vicinity. Cherry is also used, in part, for the interior wood-work of the house, which was built in the early part of this century by the Philpot family.

CHESLEY'S HILL. This hill is mentioned in the Durham records. It is at the west end of Durham village, near the railroad station. It derived its name from the old Chesley residence at the top, where lived five or six generations of this name. The Chesley lands adjoining, originally a part of Valentine Hill's Five-Hundred-Acre grant, extended south as far as Chesley's mill on Oyster river. The house and grounds, now enclosed between the old Mast road and the turnpike road, have recently been acquired by the Agricultural College. There is another *Chesley's Hill* at Lubberland. (See *Great Hill.*)

CHESLEY'S ISLANDS. These islands, two in number, are in Great Bay, off that part of the Durham shore ceded to Newmarket in 1870. The name is derived from Joseph Chesley, who, March 26, 1707, bought of Sampson Doe all the land between John Goddard's and Richard Yorke's, and with it six acres and *two islands*, which Joseph Smith had previously sold Nicholas Doe. These islands originally belonged to Richard Yorke, who, about 1652, had a grant of seven acres of marsh in the Great Bay, butting upon *two small islands*. John York, Oct. 14, 1680, conveyed to Roger Rose 80 acres of land, granted said York's father, with all meadows, flats, creek, thatch-bed, *islands*, and *islets*, belonging to said grant. Roger Rose conveyed this land to John Smith July 17, 1705.

Merrill's *Gazetteer* of New Hampshire, in 1817, mentions *Chesley's island* as "the south corner boundary of Durham at the west." When the bounds were perambulated in 1805, the line on this shore ran from the mouth of Goddard's creek to "*Chesley's little island.*" "*Chesley's great island*" is spoken of in a deed of May 18, 1743. These islands are now called *Channell's islands,* from the present owner.

CHESLEY'S MILL. See *Oyster River Falls.*

CHESLEY'S PONDS. These ponds are in the lower part of Barrington. "*Chesley's upper pond*" and "*Chesley's lower pond*" are on the Barrington map of 1805. They are now known as *Bodge's* and *Swayne's ponds.* The latter is the source of the Bellamy river. These ponds were formerly separated by a narrow isthmus, but when Sawyer's reservoir dam was built at the outlet of Swayne's pond it caused an overflow which converted them into one pond.

CHURCH'S BROOK. Mentioned Dec. 23, 1712, when a 20 acre grant to Thomas Hanson, Sr., in Ash Swamp, was laid out to Nathaniel Hanson, beginning near the S. W. corner of Robert Evans' three score acres (acquired by John Hanson in 1713), thence running N. 80 rods to a beech tree, then W. 10 rods to a birch near *Church's brook.* This brook crosses the Dover road to Madbury near Mr. O. K. Hayes's, and empties into the Bellamy. John Church and wife Mary, March 23, 1736-7, conveyed to Wm. Twombly 30 acres of land granted to John Church, Sr., deceased, and laid out in Ash Swamp in 1696, but, found to intrench on another grant, 24 acres were removed to "a place called Barbadoes" May 8, 1721, beginning at the west end of Pomfret Whitehouse's land, sold to Nathaniel Hanson, thence running N. W. 40 rods to "Bellimon's bank freshet," then N. N. E. 96 rods by the river, then E. S. E. 40 rods to a lot laid out to Thomas Hanson, deceased.

John Church, Sr., was killed by the Indians May 7, 1696. His son John, who seems to have married Mercy Hanson, was also killed by the Indians in 1711.

CLAM BROOK. This name is given to one of the two brooks that afford an outlet to Meader's swamp in South Lee, near the site of French's garrison. These brooks unite and empty into Lamprey river below Wadleigh's falls.

CLARK'S BROOK. This brook rises near the source of Wednesday brook, in the Demeritt pasture on the west side of Wednesday Hill, and empties into Lamprey river near Dame's mill, at the head of Lee Hook. Another Clark's brook rises in Rochester, and empties into Blackwater brook in the upper part of Dover.

CLARK'S FERRY. This ferry ran across the Cochecho river, above the mouth of Fresh creek. It is mentioned Feb. 26, 1730-31, when a road was ordered to be laid out thereto, "along by Ephraim Tebbetts's." This is doubtless the road to *Perkins' landing,* at the upper side of Bantom's Point, mentioned on Whitehouse's map of Dover. The name was no doubt derived from Elisha Clark, who conveyed to his daughter Katharine James, May 4, 1739, twelve acres of land, "beginning at the road running by John Bampton's down to a landing-place on Cochecho river." On one side it extended to Samuel Tibbet's fence. (See *Bantom's Point.*)

Clark's Plains. These plains, once owned by Abraham Clark, are south-east of Pudding hill, on the line between Dover and Madbury. They were formerly somewhat noted for horse-races.

Clay Point. Mentioned the 4th, 10 mo., 1656, when three acres of upland on the east side of Dover Neck, "at a poynte called *Clay poynt*," were laid out to Joseph Twamley (Twombley), and again Jan. 5, 1669, when Jedediah Andrews of Salisbury, Mass., conveyed to the Rev. John Reyner three acres of land, 22 poles square, at *Clay Point*, being the same land given Ralph Twamley as a house lot. This land was near said Andrews' house lot, also conveyed to John Reyner; and between the house of Thomas Roberts and land previously owned by John Reyner. The name of Clay Point has not been perpetuated, but it was no doubt near the Roberts land on the east side of Dover Neck.

Cleft Cove, otherwise Cliff. This cove is on the Lubberland shore, between Crummit's creek and Pinder's Point, but the name is no longer retained. It is mentioned July 1, 1669, when Thomas Roberts, Sr., conveyed to John York a tract of land " beginning at ye little poynt in *Cliff cove*, adjoining Thomas Morries, and so over the neck to a pine tree by ye path going to Lubberland." And again May 16, 1681, in a deed from John York to John Pinder. (See *Pinder's Point*.) Benjamin and Joseph Pinder conveyed to Dependence Bickford of Newington, July 2, 1763, their farm in Durham where they then lived, beginning at *Cleft cove*, so called, and running northerly by the land of John Durgin, westerly by Ebenezer Smith's, southerly by Benjn Colbroth's to the Great Bay, and thence by the bay to the first bound.

Clement's Brook. This name is given to the upper part of Twombley's brook in Rollinsford, that flows through the old Clement land. Ralph Twombley's grant next "*Mr. Clement's*" (no doubt Job Clement) is mentioned in 1725. (See *Twombley's Brook*.)

Clement's Point. Whitehouse's map of Dover in 1834 gives this name to the point at the mouth of Back river, on the west side. It is also so called in Sanford & Evert's Atlas of Strafford Co. The Clement land in the lower part of the Back River district, adjoining the lands of Samuel Emerson and Thomas Layton, is repeatedly mentioned in the early records. Job Clement had one of the twenty acre lots in that vicinity in 1652. He married Joanna, widow of Thomas Layton, July 16, 1673. March 15, 1704, he conveyed 30 acres on the west side of Back river to John Laiton. The inventory of Job Clement's estate Dec. 1, 1716, mentions 16 acres of pasture and meadow land "on the *back cove point*, on ye west side of ye Back river." This land was given his wife during her lifetime.

Cochecho. This name was for a long time given to the settlement around the lowest falls in the Cochecho river, in order to distinguish it from the settlement on Dover Neck. James Ordway testified in 1705 that sixty years previous, Major Waldron with some others began *the plantation called Cochecho*, and two or three years later built a saw-mill and corn-mill there. (Dr. Quint's ed. of Pike's *Journal*, p. 10, foot-note.) "Peter Coffin of *Cochecha, in the township of Dover*," is mentioned Ap. 1, 1673. (See *Muchadoe*.) "Lands and tenements in *Cochecho, Dover*," are mentioned Oct. 8, 1683. (*N. H. Prov. Pap.*, 1: 468.) "The road which leads to *Cochecha*" is mentioned in the will of Judge John Tuttle, Dec. 28, 1717. "Samuel Heard of *Cochecho, in the township of Dover*," Aug. 13, 1731, conveyed to Richard Rookes of "the parish of Sumersworth," schoolmaster, 30 acres of upland and swamp "in ye parish of Cochecho afores^d," on the S. E. side of the road from Salmon falls to the Cochecho boom. Thomas Roberts and Elizabeth conveyed to Benjamin Roberts, Jan. 3, 1734–5, 30 acres of land, bounded east by " ye highway y^t runs up to *Cochecho, a place in Dover*, so called." "The meeting-house at *Cochecho in Dover*" is mentioned May 22. 1754 (*N. H. Town Pap.* XI: 524). "Thomas Westbrook Waldron's mills at *Cochecho*, below ye lower falls," are mentioned Jan. 22, 1770. (*Ibid.*, p. 534.)

The Cochecho settlement is now the city proper of Dover.

COCHECHO RIVER and FALLS. This river rises among the ponds of New Durham and Middleton, and empties into the Newichawannock at Cochecho Point. The word Cochecho signifies, according to Dr. Quint, "the rapid foaming water." It was the Indian name of the falls in Dover city, but the early settlers extended it to the whole stream, and gave it to the settlement that grew up around these falls. It is now generally, but incorrectly, written *Cocheco*—the form adopted by the Cocheco Manufacturing Company, said to be owing to the error of a clerk of the N. H. legislature when that company was incorporated. The name of "freshet" was often given to that part of the river above the head of tide-water. John Waldron and Mary, Jan. 2, 1721, conveyed to John Horn 60 acres of land, running S. W. by John Hilton's land to *Cochecho river freshet*, and bounded on the N. W. by Thomas Downs' 50 acres.

COCHECHO FALLS. The *first falls*, reckoning from the mouth of the river—the "Cochecho falls" *par excellence*—are in the heart of Dover city, and now owned by the Cocheco Manufacturing Company. A mill privilege here was granted the 1st, 6 mo., 1642, to Richard Waldron, who built a mill on the north side. Another mill privilege on the south side was granted him in 1648.[1] These rights were inherited by his son, Col. Richard Waldron, in 1689. The latter bequeathed his rights to his son Richard Waldron in 1730. In 1753 they fell to Thomas Westbrook Waldron and his brother George. The former bought his brother's part and became sole owner. By his will, proved in 1785, they fell to Daniel Waldron. They were acquired, Jan. 30, 1820, by the Strafford Bank, the directors of which conveyed them, Ap. 23, 1821, to Wm. Payne of Boston, who represented the Dover Manufacturing Co.

The *Second falls*, called the *Tole End* or *Tolend falls*, and otherwise *Whitch-*

---

[1] Pike's *Journal* says, Jan. 3, 1682–3: "Col. Waldron's mills burnt down in a very Rainey night."

er's or *Whittier's falls*, were granted to Thomas Wiggin and Edward Starbuck the 4th, 5 mo., 1650. The latter, July 29, 1652, conveyed his right in the "*Cochecho upper falls*," with all privileges of water and timber, to Peter Coffin, who had married his daughter Abigail. Sarah Wiggin of Quamscott in the township of Exeter, widow, and Thomas her son, conveyed to Richard Waldron of Cochecho one full half of the *second falls* of Cochecho in the township of Dover, with half of the timber granted to Capt. Thomas Wiggin (grandfather of the above Thomas) the 5th, 10 mo., 1652.

Richard Waldron, the 6th, 10 mo., 1652, was authorized to build a sawmill on the north side of the second falls, provided it did not entrench on any former grant.

"The *Second fall* of the River of Cochecha, commonly called or known by the name of *Tole End fall*," is mentioned March 3, 1702. Richard Waldron of Portsmouth having conveyed to James Chesley, Joseph Hanson, and John Hayes, the hundred-acre grant to Thomas Wiggin in 1650, on the north side of the Cochecho, near the *second falls*, this tract was divided among them July 27, 1734. Twenty-six acres were assigned to John Hayes at the S. E. corner, adjoining the river, near the *Tolend mills*. Twenty acres fell to Joseph Hanson in the S. W. corner, adjoining the river, " at y*e* *Eleware wading-place*." This was, of course, the *Lower Eelweir*. James Chesley had the remaining 54 acres. This Eelweir above Tolend falls is again mentioned Dec. 2, 1734, when Ezra Kimball conveyed to Joseph Hanson one acre and three quarters of land adjoining the Cochecho river on the north side, " at a place call*d* y*e Ealware falls*," and also joining to y*e* S. W. corner of y*e* 100 acres granted Thomas Wiggin by the town of Dover, beginning at a small oak in a little valley on the line between said Kimball and Hanson, thence running W. to the river, by a small hemlock between y*e cove* and y*e island*, thence down the river, including said island, to the first bound.

The name of " *Whittier's mill* " was derived from Obadiah Whittier, who is called a "cloathyer" March 28, 1797, when William Brown and Abigail conveyed to him 9 acres, 16 sq. rods, bounded by "the highway in Dover called Scatuate" (Scatterwit), and by the land of the widow Conner, and that in possession of Thomas Hanson. Obadiah was succeeded by his son Moses, who had a clothing-mill, carded wool, and manufactured homespun cloth. This was on the easterly side of the river. On the opposite shore was Ephraim Ham's grist-mill. "The mills at Tolend, known by the name of *Whittier's mills*," were burned down Jan. 7, 1818. (*Dover Sun* of 1818.) Clough's gristmill is now at Tolend falls.

The *third falls* are mentioned Ap. 6, 1702, when Richard Waldron had a grant of " three score acres of land on the north side of the Cochecho river, adjoining to the *third falls*, commonly called *Hayes's falls*, or as near adjacent thereunto as it can be found in common." In 1704 he had a grant of the falls, "commonly called *haises fall*," with due regard to the falls below. Richard Waldron conveyed the above grant of 60 acres to Daniel Horn, July 15, 1729, when *Hayes's falls* are again mentioned. Joseph Twombley, Jr., conveyed to Ezra Kimball, June 14, 1733, sixty acres of land, part of a hundred-acre grant to Peter Coffin, adjoining the Cochecho river on the north side, a little above the *third falls*. Nehemiah Kimball conveyed to his brother Ezra, Dec. 2, 1734, one half of his right in "a certain pair of falls w^h unto my land doth joyne, known as *Hayes' falls*." Hence the name of *Kimball's falls* and *mill*, at one time given to the dam and mill at this place.

The third falls are now generally called *Pike's falls*, from Wm. H. Pike, who, in company with Thomas J. Dearborn, once had a saw and planing mill here. Clarissa Kimball conveyed to them, April 4, 1867, five acres of land on the northerly side of the Cochecho river, with the saw mill, mill privilege, and water power on, and pertaining to, said land, but subject to an indenture of Nov. 4, 1861, between Ezra and Clarissa Kimball on one side, and the Cocheco Manufacturing Co. on the other, allowing only a certain height to the dam. Pike's mill was afterwards sold to that Company, but was burned down soon after. The privilege remains unused.

The *fourth falls*, once known as *Kimball's falls*, are now generally called the *Upper Factory falls*, from the cotton factory, now gone, built here in 1815 by the Dover Cotton Factory Co. This Company was incorporated Dec. 15, 1812, and bought 5 acres, 8 sq. rods of land at *Kimball's falls* on the east side, from Ezra, Jonathan, and other Kimballs, Ap. 25, 1814. On this land the upper factory was built. Other Kimball land was acquired in 1818, when Wm. Kimball, Ap. 23, conveyed to Williams and Wendell 93 acres of land on the southerly side of the " Scatawit road," formerly the homestead of John Kimball. This was at the westerly side of Nathaniel Ham's homestead farm, and extended up to Joseph Waldron's land. It included an island near the bank of the river.

The "*Horne dam*," now gone, is mentioned in 1820, as a little above the Upper Factory falls, at the lower end of the Kimball farm. This is apparently the fall mentioned Dec. 14, 1820, when John Young conveyed to John Williams and Isaac Wendell (for the Dover Cotton Factory) one acre of land "westerly of the next falls or cataract" above said Cotton Factory, including the privilege on said falls. This fall disappeared when the Upper Factory dam was raised.

The *fifth falls*, properly *Waldron's falls*, but now generally called *Watson's Falls*, are the first falls below the mouth of Reyner's brook. Here once stood a "day" sawmill of which the Watsons were the chief owners. The privilege, on the east side, however, belonged to Joseph Waldron, who had a grist-mill here. These mills are mentioned Feb. 1, 1819, when Winthrop Watson and Winthrop Watson, Jr., conveyed to Moses Whittier, clothier, one acre of land, and the mill privilege attached thereto, beginning by the Cochecho river, on the southerly side, at a place called *Waldron's* and *Watson's mills*, a little westerly of a point of rocks westerly of the bridge, and running south 35 deg. E. 24 rods, including all the land between said line and said river, with all their right in the dam halfway over the river, and a right to pass and re-pass across their land and Aaron Watson's land from Tolend road, with carts, teams, and all things necessary for improving said privilege, building mills, etc.

The Dover Cotton Factory Co. acquired, Dec. 15, 1821, one acre of land at a place called *Waldron's* and *Watson's falls*, with the privilege in the dam half way across the river, being the land and mill privilege Winthrop Watson and Winthrop Watson, Jr., conveyed to Moses Whittier Feb. 1, 1819; excepting, however, and reserving to said Whittier the privilege of drawing such a quantity of water from the pond as he might have occasion for in fulling cloth or skins. This fulling-mill on the westerly side of the river is mentioned on Whitehouse's map of 1834. Whittier moved this mill down the river about 1842. John Trickey afterwards acquired the mills on the east side of these falls, which he demolished about 1853. There is no mill here now, and the whole water power is owned by the Cocheco Manufacturing Co.

The *sixth falls*, called *Hussey's falls* and the *Upper Eel-Weir falls*, are below the mouth of Blackwater brook. They are mentioned July 31, 1721, when 60 acres were laid out to Stephen Field, on the N. W. side of Long hill, granted to his father Zachariah in 1694, on the west side of the Cochecho river, "above y^e *Ealeware*," beginning at a red oak tree, one of the bounds of the land of John Winget, deceased. (See *Sandy Log Hill*.)

The name of *Hussey's falls* was derived from Timothy Hussey and his nephew Elijah, who once owned this water privilege and the adjoining land. No mention is made of any mill here. Timothy Hussey and Elizabeth, Dec. 11, 1821, conveyed to Isaac Wendell, for the Dover Cotton Factory, one acre of land " at a place called *Eelware falls*," together with the falls. This was on the easterly side of the river. Elijah Hussey and Jane, that same day, conveyed to said Wendell one acre on the west side of the falls, including all the water privilege adjoining said lot. A reservoir dam was built here by the Cotton Factory soon after this purchase.

Above the Dover line there are two falls in the Cochecho, below Gonic. The lower one, of eight feet, is not used. At the upper one, a fall of 15 ft., is a saw-mill. At Gonic is a fall of 19½ ft., 120 horse power, used by the Gonic Manufacturing Co. The next falls are in the city proper of Rochester, where there are three privileges. At the lowest is a saw- and grist mill. The next one supplies the mills of the Norway Plains Manufacturing Co., which has another mill at the dam still further up. This Company controls the reservoirs in New Durham and Middleton.

COCHECHO BRIDGE. Mentioned July 10, 1758, when Joseph Hanson conveyed to the deacons of the Congregational church a lot for their meeting-house, a quarter of an acre in extent, on the northwesterly side of ye main road from *Dover Neck* to *Cochecha bridge*, and on ye northeasterly side of ye road that leads from yᵉ aforesᵈ road to Littleworth. The town of Dover voted Jan. 22, 1770, that a *new bridge* be built " over the *upper ware,* so called, next below Capt. Thoˢ Wᵏ. Waldron's mills at *Cochecho,* below yᵉ lower falls." (*N. H. Town Pap.* XI : 534.) "The *two new bridges* lately built over Quochechaw River," are mentioned Jan. 11, 1771. (*Ibid.,* 541.)

COCHECHO LANDING. The landing-place on the Cochecho river, below the lowest falls, are so called Jan. 11, 1771, in a plan of the two bridges across the river, above it. It is now called *Dover Landing.* The adjacent school-district was called the "*Landing-District,*" by a vote of the school meeting, Ap. 7, 1806.

COCHECHO LOG SWAMP. This swamp was between the Cochecho river and Bellamy Bank freshet, and comprised *Waldron's Log Swamp,* and perhaps *Nock's Marsh, Ash Swamp,* etc. Fifty acres were laid out to Wm. Thompson March 17, 1658-9, "*beyond Cochecho log swamp,*" bounded S. E. by land then " in possession of Thomas Nocke, and South by Bellamies Banke freshett." When this tract was conveyed by John Thompson, son of Wm., to John Tuttle, Feb. 11, 1715-16, it was said to be "*at Cochecho log swamp.*" When this land was sold to Moses Wingate by Solomon and Ebenezer Hanson, it was stated to be "*in Ash Swamp.*" And Moses Wingate, Sept. 12, 1752, bought of Nathaniel Hanson 20 acres " in *Cochecho* or *Ash swamp.*" (See *Ash Swamp.*)

Cochecho Swamp seemed to extend to Barbadoes Pond, if not to Mallego river. (See *Broad Turn* and the *Saplings.*) An " ancient cartway leading from the second [Tolend] falls into the swamp till it meets the other way that leads from *broad turn,*" is mentioned March 4, 1703-4. (*Dover Records.*)

COCHECHO MARSH. This marsh, now for the most part drained, lay at the upper side of Garrison Hill, and extended into the present town of Rollinsford. It is otherwise called the *Great Cochecho Marsh* and the *Great Fresh Marsh.* It is mentioned as early as May 2, 1642, when lots of six acres therein were granted to Anthony Emery and Stephen Tedder. Twenty lots of the same size were granted to other Dover settlers June 16, 1648. A path led to this marsh as early as 1648, called the "*cartway,*" which is the present Garrison Hill road. This marsh is mentioned June 17, 1677, when Wm. Wentworth conveyed to George Ricker " a piece of marsh and swamp-land near Cochecho, near yᵉ lower part of yᵉ marsh commonly called *Cochecho Marsh,* the lower end butting upon yᵉ northern side of yᵉ brook which doth run out of yᵉ sᵈ marsh upon a *little pond* by yᵉ sᵈ brook." The only brook that answers to this description is the Styx, which flows through the marsh in the vicinity of No-Bottom pond. Faggoty brook also once drained the neighboring marshes, now for the most part dried up.

Peter Coffin conveyed to Maturin Ricker, Dec. 26, 1682, 12 acres at the lower end of the marsh commonly called *Cochecha marsh* in Dover, bounded S. by a brook of water which issues out of said marsh, and N. E. by a small stream of water which doth empty itself into said brook. A final division of Cochecho marsh was made by a vote of the town Apr. 16, 1722.

COCHECHO POINT. This point is at the junction of the Cochecho and Newichawannock rivers. It was granted to Wm. Pomfrett the 30th, 6 mo., 1643. His grant is described as "a neck of land between the mouth of Cochecha river and Nechewanick river, with the marsh to the first narrow." (*N. H. Prov. Pap.*, 9 : 153–4.) The name of Cochecho Point seems also to have comprised the lands above Pomfrett's grant. John Roberts conveyed to Joseph Austin, July 7, 1658, all his upland "commonly called and known by the name of *Cochecho poynt* in Piscataq river." Thomas Canney, Oct. 6, 1670, conveyed to his son Joseph one undivided eighth of *Cochecho Point*, bounded by the Cochecho and Newichawannock rivers, and the Newichawannock path from Fresh creek to St. Alban's cove. Richard Waldron of Portsmouth, July 24, 1729, conveyed to Benjn Mason of Dover, one half of a neck of land in Dover, granted ye 10 mo., 5th day, 1652, to his father Capt. Richard Waldron, Wm. ffurber, Wm. Wentworth, Henry Langstar, and Thomas Kenny, being the whole neck of land from St. Alban's cove to ye head of Fresh creek, and so to *Cochecho point*, except a former grant to Wm. Pomfrett, one half of which grant, and of all privileges, belonged to Capt. Waldron.

After the township of Rollinsford was incorporated, this point was often called *Rollinsford Point*, but it has resumed its ancient name since its re-conveyance to the township of Dover.

COCHECHO POND. This pond is on the borders of Dover and Somersworth. It was originally called "the *Great pond*," but is now known as *Willand's pond*. (See *Great Pond*.) It is mentioned Ap. 4, 1757, when Nathaniel Austin conveyed to John Mackelroy 30 acres of land in Somersworth, part of a tract in the plains above *Cochecho pond*, which formerly belonged to his grandfather Thomas Austin. It is called *Cochecho Pond* on Whitehouse's map of 1834. (See *Willand's Pond*.)

COCHECHO POND BROOK. Mentioned June 10, 1736, when 20 acres of land were laid out to Thomas Pinkham "up at a place called *Cochecha Pond Brook*, about 12 rods westerly of ye brook," on the N. side of a lot formerly Joseph Astin's (Austin's). (See *Peter's Marsh Brook*.)

COFFIN'S BROOK. Dr. Quint gives this name to a brook which once ran through the old Coffin field, now traversed by Washington St. in Dover city. It crossed the lot where the Masonic Hall now stands, and emptied into the Cochecho river near the Washington St. bridge. It now runs wholly through sewers, but was once of sufficient size to run a grist-mill, which stood near the above mentioned bridge as late as 1833, when it was owned by Arlo Flagg.

COFFIN'S MILL. Mentioned June 23, 1701, when 30 acres were granted to Daniel Messerve "between *Coffin's mill* at oyster Riuer and moses davis his land." Henry Marsh had a grant of 40 acres, March 23, 1701–2, "above *Coffin's mill*, over against Moses Davis his land." The Meserve land was on the mill road in Durham, above Chesley's mill. Henry Marsh's land was between Chesley's mill and the Mast road, adjoining the north side of Oyster river. His son Hezekiah Marsh conveyed his right thereto to Jonathan Thompson Feb. 7, 1737; and his daughter Dinah Marsh quitclaimed to said Thompson March 6, 1737-8. Her deed describes this land as a tract of 40 acres granted her father, Henry Marsh, deceased, laid out on the north side of Oyster river, over against ye land which was Moses Davis's, beginning at an elm tree at the river side. Where Coffin's mill stood does not appear. The only mills at that time on Oyster river, below the above lands, were Chesley's mill and those at the lowest falls. Peter Coffin, however, appears to have owned mill privileges on Lamprey river and the Pascassick within the limits of the Oyster River district.

COLE'S POND. This pond, so called in Merrill's *Gazeteer* of N. H. in 1817, is in the northeastern part of Somersworth. It is 150 rods long, and half as wide. It is called *Hurd's Pond* on Holland's map of 1784. And it is sometimes called *Lily pond*, from the profusion of lilies that grow therein. Ebenezer Cole, who married Mary, daughter of Benjn Wentworth, lived at Rocky Hills, near this pond, in the middle of the last century.

COLEMAN'S CREEK. This name is now given to a small brook that empties into Trickey's cove, Newington. It is the "little gully" mentioned in a deed from John Downing to Saml and Jno Shackford, March 5, 1713. (See Trickey's Cove.) The present name is derived from Nathaniel P. Coleman, to whom Ruel J. Bean conveyed, May 11, 1846, a tract of land adjoining Pascataqua river, formerly owned by Capt. Saml Shackford, beginning at the creek on the easterly side of Bean's land, and running southerly by the river round by Zackey's Point, so called, to the centre of the creek against Nancy Drew's land, etc. This land now belongs to Valentine M. Coleman, Esq., son of the above Nathaniel.

"*Coleman's cove*, so called, in Newington," is mentioned in the *N. H. Gazette* (Portsmouth) of Oct. 20, 1801; apparently the small cove below Dumpling cove, where James Coleman owned land at the close of the last century.

COMMON. All the land between Fresh Creek and the Cochecho, below Wm. Wentworth's and John Heard's, excepting the tract laid out to Wm. Pomfrett, was ordered the 19th, 11 mo., 1664, to be set apart as a *common* forever to the inhabitants of Cochecho. And it was voted at a public town-meeting May 31, 1675, "that all ye land ungranted above Little John's creek, on ye west side of ye way y^t goes to Belamyes bank shall lye *common* forever."

CORSEY BROOK. This brook empties into Lamprey river, between Packer's and Sullivan's falls, on the north side.

COTTERILL'S DELIGHT. This place is mentioned in May, 1653, when the inhabitants of Strawberry Bank petitioned the General Court at Boston to grant them "the necke of land beginninge in the Great Bay, at the place called *Cotterill's Delight*, soe running to the sea." This petition was "respited because of Mr. Mason's claim." (*N. H. Prov. Pap.*, 1: 208.) In the division of the Swamscott Patent (otherwise called the Hilton or Squamscot Patent), May 22, 1656, the territory assigned to Dover included " all the marsh from Hogstye Cove round about the bay up to *Cotterill's Delight*, with 400 acres of upland, as granted by the Court, bounded and laid out and possessed by the inhabitants of Dover," etc. (*N. H. Prov. Pap.*, 1 : 222–223.) This is called the *first* division of that Patent. As this division extended up the Great Bay shore to Cotterill's Delight, and the *second* division began 40 poles below Sandy Point, and extended towards Exeter, there can be no doubt as to the situation of Cotterill's Delight. It is at the upper end of the beautiful shore of Great Bay known as *Bay Side*, beginning 40 rods below Sandy Point, whence ran the old line from the Great Bay, extending down between Portsmouth and Hampton. Henry and John Sherburne and Samuel Haynes were authorized by the town of Portsmouth, Ap. 6, 1666, " to meet the neighbors of Hampton, to run the lyne between the towns of Portsmouth and Hampton, provided it be run from *Cotterill's Delight*, and from thence unto a little river about half a mile beyond Little Boar's head." (*Ports. Records*.)

The grants made by the town of Dover on the shore of Great Bay to Thomas Canney, Wm. Furber, Richard Hussey, Thomas Willey, George Webb, and perhaps others, were all above the mouth of Winnicot river, and of course below Cotterill's Delight. These grants are now owned for the most part by the Weeks family. Beyond lay the large tract which Richard Waldron and Thomas Lake reserved for themselves, which no doubt included Cotterill's Delight. That the Greenland line began 40 rods below Sandy Point Sept. 1, 1719, is shown by a deed of that date from Simon, Andrew, and Jonathan Wiggin, and John Sinkler, guardian of the children of Bradstreet Wiggin of Quamscott, deceased, conveying to Joshua Bracket of Greenland in the township of Portsmouth, 71 acres *in Portsmouth*, part of a tract of land their grandfather Capt. Thomas Wiggin bought of Mr. Richard Waldron and Thomas Lake, " bounded att a clump of trees standing on a piece of old planting land near *forty rods below Sandy Point*, as by deed of the year 1658,—which tract said Bracket is now in possession of, bounded as follows, beginning at a stake standing in a piece of *Old Indian Ground*, 15 rods from highwater mark, about *40 rods below Sandy point*, and from said stake S. E. 287 rods to an ash tree, then S. W. 40 rods to a black ash, then N. W. to two stones 3½ rods N. W. of *brandy rock*, thence N. E. to the first bound." Here no doubt was *Cotterill's Delight.*

The name of *Cotterill's Delight* cannot with certainty be traced. There was a Robert Cotterill in Providence, R. I., in 1645, and a Francis Cotterill or Cottrell at Wells, Maine, in 1668. The name may have been given by Francis Champernowne, who was connected with the Cotterells of England, through the Gorges. Sir Ferdinando Gorges' nephew, Samuel Gorges (born in 1604), married Jane, daughter of John Cotterell, Esq., of Somersetshire, Eng.

The Cotterells were also connected with the Pendletons, who had large grants from the town of Portsmouth in early times, but afterwards left the province. Capt. James Pendleton had, at least, a small grant of 15 acres " at Greenland " in Jan. 1667, " one side *joining to Dover*," and adjacent to the land of Wm. Furber. (*Ports. Records.*) His daughter, Dorothy Cotterell, widow, of " Westerly, in King's Co., colony of Rhoad Island and Providence plantations," Aug. 1, 1734, conveyed to Edmund Pendleton of said Westerly, all right and title to any lands, tenements, etc., that had or might come to her from her honored grandfather, Brian Pendleton, late of Saco, gent., deceased, and all claim to lands, etc., that belonged to her father James Pendleton, late of Westerly, deceased.

CROCKETT'S CROSSING. This is a crossing on the Boston & Maine railway, mentioned July 3, 1849, as one of the bounds between Somersworth and Rollinsford, south of the dwelling-house of Andrew Crockett. (See *Rollinsford.*) The woods near this crossing are said to be a favorite camping-place for gypsies.

CROMWELL'S CREEK. Mentioned Feb. 18, 1739–40, when Thomas and Eliza Waits conveyed to John Pearl, bricklayer, four acres of upland on the westerly side of Dover Nook, and on the southeasterly side of a small creek commonly called *Mast creek* or *Crumwell's creek;* also the thatch-bed between said land and creek, beginning at the mouth of the creek, by ye Back river, and running northerly, up the middle of said creek as it runs. The name of Cromwell's creek was derived from Joshua Cromwell, to whom the above four acres were conveyed July 4, 1727, by Thomas Roberts, to whose father (Thomas) they had been granted in 1658. This land is described as " butting on ye back river on ye west side, on a small creek on ye norwest side," and lying between Thomas Whitehouse's land and that of Abraham Nute. Joshua and " Ledea " Cromwell conveyed it to Thomas Waitt Ap. 10, 1730.

This creek is again mentioned Ap. 2, 1754, when Mary, widow of John Pearl, conveyed to Moses Varney four acres of upland on the west side of Dover Neck, on the southeasterly side of a small creek, commonly called *Mast creek* or *Cromwell's creek*, which runs into the Back river. Neither of these names has been retained. The creek is no doubt the same as *Varney's creek*, otherwise called *Little John's creek*. (See *Varney's Creek.*)

CROXFORD'S SWAMP. This was part of Moharimet's marsh, in the Packer's Falls district, Durham, so named from Daniel Croxford who was in General Sullivan's employ at the fulling-mill which stood at Sullivan's falls as early as 1774. It is now owned by Mr. Ezra Parsons. Daniel Croxford is mentioned Feb. 19, 1788, when he bought 20 acres of land of Isaac Medar, which he sold Eleazar Bennet Dec. 3, 1792.

CRUMMIT'S CREEK, otherwise CROMMET'S. This name has been given for a hundred years, or more, to the inlet from Great Bay which divides the Durham Point district from Lubberland. In early times it was variously called *Great creek, Branson's Creek, Long creek*, and finally *Mathews'* or *Mathes's creek*, which name it chiefly bore from 1653 till the latter part of the eighteenth century. It is called "Sturgeon creek" on Sandford & Everts' county atlas of 1871, but for this name there is no warrant whatever. It is otherwise called in the Durham records of March 21, 1746-7, when a petition was made for a new road by John Edgerly's "to the creek called the *Mill creek.*" This name was derived from *Mathes's mill,* afterwards *Crummit's mill,* which stood at the head of tide water. "*Crummit's mill Cove*" is mentioned in 1825. (See *Mathew's Neck.*) And *Crummit's mill-creek bridge* is mentioned in the Durham records of 1835. The name of Crummit's creek was derived from Jacob Crommet, to whom Peter Levius conveyed, Feb. 14, 1772, a farm of 140 acres adjacent to this creek, "beginning at the southerly end of *the mill dam thereon,* thence running down the creek 9 rods, thence north 26 deg. E. 13 rods, across said creek to a stone, which is an old Monument," etc. John Peirce of Portsmouth, Jan. 10, 1778, conveyed to Jacob Crommet 35 acres, "set off by execution as the estate of Peter Levius, Esq., beginning at a rock at the N. W. corner of *the mill,* thence running down the creek S. 55 deg. E. 8 rods," etc., being part of the farm then occupied by said Jacob Crommet.[1]

The Crummit lands and mill were acquired by the Kent family, by intermarriage. The mill is no longer in operation, but the water privilege is now owned by Mr. James Kent.

The name of Crummit is said to be a corruption of Cromwell, and the family claim relationship with the great Protector. Philip Cromwell was taxed in Dover as early as 1657, and Daniel in 1662. One share in the ox pasture on Dover Neck was conveyed to Timothy Carel Dec. 16, 1709, by "Samuel Cromwell" who calls himself in the deed "the heir and successor of Phillip Cromwell of Dover," to whom it had been granted. The confusion occasioned by the various ways of writing this name is shown by a letter from the army commissary in 1780 concerning a soldier from Durham, called James Crummett, Cromel, or Cromwell. (*N. H. State Pap.*, 17 : 367.)

CRUMMIT'S HILL. This hill is in Durham, on the lower side of Crummit's creek, near the site of the old mill.

There is another *Crummit's hill* in Lee, at the upper end of the Stepping-Stones road, so named from Joshua Crummit, who had 25 acres laid out to him on the south side of the Newtown road, May 19, 1749. The name of *Crummit's hill* is also sometimes given to Otis' hill in Somersworth, otherwise called Ricker's Hill. (See *Otis' Hill.*)

CURRIELL POINT. Mentioned Jan. 23, 1720, when Deacon John Hall's hundred-acre grant of 1656, between St. Alban's cove and Quamphegan, was re-surveyed for his grandson John Hall, "beginning at a poynt commonly called *Curriel Poynt.*" This land, when first laid out in 1659, was bounded on the S. E. by the Newichawannock river; S. W. by John Roberts' lot, and N. E. by the highway from the river between Hall's land and Henry Magoon's.

The name of Curriel Pt., which has

---

[1] An old newspaper of June 14, 1800, states that Jacob Crummet, returning from a walk in his field, fell down at his door and expired instantly.

not been perpetuated, seems to have been derived from Edward Cowel, who acquired the Magoon land, afterwards conveyed by his grandson Jethro Furber to Benjn Waymouth, and now forms part of the Garvin lands.

CUSHING'S CROSSING. Mentioned in the Wentworth Genealogy, Vol. II, p. 545. This is a railway station on Dover Neck, above Little John's creek, where the Portsmouth & Dover R. R. crosses the land of Mr. Jonathan Cushing.

CUSHING'S HILL. See *Madam's Cove*.

CUTT'S BROOK. This brook is so called in the division of Robert Burnham's estate, Ap. 28, 1762. It rises in the Long Marsh, Durham, crosses the highway at the foot of Cutt's Hill, and empties into Burnham's Creek on the lower side of Oyster river. It is sometimes called *Sandy Brook*.

CUTT'S HILL. This hill is on the road to Durham Point, just below the house of the late Col. Joseph Burnham. On the south side of it is *Cutt's spring*, a source of excellent water. Here is the land purchased over two hundred years ago by John Cutt or Cutts of Portsmouth, first president of New Hampshire. Thomas Doutie (written "Doughty" in President Cutt's will), "resident at Oyster River," sold John Cutt, of Portsmouth, Oct., 1657, land, marsh, dwelling-house, etc., bought of William Roberts, who was then in possession thereof. This farm and half of the "plantation" near it, which President Cutt bought of William Williams, were bequeathed to his son Samuel, and now belong in part, if not wholly, to the heirs of Col. Burnham, and the heirs of H. A. Mathes. The name is now generally written Cutts.

The highway to Durham Point formerly led around Cutt's hill to avoid its steepness, but was finally run directly across it, by way of a *short cut*. "What name can be more unluckily short?" says Benjamin Disraeli, speaking of John Cuts, commissioned by Queen Elizabeth to receive a haughty ambassador from Spain, who, accustomed to the long sonorous names of Spanish dignitaries, considered the brevity of Cuts' name a just ground of complaint.

CUTT'S MARSH. "A fresh marsh, commonly called Cutt's marsh" is mentioned Ap. 15, 1719, in a deed from James Burnham to Robert Burnham. This marsh, still owned by the descendants of said Robert, is on the west side of Cutt's brook, opposite the Burnham house, on the way to Durham Point. It is otherwise called *Adder's Swamp*.

DAME'S FALLS. This name is now given to the falls at the upper end of Lee Hook, from the sawmill there, owned by the sons of Mr. Israel Dame. They were previously called *Mathes' falls*, from John Mathes, at that time the proprietor. On the state map of Lee in 1803 they are called *Hill's falls*. (See *Hill's Falls*.)

DAME'S POINT. This point, so called on Whitehouse's map of Dover, is between the Cochecho river and the mouth of Fresh creek, at their junction, where Wm. Pomfrett had a grant of 100 acres the 5th, 10 mo., 1652, laid out June 5, 1674. Wm. Pomfrett, March 26, 1675, out of love and affection to his grandchild **Wm.** Dam, then about 20 years of age, son of John Dam, Sr., conveyed to him all the upland and meadow granted said Wm. Pomfrett the 5th, 10 mo., 1652, "lying and being from ye mouth of Fresh creek, on ye western side towards Cochecho —that is to say, it runs up from Cochecho river by said creek's side, from ye mouth thereof, the creek being the bounds thereof on ye eastern side. And from the mouth of Fresh creek it runs up the river, which is ye bound on ye south and by west side." These bounds were renewed, at the request of Pomfrett Dam (son of Wm.), June 9, 1724.

Another **Dame's Point** is on the Newington shore of Little Bay, at the lower side of Welshman's cove, where John Dam, Sr., of Dover had a grant of 40 acres of upland in 1652, laid out the 10th, 11 mo., 1656, between Richard Cater or Carter's land and that of Elder Nutter. This point is often called *Joshua's Point,* from Mr. Joshua Pickering, the late proprietor, by whose heirs it is now owned.

Dam's Windmill, otherwise **Dame's.** Mentioned May 4, 1736, when John Tebbets, Jr., "of Cochecho, in Dover," Jeremiah Tebbets, Jr., and Tamsen Tebbets, conveyed to James Clark one half of a 40 acre grant to their grandfather John Meader, March 23, 1702, laid out Feb. 28, 1705-6, on the south side of ye Back river, "which land now lyes between ye s^d Back river and *Wm. Dam's windmill,* being on ye east side of Samuel Davis's land, joining to John Twombley's, having said Twombley's on the east side joining to it at full length;" the west side of said grant, joining to Samuel Davis's, being reserved for Wm. Hill, Jr. In their deed to Wm. Hill, that same day, *Wm. Dam's windmill* is again mentioned, and this land is stated to have been given to their mother Sarah Tibbets by her father. This windmill, otherwise called *Drew's windmill,* stood on Pudding Hill, and seems to have been owned in common by Wm. Dam and Clement Drew. (See *Pudding Hill.*)

Daniel's Brook. This brook rises among the marshes in Horn's Woods, and empties into Crummit's millpond, Durham. The name is derived from John Daniel, who had land in this vicinity before April 11, 1694, when 40 acres were laid out to John Bickford, "beginning at a white oak on the hill at the south side of the *old dam* at the head of the Creek," dividing this tract from John Daniel's, and running thence W. S. W. 47 rods to the *brook* that also divided their lands. Forty acres were laid out to John Daniel Nov. 13, 1713, "on the north side of the *brook going to Lubberland,* the next brook to his home field, beginning at a black ash tree in the *grassy swamp* near the parting of the brooks." Joseph Wormwood, in 1810, conveyed to Eliphalet Daniel land on the *south branch* of Mathes's mill-pond, that formerly belonged to Gershom · and Benjamin Mathes, Jr. The Daniels farm is now owned by Mr. James Meader. (See *Edgerly Brook.*)

David's Lane. This lane, so named from David Daniels, is in Madbury, and extends from Nute's corner to the house of Mr. Charles W. Hayes, whose farm was originally owned by the Daniels family, seven generations of which are said to lie buried at the foot of the Hayes garden. The old Daniels house was a garrison.

DAVIS'S BROOK. See *Beaver Pond.*

DAVIS'S HILL. This hill is in the south-western part of Lee, and so named from Mr. Obadiah Davis, whose house stands at the foot. On the top of this hill once lived Miriam Clement, a reputed witch of local notoriety.

DEAD WATER BROOK and NECK. Tristram Heard of Dover, in his will of Ap. 18, 1734, gives his grandsons Joseph Knight and Tristram Warrin 30 acres of land at a place commonly called *Dead Water.* Tristram Warren, of Berwick, Me., conveyed to Joseph Hanson, Esq., March 19, 1754, all right to 30 acres of land in Dover, granted to his honored grandfather Tristram Heard March 19, 1693-4, and laid out on the north side of the Cochecho, between ye mouth of *Black Water brook* and *Dead Water neck*—the same land which Tristram Heard, deceased, gave Joseph Knight (son of Robert Knight) and Tristram Warren in his last will and testament. Seventeen acres of land were laid out to Joseph Hanson, Jr., Nov. 5, 1741, on the east side of the river Cochecho, in a place called *Dead Water Neck*, opposite the 37 acres laid out to him that same day on the other side of the river (see *Sandy Log Hill*), beginning at the mouth of *Dead Water brook*, and running up said brook as it goes to the head, and so along the ridge of the hill, as the hedge fence goes, to a white birch marked I. H., thence S. by W. to a large cove in said river, bounding the same by said river down to the mouth of said brook where we began—which land said Hanson had for some years improved. Oct. 28, 1765, Humphrey Hanson (and Joanna) conveyed to his brother Ephraim Hanson, innholder, 17 acres on ye east side of the Cochecho, at a place called *Dead Water Neck*, laid out to their father Joseph Hanson, Esq., Nov. 5, 1741.

Deadwater Brook empties into the Cochecho on the east side, over 40 rods above the upper Eelweir falls. The *Neck* lies between this brook and the Cochecho river.

DEAN'S MARSH. This marsh is spoken of in the Durham records of Jan. 29, 1733-4, as "above Newtown river," meaning, of course, that part of Oyster river which flows through Newtown in Lee. Its name, not perpetuated, was derived from John Dean, who was slain by the Indians July 18, 1694, as he came out of his house by the saw-mill, at the falls where is now Durham village. His wife and daughter were carried up the river and left in a spruce swamp in the care of an old Indian, from whom she made her escape with her child. This daughter afterwards married Stephen Jenkins, who, Nov. 19, 1729, with "Elizabeth his wife, daughter of John Dean, deceased," conveyed to Ann Kinket, widow, "land in Newtown, the old possession of John Dean, deceased." Ann Kincaid afterwards married Thomas Potts. "Potts' bridge" on the highway from John Snell's to Benjamin Clark's, in Newtown, is mentioned Oct. 12, 1790.

DEMERIT'S MILL. This mill is mentioned in the Dover records Dec. 8, 1734, when a petition was made for a road "from *Demerit's mill* to the Mallego road at the Saplings."

It was built in 1722 by Eli Demerit, Jr., maternal ancestor of the writer. It stood in the fork of the Bellamy and Mallego rivers, just above the bridge, and at a later day was called the *Hook mill,* from a remarkable bend in this part of the Bellamy river.

In the *Granite Monthly* of Dec., 1881, is an interesting account of a suit brought against Ely Demerit, Jr., "planter," by Capts. Timothy and Paul Gerrish, by which it appears that the said Demerit and others, supposing the Gerrish right to the rivers did not extend to the branches, had begun in May, 1719, to build a dam across the Bellamy, about eighty rods above the mouth of the Mallego. An action for trespass was brought against him, his estate was attached to the value of £100, and he was summoned to appear at the September term of the Court of Common Pleas. The trial came on at Portsmouth, Sept. 3, 1719. One of the judges on the bench was Col. James Davis of Oyster River; and among the witnesses appeared old Parson Buss and his son, and John Thompson, all of the same place. John Buss, Jr., testified that "the Damm in controversy is between six and seven miles above Capt. Gerrish's *upper* mill as the river runs." This implies that Gerrish then had two mills at the lower falls. The verdict was against Demerit, and he appealed to the Superior Court. But it was a struggle against one of the monopolies of that early day, which had existed from the time when Major Richard Waldron acquired control of the Cochecho, and his son-in-law, John Gerrish, control of the Bellamy.

Demerit lost his case again; but the Gerrishes, by an indenture of May 30, 1722, finally granted Ely Demerit, Sr., Ely Demerit, Jr., Derry Pitman, and Samuel Chesley, four parts in six of the water-privilege in controversy, for two years.

Ely Demerit strengthened his claims by acquiring land in the vicinity, ten acres of which were laid out Nov. 1, 1734, " on the north side of Bellamy river, near the *hook mill*, beginning at a stake by the road that comes down to the *wading-place* below the mill." And ten acres, part of a grant to Sylvanus Nock, were laid out to Ely Demerit, Jr., June 11, 1735, beginning at a red oak tree " near his land above the *hook mill,* said tree north of Saml Davis's house." And so persistently did said Ely retain his hold of the mill he built here, that it was still in his possession at the time of his death. In his will of Jan. 10, 1758, he gives his son Ebenezer all his " Right, Title, and Interest in and unto the *saw mill* standing upon ye falls in Bellemin's Bank freshet at *ye Hook,* commonly so called," and all his *right* in said freshet.

This mill gave an impetus to the lumber business in that part of the township, and promoted its settlement. It long bore the Demerit name, and became one of the prominent landmarks of Dover. *"Demerit's mill"* is repeatedly mentioned in the early grants and laying out of roads. The name was often abbreviated to *Merit.* Joseph Rines had 10 acres laid out Ap. 7, 1735, " beginning at a pitch pine tree on the west side of ye road that leads from *merit's mill* to the head of the township, two rods from Israel Hodgdon's north corner." Ten acres were laid out to Maul Hanson, May 12, 1735, " at the Sou West side of the road that leads from *Merrit's mill* to the head of the town at Joseph Rines's." And five acres were laid out to Wm. Hill Ap. 9, 1736, beginning at the west side of the road, about 10 rods S. W. of *Merrit's mill*, and bounded partly by *Merrit's millpond.*

A vote was passed at a town meeting " at Cochecha," Aug. 16, 1736, " that a highway be layed out from yᵉ road that leads from Madberry up to yᵉ mill now in possession of Eli Demerit and others, across over to yᵉ way that leadeth from Littleworth to Mallego, said road to be two rods wide."

The cost of rebuilding the Hook mill-dam in Oct., 1758, according to the accounts of Ely Demerit, amounted to 155 £., 15s. for the work alone, without reckoning the materials.

It is evident from the above mentioned records that the true *Bellamy Hook* is at the mouth of the Mallego, and not the bend in the river below.

Another "*Demerit mill*" was built by the same Ely, Jr., about half a mile south of his garrison, on *Demerit's brook*—a streamlet that empties into Johnson's creek at Back river. This mill was in operation till the first part of this century, and a portion of the dam still remains.

Dishwater mill, on Oyster river, in Lee, is also often called *Demeritt's mill*, as the name is now written.

DENBOW'S BROOK, otherwise DENBO'S. Mentioned Aug. 15, 1743, when Joseph Davis of Durham conveyed to John Sambon, "cordwinder," 2 acres, 42 rods, of land, beginning at said Davis's N. E. corner, at the country road near *Denbo's brook*, and running N. by W. to the *mill-pond* (at Durham falls), bounded N. E. by land said Sambon bought of James Smith. In Smith's deed to Sambon, June 13, 1743, this brook is called " *Long Marsh brook*," one branch of it taking its rise in that marsh. The other branch rises at the Moat. It is sometimes called *Horsehide Brook* where it crosses the Newmarket road, south of Broth Hill.

It was no doubt from the Moat, and partly by means of Denbow's brook, that Valentine Hill proposed to construct a canal from Lamprey river to Oyster river—probably the first canal projected in New England. The 14th, 11 mo., 1655, he obtained " free liberty to cut through the commons for drawing part of the water of lamperele River into Oyster river, for the supply of his mill," provided no injury be done other grants of land or water, and that he should build bridges wherever his new feeder interfered with the highways, and that this water-course should cease if he should throw up the grant of Lamperel river.

The name of Denbow's brook was no doubt derived from Salathiel Denbow, who owned land on the west side of Long marsh before 1713.[1] And Richard Denbo had a grant of 20 acres of upland, laid out, Oct. 14, 1713, "on the west side of Colley's marsh, near his father's place, on the east side of the road that goeth from Oyster

---

[1] Salathiel Denbow served in the French and Indian wars of that period. A pension for a "hurt" received was granted him Dec. 1, 1730. (*N. H. Prov. Pap.*, 4: 581, 723.)

River to Lubberland." This name is now written Dinsmoor.

DIRTY BROOK. Mentioned March 19, 1693-4, when John Bickford had a grant of 60 acres on "the south side of the *durty brooke*, going to the *second falls*," at the upper side of Benj[n] York's land. John Bickford conveyed this land to John Smith Ap. 8, 1703, when *dirty brook* is again mentioned. Part of John Smith's grant of 50 acres, June 23, 1701, was laid out Ap. 3, 1705, "on the north side of the *durty brook*," bounded one side by "*follet's path*," thence running westward to the brook. This land was near the second falls in Lamprey river. He had another grant of 20 acres Oct. 2, 1729, at the upper side of his grant of 1701, "lying between *Follet's bridge path* and the *Durty brook*." It joined the lands of Burnum, Goddard, and Stevenson.

Dirty brook is in the Packer's Falls district, Durham, and empties into the Moat. It once had sufficient power to run a shingle-mill.

DIRTY GUT. Mentioned Ap. 11, 1694, when George Braun had a grant of 20 acres " at the *durty gutt*." Geo. Brawn, March 10, 1703, conveyed to John Downing a tract of land near Bloody Point, on the westerly side of Pascataqua river, "on y[e] place called the *dirty gutt*," granted him by the town of Dover in 1694. This land was laid out to John Downing with 140 acres he bought of Joseph Hill. James Place of Newington, Ap. 26, 1736, conveyed to John Hodsdon one acre on the south side of Capt. Downing's land, formerly Jos. Rawlins', beginning at a place called the *durty gut*, joining on the north easterly side land at s[d] gut that formerly belonged to Jos. Richards, and running up towards the Pitch-Pine plains, which said acre James Place bought of Samuel Benson, and Benson of Jos. Rawlins. Wm. Vaughan conveyed to Geo. Huntress, Sr., Feb. 5, 1708, a tract of land in the Long Reach, beginning at y[e] river's side at Canney's cove, and running W. S. W. to a certain place called the *Durty Gutt* in the way that goes from Rawlins's to the Pitch-Pine plains, etc. (See the *Gore.*)

The name of Dirty Gut has not been perpetuated, but it is apparently the brook, or a branch of it, which empties into Pickering's cove near Birch Point. This brook has two branches, both of which rise in the old Pitch-Pine plains of Newington. One rises in the so-called "Langdon pasture," in the lower plains; and the other above, east of the parsonage land, but is fed chiefly by Coleman's spring. They both cross the road from Fox Point to Portsmouth, one a little below Stony hill, now Pine hill, and the other further down. They afterwards unite in one brook which finally empties into Pickering's Cove.

Another *Dirty Gut* is mentioned Ap. 9, 1703, when a highway was laid out "from the Oyster bed at Oyster river to the country road at the *durty gutt* by Abraham Clark's." Abraham Clark lived near the dividing line between the Oyster River precinct and Dover proper, as appears from a vote at the town-meeting of Ap. 22, 1706, that the inhabitants of Dover Neck should keep in repair the road from Hilton's

Point to Abraham Clark's; and the inhabitants on the north side of Oyster river should keep the road in repair from said Clark's to Oyster River falls.

DIRTY LANE. Mentioned Oct. 7, 1713, when Joseph Beard conveyed to Ralph Hall all right to his father's land, bounded S. by the lane from *high street* to the *back cove*, and W. by the lane formerly called *Dirty lane*. This lane was at the lower part of Dover Neck, between high street and Back river. It seems to have been a part of Low street.

DIRTY SLOUGH. Mentioned March 19, 1693-4, when 30 acres of land were granted to "Isaac gold by the *durty slow*, below beach hill." And again Jan. 9, 1721, when Wm. Leathers gave his son Thomas a tract of land on the northwest side of the way to Beech Hill at ye place called the *Dirty Slough*. This slough is a gully on the borders of Durham and Madbury, a little west of the Tom-Hall road, on the way to Beech Hill.

The name of *Dirty slough* is sometimes given to the brook that empties into Bunker's creek, in Durham.

DISHWATER FALLS and MILL. See *Oyster River Falls*.

DOE'S NECK. This neck, now in Newmarket, but once a part of ancient Dover, was so called from Sampson Doe, to whom Richard Waldron conveyed, March 22, 1709, all that neck of land between Lamperell river and Goddard's creek in the township of Dover, formerly granted by said town to Peter Coffin of Exeter. (See *Lamprey-River Neck*.) Nathaniel Doe, Ap. 19, 1745, conveyed to Ralph Cross of Newbury half of a farm commonly called *Doe's Neck*, consisting of 120 acres, with dwelling-house, and barn southward of the house, the land extending from the barn to Lamperel river, then E. on said river to the Great Bay, and by said Bay northerly to a fence northward of *Martain's layn*, so called, then up the creek (Goddard's) to a rock eastward of *Burch Point*, near the place where people commonly pass over, and from said rock to a large red oak by the upland above *Burch point*, then along said creek to the fence between said Doe's land, and that of Samuel Smith of Durham. (See *Lamprey River Neck* and *Martin's Lane*.)

DOVER. This name was given to the settlement at Hilton's Point as early as 1639, if not before. It was changed to *Northam* in 1641, but the name of *Dover* was restored in 1642. "A Combination for government" was formed by the inhabitants of Dover, Oct. 22, 1640, and the settlement remained independent till its union with Massachusetts, which was consummated Oct. 9, 1641. C. W. Tuttle, in his *Historical Papers* (p. 333) says it is an error to give the name of "*Dover Combination*" to the local form of government of 1640, because the word "Dover" does not appear in the document. It was merely endorsed, "The Combination for government by ye people at Pascataq." The name, however, is in constant use, and serves to distinguish it from the combinations at Exeter and Strawberry Bank. And it is appropriately so called, because it was formed by and for the Dover settlers. This Combination was the only charter of incorporation Dover ever had, till it was made a city June 18, 1855. The township of Dover formerly comprised, not only Dover proper, but the present townships of Durham, Lee, Madbury, Somersworth, and Rollinsford, the greater part of Newington, and a portion of Greenland and Newmarket.

The name of Dover, in a restricted sense, was sometimes given in early times to the settlement on Dover Neck, by way of distinction from that called "Cochecho," around the lowest falls in the Cochecho river. "The road from *Dover* to *Cochecho*" is mentioned May 5, 1718, meaning the road from Dover Point. (See *Cochecho*.)

DOVER GARRISONS.

I. PETER COFFIN'S GARRISON. The N. H. government ordered, March 13, 1683–4, that the houses of Peter Coffin, Esq., and Richard Otis be immediately fortified as "by-garrisons for Cochecho," for the security of the inhabitants in their vicinity. (*N. H. Prov. Pap.*, 1:499.) Coffin's house is mentioned May 27, 1671, when Richard Waldron conveyed to Peter Coffin one fourth of the sawmill works on the south side of the river Cochecho, with one fourth of all grants and privileges thereunto pertaining. Also six acres of land on the south side of the river, adjoining "ye two acres of land upon part whereof "ye s^d *Peter Coffin's house* now stands, which s^d Peter formerly bought of his father-in-law Edward Starbuck." Coffin's garrison and mill were burnt by the Indians June 28, 1689. The Rev. Joshua Moodey of Portsmouth implies that this was a judgment on Peter Coffin, who was one of the Justices at Moodey's trial in 1684. (*Ibid.*, 1:523.) Coffin himself, however, escaped the fate of Col. Waldron, having treated the Indians more equitably, as shown by his securing from them a title to his lands at Squamanagonick and at the second falls in Lamprey river. Coffin's garrison is said to have stood on an elevation, now cut down, between Orchard and Waldron streets, in the rear of Varney's block, about sixty feet from the line of Central Avenue.

II. TRISTRAM COFFIN'S GARRISON. This garrison, built by Tristram, son of Peter Coffin, escaped destruction in the Indian attack of 1689. Where it stood is uncertain, but it is supposed to have been on the high land near the present Belknap schoolhouse on Silver street, which is part of the old Littleworth road. Eliphalet Coffin conveyed to Joseph Hanson, Sept. 5, 1735, two acres of land in Dover, bounded S. by the highway to Littleworth, W. by David Watson's two-acre home lot, N. by *Leah's field*, so called, and E. by "a small gore claimed by Mr. Richard Waldron y^t lies over against *ye pound*, being the *very same land where Tristram Coffin*, father of Eliphalet, *formerly lived*." Tristram's son of the same name, however, lived near the lowest falls in the Cochecho. Peter Coffin, son of Eliphalet, conveyed to John Gage all right and title to the mill privilege at the lower falls in Cochecho river, on the south side, "being near *ye dwelling house of Capt. Tristram Coffin*."

III. GERRISH'S GARRISON. Mentioned in the Journal of the Rev. John Pike, Dec. 25, 1692, when, as he states, "A dolefull and tremendous noise was affirmed to be heard in the Ayr nigh *Capt Ger: Garrison,* which Continued (with a little intermission) near half an hour."— "Money p^d for diating of soldiers at *Capt. John Gerrishes Garason*" is mentioned in 1692. (*N. H. Prov. Pap.*, 17: 621.) Two soldiers are mentioned as "serving his Majesty" in *Capt. Gerrish's garrison* from Jan. 7, 1695, till Feb. 6, following. (*Ibid*, 17: 648.) This garrison no doubt stood near Gerrish's mills at the lowest falls in the Bellamy river, but the precise spot is not known.

IV. HAYES'S GARRISON. This was a minor garrison of a later day, which, according to Sanford & Evert's atlas, stood west of the Cochecho river at the foot of Winkley's hill, at the junction of the road to Barrington and that to Tolend falls. It is elsewhere spoken of as "the garrison of Lieut. Jonathan Hayes," who died Ap. 15, 1787. It was taken down in 1812.

V. HEARD'S GARRISON. This garrison, built by Capt. John Heard of the Dover Combination of 1640, stood on a small hill, west of Garrison Hill, at the lower side of the ancient cartway, where is now the garden of the Bangs residence. It escaped destruction in the attack of 1689, at which time John Heard was already dead. The allowance made by the government for the subsistence of soldiers at *Dame Heard's garrison* in 1692 and 1693, is given in the *N. H. Prov. Pap.*, 17: 621, 629. Five soldiers were ordered to be stationed at "*Samuel Heard's garrison*" in 1693. (*Ibid.*, 2: 103.) Orders were given Oct. 20, 1693, that only two soldiers be left at *Heard's garrison*. This seems to have been the only fortified garrison on the north side of the Cochecho river Feb. 17, 1696-7, when the government ordered that the bridge (boom) "broken and gone," should be speedily repaired, in order that *Heard's garrison* might be relieved in case of an attack by the enemy. Six men were ordered to be sent to *Heard's garrison* Ap. 15, 1697. (*Ibid.*, 2: 223, 227.) This garrison is mentioned Jan. 16, 1721, when Stephen Varney conveyed to Wm. Welland "30 acres of land, which was the homestead of John Heard, deceased, lying in Cochecho, beginning at the highway at the back side of Lt. Tristram Heard's house, and running W. by N. to the end of the lot, taking in the *Old Garrison House.*"

VI. MEETING-HOUSE FORT or GARRISON. Capt. Peter Coffin agreed, the 4th, 5 mo., 1667, to build a fort about the meeting-house on Dover Neck, 100 feet square, with two Sconces 16 feet square, all the timbers to be 12 inches thick, and the wall to be 8 feet high, with sills and braces. It was ordered by the Governor and Council, March 13, 1683-4, "that the meeting-house at Dover be immediately fortified, and a line drawn about it, which meeting-house shall be the *main garrison* for defending the inhabitants against the attacks of the enemy; also that the house, formerly called the *Watch House,* be a by-guard." (*Ibid.*, 1: 499.) "The *garrison about ye ministry house* on Dover Neck" is spoken of May 11, 1697. (*Ibid.*, 17: 656.) This house and its fortifications are now gone. The land where it stood was purchased a few years ago by the Hon. C. H. Sawyer and Mr. E. R. Brown, and presented by them to the Congregational Society of Dover. (See *Nutter's Hill*.) The *guard house*, mentioned above, is referred to in Job Clement's will of Sept. 4, 1682, in which he gives his grandchild Jane Kenney a part of his six acre lot " near the *watch house* on Dover Neck."

VII. OTIS' GARRISON. This garrison stood about half way between Heard's and Waldron's garrisons, on the brow of a hill on the west side of what is now Central Avenue, near Milk St. It was built by Richard Otis, ancestor of the present writer, who settled in Dover as early as 1655. The N. H. authorities ordered, March 13, 1683-4, that his house should be immediately fortified, as one of the " by-garrisons " of Cochecho, for the security of the neighboring inhabitants. (*N. H. Prov. Pap.*, 1:499.) It was destroyed by the Indians June 28, 1689, on which occasion Richard Otis was killed, together with his son Stephen and daughter Hannah. His wife, and twenty-eight other inmates of the garrison, were taken captive.

VIII. PAINE'S GARRISON. Mention is made of *Thomas Paine's garrison* being surrounded by a band of Indians in the night of June 27-28, 1689. (*Ibid.*, 2:51.) It was probably destroyed on that occasion, for no mention is made of it subsequently. Dr. Quint says it stood close to the house of the late Capt. James Varney, on the turnpike road (Portland St.), near the corner of Rogers St.; but on what authority does not appear. It was undoubtedly on that side of the Cochecho river, however—probably on Mt. Rawlings, where Thomas Paine acquired land and a dwelling-house March 5, 1673. (See *Mount Rawlings*.)

IX. PINKHAM'S GARRISON. This garrison was built by Richard Pinckhame, of the Dover Combination. It stood on the west side of Dover Neck, on gently sloping land overlooking Back river, that for six generations remained in possession of the Pinkham family, covering a space of about 250 years. It is now owned by Mr. Charles Thompson. About four rods west of his house stood the garrison, which was taken down about 1825.

X. SAMUEL TIBBET'S GARRISON. Mentioned in 1696, when Richard Clay was stationed there from Ap. 13 till June 8. This garrison was on Dover Neck. Samuel Tibbet's land in the upper part of Dover Neck, on the east side, is mentioned in 1702. He was still living Feb. 9, 1733-4, when he declared himself to be 67 years old. " Capt. Samuel Tibbets " is spoken of Ap. 17, 1742, as " deceased."

XII. VARNEY'S GARRISON. This garrison was on the Blackwater road in Dover, some distance N. W. of Willand's pond. It was no doubt built by Stephen Varney, who, Oct. 24, 1719, acquired part of Wm. Pomfrett's hundred-acre grant in Cochecho woods, bordering on Mr. Reyner's 400 acre grant, at the east. It was a large garrison of two stories, the second story projecting about three feet beyond the first. During the French and Indian wars of the last century it is said to have afforded shelter to all the neighboring farmers. It was still standing in 1834, in which year it is mentioned as the " Old Garrison " on Whitehouse's map of Dover. It was taken down not long after, and some of its timbers were used in the construction of the Bickford house near Faggoty bridge, now owned by Mr. Moses Hussey. The cellar, however, can still be traced.

XIII. WALDRON'S GARRISON. This garrison was built by Major Richard Waldron, founder of the Cochecho settlement. It stood north of the Cochecho river, on the west side of Central Avenue, between First and Second streets, directly behind the National Block, which, as Dr. Quint says, should have been called Waldron's block. The present Court House stands on a part of this garrison site. This garrison was destroyed in the attack of 1689, on which occasion the Indians, by way of revenge for numerous wrongs, put Major Waldron to death in the most barbarous manner.

There were other Dover garrisons on the west side of Back river. (See *Back River Garrisons.*)

DOVER LANDING. See *Cochecho Landing.*

DOVER NECK. This neck is mentioned in 1643, when Wm. ffurber had a grant of "two house lots containing six acres, on the east side of y^e *neck of Dover*, butting on ye fore side of the river, next Joseph Austin at the north." Dover Neck and Point constitute a tongue of high land that extends between Fore and Back rivers to the main body of the Pascataqua. Belknap describes it as a ridge "about two miles long, and half a mile wide, rising gently along a fine road, and declining on each side like a ship's deck."

DOVER POINT. This name is now given to Hilton's Point, at the lower end of Dover Neck.

DOVER POINT FERRY. This name was given to a new ferry from Dover Point to Newington, established by the Pascataqua Ferry Co. in 1856. It was connected with Dover city and Portsmouth by means of a daily stage-coach. The ferry here in early times was called the *Bloody Point ferry* and *Knight's ferry.*

DOVER RIVER. This name is given to the Cochecho river on Pike's map of Somersworth in 1805. "Cochecho or *Dover river*" is mentioned in Merrill's *Gazeteer* of N. H. in 1817.

DOW'S HILL. This name is now given to the highest point of land in Newington, from Amos Dow, to whom Seth Walker conveyed, Sept. 25, 1816, a tract of land on the N. W. side of the road to Bloody Point ferry, adjacent to the Huntress and Rollins lands.

DOWNING'S CREEK. See *Uncle Siah's Creek.*

DOWNING'S PLAINS. So called from John Downing, who acquired land in the Pitch-Pine plains of Newington Feb. 14, 1723-4. (See the *Gore.*) Richard Downing's land in the upper Pitch-Pine plains of Newington is mentioned in 1770. (See *Pitch-Pine Plains.*) And Feb. 27, 1799, Bartholomew Downing and Richard D. Hart advertised for sale "100 acres of corn land on *Downing's Plain* in Newington."

DOWNS' BROOK. This brook is in Somersworth, below Great Falls, and so named from an old family in that vicinity. A quitclaim to 60 acres of land at Indigo Hill, lying between the lands of Wm. Downs and Paul Brown, joining the river at the northeast, was given to Samuel Downs March 13, 1750, by the other children of Thomas Downs, who, says the deed, "upward of thirty years ago was killed by ye Indians." A part of the old Downs land is now owned by Mr. Morrill.

DRAM ROCK. This rock, according to Dame's map of Newington in 1805, is in the Long Reach, off the Newington shore, about half way between Bloody Pt. and the Portsmouth line. It is apparently the same as *Shag Rock*, and no doubt derived its name from the boatmen who regarded it as a signal for a dram when they ascended the river.

DREW'S HILL. This is a steep hill in the Back River district, about a mile below Sawyer's bridge across the Bellamy. Along the upper side of this hill runs the old mast road from *Wingate's Slip* (now *Ford's Landing*) to Madbury. The name is derived from John Drew, who acquired several of the twenty-acre lots on the west side of Back river, granted in 1642. His land here is mentioned Nov. 22, 1698, when John Laighton of Rochester sold Shadrach Hodgdon 20 acres on the west side of Back river, where said Laighton had built a house in which he then lived, bounded northeasterly by Back river, S. E. by Hodgdon's land, S. W. by *Drew's land*, and northwesterly by the highway " from *mast bridge* to ye river, at a place cal^d y^e *Slip*"—being lot No. 21, granted Henry Beck in 1642, and laid out to Thomas Layton, his successor.

DREW'S MARSH. This was a small marsh in a bend or bow of Johnson's creek, on the south side; and northeast of a little run of water from a spring near the Jones house in Durham. It is mentioned in some depositions of Aug. 1, 1776, made by Stephen Pinkham and others, who testified that this marsh had long been owned by the Drews of Back River.

DREW'S POINT. Mentioned Sept. 7, 1738, when John Downing of Newington and his wife Elizabeth conveyed to Benjamin Mathes 50 acres of land in Durham, "beginning at Oyster river, near ye Pint cal^d *Drew's Point*," and running along a highway from the river between said land and the lands of Joseph Stevenson and Thomas Footman till it came to the highway "from ye falls to ye ferry called *Bickford's ferry*," bounded north by the river, and east by Caleb Wakeham's land,—which fifty acres formerly belonged to James Langley, and was part of the estate of his father James Langley. (See *Langley's Point*.)

DREW'S WINDMILL. See *Dam's Windmill*.

DRY HILL. This name is given to Gage's hill in the Dover *Sun* of Ap. 17, 1813, when mention is made of land on *Dry Hill* belonging to the estate of Samuel Bragg, Jr., formerly editor of that newspaper. And Capt. Moses Paul also speaks of "*Dry Hill*" in his diary of 1852. It is otherwise called *Faggoty hill* and *Gage's hill*.

DRY PINES. Mentioned March 19, 1693-4, when Richard Pinkham had a grant of 30 acres of land "between ye drie pines and Abraham Clark's." And that same day Zachariah Pitman had a grant of 20 acres "in y^e *Dry Pines*, between Jno Knight's and Zacharias field's." Pitman conveyed this land to John Drew Aug. 16, 1697.

Elijah Drew and wife Abigail, Nov. 29, 1762, conveyed to Shadrach Hodgdon 25 acres of land, bounded northerly by the highway that leads from the country road to Clement Meserve's, westerly by said Meserve and Samuel Hayes, and easterly by part of the estate of John Field, deceased; which land, called the *Dry Pines*, formerly belonged to Joseph Drew, father of said Elijah. John Knight's land at Mast bridge was afterwards acquired by Benedictus Torr. And Samuel Hayes' land, above mentioned, was conveyed to him Dec. 3, 1737, by Daniel, son of Zacharias Field. The *Dry Pines*, a portion of the tract generally called *Field's plains*, were in the upper part of the Back River district. (See *Field's Plains*.)

The DUMP. This name is now given to a deep ravine at the eastern side of the Waldron cemetery on Chapel St., Dover, into which, for a time, was dumped the refuse of that vicinity. A small brook flows through this ravine and empties into the Cochecho river.

DUMPLING COVE. This cove is on the Newington shore of Little Bay, at the lower side of Dame's Pt., now Joshua's Pt. It is mentioned the 11th, 10 mo., 1656, when Richard Catter's (Carter's) grant of 40 acres of upland in 1652, was laid out "south of the freshett at *Dompline Cove*," bounded north by Henry Lankstar's land, and south by that of John Dam. Henry Langstar's grant of 200 acres in 1652 was laid out in 1659, " beginning at *Doempling Coue* in the letell Bay, and so up the freshett to the parting of it," thence over to " the freshett that goeth into the *broad Coue* below *foxe poynt*, thence over the mouth of the crike to a maple tree, thence to the north side of a little swamp, thence to a Rock a little below *Terning Poynt*, and up the little bay to *Doompline Cove*." Henry Langstar, Oct. 27, 1704, conveyed to his daughter Mary all his land on Little Bay, beginning at the mouth of a creek in Broad Cove, and running up Little Bay as far as *Dumpling Cove*, to the southwest side of the freshet; which land was granted said Henry Langstar the 9th, 5 mo., 1652.

Sarah Levett, "widow and relict of James Levett," conveyed to Joseph Adams, "preacher of the Gospel," March 15, 1721, a tract of 40 acres, " bounded somewhat northerly on ye lands that were formerly old Mr. Langstar's, now in ye possession of Mr. Eleazar Coleman, somewhat westerly on ye river that runs into ye Great Bay, somewhat southerly by the lands of Mr. John Dam, and somewhat easterly by the lands of said Adams ;"—the land thus bounded being " at or near a place called *Dumpling Cove*, and formerly granted by the town of Dover to one Richard Cater" (Carter.)

Joseph Adams of Newington, Dec. 18, 1783, conveyed to John Gee Pickering 20 acres of land in Newington, " supposed to be half of the farm where said Adams then lived," beginning at Joseph Dame's land, and running along Little Bay to the land of James Coleman. This land is now owned by Mr. Gee Pickering of Portsmouth, and the Dame land adjoining by the heirs of Mr. Joshua Pickering.

Dumpling cove is sometimes called *Sow-Pit cove*, probably a corruption of *Sow and Pigs*, a name given to a cluster of rocks in the river near this cove.

DUNN'S WOODS. These woods are in Dover, adjoining the road to Durham. They were acquired early last century by Benedictus Torr, and now belong to Mr. Simon Torr. For the last fifty years they have been known as "Dunn's woods," for the strange reason that Samuel Dunn, of Dunn's tavern, Dover, owned land adjoining, that was almost entirely woodless. In days by no means distant, these dark, damp, lonely woods, enclosed by hills, and remote from any dwelling, were said to be the scene of many a robbery by day and supernatural occurrence by night, stories of which at once delighted and terrified the neighboring children. The ghost stories sprang chiefly from the delusive phosphorescent lights which on dark nights were often seen gleaming here and there among the bogs and decayed wood. *Torr's woods*, as they should be called, are now fast disappearing, and with them the nocturnal lights which once startled the belated traveller.

DURHAM. This name was given to the Oyster River parish when it was incorporated as a town May 15, 1732. It included the present township of Lee till the latter was incorporated Jan. 16, 1766, and a part of Newmarket, ceded to that town July 2, 1870. The name of Durham was apparently given at the request of the Rev. Hugh Adams, then the minister at Oyster River. In his address to the General Court in 1738, he says this parish "was chartered into the township of *Durham*" in answer to his petition " for its privileges and *said name*, as therein pleaded for." (See *N. H. Prov. Papers*, V : 35.) The name of Durham may have been chosen in order to commemorate the palatine form of government originally accorded to the New Hampshire settlement, if credit is to be given to the so-called Charter of Charles I to Capt. John Mason, Aug. 19, 1635, granting him the province of New Hampshire, " with power of government and as ample jurisdiction and prerogatives as used by the bishop of Durham." (*Ibid*, 1 : 37.) The bishops of Durham, England, it will be remembered, formerly exercised the semi-regal powers of a count palatine. It does not appear, however, that Capt. Mason or his heirs ever attempted to exercise such prerogatives in New Hampshire.

Similar powers were also conferred on Sir Ferdinando Gorges in the Royal Charter of April 3, in the fifteenth year of the reign of Charles I, granting him the Province of Maine, with " all the Powers, Rights, Franchisses, Immunities, Royalties, & Priviledges wch are enjoyed or ought to be enjoyed by the Bishop of Dureseme in the County Palatine of Duresme." (See Baxter's *Sir Ferdinando Gorges*, 3 : 304.)

The first government established in Maryland was also palatinate, according to the charter from Charles I to Cecilius, the second Lord Baltimore, June 20, 1632, conferring on him prerogatives as ample as those exercised by the Bishop of Durham, which, as implied above, fell little short of royalty itself.

DURHAM CORNER. This corner is at the centre of Durham village, where three roads meet, coming from Dover, Lee, and Newmarket.

DURHAM FALLS. This name is often given to the lowest falls in Oyster river, and to the village of Durham itself. (See *Oyster River Falls.*) A road, laid out "from *Durham Falls* to Coos," is mentioned July 13, 1768, as "beginning at *Durham Falls*," and thence running to Madbury Meeting-house, thence through Barrington by Levi Daniels' house, etc. (*N. H. State Pap.*, 18 : 584.)

Durham Falls bridge, across Oyster river at the foot of the lowest falls, is mentioned Oct. 8, 1770, when Wm. and Avis Odiorne conveyed to Timothy Meder the "Mansion House" where they then dwelt, together with a barn and warehouse, and one acre of land, bounded S. by land of Abraham Perkins, deceased, E. by the road from *Durham Falls bridge* to Nottingham, and N. and W. by John Hanson's land.

DURHAM LANDING. A landing-place at the head of Oyster river, according to a vote of the town of Dover, Oct. 27, 1701, was laid out June 14, 1703, beginning at high-water mark by Geo. Chesley's fence, and running by. his fence to the top of the hill by Bartholomew Stevenson's house, (now Mr. Wm. P. Ffrost's), "thence N. N. W. to a pitch pine on the *east side* of the mast path which leads from Oyster river, thence to the fence on the *west side* of the aforesaid path, then southward, as the fence goes, till it comes to the fresh river above the saw-mill, all which land thus laid out is to lay open for a public landing-place." (*Dover Records.*) This landing-place included, not only the slope of Log hill in front of the Ffrost residence, but all the land on the south side of the road immediately above the saw-mill, now enclosed as house-yards, which, within the writer's recollection, lay open as a place for lumber for the convenience of the mill, and still properly belongs to the town or the mill privilege.

DURHAM POINT. This name is now given to the entire district between Little Bay and the lower part of Oyster river, but strictly speaking the point itself is at the mouth of the river on the south side. It was originally called *Oyster River point* or *Bickford's point*.

DURHAM RIVER. D. Smith, on his map of 1805, gives this name to the fresh-water part of Oyster river. He confines the name of "Oyster river" to the tidal or salt-water portion, below Durham falls.

EDGERLY BROOK. This name is often given to Daniel's brook, the southern branch of Crummit's creek, from Samuel Edgerly, to whom 30 acres were laid out Oct. 15, 1714, "beginning at a hemlock tree on a little hill on the west side of a path that leads from Oyster River to John Daniel's." This land is still owned by the descendants of the above Samuel. (See *Daniel's Brook.*)

EEL-POT CREEK. This creek runs through the land of Mr. Rufus W. Weeks of Greenland, and empties into the Great Bay, about fifty rods above the mouth of Winnicot river. It is mentioned Nov. 22, 1716, when Henry Langstar, of Piscataqua, New Jersey, by virtue of a power of attorney from his father John Langstar, son of Henry Langstar (otherwise Langstaffe) of Dover, deceased, conveyed to Henry Nutter a tract of 20 acres in Portsmouth, on y͏ᵉ westernmost side of *Greenland river*, in y͏ᵉ Great Bay, bounded upon *Ealpole creek.*"

EELWEIR FALLS. (See *Cochecho Falls.*)

EELWEIR PLAINS. Mentioned Nov. 5, 1741 (see *Sandy Log Hill*), and again Nov. 2, 1773, when John Twombley and Sarah conveyed to Thomas Hayes 37 acres on the westerly side of the Cochecho river, " at or near the *Eelware Plains*, so called," formerly laid out to Joseph Hanson, which land said Twombley bought of Ephraim Hanson, deceased.

EGG POND. This name is sometimes given to *No-Bottom pond*.

ELIJAH'S LEDGE. This is a quarry in Horne's woods, so called from Elijah Edgerly, who sold it to the Newmarket Manufacturing Co.

EMERSON'S BROOK. This brook, otherwise called *Great Brook*, is in the southwestern part of Lee. It flows through the lands acquired by Samuel and Solomon Emerson in the middle of last century (see *North River*), and empties into North river a little below Harvey's mill. A place in the channel, called the *Round Hole*, seems to indicate that there was once a dam here. The Emersons, however, acquired the neighboring privilege on North river, where Samuel Emerson had a mill at the beginning of this century.

FABYAN'S POINT. This point of land, originally called *Starbuck's Pt.*, is on the Newington shore of Great Bay, at the upper side of Herod's Cove, otherwise Laighton's. It is mentioned May 30, 1721, when Mary, widow of Thomas Pickering, and her three sons, James, Joshua, and Thomas, conveyed to John Fabins all right to a tract of land, commonly called *Starbuck's Point*, on Great Bay, with one half of y͏ᵉ salt marsh thereto adjoining. John Fabyan is mentioned in 1713 among the petitioners for Newington to be made a separate parish.

FAGGOTY BRIDGE. This is a small bridge across *Faggoty brook*, on the road from Dover to Rochester, at the foot of *Faggoty hill*, now Gage's hill. It was so named because the road at this point lay across a bog that had to be filled in with faggots and small trees, to give it stability. It is mentioned Dec. 22, 1720, when 60 acres of land, granted Tobias Hanson in 1702, were laid out to him " between *fagote bridg* and the *old bold spit*," on the east side of Wm. Pomfrett's grant, then in possession of Ephraim Wentworth, Thomas Downs, and Stephen Varney. Tristram Heard, in his will of Ap. 18, 1734, gives his son John 30 acres of land " above *Faggoty bridge.*" And June 23, 1736, eleven acres were laid out to Thomas Varney on the N. E. side of *Faggoty bridge*, beginning at the S. corner of Jos. Heard's land, north of said bridge, and thence running S. E. by y͏ᵉ road 47 rods.

FAGGOTY BROOK. This brook rises in a marsh in the Page pasture, Dover, and crosses the Rochester road at the foot of Gage's hill, then flows through the lands of Mr. Freeman Babb and Andrew Rollins, and crosses the road above Mr. Andrew Rollin's house. in Rollinsford, and empties into Rollin's brook.

FAGGOTY HILL. This name was generally given to Gage's hill till the middle of this century. In an advertisement of 1802 it is called "*Faggotty bridge hill*."

FALLS HILL. The hill in Durham village on which the Congregational meeting-house now stands is repeatedly called by this name in the records of last century. May 25, 1736, Nathaniel and Valentine Hill sold Thomas Pike, Jr., of the bury Newtown, three acres on the west side of *Falls hill*, bounded northerly by the mast way, and westerly by the way leading towards ye spruce swamp and little mill (Chesley's mill). This land Thomas Pike conveyed to Joseph Atkinson Sept. 12, 1738, when *Falls hill* is again mentioned, as well as the other bounds. Timothy Jones of Stratham, innholder, and Elenor his wife, Sept. 4, 1747, conveyed to Abednego Leathers of Durham, mariner, three acres of land, with dwelling-house, barn, and malt-house thereon, which land and buildings Jones had bought of Dr. Joseph Atkinson, " lying on the west side of a hill called and known by the name of *Falls hill*, bounded N. by the mast path, W. by the usual way leading to the spruce swamp, and S. and E. by the land of Nathaniel and Valentine Hill." This land was afterwards acquired by James Laighton, and is now owned for the most part by Mrs. Cook.

Deacon Hubbard Stevens of Durham conveyed to Moses Emerson[1] of Haverhill, Mass., May 23, 1751, a quarter of an acre of land, with a dwelling-house on it, on the west side of a hill called by the name of *Falls hill*, lying between the country path (the road to Madbury) and the mast path, which land said Stevens bought of Nathaniel Hill. Here, at a later period, stood Ballard's tavern, now owned by Mr. Hoitt.

Both of these tracts originally belonged to Valentine Hill's grant of 500 acres, which comprised all the land from Durham falls, including the greater part of the present village, to the western boundary of the land owned by the late Benjamin Thompson.

FANCY HILL. Mentioned July 23, 1735, when 20 acres of land were laid out to Ichabod Canney on the S. W. side of the road from Littleworth to the Saplings, at a place called *Fancy Hill*, beginning at Joseph Hanson's east corner, and running along his land S. W. to his south corner, then along the commons and Wm. Twombley's land to the road, and by the road to the first bound. The name of Fancy hill has not been perpetuated, but it seems to have been the hill a little west of Barbadoes Pond, which affords a pleasant view across the pond, with the city of Dover farther east, and Garrison Hill and other heights in the distance.

FIELD'S MARSH. This was a small marsh in the Durham Point district, mentioned in the Durham records of 1764 as next the parsonage lands.

---

[1] Moses Emerson was appointed commissary in the Revolutionary army in 1775. He had four brothers in the army, one of whom was Capt. Nehemiah Emerson of Haverhill, Mass. They descended from Jonathan Emerson, of Haverhill, brother of Capt. Samuel Emerson of Oyster River. The second wife of Moses Emerson was a Taylor, a great granddaughter of Gov. Edward Winslow of Mass., and a near relative of Gov. John Taylor Gilman's mother, of Exeter. She died in Durham, and lies buried in the Thompson burial-ground, near the residence of Mr. Lucien Thompson.

The county records speak of Nicholas Follet's dwelling-house, July 22, 1680, as standing on land adjoining *Joseph Field's marsh.* Joseph was the brother of Zacharias Field who settled in the Back River district. He was taxed at Oyster River in 1657. They are supposed to have been the sons of Darby Field, who is noted as the first of our colonists to make the ascent and give an account of the White mountains. Gov. Winthrop speaks of him as an Irishman, but Bell's History of Exeter says there is some reason to suppose him connected with the Hutchinson's of the Antinomian controversy in Massachusetts. Most writers regard him as one of the early settlers at Exeter, N. H., but there is no proof that he ever lived there. Like Francis Mathews, he subscribed to the Exeter Combination of 1639, but they both settled on what was then debatable land between Exeter and Dover proper, known as the Oyster River settlement, now Durham, where Darby Field owned land as early as 1639. Wm. Beard conveyed to Francis Mathews, June 16, 1640, his house and land at Oyster River " next adjoining ye land of Darbey ffield." Darby Field was still living at Oyster River in 1644, when he was licensed to sell wine. This was no doubt at Durham Point, where stood his dwelling-house, which, with part of his land, he conveyed to John Bickford June 17, 1645. (See *Bickford's Garrison.*) He was still living at Oyster River, however, in 1649, when he had a case in court. And here he no doubt died about two years later. Ambrose Gibbons was appointed " administrator of ye estate of darbey ffield, deceased, at ye court holden in Dover ye 1, 8 mo., (16)51."

FIELD'S PLAINS. This name is generally given to the level sandy tract between Dover and Durham, in the upper part of the Back River District. It includes the *Dry Pines* and *Pitch-pine plains* of early times, and *Clarke's plains* of a later day. They are so named from Zacharias Field, who acquired land on these plains more than 200 years ago, and here built his garrison. Mention is made of them May 9, 1768, when Paul Giles conveyed to Stephen Evans three acres of land on the westerly side of the main road from Cochecho to Durham at a place called *Field's Plains,* beginning at the northerly corner of Clement Meserve's land, adjoining said road, and running westerly by his land to Evans' other land, which three acres said Giles purchased of his honored father-in-law John Field, deceased. Stephen Evans and wife Lydia conveyed to Clement Meserve, Ap. 7, 1773, 58 acres at a place called *Field's plains,* on the right hand side of the road from Dover to Durham, bounded westerly by said Meserve's land, southerly by Capt. Shadrach Hodgdon's, northerly by a highway, and easterly by the aforesaid road to Durham. (See *Dry Pines* and *Field's Garrison.*)

FIELDEN'S BROOK, otherwise FIELDING'S. Mentioned in the Report of the committee for the supply of water in Great Falls, Dec. 2, 1890. It is a small brook that runs through the old Hanson lands on the west side of Prospect Hill, at the upper end of Great Falls village, and empties into the Salmon Falls river. The name is derived from a family that lived there the first half of this century. It is properly *Hanson's brook.*

FLAGGY HOLE. This place is mentioned in the Madbury records. It is a " bog-hole," or low swamp, at the foot of Perry's hill, nearly a mile above Hicks's hill. Two brooks have their source in this bog, on the south side of the road to Barrington. One flows south-west into Oyster river, and the other flows north into the Bellamy. The latter crosses the road, and the bridge over it is called in the town records "*Flaggy Hole Brook bridge.*"

FLAGGY SWAMP. Mentioned July 13, 1721, when one half of Joseph Jenkins' grant of 40 acres near Gallows Hill, afterwards removed, was laid out to his son William. One bound of this land was a maple tree in *Flaggy swamp.* Wm. Jenkins seems to have settled in the vicinity of Wednesday Hill, but he also owned land near the Frog pond, Back River, mentioned in 1771. Joseph Jenkins, however, had land in 1751 in the vicinity of *Flaggy Hole* in Madbury.

FOLLET'S BROOK. This brook rises in Lee, on Mr. Geo. Yorke's land, at a source called *Sam's spring* from Samuel Davis, a former owner of the land. It flows through *Follet's marsh* in the Packer's Falls district, Durham, and finally empties into the Pascassick river near the Boston & Maine railway.

FOLLET'S PATH, otherwise FOLLET'S BRIDGE PATH. (See *Dirty Brook*).

FOLLET'S ROCKY HILL. Mentioned Ap. 9, 1703, when a road from the Oyster bed was laid out along the west side of *Follet's Rocky hill,* above Follet's barn, then along the east side of the next rocky hill to Abraham Clark's. This hill is on the upper side of Oyster river, near the head of Bunker's creek, so called from Wm. Follet, who, with James Bunker, had a grant of a point of land, afterwards called Bunker's neck, Oct. 10, 1653. Follet's share was sold to James Bunker March 28, 1707, by Nicholas Follet of Portsmouth. (See *Bunker's Neck.*)

FOLLET'S SWAMP. This swamp is frequently mentioned in the old grants and deeds at Dover and Exeter, and in the early records of Durham. Ap. 2, 1694, John Thompson, Sr., had a grant of land from the town of Dover in *Follet's swamp* at Oyster River, on the north side of the mast path. And this John Thompson, in his will of Ap. 12, 1733, gives his son Jonathan his land at *Follet's swamp* on the south side of the mast path " where he (Jonathan) now dwells." Forty acres of land, granted to Eli Demerit[1] Ap. 11, 1694, were laid out to him May 31, 1699, at the south-east side of *ffollet's swamp,* bounded north by Jonathan Woodman's land, leaving a path 4 rods wide on one side, for cattle to go into the woods. Eli Demerit, in his will of Nov. 12, 1739, gives his son Ely all his lands " at a place commonly called and known by the name of *Follet's swamp,* in the town of Durham." This land formed part of the estate afterwards inherited by his great-grandsons, Nathaniel and Israel, and still owned by their

---

[1] This name, in one record of the original grant, is written (no doubt phonetically) "Eli Demrey;" and in another record of the same grant " Eli De Miret." The Rev. Hugh Adams, a contemporary of said Eli, writes it " De Merit " in his church records.

descendants. Thomas Johnson's 100 acre grant near Philip Chesley's, laid out to Stephen Jones July 19, 1715, was, when re-surveyed for Joseph Jones, March 14, 1745-6, declared to be "at a place commonly called *follet's swamp*." "Lieut. Jones' fence near *follet's swamp*" is mentioned Ap. 4, 1752. His land was above the Demerit farm, on the borders of Oyster river. This shows that Follet's swamp not only extended along the Mast road, but up the river, and in the direction of Beech Hill.

This swamp is again mentioned June 5, 1764, when Ebenezer Jackson conveyed to Jonathan Thompson 24 acres of land in Durham, "being one half of the land that belonged to his honored grandfather Ichabod Follet, deceased, lying at a place commonly called and known by the name of *Follet's Swamp*," reserving the rights of the widow Prudence Follet during her natural life. Robert Leathers and wife Deborah (Follet) conveyed to Jonathan Thompson, Nov. 21, 1763, one half of the farm where lived Ichabod Follet, deceased, beginning at said Thompson's land, and running along the Mast road to Oyster river, then by said river and John Laskey's land to the land of Joseph Smith, and by Smith's land to that of Jonathan Thompson, also reserving said Prudence's rights.

"*Follet's Swamp* (school) *district*" is mentioned in the Durham records of 1794. It is now called the "*Mast-road district.*"

Another FOLLET'S SWAMP is in the vicinity of Packer's falls, on the upper side of Lamprey river, where Wm. Follet had a grant of six acres in "*Mahomet's Marsh*" the 7th, 6 mo., 1661, and another grant of 100 acres of upland near "*Mohermit's marsh,*" the 18th, 10 mo., 1663. (See *Moharimet's Marsh.*) William Follet was in Dover as early as 1649, and John Follet belonged to the Dover Combination of 1640.

A third FOLLET'S SWAMP is mentioned in the Durham records of 1820, when the heirs of Jeremiah Brackett were taxed in Durham for land "at *Follet's swamp* in Packer's Falls." This land is on the south side of Lamprey river, and is now owned by Mr. James McDaniel. But in the middle of the last century it was in the possession of a Follet, whose cellar may still be traced. The name, however, has been corrupted, and the swamp and a neighboring brook are now often called *Follard's marsh* and *brook*. (See *Follet's Brook.*)

FOOTMAN'S ISLANDS. These islands, two in number, are near the Lubberland shore of Great Bay, not far above Crummit's creek. They are now owned by Dr. Elkins of Newmarket. The name was derived from Thomas Footman, who, the 10th, 8 mo., 1653, had the grant of *an island* containing one acre of land, more or less, in the mouth of the Great Bay. In his will of Aug. 14, 1667, he mentions his house, with 80 acres of land adjacent, and the "*island* laying against the house." The other island is insignificant.

FORD'S CROSSING. This is a crossing on the Portsmouth and Dover R. R., at the lower end of Dover Neck, adjoining the land of Mr. George Ford.

FORD'S LANDING. See *Wingate's Slip.*

FORE RIVER. This name was given by the early settlers on Dover Neck to that part of the Newichawannock on the fore or east side of this Neck. Fore river is repeatedly mentioned in the old grants and deeds of land adjacent.

FOWLING MARSH. Mentioned Aug. 6, 1691, when John Roberts gave his grandsons, Wm. and John Roberts, "a piece of marsh lying on Nechowanuck side, commonly called ye *fowling marsh*," with the flats belonging thereto. This name has not been perpetuated, but the land referred to was evidently in the lower part of Rollinsford.

FOX BROOK. "Edward ffox of Greenland, belonging to Portsmouth," conveyed to Joshua Weeks May 14, 1698, 30 acres of upland "lying *within ye bounds of Portsmouth or Dover*," bounded N. W. and N. E. by Great Bay, S. W. by land in possession of Samuel King, and east by Wm. Shackford's, then in possession of Joshua Weeks. John Dockum conveyed to his oldest son John, June 6, 1713, a tract of land southeast from ye corner of ye road opposite Christopher Keniston's, running W. S. W. by Alexander Keniston's to *ffox brook*. This was, of course, above Winnicot river, but the name of Fox brook is no longer in use.

FOX POINT. This point is so called Sept. 14, 1642. (See *Royall's Cove*.) It is on the Newington shore of the Pascataqua river, between Little Bay and Broad Cove. It is nearly half a mile long, and is the most prominent headland on that side of the river. Its name is supposed to have been given by the hunters of early times, who drove the foxes they pursued into this long narrow neck, whence it was impossible to make their escape. It is said to have been an old Indian "drive," where the aborigines brought the wild deer to bay in a similar manner.

This point was originally owned by John Bickford of Oyster River. "Thirty acres of upland on *fox poynt*" were granted John Bickford, Sr., by the town of Dover, the 10th, 8 mo., 1653, and laid out by Robert Burnum and John Davis, beginning at a marked tree near Thomas Trickey's marsh on "the *letell baye* sied," and extending to "a marked tree at the broad cove on the other sied of the necke."

May 13, 1677, John Bickford and Temperance his wife, "out of love and affection to their daughter Mary, wife of Nicholas Harryson of Oyster River," conveyed to her "twenty acres of land in Dover, bounded on one part by the river of Piscataqua where it leads into Little Bay, said land known by the name of *ffox poynt*, granted unto said Bickford by the town of Dover." Nicholas Harrison, in his will of March 5, 1707,[1] gives his son-in-law John Downing and wife Elizabeth, as his eldest daughter, "all his housing, orchards, and lands, at *ffox pointe*," given him by his father-in-law John Bickford. James Burnam of Oyster River, and Temperance his wife, July 8, 1713, conveyed to John Downing of *ffox point* in ye township of Dover, two lots at or near ye head of broad Cove at *ffox point*, one containing 11 acres, and the other 19 acres, which lots were granted by Dover to Mr. Nich-

---

[1] The Rev. John Pike says, "Nicholas Harrison died strangely insensible of any spiritual good," Ap. 11, 1708.

olas Harrison, and bequeathed by him to Temperance his daughter.

Fox Point was the Newington terminus of the old Pascataqua bridge from the Durham shore. Richard Downing of Newington, Nov. 12, 1793, "for the sum of five shillings, but more especially for the encouragement of building a bridge over the Piscataqua river at and from *Fox Point*," conveyed to the proprietors of said bridge " one acre, to be laid out in square form, upon any part of my farm at *Fox Point*, now in possession of my son Bartholomew, where said proprietors may think proper to build said bridge and from my farm," on condition that the deed be null and void if the bridge be not commenced within two years and completed as directed by the act of incorporation.

Fox Point[1] remained in possession of the Downing family till the present century. It is now chiefly owned by the heirs of Dr. F. E. Langdon. The view from the ridge above the Langdon house is fine, with Little Bay at the left; Durham shore, with the intermediate islands, in front; and the mouth of Back river at the northwest, out of which pours a stream to quicken the course of the turbulent *Horse Races* of the Pascataqua, which may be seen swiftly coursing towards the Long Reach. Dover Point is in full sight. It is a page full of historic interest.

Charles W. Tuttle, in his "*Historical Papers*," pp. 163–171, endeavors to prove that no Indian attack on Fox Point was made May 28, 1690, as generally believed. His reasoning, however, is wholly negative. On the other hand, Wm. Vaughan, a prominent man of Portsmouth, in a letter written *that very night* at ten o'clock, asserts that the neighborhood of Bloody Point had that afternoon been ravaged by the Indians under Hopehood, who had been killing and burning *within three or four miles of Portsmouth*. Belknap, in his *History of N. H.*, gives an account of this attack without expressing the slightest doubt as to its occurrence. And the constant tradition in Newington is supported by the marks of assault on the Downing garrison at Fox Pt., and the tradition of the massacre at Bloody Point, near Langstaffe's garrison.

Fox Point ferry ran to *Meader's landing* at the mouth of Oyster river, on the upper side. It is mentioned Aug. 21, 1771, when Lemuel Meader conveyed his ferry place and privilege to George Knight, son of John Knight of Portsmouth, from whom it was sometimes called *Knight's ferry*. "*Fox Point ferry* to Durham Point" is mentioned in 1792, no doubt the same as *Bickford's ferry*, which is spoken of Aug. 23, 1764, when Stephen Willey conveyed to his son Stephen his homestead at or near this ferry. This land was at Durham Point.

FRANCE. This name is given to a neighborhood in Barrington, westerly of Swayne's pond.

FRANK'S FORT. This is an island

---

[1] As you turn down from Broad Cove to Fox Point, there is a fine wood at the right, in which is a remarkable oak, or series of oaks—four in number—that spring from a common base of oval shape, with a space between each bole like a seat. These three spaces are delightfully umbrageous, and being well adapted for sweet converse, have been popularly named the *Lovers' Seats*.

in the Long Reach of the Pascataqua river, just above Eliot Neck. It was once a steep gravelly height, flat on the top, with the aspect of a fortification, but has been greatly worn by the elements, and partly carried away by vessels for ballast. *Frank's Fort* is mentioned Feb. 14, 1648, in a grant to John Gren. (*York Records.*) In a deed from George Smith of Dover to Dennis Downing of Kittery, Dec. 18, 1650, *ffrankes fort* and *watts fort* are mentioned. Land on the east side of the Pascataqua river, "betwixt *Franke's fort* and *Darby's fort*," was granted, July 14, 1659, by the General Court of Mass. Bay to Wm. Hawthorne of Salem. *Frank's fort* is also spoken of Dec. 4, 1663, when James Emery of Kittery conveyed to Stephen Robinson of Oyster River a tract of land between Richard Rogers and Richard Green, Sr. ;[1] and again, May 16, 1695, in a grant of land to Maj. Thomas Clark, "between *ffrankes fort* and *Wat's fort.*"[2] The name of *Frank's fort* has been perpetuated to this day, but its origin is not known. Boatmen on the river invariably call it by this name. "Frankfort" is a corruption that should be ignored. A Newington tradition says the powder from Fort William and Mary was first stored on this island, whence it was conveyed farther up the river for greater security.

FRANKLIN CITY. This name was given to a projected settlement or town, laid out in Durham, at the end of Pascataqua bridge, towards the close of last century, by a company of men belonging to Dover, Portsmouth, Durham, etc., two of whom— Nathaniel Coggswell and Thomas Pinkham, in behalf of themselves and their associates—petitioned the New Hampshire legislature in 1796 to be incorporated under the name of the *Franklin Proprietary*, to " continue a body politic and corporate by that name forever." The act of incorporation was passed Dec. 15, 1796, and approved the next day. This bill authorized Ebenezer Thompson of Durham to call the first meeting of the proprietors, or, in case of his failure, Ebenezer Smith of the same town.

Thomas Pinkham of Durham, Dec. 30, 1797, conveyed to Wm. King Atkinson of Dover all right, title, and interest, in fourteen lots in "*Franklin Propriety*, so called," in Durham, also three lots in the flats, and "one third of all the land at *Tittle*, or *Tickle*, or *Trickle Point*, so called, in said propriety, not laid out and drawn, and one third of the flats not heretofore conveyed, lying near Pascataqua (river) and one third of any common land of said Franklin," etc. Each of these lots contained one fourth of an acre.

The Portsmouth *Gazette*, of April 11, 1801, gives notice of a meeting to be held by the proprietors on Thursday, May 7, of that year, among

---

[1] Ap, 28, 1697, "John Hall, Sen., drowned coming up the River in a little float, near *Green point*." Rev. John Pike's *Journal*.

[2] *Watt's fort*, otherwise *Joslin's fort*, was about a mile farther up the river, on a point of land where Henry Joselyn or Josselyn is said to have lived for a time before going to Scarborough. Wm. Leighton, mariner, bought land at or near Watt's fort June 20, 1656, and his son Capt. John Leighton, the Sheriff, built a garrison there in 1690, generally called *Leighton's fort*. This point is in Eliot, and still owned by the Leighton family.

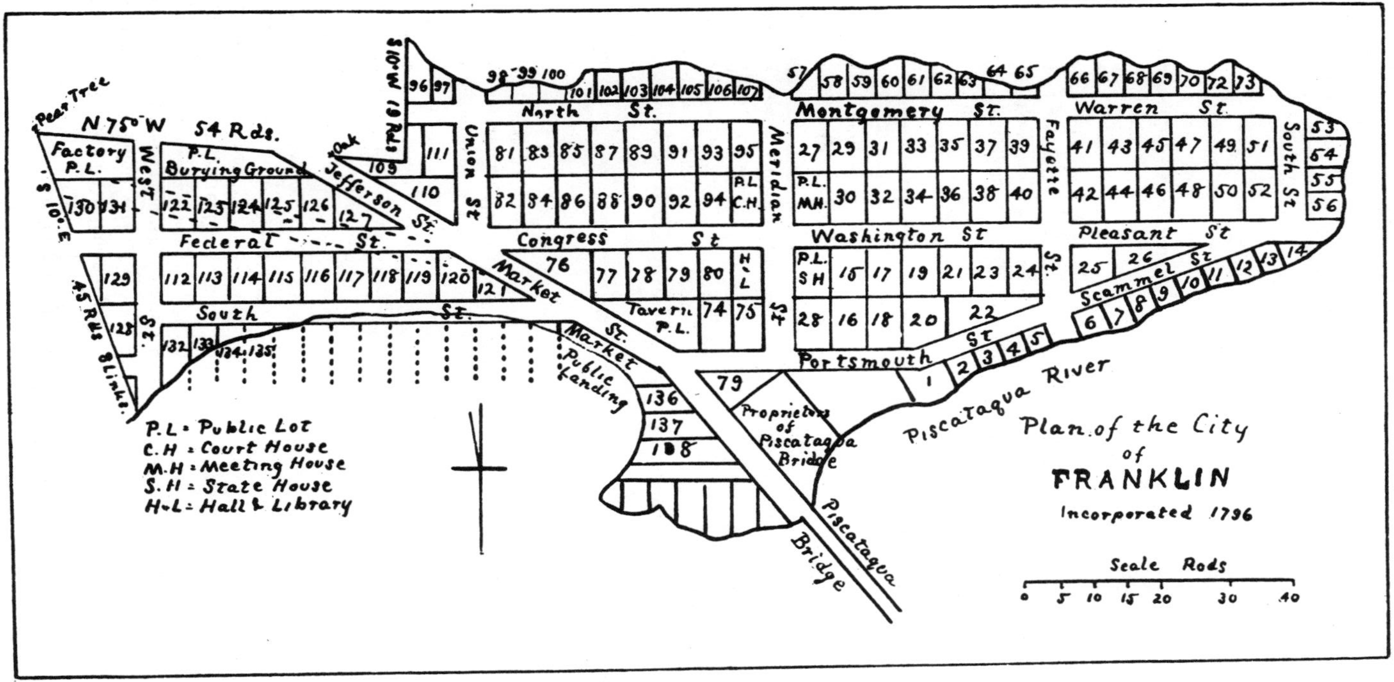
Plan of the City of FRANKLIN
Incorporated 1796
Scale Rods
0 5 10 15 20 30 40
P.L = Public Lot
C.H = Court House
M.H = Meeting House
S.H = State House
H.L = Hall & Library
Pear Tree
N 75° W 54 Rds.
S 10° E
45 Rds 8 links
S 10° W 19 Rds
Oak
Factory P.L.
P.L. Burying Ground
West St.
Jefferson St.
Union St
North St.
Meridian St
Montgomery St.
Fayette St.
Warren St
South St
Federal St.
Congress St
Washington St
Pleasant St
Scammel St
South St.
Market St.
Market St.
Portsmouth St
Tavern P.L.
Public Landing
Proprietors of Piscataqua Bridge
Piscataqua River
Piscataqua Bridge

other purposes, to see what should be done about the New Hampshire turnpike road passing through some of their lots, and to renew the boundaries. This notice is signed by eleven of their number, among whom are Wm. K. Atkinson of Dover, Mark Simes of Portsmouth, etc.

The founding of Franklin City was projected by men specially interested in trade and shipping. In the first quarter of this century many vessels were built, not only on the wharves in Durham village, but at Pascataqua bridge. The embargo and the war of 1812 were a great check to this business, but mention is made of two privateers built at this bridge by Andrew Simpson of Durham during that war, the contracts for which are in the writer's possession. The decline of shipping was a serious blow to the settlement of the proposed city, and the idea was gradually abandoned. Ballard Pinkham, administrator of the estate of Thomas Pinkham, advertised the sale of "seventeen lots in *Franklin city*," Jan. 2, 1812. The "Winkley estate in *Franklin city*, so called," is mentioned in the *Strafford Register* (Dover) of Feb. 15, 1820. Mention is made of the owners of 36 lots in 1825. And May 28, 1829, Andrew Simpson sold 25 lots. But their decrease in value is shown by the abatements in the rate-lists. The Durham records of 1821 mention an abatement of $3.15, on Timothy Pinkham's "land in *Franklin City*."

Franklin City was laid out by Nathaniel Coggswell and Thomas Pinkham. The plan was drawn by Benjamin Dearborn, one of the proprietors, who was a teacher in Portsmouth, and a man of much mechanical genius.[1] This plan, beautifully executed, is still preserved, and in the possession of Mrs. Alley, the present owner of the site of Franklin City. But no one can behold it, with its wharves, streets, and house-lots, all marked out in imposing array, without being reminded of that which young Martin Chuzzlewit found adorning one side of Mr. Zephaniah Scadder's office, and, like Eden City, with nothing yet built, and in nearly as low and unpromising a situation as that renowned settlement. (See *Meader's Neck* and *Tickle Point*.)

FREETOWN. This name has long been given to a part of Madbury, north of Hicks's hill, now in school-district No. 3. It is mentioned in Feb., 1730, when twenty acres of land were laid out to Derry Pitman, "a little above the west end of Mehermett's Hill," beginning at the corner of Wm. Demerit's land, and running N. by it 60 rods, then E. by the common, then S. "on a road leading to the road commonly called *Freetown road*." Derry Pitman and wife Dorothy[2] conveyed to Wm.

---

[1] Benjamin Dearborn is mentioned in 1786 as an inventor of a certain balance or scales, and an engine for throwing water. (*N. H. State Papers*, 18 : 779.)

[2] Sir William Pepperrell, in his will of Jan. 11, 1759, mentions his "kinswoman Dorothy Pitman," and gives her "all the money which her husband Derry Pitman oweth me." The Durham records have the following entry: "The ages of Mr. Derry Pitman's children, born in the year 1749, in March ye 22, *andrew pepral Pitman*, and Mary Pitman." These twin children were evidently both named for the Pepperrell family. An interesting account of the captivity of Derry Pitman's parents is to be found in the *N. H. Town Papers*, 17 : 682. His sister Tabitha married Eli Demerit, Jr., and Abigail, another sister, married Wm. Demerit, brother of said Eli.

Fowler, June 25, 1748, one acre of land in Madbury, part of a 30 acre grant to his father Nathaniel, June 23, 1701, beginning at Zachariah Pitman's fence, near said Fowler's house, on the same side of the road leading from Madbury to the place commonly called *Freetown*.

Twenty-eight acres were laid out to Nathaniel Davis Nov. 14, 1749, at a place called *Freetown*, where said Davis then lived, being part of a thirty acre grant to his father John Davis, deceased. Samuel Emerson of Dover and Dorothy his wife, Wm. Allin of Rochester and Hannah his wife, Joseph Tibbets of Rochester and Sarah his wife, and John Tompson, Jr., of Durham and Abigail his wife, conveyed to Wm. Dam, Jan. 10, 1751, 25 acres of land in that part of Dover called *freetown*, granted "Michal" Emerson of Dover, deceased, in the division of the common lands, bounded on the S. E. by Joseph Jenkins, and joining Nathaniel Davis, and the Hayes lands, on the S. E. and S. W., and running north to a rock called *John Foy's*. The inventory of Mrs. Sarah Dam's estate, July 16, 1767, mentions her land "at a place called *Freetown*, in Madbury."

At a public meeting in the parish of Madbury, March 31, 1757, it was voted that a school be kept two months "at Mr Hill's House at *Freetown*."

FRENCHMAN'S CREEK. This creek is one of the bounds of the old Emerson and Leighton lands, in the lower part of the Back river district. The origin of the name is uncertain. John Winthrop, in his Journal, June 25, 1631, speaks of an English ship that had brought to Pascataqua some Frenchmen to make salt. Henry Frenchman was taxed in Dover in 1665. John Frenchman, "smith," is on the Portsmouth rate-list of Sept. 24, 1681. Frenchman's creek is mentioned the 6th, 10 mo., 1656, when Thomas Layton's grant of 100 acres was laid out on the south side of "*the frenchman's creek.*" (See *Royall's Cove*.)

Nicholas Harford conveyed to Samuel Emerson, March 20, 1711–12, land on the west side of Back river, near *Frenchman's creek*, which land had been bought of Moses Davis, to whom it was granted in 1701. It was between the land of Thomas Layton and the land Samuel Emerson bought of Joseph and Thomas Hall, Dec. 18, 1700. May 17, 1714, Thomas Laiton sold Samuel Emerson the eastern portion of his land at Back river, "beginning at rocky Hill at ye turn of the fence, and so running straight down to a white oak standing against a little orchard y^t was Nich^{ls} Harford's on ye west, then straight to the turn of ye marsh and so to ye river." These tracts became the homestead estate of Capt. Samuel Emerson, and remained in the possession of his descendants about 175 years. The buildings, with part of the land, now belong to Mr. Mark Chase. Capt. Emerson, a direct ancestor of the writer, was a native of Haverhill, Mass., and a brother of Hannah Dustin, famous for her escape from the Indians in 1697. He married Judith, sister of Col. James Davis of Oyster River, who, after her marriage, was for several years a captive among the Indians. Capt. Emerson removed, early last century, to Oyster River, where he was appointed one of the first deacons of the church, April 3, 1818, the Sunday after its organization, and his wife was the first person admitted as a member, that same day. He was ordained "Elder" Nov. 16, 1721. The grave of Samuel Emerson,—captain, deacon, and elder,—and that of his wife, Judith, may still be seen near the residence of his descendant, Deacon Winthrop S. Meserve, of Durham.

FRESH CREEK. This stream is a tributary of the Cochecho river, into which it empties on the east side, not far above the mouth. It is mentioned in the Dover records as early as 1648. The mill privilege on this creek was granted the 5th, 10 mo., 1652, to Wm. Furber, Wm. Wentworth, Henry Langstar and Thomas Canney, together with the timber "from the head of tidewater three miles up into the woods betwixt the *two freshets*, the southernmost freshett coming out of the marsh beside the Great hill at Cochecho, the northernmost freshett bounding Capt wiggins and M^r broadstreet's grant at Quomphegan," etc. (*N. H. Town Pap.*, XI: 530.) Henry Tibbets, June 29, 1713, conveyed to John Drew, Sr., one half of the mill privilege at the head of Fresh creek, and half of his labor in building the saw-mill there, with the privilege of erecting a dam for the convenience of said mill, together with land for a *log hill*. This fall was within the line of Samuel Croumel's (Cromwell's) land, near ye place where Joshua Croumel's house formerly stood.

The name of Fresh creek is still retained, but the water power is now small. The lowest saw-mill thereon was at the crossing of the present road to Eliot. *Flagg's mill*, a tide mill, was the last that stood here. The tide, however, extends up to the old road laid out in 1709, where stood *Fielding's mill*. Another mill once stood farther up the stream, where it is crossed by the road of 1733. Between the site of Flagg's and Fielding's mills are the remains of an old beaver dam in a cove, at the foot of a hill covered with alders, poplars, and red oaks. The part of Fresh creek above the head of tide water to the mouth of Twombley's brook is often called *Willow brook*, from the number of ancient willows that border the stream for some distance; and sometimes *Barbel brook*, because in spring it is full of barbels, as well as lamprey-eels, etc. Barbel brook is crossed by the turnpike road to Portland. Above the mouth of Twombley's brook, it is called *Rollins brook*, to its source among the springs in the vicinity of *Otis' Hill*. (See *Rollins'* and *Twombley's Brooks*.)[1]

The whole brook above the head of tide water was in early times called *Fresh creek brook*. This name is given it Dec. 16, 1720, when Gershom Wentworth conveyed to Thomas Downs ten acres of land near said Downs' house, extending up *fresh creek brook* 31 poles. Ebenezer Wentworth conveyed to Benjamin Wentworth, June 27, 1737, all right and title to the estate of their

---

[1] A description of Fresh creek and its tributaries, written with charming freshness (as the subject required) by Mrs. Baer of Rollinsford, is to be found in the *Granite Monthly*, Dec., 1883.

honored father Benj[n] Wentworth, bounded northerly by Ephraim Wentworth's land, easterly by *Fresh creek brook*, etc.

FRESH CREEK WOODS. Mentioned Nov. 28, 1729, when Ephraim Wentworth conveyed to Gershom Wentworth ten acres in a place called *Fresh Creek woods*, beginning at the highway side, near John Heard's land, and extending along said way over *Fresh creek head* 46 rods to Daniel Plummer's land; and two acres more on the north side of said highway, beginning at a heap of stones near Richard Goodwin's easterly corner.

FRESH CREEK NECK. This neck of land is in the lower part of Rollinsford, between Fresh creek and the Newichawannock river. It is mentioned March 19, 1693-4, when Thomas Tibbets had a grant of 40 acres "on *Fresh creek neck*." And Ap. 2, 1694, Joseph Jenkins had a grant of 20 acres "on *Fresh creek neck*, to butt on y[e] fore river." The lower part of this neck was granted Wm. Pomfrett in 1643, and the remainder to Richard Waldron and others in 1652. (See *Cochecho Point*.)

FRESHET BRIDGE. This bridge is across Johnson's creek, in the lower part of Madbury, and is so called in the town records to distinguish it from "*Johnson's Creek bridge*," which is not far off, on the boundary line between Durham and Madbury. The road from the Dover line above Daniel Pinkham's house is spoken of Ap. 6, 1815, as leading down by his house over *freshet bridge*.

FROG POND. Mentioned in Col. James Davis's will of Oct. 18, 1748, in which he gives his son Ephraim 15 acres of land granted to his father, laid out adjoining "a place commonly called and known by the name of *Frogg Pond*." This is probably the pond referred to July 24, 1771, when Nathaniel Lamos conveyed to James Lamos 15 acres and 100 sq. rods, part of a pasture near Johnson's creek, beginning at a *Frog Pond* by the land of Wm. Jenkins.

FURBER'S BRIDGE. So called in the town records of Lee in 1785. It is across Little river, on the road from Lee Hill to Wadleigh's falls. Its name was derived from Jethro Furber, whose land on Little river is mentioned when the above road was laid out in 1755. (See *Little River*.)

FURBER'S POINT and FERRY. Furber's Point is on the Newington shore, at the Narrows between Great and Little Bays. The name is derived from Wm. Furber, who came from England in the "Angel Gabriel," which was wrecked at Pemaquid in August, 1636. He was at Dover in 1637, and belonged to the Combination of 1640. He had a grant of land at Welsh Cove as early as 1652. In 1657, he had a grant of thirty acres more, which must have been beyond the boundary line at Hogsty Cove, as they were a part of the 400 acres along Great Bay granted to Dover by the government of Mass. Bay in 1643, and confirmed in May, 1656. These 30 acres were doubtless part of the land he afterwards gave his son Jethro. June 17, 1674, he gave his homestead to his oldest son William (see *Pascataqua Rock*), who, Dec. 11, 1694, was licensed to keep a ferry "from his house at Welchman's cove over to Oyster River." (See *Mathew's Neck*.) Furber's ferry, however, was in operation before May, 1694. (See *N. H. Prov. Pap.*, 17: 668.) The ferry place on the Newington side is mentioned May 19, 1708, when "Joshua ffurber of Portsmouth, mariner, now bound to sea, upon a voyage to the West Indies, and not knowing how the Lord may dispose of me," gives, in his will, unto his "dear and loving wife Elizabeth," till her son Joshua should be of age, his dwelling-house at Welch cove, and all his lands, " beginning at a pitch-pine tree standing below *the point*, about fifteen rodds or thereabouts below the *ferry-place*, where the turn of the tide begins at ebb and flow, and from there to a stake in the field, on the south side of the old barn, and so on to William's line, and from thence to the elm tree by the brick-yard home to the meadow of Thomas Roberts, being the house and land which my father William ffurber, deceased, gave me by his deed of Sept. 13, 1707." The old Furbers lie buried at the right, as you drive down to the point where Furber's wharf formerly stood. The way, now seldom traversed, is rough, but bordered with many fine walnut trees, and the view up Great Bay and down Little Bay amply repays all fatigue. Across the Narrows may be seen, amid the trees, the white house on Adams' Point, once called Mathews' Neck, the Durham terminus of Furber's ferry.

FURBER'S STRAITS. This name is sometimes given to the *Narrows* between Great and Little bays, across which Furber's ferry once ran.

GAGE'S HILL. This name is now generally given to Faggoty hill, from Capt. John Gage, who lived at the foot of it, on the place now owned by Mr. Joseph Hutchins. It is otherwise called *Dry Hill*.

GAGE'S POINT. This name is given on Whitehouse's map of 1834, to a point at the mouth of the Cochecho on the west side. It is derived from Col. John Gage of Beverley, Mass., who came to Dover before 1725, and married Mrs. Elizabeth (Roberts) Hubbard, great-granddaughter of Thomas Roberts of the Dover Combination of 1640. He acquired land below the mouth of the Cochecho, on the west side, before Feb. 12, 1742, on which day Love and Mary Canney confirmed to him all right to 70 acres in Dover, bounded southerly on Gage's land to the mouth of the Cochecho, westerly on said river to Thompson's Point, and northerly by said river to a place commonly called Long creek, etc.

GALLOWS HILL. This hill is mentioned May 30, 1699, as a little below the falls in Oyster river, where Samuel and Philip Chesley and others had liberty to build a saw-mill. (See *Oyster River Falls*.) This mill became known as "Chesley's mill," and was so called as early as 1701. At a later period it became a grist-mill. Gallows hill is just below, on the so-called "Mill road," that leads from Durham village to Packer's Falls. This sinister name is derived from some residents of former days, supposed to be morally qualified to undergo the *highest* penalty of the law.

Swazey's hill in Dover, just below Central square, between Central avenue and the Cochecho river, was often called *Gallows hill* after the execution of Elisha Thomas, who was hung in 1788 for the murder of Capt. Peter

Drowne of New Durham. The spectators assembled on this hill, but the gallows stood at the foot—where the print-works now are.[1]

GARRISONS. The garrisons mentioned in this work are classified under the following heads: *Back River, Dover, Greenland, Lee, Madbury, Newington, Oyster River* (Durham), and *Rollinsford Garrisons.*

GARRISON HILL. This name was originally given to the small hill in Dover on which Heard's garrison once stood, but for more than half a century has been transferred to the height at the eastward, called in early times the *Great Hill,* and at a later period *Varney's hill.* If no garrison ever stood on the Garrison Hill of the present day, it was at least surrounded by garrisons. Heard's was on the westerly side; Otis's farther off, at the south; and a little later, one, if not two, Wentworth garrisons were built at the eastward. And Varney's house probably had defences. Ebenezer Varney acquired land here in 1696, after which it was generally called " *Varney's hill.*" This name is given to it as late as 1834, on Whitehouse's map of Dover. (See *Great Hill* and *Varney's Hill.*)

Garrison Hill is about a mile above the Dover railway station. Eight and a half acres thereon were bought by the city in 1888, for a public park and a reservoir to supply the city with water. The reservoir, which contains about two million gallons, is supplied from Page's springs, and, when necessary, from Willand's pond. The Hussey springs have also been recently acquired. The Park has deservedly become a popular resort. The view from the top of the hill, which is 298 feet above the head of tide-water, extends from the White Mountains to the Isles of Shoals. In every direction is a glorious range of hills—among them the Northwood hills and Saddleback mountain, the three Pawtuckaways in Nottingham, the Blue ridge in Strafford, with Blue Job at the head,[2] Otis' or Ricker's hill in Rollinsford, Frost's hill in Eliot, and, further east, Mount Agamenticus of legendary fame.

GARRISON HILL VILLAGE. This name is given, on Whitehouse's map of Dover, to the settlement northwest of Garrison Hill.

GEEBIG ROAD, otherwise CHEBEAGUE and JEBUCTO. The first of these names is popularly given to a road that leads through the northeastern part of Nottingham to *Geebig mill,* on North river. It is called *Jebucto road* on Tuttle's map of Nottingham in 1806. " *Jabeague upper mill* " is mentioned Oct. 31, 1765, when Solomon Davis conveyed to Wm. Drew a tract of land on Cross street in Nottingham, adjoining this mill. The name is said to have been derived from Chebucto, an Indian chief in the vicinity of North river, the first half of last century. Chebucto or Jebucto was also the ancient name of the place where is now the city of Halifax, N. S. Great and Little Chebeague islands on the coast of Maine have names akin.

---

[1] Capt. Peter Drowne was a revolutionary officer in Col. Stephen Peabody's regiment, that went to Rhode Island in 1778. He was murdered Feb. 4, 1788, by Elisha Thomas, who had served as a private in Col. Tash's regiment in 1776.

[2] The name of *Blue Job* is given to the highest part of the Blue Hill range in Farmington, from Job Allard, a former proprietor.

GEORGE'S CREEK. This creek, menioned in the Dover records of 1803, empties into the Cochecho river near Beach's soap-factory.

GERRISH'S BRIDGE. This is a well known bridge across Bellamy river in Madbury, below the Hook. A petition for a bridge across Bellamy Bank freshet, "a little above *Capt. Paul Gerrish's saw-mill*," was made Oct. 12, 1756. This bridge is spoken of in 1787 as standing by "Benjamin Gerrish's corn-mill." Being long and high and difficult to keep in repair, Gerrish's bridge is repeatedly mentioned in the town records of Madbury.

GERRISH'S MILLS. The first mills of this name were at the lowest falls in the Bellamy river. Capt. John Gerrish, through his wife, daughter of Major Richard Waldron, acquired one half of the water privilege here, Oct. 17, 1683, and became sole owner at a later day. At his death this property fell to his sons Timothy and Paul, who had two mills on the lower part of the Bellamy in 1719, and seem to have acquired exclusive possession of all the mill privileges on the river, within the limits of ancient Dover. (See *Demerit's Mill* and *Bellamy Falls*.)

Another *Gerrish mill*, frequently mentioned in the Dover and Madbury records, also stood on the Bellamy. It was in Madbury, below the Hook, directly southwest of Barbadoes Pond. A record of Jan. 7, 1758, speaks of it as "set up by Capt. Paul Gerrish and others." Among these was John Hanson, of Dover, who, that same day, sold Daniel Hayes, of Madbury, one sixteenth part of this mill. "*Log hill*, adjacent to the mill," is spoken of in the deed of conveyance. A grist-mill was also erected here. One of these mills was swept away by a flood in 1798, and the other, June 24, 1799; but they were both rebuilt soon after. Mrs. Sarah Meserve, of Dover, March 28, 1804, sold Daniel Hayes of Madbury, one twenty-fourth part of *Gerrish's saw-mill*—"the same," she says in her deed, "that was set up by my father, Benjamin Gerrish." Benjamin was the son of Paul. This saw-mill became a day-mill in time, and was taken down about 1833.

"The grist-mill and falls, with the privilege belonging to the same," were, in the early part of this century, acquired by Eli Demerit,[1] who sold them at auction in 1832. This mill is now gone. The dam was removed in 1865 by the Messrs. Sawyer of Dover, who had acquired control of all the mill privileges on the Bellamy.

GILES'S CREEK. This creek, the first below Stevenson's, on the south side of Oyster river, is mentioned May 26, 1719, when James Davis, son of Moses, and Mary his wife, daughter of Bartholomew Stevenson, sold James Langley fifteen acres of land granted Joseph Stevenson March 19, 1693-4, beginning at an oak tree near the highway that goeth from a creek called *Giles's creek*, thence E. S. E. to a pine tree by *the pen*.[2] This name, now discontinued, was derived from Matthew Gyles, who was taxed

---

[1] This Eli Demerit was the great-grandson of the Eli who built the first saw-mill at Bellamy Hook.
[2] Several "*pens*" are mentioned in the neighborhood of Durham Point and Lubberland. A tract of four acres called "*the Pen*," on the north side of the road to Durham Point, originally part of the parsonage land, was conveyed to Valentine Mathes by Robert Mathes, May 3, 1832.

at Dover in 1648. He died before June 30, 1668, when his estate was divided between Richard Knight and Matthew Williams. His land was afterwards acquired by William Pitman, whose son Francis sold it to Edward Wakeham, May 2, 1695. The deed of conveyance describes it as " situate and lying, and being in ye place known by ye name of *Gile's old field*, lying between two creeks." (See *Wakeham's Creek*.)

GILMORE'S POINT. This point is on the upper shore of Oyster river, between the Smith land and the mouth of Bunker's creek. It was so named from James Gilmore, who lived in that vicinity the middle of last century. He seems to have married Deborah, widow of Joseph Smith, who died before Ap. 3, 1766. James Gilmore conveyed to Daniel Smith, July 23, 1792, the whole share that fell to Samuel Smith out of that part of his father Joseph Smith's estate that was set off to his mother Deborah Gilmore for her thirds. Daniel Smith married Mary Gilmore Dec. 7, 1780. This tract is now owned by Mr. Geo. Fowler.

GOAT ISLAND. This island is in the Pascataqua river, a little below the mouth of Oyster river, and, like Rock island, belongs to Newington. Wm. Pomfrett, the 5th, 5 mo., 1652, had the grant of " one island, lying in the river that runneth toward Oyster river, commonly called by the name of *Gooett Iland*, having *Seder* (Cedar) *point* on the north, and *Redding Point* on the east and *Fox poynt* on the southwestward." William Pomfrett gave this island to his grandson, Wm. Dam. " William Damme of Dover," and wife Martha, Aug. 5, 1702, gave their son Pomfrett Dam the island " commonly called and known by ye name of *Goat Island*, lying between *Fox point* and ye neck of land formerly granted unto Mr. Valentine Hill, deceased." In the appraisal of the estate of Samuel Dam, Ap. 18, 1751, mention is made of " one small island of about three acres, called *Goat Island*," valued 20 £. It is also mentioned in the inventory of Timothy Emerson's estate in 1755, and valued 60 £. It now belongs to Mr. Cyrus Frink and others.

According to Dame's map of Newington, Goat island is 48 rods long. At the west end it is 11 rods wide. Its greatest width is 12 rods, whence it tapers to the east end, where it is only 2 rods wide. This island was one of the links in the old Pascataqua bridge. On it was built the " Pascataque-bridge tavern " before Oct. 24, 1794, on which day the agents of the Bridge Co. advertised it " to be let," describing it as " a new, commodious, double house, with a large, convenient stable, and a well that afforded an ample supply of water in the dryest season." This tavern was burned down many years ago, and no buildings now remain on the island. There is another *Goat Island* in the Pascataqua river, off the Kittery shore.

GODDARD'S CREEK. This creek is on the southern shore of Lubberland, and was, till 1870, one of the boundaries between Durham and Newmarket, and, of course, between Strafford and Rockingham counties. The dividing line, when perambulated March 4, 1805, " from Lampreyeel River Bridge to the great bay," began " at the *picked rock* under said bridge, and ran S. 56½° E. 264 rods, to the head of *Goddard's creek*, so called, thence by the channel of said creek to the mouth at the bay aforesaid."

The name of this creek was derived from John Goddard, one of Capt. Mason's colonists, who came over with Henry Jocelyn and others in the *Pied Cow*, in 1634, and arrived at Newichawannock July 13, where he aided in erecting a saw-mill and corn-mill. (Tuttle's *Capt. John Mason*, p. 325.) He acquired land on the creek that afterwards took his name Sept. 22, 1647, when Joseph Miller conveyed to him the house where Miller then lived, together with 30 acres of marsh on the west side of Great Bay, near the Great Cove, and 100 acres of land on the west side of said marsh, all of which had been originally granted to Thomas Larkham. John Goddard died before June 27, 1667, on which day the inventory of his estate was made. "The *old way* from Lamprill-river falls to John Godder's," is mentioned the 28th, 2 mo., 1664, in the laying out of a road from said falls to the Great Bay. His creek is mentioned June 25, 1675, when all of Lamprey river neck was conveyed to Peter Coffin, extending from the head of "*John Goddar's creek*" to the head of tide water below Lamprey river falls, where Mr. Hill's works stood. An error having been made in laying out "a lot at Lubberland for old Richard York," and the old return being lost, the bounds were renewed Dec. 11, 1683, beginning at a marked tree by the creek called *Goddard's creek*, and running N. N. W. 60 poles to a valley or gutter, etc. Four acres of thatch-ground on the south side of "*Gothard's creek*," joining the south side of "Lampreel river neck," were granted Wm. Furber, Sr., June 23, 1701.

This creek is called *Lubberland creek* March 10, 1740–41, when Sampson Doe of the parish of Newmarket, in the town of Exeter, conveyed to his son Samuel, one fourth of a piece of salt marsh and flats in "ye creek commonly called *Lubberland creek*." There appears to have been a mill on this creek in early times. "Samson Doe" conveyed to Nathaniel Doe, Ap. 22, 1742, his land and marsh "between ye fence and *Goddard's creek*, from *ye old mill*, so called, up to an elm tree at Drisco's field."

GOLDING'S BRIDGE. Mentioned Dec. 21, 1721, when Maturin Ricker's grant in the "Trunnel country" was laid out to his son Joseph on the "east side of a way that leads from Quamphegan to *goldins bridge*." This name may be a corruption of Gooding. Maturin and Hannah Ricker Aug. 29, 1721, conveyed to Richard Gooding 12 acres, part of a 20 acre grant to Joshua Cromwell, and laid out to said Maturin Dec. 14, 1720, on the north side of the way from Cochecho to Salmon falls, and two acres more on the south side of said way, beginning at an elm tree standing by *a bridge*. This was no doubt Golding or Ricker's bridge. (See *Fresh Creek Woods*.)

Maturin Ricker conveyed to Gershom Wentworth, Oct. 27, 1729, twelve acres of land on the easterly side of the road from Cochecho to Salmon falls, beginning at an elm tree near a certain bridge called *Ricker's bridge*, and running S. by E. to Joseph Ricker's fence, and thence easterly to Jeremiah Rawlin's fence.

This bridge was no doubt across Fresh creek brook, now Rollins' brook.

GONIC. See *Squamanagonic.*

GOOSEBERRY MARSH. This marsh is in the upper part of Madbury, on the south side of Bellamy river. It is so called May 30, 1738, when John and Sarah Giles conveyed to Wm. Dam 20 acres on " the S. E. side of y^e *Hook marsh,* beginning at a hemlock tree near ye place called y^e *goosbery marsh.*" Timothy Moses conveyed to Timothy Emerson, Aug. 24, 1741, five acres at the east end of *Gooseberry marsh,* on the south side of Belleman's Bank river.

THE GORE. This was a section of land on the borders of Portsmouth and the Bloody Point district that remained ungranted till 1693. It did not form part of Ancient Dover, but it is often mentioned in the conveyances of the Dover lands adjoining, and now belongs for the most part, if not wholly, to Newington. The selectmen of Portsmouth, March 22, 1693, conveyed to Wm. Vaughan "*a gore of land* between the land formerly granted Capt. Bryan Pendleton and the line y^t is ye bounds betwene the towns of Portsmouth and Dover y^t runs from Cannyes Coue to hoogsty Coue, and runs from Cannyes Coue to (the) Bloody point roode waye that leads to Greenland." William Vaughan of Portsmouth, Feb. 1, 1708, conveyed to George Huntris of Dover, a tract of 40 acres "*in Portsmouth,* adjoining to *Cannyes Cove,* near said George Huntris' house in Piscataqua river, in that part which is called the Long Retch, beginning at the river's side, at said cove, and running W. S. W. from the river by a tract of land which was formerly given and laid out to Capt. Pendleton by the town of Portsmouth, which said Pendleton sold to Christopher Jose, and now belongs to Capt. Richard Gerrish, to run on a W. S. W. line by said Gerrish's land to a certain place called the *Durty Gutt,* in the way that goes from Rawlins' to the *pitch-pine plains,* and from said *durty Gutt* in said way to run N. W. by ye edge of the swamp to the line that bounds Portsmouth and Dover, and thence upon said Portsmouth and Dover line to ye first bounds, being a gore, and is *part of that gore* which the said Wm. Vaughan bought of the town of Portsmouth, which lott contains about 40 acres, reserving unto said Wm. Vaughan, his heirs and assigns, a cartway down to Canney's cove, and 40 feet at the foot of the hill at said cove."

William and Abigail King of Portsmouth, Feb. 14, 1723-4, conveyed to John Downing, Jr., of Newington, his part of *the gore in the pitch-pine plains in Newington,* which land lay in equal partnership between Capt. Nathaniel Gerrish, Mrs. Margret Vaughan (then Mrs. Margret ffoye), Mrs. Abigail Shannon, Mrs. Elizabeth Vaughan, and the said Wm. King.[1] Bridget Gerrish of Berwick, widow of Nathaniel Gerrish, March 25, 1730, conveyed to Margaret, " ye now wife of John ffoye of Charlestown, Mrs. Abigail Shannon, widow,[2] Mrs. Eliz-

---

[1] Wm. King was the son of Mary Vaughan, who married Daniel King of Salem.

[2] Capt. Nathaniel Gerrish of Berwick married Bridget Vaughan. Abigail Vaughan married, 1st, Nathaniel Shannon, and secondly, Capt. George Walker. Margaret Vaughan married, 1st, Capt. John Foye, and 2dly, the Hon. Charles Chambers, both of Charlestown, Mass.

abeth Vaughan, single woman, and Wm. King, mariner, all of Portsmouth, her fifth part of *the Gore* of land which her father Wm. Vaughan had of the town of Portsmouth—which fifth part was 52 acres. The whole tract was bounded S. E. on the land of Wm. Vaughan, then in possession of John Vincent; W. by Jos. Johnson and Alex[r] Hodgden; S. by land of Capt. Henry Dering and Lt. Gov. Wentworth, then in possession of Samson Babb and John Stevens; N. W. on Mad. Grafford's common right, Mr. Ephraim Dennet and others; and " on y[e] east, northerly, on y[e] road that leads from Islington to Newington ferry."

GOSLING ROAD. This name is popularly given to the long straight road leading from the Pascataqua river two miles along the dividing line between Newington and Portsmouth. Richard Dame, on his map, calls it the "*Road to Boiling Rock.*" It is called the "*New Road*" May 12, 1759, when David and Charles Dennett conveyed to John Hart eleven acres of land in Portsmouth, on the southeasterly side of y[e] *new road*, so called, which divides y[e] town of Portsmouth and y[e] parish of Newington, and on y[e] southwesterly side of y[t] road that leads from Portsmouth by Islington to Knight's ferry, having the land of Benj[n] Miller on y[e] S. E. side, and the land of John Shackford on the southwest. It was still called the "new road" in 1772, when Joseph S. Hart, the 11th of June, conveyed to Richard Hart 150 acres of land in Newington, beginning at the river, and running westerly by the *New Road*, so called, to the land of Samuel Ham, etc., being the land on which his father John Hart then lived. This land was acquired by Richard Pickering in 1808.

GRANITE STATE PARK. This park is on the N. W. side of Willand's pond, partly in Dover and partly in Somersworth. It was laid out in 1876, on land acquired from Mr. Frank Bickford and Mr. Howard Henderson. A " Race Course " here is mentioned on Chace's county map of 1856. There is still a trotting ground, and agricultural fairs are held in the park.

GREAT BAY. This beautiful basin of water, four miles wide in one part, enclosed between Durham and Newmarket on the north, and Greenland and Newington on the south, was so named as early as 1643. It was otherwise called the Bay or Lake of Pascataquack. It is generally supposed to be formed by the union of the Winnicot, Squamscot, and Lamprey rivers, but it is by no means dependent on them for its supply of water. It is a tidal basin that depends chiefly on the ebb and flow of the ocean. "At high tide," says Mr. J. S. Jenness, " when this large basin is filled by the sea, the prospect over its pellucid surface, framed all around with green meadows and waving grain and noble woods, is truly enchanting. But when the tide is out, a vast bed of black ooze is exposed to view, bearing the scanty waters of several small streams which empty into this great lagune."

GREAT BEAVER DAM. See *Beaver Dams.*

GREAT BROOK. See *Emerson's Brook.*

GREAT CREEK. Mentioned the 23d, 10th mo., 1644, when, at a public town meeting in Dover, a grant was made to Mr. ffrancis Mathes[1] of "all the marsh in the *Great creek* on the norwest side of the Great bay, being the first creek, and one hundred acres of upland adjoining to it." The inventory of his estate, made "50 or 60 years" after his decease, and sworn to by his son Benjamin, March 6, 1704, mentions, among other lands, 100 acres adjoining the N. W. side of the first creek in the Great Bay, together with three acres of salt marsh. Francis Mathes, Dec. 5, 1749, conveyed to his grandsons Gershom and Benjamin Mathews, Jr., 100 acres of land in Durham, adjoining the *Great Creek*, commonly called *Mathews' Creek*, then in possession of said Gershom and Benjamin, with all his right to the said *Great Creek*, etc. This creek is now called *Crummit's creek*.

GREAT FALLS. This name was given at an early day to the chief natural falls in the Salmon Falls river. Richard Hussey, March 19, 1693–4, had a grant of 50 acres above the *Great Falls*, laid out Dec. 9, 1729, beginning above said falls at a pitch-pine tree on the west side of a brook, thence running N. 45° W. 100 rods, to a small white oak in sight of Peter's marsh, then 49° E. 80 rods, to land belonging to the heirs of John Hanson, deceased. Job and Joseph Hussey conveyed part of this land to Thomas Wallingford July 5, 1743, giving the same bounds. Forty acres, "near adjatiant to the *Great falls* on Salmon fall Riuer," were granted to "Henry hobs" Ap. 11, 1694. Benjamin Mason of Dover, son of Peter, conveyed to Thomas Hanson, Oct. 8, 1727, a quarter part of "ye new mill upon Salmon falls river, on that part of ye river commonly called by ye name of the *Great Falls*, distinguished and known by that name, built in ye year 1727, joining to the old mill, or near to it, with a quarter part of all the privileges, and ye dam thereto, with ye falls and water and water courses thereto belonging," etc.

Ten acres of land, acquired by Benjn Waimouth in 1734, were laid out to Joseph Wentworth Ap. 2, 1747, "beginning at a small white oak near Hogges fence above s^d Wentworth's house at y^e *Great falls* where he now lives." Thomas Westbrook Waldron, administrator of the estate of Joseph Wentworth of Somersworth, Ap. 10, 1766, conveyed to Andrew Horne of Dover, blacksmith, (the highest bidder at a public sale), $\frac{2}{3}$ of the homestead estate of said Wentworth, situate, lying, and being at a place called the *great falls* in Somersworth, being $\frac{2}{3}$ of 53 acres and 120 rods of land, with $\frac{2}{3}$ of the house and barn, and $\frac{2}{3}$ of a grist-mill, and $\frac{2}{3}$ of $\frac{5}{24}$ of the stream saw in the double saw-mill there, together with the proportionable part of all the machinery and privileges belonging to said mill as then situated on Salmon falls river.

The water privilege here was acquired between 1820 and 1823, by Isaac Wendell of Dover, who also bought of Gershom Horn a tract of land adjacent. This purchase was made for the Great Falls Manufac-

---

[1] This Francis Mathes or Mathews was one of Capt. John Mason's colonists sent over between 1631 and 1634, and asigner of the Exeter Combination of 1639. His descendants are still numerous in Durham and the neighboring towns.

turing Co., which was incorporated June 11, 1823. This Company now has control of the whole water power from the various sources of the Salmon Falls river to the third level at Great Falls, including Great East, Horn's, and Wilson's Ponds on the East branch; Cook's, Lovell's, and Cate's, on the West branch, and the Three Ponds at Milton. Around the extensive cotton mills belonging to this Company has grown up the flourishing village of Great Falls, the only village in Somersworth since the incorporation of Rollinsford.

The name of *Great Falls* was also formerly given to the falls in North River, at South Lee, where Harvey's mill now stands. (See *North River*.)

GREAT HILL. Mentioned the 5th, 10 mo., 1652, when John Heard had a grant of 50 acres under the *Great Hill of Cochechoe*, on the south side, below the cartway. A freshet is mentioned the same day as " coming out of the marsh beside the *great hill* at Cochecho*." Thomas Paine of Dover, in yᵉ *county of Dover and Portsmouth*, conveyed to Ginking Jones, July 9, 1673, twenty acres of land at Cochecha near yᵉ *Greate hill*, bought of Wm. Wentworth March 6, 1666, being part of 50 acres granted said Wentworth the 1st, 10 mo., 1652, beginning at a gutt at yᵉ lower end of said Wentworth's field, on yᵉ east side of the *Greate hill*, and running by yᵉ cartway to a marked tree. This hill is otherwise called the *Great Cochecho hill* and *Cochecho Great hill*. The Rev. John Pike calls it simply "*the Hill*" May 28, 1704. It is now called *Garrison Hill*.

The name of *Great Hill* is also given to a hill in Lubberland near the head of Goddard's creek. It is mentioned the 10th, 2 mo., 1674, when 100 acres of land on the Great Bay, bought by John Goddard of Thomas Larkham, were laid out, beginning ·t the corner of the orchard and running N. by W. to a marked tree under the *Great Hill.* "Yᵉ *Great Hill*" is again mentioned in a deed from Martha, widow of Elias Critchet, Sr., and daughter of John Goddard, Sr., to her grandson Joseph Thomas, Aug. 4, 1729. It is called *Chesley's Hill* in a deed from Elias Critchet to Samuel Smith Ap. 5, 1731. It is otherwise called *Rocky Hill*. (See *Birch Point, Doe's Neck,* and *Stony Brook.*)

GREAT POND. So called in the Dover grants of 1650. Joseph Austin's land near the *Great Pond* is mentioned the 23d, 10 mo., 1658. Thomas and Sarah Downs, Dec. 16, 1720, conveyed to Gershom Wentworth 50 acres of land near yᵉ *Great Pond* above Cochecho, half of a hundred-acre grant to Wm. Everit, deceased, " beginning at a pitch-pine tree near yᵉ pond, on yᵉ west side of yᵉ road yᵗ leads to *Whitehall*." Gershom Wentworth conveyed this land to his "loving son Ezekiel" Nov. 10, 1730, when the *Great Pond* is again mentioned. Moses Stevens had 6¼ acres laid out March 27, 1736, on the north side of the brook that comes out of the *Great pond,* below the *stepping-stones,* so called, joining to the marsh line, beginning at an alder bush near the old bridge.

This pond is now called *Willand's Pond*. (See *Cochecho Pond*.)

GREAT SWAMP. This swamp, partly in Greenland, and partly in

Portsmouth, is crossed by the Portsmouth and Concord railway. It is the source of several streams that flow through a part of ancient Dover.

GREAT TURN. Mentioned June 10, 1719, when 100 acres of land, granted to Wm. Follet in 1658, were laid out to Ichabod Chesley "near y[e] Place called the *Grate Turn*." This land adjoined the S. W. side of "Belloman's Bank freshett." Thirty acres were laid out to Daniel Messerve June 12, 1719, beginning "at the south side of the way that leads to the *hook*, at a pine at the *great turn*," and thence running N. N. W. 60 rods by the path to a white pine. A highway into the woods was laid out May 31, 1733, "beginning on y[e] west side of the road at y[e] *great turn*, as y[e] way was formerly laid out by Capt. Jones and Jonathan Thompson," and running "as y[e] way now goes on y[e] north side of John Davis's house, and so along y[e] same way till it comes to Durham line." Ichabod Chesley and wife Temperance, Ap. 4, 1748, conveyed to Joseph Daniel 25⅝ acres of land in Dover, near the place called the *great turn*. May 28, 1748, he conveyed to Eli Demerit 13¼ acres in Dover, on the S. W. side of Belliman's Bank freshit, near the place called the *Great turn*, being part of 100 acres granted to Wm. Folliott of Oyster River the 5th, 2 mo., 1658.[1] And that same day Ichabod Chesley conveyed to Solomon Emerson 9½ acres of Follet's grant, near the *great turn*, beginning at the S. E. corner of the land Zachariah Pitman bought of said Chesley, near said Emerson's orchard. (See *Long Turn*.)

GREEN HILL. The road to Green Hill is frequently mentioned in the Dover and Madbury records. It is in the eastern corner of the Two Mile Streak, adjoining the Dover line. It is so called on an old plan of July 10, 1753, executed by Thomas W. Waldron, and on Holland's map of 1784. At the foot of this hill is *Fly Market*. (See the *Heath*.)

GREENLAND. The entire shore of Greenland, beginning 40 rods below Sandy Point, appears to have formed part of ancient Dover. At the Court held in Boston the 19th, 7 mo., 1643, it was ordered "That all the marsh and meadow ground lying against the great bay on Strawberry bank side shall belong to the towne of Dover, together with 400 acres of upland adjoining." (*N. H. Prov. Pap.*, 1: 172.) This grant was more clearly defined in the division of the Squamscot Patent, May 22, 1656, when all the marsh was assigned to Dover from Hogsty Cove, near the mouth of Great Bay, round about the Bay up to Cotterill's Delight, together with 400 acres of upland, as granted it by the Court. (*Ibid*, 1: 222. See also *Cotterill's Delight*.)

Among the Dover grants on the Greenland shore are those to Thomas Canney, Richard Carter, John Hall, John Heard, Richard Hussey, Henry Langstaffe, John and Thomas Roberts, Henry Tibbets, Thomas Willey, George Webb, etc. The grants to Thomas Canney and Thomas Willey were at a considerable distance above the mouth of Winnicot river. (See *Canney's Marsh* and *Willey's Island*.) And still farther above was the large tract which Richard Waldron and Thomas Lake reserved for them-

---

[1] Foliot was the name of a Devonshire family, allied with the Gorges. (Baxter's *Sir Ferdinando Gorges*, 2: 152.)

selves. The Dover grants on this shore seem to have been for the most part purchased by the Portsmouth settlers, and the whole shore was finally relinquished when Greenland was made a separate parish.

Greenland is mentioned in the Portsmouth records as early as July 10, 1655, when 300 acres of upland and meadow were granted to Capt. Champernoun,[1] "adjoining his now dwelling house at *grenland*." In July, 1657, Francis Champernoone conveyed to Valentine Hill his "farm in y⁰ Great Bay called by y⁰ name of *Greenland*," which had been in his possession 16 or 17 years, with all right to "400 acres in said farm granted him by Mr. Robert Saltonstall and others of y⁰ Patentees." Valentine Hill of Dover conveyed to Capt. Thomas Clark and Wm. Paddy of Boston, merchants, his "farm called *Greenland*, lying in y⁰ bottom of y⁰ Greate bay in y⁰ river of Piscataqua."

March 12, 1713, Edward Hutchinson of Boston, merchant, and Mary, wife of Josiah Wolcot of Salem—son and daughter of Eliza Hutchinson, lately deceased, the heir of Major Thomas Clark, late of Boston, deceased—conveyed to Col. Wm. Partridge in the name of said Clark and of Wm. Paddy, deceased, a certain neck, tract, or parcell of land commonly called by the name of *Greenland* or *Champernoun farm*, butted and bounded on the Great Bay, and lying between two creeks, purchased by said Clark and Paddy before released from Valentine Hill, long since deceased, who derived his title from Capt. Francis Champernoun, the first and original proprietor of said farm.

Wm. Partridge, Esq., of Newbury conveyed to Thomas Packer of Portsmouth, chirurgeon, one half of all his right unto *ye old* and *new ffarme* at *Greenland*, called Champernowne ffarme or ffarmes, as sold by ffrancis Champernoun to Nathaniel Fryer, Henry Langstaffe, and Philip Lewis, March 27, in y⁰ one and twentieth year of y⁰ late reign of our sov. Lord, Charles y⁰ Second.

John Davis of Oyster River, in his will of May 25, 1686, gives his son Joseph "one half the marsh which I bought of Mr. Valentine Hill, situate and lying in *Greenland*."

Francis and Mary Drake of Portsmouth, Aug. 5, 1686, conveyed to John Johnson and Thomas Bracket "my now dwelling-house" and 84 acres of land in *Greenland* in y⁰ township of Portsmouth, obtained partly by grant, and partly from Capt. Francis Champernoon. Sept. 20, 1717, Wm. Partridge and Thomas Packer conveyed to Matthias Haynes 66 acres in the parish of *Greenland*, part of *the Champernoon new farm*, joining the road from Greenland to Hampton, at the turn of the road against Neel's. Capt. Champernowne was a member of the Dover Combination of 1640, and a portion of his land at Greenland

---

[1] This was Francis Champernowne of royal descent, the friend and relative of Sir Walter Raleigh, and, as Mr. J. S. Jenness says, "the noblest born and bred of all New Hampshire's first planters." On Champernowne's island, now called Gerrish's island, at Kittery Point, may be seen his grave, with its rude cairn, over which Dr. Wm. Hale of Dover has recently sung so plaintive a dirge :

"Where, wind to wave, and wave to echoing rock,
 Their endless dirges chant for lost renown;
With every bursting wave sounding a knell
 Above the lonely grave of Champernowne."

fell within the limits of ancient Dover. The part acquired by Capt. Thomas Packer became known as the *Packer farm*. A portion of this is now generally called the "Peirce[1] farm," from the late Col. Joshua W. Peirce, by whose heirs it is still owned.

It was voted at a town meeting in Portsmouth, June 4, 1705, that "ye bounds of Greenland be on ye south side of *Col. Packer's farme*." And a petition of May 26, 1725, mentions a vote of the town "that Greenland bounds should be on the south side of *Packer's farm* (which suppose is now Doctor Marches)."

The name of Greenland, originally confined to the Champernowne farm,[2] was finally given to all the western part of Portsmouth, which was set off as a separate parish in 1706, but continued to be assessed as a part of Portsmouth till March 21, 1721, when, at the petition of Samuel and Joshua Weeks and James Johnson, it was allowed to be taxed separately (*N. H. Prov. Pap.*, 2 : 739-40.) The privilege of sending a representative to the General Assembly was granted to the Parish of Greenland May 12, 1732. (*Ibid*, 4 : 618, 785.)

GREENLAND GARRISONS. It is one of the boasts of Greenland that it never had any garrison, or any need of one, the land having been peaceably acquired from the Indians. The house of John Keniston at Greenland, however, was burned by the Indians, and he killed, Ap. 16, 1677. And there appears to have been one garrison at least, no doubt *Neale's Garrison*. In the Portsmouth records of 1692, among the accounts of ammunition furnished the various *garrisons* that year, mention is made of "17 lbs. of of powder and 18 lbs. of bullets to *Capt. Nele, for Greenland*." His house was on Heard's Neck, near the mouth of Winnicot river, on the upper side. The Portsmouth authorities ordered July 22, 1665, that Walter Neale's home lot should extend "from goodman hayins his house due north and by east unto Winicont Riuer, leaving a way for Capt. Champernoune between his houses." (*Ports. Records.*) Brewster's *Rambles* says the Weeks house in Greenland, one of the oldest houses in the state, "was evidently built as a sort of garrison." It was erected by Leonard Weeks, "over against" whose house a road was laid out in 1663. (*Ports. Records.*)

GREENLAND RIVER. This name is given on Merrill's map of Greenland, in 1806, to the tidal portion of Winnicot river. It is mentioned Ap. 19, 1746, when Samuel Nutter conveyed to Ebenezer Johnson all right and title to half a tract of salt marsh and thatchbed, bounded northerly by Great Bay, easterly by *Greenland river*, and south by a creek parting said marsh from that of Matthias Haines. Thirty acres of land were laid out to Henry and Sylvanus Nock, June 29, 1702, being the divi-

---

[1] This form of the Pierce name reminds one of the Feilding family of Great Britain. When one of its members, a peer of the realm, who retained the old usage of placing the *e* before the *i* asked his kinsman, Henry Fielding, the great novelist, why they wrote their names differently, the latter replied that he could not tell, unless because his own branch was the first that knew how to spell.

[2] The editor of Mr. G. W. Tuttle's *Historical Papers* says there was anciently a cove or dock in the harbor of Dartmouth, England, called *Greenland Dock*—a name that must have been familiar to Capt. Champernowne, who undoubtedly gave it to his farm on Great Bay.

dend land belonging to their grandfather Tibbets' marsh, adjoining their marsh on the S. side of the Great bay, about half a mile to the westward of *Greenland river.* (*Dover Records.*) Thomas Roberts conveyed to Mark H. Wentworth, Ap. 20, 1750, his marsh, bounded northerly by Haines' marsh, and easterly and southerly by *Greenland river.*

The GULF. Mentioned the 30th, 6 mo., 1643, when 20 acres were granted Wm. Furber, "abutting upon a certain place called y^e *Gulfe.*" And again the same year mention is made of William ffurber's twenty acres of upland, lying north of the river Cochechoe, below ye falls, abutting on a certain place called y^e *Gulfe.* These twenty acres were conveyed to Thomas Nock July 2, 1657, —James Kid, Oct. 28, 1714, conveyed to Job Clement 20 acres joining the Cochecho river at a place called the *Gulf.* This name is still retained. The Gulf is an enlargement of the Cochecho river, just below the head of tide water.

GUPPY'S HILL. This hill is in Dover, on the Portland turnpike road. On the west side are *Guppy's woods*, formerly *Paine's woods.*

GUPPY'S POINT. This is the first point below St. Alban's cove, on the Newichawannock river. So named from James Guppey, who conveyed to James Philpot, Aug. 3, 1736, 30 acres of land in Dover, bounded northerly by the road from Fresh creek to St. Alban's Cove, easterly by Wm. Stiles' land, S. by Joseph Hussey's, and W. by that of Thomas Downs and Joseph Ricker; being the place where said Guppey then lived. To his son Joseph he conveyed his undivided eighth of Cochecho Point, bounded by the Cochecho and Newichawannock rivers and the path that led from Fresh Creek to St. Alban's cove. Joseph Guppy conveyed part of his land, including *Guppy's Point* to Wm. Styles. This point was sold by Moses Styles to Judge Doe, who uses it for a family burial-place.

HALF-WAY SWAMP. Mentioned the 5th, 10 mo., 1652, when Wm. Wentworth had a grant of 40 acres of upland, northward of the *Half way swamp*, on the north side of John Heard's 40 acre lot, and so along the *cart-way.* And again March 10, 1665, when James Ordway of Newbury, and wife Ann, conveyed to John Heard of Cochecho 20 acres granted him by the town of Dover, on the further side of the *half way swamp* going to the marsh of Cochecho aforesaid, joining on one side to y^e *cart path*, and at ye other end by a freshet or swamp. This swamp, now drained, was southwest of Garrison Hill, on the west side of the old cartway, now the Garrison Hill road. It was so called because it was about halfway between Cochecho falls and the Great Cochecho marsh.

HALL'S MARSH. Mentioned the 12th, 10 mo., 1658, when 250 acres were laid out to John Hall (see *Robert's Creek*), butting partly on the Great Bay. This was in Greenland. And again Aug. 14, 1698, when Richard Cater (Carter) of Kittery conveyed four acres of fresh and salt meadow at the bottom of the Great Bay in Pascataqua river, near the upper end of *John Hall's marsh*, and on the north side of a creek over against *Capt. Champernoon's meadow;* also 30 acres adjoining, granted by the town of Dover to James Rawlings. This land now belongs to the Peirce farm in Greenland, part of which is called the *Hall field* to this day.

HALL'S SLIP. Mentioned in a deed from Ephraim Tibbets to John Clement Sept. 4, 1766, as below Tibbet's homestead on Back river, the westerly side of Dover Neck.

HALL'S SPRING. This name is still given to a spring near the spot where Deacon John Hall lived over 200 years ago. It is S. W. of the site of the old fortified meeting-house on Dover Neck, towards Back cove.

HAM'S MARSH. John Ham's marsh is mentioned Nov. 23, 1735. It was at Oak Swamp. Eleven acres were laid out to Peter Hayes, Oct. 15, 1748, beginning at a pine tree on the west side of the mast road that goes from Tolend to Rochester, " about 16 rods above the crotch of the way that comes over *Ham's marsh.*" Oct. 15, 1748, 21 acres were laid out to Joseph Hanson, Jr., beginning at a pitch pine on the west side of the old mast path, leading from *Ham's marsh,* so called, to the "Ealware plains," about 10 rods above the path that leads to Tolend. (See *Oak Swamp.*)

HARDSCRABBLE. This name is given to a rough district in the eastern part of Barrington.

HARFORD'S FERRY. So called from Nicholas Harford, who, in 1717, was licensed to keep a ferry across Fore river from Dover Neck to Kittery. He petitioned March 26, 1726, that his license might be renewed. This ferry ran from Beck's slip to what is now known as *Morrill's point* on the Eliot shore, originally a part of Kittery. At a later day it was called *Morrill's ferry.* (See *Beck's Point* and *Slip.*) The name of Harford is otherwise written Hartford.

HARRUD'S SPRING, otherwise HEARD'S. Mentioned May 25, 1735, when James Hanson conveyed to Joseph Hanson, Jr., 5 acres of land in Dover, at the north end of James Hanson's pasture, called *Hard Spring pasture,* on the east side of Richard Scammon's pasture, and partly on the S. W. side of the highway that leads down to widow Cloutman's, and partly on ye west end of Joseph Hanson's own land, on the south side joining to James Hanson's land. This spring is again mentioned April 9, 1737, when James Hanson conveyed to Joseph Hanson 8 acres and 100 rods of land in Dover, adjoining s^d Joseph's land on the S. E., beginning " southward of *Harrud's spring,* by said Hanson's land which contains ye s^d *Harrud's spring,*" thence running N. 27 deg. E. by s^d Joseph's land 46 rods to the land of Joseph Hanson, Jr., and 31 rods to Richard Scammon's. This was apparently on the Upper Neck, where John Heard acquired land in 1669. (See *Campin's Rocks.*)

HARVEY'S HILL, otherwise MESERVE'S. This hill is at the upper side of Freetown in Madbury, on the road to Barrington. It was so named from Daniel "Messerve," who had a grant on the south side of the way that leads to Bellamy Hook, June 12, 1719. He is called "Daniel Misharvey" in a deed from James Huckins to Eli Demerit Dec. 19, 1746. Meserve's garrison stood on this hill.

HARWOOD'S COVE, otherwise HARROD'S, HEROD'S, HEARD'S, etc. This cove, now called *Laighton's Cove*, is on the Newington shore of Great Bay, below Fabyan's Point. It is referred to the 20th, 8 mo., 1651, when Wm. Pomfrett of Dover conveyed to Anthony Nutter a marsh on the N. E. side of Great Bay, at *the great cove* there, above *long point.* Anthony Nutter and wife Sarah, in exchange for land at Welsh Cove, conveyed to Thomas Roberts, June 6, 1664, " a parcel of marsh in y⁰ Great Bay in Dover, in a certain cove usually called by yᵉ name of *Harrod's Cove,* bounded by yᵉ mouth of a *small trench,* and so upon a straight line down to yᵉ middle of a *small island* betwixt yᵉ marsh of John Dam, Sr., and yᵉ aforesaid marsh of Anthony Nutter." Thomas Roberts, in his deed of land on Welsh Cove, exchanged for the above tract, speaks of the latter as " in *Hard's Cove.*" " The freshett called *Harwood's creek* or *cove,*" is mentioned in Mr. Moody's grant of May 10, 1668. (See *Harwood's Creek.*) It is called *Herd's cove,* July 5, 1700, when Thomas Tibbets of Dover and Judith his wife conveyed to George Huntress all his salt marsh (about two acres) on yᵉ east side of the creek running out of yᵉ gutt commonly called by the name of *Herd's Gut* into the great bay, bounded by John Dam on the west, north-west by said creek, and so to *Herd's cove,* with the privilege of the flats from the lower point of the marsh at the creek's mouth on a S. S. W. direction into the bay. This adjoined the tract conveyed to George Huntress, Dec. 13, 1699, by James and John " Leitsh " (Leach), who, in the deed, speak of it as " land *in Portsmouth* at great bay, at a place called by y⁰ name of *Harwoods cove,*" on the north side of George Walton's land, which tract had been granted their father James " Leith " by the town of Portsmouth.

Shadrach and George Walton of New Castle conveyed to Nath Knight in 1708, a tract of " 136 acres *in Portsmouth,* on the N. E. side of the Greate Bay, at a place called and known by the name of *Harwood's cove,*" beginning at a white oak by the water side in said cove, and running to a red oak near John Hall's fence, joining John Jackson. Nathan Knight of Dover conveyed to John Downing, Jr., Ap. 12, 1712, " thirty acres of land *in Dover,* part of 136 acres laid out to George Walton, Sr., in 1665, beginning at a white oak by the water side in *harrold's cove,*" etc. Thomas and Ephraim Tibbets, Dec. 2, 1735, conveyed to John Nutter of Newington a tract of marsh (four acres) in *Harrod's cove* in Great Bay, bounded on the upper end by the marsh of Deacon Moses Dam, west by the marsh of Anthony Nutter, deceased, and easterly upon " yᵉ crick that runs between yᵉ marsh of Christopher Huntress " (grandson of the above George) and the premises then conveyed, with the thatch-bed adjoining, running over to " yᵉ loor paint [lower point] of yᵉ salt marsh formerly sold to sᵈ Huntress." John Perry conveyed to John Vincent May 12, 1735, " a parcel of fflatts or thatch-bed in *Harwood's Cove,* Newington," on the S. side of Christopher Huntress. (See *Laighton's Cove.*)

The name of Harwood's cove was probably derived from Andrew Harwood, who is mentioned in 1643, when he and Thomas ffurson were brought before the authorities " for neglecting to come to the ordinances of God this last winter." He was engaged in the lumber business. A suit at court concerning the sale of timber, clapboards, and pipe-staves, by Philip Swadden, Thomas Johnson, *Andrew Harwood*, and Thomas ffurson is mentioned the last of the 6th mo., 1643. (*County Records*, Exeter.) See *Herod's Point* and *Wigwam.*

HARWOOD'S CREEK, otherwise HARROD'S, HEROD'S, etc. This name was given, not only to the inlet called *Harwood's* or *Herod's cove*, but to the freshwater stream which empties into it, now usually called the *Trout brook.* It is mentioned Jan. 11, 1657, when the town of Portsmouth granted to Henry Sherburne and others the land from *Harrod's creek* northward to Welshman's Cove, excepting the 400 acres belonging to Dover. (See *Hogsty Cove.*)

A part of this tract (141 acres) was afterwards re-granted to the Rev. Joshua Moody of Portsmouth, and laid out Jan. 21, 1666, beginning at "a white oak by the freshet called *Harrod's cove* neere Jn°. Dam's marsh," thence running N. E. by E. to a small asp tree, and thence by that point towards Bloody Point, to "a *three forked pine* tree which is *Dover bounds*, standing in the road way, thence S. W. by W. down to the aforesaid ffreshet called *Harrod's Creeke* to a hemlock—Bloody Point or Hampton path being the eastern bound, *Dover bounds* the northern, and the freshet called *Harrod's creeke* aforesaid the western."

Wm. Furber, Sr., Anthony Nutter, and John Dam, Jr., having been appointed by the town of Dover to meet the lot-layers of Portsmouth, to settle " the line in the woods between Cannyes Coue and hogsty Coue," made their report under oath before Richard Cutt at Portsmouth, May 10, 1668, " that the great *three-forked pine* should be the bound tree," whence the line should run straight to the middle of the mouth of each cove, " which said *forked pine* stands in ye way y^t goes from bloody Point to Portsm° & is too (two) hundred rod to the northward of y^t path y^t turns out of said way wch goes to goodman Pickering's and goodman Hall's farms; and nere said *three forked Pine* is a little dry round gully, not above two or three rod distance."—"And at the same time ye lott-layers of Portsmouth laid out a pcell (parcel) of land to Mr. Joshua Moody, (w)hose northern bound was the *three forked pine*," and thence ran in a straight line " to the freshett called *Harwood's creek* or *Coue*, nere John Dam's marsh. And the gore of land that remained between dover and Mr. Moodyes line ye said lott-layers laid out to Capt. James Pendleton, and is bounded at one end by the said Willm Furber Senr his land."

The road above mentioned, on which stood the three-forked pine, must not be confounded with the present road from Bloody Point to Portsmouth. It must have meant the road to Greenland, then belonging in part to Portsmouth, or less probably the old road to Portsmouth called the *Narrow lane* that seems to have led from Welsh Cove or Furber's ferry. Samuel Moody of Boston, Sept. 10, 1704, conveyed to Thomas Row of Welsh Cove 36 acres of land formerly belonging to his honoured father, the Rev. Joshua Moody, lying at or near Welch Cove in ye town of Portsmouth, adjoining the brook that runs into *Harwood's Cove*, beginning at a hemlock tree near the way that leads from Welch Cove to said Row's house, thence running 136 rods E. by N. to the *antient bounds* wch is a *pine tree adjoining the road which leads from Bloody Point to Greenland*, thence 60 rods along the road to another pine, thence 130 rods S. by W. to a pine 8 rods from the brook, and thence to the first bound. This land seems to have extended to the vicinity of *Sam Row's hill*, near which is the source of Harwood's creek. Twenty acres of the above tract were conveyed by Thomas Row, Ap. 10, 1733, to his son-in-law, John Quint, beginning at a small white oak by the road from Newington meeting-house to Greenland, and running along this road 30 rods to a pitch pine, then 130 rods S. W. to a pine tree, 8 rods from the brook. One bound is a small hill at the corner of Thomas Row's orchard.

Joseph Richards, planter, of "Welsh-mans cove," and Abigail his wife, conveyed to Benjn Richards, March 20, 1702, ten acres of land which said Joseph's father purchased of Wm. ffurber, lying and being on the S. E. side of the road which goes to Portsth from Welsh man's cove, bounded on the north side by *Dover bounds*, and on the east side by Mr. Moody's land. Samuel Moody quit claim to Clement Messervey of Portsmouth, July 29, 1703, to a tract of 25 acres, lying and being in Portsmouth, at or near Welch cove, beginning at a white oak by y^e *freshett* called *Harrod's cove*, near John Dam's marsh, and running along ye brooke 116 rods to a maple that stands near ye road that goes down to Mr. Wm. Furber's, thence 120 rods along *ye road towards Portsmouth* to a flat rock that stands near ye path, and thence 160 rods to the first bound. "Clement Misservie, late of Newington, now of Scarborough, Maine," (son of the above Clement) conveyed to John Vincent, Oct. 26, the first year of the reign of our sovereign lord, George the second (1727), 25 acres in Newington, beginning at a white oak by y^e *ffreshet* that runs into *Harrods Cove* near the land of Deacon Moses Dam, and extending along the brook 116 rods to a maple that stands near the road to Welch Cove, thence 120 rods along y^e *road towards Portsmouth* to a flat rock that stands near ye path, and thence 160 rods to the first bound.

Harwood's creek is called "*Herds gut*" July 5, 1700. (See *Harwood's Cove*.) It is otherwise called "*Stony brook*" in Geo. Huntriss' will of June 8, 1715. (See *Stony Brook*.)

HAVEN'S HILL. This hill is in Rochester, on the main road from Dover to Norway Plains. Here stood the first meeting-house in Rochester, built in 1731. Its name was derived from the Rev. Joseph Haven of Portsmouth, who was installed at Rochester Jan. 10, 1776, and there died Jan. 27, 1825, after a pastorate of forty-nine years.

HAYES' FALLS. See *Cochecho Falls.*

HAY STACK. Mentioned in 1654, when Jonas Binn had a grant of ten acres on the S. W. side of Branson's creek, joining Geo. Webb, and next to Charles Adams' lot, " the east side coming to a little gutt right over against a place called the *hay stack*." This was near the upper shore of the Great Bay, above Crummit's creek, but the name has not been retained. It may have been a place where the early settlers stacked their salt hay or thatch. (See *Branson's Creek*.)

HEARD'S NECK. Mentioned Dec. 5, 1653, when Walter Neall had a grant of " eaight acres to his house upon the neck of land by Winacont river, commonly called *John Heard's necke*." (*Portsmouth Records*.) This was in Greenland.

HEARD'S POND, otherwise HERD'S. Holland's map of 1784 gives this name to Cole's pond, in the N. E. part of Somersworth. It was perhaps derived from John and Samuel Heard, who were engaged in the lumber business on the Salmon Falls river in the middle of last century.

The HEATH. A heath in the upper part of Dover is mentioned July 5, 1736, when 20 acres—part of a 30 acre grant to Thomas Wille, July 8, 1734—were laid out to his son Thomas " at a place called y* *Eleware plains*," on the north side of the road from the *heath* to *Green Hill*. This land was conveyed to Stephen Hawkins March 29, 1743. Ichabod Canney's seven acres of land, conveyed to Paul Hayes Ap. 1, 1741, were laid out above the *heath*, on the S. W. side of Cochecho river, beginning at Stephen Wille's W. corner bound. Joseph Roberts' share of the common lands in 1734, was laid out to him Nov. 10, 1741, above the *heath*, beginning at the head line of Dover, at the N. W. corner of Ichabod Canney's land.

The marsh adjacent to Willand's Pond, between Peter's Marsh brook and the Dover road to Whitehall, is commonly called "the *Hathe*" or *Heath*. Peter Austin of Somersworth, and wife Betty, conveyed to Moses Carr, Jan. 16, 1788, 26 acres of land, bought of Nicholas Austin, bounded E. by the road from Dover to Great Falls and the land of Ichabod Rollins, southerly by Daniel Randall, and westerly by the *heath brook*, so called.

There is also a heath on the upper side of Wheelwright's pond. (See *Langley's Heath*.)

HEN ISLAND. This is an islet at the lower side of Fox Point, Newington, near the shore. It bears a single pine tree—verdant, broad-spreading, and somewhat picturesque.

HENDERSON'S POINT. This point is on the Rollinsford shore of the Newichawannock, below Middle Point. It is the terminus of the bridge from Eliot, at the lower side of Jocelyn's cove. The name is derived from Wm. Henderson, who had a grant of land on this shore March 19, 1693-4. (See *Jocelyn's Cove*.) It is now owned by Mr. Hiram Philpot.

There was also a *Henderson's point* on the east side of Dover Neck, to which led a road, mentioned in 1812. This was apparently above Morrill's ferry, formerly Beck's slip. *Henderson's spring* in that vicinity is mentioned in Sanford & Evert's Atlas.

HEROD'S POINT and WIGWAM, otherwise HARROD'S. Herod's wigwam is mentioned the 15th, 4 mo., 1646, when "John Damme" had a grant from the town of Dover of "six acres of marsh on ye Great Bay, bounded w^h ye creek at ye mouth on the northwest side, the upland on ye southeast side, & ye island of ye northwest nere to a *wigwam* on the south east side of said marsh, commonly called by the name of *Herod's wigwome.*"

Thirty acres of upland were laid out to John Dam, Sr., the 10th, 10 mo., 1656, "on the south side of his marsh towards *Harroed's Poynt*, 6 acres and 24 acres at the head of his marsh, bounded by the freshet that goeth towards Bloody Poynt." Another record of the same date says: "Whereas by order of the General Court, 400 acres of upland were given to the inhabitants of Dover that have marsh in the Great Bay, Elder Nutter, Wm. Story, Wm. ffurber, and Henry Lankstar, laid out and bounded unto John Dam, Sr., 30 acres of upland as follows, 6 acres and 24 acres at the head of his marsh towards *harrods wigwame* —the upland bounded by the freshet that goeth towards Bloody Point; that is, 16 poles up the freshett, and 26 pooles wide." This tract joined the Layton and Nutter lands, and being part of the 400 acres, was of course *above* Hogsty Cove—that is, "above" with reference to the course of the river or bay, not to the points of the compass.

Herod's Point seems to have formed part of the Fabyan lands. (See *Swadden's Island.*) The mention of a wigwam has led to the supposition that the name of this Point, and of Herod's Cove, was derived from an Indian sagamore. It may, however, have been a variation of Heard, pronounced with a brogue. But it was more probably a corruption of Harwood. (See *Harwood's Cove.*)

The word "wigwam" does not necessarily imply an Indian cabin. It was a name often given by the early pioneers to a logging shanty in the forest. Mention is made of one, Nov. 21, 1706, when land was laid out to Thomas Goodwin in Kittery, near the Salmon Falls river, above the *Nine Notches*, "beginning about 30 or 40 poles below the *logging house* or *wigwam* that Wm. Grant, Thomas and Daniel Goodwin, and Joseph Hodsden, kept in, the last winter." (*Kittery Records.* See *Historical Mag.*, Oct., 1868, p. 192.) "*Young's wigwam*" in Hampton is also mentioned Ap. 5, 1710.

Herod's wigwam was probably the logging camp of Andrew Harwood, who was undoubtedly engaged in the lumber business. Thomas Johnson brought a suit against him in 1644, for "6000 hogshead staves to be delivered at highwater mark in ye river of Pascataway." (*County Records*, Exeter.)

HICKS'S HILL. See *Moharimet's Hill*.

HIGH POINT. This is the first point on the Rollinsford shore of the Newichawannock river below the Eliot bridge. It formerly belonged to the Cate family, but is now owned by Mr. John Bennett.

The name of *High Point* is also given to a subdivision of Long Point, on the Newington shore of Great Bay. (See *Long Point.*)

HIGH STREET. This name was given in early times to the main road along Dover Neck to Hilton's Point. It is mentioned Sept. 11, 1733, when Thomas and Ephraim Tibbets sold Richard Plummer[1] a small strip of land at the S. E. corner of their field, adjoining "ye little Logg House yt Jn° Foy lived in," extending from said house six rods northerly, joining on *high street*.[2]

It is called *Great street* Oct. 6, 1670, when Thomas Canney, Sr., conveyed his dwelling house and lot to his son Joseph, bounded E. by Fore river, W. by "*ye great street* on Dover Neck," etc.

HILL'S COVE or CREEK. This inlet, no doubt the *Pine Cove* of early times, is on the Newington shore of the Long Reach, below Paul's creek; so called from Samuel Hill, who acquired part of the Folsom farm, which his son William Hill conveyed in 1869 to Mr. de Rochemont, the present owner. It was previously called *Stoodley's creek*.

HILL'S FALLS. The State map of Lee in 1803 gives this name to the falls in Lamprey river at the head of Lee Hook, where at that time stood a saw-mill and grist-mill, owned by the heirs of Capt. Reuben Hill, who acquired this water privilege and the adjoining farm in the middle of last century. He was one of the selectmen of Lee in 1769. His mill is mentioned in the records of that town; and the neighboring bridge across Lamprey river is repeatedly called *Hill's bridge* in the town accounts from 1771 till 1800, and doubtless much later. For instance, 5 £., 1s., were " p{d} Ensign Reuben Hill on *his bridge*" in 1771. This name is still retained, though Reuben Hill died about 1794, and his heirs sold the water privilege here at the beginning of this century. Chace's county map of 1856 mentions "J. Mathes's shingle and grist-mill" at Hill's falls. There is now a sawmill here, owned by the Dames. (See *Dame's Falls*.)

HILL'S FIVE HUNDRED ACRES. Frequently mentioned in the old conveyances of Durham lands, referring to Valentine Hill's grant of 500 acres from the town of Dover, the 14th, 5 mo., 1651, for a farm adjacent to his mills at Oyster River. This tract comprised the whole site of the present village of Durham on the upper side of Oyster river, and extended from the lowest falls westward as far as Follet's swamp. It was bounded on the south by the fresh part of Oyster river, and on the north by the Woodman, Thompson, and Demeritt lands. It is mentioned June 15, 1719, when 30 acres of land, laid out to Bartholomew Stevenson May 31, 1699, found to intrench on "*Capt. Hill's five hundred acre lot*," were, at the request of Abraham Stevenson, laid out anew, "beginning at Hill's line, near the north corner of Hill's land." This land was conveyed by Abraham and Mary Stevenson to Jonathan Thompson Feb. 24, 1732-33, " beginning at ye north corner of

---

[1] Richard Plummer's wife was Elizabeth, daughter of Joseph Beard. She quit claim to all right in her father's estate in favor of her brother Samuel, May 25, 1737. And her sister, Esther Dolloff, did the same Ap. 8, 1731.

[2] John Foy married Mary, widow of Ralph Hall, before Feb. 26, 1717-18. She was the daughter of Philip Chesley of Oyster River. *John Foy's Rock* is mentioned in article *Freetown*. (See p. 78.)

Capt. Nathaniel Hill's *five hundred acres*, at a stump in said Hill's line."
Joseph Buss and wife Lydia conveyed to Thomas Chesley, Feb. 21, 1739-40, one half of two thirds of one third part of *five hundred acres* in Durham, granted to Valentine Hill by the town of Dover the 14th, 5 mo., (16)51, "for a farm adjacent to his mills at Oyster River, provided it doth not not annoy the inhabitants, and laid out and bounded in ye year 1660, ye 3d day of ye 11th mo., bounded upon a N. and S. line from Oyster River 200 rods, and from that bound N. W. half a point westerly 320 rods, and from y^t to Oyster river upon a S. W. and by S. line 210 rods to ye river, and so ye river is ye bounds."

Valentine Hill of Nottingham and Robert Hill of Durham conveyed to Joseph Smith, Feb. 23, 1765, part of that land in Durham "commonly known by the name of *the five hundred acres*," beginning at the N. W. corner of Samuel Hill's homestead farm by the land of Samuel Demerit, etc. (See *Warner Farm*.)

Valentine Hill, who had this grant of 500 acres, was the most enterprising of the early settlers at Oyster River. He was in Boston as early as 1638, a freeman in 1640, and was ordained deacon in Boston "by ye laying on of ye hands of ye presbytery," May 7, 1640. He was also a member of the Ancient and Hon. Artillery Co. He had a grant at Oyster River the 5th, 5 mo., 1642, and another the following year. And further grants of lands and mill privileges on Lamprey and Oyster rivers were made to him in 1649, 1651, 1652, etc. He was apparently the first to erect mills at Oyster River, and it was he who built the first meeting-house here in 1656-7. He was the representative from Dover to the General Court at Boston in 1652-3-4-5 and 7. The freemen of Dover petitioned, May 27, 1652, that Mr. Valentine Hill might be appointed one of the Associate Judges of the Court that year. Their petition was granted. (N. H. *Prov. Pap.*, 1 : 198, 207.) He died in 1661, leaving two children, Nathaniel and Mary, by his last wife, who was Mary Eaton, daughter of Gov. Theophilus Eaton of New Haven. She survived him, and afterwards married Ezekiel Knight.

Mary, daughter of Valentine Hill, married John Buss, son of Parson Buss of Oyster River. Nathaniel Hill, the only son left by Valentine, married Sarah, daughter of Anthony Nutter of Welshman's cove. He inherited the greater part of his father's lands at Oyster River, on which he settled. He was appointed deacon of the Oyster River church. He had two sons, Valentine and Samuel. The latter married Sarah, daughter of John Thompson, Sr., of Oyster River, and lived a short distance above the present railway station. Sarah Hill, daughter of Nathaniel, married Daniel Warner of Portsmouth, who afterwards acquired a part of Hill's Five Hundred Acres. (See *Warner Farm*.) Abigail Hill, another daughter, married Benjamin, son of Capt. Francis Mathes, Dec. 17, 1716. The name of Valentine, from her grandfather Valentine Hill, became henceforth a favorite name in the Mathes family, where it is perpetuated to this day. Among those who still bear it may be mentioned Mr. Valentine Mathes of Dover, and Valentine Mathes Coleman, Esq., of Newington.

HILL'S MILL POND. This name, derived from Valentine Hill (see *Hill's Five Hundred Acres*), is given to the mill-pond above the lowest falls in Oyster river (now Durham Falls) the 25th, 9 mo., 1661, when 20 acres of upland were granted to John Woodman " betwixt the freshett that runneth to *Mr. hill's mill pond* and the upper end of the pond, whear the sayd John Woodman shall see gode to make choyse of, not intrenching apon ani former grant."

HILL'S PAN or PEN. See *Stony Brook*.

HILL'S SWAMP. Mentioned in 1656, when John Bickford, Sr., had a grant of 100 acres of upland adjacent to Thomas Footman's hundred acres, on the N. W. side of " the swampe sometimes called *Mr. hill's swampe*." This Bickford land was afterwards acquired by Joseph Hix, for whom it was laid out anew Ap. 12, 1718, on the N. W. side of *hill's swamp*. This swamp was apparently the low land in Madbury, adjoining the Boston & Maine R. R., between Hicks's Hill and Pudding Hill. The name may have been derived from Valentine Hill of Oyster River, the only person of the name in Dover at the time of Bickford's grant, who appears to have had the prefix of " Mr." A timber grant to " Mr. Hill " (no doubt Valentine) " on ye north side of ye path from Bellamies Bank towards Oyster River," is mentioned in a grant to Richard Waldron in 1652. In the time of Joseph Hix (or Hicks), however, Wm. Hill lived at the lower side of Pudding Hill. "The mast path that leadeth from Knight's farm to *William Hill's*," is mentioned Feb. 28, 1705–6. Thirty acres were laid out to Henry Marsh Ap. 4, 1709, " eastward of Mahorramet's hill, beginning at a hemlock tree on the poynt of the plain to the westward of *William Hill's plantation*."

HILTON'S COVE. This cove is on the Newington shore, adjoining the old terminus of Knight's ferry, but the name is no longer in use. It is mentioned the 9th, 5 mo., 1652, when John Hall had a grant of 18 acres " a little above *Hilton's Cove*." It is again mentioned the 5th, 10 mo., 1674, when Thomas Tricke's grant of 18 acres in 1656, " on Bloody poynt side," was laid out " aboue *hilltones coue*, joining to henery Lankster his land westerly, bounded up the gutt to a rock, and from the rock to A wall nutt Tree marked with an H and a T, and soe to a Beich Tree marked with A and T, and so to the freshett that runs in too *Thomas Trickey his coue aboue his house* at high-water mark."

John Hall conveyed to Henry Langstaffe, the 1st, 4 mo., 1668, 12 acres of land granted him by the town of Dover, together with house, goods, and chattels within doors and without. Henry Langstar, grandson of the above Henry, conveyed to John Shackford, Nov. 23, 1716, ten acres of land called *Hall's field*, bounded N. W. by a little mead, W. by land formerly Zachariah Trickey's but then in possession of Capt. John Knight, and E. by the highway to the ferry. George Walton and Frances conveyed to John Knight, Feb. 27, 1718–19, ten acres of land " in y^e

town of Newington," bounded northwesterly by land formerly Zachariah Trickey's, then yᵉ said Knight's, and easterly by the highway from the ferry to the meeting-house—" which ffield is called *Hall's ffield*, and formerly belonged to Henry Langstar, deceased."

John Knight, Sr., and wife Bridget, conveyed to their son John, Feb. 7, 1717–18, a tract of 18 acres at Bloody Point, bought of Zachary Trickey, bounded N. W. by the main river, east by John Hoyt's land (previously Geo. Brawn's), south by the Bloody Point highway to Nutter's, and west by Ephraim Trickey's land,—together with the dwelling-house, and all interest in the ferry at Bloody Poynt.

HILTON'S POINT. This name was given for more than a century to the lower extremity of Dover Neck, from Edward Hilton, who founded a settlement here as early as 1623, that proved, however, unsuccessful. It is so called March 12, 1629–30, in the new patent he obtained from the Plymouth Council. He afterwards settled in Exeter, but this point continued to bear his name till the second half of the 18th century. (See *Hilton's Point Ferry*.) The Dover records make mention of it repeatedly. It is so called by Robert Mason in 1681. Thomas Mason of Dover, trader, and Magdalen his wife, Sept. 13, 1733, conveyed to John Wheelwright and others, of Boston, merchants, his dwelling-house on Dover Neck, " on the westerly side of the road that leads down to *Hilton's Point*, commonly so called," together with the land adjacent. It is now called *Dover Point*. (See *Wecanacohunt*.)

HILTON'S POINT FERRY. Mentioned Sept. 4, 1766, when Ephraim and Hannah Tibbets conveyed to Job Clement 12½ acres " on Dover Neck the westerly side of the road to *Hilton's Point ferry*, so called," extending to the upper side of the way that leads to *Hall's slip* on Back river. This was the ferry from Hilton's Point to Newington, generally called *Knight's ferry*.

HILTON'S POINT SWAMP. Mentioned in 1652, when this swamp was laid out as an ox pasture. Humphrey Varney conveyed to John Knight, Nov. 8, 1711, his share in the ox pasture " granted him in *Hilton's Point swamp* at yᵉ loer end of Dover Neck."—" The ox pasture in *Hilton's Point swamp*" is again mentioned in Judge John Tuttle's will of Dec. 28, 1717. Joseph Hall of Newmarket conveyed to Thomas Millet, Feb. 11, 1736, two tracts of land in Dover; " one known by yᵉ name of yᵉ *Swamp* or *Ox common*, and callᵈ by some *Hilton's Point;*"—" yᵉ other known by yᵉ name of yᵉ *Calves Pasture*." These lots were originally laid out to " Lt. Ralph Hall," grandfather of said Joseph. This swamp is now called *Huckleberry Swamp*.

HOBBS'S HOLE. Mentioned Nov. 20, 1722, when Samuel Kenney confirmed to Capt. Ichabod Plaisted all right to three acres of land at a place in the township of Dover called *Hobbs's hole*, bounded southward and eastward by " Nichewanock" river, north by said Plaisted's land, and west by that of Henry Hobbs, deceased. The significance of the word " *Hole*" does not appear.

Henry Hobbs married Hannah, daughter of Thomas Canney, Sr.,

and received as part of her portion, July 12, 1661, six score acres of land between St. Alban's cove and Quamphegan, bounded S. E. by the "Nechewannick" river in part, and partly by land that was sometime possessed by Capt. Mason's agent; N. E. by the highway that goeth from ye south end of ye s^d lot up into ye woods towards the N. W.; N. W. by Thomas Hanson's land, and S. W. partly by James Grant's, and partly by the commons. Henry Hobbs conveyed to Thomas Hobbs, Ap. 12, 1720, one half of all his land at Sligo, bounded easterly by the "Nechawonack" river, southerly by Sylvanus Nock's land, and northerly by that of James Stackpole. On this shore, in the upper part of the "Point district," not far above St. Alban's cove, the Hobbses built ships in early times, which were easily launched at high tide, this part of the river being deep. "The road that passes by the meeting-house down to Capt. Hobbs's by the river" is mentioned July 26, 1764, in a deed of six acres of land which Thomas Wallingford sold Benjamin Warren, part of a tract said Wallingford had purchased of Thomas Hobbs.

HODGDON'S POINT. This point is on the shore of the Pascataqua, below Bloody Point, but the name has not been retained. It was so called from John Hodgdon, who conveyed to John Knight, in three parcels, all his lands on the southerly side of the road from Bloody Point, part of which adjoined Henry Langstar's ten-acre grant. The last of these was conveyed March 7, 1736, when John and Mary Hodgdon sold John Knight "all the land where we now dwell, beginning at the lower end of our garden, and running along the land we sold s^d Knight to Mr. Geo. Walton's line, then somewhat southerly by Walton's line up to ye road." John Knight, son of the above John, in his will of 1770, speaks of his land at *Hodgdon's Point*, on the east side of the lane leading from his dwelling-house to Portsmouth, adjoining the land of Geo. Walton.

HOGSTY COVE. This cove is mentioned as one of the bounds of ancient Dover the 8th, 7 mo., 1652, when the line ran "from a creek next below Thomas Canney his house, to a certain cove near the mouth of the Great Bay called *Hogsty Cove*. In the division of the Squamscot Patent, May 22, 1656, the General Court at Boston granted to the town of Dover "the land from Kinges (Kenney's) Creeke to a certain Cove neere the mouth of the great Bay called *Hogstye Cove*, with all the marsh from that place round about the bay up to Cotterill's Delight, with 400 acres of upland, as granted it by the Court," etc. (N. H. *Prov. Pap.*, 1:222.) This was a confirmation of a previous decree the 19th, 7 mo., 1643, when the General Court at Boston ordered "that all the marsh and meadow ground lying against the great bay on Strawberry bank side shall belong to Dover, together with 400 acres of upland adjoining." (*Ibid*, 1:172.) The Dover bounds, as defined by the N. H. General Court, Sept. 12, 1701, ran "from *Cannye's Crike* on a Directe Line to *Hoogstie Cove*, with the Mashes on the Grete Baye and foure Hundred Acres of Upland Adjoininge thereto, as formerly laid out, and from *Hoogstie Cove* over to Lamperill River mouth," etc. (*Ibid*, 3 : 227.) That Hogsty Cove was the lowest cove on the Newington shore of the Great Bay—that is, the cove immediately above Furber's Point or Ferry-place—is proved by the fact that all the lands above this cove—that is, up the Bay side—were, according to the Dover records, a part of the 400 acres granted to Dover *above* Hogsty Cove, as will be seen by reference to *Furber's Point, Harwood's Creek, Herod's Point, Laighton's Cove, Long Point*, etc.

When George Snell and Wm. Vaughan surveyed the bounds of Portsmouth, the 28th, 8 mo., 1695-6, they ran the line "from Cannye's Coue in the longe reche to *Hogg Stye Coue at y*^{e} *mouth of y*^{e} *great Bay*, and from the midle of the mouth of one Coue to ye midle of the mouth of ye other, is west, & by South and East & by north & strikes *Mr. Williame ffurbers Barne*." (*Portsmouth Records.*)

This clearly defines the position of Hogsty Cove. It was "*at* ye mouth of ye Great Bay," and the line thereto from Canney's creek struck the barn of Wm. Furber, who then lived at the Narrows between Great Bay and Little Bay, having been licensed, Dec. 11, 1694, to keep a ferry "from his house at Welchman's Cove over to Oyster River." (*Ibid*, 2 : 147.) His farm at the ferry-place was given him by his father, Wm. Furber, in 1674, together with two dwelling-houses, a *barn*, etc., thereon. (See *Pascataqua Rock.*) The line from Canney's Creek through Wm. Furber's barn could only terminate at the first cove above the Narrows or ferry-place.

Wm. Furber of Welch Cove, in the township of Dover, conveyed to his son Jethro, Ap. 3, 1706, a tract of 60 acres on which said Jethro then dwelt—being all the land from a white oak, called by the name of *the bound tree between Dover and Portsm*°, to a white oak near the line of the land given by said William to his son William by deed,—that is, all his land south of that line, which said Wm., senior, had of his father by a deed of gift, and so home to the land which his father gave his brother Jethro.

Jethro Furber of Portsmouth, Aug. 1, 1706, conveyed to John Bickford of Welch Cove in the township of Dover 100 acres of upland *in the township of Portsmouth, at Long Poynt*, bounded S. W. by the land of said John Bickford, S. E. by that of Thomas Laiton, E. by that of Wm. ffurber, Jr., and W. N. W. by that of Jethro ffurber, son of William.

The map in C. W. Tuttle's *Historical Papers*, edited by Mr. A. H. Hoyt, (1889), supposes Laighton's Cove to be the ancient Hogsty Cove. And the present writer, in the first edition of "Landmarks in Ancient Dover," deferring to the opinion of others, makes the same statement. This, however, is certainly an error, for the old Laighton, Nutter, Dame, and Bickford lands, around and below Laighton's cove—that is, below in the sense of going down stream, though really in a northerly direction—and even the southern portion of Wm. Furber's land, (see *Furber's Point*), are clearly stated in the Dover records to have been part of the 400 acres granted to Dover *above* Hogsty Cove. As the only cove between these lands and the mouth of the Great Bay is the one immediately above Furber's Point or Ferry-place, this is undoubtedly the ancient Hogsty Cove.

Moreover, the town of Portsmouth, Jan. 11, 1657, granted to Henrie and John Sherburne, Wm. Cotton, John Pickering, Geo. Walton, and Philip Lewis, "the tract of land more or lesse *from Harrod's creek northward to Welchman's cove, excepting the grant by dover on the 400 acres*, wth this p^{ro}viso, they maintaininge all sutts (suits) of law against any that aposeth them, of there own proper cost, always acknowledging Portsmouth as there towne in paying all publike charges thereunto." (*Portsmouth Town Records*.)

A foot-note in the N. H. *Prov. Papers*, (Vol. 3 : 227,) says Hogsty Cove was "a place where swine were driven from Exeter every spring." The court at Exeter, the 30th, first mo., 1641, ordered "that all the swine above ½ a year old and upwards are to be sent down into the great bay by the 10th day of the second month." (*Ibid*, 1 : 142.)

HOGSTY POINT. Mentioned in 1652, when 40 acres of upland at Welshman's cove were granted to Thomas Layton in 1652, ten acres of which were laid out on *hoggstie poynt*. No further mention of these ten acres of upland is made. They perhaps intrenched on the Furber grant at the mouth of the Great Bay. The other 30 acres were laid out at the head of Thomas Layton's marsh, the south bound being a *Great Rock* towards *longe poynt*. The name of Hogsty point has not been perpetuated, but it was probably on one side of Hogsty cove.

HOITT'S CROSSING. This is a railway crossing on the turnpike road in Lee, near the Hoitt homestead, now belonging to Mr. Layn. A great amount of lumber is conveyed to market from this crossing, and it will probably be soon made a passenger station. There are five other railway crossings in Lee, but none of them stopping-places, viz: *Pinkham's*, on Newtown Plains; *Pendergast's*, at the head of Wheelwright's pond; *Thompson's*, between Little river mill and Nottingham; and *Obadiah Davis's*, near the South Lee station.

HOLMES' BRIDGE. Mentioned June 23, 1701, when Edward Cloutman had a grant of 30 acres "between Cochecha and Nechewanick, as near *holmes his bridge* as may be." That same day 30 acres were granted to Benjn Waymouth, joining Edward Cloutman's land "near *holmes bridg*." Joseph Roberts conveyed to Samuel Randle, Feb. 27, 1726-7, 30 acres on the south side of the Salmon falls road (from Cochecho) "near *Home's bridge*," thence running S. S. E. to a hemlock in Jeremy Rollins' fence, then E. to an elm in a hollow near Thomas Nock's. This bridge seems to have been across the Twombley brook in Rollinsford, but the name is no longer in use. (See *Otis' Bridge*.)

HOOK-ISLAND FALLS, otherwise HOOK FALLS. These falls are in Lamprey river, on the east side of Lee Hook. They are called the "*Hook falls*" on the State map of Lee in 1803, but are now generally called *Hook Island falls*, from an island that divides them.

HOOK MARSH. This marsh is in Madbury, in the vicinity of Bellamy

Hook. It is mentioned May 30, 1738. (See *Gooseberry Marsh*.)

HOOPER'S POND. This is an artificial pond on the Hooper farm in the Back River district, made by enlarging the bed of Johnson's creek, which rises among the marshes not far beyond.

HOPE HOOD'S POINT. This point, so called, according to the late C. W. Tuttle, as early as 1694, is on the western shore of Back river, above the Three Creeks. It is mentioned March 1, 1701, when John and Mary Tuttle conveyed to Richard Pinkham a parcel of land and marsh " lying and being at ye hed of the crike runninge upon the west side of *Hoope Hood's Poynte,* so called, and so through said Pinkham's 20 acres bought of Philip Cromwell on ye west side of ye Bake river, and lying wthin ye southernmost line of that Twenty Acre loat by anny waies or menes whatsoever." Thomas Tuttle conveyed to James Tuttle, May 3, 1740, a tract of salt marsh and upland in Dover, at *a place commonly called Back River,* beginning at a rock at *Hope Woods Point,* and running W. N. W. 34 rods by Pinkham's land.

The name of this point is derived from a noted Indian chief, said to have belonged to the Abenaki tribe. Dr. Quint says he was the sagamore Wahowah or Wohawa, chief of all the lands from Exeter to Salmon Falls. Hubbard, in his *Narrative,* calls him *Hope Hood,* and says he was the son of Robin Hood. The name of " mr. hope hoth " and that of " Old Robin " are affixed to a letter from John Hogkins May 15, 1685. (*N. H. Prov. Pap.,* 1 : 583.) "*Hoope Whood*" and " Ould Robin" are also among the signers of a deed of land at " Squammagonake " to Peter Coffin Jan. 3, 1686. It was Hoop Hood who led the attack on the Newichawannock settlement in 1690, as well as that on the Bloody Point shore soon after, which Mr. Tuttle endeavors to disprove. So noted did he become for his ferocity to the English settlers that Mather, in his *Magnalia,* loads him with opprobrious epithets, such as " that memorable tygre," " that hellish fellow," etc. According to a local tradition he was killed in 1690, and buried on this point of land, which has ever since borne his name. It is a spot as wild and solitary as it was 200 years ago, covered with thickets where the wild grape runs from tree to tree, and where, it is affirmed, the groans of the Indian warrior are still to be heard from time to time among the moaning branches.

HOPPERS. There are several " hoppers " within the limits of ancient Dover. The most important of these is mentioned Nov. 10, 1753, when the head line of Dover was perambulated. This line, in its course, is stated to lead " through a Vault in the earth, commonly known and called by the name of the *Hopper,* on the westerly side of Cochecho river, to the edge of the hill on the westerly side of the said Vault." This Hopper is on the line between Dover and Barrington, on the Ezra Hayes farm, now in the tenure of his son-in-law, Mr. John Grey. The farm house itself is within the Barrington line, at the southeast side of Green hill. There are three hoppers in this vicinity, the largest of which is the one above mentioned. It is a remarkable hollow in the woods, about 100 feet in depth, and 500 feet across. Full grown pines have been cut in this Hopper for timber.

Another Hopper is in Madbury, near the site of Clark's garrison. It is a natural, funnel-like hole in the ground, somewhat curious, but less remarkable than the three above mentioned.

HORNE'S HILL. Mentioned in 1834, when it is related that the Strafford Guards of Dover, returning from the inauguration of Gov. William Badger, were met at *Horne's hill* by Captain Moses Paul and a cavalcade of citizens, who escorted them into town. This hill is on Sixth street, at that time called the "new upper Factory road," and afterwards "Brick street," from a brickyard where is now Snow's tenement house. The name is derived from Wm. Horne, to whom Nathaniel Starbuck conveyed 240 acres of land between Cochecho and Tolend Sept. 20, 1661. This land was originally granted to Elder Edward Starbuck in 1643.

Before the Cochecho railroad was built, the intervale on this shore was used by the Dover military companies for target practice, with Horne's hill for a background. The river at this place was long used by the Free Will Baptist Society for the rite of immersion, the bank being low, and the water shoal. It is now a favorite bathing-place.

HORN'S WOODS. The woods which have borne this name for two hundred years or more, are in the heart of the Lubberland district, below the present road from Durham village to Newmarket. Thirty acres of land were granted to "Mr. Thomas Edgerlie, Sen'., between Collies marsh and the *hornes*," March 19, 1693–4, laid out March 29, 1699. The Edgerly family still own part of these woods. Ten acres, part of a 40 acre grant to John Doo (Doe) in 1694, were laid out to John Smith, Jr., Aug. 12, 1732, "beginning at a black oak in *Horn's woods*, so called." (*Durham Records*.) Capt. John Smith's ten-acre lot "in the *horn's woods*, by the *grassy swamp*," is mentioned Oct. 31, 1749. John Mason conveyed to Abraham Mathes Aug. 5, 1747, 16 acres of marsh and upland, commonly called *Doe's marsh*, "lying in a place commonly called the *Horne's woods* in Durham, being part of the estate of my honored grandfather John Doe, set off to my mother Mary Mason of Durham, widow." Ninety acres in *Horne's woods* are mentioned in the inventory of Abraham Mathes' estate, Feb. 9, 1762. A highway from "Wormwood's into *Horn's woods*," bordering on the Edgerly lands, is mentioned Dec. 26, 1743.

No Horns appear in the early rate-lists of Oyster River, but there were Hornes in Dover proper. The name may have been derived from John Haunce, who was taxed at Oyster River as early as 1655. Geo. Walton, May 24, 1665, conveyed land on Great Island to "John Haunce of Oyster River, carpenter."

HORSEHIDE BROOK. This name is sometimes given to that part of Denbow's brook, where it crosses the Newmarket road at the south side of Broth Hill, in Durham. It was so named from a tan-yard formerly adjacent, belonging to Robert Jones. This brook has two branches, one of which rises at the Moat. It is perhaps "the little brook that cometh out of the mooet," mentioned in old grants. This unites with Denbow's brook, which rises in the Long marsh, and empties into the mill-pond above Durham falls. (See *Denbow's Brook*.)

HUCKINS' BROOK. This brook rises in Madbury, above the town-house, passes through the old Tasker lands— whence this part of it is often called the *Tasker* or *Tasket brook*,[1]—crosses the highway below the Miles house, and, after being fed by the Pendexter springs farther down, comes into Durham, where it flows through the old Huckins land, east of the spot where stood the Huckins garrison, destroyed by the Indians in 1689. It is joined by the "Tom-Hall brook" a little below the place where the Huckins massacre occurred, and empties into Beard's creek.

Huckins' Mill was built on this stream at an early day. It is mentioned Jan. 10, 1697-8. Among the Dover grants is recorded, Jan. 23, 1701, "libbertie of a Remoue of ten Acres of land granted Robbart Huckins in 1664 at the head of his twenty acre lott on the west side of back riuer, to be laid out adjoining to his home land at oyster Riuer, on the west side of *the brooke that driues his mill.*" This removal of Robert Huckins' grant seems to have been made in favor of his grandson Robert, son of James Huckins who was killed by the Indians in 1689. One fourth of this mill was sold by John Huckins to Capt. Samuel Emerson, Oct. 24, 1727, for £30. The receipt for this sum, still extant, declares,—"The said mill standeth on the stream called *Huckins' brook*." The entire mill and the Huckins lands were finally acquired by Capt. Emerson and his sons. The mill is now gone, but the remains of the dam are still to be seen on that part of the brook which flows through the land of Mr. Ebenezer T. Emerson.

HUCKLEBERRY HILL. This is a high ridge on Dover neck, about three quarters of a mile below the bridge across Little John's creek. It is mentioned the 5th, 10 mo., 1659, when it was ordered that *huckleberry hill*, which had been laid out for a sheep pasture, should be divided for a public training place for the township of Dover. "The way which doth lead from *huckleberry hill* to Cochecho" is mentioned in a conveyance of land from the town to John Tuttle, March 5, 1674-5. This hill commands an extensive and magnificent view across the Newichawannock on one side, and Back river on the other. And far down the Long Reach of the Pascataqua may be seen the spires of Portsmouth rising beyond the fair shores of Newington, with beautiful hills and gleaming waters in every direction.

HUCKLEBERRY PLAIN. Mentioned March 19, 1693-4, when the town of Dover granted to Zachariah Trickey "that ffield he hath ffenced on ye *horttleberry plain*, with as much joining it as to make it twenty acres." This land was no doubt "zachery trickey's twenty acres in the *pich pine plains*"

---

[2] The name of Tasker seems to have been thus corrupted at a very early period. Or Tasket may have been the original name. At any rate, it is written Tasket in the Dover rate-list of 1675, and in the court records of 1686. (See Farmer's Belknap, page 169, foot note.) John Tasket's name is on the muster-roll of Capt. James Davis's scouting party in 1712. And the name is frequently so called to this day in Madbury

(in Newington), next Richard Pomeroy's grant, mentioned Ap. 2, 1694. (See *Pitch-Pine Plains*.)

HUCKLEBERRY SWAMP. This name is now given to *Hilton's Point swamp*, which was laid out as an ox pasture in 1652. It is at the lower end of Dover Neck.

HULL'S MEADOW. So named from Benjamin Hull, who had a grant adjoining the Pascassic mill in 1659. (See *Indian Graves*.) Benjamin Hull of Dover, Dec. 12, 1678, conveyed to John Rand 120 acres of land *in Dover*, bounded N. E. by Lamperel river, and S. W. by the *Dover line*. John Rand of ye township of Dover, in y^e *county of Portsmouth*, conveyed to Robert Wadley of Dover, Aug. 26, 1679, "120 acres of land and meadow ground, lying by Lamperell river, between y^e *Island Falls* and y^e *second Falls* of ye afores^d river, commonly called by ye name of *Benjamin Hull's meadow*."

The Hull land was acquired Jan. 12, 1695, by Richard Hilton, who, Dec. 5, 1735, conveyed to Thomas Darling of Portsmouth 120 acres of upland and Meadow in Durham, beginning at a pitch-pine tree on or near the line between Durham and Exeter, thence up said line W. and by N. 170 rods to a black oak on said line or town bounds, then north 160 rods to a hemlock on the bank of Lamperel river, then down said river as far as it bears east nearest, then E. and by N. six score rods to a pine, thence to ye pitch pine first mentioned, standing on ye town bounds, near to y^e *Indian graves*. Thomas Darling of Durham, Oct. 27, 1742, out of love, good-will, and affection to his well-beloved son-in-law, John Frost of Portsmouth, conveyed to said Frost one half of his homestead estate—that is, half the upland he bought of Richard Hilton, except 40 acres then owned by Nathaniel Frost, together with one half of ye meadow commonly called *Hull's meadow*. That same day Thomas Darling conveyed to his beloved son-in-law Nicholas Tuttle the other half of his homestead estate, and half of ye meadow commonly called *Hull's meadow* on the north side. Nicholas Tuttle conveyed his part to Jeremiah Folsom, Jr., Feb. 10, 1752. John Frost, Sept. 20, 1752, conveyed to Thomas and John Tash, both of Durham, a tract of upland and meadow in Durham, part of the land formerly granted to Benjamin Hull, bounded N. by Nathaniel Frost's land, and S. and W. by that of Jonathan Stevens and David Davis ye 3^d. The Tash land, between the Pascassic river and Lee Hook, is still pointed out.

HUMPHREY'S POND. This name is given to Willand's Pond in the Somersworth records of March 16, 1793; also in Merrill's *N. H. Gazetteer* of 1817, and in Hayward's *New England Gazetteer* of 1839. The origin of the name is uncertain, but it may have been derived from Humphrey Varney, who was received an inhabitant of Dover, Aug. 2, 1659, and married Sarah, daughter of Elder Edward Starbuck, who owned land around Cochecho pond, now Willand's.

HUNTRESS LANDINGS. There are two landing-places of this name on the western shore of the Long Reach, called by the river boatmen the *Upper* and *Lower Huntress*.

The UPPER HUNTRESS is in Newington, a short distance above Paul's creek, at the foot of an old road along the east side of a point of land owned by Miss Mary Huntress, to whom the landing-place also belongs. This is a remnant of the old Huntress estate on this shore, acquired by George Huntress about 200 years ago, half of which was inherited by his son Samuel, whose grave is still to be seen not far from the landing-place that bears his name. Here he doubtless moored his gundelows and other craft, mentioned in the public records. It was voted by the N. H. General Assembly, Dec. 13, 1746, "that Saml Huntriss be allowed fifteen shills and nine Pence in full for ye use of his Gundloe 18 days at ye Fort." And the "Acc^t of Saml Huntress for gundaloe hire at N. Castle" is again mentioned the same day. (*N. H. Prov. Pap.*, 5 : 475, 855.)

The LOWER HUNTRESS is in Portsmouth, just below the Newington line, at the foot of the Gosling road. The name is derived from Clement Huntress, to whom Alice Thompson conveyed, Oct. 5, 1831, four acres and two rods of land in Portsmouth, at the northwesterly corner of the premises adjoining the road which separates Newington from Portsmouth, bounded on one side by the Piscataqua river, and adjacent to the Elliot farm, so-called, then belonging to Stephen Pearse. This land is now owned by Mr. Nathaniel Huntress, nephew of the above Clement. The landing-place here is sometimes called *Thompson's Point.*

HUSSEY'S BROOK. This is the first brook that empties into the Newichawannock river above Cochecho Point. So named from Joseph Hussey whose land below St. Alban's cove is mentioned in 1736. (See *Guppy's Point.*)

HUSSEY'S FALLS. See *Cochecho Falls.*

HUSSEY'S POND. This name is sometimes given to Willand's pond, from the Hussey families that own land in its vicinity.

HUSSEY'S SPRINGS. The largest of the Hussey springs is on the farm of Mr. Benjamin Hussey, but those acquired by the city of Dover for the public water-works are on the farm of Mr. John S. Hussey, between Gage's Hill and Willand's Pond, partly in Dover and partly in Somersworth.

INDIAN BROOK. Mentioned June 23, 1701, when John Varney had a grant of 30 acres "near the *Indian brook.*" This brook, which is opposite the old *Indian corn ground*, crosses the Scatterwit road in Dover, and empties into the Cochecho river, a little above the Upper Factory falls. The name is still retained. It is mentioned in 1865, as one of the bounds of Dover "highway district No. One."

INDIAN GRAVES. Mentioned the 4th, 9 mo., 1652, when Philip Chesley had a grant of 100 acres "at the *Indian graves,*" which was laid out in 1661. Of this land 78 acres were laid out for his grandson, Lieut. Philip Chesley, July 21, 1715, beginning at "the south end of the *Indian graves* att beach hill, att a hemlock marked P. C. on the south side of the road, thence running S. S. W. 52 rods to a hemlock, thence S. S. E. 240 rods along by Mr. Woodman's land to a beach tree, thence N. N. E. 52 rods, to a red oak by a *grate rock* by the road, thence by the highway to the first bound."

This land is on the western side of Beech Hill, and is now owned in part, if not wholly, by Mr. I. Blake Hill.

Another Indian burying-ground is mentioned the 5th, 8 mo., 1659, when Benjamin Hull had a grant of 100 acres from the town of Dover, "adjacent to the bounds of Puscassick mill, on the S. W. sied of Lamprill River fall," which was laid out the 12th, 11 mo., 1660, "beginning at a marked tree in the *town bounds*, by the *Indian graves* that are thear," and running W. by S. 12 rods, "then N. to Lamprill river, and along the river side as long as the river bears away east, making the line 120 rods, till you come to a marked tree, then S. to the town bounds next Exeter side near the *graves*." Exeter, it will be remembered, then included Newmarket. (See *Hull's Meadow*.)

The tongue of land on the west side of Beard's creek, where the Woodmans lie buried, not far from their garrison, has always borne the name of the *Indian burying-ground*, derived perhaps from a tradition that they were partly of Indian descent, through an early member of the family said to have married a dusky maiden of the Mohawk race. Nothing has been found in the records, however, to justify this romantic tradition.

INDIAN GROUND, or CORN GROUND. Mentioned the 7th, 10 mo., 1659, when sufficient land to make up Peter Coffin's lot of 100 acres, was laid out a little above the third fall in the Cochecho river, beginning at a pine tree by the river side and extending up the river to a white oak on a little hill, thence northward to the swamp by the *Indian ground*. This planting-ground seems to have been abandoned by the Indians after the disturbances occasioned by Major Waldron's treachery to them in 1676, and it was afterwards divided among the Dover settlers. Among others, John Horn, Sr., had a grant of 30 acres " on the *Indian Corne ground* on the west side of Cochecho river," March 19, 1693-4. It was laid out Feb. 16, 1711, beginning at the *Indian Corn ground*, upon the north side of burbadus (Barbadoes) way that leads to tole end." Wm. Hartford Ap. 1, 1712, conveyed to John and Peter Haise 20 acres of land " between Cochecha river and Barbadoes, beginning at a red oak on y^e *Indian Corn Ground*." (See *Moharimet's Planting-Ground*.)

INDIAN HILLS. These hills are on the neck of land between Fresh creek and the Newichawannock river. Robert Huggens conveyed to James Guppy, Oct. 19, 1713, 20 acres of land, with a parcel of marsh and flats belonging thereto, "from the lower point, where the *Indian hills* are, to ye head of ye Fresh creek on Cochecho point." John Meader, aged 70 years, or thereabouts, testified before John Woodman, Justice of the Peace, Sept. 17, 1702, that "all the marsh flats from the lower point where the *Indian hills* are, to ye head of ye crick, on both sides of the crick which is commonly called Fresh crick, on ye north side of Cochecho river, as also a parcel of planting land on the west side of said creek" were, in the year of our Lord 1647 or 8, in the possession of Robert Huckins, grandfather of Robert Huckins, Jr., then claiming title to said marsh.

James Guppy, Aug. 21, 1733, conveyed to Thomas Downs 35 acres of his land " on a certain neck commonly called by ye name of Cochecho Point, beginning at a rock on the south side of the way leading to Nechowannuck, near a brook y^t runs out of Cromwel's land into Fresh creek." Another portion he conveyed to Joseph Ricker, Nov. 21, 1733, beginning at the S. E. corner of Thomas Downs' land on Fresh creek. And Aug. 3, 1736, he conveyed 30 acres to James Philpot. (See *Guppy's Point.*)

INDIAN OVEN. This is a cave in the side of a steep ledge near the top of a hill in the Caverno pasture, in Lee, overlooking the lower side of Wheelwright's pond. The opening is five or six feet high, and the depth perhaps four feet. Traces of fire within still bear witness to its having been used for domestic purposes. In this vicinity took place the battle of Wheelwright's pond.

INDIAN PATH. Mentioned May 4, 1657, when 200 acres of land were laid out to "Mr. Edward Rawson, secretary;" one half of it on "the east side of the Quochecho river," and the other half on the west side, "a little below the *Indian path*," which path "lyeth about three miles above Peter Cofyns house." (*N. H. Prov. Pap.*, 1 : 229.) This land was afterwards acquired by Richard Waldron, who conveyed it in part, if not wholly, to Peter Coffin May 27, 1671. It apparently joined the Indian reservation above Tolend, called in the early records the "Indian cornground." Peter Coffin of Exeter, June 2, 1696, conveyed to his son Peter of Nantucket a tract of 200 acres on "the north side of Cochechow river, at a place called "*ye six Indian wigwams.*" (See *Indian Cornground.*)

INDIGO HILL. This is a well-known hill in Somersworth, about three quarters of a mile below Great Falls, between the river and the new road to Salmon Falls. It is mentioned March 19, 1693-4, when Ezekiel Wentworth had a grant of land on Salmon Falls river, above *Indigo Hill.* John Tuttle had a grant of 60 acres June 18, 1694, between *Indigo Hill* and Antonies (brook), which, in his will of Dec. 28, 1717, he gives his son Ebenezer. Over 23 acres of this land were conveyed to Robert Cole Sept. 4, 1730, when it is spoken of as on the north side of John Hall's lot. A road was laid out in 1720 from Quamphegan to *Indigo Hill* and the commons. This road is now partly closed up. The name is found variously written *Indigo*, *Indego*, and *Endego*. Its origin does not appear, but the suggestion has been made that it may be a corruption of Endicott. John Endicott was governor of Massachusetts for many years between 1644 and 1665, at which time New Hampshire was under the jurisdiction of the Massachusetts government. Others suppose it to be a reminiscence of commercial relations with Antigua, the name of which is found corrupted to Antegoe in the old records, not dissimilar in sound to Indigo.

ISINGLASS RIVER. This is a branch of the Cochecho, that rises at Bow pond, Strafford. On the state map of Barrington in 1805, mention is made of *Foss's mills* on this stream, not far from the source, with a bridge just below. Then come *Roberts' saw-mill* and *Nat'l Foss's grist-mill*. Farther down is *Caverly's bridge*, on the *Ridge road*, with *French's mill* just below, at the outlet of *Long pond*. In the bend below is Judge Hale's house, east of *Nippo pond*. At the next bend stand *Twombley's mills*, above the mouth of a brook that connects Isinglass river with *Ayer's pond*. A little below the mouth of this brook is *Tuttle's fulling-mill*, with *Blake's bridge* below. Farther down, on the *Green Hill road*, is *Babb's mill*. *Locke's mill* is on or near the line between Barrington and Rochester. Coming into Rochester, Isinglass river flows along the west side of *Blind Will's Neck*, and empties into the Cochecho on the west side.

The Isinglass river is fed, not only by Bow pond in Strafford, where it takes its rise, but through its tributaries by Ayer's, Nippo, Round, and Long ponds, in Barrington. These ponds are the chief reservoirs of the Cocheco Manufacturing Co., which has a dam at the outlet of the three first, if not all.

ISLAND FALLS. So called in 1669, when Robert Wadley's claim to these falls was confirmed by a grant from the town of Dover. And again Aug. 26, 1679, when John Rand conveyed to Robert Wadley 120 acres of land " between y^e *Island Falls* and ye second falls in Lamperell river." They are now called *Wadleigh's falls*. In an old plan of 1739, five islands are represented at these falls.

JACKSON'S CREEK. Mentioned March 6, 1710–11, in connection with a road from Lamprey river to the Salmon Falls river, which, in its course, ran near Robert Huggins' house, at the south; thence to Wm. Jackson's pasture and to the head of *Jackson's creek*, straight as ye old road went, then "Joseph Jenkins to open at ye left," etc. Evidently the same as Johnson's creek, near which Walter Jackson had a grant of land the 19th, 1 mo., 1665.

JACKSON'S POINT. Mentioned Jan. 26, 1773, when a tract of upwards of 47 acres, belonging to Jonathan and Robert Leathers, is described as running southerly along the land of Samuel Chesley and Wm. Jackson to highwater mark at *Jackson's Point*, so called, then easterly by the upland 4½ rods to Robert Leathers' thatch-bed, and along this bed S. 13 deg. W. to the channel of Oyster river, westerly by this channel to the land of Mary and Jonathan Chesley, and northerly to the highway. The name of this point has not been retained, but the tract referred to appears to be the Leathers land in Durham, now owned in part by the heirs of the late John T. Emerson.

JEEMS'S COVE, otherwise JAMES'S. This is the first cove below Paul's cove, on the Rollinsford shore of the Newichawannock river, so called from a family that once lived adjacent thereto. The boatmen on the river in those days, when they came abreast of this cove, hailed it with the cry: "There's Mother Jeems!" and laid down their oars to take their turn at the jug which was passed around. The land here is now owned by Mr. Henry Paul.

JEWELL'S POINT. This point, so called on Smith's map of Durham, is on the Lubberland shore, at the lower side of Broad Cove. It was originally called *Needham's Point*, but is now known as *Long Point*, and forms part of the present Randall farm. The name was derived from Bradbury Jewell of Tamworth, to whom Thomas Stevenson of Durham, and wife Agnes, Feb. 10, 1785, conveyed all his homestead plantation of 64½ acres, where he (Stevenson) then dwelt, together with another tract of 30 acres called *Ambler's marsh*, bounded S. by the lands of Benjamin and John Smith, westerly by the highway to Durham Falls, and northerly and easterly by the lands of Ephraim Davis and the heirs of Wm. Durgin. (See *Red Rock* and *Needham's Point*.) Bradbury Jewell, after living for some years on this shore, removed to Sandwich, N. H. The Rev. Curtis Coe of Durham records the marriage of Bradbury Jewell, Esq., of Sandwich and Ann Elizabeth Edgerly of Durham, Jan. 4, 1804. She was the daughter of Moses Edgerly, who seems to have bequeathed her 30 acres of land in Durham.

JOCELYN'S COVE. Mentioned Dec. 12, 1701, when 30 acres of land were laid out to Wm. Henderson, Sr. (granted March 19, 1693-4), beginning at a small white pine near Cornelius Courson's fence, on the south side of *Josling's Coue*. This cove is on the western shore of the Newichawannock, just above the bridge to Eliot. The name was no doubt derived from Henry Jocelyn, who was appointed Capt. John Mason's agent in New Hampshire in 1634. He was the son of Sir Thomas Josselyn, whom Sir Ferdinando Gorges appointed Deputy Governor of Maine in 1639. A list of the goods left with "Mr. Joslyn" in the house at Newichawannock, Aug., 1634, is given in the *N. H. Prov. Pap.*, 1: 93-94. He seems to have written his name "Jocelyn." Henry Jocelyn afterwards went to Black Point, Scarborough, Me., where he built a garrison, which, in spite of the vigilance implied in Whittier's line,

"Grey Jocelyn's eye is never sleeping,"

was captured by Mogg Megone or Hegone Oct. 12, 1677.

JODY'S SPRING. This name is given to a "boiling spring" at the lower end of the Rollins farm, in Newington, from Joanna Rollins, a former proprietress. It is in a thicket near the railway.

JOHNSON'S CREEK. This is the first inlet from Oyster river above Bunker's creek, in Durham. The name, however, was generally given at an early day, not only to the tidal portion, but to the fresh-water brook above it. This brook rises in the marshes above the Hooper land in the Back River district, Dover. The name is derived from Thomas Johnson, who was in Dover as early as 1639, and afterwards had a grant of 100 acres of upland next Philip Chesley's. Thomas Johnson of Pascataway, planter, conveyed to Nicholas ffollett house, field, marsh, goods, cattle, etc., Sept. 6, 1652. This was perhaps a mortgage, for the inventory of Thomas Johnson's estate, made July 1, 1661, mentions his house, land, and marsh.

"The path at the head of *Johnson's Creek*" was one of the old bounds between the Oyster River precinct and Dover proper, when defined Dec. 21, 1657. Permission was granted Ambrose Gibbons the 5th, 10 mo., 1659, to erect a sawmill at the head of *Thomas Johnson's creek*—that is, at the head of tide water. Twenty acres of land, granted to Valentine Hill the 5th, 10 mo., 1652, were laid out Dec. 2, 1709, to Nathaniel Hill, only son of said Valentine, on "the east side of *Thomas Johnson's creek*, between Wm. Stories 100 acre lot and the swamp."

Johnson's creek bridge is often mentioned in the Durham and Madbury records, generally referring, not to the bridge near the mouth, but to the one on the road to Back River, on the line between Durham and Madbury. When this line was perambulated Jan. 9, 1802, it ran from Cedar Point in a westerly direction " to the middle of *Johnson's creek bridge*." (*Durham Records.*)

The name of Johnson's creek is still retained, but the tidal portion is sometimes called *Jones's creek*.

JOHNSON'S CREEK HILL. This hill is mentioned in the Madbury records of 1803, when $14 were paid Wm. and Thomas Jones for land taken for a highway on " *Johnson's Creek Hill*, so called." This was no doubt the road laid out Oct. 20, 1800, across a corner of land belonging to the heirs of Stephen Jones, on the hill below Johnson's creek bridge, to avoid the steepness of the hill on the old road. This, of course, was in the lower part of Madbury.

JONAS' CREEK, otherwise JONAS BINE'S. Mentioned the 10th, 8 mo., 1653, when Wm. Follet and James Bonker had a grant of " tenn acres of land above the head of *Jonas his creek*, called the *Vinyeard*."

Ap. 2, 1711, Nicholas ffollett of Portsmouth, heir and successor of Wm. ffollett, late of Dover, deceased, conveyed to James Bunker 20 acres of land, " being one moyetie or part of a forty acre grant to Wm. Story in the year 1650: 29: 5 mo., lying upon the neck of land between Johnson's creek and *Jonas Bine his creek*." This inlet is now called *Bunker's creek*.

Jonas Bine's marsh at the head of his creek is mentioned in 1653.

JONAS' POINT. So called from Jonas Binn or Bine, who, in 1651, had a house and lot of six acres which he bought of Thomas Stevenson, on the point at the entrance into Oyster river, compassed with the river every way except the south side, which joined the land of Mr. Francis Mathes. Francis Mathes, Dec. 20, 1748, conveyed to Valentine and Abraham Mathes, Jr., the homestead where he then lived, " beginning at John Bickford's orchard point, so the salt water is ye bounds to *Joneses Point*, and Oyster river and said point is on ye northerly side," etc. John Bickford, June 8, 1771, conveyed to his son Winthrop Bickford 25 acres of land, bounded northerly and westerly by land of Valentine Mathes, easterly by the water, and southerly by the land of Stephen Willey. Also another parcel of land near the above, commonly known by the name of *Jonas's Point*, containing six acres, bounded southerly by land of Valentine Mathes, and westerly, northerly, and easterly by the salt water.

Jonas' Point is on the south side of Oyster river, at the very mouth, and now belongs to Miss Dorothy Mathes. The name is still retained, but is generally corrupted to *Jones's Point.*

JONES'S CREEK. This name is now generally given to the tidal portion of Johnson's creek, in Durham, from Stephen Jones, who was at Oyster river as early as 1663, and acquired the lands of Thomas Johnson. "*Jones's creek*" is mentioned in the Durham records as early as March 27, 1785. *Jones's bridge* is also frequently alluded to in the town accounts, meaning the bridge near the mouth of Jones's creek, on the turnpike-road.

KELLEY'S SPRINGS. This name is now given to Barbadoes springs, which supply the Dover aqueduct with water. They are southeast of Barbadoes pond, and originally belonged in part to the Evans family. Samuel and Nathaniel Evans, Dec. 22, 1812, conveyed to Benjamin Kielle 24¼ acres of land in that part of Dover called Littleworth, on the southerly side of the road from Dover to Barrington, "commonly known by the name of the *spring pasture.*" This pasture is said to contain scores of springs. The old name of Kielle is now written Kelley.

KENNEY'S COVE, CREEK, etc. See *Canney.*

KIMBALL'S FALLS. See *Cochecho Falls.*

KINCAID'S BROOK. This brook is mentioned several times in the Durham records previous to the incorporation of the township of Lee. In 1765 the town paid Simon Randall 1£, 6s., 3d., for timber furnished Thomas Leathers for "the bridge over *Kincaid's brook.*" This appears to be the trout brook that rises among the marshes in Newtown, crosses the turnpike road above Mr. S. E. Demeritt's, and finally empties into Oyster river. It is now generally called *Demeritt's brook.*

KNIGHT'S FERRY. This ferry, under the name of *Trickey's ferry* or *Bloody Point ferry*, was in operation at an early day. It ran not only from Bloody Point to Hilton's Point, but also to the Kittery shore, and was originally owned by Thomas Trickey, who was in Dover as early as 1640, and was living at Bloody Pt. before 1657. He died before 1680, in which year, on the 16th of June, his widow Elizabeth renounced all claim to the Trickey plantation and the *ferry* belonging to it, in favor of her son Zachariah. Zachariah Trickey of Bloody Point, Aug. 1, 1705, conveyed to John Chevalier, *alias* Knight, 14 acres of upland at Bloody Point, *where ye ferry is kept*, part of yᵉ land formerly granted Thomas Trickey, bounded east by Zachariah's homestead, of which this tract was a part, south by the highway going to Nutter's (Welsh Cove), and northwest by other Trickey lands and the "maine river." This deed was confirmed Nov. 22, 1705, when mention was made of the boats, "gondeloes," and other equipments for the ferry.

"Capt. John Knight of Dover, near Bloody Point," petitioned to the N. H. General Assembly, Dec. 18, 1705, for a license to carry on the Bloody Point ferry, "setting forth that the *ferry* there kept *to Hilton's Point* belonging to Dover Neck, and the other from the said Bloody Point to Kittery Neck, were always holden by the inhabitants of Trickey's farm, which is now his by purchase, and thereupon humbly prays that the right of the said ferrys may be conferred upon him." It was "accordingly agreed that the Governor be desired to give him a patent for the said ferrys, he not demanding more than twelve pence for every horse and man at each ferry, and three pence for every single person without Horse, he always taking care that there be Boats always ready, that there be no complaint thereupon." (*N. H. Prov. Pap.*, 3 : 322–323.)

John Knight was a Huguenot refugee, who changed his French name of Chevalier for its English equivalent of Knight. "John Chevalier and man" are on the Portsmouth rate-list of 1681. "John Knight of Portsmouth, *alias* Chevalier," Oct. 18, 1702, bought the Carter farm at Pine Point, adjacent to the mill-stream below Bloody Point. (See *Pine Point*.)[1]

The Knight place at Bloody Point, whence the ferry ran to Hilton's Point and Kittery, was acquired by Miss Nancy N. Drew July 16, 1831. (See *Nancy Drew's Point*. It now belongs to Mr. Charles Dame.

There was another *Knight's ferry* between Fox Point and the Durham shore. (See *Fox Point*.)

LAIGHTON'S COVE. This cove, originally called *Harwood's*, *Harrod's*, *Herod's*, *Herd's*, etc., is on the Newington shore of Great Bay, between Fabyan's Pt. and Long Pt. Its present name was derived from Thomas Layton of Dover, who, the 15th, 4 mo., 1646, had a grant of ten acres of marsh in the Great Bay, upon the other side of ye creek west of ye land of Wm. Pomfrett. (Pomfrett's land was sold to Anthony Nutter in 1651.) Thirty acres of upland were laid out to Thomas Layton in 1656, adjoining his marsh in the Great Bay, towards Long point. Elder Nutter's land was on one side. This tract is specified as part of the 400 acres granted to Dover on Great Bay, which proves, beyond all dispute, that Hogsty cove was further down the shore, and not Laighton's cove itself, as some have supposed. (See *Hogsty Cove* and *Long Point*.) Thomas Laighton, descendant of the above Thomas, Jan. 26, 1741, conveyed all his lands, marsh, and flats, in Newington, to Thomas Laighton, Jr., who, about thirty years later, sold them to Nicholas Pickering.

LAIGHTON'S HILL. This hill, so called in the Madbury records, is in the southwestern part of the Back River district, on the borders of Dover and Madbury. It is crossed by the road to Dover from the old Pascataqua bridge, and is now generally called *Atkinson's Hill*. Its old name was derived from Thomas Layton, who, the 6th, 10 mo., 1656, had a grant of 100 acres on the west side of Back river, which was laid out at the head of a 20 acre lot he bought of Ambrose Gibbons, running along the northern branch of Royall's cove and up the freshet. (See *Royall's Cove*.) This land was still owned by his descendants Ap. 1, 1762, when Thomas Laighton conveyed to Thomas Wallingford of

---

[1] The marriage of Elizabeth, daughter of John Knight and Bridget his wife, to John Janvrin, is thus recorded by the Rev. John Pike: "Mr. John Jambrin of Jersey (belonging to England) was legally married to Elizabeth Knight, alias Sheavallier, of the town of Dover in New England, upon the 12 of September, 1706." The Knights and Janvrins are connected with the present writer through her paternal grandmother.

Somersworth 100 acres of land in Dover, on the west side of Back river, extending from Royall's cove about 40 rods westward to the land of Joseph Meader, and running along his land and that of Ephraim Davis to Paul Nute's. Isaac Lord gave a quit claim deed to Wm. King Atkinson, Feb. 3, 1798, of 100 acres of land in Dover, Durham, and Madbury, that belonged to his grandfather Thomas Wallingford. Other heirs quit claim that same year. Atkinson also bought 30 acres of Ephraim Davis's land adjoining, July 17, 1799, bounded west by the road to Pascataqua bridge. (See *Atkinson's Hill*.)

LAIGHTON'S POINT. This name is sometimes given to the point at the lower side of Laighton's cove, in Newington, generally called *Long Point*.

LAMOS BRIDGE. This bridge is at the foot of Guppy's hill in Dover, across a large culvert on the turnpike-road to Portland, so called from a workman named Lamos, who was killed in the course of its construction.

LAMPREY RIVER. The Indians called this river the Pascassick, a name now confined to the lowest western tributary, and generally written Piscassick. In the Exeter records of 1639 it is called *Lamprill* and *Lamprel river*, and elsewhere *Lampereel*, *Lampreel*, etc. It is called " *Lamprey River* " March 20, 1641, in the inventory of the estate of John Phillipps. (*County Records*, Exeter. Vol. 1, p. 16.) And again in 1652, when "*Lamprey river*" was declared to be the lawful boundary between Dover and Exeter.

This river rises in Northwood, west of Saddleback mountain, and, after a circuitous course through Deerfield, Candia, Raymond, and Epping, it enters Lee above Wadleigh's falls, and after a deep bend, called the Hook, it enters Durham below Hook Island falls. It crosses the Durham line into Newmarket near the mouth of the Pascassick river, and finally empties into the Great Bay.

The name of "*Lamprey River*" was generally given to the village of Newmarket till 1849, to distinguish it from another village in the same township called "Newfields," now South Newmarket, which was not incorporated as a separate township till June 27, 1849.

LAMPREY RIVER FALLS. There are several falls in this river within the limits of ancient Dover where mill-dams have been erected. The uppermost are *Wadleigh's falls*, often called the " *upper falls* " in early times, and previously known as *Island falls*, from the number of islets adjacent. The latter name is mentioned as late as Dec. 30, 1736, when Robert Wadleigh of Exeter conveyed to Ebenezer Smith of Durham one half of a certain grant of 120 acres, with ye Falls and privilege of timber, at a place (formerly) call^d y^e *Island falls*, but now by ye name of *Wadly's Falls*, which land, falls, and timber were granted by the town of Dover to his father Robert Wadley, deceased. Below are *Dame's falls*, formerly *Mathes's*, called *Hill's falls* on the state map of 1803. On the easterly side of the Hook are *Hook-Island falls*, so called from the islet that divided the dam. Below are *Long falls*, and another fall apparently unnamed. Then come *Wiswall's falls*, where stood the paper-mill of Mr. Thomas H. Wiswall, formerly called *Wiggin's falls*. Just below the Packer's falls bridge, on the road to Newmarket, are the falls to which the name of "*Packer's*" is now confined, and a little below are *Sullivan's falls*. There are no others in the river till you come to Newmarket falls at the head of tide water.

The lowest falls, generally called "*Lamprey River falls*," by way of superiority, are in Newmarket village, and now belong to the Newmarket Manufacturing Company. In early times the water privilege here, on the easterly side, belonged to the town of Dover, and the 19th, 10 mo., 1647, was granted to Elder Nutter and Elder Starbuck, who were authorized to build a sawmill at the upper or lower falls in Lamprell river. And the 7th, 5 mo., 1652, Mr. Valentine Hill of Dover had a grant of the whole accommodations of Lamprell river for the erecting and setting up of a sawmill or mills, with all the timber on the south side of the river within the Dover line, a mile in breadth, not infringing on the Piscassick grant, and all the timber on the north side a mile in breadth, and all the land in length, at the rent of twenty pounds a year.

Peter Coffin afterwards acquired this water privilege. The mill at Lamprey river lower falls, " built by Capt. Coffin, but carried away by a freshet," is mentioned in a deed from Dyer to Hilton, Apr. 11, 1715.

LAMPREY RIVER NECK. This neck is mentioned April 26, 1675, when all the town right of Dover " in *Lamper-Eel River Neck*, both land and timber " was conveyed to Peter Coffin, " from the head of John *Goddar's Creek* so far as the tide flows upon a strait line to the Cove at high-water mark below *Lamper Eel fall*, where Mr. Hill's works stood." (*N. H. Prov. Pap.*, 17 : 604, 605.) " Hill's works " were the mills of Valentine Hill, who had a grant of the privilege at Lamprey river falls in 1652. The neck " between Lamper-Eel river and Goddard's creek " was conveyed by Peter Coffin to Capt. Richard Waldron, June 25, 1675. (*Ibid*, 17 : 605.) Richard Waldron, March 22, 1709, conveyed to Sampson Doe of Lubberland all that neck of land between Lamperell river and Goddard's creek in the township of Dover, formerly granted by said town to Peter Coffin of Exeter.

The bounds of this Neck were defined May 15, 1711, when Jn° Tuttle, Sen', Jn° Bickford, and Tristram Heard, " lott layers of Dover," at the request of Sampson Doe, drew " the *neck line* from the head of *goddard's Creek* to Lampreele Riuer as followeth, beginning at the head of *goddard's Creek* at the flowing of the tide there, at about Eight Rods southward from *Abraham benick's mill*, and from thence to run nor west and be west ¾ westerle cours to *Stony brook*, a little below Lamprele Riuer first falls. Lamprill Riuer bounds *this Neck* on the westward side, the great bay upon the southward side, and *Goddard's Creek* on the eastward side up to the place where we begun." (See *Doe's Neck*.)

LANGLEY'S HEATH. This heath is on the borders of Wheelwright's pond in Lee, just below the outlet, or source of Oyster river. It is now owned by Mr. Cummings. It is commonly called "*the Hathe.*"

LANGLEY'S POINT. Mentioned March 8, 1770, when Benjamin Mathes and wife Ann conveyed to the "Hon. Jonathan Warner, Esq.," 50 acres of land in Durham, beginning at Oyster river, near the point called *Langley's Point,* thence running southerly on the east side of a highway between said land and the lands of Abraham Stevenson and others, leading from the river to the country road from Durham Falls to Bickford's Ferry or point; thence by said country way to said Mathes's land, formerly Caleb Wakeham's, and by this land to Oyster river to the head of the creek there, and down through the channel of said creek to the place where we began.

Langley's Point, otherwise called *Drew's point,* and sometimes *Warner's point,* was so named from James Langley, who was appointed deacon of the Oyster River church June 17, 1724. The Rev. Hugh Adams, in his parish records, May 12, 1728, speaks of "Deacon Langley and Mary his Godly wife." Mary was the daughter of Job Runnells or Reynolds of that part of Oyster River parish now the township of Lee. Drew's Point was acquired by James Langley Nov. 5, 1714, when Stephen Jenkins and wife Elizabeth conveyed to him "all the lands, tenements, and messuages," which said Jenkins bought of John Drew, and he of Richard Elliot, and was "the estate of William and Thomas Drew on the south side of Oyster river, and not elsewhere," reserving to said John Drew the whole length of his marsh two rods wide. James Langley petitioned July 25, 1715, for "a highway out to the country road that goeth from Willey's creek to Oyster river falls," as he was "penned up by Bartholomew Stevenson to eight foot or thereabout." This road was laid out two rods wide May 28, 1716, "beginning at Will Drew's old possession, joining to the *bond highway,*" and running W. S. W. and by W. to a little hill, leaving the *spring* seven rods on the N. W. side, and so to Willey's way. This "bond highway" is referred to Aug. 22, 1719, when Thomas Stevenson and wife Sarah, out of love and tender affection to his brother Joseph, quitclaimed to him the land whereon their father Bartholomew Stevenson did both live and die, except said Thomas' part of the marsh and flats. This land was on the westerly side of Oyster river, on the upper side of "*ye covenant highway* maintained between Thomas Drew and his successors."

The above mentioned spring is still to be seen, full to the brim, a few rods westerly of the road branching off the highway towards the residence of Mr. Nathaniel Stevens, the present owner of Langley's or Drew's Point and of part of the Stevenson land. This road extends to Oyster river, where the Durham packet to Portsmouth formerly stopped for passengers, announcing its arrival here by the blowing of a conch (shell).

LANGSTAFFE ROCKS. These rocks are in the Pascataqua river, off the Newington shore below Bloody Pt. They are hidden beneath the current, and are carefully avoided by boatmen, for more than one schooner has been driven thereon and wrecked.

The name is derived from Henry Langstaffe or Langstar, who acquired land on the neighboring shore as early as 1652.

LAOMI'S POND, otherwise LOMY'S. This is a little pond at the easterly side of the road from Fox Point to Portsmouth, on Mr. Charles Lamprey's land. Its name was derived from a woman named Laomi or Lomy (perhaps Salome), who, supposed to have strayed from the path in a cold, dark night, was drowned in this pond.

LASKEY'S BRIDGE. This bridge is mentioned in the Durham records March 21, 1798, as one of the bounds between Durham and Lee. It is across Oyster river, on the Mast road, near the old Laskey farm, now Mr. Charles W. Bartlett's. It is called "*Mast bridge*," in a deed of neighboring land from Moses Davis to David Kincaid Nov. 18, 1713. It was voted at the Durham town-meeting, March 27, 1786, "to build a causeway at the head of the town near the bridge by Mr. Wm. Laskey's."

LAYN'S MILL. See *Newtown Mill*.

LEATHERS CITY. This name is given to the once noted Leathers settlement in Barrington, above Bodge's pond. It is divided into Upper City and Lower City, which are not far apart. In this region are to be found *Hopping Pat's Lane*, so called from one of the most notorious of the Leathers tribe; *Pig Lane*, where the swine once had free range; and other places with equally significant names. Dr. Quint supposes this tribe to have sprung from the Leathers family of Durham. This is doubtful, however, though some members of that family may have drifted into the Barrington tribe.

LEDGE WHARF. This wharf is on the upper side of Oyster river, below the mouth of Beard's creek. Its name was derived from the "Cleft Ledge Granite Co.," that once owned a quarry in Durham, and shipped their blocks of granite from this wharf, to which led a wheel-path from the turnpike road. This path and wharf now belong to the heirs of the late John T. Emerson, to whom they were conveyed March 21, 1842, by Thomas A. Adams of Portsmouth, by virtue of an execution in his favor against said company in 1840.

LEE. The upper part of Durham was set off as a separate parish, with town privileges, under the name of Lee, by an act of the N. H. legislature, passed Jan. 10, 1766, and approved Jan. 15, following. (*N. H. Prov. Pap.*, 7 : 97.)

LEE GARRISONS. Only three garrisons are mentioned within the limits of the present town of Lee.

I. The DOE GARRISON, generally called the FOX or FRENCH GARRISON. This garrison stood in the southwestern part of Lee, "District No. 7." It was no doubt built by Joseph Doe, who, June 23, 1737, bought land here of John Bickford, which had been assigned the latter as his share of the common lands in Durham in 1734. After the death of Joseph Doe and his wife, this place fell to their daughter Elizabeth, wife of Elijah Fox, from whom the garrison became known as the *Fox garrison*. Ann, the granddaughter of Elijah and Elizabeth Fox, and wife of Daniel Cartland, inherited this dwelling-house, but after her death it was sold to Samuel French, from whom it was often called the *French garrison*. It was taken down a few years ago by Mr. Kenerson, the present owner of the Doe land.

II. A *Jones garrison* in Newtown is said to have stood on the land now owned by Mr. Nehemiah Snell. An old road from Madbury to Snell's mill, now disused, passed by this garrison.

RANDALL'S GARRISON. This garrison, taken down towards the middle of this century, stood between Durham and Lee Hill, on the south side of the Mast road, two or three rods east of Mr. A. D. Wiggin's house. It was built of logs, with loop-holes in the thick walls for the discharge of guns, and naturally became the centre of a neighborhood. It was erected by Capt. Nathaniel Randall, son of Richard Randall and of Elizabeth Tozer, his wife. Capt. Randall's grandfather Richard Tozer was, May 5, 1657, married to Judith Smith in Boston, by Gov. Richard Bellingham. He afterwards settled near Salmon Falls, on the Berwick side, where he was killed by the Indians, Oct. 16, 1675. Nathaniel Randall married Mary Hodgdon of Dover, and settled in Lee, where he had several grants of land, and acquired a large estate. He died March 9, 1748-9, in his 54th year. His grave may be seen in the Lee cemetery, near his lands, with that of " Mary, his consort," who died Jan. 3, 1775, in her 76th year. They were the maternal ancestors of the writer, through their daughter Elizabeth, who married Capt. Samuel Demerit of Durham.[1]

The Randall garrison was inherited by his son, Miles Randall, a man of energy and ability, who was made a county magistrate by the Exeter authorities in 1775. At the Revolution he obtained a large quantity of nitre beneath his garrison, which he sent to the Committee of Supplies for the manufacture of gunpowder.

LEE HILL. This elevation, or table-land, is in the central part of Lee, where five or six roads meet, coming from Durham, Epping, Newmarket, Nottingham, etc. Here is a hamlet, rather than a village, with a meeting-house, town-house, post-office, variety store, and a grave-yard. And in the days of stage-coaches there was a tavern. In the time of the Federalist and Republican parties this height was often called " *Federal hill*," from the number of Federalists in the vicinity. No name is given to this hill on the State map of 1803, but it is called " *Lee Hill* " on Chace's County map of 1856.

LEE HOOK. This is a remarkable bend or bow in Lamprey river, in the southern part of Lee, below Lee Hill. A saw-mill was built here at an early day. The inventory of Geo. Chesley's estate, of Durham, Aug. 27, 1724, mentions part of the mill " at y^e *hook of Lampreel river*." It is called " the *Hook mill* " in a deed of 1728. Ephraim Foulsham, Dec.

---

[1] Capt. Samuel Demerit was appointed quarter-master in Col. John Downing's regiment of troopers, by Gov. Benning Wentworth, Sept. 29, 1755, and was efficient in raising and equipping men for the Seven Years war, as shown by documents still extant. In view of his services, he received from Gov. Benning Wentworth Ap. 5, 1765, the commission of Captain in Col. Clement March's regiment of " Gentlemen Troopers." Both of the above commissions are in the writer's possession.

4, 1742, conveyed to his son John sixty acres of land in Durham, bought of Maj. Peter Gilman Dec. 8, 1739, lying next ye highway below y^e *Hook mill*, beginning 20 rods above ye second brook from ye house formerly Capt. John Gilman's, towards y^e *Hook mill*. Peter, John, Saml, and Nathl Gilman, May 2, 1749, conveyed to Joseph Smith 190 acres at a place commonly called *the Hook*, beginning by the side of Lampereel river, in the turn below the falls where the *Hook mill* stood.

John Thompson of Durham, "one of the proprietors of the *Hook land*, and ye proper owner of one whole share," conveyed this share, Aug. 30, 1748, to Abner Clough of Salisbury, Mass.

The Durham grants of land at the Hook conflicting with the Gilman claims, Samuel Smith and Capt. Jonathan Thompson were appointed agents of the land proprietors in Durham Nov. 28, 1748, to agree with Col. Peter Gilman and others about "the parcel of land in Durham, on the south side of Lampreel river, commonly called and known by the name of the *Hook land*." In a deed of Aug. 30, 1748, this district is called "*Durham Hook*," Lee being at that time a part of Durham. The Rev. John Adams of Durham records, June 10, 1750, the baptism of "Nicholas, son of Nat Frost, in *ye Hook*."

The "*Hook road* to Northwood" is mentioned on the State map of 1803. It runs from Newmarket through the Hook, and crosses Lamprey river at Hill's bridge, near the falls where now stands Dame's mill.

LIBBEY'S BRIDGE AND MILL. The bridge across Bellamy river, near Ex-Governor Sawyer's residence, is frequently called Libbey's bridge in the Dover and Madbury records. "The road from *Libbey's bridge* to Durham as far as Pinkham's hill" is mentioned in 1812. It afterwards acquired the name of *Dunn's bridge* from its proximity to Dunn's tavern— previously the Titcomb place, where Col. Benjamin Titcomb, a Revolutionary officer who was wounded in three different battles, ended his days. Sawyer's village and the château-like mansion, built by the late Jonathan Sawyer, stand on the Titcomb land. Libbey's bridge is now called *Sawyer's bridge*. The former name was derived from Benjamin Libbey and his son Enoch, who lived just below, on the Back river road, and successively owned the privilege at Sawyer's upper mill. (See *Bellamy Falls*.) Benjamin Libbey first acquired land here Sept. 26, 1752, when Timothy Gerrish conveyed to him three quarters of an acre of land in a triangular form, on the southerly side of Bellamin's Bank river, a little below ye bridge made over s^d river in ye Road y^t leads from Cochecho to Durham, beginning at a certain rock by s^d river four rods below to ye southerly side of s^d bridge, thence running southerly by the road 18 rods, leaving out ye spring and ye brook to ye river. This land was probably sold Libbey that he might operate the grist-mill here, which he afterwards acquired. "*Libbey's grist-mill*" is mentioned in 1820. The Dover *Sun* of 1824 gives notice of clothing business carried on "near the village of Dover, at the place formerly known as *Libbey's* mills," but then owned by the Great Falls Manufacturing Company.

LIMMY'S LEDGE. This is a rocky islet on the upper shore of Great Bay, at the south side of Adams Point, Durham. It is said to have derived its name from Lemuel Furber, who was left on this ledge and forced to swim ashore at the risk of his life. On Smith's map of Durham it is called *Nutter's Island*.

LINE HILL. This name is sometimes given to a hill on the line between Dover and Rochester, west of the river Cochecho. It is crossed by the highway from Tolend, below Blind Will's Neck.

LITTLE BAY. So called as early as Sept. 14, 1642. (See *Royall's Cove*.) It is the basin between Newington and the Durham Point district, into which the waters of the Great Bay pour, on their way to join the main body of the Pascataqua. At the upper extremity of Little Bay is the strait between Adams Point and Furber's Point, generally called the Narrows. At the lower end is the headland from the Newington shore, called Fox Point.

LITTLE FALLS. These falls are in the Salmon Falls river, and are sometimes called *Mast Point falls* from their vicinity to Mast Point. They are mentioned in the Dover records of 1753 (see *Mast Point*) and much earlier in the Kittery records. They probably acquired the name of Little falls because they are not far below the mouth of Little river on the Maine side, or in contradistinction from Great Falls in the Salmon Falls river below.

LITTLE JOHN'S CREEK. This is an inlet from Back river, on the eastern shore of Dover Neck, where Joseph Austin had the grant of a saw-mill privilege the 5th, 10 mo., 1652. In 1656 he had a grant of 30 acres of land, bounded southeasterly by this creek and *Little John's Marsh*, southwesterly by the river, and on the other sides by the common.

Richard York sold Joseph Austin, Aug. 7, 1661, 50 acres of land at *Little John's Creek* which he bought of Wm. Hilton. *Austin's Mill* stood near the mouth of this creek, and a road led thither from the main thoroughfare along Dover Neck. Thomas Austin conveyed to his son Nathaniel, Dec. 23, 1720, the land where said Nathaniel then lived, bounded northeasterly by the road y^t leads down to Dover Neck, northwesterly by *Little John's creek*, and southerly by Thomas Robert's land, with all the meadow on ye eastern side of said creek, from said road down to ye lower side of ye cove y^t is next s^d creek's mouth, except 1½ acre on the easterly side of the creek, adjoining the road. Thomas Austin conveyed to his son Joseph, Jan. 2, 1720–21, his home estate, together with y^e *mill creek*, mill, etc. The mouth of this creek has been greatly disfigured by the Portsmouth and Dover railway. It is entirely filled up with an embankment, leaving only a small archway for the current, that looks like the opening of a sewer. The old banks are still to be traced, however, showing the original width of this creek at the mouth. The main road to Dover Point crosses Little John's creek about two miles below Central Square in Dover city. The head of tide-water is still further above, where it is met by a fresh water brook, formed by the union of

Canney's and Varney's brooks. Little John's creek is called "*Varney's Creek*" on Whitehouse's map of Dover. (See *Varney's Creek*.)

"Little John" is supposed to have been an Indian, so named from the celebrated English outlaw of the greenwood, who was the boon companion of Robin Hood. And, as the father of Hope Hood, the ferocious Indian warrior, was named Robin Hood, it is not unreasonable to suppose there may have been another son of the forest named "Little John." The "Little John" of English lore was so-called by way of anti-climax, on account of his stalwart frame. He is said to have been seven feet tall, and according to an old ballad his original name of John Little was transposed by Robin Hood when received into his band.

"This infant was called John Little, quoth he,
Which name shall be changed anon;
The words we'll transpose, so wherever he goes,
His name shall be called *Little John*."

LITTLE JOHN'S FALLS. Mentioned July 3, 1717, when Jeremiah Tibbetts conveyed to Samuel Tibbetts, Jr., land on the Newichawannock river "at the mouth of the first cove above *Little John's falls*"—part of a hundred acre grant to Henry Tibbetts in 1656, bounded N. by Ralph Twombley's land, N. E. by John Dam's, S. W. by Joseph Austin's, and S. by said river. These falls are below the Samuel Hale place in Rollinsford. They begin in the Newichawannock above the mouth of the Great Works river,[1] and extend down an eighth of a mile or more to Madam's Cove.

LITTLE RIVER. This stream is frequently mentioned in the early records of Dover and Durham. It rises at Mendum's pond, in Barrington, and empties into Lamprey river, south of Lee Hill. Three score acres of land were granted to Jethro Furber, June 23, 1701, "adjacent to *Lampereal Little River*," laid out Feb. 2, 1726-7, "beginning on the northeast side of said *Little river* above the *old mast way*." (*Dover Records*.)

A highway was laid out July 31, 1755, beginning "at the northeast side of the *spruce hole* by the *mast rode*," extending to Jethro Furber's land, then "by his land to *Litel River*, then across *litel River* by Furber's land, then southerly to Lampreel river, and along this river as far as the bridge"—evidently the bridge at Wadleigh's falls. Communication was opened between this stream and the lowest falls in Oyster river at least 200 years ago, by means of the Mast road, which is mentioned in a grant to John Thompson, Sr., Ap. 2, 1694. This road comes to the upper side of Little river a short distance above Lee Hill, where a sawmill was erected at an early day. "Little river mill" is mentioned in the will of said John Thompson Ap. 12, 1733. And again Jan. 1, 1750, when John Follet conveyed to Samuel Demerit of Durham

---

[1] *Great Works river* rises in Bonny Bigg Pond, North Berwick, or among the ponds above, and empties into the Newichawannock below Salmon Falls, on the South Berwick side. It is mentioned Dec. 18, 1674, when Moses Spencer conveyed to Daniel Goodwin, Sr., a tract of land "on ye North side of *great work river* and is a little above the place called the *great Eddy*." The Great Eddy is mentioned Ap. 26, 1672, when 1,282 acres of land were laid out to Capt. Richard Waldron and others on the S. side of the Newichawannock, about a mile above the head line of Dover, "beginning at a certaine elbow of the said river knowne by the name of the *Great Eddy*, neare to a point of land called *Goljabs Neck*." (*N. H. Prov. Pap.* 1: 314–315.)

₁⁄₁₆ part of *Little River mill*, with all his rights in the falls, mill-pond, etc.

Jonathan Thompson of Durham, in his will of Sept. 10, 1756, gives his son Jonathan one half his right in *Little River sawmill* and the falls. And to his son Joseph his right in the *gristmill* and *fulling-mill* at *Little river*, with all his right to the falls where said mills stood. The two last mills were a short distance below the saw-mill, at *Thompson's falls*, afterwards called *Bartlett's falls*. (See *Mendum's Pond*.)

There is a Little river which rises in Acton, Me., and empties into the Salmon Falls river on the Berwick side, opposite Rochester.

LITTLE WATER BROOK. Mentioned the 30th, 6 mo., 1643, when Edward Starbuck had a grant of four score acres of upland "at Cutchechoe, next above the Lott of John Baker, at the *little water Brook*," forty of which were on one side of the fresh river (the Cochecho), and forty on the other. The name has not been perpetuated.

LITTLEWORTH. This is a district in Dover, between the Cochecho river and Barbadoes Pond. It is so called Aug. 15, 1721, in a deed from John to Ichabod Haise. (See *Broad Turn*.) "Yᵉ mast path yᵗ goes to a place called by yᵉ name of *Littleworth*" is mentioned Dec. 9, 1722. "The road from *Littleworth* to the Saplings" is mentioned Sept. 20, 1734. (See the *Saplings*.) It is miscalled *Trueworth* on Whitehouse's map of 1834. Littleworth is the name of one of the present school-districts in Dover.

LOG HILL. This name was commonly given in former times to a hill in the vicinity of a saw-mill, from which logs could be rolled down to the waterside. One is mentioned Dec. 25, 1695, when Peter Coffin of Exeter conveyed to his grandson Tristram Coffin all his lands " at *logg hill* " at Cochecho. The log hill above the Cochecho first falls is said to have been the high bank where the Portsmouth and Dover R. R. crosses the old bed of the Cochecho river. From it led the *Great Mast path*, southward, in the line of Lexington St., into the "logg swamp."

"A conueniant *Logg hill* accommodable to the mill " at the second falls on the Cochecho, was laid out March 4, 1703–4, " beginning att the Taill of sᵈ mill " and extending five rods by the river side. On the same day were renewed " the bounds of the ancient cartway leading from the falls into the swamp " till it met the other way leading from the *broad turn*.

Sandy Log Hill, in the upper part of Dover, on the west side of the Eel-Weir falls, is mentioned Nov. 5, 1741. (See *Sandy Log Hill*.)

A *log hill* at Quamphegan falls is mentioned Dec. 7, 1732, when Thomas Tebbets conveyed to Nathan Lord one third part of the saw-mill at Quamphegan, on the west side of the river, called " yᵉ shere mill " (share mill), with one third of " the privilege of the land called yᵉ *logg hill*." (See *Quamphegan*.)

A *logg hill*, adjacent to Gerrish's mill in Madbury, is mentioned Jan. 7, 1758. (See *Gerrish's Mill*.)

The *log hill* at Durham falls is still in use.

There is also a *log hill* at Wadleigh's falls in Lee.

LOG SWAMP. See *Cochecho Log Swamp* and *Waldron's Log Swamp.*

LONG CREEK and LONG CREEK BROOK. Long creek is mentioned the 10th, 8 mo., 1653, when John Hill had a grant of land on the northwest side of the Great Bay, between Thomas Footman's and the *long creek.* Thomas Wille, the 10th, 2 mo, 1654, had a grant on the N. W. side of Little Bay, beginning " at the mouth of the *Long creek*, and so upwards into the woods." It is again mentioned Oct. 26, 1658, when a grove of pines, reserved by the town, was laid out on the N. W. side of Little Bay, about half a mile from a creek " commonly called the *long creek,"* bounded on the south by Thomas Wille's grant. Wm. Perkins and wife Elizabeth conveyed to Thomas Edgerly, Jan. 28, 1669, twenty acres previously a part of Thomas Wille's 60 acres on the S. W. side of the *Long creek.* " John Alt's *Long Creek* near *ye mill"* is mentioned in 1678. Thomas Edgerly, Sr., and wife " Rebeckah " (daughter of John Alt,) conveyed to their son Samuel, May 1, 1700, fifteen acres of land " beginning at the head of *ye old dam* seated between the *long Crike brook* and the highway that goeth into y⁶ commons, lying to the west of the little Bay in Oyster River."

Long creek, properly speaking, was the inlet from Great Bay now called Crummit's creek, in Durham, but the name appears from the above grants and conveyances to have been also given to a branch of it that crosses Long marsh.

Another *Long Creek* is on the eastern side of Dover Neck, just below the mouth of the Cochecho river. It is mentioned the 6th, 10 mo., 1656, when Thomas Canney's grant of 16 acres of upland to join his land *at Tomson's poynt* was laid out from the outmost point turning up to Cochecho, 50 rods to the *long creek* westward below *Tomson's poynt* butting on Fore river, thence running three score and ten rods up the *long creek* side, reserving a cartway from the woods to the water side, at the head of the creek, and up Cochecho river three score and ten rods, and from the end of that three score and ten rods upon a straight line over to the bound at the head of the *long creek.*

Love and Mary Canney, Feb. 12, 1742, confirmed to John Gage all right to 70 acres in Dover, bounded southerly on Gage's land to the mouth of the Cochecho river, and westerly on said river to *Thompson's Point*, extending downward to a place commonly called *Long Creek*, and running up said creek to Benjⁿ Roberts, Jr., his land, which he bought of Randall.

LONG FALLS. These falls in Lamprey river are mentioned Jan. 29, 1718, when Geo. Jeffrey and Henry Dyer conveyed to Andrew Glidden and others all right and title to " certain falls between Wadleigh's falls and Packer's falls, called the *long falls,"* with the use and improvement of the water privilege " where the present saw-mill standeth, on yᵉ south side of Lamperill river, and no other part thereof, all the rest being reserved, being part of the grant to Mr. Valentine Hill in 1652 of 100 acres of land adjoining each mill that should by him be erected on the falls in said river."

Forty acres, granted to Francis

Pitman in 1702, were laid out to Joseph Jenkins Oct. 9, 1726, on the north side of Lampreall river, on the west side of a lot laid out to Samuel Smith adjoining to the *long falls*. (See *Lamprey River Falls.*)

The name of "*Long Falls*" is also given on the State map of Lee, in 1803, to the falls in North river in the southwestern part of Lee, formerly called "*Great Falls.*"

LONG GUT. A name formerly given to the run at the lower end of the Canney portion of the Calves' Pasture on Dover Neck, a short distance below the run from Pinkham's spring.

LONG HILL. This hill is mentioned July 31, 1721, when 60 acres of land, granted to Zachariah Field in 1694, were laid out to his son Stephen on ye northwest side of y^e *Long Hill*. The "*mast way to Long Hill*" is mentioned June 24, 1738. "*Long-hill road*" is mentioned in the surveyor's warrant of 1810, as "crossing Reyner's brook at the bridge." *Long Hill school-district* is mentioned as early as 1790. This hill is in the upper part of Dover, on the east side of the river Cochecho.

There is another *Long hill*, which deserves its name, in the upper part of Madbury near Mr. Reuben Hayes's.

LONG MARSH. This marsh is chiefly in the Durham Point district. It is mentioned the 10th, 7 mo., 1663, when "all the *longe marsh* wich layes joining too *Antoney nutters marsh*, and soe towards Oyster River falls," was laid out "for the ministrie" at Oyster River. Twenty acres of land were granted to Ezekiel Pitman, Ap. 2, 1694, at the lower end of the *long marsh* above the head of John Davis's land. And Feb. 22, 1720–21, a road was laid out across the *long marsh*, beginning at Team Hill, and extending to "the King's thoroughfare road to Lamprey river." The name of Long marsh is still perpetuated; and the old road, mentioned above, is still known as the "*Long Marsh road.*"

A *Long marsh* on the Greenland shore of Great Bay is mentioned Ap. 9, 1729. (See *Wigwam Point.*)

LONG MARSH BROOK. This brook rises in the Long marsh, Durham, and empties into Crummit's creek. In a deed from Joseph Smith to John Sambon, June 13, 1743, this name is also given to *Denbow's brook*, which rises in the Long marsh, and after uniting with a brook from the Moat, empties into Oyster river mill-pond. (See *Horsehide Brook.*)

LONG POINT. This point is on the Newington shore of Great Bay, at the lower side of Laighton's Cove. It is mentioned July 17, 1645, when "Darby ffield of Oyster River, planter," sold John Bickford (also of Oyster River) "seven or eight acres of marsh at *Long Poynt* in the great bay, together with one poynt of land thereunto adjoining."

By virtue of an order of the general court "that *400 acres of upland* should be given to the inhabitants of Dover who had marsh in the Great Bay, Elder Nutter, Wm. Storey, Henry Lancaster, and Wm. Furber, appointed to lay out and bound unto the particular inhabitants their division of upland to their marsh, laid out the 27th, 11 mo., 1656, thirty acres of upland to John Bickford, Senior, joining to his marsh upon the northeast end over the neck from water to water, joining to Tho. Layton's upland within twoel (12) poll or thereabouts." (*Dover Records.*)

The order of the General Court, above mentioned, refers to a grant to the town of Dover of all the marsh from Hogstye Cove round about the bay up to Cotterill's Delight, with *400 acres of upland* adjoining (*N. H. Prov. Pap.*, 1 : 222.) The fact that the Bickford land at Long Point, as well as the Laighton land adjoining, was a part of these 400 acres, proves conclusively that the ancient Hogsty cove was not the present Laighton's cove, as many writers have supposed, but must have been below Long Point; that is, farther down the shore of the Great Bay. Anthony Nutter bought of Wm. Pomfrett of Dover, the 20th, 6 mo., 1651, a marsh on the N. E. side of Great Bay, at the *great cove* there, above *long point*. This was at the head of Herod's cove, now Laighton's. Thirty acres of upland (part of the 400 acre grant to Dover) were laid out to Elder Nutter, the 10th, 10 mo., 1656, adjoining his marsh : 22 acres of it on the easterly side of John Dam's upland, and four acres at the head of the creek that runneth through Elder Nutter's marsh, and four acres adjoining Thomas Layton's upland on the S. W. side of the creek. As this grant was part of the 400 acres, it was, of course, above Hogsty cove.

Wm. Furber, Sr., " of Dover, in Piscataqua River, in consideration of ye natural love and tender affection to his dutiful and well-beloved son Jethro," conveyed to him, Feb. 14, " in ye year of o^r Lord God, according to ye computation of ye church of England, 1677," a neck of land, containing 100 acres or thereabouts, within ye mouth of ye Great Bay, in ye township of Dover, commonly called and known by the name of *Long Point*, bounded on ye N. W. by the land of Wm. Furber, Jr.; on ye S. W. by John Bickford's, on ye S. E. by the land of Thomas Layton, late of Dover, deceased, and on ye N. E. by Anthony Nutter's land.

As this land was between the Ferry Farm and the Bickford land, it is evident that the name of Long Point, like that of Durham Point, Welch cove, etc., was given, not merely to the point itself, but to the neighboring district.

Anna Walker, relict of Samuel Walker of Newington, May 22, 1731, conveyed to her well beloved brother Lemuel Bickford, shipwright, all right to a tract of land in Newington " at a place called or known by ye name of *Long Point*, and is part of ye farm my honour^d father Mr. John Bickford, late of Newington, dyed possess^d of, and is yet in ye possession of my hon^{ed} mother Mrs. Susan Bickford." Joseph Bickford of the city of Bristol, mariner, gave a power of attorney, dated at London, Ap. 12, 1740, to his brother Eliakim Bickford, mariner, to receive from his brother Lemuel Bickford of Newington, shipwright, all money and rents due from one ninth part of the land in Newington, adjoining Great Bay at *Long Point*, and all other lands that belonged to his father John Bickford, deceased.

Lemuel Bickford of Newington, shipwright, and wife Temperance, for 1250 pounds, new tenor, conveyed to Thomas Pickering, gentleman,

May 2, 1751, 100 acres of upland, marsh, and thatch-beds, with buildings thereon, bounded northerly by the land of Jethro Bickford and Richard Dam, east by Thomas Layton and said Dam, and on all other sides by the Great Bay, being all the tract on which the said Lemuel then lived, except one acre of salt marsh and flats belonging to Jethro Bickford. Thomas Pickering, in his will of Ap. 4, 1782, gives his son Nicholas the farm whereon the said Nicholas then lived—the same which said Thomas bought of Lemuel Bickford.

Nicholas Pickering, in his will of Nov. 21, 1807, gives his grandson Nicholas Woodman (son of his daughter Betsey, who married a Woodman) "all the farm whereon I now live." It was from this Nicholas Woodman that Long Point acquired the name of *Woodman's Point*, by which it is sometimes called. Richard Dame calls it *Long Point* on his map of Newington. Properly speaking, Long Point is the whole neck of land on the north side of Laighton's cove, between that cove and Great Bay. At the upper side is a small bluff, called *High Point*, which is surrounded by marshes and becomes an island at high tide. Both points are now owned by the heirs of Mr. James Alfred Pickering.

A pine grove covers the ridge as you go to the end of Long Point, and beyond are oaks, and tall tapering cedars of funereal aspect, that skirt the point itself, which terminates in a broad slaty ledge, from which there is a fine view up and down the Great Bay. Off the point is *Nanncy's island*, green with low shrubs, and all along the shore the wild convolvulus blooms profusely in every direction, lighting up this romantic, but somewhat desolate point.

There is a *Long Point* on the Lubberland shore of Great Bay, at the lower side of Broad Cove. (See *Jewell's Point*.)

LONG REACH. This name is given to that portion of the Pascataqua river between Dover Point and the narrows below Boiling Rock. It is so called on Holland's map of 1784, and is in common use among the river boatmen to this day. The name was also given in early times to the adjacent shores. James Rawlins, in 1662, mortgaged 100 acres of land "lying in y^e *Long* Reach, back from Canney's cove upward." Pike's Journal of Aug. 24, 1694, says "8 persons were killed and captivated at *Long Reach*: 5 at Downing's and 3 at Toby's."[1] This was in Kittery, which then extended up the river as far as the Berwick townships. Richard Cutts, in his will of May 10, 1675, gives his daughter Bridget his land "in the *long reach*," next Capt. Pendleton's, "thirty three pole broad front on the river, and so back the whole depth." This was in Portsmouth.

That part of the Long Reach in the vicinity of the Pulpit is often called the *Pulpit Reach*, which is, of course, below the bounds of ancient Dover. Theodore Atkinson, administrator of the estate of Dr. Robert Pike of Portsmouth, conveyed to Christopher Rymes, mariner, a parcel of land said Pike bought of Samuel Cutt, deceased, June 30, 1720, fronting on

---

[1] James Tobey's land "near *ffrankes fort*" is mentioned Jan. 13, 1695-6; Joshua Downing of Kittery is mentioned in 1717.

the Pascataqua "at a place commonly called by y⁶ name of y⁶ *Pulpit Reach*, 60 poles on the river, and carrying the same breadth back into the woods 266 rods, being y⁶ farm commonly called Cutt's farm, and the westerly half of 200 acres granted by Portsmouth to John and Richard Cutt." (For the *Pulpit*, see *Pascataqua River*.)

LONG TURN. Mentioned Ap. 19, 1725, when John Pitman (and Elisabeth) conveyed to Benedictus Torr 20 acres of land granted to his father Joseph Pitman on the north side of Mahorimet's hill, but afterwards removed to the *long turn* on the westerly side of y⁶ mast way yᵗ leads up to y⁶ Hook timber at or near y⁶ place in y⁶ way commonly called y⁶ *long* or *broad turn*, beginning at a red oak by y⁶ above said way. Benedictus Torr and Leah conveyed this land to Benjⁿ and Ralph Hall Nov. 29, 1726. Ralph Hall conveyed to Benjⁿ Hall, Nov. 21, 1749, all right and title to 13¾ acres in that part of Dover called *Madbury*, on the westerly side of the *mast way* that leads along by said Benjamin's dwelling-house, part of a grant to 'Joseph Pitman, and purchased by said Ralph and Benjⁿ, as tenants in common, of Benedictus Tarr of Dover, deceased. Benjⁿ and Frances Hall of the parish of Madbury conveyed to Joseph Masarve, Sept. 6, 1756, half of the homestead where they then dwelt (17 acres), reserving one square rod where their children lay buried, beginning at the N. E. corner of the lot which Wm. Hill purchased of Ralph Hall.[1]

The names of *Broad Turn*, *Great Turn*, and *Long Turn* are supposed by some to apply, not to the highways, but to the long bend in the Bellamy river, in its course through Madbury. (See *Great Turn*.)

LUBBERLAND. This name was given to the upper shore of Great Bay as early as 1669. (See *Cleft Cove*.) It then formed part of the Oyster River precinct, but the greater part of it now belongs to Newmarket. It is frequently mentioned in the public records of the last two hundred years. A right was reserved for two highways "from *Lubberland* to Oyster River" when John Alt's grant of 80 acres on Great Bay was laid out Dec. 9, 1679. "The path to *Lubberland*" is mentioned in a deed from John York to John Pinder, May 16, 1681. The Rev. John Pike records the death of "Roger Rose of *Lubber-Land*" Aug. 6, 1705. The Rev. John Buss, in his "humble petition" of May 26, 1716, speaks of his thirty-acre grant between the minister's lot and "*Lubber Land*." Twenty acres were laid out to him July 25, 1716, "on the west side of the path or high way going to *Lobber Land*." The Rev. Hugh Adams in 1717 calls it "*Lover Land*," for which there appears no precedent. Since his day, however, this form of the name is occasionally found, sometimes absurdly varied to *Loving-land*. In a few instances *Lobberland* and *Louberland* are mentioned. But the prevailing form from the beginning is *Lubberland*.

Lubberland brook is mentioned

---

[1] Ralph Hall and Elisabeth, conveyed to Wm. Hill, June 13, 1744, eight acres of land, part of his right from the town of Dover, beginning at a rock at a place called *freetown* in Dover, on the north side of a road that runs from James Huckins' to Joseph Daniels', Jr.

June 23, 1701, when John Daniel's grant was laid out between Thomas Morris's land and John Bickford's, on the north side of *Lubberland brook*—apparently the brook that empties into Crummit's creek.

Lubberland creek, for Goddard's, is mentioned March 10, 1740–41.[1] (See *Goddard's Creek.*) *Lubberland marshes* are mentioned June 15, 1734. (See *Birch Point.*)

Lubberland school-district is mentioned in the Durham records of 1784.

The name of Lubberland was perhaps given by the sailors or fishermen of early times, by way of deriding the peaceful farmers along the Great Bay.[2]

"A cup of welcome to thee out of *Lobby-Land*," cries Lord Saville to Chiffinch in Scott's *Peveril of the Peak*. "Why, thou hast been so long in the country that thou hast got a bumpkinly clod-compelling sort of look thyself."

It has been kindly suggested to the writer by the author of "*New Castle, Historic and Picturesque*," that the name of Lubberland may have been derived from some old tale of English folk-lore, brought over by our early settlers, and he refers to the use of the name in Ben Jonson's "Bartholomew Fair" by John Littlewit: "Good mother, how shall we find a pig if we do not look about for 't: will it run off o' the spit into our mouths, think you, as in *Lubberland*, and cry, wee, wee!"

This Lubberland of Jonson's may be the "*Lob's pound*" of pixy-land, mentioned by Massinger and the author of "Hudibras," or the "pond-fold" of Phooka or Pouka, the Irish Puck. Pixy-land is Puck's land, and Puck himself, in the "Midsummer-Night's Dream," is addressed as "Thou *lob* of spirits!" Grimm tells us of a German sprite, whom he calls "*Good Lubber.*" *Lob's pound* seems to be a place or condition into which one is led by a kind of elfish enchantment or *diablerie*, worthy of the "*Lubber-fiend*" of Milton's "L'Allegro."

But, Pixy-land or not, the drive along the shore of Lubberland from Newmarket to Jewell's Point, when the waters of the Great Bay are at high tide, and the sun is turning to the west in a cloudless sky, is one of constant delight.

LOW STREET. This name was given in early times to a road in the lower part of Dover Neck, nearly parallel with High street, between that street and Back river. It is mentioned Ap. 5, 1701, when Sylvanus Nock (and Eliza) conveyed to Wm. Harford his dwelling on Dover Neck, with seven acres of land, bounded E. by *high street*, W. by *low street*, N. by a lane separating it from John Pinkham's land, and S. by Philip Cromwell's land. John

---

[1] There is a *Lubber's Creek* at New Castle, so called in an advertisement of Nov. 15, 1800.

[2] *Land-louper* and *louper-lan*, Scotch words from which Louberlan or Lubberland may have been derived, has a more invidious signification, as is evident from the application of the name of "landlouper" to Capt. Waverley by the Laird of Balmawhapple, and to the German adventurer Dousterswivel by Mr. Jonathan Oldbuck. The Zetlanders also called the pirate Cleveland a "landlouper," though for many years he had been a cruiser in the Spanish main. And Scott, too, makes King James I use the word "dyke-louper" in reference to the escapades of the Duke of Buckingham. A *louper* is evidently a person given to overleaping the proper bounds of moral restraint.

Pinkham conveyed to his son Amos, June 19, 1715, his dwelling-house and four acres of land on Dover Neck, bounded E. by *high street*, W. by *low street*, and S. by a lane between this lane and Wm. Harford's. Amos Pinkham and Elizabeth conveyed this house and land to Otis Pinkham Aug. 8, 1720.

The *first Meeting-House* on Dover Neck was on Low Street. Richard Yorke's lot was on the south side of Nutter's lane, and measured 28 rods on Low Street. Next below him was John Dam's lot, 14 rods on Low St. Next came the lot on which stood the meeting-house and Mr. Maud's parsonage, which was 28 rods on Low St., and 20 rods on a cross lane.

MADAM'S COVE. This cove is at the foot of Little John's falls, on the Rollinsford shore of the Newichawannock. So called, it is said, from Madam Wallingford, probably the third wife of Col. Thomas Wallingford, who outlived her husband nearly forty years. Her daughter Olive married John Cushing of S. Berwick, from whom the name of *Cushing's hill*, below the S. Hale place in Rollinsford, is said to have been derived.

MADBURY. This name was given to a part of Dover as early as March 19, 1693–4, when 40 acres of land were granted to Francis Pitman, "on the N. W. side of Logg hill, on the N. E. side of the path going to *Madberry*, where he had all Reddy begun to improve." And that same day, 30 acres were laid out to Stephen Willey "on ye north side of ye mast path which comes from *Madberry*." (*Dover Records*.)

According to the late John Elwyn of Portsmouth,[1] the name of Madbury was derived from Modbury, in Devonshire, Eng., the seat for centuries of the Champernowne family, to which belonged Capt. Francis Champernowne of the Dover Combination of 1640. He acquired a large tract of land on the eastern side of Great Bay, part of which fell within the limits of Ancient Dover. (See *Greenland*.) He married the widow of Robert Cutt, brother of President John Cutt, and was one of the most influential men in the Province. He was a member of the provincial Council in 1686, about which time Madbury received its name. Capt. Champernowne was of royal descent, and a nephew, by marriage, of Sir Ferdinando Gorges. His great-grandfather, Sir Arthur Champernowne of Modbury, took part in the battle of Bosworth Field, and was vice-admiral in the English navy.[2]

---

[1] John Elwyn, who was thoroughly versed in everything relating to the early history of the Pascataqua region, was the grandson of Gov. Langdon, and a descendant of Ambrose Gibbons the early pioneer, who died at Oyster River, July 11, 1656.

[2] Sir Arthur Champernowne acquired the barony of Dartington two miles above Totness, Devon, whence came some of the early settlers along the Pascataqua, such as the Coffins of Dover and the Shapleighs of Kittery. The name of *Dartington* was given, June 14, 1638, to a neck of land, containing 500 acres, east of the mouth of the Pascataqua river, and extending northeasterly to Braveboat Harbor, granted by Sir Ferdinando Gorges to Arthur Champernowne, father of Capt. Francis. This was in Kittery, and included the island afterwards called Champernowne's Island, where Capt. Francis Champernowne now lies buried. *Kittery* is another Devonshire name, probably given by Capt. Champernowne in memory of *Kittery Court*, on the River Dart, near Dartmouth, Eng. And there is a bend of the river at Kittery Court that still bears the name of *Kittery Point*. Not far from Modbury is Portledge, where, as Kingsley says in *Westward Ho!* "The Coffins had lived ever since Noah's flood, if indeed they had not returned merely thither after that temporary displacement." Peter Coffin of Dover was born in Devonshire in 1630.

At Modbury was born Katherine Champernowne (great aunt of Capt. Francis Champernowne), who, by different marriages, was the mother of Sir Humphrey Gilbert and Sir Walter Raleigh.

The Champernowne house at Modbury, where the royalists had entrenched themselves under Sir Edmund Fortescue, was taken and devastated by the Parliamentary troops in 1642.

Modbury is midway between Dartmouth and Plymouth. Some ruins are still left of the ancient manor-house, where, according to the expression of an old chronicler, "the clarious family of Champernon" once lived in dignity and splendor. But alas, as John Elwyn laments,

"No crusader's war-horse, plumed and steeled,
Paws the grass now at Modbury's blazoned door."

It is to be deplored that this historic name should have been corrupted to Madbury by our early settlers. The original name should be restored. Modbury is more agreeable to the ear, and its association with the Champernownes would give it a significance not to be regarded without pride.

Madbury was made a separate parish, with town privileges, May 31, 1755, and a township May 26, 1768. There is no village in Madbury.

MADBURY GARRISONS. These garrisons all appear to have been of the eighteenth century, or at least erected after 1694.

I. *Clark's Garrison.* This garrison stood on Clark's plains, near the borders of Dover and Madbury, where Mr. Biederman's house now is. It was built by Abraham Clark, who owned land in this vicinity, March 19, 1693-4, when Richard Pinkham had a grant of 30 acres "between Drie pines and Abraham Clark's." It was taken down about the year 1836.

II. DANIEL'S GARRISON stood near the present residence of Mr. Charles W. Hayes. (See *David's Lane.*)

III. DEMERIT'S GARRISON. This garrison was built by Eli Demerit, Jr., about 1720. It stood where is now the house of Mr. Alfred Demeritt, his direct descendant, and was taken down in the spring of 1836.

IV. GERRISH'S GARRISON stood on the first hill west of Gerrish's mill, near the present dwelling-house of Mr. B. F. Hayes. It was probably built by Capt. Paul Gerrish, who erected the first mill at the neighboring fall in the Bellamy. It must not be confounded with the old Gerrish garrison built the previous century by Capt. John Gerrish, probably near his mill at the lowest falls on the same river.

V. MESERVE'S GARRISON. Traces of this garrison are still to be seen on Harvey's hill, that formed part of the old Meserve lands. The land of Daniel Misharvey, Jr., (Meservey or Meserve), at a place called Freetown, is mentioned Dec. 19, 1746, in a conveyance to Eli Demerit. There was another Meserve garrison in the Back River district, Dover.

VI. TASKER'S GARRISON. This garrison was at the foot of Moharimet's hill, now Hicks's hill, on the south side, where now stands the house belonging to the heirs of the late E. E. Demeritt. The land here originally belonged to Charles Adams of Oyster River, who had a grant of

100 acres, laid out Nov. 1, 1672, at the foot of "Maharmett's hill," half of which he conveyed, March 11, 1693-4, to his daughter Mary, wife of Wm. Tasker. The Taskers were living here when their house was attacked by the Indians not long after, but they succeeded in making their escape to Woodman's garrison. As their house was then in a defence-less condition, the garrison was no doubt erected subsequently. It was taken down about 1820, soon after it was acquired by Eben[r] T. Demeritt.

VII. *Twombley's Garrison.* This garrison stood a few rods above the present residence of Judge Young. It was no doubt built by Wm. Twombley, who acquired land near the Saplings before April, 1734. It was taken down in the spring of 1842 by Mr. Nathaniel Twombley, and some of its timbers were used in framing the barn now owned by Judge Frost at the corner of Locust and Nelson streets, Dover.

MADBURY MEETING-HOUSE. This meeting-house is often mentioned in the records of last century. It stood near the present brick school-house, a short distance south of Hicks's hill. John Tasker and "Judah" his wife, Sept. 23, 1735, conveyed one acre of land to the inhabitants of the western side of Dover township for a meeting-house, "beginning at y[e] turn of y[e] way that leads from Madberry road to beach hill;" acknowledged Sept. 6, 1759. The "meeting-house now at Madbury, standing almost home to Durham line," is mentioned in a petition of May 8, 1744. (*N. H. Prov. Pap.*, 9 : 176-177.)

A plan of this large old-fashioned meeting-house, with its interior gallery around three sides, is to be found in the Madbury records. It was taken down within the writer's recollection.

MAINE. The territory comprised in Ancient Dover formed part of the *Province of Maine*, as granted by the Council for New England to Sir Ferdinando Gorges and Capt. John Mason, jointly, Aug. 10, 1622. This grant comprised all the land along the sea-coast between the Kennebec and Merrimac rivers, with all the islands within five leagues, and extended 60 miles inland—which territory, says the patent, is "to be called the *Province of Maine.*"

But no part of New Hampshire was included in the Province of Maine, as granted Sir Ferdinando Gorges in the charter of Charles I, Ap. 3, 1639. It began "at the entrance of Piscataqua Harbour," and extended up the river into the Newichannock, to the head thereof, till 120 miles were accomplished; and from the mouth of Piscataqua Harbour north-eastward along the sea-coast to Sagadahoc, thence up stream, through the "Kynybequy" river[1] to the head thereof to the distance of 120 miles, thence across to the head of the Newichawannock line; together with the north half of the Isles of Shoals, and all the islands within five leagues of the coast, etc. (See Baxter's *Sir Ferdinando Gorges*, 2 : 124-5.)

The Indian name of this district was *Mawooshen* or *Maroshen*, which, according to Purchas's *Pilgrimes*,

---

[1] The Kennebec river was called in early times the Quinnebequi, from the Indian words *quinne,* " long," and *bequi,* " still water," referring to its long stretches of still water.

lay between 43 and 45 degrees, 40 leagues in breadth and 50 in length, containing nine rivers, among which was the Sagadahoc (Kennebec), which had six islands and two branches. The Portsmouth Oracle of May 18, 1799, publishes a proposed Bill to the Massachusetts legislature of that year that all the portion of the Mass. commonwealth, called by the aborigines *Maroshen,* but " now commonly called the District of Maine, lying between the state of New Hampshire and the province of New Brunswick," should be made a separate state under the name of the *State of Maroshen.*

MALLEGO. This name has been given for nearly two hundred years to the north easterly branch of the Bellamy river[1], which rises at Cate's pond in Barrington, and empties into the Bellamy at the Hook. The extensive forests in this region led to the opening of a mast road hither at an early day. " *Mallego way* " is mentioned in the Dover records, Feb. 16, 1710–11. And " *the Mast road to Mallego* " is mentioned in 1717. Mallego brook or river is repeatedly spoken of in the depositions concerning Demerit's dam at the Hook in 1719, (*Granite Monthly,* Dec., 1881.) *Mallego woods* are referred to Jan. 12, 1742, when Ichabod Canney conveyed to Robert Hanson 35¾ acres in *Mallego woods,* " at a place called y[e] Saplings," on the southerly side of the road from Littleworth to Barrington, beginning at an asp tree at the S. E. corner of ten acres laid out to the Quakers. Ichabod Cate of Barrington conveyed to David Waldron, Ap. 19, 1810, land in Barrington, in the *Two-mile Streak,* so called, beginning at land owned by Isaac Waldron at the east side of a river that runs through said land, called *Malago river* or *Huckins brook,* and running E. by said Waldron's land 7 rods, then turning and running up by said river, carrying the same breadth of 7 rods till it comes to a place called *Cate's dam,* 20 rods more or less, then turning and running across said river till it comes to the *province road,* so called, then down by said road to Isaac Waldron's land, then by said land across said river to the first bound.

The *Mallego bridge* in Barrington is on the old stage road from Dover, which crosses this river not long after it issues from Cate's pond.

The name of Mallego, like that of Barbadoes, was no doubt given by the early lumber-men engaged in supplying the foreign market with lumber. Lt. Gov. Partridge, among others, certainly furnished timber for the Mediterranean coast at the end of the xvii century. (*N. H. Prov. Pap.,* 2 : 247.) Our intercourse with Spain at an early day is evident from the accounts of Capt. John Smith and Sir Ferdinando Gorges (the latter in his *Narration*) of a merchant named Hunt who treacherously seized 20 of our Indians in 1614 and carried them to Spain, where he sold a part as slaves, and the rest were taken from him by the friars to be brought up in the Christian faith. An interesting account of one of them, named Tasquantum, who made his escape from Malaga and returned

---

[1] Stephen Newt's map of Madbury in 1805 erroneously gives the name of " Bellamy river " to the Mallego branch.

to this country, is given in Baxter's *Sir F. Gorges*, 1 : 103–106.

The name of Mallego is akin to *Malagoe*, one of the isles of Shoals, which is otherwise written " *Mallago* " in a letter from Capt. Willey to the Mass. government, March 11, 1691-2. (Jenness' *Isles of Shoals*, p. 201.) Cargoes of fish, and also clapboards, pipe-staves, etc., that must have come from the main land, were sent from the Shoals in the middle of the xvii century to the Mediterranean; and wines and other foreign products were brought back. (*Ibid, p.* 91.) The name of Malaga island may therefore have been given by merchants in traffic with the Spanish city of that name. Nor is it so inappropriate as might at first seem, if the name is derived, as some say, from the word *Melach* which signifies *salt fish*—the great staple at the Shoals.

The island of Malaga was bought in 1647 by Henry Sherburne, son-in-law of Ambrose Gibbons, the early pioneer on the Newichawannock, who had grants of mill privileges and forest lands in ancient Dover, and died at Oyster River July 11, 1656.

MAPLE BROOK. This brook rises in Barrington, and empties into Oyster river not far from Wheelwright's pond. It is often mentioned in the Durham records of last century; as Aug. 10, 1745, when a road was laid out " from a peaked rock by Thomas Willey's new house where he now dwelleth," past James Bunker's, etc., to *Maple brook*, so-called. And Nov. 18, 1758, a road was laid out from the north-east corner bound of Nottingham, running along the Barrington line, etc., to *Maple brook*, so-called. (See *Caldwell's Brook.*)

MARSH BROOK ROAD. This road is mentioned in the Dover records of 1819, as extending to the Madbury line. It is apparently the way leading from the Littleworth road to the head of Barbadoes pond, where it crosses a brook running through the marsh into the pond. The bridge across this brook is on the bounds of Dover and Madbury.

MARTIN'S BROOK. Mentioned Ap. 1, 1721, when Samuel King of the parish of Greenland, and wife Elizabeth, conveyed to Capt. Joshua Weeks a tract of 40 rods on the west side of *Martin's brook*, in a convenient place to set a mill near the mouth of said brook, where Capt. Weeks might choose, with his privilege of land on the east side of the brook, adjacent to Robert Davis's land, and all the land the dam of said mill might cause to overflow. Eight acres adjoining this land were conveyed to Joshua Weeks by Samuel King, June 5, 1724, bounded North by the Great Bay, and South by *Martin's brook*. John Dockum, Jr., conveyed to Capt. Joshua Weeks, Ap. 6, 1726, 13 acres on the south side of *Martin's brook*, adjacent to the lands of Tucker Cate and John Vrin, where the road leads to the Great Bay.

George Keniston conveyed to said Weeks, July 25, 1727, one acre, beginning at *Martin's brook* on the west side, and running down to the Great Bay. Martin's brook is just above the Bay-side railway station. It flows through the old King land, now owned by Messrs. G. and J. P. Weeks, and empties into the Great Bay near Mr. J. H. Brackett's house.

MARTIN'S LANE. So named from John Martin, whose house and lane (at Lubberland) are mentioned as early as the 28th, 2 mo., 1664, in connection with a road "from Lamprill river fall to the water side in the great bay," which passed " betwixt a letell swampe and the *Rocky hill* side that lieth behind John Martin's house, and soe strait to the *laen* (lane) that is betwixt John Godder's fence and John Martin's fence." Martin's lane is again mentioned Ap. 19, 1745. (See *Doe's Neck*.)

John Martin (and Hester) conveyed to Thomas Mounsell, Sept. 20, 1667, his dwelling-house " now standing in Luberland in y⁶ Great Bay," together with 40 acres of upland granted him by the town of Dover, bounded on one side by Richard York from y⁶ high-water side, and on y⁶ other by y⁶ land of John Goddard. Also two acres of salt meadow adjoining s^d upland, and 12 acres of fresh meadow about ¾ of a mile from the house. Also six score acres of upland, lying by the side of Lamperil river near y⁶ mill, with all rights, privileges, etc.

Thomas Mounsell conveyed the above lands to Nicholas Doe, Feb. 14, 1667-8. Nicholas Doe was received as an inhabitant of Dover the 21st, 7 mo., 1668, "upon the same terms Thomas Whitehouse was received in 1665." John Martin went to Piscataqua, New Jersey.

MAST BRIDGES. A Mast bridge on the Mast road to Madbnry is mentioned Ap. 11, 1694, when John Knight had a grant of 40 acres " joyning to his plantation at *mast bridge*

all Reddy Improved." This land was laid out to Leah Knight, widow of said John, June 17, 1700, four rods being allowed for a highway to Johnson's creek. Thomas Hanson of Dover, in his will of Sept. 18, 1728, gives his well-beloved sons Maul and Jonathan 97 acres of land " near the river, near *mast bridge*." This tract was confirmed to them March 20, 1741-2, in a deed from Geo. Jaffrey of Portsmouth, executor of the estate of Jane Gerrish, widow of Richard Gerrish of Portsmouth, giving Maul Hanson, husbandman, and Jonathan Hanson, blacksmith, a quit claim to 97 acres of land in Dover, on the westerly side of Bellamy's bank river, running southwest to y⁶ *mast Road*, thence northwest to y⁶ land of Benedictus Torr, deceased, bounding on y⁶ said mast road y⁶ whole breadth of said Torr's land.

Henry Hill and wife Hannah, and Clement Bunker and wife " Rebeck," all of Durham, conveyed to John and Daniel Twombley of Dover, March 24, 1738-9, 168 acres of land on the west side of " Bellemins Bank river near *y⁶ windmill*, (see *Drew's or Dam's Windmill*), bounded north by John Twombley's land, east by that of John Ham, Jr., south by y⁶ road y^t leads down from said *windmill* over *mast* bridge, and west by the town's common.

Tristram Pinkham and wife Martha conveyed to James Tuttle, Jan. 8, 1745-6, one acre and a half of land which said Pinkham bought of Nathaniel Randal, " beginning at *Mast bridge bruck*."

Catharine Tibbetts, single woman, and Jacob Allin and wife Hannah, all of Dover, conveyed to Maul Hanson, Feb. 1, 1760, four acres of land on the west side of "Bellemin's Banck river," and on the easterly side of the road that leads over *mast bridge* to Madbury, which land formerly belonged to Joseph Tibbetts, father of said Catherine and Hannah, commonly called the *mast bridge land.*

This bridge crosses the upper part of Johnson's creek, near the Hooper land in the Back River district, Dover. (See *Reynold's Bridge.*)

A *mast bridge* across Oyster river is mentioned Nov. 18, 1713, in a deed from Moses Davis to David Kincaid. It is otherwise called *Laskey's bridge* in the Durham records. It is on the Mast road from Durham falls to Nottingham, and is one of the boundaries between Durham and Lee, near Mr. Charles W. Bartlett's.

A *Mast bridge* across the Blackwater is mentioned June 23, 1701, when Tristram Heard had a grant of 30 acres "between the *Mast bridge* and *Hodsdon's Cole pitt.*" This grant is elsewhere spoken of the same day as "between *blackwater bridg* and the *pitch pine plains.*" This was on the Mast road to Whitehall.

MAST CREEK. See *Cromwell's Creek.*

MAST PATHS or ROADS. Several mast roads were laid out at an early day from the Bellamy, Cochecho, Lamprey, Oyster, and Salmon Falls rivers, for the conveyance of timber suitable for masts and other shipping purposes, especially for the Royal navy, to be sent down the river to Portsmouth. Mention is made in 1667 of masts sent his majesty from the lands of Robert Mason two years before. (*N. H. Prov. Pap.*, 17: 519.) The course of these mast paths into the forests was no doubt varied at first to suit the convenience of the lumbermen, but in later years was straightened and perhaps otherwise changed, by order of the town.

The GREAT MAST PATH is mentioned the 17th, 12 mo., 1672, when 50 acres were laid out to Peter Coffin "on ye north side of y^e *Great mast path* going into ye swamp." (See *Plum-Pudding Hill.*) This path began at Log hill, near the first falls in the Cochecho, and ran south in the line of Lexington St., leaving Plum-Pudding hill at the right. It then curved a little to the west, and crossed the road from Cochecho to Tolend into the Cochecho swamp. It afterwards extended to Barbadoes, and finally to Bellamy Hook and the Mallego. It is the present Littleworth road. "The *Mast path to Littleworth*" is spoken of Dec. 9, 1722. The "*Mast path to Mallego*" is mentioned in 1717.

The *Mast Path to Long Hill* is mentioned June 24, 1738. This is on the easterly side of the Cochecho river. "The *mast road that goes from Tolend to Rochester*" is mentioned Oct. 15, 1748. (See *Ham's Marsh.*) It is again spoken of that same day when 21 acres of land were laid out to Joseph Hanson, Jr., beginning at a pitch pine tree on the west side of the *old mast path* leading from Ham's marsh, so called, to the Eelware plains, about ten rods above the path that leads to Tolend. This is the road on the west side of the Cochecho river. (See *Sandy Log Hill.*)

The MAST PATH TO WHITE HALL is

mentioned Dec. 20, 1714, when Ebenezer Downs conveyed to John Hurd half the land given his brother Thomas by their grandmother, Martha Lord, beginning at a pine tree near the great Pond above Cochecho (Willand's pond), on y⁰ west side of the *mast path yt leads to White Hall.* Thomas Horn, June 18, 1728, conveyed to Stephen Varney 46 acres of land that were Edward Starbuck's, "on y⁰ south side of y⁰ way or path y⁰ is called by y⁰ name of *ye mast way that leadeth to Whit Hall.*" (See *Whitehall.*)

The MAST ROAD TO MADBURY is mentioned May 8, 1682, when Richard Waldron conveyed to John Knight 20 acres of land, part of a tract of 400 acres, 300 of which said Waldron acquired from the town of Dover, and 100 he bought of Wm. Follet, all laid out on the west side of Belloman's Banke river. The 20 acres sold John Knight began on "the west line of said tract, nere the *masting way,* and so Este by said *masting way* 40 perches, and so south south west four score and six perches the like breadth." This land was afterwards acquired by Benedictus Torr, who married Leah, the widow of John Knight. (See *Torr's Garrison* and *Mast Bridge.*)

Forty acres were laid out to John Bussell, June 13, 1694, on "the south side of the *mast path that goes from John Knight's to New towne,* beginning at a beech on the side of a brook." Fifty acres were laid out to Stephen Wille, March 19, 1693-4, joining his house, thirty acres on "y⁰ south side of y⁰ *mast path which comes from Madberry,*" and twenty on y⁰ north side. Stephen Wille lived at Newtown. That same day 50 acres were granted Joseph Jones "on the north side of the *mast path that goes to William Tasker's,* below Stephen Wille's." Wm. Tasker lived at the foot of Moharimet's hill, otherwise Hicks's hill, on land now owned by the heirs of Edric E. Demeritt. John Drew's land, "on the north side of y⁰ *mast path* above Knight's farme," is mentioned in the Dover records June 23, 1701. Thirty acres were granted Thomas Perkins Ap. 5, 1703, "beginning at a hemlock on the north side of the *mast path* at the northwest of *Mahorramit's hill*"—a highway of four rods to go through this land, as the *mast path* then went. *The mast-road through Madbury* is spoken of in the Dover records, March 24, 1728-9, when the town voted to lay out a road "from y⁰ place commonly called by the name of *Winget's Slip* to y⁰ end of y⁰ township." The surveyors testified, Dec. 27, 1729, that they had laid it out "as y⁰ *mast way* now goes." And the same day they laid out "a cross road four rods wide from y⁰ above said *mast way to Newtown way,* beginning at a pine tree between Philip Chesley's land and John Tasker's land."

Thomas Laighton and Susanna conveyed to John Ham, Jan. 21, 1722-3, 14 acres in Dover, on y⁰ plains, by y⁰ highway y⁰ goeth from *Winget's slip to Madbury,*" part of a grant to John Drew. This land was on the north side of said highway.

"Mr. Deary Pitman's house" (see *Freetown*) "on the west side of the *mast path* that runs from Winget's slip through Madberry to the end of the township," is mentioned June 30, 1736.

The mast road to Madbury begins at Wingate's slip, now Ford's landing, on the west side of Back river, and runs along the upper side of Drew's hill. Soon after, it crosses the old *mast bridge brook*, sometimes called *Reynold's brook*, but really the upper part of Johnson's creek, through the old Knight and Torr lands into Madbury.

The Madbury mast road appears to be the one referred to March 19, 1693-4, when 20 acres of land were granted James Jackson " near where the *mast wheels* whare (were) broken, on the no: west side of the way." The bounds of James Jackson's land, granted to his father James in 1693-4, were renewed Oct. 14, 1732, "beginning at the *mast way*, so called, *at a turn of said way*, above where his house now stands." Ten acres of this land were laid out on the west side of said *mast way*, running along this way 52 rods, near Eli Demerit's land. The other ten acres were laid out on the east side of said *mast way*, beginning at a pine root, a former corner bound of Eli Demerit's land, and running 40 rods northeasterly along by said Demerit's land to a heap of stones, then 40 rods S. W. to a beech tree standing in the fence by said way N. Westerly of his house, thence S. easterly to the first bound. This land was in Madbury, and is still owned in part, if not wholly, by said James's descendants.

A mast road is mentioned the 7th, 9 mo., 1682, when 20 acres of land, granted Walter Jackson the 19th, 1 mo., 1665-6, " at the head of his own lott betwixt the *cow-path* and the swampe," were laid out adjoining the land he bought of Thomas Johnson, " lying betweene William Beard's crick, and the crick called Thomas Johnson's." This land ran along the *mast path* from the west end to the south. It does not appear what mast path this was. Walter Jackson of Oyster River and wife Jane conveyed to Robert Watson, Dec. 14, 1668, a tract of land on the north side of the river, (27½ rods on the river), and extending the same distance to " the *Cochechow path* from Wm. Beard's, bounded E. by Philip Chesley's land, and W. by said Jackson's." The Jackson land last mentioned was east of the Beard land, afterwards acquired by Edward Leathers. The commissioners appointed to measure a tract held in common between Robert Leathers (deceased) and Jonathan Leathers, Jan. 26, 1773, began at the N. E. corner of Mary and Jonathan Chesley's land at the highway, thence ran easterly by said way to the land of s^d Robert and Jonathan Leathers, and by their land about S. 5 deg. 52 rods, then N. 55 deg. E. 22 rods, to the land of Samuel Chesley and Wm. Jackson, and along s^d land southerly to highwater mark at *Jackson's point*, so called. (See *Jackson's Point*.)

The MAST PATH TO OYSTER RIVER was laid out at least two hundred years ago. It is mentioned Ap. 2, 1694, when John Thompson, Sr., had a grant of fifty acres in Follet's swamp at Oyster River, on the north side of the *mast path*. And John Tuttle of Dover conveyed to John Thompson, Sr., Feb. 18, 1715-16, forty acres in *Oyster River woods*, on the south side of the *Mast path* that leads to Little river. This path was declared, June 6, 1701, to be a highway of four rods wide, "as first laid out," beginning at the foot of Oyster River falls, and extending "to the utmost bounds of the town." John Pitman of Durham, Nov. 20, 1744, conveyed to Jonathan Thompson, Jr., 25 acres in Durham (which then included Lee), on the north side of *ye mast way yt leads* up to Wm. Kelsey's at Nottingham, with dwelling-house, etc., beginning at a stake on the north side of said way near y[e] *Little river mill.*

Fifty acres of land, granted to Capt. Thomas Packer, Ap. 11, 1694, "on the south side of *Lamprell river fourth falls*, or elsewhere for his conveniency," were laid out to Jonathan Chesley, beginning at a white oak on the south side of the *mast path* that leads from y[e] Little river to Oyster River Falls, and from said tree S. S. E. 100 rods to a pine stump near *Wednesday Hill.*

Fifty acres of land were laid out Dec. 17, 1723, to Jonathan Woodman, James Davis, Joseph Meder, and Mary Thomas (widow of James Thomas, who was one of the original grantees), beginning at a white oak standing by the *mast path*, the westward bound of Capt. Packer's land, and running 84 rods by the *mast path.* Joseph Thomas conveyed to Samuel Smith, July 21, 1730, 15 acres of land (part of the above tract), beginning 35½ rods from Packer's west corner bound standing by y[e] *mast path* and extending up to y[e] Little river.

In the warrant for a town-meeting in Durham, Nov. 9, 1744, is the proposal of a highway from Little river mill to Nottingham "where the *mast path way* now goeth." At a town-meeting held Dec. 24, 1744, it was voted "that the *mast way* from litel Riuer to Sam[u] Siases, and so to the head of the township, be made and maintained."

This mast road begins at the Durham Landing, at the lowest falls in Oyster river, and constitutes the principal street through Durham village as far as the foot of Chesley's hill, where it bends to the right, leaving the turnpike road, but joining it again at the top of the hill. A quarter of a mile further west, it again leaves the turnpike road, and bends around northwesterly, and then southerly, to the mast-road schoolhouse, where it crosses the turnpike road in the direction of Lee Hill. The portion of this road between the schoolhouse and the Lee boundary constitutes a neighborhood, now popularly called "the *Mast Road*," inhabited chiefly by the Bunker, Wiggins, and Chesley families. On the bounds of Durham and Lee this mast road crosses Oyster river at the old *mast bridge*, otherwise called *Laskey's bridge* in the Durham records.

MAST POINT. This point is on the westerly side of the Salmon Falls river, on the confines of Somersworth and Rochester. It is mentioned Nov. 10, 1753, when the bounds between Dover and Rochester were perambulated, "beginning at a dry pitch-pine tree at *Mast Point* by Salmon Falls river, three rods S. W. of a certain cove next adjacent to the uppermost head of the *Little falls*, so called." (*Dover Records.*) "The road from y[e] *Mast Point* to Cochecho landing," is mentioned last century in a deed from Benjamin to Jonn Wentworth. A bridge across the river at Mast point once connected Berwick with Rochester and Dover, but this is now gone, and in its place is Mast Point dam, built by the Great Falls Manufacturing Co. in 1835. The river above, for several miles, is broad and deep, and in early times afforded a natural highway for the transportation of masts and other timber. The "Landing-place for masts," is mentioned on Holland's map of 1784, just above the junction with Little river. The cove at the upper side of Mast Point is said to have been another landing-place whence the timber was conveyed by teams to Cochecho landing, and sent to Portsmouth by water. The name of *Mast Point falls* is sometimes given to Little falls.

MATHEWS' CREEK, otherwise MATHES'S. This creek was called "the *Great creek*" in 1644, when Francis Mathews had a grant of marsh and upland on its northwest side. (See *Great Creek*.) It is mentioned the 10th, 8 mo., 1653, when John Bickford and Thomas ffootman had the grant of a neck of land "on the southwest side of *Mrs. Mathews' creek*, from the flowing of the tide of the southernmost branch of *Mrs. Mathews' creek* to the flowing of the tide in the creek at the old tree." This was Mrs. Tamsen or Thomasine Mathews, widow of the above Francis Mathews.

Three score and ten acres of land, or thereabout, were laid out to Oleuer (Oliver) Kent the 3d, 2 mo., 1658, bounded by Wm. Drew and Mr. Mathews and Charles Adams, "by the creek side, commonly called *Mr. Mathewses Creek.*"

Francis Durgin of Exeter conveyed to John Smith, Dec. 25, 1723, all right and title to "a certain neck of land on the N. W. side of y[e] Great bay, aioyning to *Matheses Creek*, so called, being half of said neck of land which his father Wm. Durgin lived on in his life-time."

James Durgin of Dover, in Oyster River parish, conveyed to John Smith, Jr., March 9, 1729-30, one third of a tract of 20 acres on the N. W. side of Great Bay, "adjoining the creek commonly called *Mathewes Creek*, which land the Governor and council heretofore settled on y[e] heirs of my father Wm. Durgin, deceased, Oct. 19, 1706."

Lemuel Bickford of Newington, Oct. 10, 1733, conveyed to John Smith a tract of land on the southwest side of "*Mathises creek*, so called," originally granted to his grandfather John Bickford and Thomas Footman.

Robert and Joseph Kent, and others of the same family, conveyed to John Kent, Ap. 1, 1748, a tract of land, formerly the estate of Joseph Kent, father of said Robert, and grandfather of said John— which land joined Thomas Drew's land where he then dwelt, and "the land of Capt. Francis Mathes in y[e] possession of Abraham Mathes, which is called by the name of *Mathes Neck*," and thence ran to "*Mistress Mathes' creek*, commonly called and known by said name." A mill on this creek is spoken of in 1678. (See *Long Creek*.) The "old dam" at the head of it is mentioned

Ap. 11, 1694. (See *Daniel's Brook.*) Eliphalet Daniel, March 13, 1755, conveyed to Daniel Rogers and Benj[n] Jenkins 100 acres of land in Durham, bounded northeasterly by land in possession of Gershom and Benj[n] Mathes, and running by their land to *Mathes's mill-pond*, so called.

Gershom Mathes conveyed his rights here to his brother Benjamin Feb. 13, 1756, and afterwards went to Loudon. Benjamin Mathes, Nov. 8, 1756, conveyed to Joseph Sias a tract of 60 acres in Durham, part of the farm where his father Francis Mathes, deceased, formerly dwelt, beginning at a *stone* at high-water mark, about 6 rods N. E. from the *corn-mill*, thence running N. 63 deg. W. 80 rods to the *well marsh*, so called, thence N. 33 deg. E. 126 rods, to the road; together with one half of the *corn-mill* adjoining thereto.

Benjamin Mathes, Jr., conveyed to Joseph Sias, Aug 15, 1765, all right and title to the creek or mill privilege, joining to that farm in Durham which he sold said Sias, with the mills thereon, and utensils, etc.

This mill and part of the Mathes land were afterwards acquired by Jacob Crommet or Crummit, from whom Mathes' creek derived the name of *Crummit's creek*, by which it is now known. (See *Crummit's Creek.*)

MATHEWS' NECK. This name is given on Smith's map of Durham in 1805, to the small peninsula at the Narrows, between Great and Little Bays, now called *Adams' Point*. Benjamin Mathews or Mathes, the 10 th, 2 mo., 1654, had a grant " on (of a ?) Little Plott of marsh at the head of the little bay, with *the neck* of land there." It is mentioned Dec. 11, 1694, when Wm. Furber was licensed to "keep a ferry from his house at Welchman's cove to transport travellers over to Oyster River," at the rate of three pence for each person, and eight pence for man and horse, if landed " at *Mathews his neck*," and six pence for each person, and twelve pence for man and horse, if landed " at *Durgin's*, on the west side of *Mathews his neck*." (*N. H. Prov. Pap.*, 2 : 146–7.)

Francis Mathes of Durham conveyed to Jabez Davis, Sept. 13, 1769, eighty acres of land in Durham, being all that tract between Great bay and Little bay in Piscataqua river commonly called by the name of *Mathes Neck*, bounded on every part by water, except the northwest part which is bounded by land in possession of John Kent. Mathews' Neck was afterwards acquired by Richard Dame. (See *Adams' Point.*)

Seth Shackford of Newmarket, and others, petitioned the N. H. legislature in June, 1825, for a bridge across the Pascataqua river at a place called the *narrows*, or *Furber's ferry*, commencing at land belonging to the heirs of William Furber in the town of Newington, and crossing the Pascataqua river in a westerly direction to the east side of *Mathes' neck* in Durham, at land belonging to the heirs of Richard Dame, and extending from the west side of said *Mathes' neck* across a small cove, called *Crummit's Mill Cove*, to land owned by James Furnald, Esq. A bridge here, it is stated, in the petition, would offer no obstruction to the navigation of the Pascataqua, and the current is less rapid than at any other place in the river below. The length of the bridge from the Newington shore to the east side of *Mathes' Neck* would be about 60 rods, and from the west side of *Mathes' Neck* across Crummit's Mill cove about 40 rods.

A similar petition was presented by Wm. Claggett and others in 1832, but the town of Durham instructed its representative to oppose this movement, and the petition was not granted.

Mathews' Neck, until the construction of the present causeway, became an island at high tide. An inlet on one side is now called *Island cove*. Beneath the banks of this Neck may be seen some half-ruined caves, said to have been used by the aborigines in pre-historic times. At a later day they often served the early settlers as places of concealment from the Indians. There is a similar cave lower down, on the shore of the Emerson farm on Little Bay. Belknap says that four sons of John Wheeler, who with his wife and two children was killed by the Indians Ap. 27, 1706, "took refuge in a cave by the bank of the Little Bay, and though pursued by the Indians, escaped unhurt." (See *Shooting Point*.)

MEADER'S BRIDGE. Mentioned on Sanford & Evert's Atlas. This bridge is on the highway where it spans the Dover and Winnipiseogee R. R. near Mr. Moses Meader's in the upper part of Dover.

MEADER'S NECK. This neck of land is on the upper shore of the Pascataqua, between the mouth of Oyster river and Royall's cove. It is mostly in Durham, and includes Cedar Pt. and Tickle Pt. Franklin city was laid out on this neck. Part of it was conveyed to John Meader by Valentine Hill and Mary his wife, Sept. 20, 1660, and part was acquired by a grant of 150 acres to John Meader and Wm. Sheffield in 1656. Wm. Sheffield's half was conveyed to James Davis, John Meader, Sr., and John Meader, Jr., in equal shares, by "Joseph Sheffield of Shurbury, Middlesex Co., Prov. of Mass. Bay," Nov. 11, 1701. John Meader, Sr., out of love and affection to his son John, conveyed to him, June 17, 1679, as his portion and patrimony in full, three score acres of land on *the neck* that lyeth between Oyster river and ye Back river, being a part and moitie of a greater tract granted ye s^d John Meader, ye father, and Wm. Sheffield at a public town-meeting in ye year of our Lord God 1656, —which three score acres begin at an aspe tree some four rods from ye flowing of ye tide at ye head of *Rial's Cove*, so north and by west 142 rods by ye lands lately Thomas Laiton's, and by ye land latelie Elder Nutter's[1] to a red oak, and thence W. by S. 68 rods to a hemlock, thence S. and by E. to a great white oak, ye N. E. corner bound of ye land which John Meader, ye father, bought of Mr. Valentine Hill, and so from s^d oak to ye aspe tree at ye head of *Rial's Cove* afores^d, always provided there be a highway one rod wide from ye s^d oak to ye aspe tree at ye Cove afores^d for a watering way to s^d Cove.

---

[1] Elder Hatevil Nutter had a grant of 200 acres of upland for a farm, next adjacent to Wm. Sheffield's, the 2d, 12 mo., 1658.

There was a fulling mill on this neck early last century, mentioned Nov. 10, 1724, when John Meder of Dover, weaver, for ye natural love and affection for his well beloved son Nicholas Meder, planter, conveyed to him, on certain conditions, Nov. 10, 1724, "a parcel of land and meadow in Dover, beginning at *ye ould fulling mill*, commonly so called, and running thence west to a great rock, thence to the dwelling house of s^d John Meder where he now liveth, and from s^d house to ye bridge that is over the gully or small brook that goeth out to ye commons—that is, all the land on the north side of the line from the *fulling-mill* to ye bridge, and from ye bridge to s^d John Meder's fresh marsh on a N. W. by N. line from the head of the marsh to the land of John Laighton, thence to the afores^d *fulling-mill*, together with the moitie or half of his other lands in Dover, and also one half of the barn Joseph Meder built." (See *Meader's Garrison, Royall's Cove,* and *Stony Brook.*)

MEADERBORO' ROAD. Meaderborough is a prosperous farming region in the northwestern part of Rochester, so named from Benjamin Meader and his four brothers, who were among the first settlers in that part of the town. They were Quakers. Meaderboro' road extends along the ridge through this district into Farmington.

MECHANICSVILLE. The *Dover Directory* of 1843 gives this name to a hamlet or neighborhood about halfway between Garrison Hill and Willand's pond, in the vicinity of Gage's hill. It was at that period chiefly inhabited by people of industrial pursuits, such as George and John Gage, wheelwrights; John Gould, baker; Daniel K. Webster, tanner and currier, etc. The name is no longer in use.

MENDUM'S POND. This pond is in the western part of Barrington, next the Nottingham line. It is the source of Little river. The name was derived from Capt. Nathaniel Mendum of Portsmouth, whose sawmill on this river is mentioned Oct. 7, 1742, when Daniel Davis of Durham conveyed to John Burnum 12 acres of land, together with "one fourth of a sawmill in Nottingham, below *Capt. Nathaniel Mendum's sawmill* on Little river." The Newmarket Manufacturing Co. have a dam at the outlet of Mendum's pond, and the sawmill here is now called the *Factory-Dam mill*. The next mill below is owned by Mr. Samuel Thompson. *Marston's mill,* also in Nottingham, is further down the river, on the highway to Lee, not far from the boundary line. (See *Little River.*)

MERIT'S MILL. See *Demeritt's Mill*.

MESSENGER'S POND. See *Cochecho Pond*.

MIDDLE POINT, MIDDLE POINT BRIDGE, and MIDDLE POINT BROOK. There is a Middle Point on the Rollinsford shore of the Newichawannock river at Jocelyn's Cove, between Pine point and Henderson's point. And the brook which empties into this cove is called "*Middle Point brook*." A point of this name in Dover is mentioned May 12, 1736, when Timothy Tebbets conveyed to Howard Henderson six acres of land laid out to said Tebbets in 1736, where he then dwelt, at or near "*Middle pinte Brook,*" in Dover.

And again Jan. 20, 1743-4, when Howard Henderson mortgaged to Abraham Nute six acres of land at or near a place called by ye name of *Middle Point brook*, in Dover. This name is no longer in use, and the bridge, formerly known as *Middle Point bridge*, has ceased to bear this name, but it appears to be the one across Canny's brook, on the socalled "*Middle road*" across the Upper Neck, about midway between Fore river and Back river. It is mentioned Dec. 7, 1737, when Samuel and Patience Carle conveyed to Jonathan Cushing ten acres of land adjoining the road that leads down from Cochecho to Dover over *Middle Point bridge*, a little above Joseph Hanson's. Wm. Twombley, Jan. 23, 1771, conveyed to Caleb Hodgdon his homestead farm of 60 acres, adjoining the main road from Cochecho to Dover neck, bounded "southerly by the land of Moses and Aaron Wingate, and northerly adjoining the road that leads from the aforesaid road over *Middle point bridge*, so called, to Dover." Benjⁿ Watson and wife Lydia, Jan. 29, 1785, conveyed to Moses Wingate 8¼ acres of land, set off as said Lydia's portion of the estate of her honored father Isaac Hanson, on the west side of the road that leads from Major Hodgdon's to *Middle point* (*bridge?*), so called, bounded northwesterly by said Hodgdon's land, southwesterly by said Wingate's, southeasterly by Thomas Kinney's, and northeasterly by the aforesaid road.

MILES' HILL. This hill is on the borders of Lee and Nottingham, at the upper side of North river, on the road from Nottingham to Newmarket. The name is derived from Miles Reynolds, who once lived on the top. He served in the Revolutionary war, and in that of 1812. "Miles Reynolds of the North River district" is mentioned in the Lee records of 1807.

MILL CREEK. Mentioned Feb. 21, 1711, when John and Elizabeth Edgerly conveyed to Samuel Edgerly a tract of land on the north-west side of Little Bay, "bounded N. by the creek called and known by the name of the *mill creek*, E. by Little Bay, and S. by the land of John Wheeler, lately deceased." And again in the Durham records of March 21, 1746-7, when a petition was made for a highway "by John Edgerly's land to the creek called the *Mill creek*." This creek is in Durham, at the easterly side of the Lubberland district. The name was derived from a mill that once stood thereon at the head of tide water. It was otherwise called *Mathews' creek*, but is now generally known as *Crummit's creek*.

Another *Mill creek* is in Newington, above Fabyan's point, so named from a mill that once stood at the head of tide water, the remains of which can still be seen, on the Thomas Pickering farm, now owned by Mr. J. S. Hoyt. (See *Swadden's Creek*.)

MILL ROAD. So called from Chesley's mill on Oyster river, to which this road once led on its way from Durham village to Packer's falls. The mill is now gone, but the road retains its name, which is often mentioned in deeds of adjacent lands. (See *Warner Farm*.)

MILL-ROAD BROOK. This brook rises in Follet's swamp, above the

Mast-road school-house, and empties into the Durham mill-pond on the west side. Its name is derived from the so-called *Mill road*, which it crosses near the Oyster River creamery, at which point it is a watering-place for cattle, and in rainy weather often swells to a considerable size.

MINNOW BROOK. This name—derived from the abundance of minnows therein, used by fishermen for bait—is now given to a small run from Hall's spring that empties into Back cove on the western side of Dover Neck.

MIRY GUT. This is a channel twenty feet deep at the mouth of Reyner's brook, where it is crossed by the Dover and Winnipiseogee Railroad and the Scatterwit highway. There is a stone culvert at this point, forty feet in length, affording room for both roads to cross. This part of the brook is often called *Miry Gut brook;* and the cove above, on the easterly side of the Cochecho, is called *Miry Gut cove.*

The MOAT. This is an outlet or arm on the left side of Lamprey river that encircles an island generally called the *Moat island,* otherwise *Doe's island.* It is in the Packer's Falls district, Durham, below the so-called "*Diamond bridge*," on the Boston and Maine railway. Mention is made of it the 11th, 7 mo., 1649, when Anthony Nutter's grant at a place called "*the moote*" is spoken of in the county records. It is again mentioned the 11th, 11 mo., 1660, when Robert Burnum's 100 acre grant in 1656 was laid out, one head line "joining to the *moet,*" and the other bounded by "a marked tree at a lettell Brook that cometh from the *moett,* joining to Elder Nutter's land." (See *Broad Marsh.*) It is again mentioned Aug. 14, 1667, in the will of John Footman. Peter Coffin conveyed to Samuel Allin of New Castle, Nov. 28, 1698, thirty acres of land "called by y[e] name of y[e] *mote, which* s[d] *Peter Coffin purchased of* y[e] *Indians.*" (See *Moharimet's Planting-Ground.*) Six score acres of land adjoining "the *mote*" are mentioned in the inventory of Nicholas Doe's estate, March 30, 1706. A road was ordered to be laid out, March 6, 1710–11, "from Lampereel river as straight as it may be to y[e] old Bridge by y[e] *moat* so as y[e] way goes to Graves[1] his land, thence to the falls," etc. (*N. H. Prov. Papers,* 17 : 710.) John Rawlins of Durham, Ap. 24, 1733, conveyed to "Joseph Smith of Newmarket in Exeter," all his homestead estate in Durham, beginning at the east side of the country road to Durham falls. One side extended to "y[e] mouth of y[e] *mote river.*" The Moat and Moat river are repeatedly mentioned in the division of John Doe's estate, Ap. 24, 1742. His widow Elizabeth's dowry was set off from the homestead, beginning at the north corner of Joseph Smith's land, one side running along Lamprey river to a pitch-pine "standing by a hollow that runs into the river commonly called the *mote river.*" Mary Mason's part was on "the southerly side of that land called the *mote.*" Elizabeth Woodman's part

---

[1] This was Wm. Graves, who married Elizabeth, the widow of Richard York. He was wounded by the Indians and his estate devastated in 1694, as appears from his petition of January 8, 1694-5. (*N. H. Prov. Pap.,* 2: 147.)

(wife of Joshua) was on the *moat river*, and extended to the "east side of the *mote*." Joseph Doe's portion was "on the *mote*," between the portions of John and Benjamin. And Daniel Doe's part began at Deacon John Yorke's land, 109 rods N. E. from Lamperel river, and ran S. E. to the "*mote river*," near Joseph Smith's land at the pine tree boundary, and up by said Smith's land to the country road. The Moat still retains its ancient name. *Moat island*, otherwise *Doe's*, now belongs to Mr. Olinthus Doe, a descendant of the above mentioned John Doe.

MOHARIMET'S HILL, otherwise HICKS'S HILL. This beautiful hill, wooded to the very summit, is at Madbury corner, west of the railway station. Its original name was derived from Moharimet or Mahomet, an Indian sagamore of the seventeenth century. (See *Moharimet's Marsh* and *Wadleigh's Falls*.) Charles Adams, of Oyster River, had a grant of 100 acres of land at the foot of *Moharimet's hill*, in 1656, one half of which he conveyed, March 11, 1693-4, to his daughter, Mary, wife of William Tasker. Derry Pitman, Jan. 1, 1723-4, sold Eli Demerit, Sr., thirty acres of land on the south-west side of *Meharmet's hill*. Thomas Footman's hundred acre grant in 1656, was laid out anew, at the request of his son John, June 23, 1715, beginning at a white pine bound tree on John Bickford's lot, near the lower end of *Maharimutt's Hill* on the west side. This land, when re-surveyed for John Roberts, July 25, 1729, ran from a white oak W. S. W. 120 rods, to "a heap of stones on the S. E. end of *Moharmot's hill*, about a rod from the way leading through Madberry, leaving the space of one rod between the land and the way where it goes down to the turn about 4 rods from *Archabel Smith's pit*," etc. Col. James Davis, in his will of Oct. 18, 1748, gives his sons, James and Samuel, twenty acres of land on the northwest side of *Maharrimet's hill*. James Davis of Dover, gentleman, conveyed to Joseph Hicks, March 5, 1761, ten acres on the north side of *Mahomet's Hill*, being half of twenty acres given him in his father's will.

The name of *Hicks's hill* was derived from Joseph Hicks, who, early last century, acquired the greater part, if not all, of this hill, and erected a garrison on the eastern side, traces of which can still be seen. April 15, 1718, John Underwood, of Newcastle, and Temperance his wife (granddaughter of John Bickford of Oyster River), conveyed to Joseph Hix 100 acres on the east side of *Maharimet's hill*, originally granted John Bickford by the town of Dover. Joseph Hicks is called "captain" in the rate-list of 1758. He married Sarah, daughter of Col. James Davis, who outlived her husband, and died at the age of ninety-one. Letters of administration were granted on her estate Jan. 14, 1794. She and her husband lie buried at the foot of Hicks's hill, at the east. A large part of this hill is still owned by their descendants, among whom may be mentioned the Kingman, Miles, and Young families.

MOHARIMET'S MARSH. This marsh is on the upper side of Lamprey river, in the Packer's Falls district, but the name has not been perpetuated. It was so named from the

THE MOAT

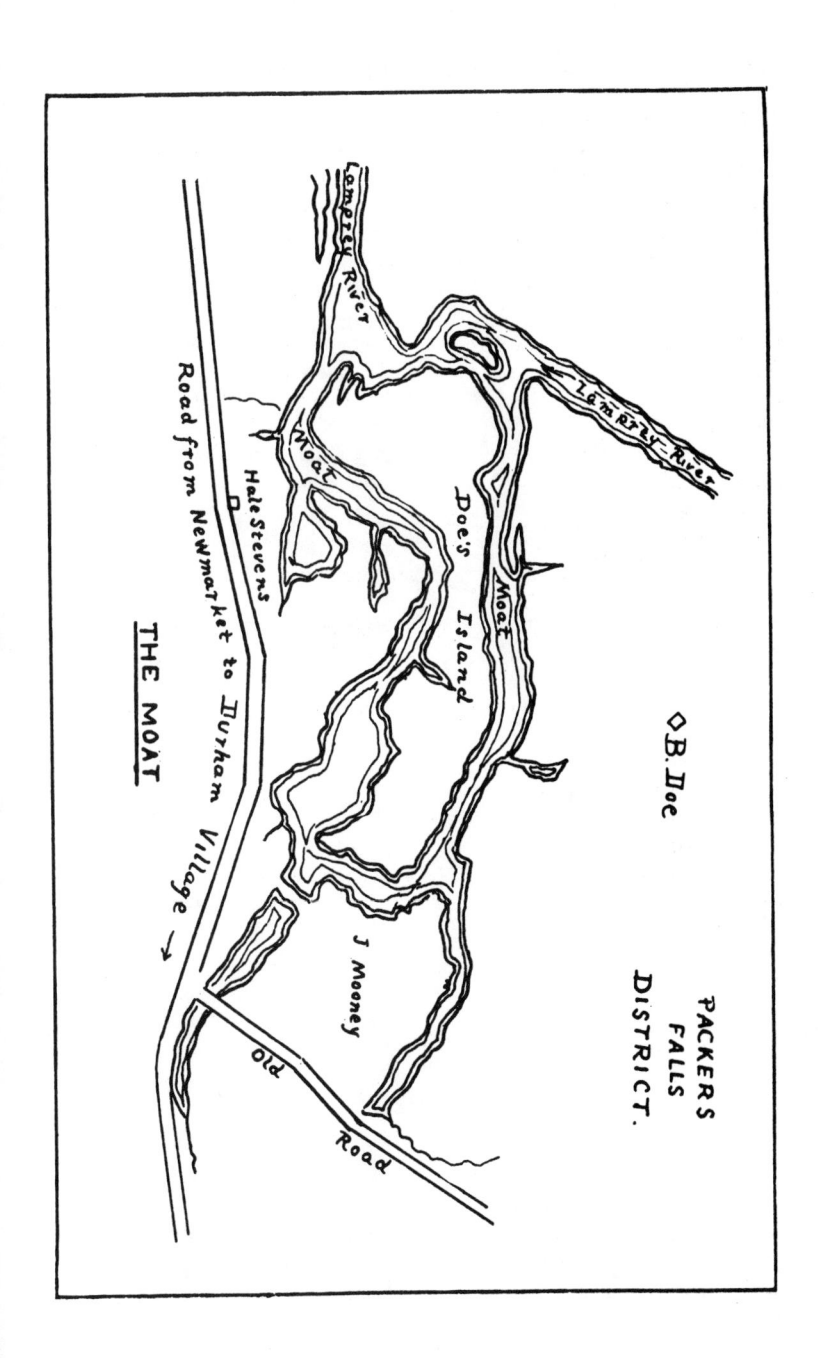

PACKERS FALLS DISTRICT.

Indian sagamore of that region, in whose presence, and with whose consent, Samuel Symonds took possession of his grant at *Island falls*, now *Wadleigh's*, June 3, 1657. The name is otherwise written, Mahorimet, Mohermite, Moharmet, etc., and is no doubt a corruption of Mahomet. In fact, it is to be found so written in a Durham record of 1735, which runs as follows:

"Whereas there was a Certain tract of Marsh laid out unto William Follet of six acres in the Marsh called *Mahomet's Marsh* the 7th day of the 6mo 1661. And also a Certain tract of land laid out to the said William Follet and bounded the 18th 10 month 1663, near a Marsh called *Mahomet's Marsh*, and we whose names are under written being Called by Nicholaus Medar[1] the Possessor of the afor^{sd} Lands to renew the bounds, we have Run the Points of Compass as before. That is to say, beginning at a White Oak stump, one of the Old bounds next Thomas Footman's land," etc. This land was laid out Aug. 30, 1735.

July 1, 1710, Nicholas Follet and Mary his wife conveyed to Nicholas Medar two lots—one of six acres and the other of one hundred acres—in *Moheremet's fresh marsh* next Thomas Footman's land. March 30, 1749, Nicholas Medar conveyed to his son Samuel eighty-six acres of land, "part of the marsh formerly granted to Wm Follet." May 23, 1763, Nicholas Medar sold Timothy Medar thirty acres, "part of the one hundred acres formerly laid out to Wm Follet." This lot was bounded N. E. and S. W. by Joshua Woodman's land, and joined the lands of John and Samuel Medar.

Timothy Medar, shipwright, conveyed the same thirty acres to Isaac Medar June 12, 1772. This land, after various owners, was purchased Sept. 1, 1820, by Capt. Edward Griffiths, whose son still owns it. Mention is made in the Dover records of a highway laid out on the south side of Oyster river freshet, June 13, 1719, beginning at Chesley's mill, and following the old way past the land of Moses Davis, Jr., etc., to Wm. Follet's hundred acre lot at *Maharimut's Marsh*. This marsh, most of which is now drained and cultivated, no doubt extended beyond Mr. Fogg's farm, and included the so called "Croxford swamp." (See *Follet's Swamp*.)

MOHARIMET'S PLANTING-GROUND, otherwise MAHOMET'S. Mentioned Nov. 28, 1698, when Peter Coffin conveyed to Samuel Allen 210 acres of upland on the south side of Lamprill river, beginning at the mouth of the Pascassick river, and running up Lamprey river to a red oak "about 20 rods above the run of water that runneth into Lamprill river, near ye land called by ye name of old *Mahormett's planting ground*." Eliphalet Coffin of Exeter conveyed to Stephen Pendergrass, Oct. 9, 1735, 84 acres of land in Durham, adjoining Lampereel river, beginning at, or near about, 20 rods above ye run of water near ye land formerly called *Mahermit's planting ground*, which land said Eliphalet had of his grandfather Peter Coffin, late of Exeter. Stephen Pendergast of Newmarket, July 12, 1740, conveyed to Nathan Mendum 84 acres of land in Durham, beginning at Lamprel river, about 20 rods above ye run of water near ye land formerly called

Mahermit's planting ground, thence along said river to the west side of a spring by the river. This land is in the Packer's Falls district, Durham, on the south side of Lamprey river. The Pendergast garrison is still standing.

MORRILL'S FERRY. See *Beck's Slip*.

MORRIS'S CREEK. Mentioned Jan. 2, 1734-5, when Francis Durgin sold John Smith, Jr., a dwelling-house and tract of land in Durham, on the shore of Great Bay, bounded by John Pinder on ye S. W., and on the N. E. by a creek " called *Thomas Morry's creek*." This land now belongs to Mr. Channell.

MORRIS'S POINT. This point, miscalled *Maurice's Point* on Smith's map of Durham, is just below Pindar's point, on the Lubberland shore of Great Bay. The name, no longer in use, was derived from Thomas Morris, who was taxed at Oyster River as early as 1663, and owned a tract at Lubberland before 1681. The Rev. John Pike, in his journal, records the death of " old Tho. Morris of Lubberland " July 30, 1707. He seems to have left no wife or children. In his will of Dec. 1, 1701, (proved June 5, 1710) he gives his friends, James and William Durgin, his house and land to be divided equally among them, and he distributes his personal effects among various neighbors on the Lubberland shore.

MOUNT BURROUGHS. This hill, so named from Jabez Burroughs, to whom it once belonged, is in the eastern part of Dover, below the Portland turnpike road. It is now owned by Mr. Geo. Yeaton, Mrs. Dana, and others. It is well-wooded on the southeast side, but is chiefly a ledge of granite.

MOUNT HUNGRY. Mentioned March 7, 1764, when Dependence and Olive Bickford conveyed land to Richard Furber in Newington, bounded westerly by the highway from the late dwelling-house of Hatevil Nutter to the hill called *Mount Hungry*, north by the lands of James Nutter and Rachel Row; east by said Row, John Quint, and Moses and Nehemiah Furber; and south by the highway aforesaid; which land had been purchased by said Dependence Bickford of Richard Furber.

Wm. Furber, in his will of Nov. 12, 1741, proved May 25, 1751, gives his grandson Richard Furber all his land in Newington on the easterly or upper side of the road from Ensign Hatevil Nutter's to Mr. *Vincent's windmill*. And he gives his sons Moses and Nehemiah all his land on the lower or westerly side of the highway that runs from Ensign Hatevil Nutter's to *Vincent's windmill*.

It is evident from the above conveyances that this windmill stood on Mt. Hungry, which probably derived its name from this circumstance. Vincent's windmill was no doubt so called from John Vincent, who bought land of Clement Messervey Oct. 26, 1727, originally granted to the Rev. Joshua Moodey. (See *Harwood's Creek*.) Part of this land was conveyed July 22, 1783, by Anthony Vincent to Ephraim Pickering, beginning at a flat rock by the road leading to Furber's ferry, at the land of Noah Huntress and running by said land to that of Moses Dame. Another part was conveyed to Wm. and Levi Furber Oct. 21, 1783.

Mount Hungry no longer retains its ancient name, but it could not have been far from the source of the Trout brook, formerly Harwood's creek.

MOUNT MISERY. This mount is in Barrington, just above the Judge Hale place.

MOUNT PLEASANT. This elevation is in Dover, east of Pine Hill, between the cemetery and the river Cochecho.

MOUNT SORROWFUL. Mentioned March 23, 1702, when 30 acres of land were granted to Paul Wentworth " near the place called *Mount Sorrowful*, not intrenching on any former grants." No commons being found here, this grant was laid out in 1718, " between Salmon fall river and Cochecha, att a place called the *great ash swamp*." The name of Mount Sorrowful is still retained. It is a steep gravelly hill in Rollinsford, near Rollins' brook, crossed by the Boston and Maine R. R. It formerly belonged to the Ricker family, but is now owned by Messrs. Samuel and Wm. Rollins.

MOUNT RAWLINGS. Mentioned March 26, 1683, when Richard Waldron of Dover conveyed to Thomas Paine a tract of land, with a *dwellinghouse* thereon, situate lying, and being, at or near Cochecho, commonly called or known by the name of *Mount Rawlings*, bounded on the south by the Cochecho river, and running from a great pine tree on the brow of the hill N. by W. 44 perches to a pine tree on the brow of another hill, being a parcel of land said Richard Waldron bought of James Rawlings March 5, 1673. This land was conveyed to Richard Waldron of Portsmouth, June 17, 1705, by Thomas Paine of Newcastle (son of the above Thomas), who in the deed of conveyance repeats the same bounds, and also gives to this tract the name of *Mount Rawlings*. This name has not been perpetuated, but it appears to have been given to one of the hills near the Cochecho river in the vicinity of Rogers street, at the head of which Paine's garrison is said to have stood. Further east are *Paine's woods*, now called *Guppy's woods*.

MUCHADOE. Mentioned in the Dover records of 1672, when Peter Coffin had ten acres laid out on the south side of the *Great Mast path*, bounded east by land previously laid out to said Coffin " to ye path y^t goeth to *Muchadoe*" (the Tolend road). And again Ap. 1, 1673, when Peter Coffin conveyed to Nathaniel Stevens a quarter part of a tract of land near Cochecha, bounded north by the highway from *Muchadoe* to Plum-Pudding hill. (See *Trumbelow Swamp*.)

The *Muchadoe* of the present day is a steep hill in Barrington, about a mile N. E. of the Congregational meeting-house. On the top are two pines, a remnant of the woods which once covered it; and at the foot is a huge rock tapestried with moss and vines, near which, according to the " Wild Artist," once lived a witch named Moll Ellsworth, whose sole companion was a black cat without a single white hair. The devil is said to have flown away with her in a gale of wind one dark, tempestuous night. At all events, she mysteriously disappeared, and with her the black cat, said to have embodied a still darker fiend.

MUD BROOK. This brook is in

Lee and empties into Lamprey river, between the mouth of Little river and Wadleigh's Falls. It is crossed by the road from Lee Hill at Mud bridge, now a mere culvert.

MUNSEY'S BRIDGE. Mentioned March 21, 1798, when the bounds between Durham and Lee were perambulated. It is on the back road across Oyster river, below Dishwater falls, and is no doubt the bridge mentioned March 19, 1693-4, when Joseph Meader's grant was laid out on the S. W. side of the path to the *burnt ground bridge*, in Follet's swamp. (See *Burnt Ground*.) The Meader land was afterwards acquired by "John Muncey." A highway was laid out Ap. 4, 1752, "beginning at Moses Davis's fence, 79 rods from Lieut. Jones's fence near folet's swamp, at the head of John Woodman's land, next to or near Jonath Monses land." (*Durham Records*.)

The Woodman land above mentioned, originally granted to John Woodman and his sons (see *Beech Hill*), was inherited by his son Jonathan, who, in his will of Jan. 2, 1749, gives his son Jonathan " 100 acres of land where he now lives, at a place called the *burnt ground*, at the eastern end thereof." This land is now owned by his descendant, Mr. Moses G. Woodman. And he gives to his son Archelaus 100 acres at a place called the *burnt ground*, at the western end thereof, reserving a highway two rods wide for his son Jonathan to pass and re-pass from his land to the mast road.

The land of Moses Davis, whose fence is mentioned above, is now owned by Mr. Israel Demeritt. In his neighborhood is Munsey's bridge, on the bounds between Durham and Lee. A nocturnal meeting of the "Know-Nothings" is said to have been held on this bridge in the heyday of that party—a singularly appropriate place for such a gathering.

NANCY DREW'S POINT. This name is now popularly given to the Newington terminus of Knight's ferry, from Miss Nancy N. Drew, to whom John Knight conveyed, July 16, 1831, 44 acres of land adjoining the road from Bloody Point ferry, so called, to Newington meeting-house, running northerly to the land of Samuel Shackford, deceased, then northeasterly by said land to Pascataqua river, and by said river to the *ferry*, thence to the first bound.

Miss Nancy Drew died in 1889 at her residence on this point, at the age of 93 years, and her homestead was sold at auction, May 31, 1890, to Mr. Charles Dame.

NANNEY'S ISLAND. This island is in Great Bay, off Long Point, and now belongs to the heirs of Mr. James A. Pickering. It no doubt derived its name from Robert Nanney of the Dover Combination of 1640. His name is on the Dover rate-list of 1649. He afterwards became a merchant in Boston, where he died Aug. 27, 1663, leaving among other property, part of an estate in Barbadoes. His wife was Katherine, daughter of the Rev. John Wheelwright, founder of Exeter.

The NARROW LANE. Mentioned Ap. 28, 1779, when Jonathan Quint conveyed to Jonathan Hight (Hoyt), both " of Newington, at a place commonly called the *Upper plains*," half an acre of land, 16 rods on the road leading from Newington meeting-house to Greenland, and 10 rods upon a road called the *narrow lane*, leading to Portsmouth.

Daniel Walker of Portsmouth conveyed to Gee Pickering, Ap. 26, 1806, one acre of land on the north side of the *Narrow Lane*, so called, bounded west by Lieut. Richard Dame's land, and N. and E. by said Pickering's land, being the same land said Walker bought of John Stevens, Dec. 11, 1787. John Stevens' land is spoken of in 1730 as at the south end of the Gore. (See the *Gore*.) Richard Dame gave a quit-claim to Gee Pickering, May 15, 1811, of 3½ acres, bounded "southwardly by the *narrow lane*, so called, which adjoins *Downing's Plains*, as formerly called."

NARROWS. The Narrows in the river Cochecho are at Campin's Rocks, about a mile below the first falls.

Furber's Straits, between Great and Little bays, are also called the Narrows. And farther down the Pascataqua, at the end of the Long Reach, below Boiling Rock, are the Narrows, so called by boatmen. There are also Narrows in Wheelwright's Pond.

"The *Narrows*" and "*Lower Narrows*" in Lamprey river, between the lowest falls and Goddard's creek, are on Smith's map of Newmarket in 1805. The latter are mentioned Feb. 22, 1714-15, when Sampson Doe conveyed to Cornelius Driscoe 60 acres of the neck of land (Doe's neck,) between Lamprill river and Goddard's creek, in the township of Dover, bounded by a little watercourse to said river a little above or near ye low^r *narrow* in s^d Lamprill river, and near s^d Driscoe's house, running along s^d water-course to a red oak about three rods from a spring in said water-course, thence northerly to an elm near the highway to Lamprill river low^r falls, etc.

NEEDHAM'S COVE. This cove, now called *Broad cove*, is on the Lubberland shore of Great Bay. The name was no doubt derived from Nicholas Needham, "Ruler of Exeter" from 1639 till 1642, at which time Exeter laid claim to Oyster River lands. It is mentioned Aug. 18, 1670, when John Alt of Oyster River, and wife Remembrance, conveyed to John Cutt of Portsmouth 80 acres of land "in ye greate Bay, in *Needum's Cove*," granted him by the town of Dover. And again, Nov. 11, 1715, when Joseph Roberts, Sr., conveyed to John Footman four score acres of land on the N. W. side of Great Bay, adjoining *Needum's Cove*, beginning at a white oak next Pinder's fence. (See *Needham's Pt.* and *Broad Cove*.)

NEEDHAM'S POINT. This point is mentioned the 10th, 8 mo., 1653, when, "at a public meeting of ye select men at oister river," 80 acres of land were granted to John Alt, at "ye Great Cove above *Needum's poynt*, 40 rods in length upon ye Cove." This point is at the lower side of Broad Cove. It is called *Jewell's Point* on Smith's map of 1805, but is now called *Long Point*.

NEW ENGLAND. This name was first given by Capt. John Smith, who explored our coast in 1614, and afterwards published an interesting account of his voyage, together with a map or chart of this region. The name of New England was subsequently confirmed by the so-called "*New England Charter*" to Sir Ferdinando Gorges and his associates in 1620.

NEWFIELDS. This name was given to South Newmarket until its incorporation as a separate township, June 27, 1849. Here lived Richard Hilton, son of William, and grandson of Edward Hilton. John ffoullsam and Abigail conveyed to Edward Hall, May 26, 1707, 12 acres in Exeter, " beginning at the water-side in the field commonly called *Mr. Hilton's new field*." The name is mentioned Nov. 25, 1755, in a petition about " a bridge over the river (Squamscot) from Stratham to a place called *Newfields*, in Newmarket."

Joseph Merrill of Newmarket conveyed to John Moody, March 4, 1771. 36 acres of land on the N. E. side of the road from the *Newfield Landing-place*, so called, to Nottingham, running N. W. as the fence runs to Piscassick river. This landing was probably at the ferry-place. Richard Hilton petitioned to the N. H. government June 12, 1700, " for a ferry to be granted to him for transporting horse and man over the river (Squamscot) against his house for 50 years' time." This petition was granted. (*N. H. Prov. Pap.*, 3 : 99–102.)

NEW HAMPSHIRE. The late C. W. Tuttle, in his "Memoir of Capt. John Mason," says the Council of Plymouth granted Capt. Mason Nov. 7, 1629, " all that part of the province of Maine lying between the Merrimack and Pascataqua rivers, and Mason called it *New Hampshire* out of regard to the favor in which he held Hampshire in England, where he had resided many years." And that Council, by an indenture of Ap. 22, 1632, declared that the lands granted Capt. Mason should henceforth bear this name.

New Hampshire was styled a *Province* till Jan. 5, 1776, and a *Colony* from that time till Sept. 11, 1776, on which day it was enacted by the General Assembly and Council at Exeter that henceforth " this Colony should take the name of the *State of New Hampshire*."

NEWICHAWANNOCK. This name, according to Mr. J. S. Jenness, is derived from the Indian word *nee-week-wan-auke*, signifying " my wigwam place." It was the name of an Indian village near Salmon falls, but the English pioneers gave it also to the adjoining river, from the head of tide water down to the main body of the Pascataqua. They seem to have pronounced the name *Ne-ge-won-nuck*. (See Belknap's *Hist. of N. H.*, Farmer & Moore's ed., p. 10, foot-note.) It is called *Nechewanick* in a grant to Wm. Pomfrett in 1643. (See *Cochecho Point*.) Capt. Dantforth, an eminent surveyor, wrote it *Negewonnick* in 1679. It is called *Nechowanuck* in 1691 (see *Fowling Marsh*), and *Nichewanock* in 1722. (See *Hobbs's Hole*.)

Above the head of tide water this stream was generally called the *Salmon Falls river* by the early settlers, which name it still retains. The part between the mouth of the Cochecho river and Hilton's Point was called *Fore river* by the people on Dover Neck. (See *Salmon Falls*.) The Newichawannock or Salmon Falls river is the eastern branch of the Pascataqua. It rises at East pond, on the borders of Newfield and Wakefield, Me., and unites with the western branch of the Pascataqua at Hilton's Point, now Dover Point.

A trading-post was established on the Newichawannock in 1631 by Ambrose Gibbons, agent of the Laconia Company. A letter to him from this Company, Dec. 5, 1632, speaks of "our house at *Newichewanick.*" (Tuttle's *Capt. John Mason*, p. 305.) There was not only a store-house here, but a large dwelling-house, palisaded and furnished with an ample supply of arms and ammunition. (*N. H. Prov. Pap.*, 1 : 116.) These buildings were burned to the ground about 1645. (*Ibid*, 1 : 45.)

A saw-mill and grist-mill, "the first set up on the Pascataqua," were erected here in 1634 by Henry Jocelyn, who was sent over, by Capt. Mason in the spring of that year. They were " at a small fall at a place called by the Indians *Assabenbeduck* on the *little Newichwannock*, now South Berwick." (Tuttle's *Capt. John Mason*, p. 25.) Three excellent saw-mills at the falls of "*Nichiquiwanick*" are mentioned in the Ms. supposed to have been written in 1660 by Samuel Maverick, who adds that down that side of the river had been procured most of the masts brought over to England; among them " that admired mast which came over some time last year containing neere 30 Tunes of timber." (*Maine Hist. and Gen. Register*, 1 : 159.)

Newichawannock is mentioned as a locality on the west side of the river. Oct. 7, 1699, when James Grant of York (Me.) conveyed to David Hambleton[1] of *Newechewannuck* 20 acres of land in the township of Dover, at *a place called Newitchewannuck*, granted said James Grant by the town (in 1657-8), lying between a place called St. Alban's cove and Quamphegan falls, bordering on the river at the S. E. ; on Thomas Canney's lot at the N. E., on ye commons at the N. W., and on Henry Magoun's lot on the S. W.

The selectmen of Dover granted Thomas Pots, March 28, 1698, in consideration of his keeping and maintaining David Hamilton, eldest son of David Hamilton, the whole term of his life, 20 acres of land at *Newchewanake*, below a lot granted to Mary Mason and the lot of Thomas Canney, being all that tract of land formerly in the tenure of David Hamilton, Sr., deceased. Thomas Potts conveyed this land to Job Clement, Esq., Jan. 19, 1698-9. Job Clement conveyed it to Henry Nock Oct. 15, 1700. Nock's widow married Eleazer Wyer, and conveyed this land to her son-in-law of the same name.

NEWINGTON. The Bloody Point settlement was incorporated as a parish July 16, 1713, but its name was not changed till May 12, 1714, when, according to the records of the Council, " Bloody Point was named NEWINGTON this day by his Excellency the Governour." (*N. H. Prov. Pap.*, 3 : 549–551, 562.) This parish had town privileges from the first. In a petition of March 30, 1784, it is stated that the inhabitants had exercised the right of sending a representative to the General Assembly for more than 60 years. (*N. H. Town Pap.*, 12 : 727.) John Dam was the representative in 1715. In 1718 Capt. John Downing presented a petition to the Governor and Council from John Fabyan, Hatevil Nutter, and Moses Dam, the *selectmen* of

---

[1] David Hamilton was killed by the Indians " at *Newick*," Sept. 28, 1692. (Pike's *Journal*.)

Newington, praying that as the *township* of Newington was a small neck of land made out of Dover and Portsmouth, with no distinct line between it and the latter town, a line might be run from the south side of Mr. Thomas Pickering's farm, fronting on the Bay, down to Joseph Dennet's farm, then in possession of Henry Bennet, and thence in a direct line to the main river. (*N. H. Prov. Pap.*, 17 : 737.)

Newington seems never to have been formally incorporated as a town. For years it was indiscriminately called a parish and a township. The "*town of Newington,*" the "*town-meeting* held in *sd town*" Jan. 21, 1744, and the "*Town Clerk of Newington,*" are all mentioned in the Journal of the House of Assembly Jan. 25, 1744, (*N. H. Prov. Pap.*, 5 : 267.) John Fabyan was chosen to represent the "*Town or Parish of sd Newington*" in 1745. (*Ibid*, 5 : 288.) In a petition of Sept. 17, 1755, it is called "the *Township* of Newington." In another of Dec. 13, 1763, it is called "the *Parish* of Newington." (*N. H. Town Pap.*, 12 : 721.) But it seems to have been fully recognized as a township from the time of the Revolution.

NEWINGTON GARRISONS. There were at least five garrisons on the Newington shore.

I. DAM'S GARRISON, otherwise DAME'S, is mentioned Sept. 26, 1696, when Sergeant John Dam was summoned to appear before Gov. Usher for dismissing sundry soldiers posted at his garrison. Their dismissal was perhaps owing to a lack of provisions, of which Sergeant Dam had previously complained in a letter dated "Welch Cove, July 27, 1696." (*N. H. Prov. Pap.*, 2 : 194–200.) His garrison is again mentioned in 1797, when one soldier was stationed there. John Dam petitioned for relief to his garrison Ap. 7, 1698. This garrison stood near Dame's Point, but the precise spot is not known.

II. The DOWNING GARRISON was on Fox Point. It was probably built by Nicholas Harrison, who, in his will of March 5, 1707, gives his son-in-law John Downing and wife Elizabeth, "as his eldest daughter," all his housing, orchards, and lands, at ffox pointe, given him by his father-in-law John Bickford (see *Fox Point*) ; also half of his lands in New Jersey. John Downing, who married Elizabeth Harrison, died Sept. 16, 1744, aged 85. His will of Feb. 23, 1743, proved Sept. 26, 1744, mentions his wife Elizabeth. He is called "Esquire" in the letters of administration. His son was the Hon. John Downing, generally called "Col. Downing," who was a man of wealth and political influence. He was a member of the Provincial Council of N. H. under the administration of Gov. Benning Wentworth, from 1742 to 1763. He was an extensive landowner in Newington, Portsmouth, Rochester, and Nottingham, besides owning 300 acres in Arundell, Maine, bequeathed him by his father. At his death he gave land for a schoolhouse in Newington, and 500 pounds "put at interest" for the maintenance of a teacher. His will, dated September 5, 1755, was admitted to probate March 12, 1766. In it he mentions his son John as "deceased." The latter died about 1750, in which year, Nov. 28, letters of administration were granted his widow Patience. Mr. Brewster, in his notes to the "Atkinson Silver Waiter" (see *Rambles about Portsmouth*, Vol. II) wrongly supposes John Downing, 3d, husband of Patience, to have been the Councillor and the same John who died in 1744. Mary, daughter of Col. John Downing, the Councillor, married Thomas Pickering Feb. 7, 1727. They were the great-great-grandparents of the present writer.

The Downing land at Fox Point was still in possession of the family, at least in part, Nov. 12, 1793, when Richard Downing conveyed one acre of it to the proprietors of Pascataqua bridge. The garrison was no doubt then occupied by his son Bartholomew, who, at that time, was living on the Fox Point farm. (See *Fox Point*.) It was built of logs, with four large rooms, each said to have been occupied by a family at one period. It was attacked more than once by the Indians, who, on one occasion, set fire to it, traces of which could still be seen when it was taken down about fifty years ago by Col. Isaac Frink, who had acquired it.

III. FURBER'S GARRISON. This garrison stood near Furber's Pt., and must have been built before 1689, in which year Wm. Furber was appointed "Ensign" by the Mass. government. He was promoted to to be "Lieutenant" Sept. 20, 1692.

Lieut. Wm. Furber speaks of his garrison at Welch Cove, July 27, 1696. He was tried by a court-martial that year for dismissing his soldiers (perhaps for lack of supplies), and not only fined for that and other offences, but forbidden to hold office.

He was, however, a representative to the General Assembly in 1703 and 1704, and in 1707 he was one of the men appointed to run the boundaries of the five townships of the province. The Rev. John Pike, in his journal, records the death of "Lt. William Furber of Welch Cove," Sept. 14, 1707. He was an ancestor of the present writer, through her great-grandmother Deborah Furber, who married John Gee Pickering of Newington.

IV. LANGSTAFFE'S GARRISON. This garrison is mentioned by Major Pike as attacked in 1789. It stood on Bloody Point itself, which seems to have verified its name if credit is to be given to a tradition that many people lie buried here who were massacred by the Indians. It was built by Henry Langstaffe or Langstar, who was one of the colonists sent over by Capt. John Mason in 1631. The Rev. John Pike, in his *Journal*, records the death of Henry Langstar at Bloody Point, July 18, 1705, at the age of about 100 years, "from a fall down four steps into his Lean-to." The Langstar homestead is mentioned Nov. 23, 1716, when Henry Langstar of Piscataqua, New Jersey, attorney of his father John Langstar, conveyed to John Shackford *one half of the homestead at Bloody Point*, on the west side of the Piscataqua river—then in possession of Henry Langstar, son of Henry Langstar, deceased—bounded south by Capt. John Knight's land, formerly Benjn Bickford's, west by ye highway leading to ye ferry, and so bounded upon ye land formerly George Braun's down to ye river, thence upon ye river to said Knight's, where we first began.

Benjamin Bickford's land was at the upper side of Pine Pt., adjoining Geo. Braun's.

V. NUTTER'S GARRISON. This garrison stood near Welsh Cove, on land now owned by the heirs of Col. Isaac Frink, whose mother was a Nutter. It was no doubt built by Anthony Nutter (son of Hatevil of Dover), who is mentioned in 1663 as a "planter at Welshman's cove." He is noted for aiding and abetting Thomas Wiggin, of Squamscot, in his assault upon Deputy-Governor Barefoot in 1685, on which occasion he is described as "a tall, big man, walking around the room in a laughing manner." (See *N. H. Prov. Pap.*, I : 578-9.) He married Sarah, daughter of Henry Langstaffe. Pike's Journal says, Feb. 19, 1685-6 : "Lt. Anthony Nutter of Welch Cove deceased of the smal-pox bef : it came out."

NEWMARKET. The north part of Exeter was made a parish under the name of Newmarket, Dec. 15, 1727, but it did not have a grant of town privileges till Aug. 19, 1737. (*N. H. Prov. Pap.*, IV : 739.) It was still called a "parish" in 1745, when Capt. Israel Gilman was chosen representative (*Ibid*, V : 339), and seems never to have been formally chartered as a township. A part of ancient Dover now belongs to Newmarket.

NEWTOWN. This name has been given for more than two hundred years to a district in the upper part of Lee, between Wheelwright's pond and Madbury. The Dover records speak of a highway laid out in 1688 from the head of Beard's creek to *Newtown*. The name itself implies a settlement. That there was one here at an early day, doubtless first made for logging purposes, is confirmed by the mention of an orchard May 31, 1721, when 60 acres of land (half of a grant to Patrick Jemison the 17th, 10 mo., 1663), were laid out to Capt. Samuel Emerson about a mile and a half from Wheelwright's pond, down the river on both sides, beginning below *Newtown Orchard*, at a red oak on the south side of Oyster river by the river side. One bound was from a tree about ten rods on the north side of the river, extending to the *upper falls*. This land was conveyed to Capt. Emerson by John Webster and wife Bridget of Salisbury, Mass., Jan. 27, 1719-20. The other half of the Jemison or Jameson grant was conveyed to Nathaniel Randall by John and Bridget Webster Jan. 27, 1719-20, and laid out to him May 31, 1721, beginning at an oak on the south side of the mast path. This was, of course, the mast path from Madbury.

NEWTOWN MILL. A mill was erected at the uppermost falls in Oyster river at an early day—no doubt the mill Belknap mentions as burnt by the Indians in 1712, together with a large quantity of boards. It must have been rebuilt soon after. It is probably the mill referred to in the inventory of the estate of Robert Huckins of Oyster River, April 22, 1720, in which "half a quarter of the saw-mill at *Webster's falls*, so called," is mentioned. (See John and Bridget Webster's conveyance at Newtown mentioned above.) This mill, however, was generally known as the *Newtown mill* down to the beginning of the present century, when it took the name of *Layn's mill*, which it still bears. Nathaniel Lamos had 40 acres of land laid out to him May 19, 1729, " beginning on Oyster river, a littel above the mill called *New Town mill*." A highway "from *New Town mill* up into the woods" is mentioned Oct. 20, 1735, when 25 acres were laid out for Robert Huckins on the south side of this road " at a place called *Maple brook*." A highway was laid out from *Newtown sawmill* on the south side of Oyster river, June 9, 1738, extending to the road that leads from Little river. (*Durham Records*.)

Wm. Clay conveyed to his sons Samuel and Joseph, Oct. 23, 1742, " one full quarter part of a sawmill situated in Durham, upon ye stream or river called *Newtown River*, being ye uppermost mill standing upon ye s^d stream, and is next to ye pond called Wheelwright's Pond, out of which s^d stream issues," with a quarter part of " ye running geer," dam, stream, and all privileges thereunto belonging. " Newtown river " is, of course, that part of Oyster river which flows through Newtown. Wm. Clay, " cordwainer," and Samuel Clay, husbandman, conveyed to Daniel Rodgers and Benjamin Mathes, July 20, 1754, 80 acres of land at or near *New Town Saw Mill* in the town of Durham, beginning at the S. E. corner of said Clay's land, next Eli Clark's, thence running by the highway to said saw-mill, and over the freshet by s^d highway to the end of Clay's fence, thence northerly to the land of widow Joanna Snell and John Jonknes (Jones?), then easterly by the highway to the first bound, with all buildings, orchards, etc. Edward Leathers, Jr., of Durham, conveyed to David Munsey, Sept. 12, 1761, one sixteenth part of *Newtown sawmill*, so called, in said Durham, also one sixteenth of the falls and privileges belonging to said mill, and a sixteenth part of all the iron work in partnership belonging thereto. Edward Leathers conveyed to John Leathers, March 5, 1790, forty acres of land in Lee, beginning at the S. W. corner of John Snell's land, and running on the road that leads to *Newtown sawmill* until it comes to *Clarke's yard*, so called, etc., excepting however the land lately sold his daughter Hannah (afterwards the wife of Lemuel Chesley.) Also a sixth part of *Newtown sawmill* and *gristmill*, so called, in said Lee, together with one sixth part of the dam and privilege of said mill. Edward Leathers, Ap. 7, 1801, conveyed to David Monsey one sixteenth part of a sawmill in Lee, known by the name of *Newtown sawmill*.

The first time the writer finds the Newtown mill called *Layn's mill* is on the State map of Lee in 1803, where mention is made of " *Layn's mill road*." This name was derived from Capt. John Layn, who was in Durham as early as March 8, 1760, when he enlisted in Capt. Samuel Gerrish's company, Col. John Goffe's regiment, for the Canada expedition. " John Layn of Durham, gunsmith," in a petition of May 26, 1761, states that he was employed as armorer for that regiment, and furnished his own tools, but had received no extra pay for this service. He was allowed 4 £ sterling. (*N. H. Town Pap.*, XI: 581–2.) He was appointed captain in Col. John Waldron's regiment, March 6, 1776, for six weeks service at Winter Hill. He acquired land at Newtown in 1763, and again June 9, 1766, when Thomas Leathers conveyed to him ten acres of land where said Thomas then lived, at the corner of the roads that led to Durham falls, Madbury, and Newtown. He established an inn in this vicinity, probably the first in Newtown. The old sign-board, bearing the name of WASHINGTON and the date of "1779," is still to be seen, but the painting of Washington on horseback, once emblazoned thereon, has been entirely effaced by the elements. John Layn calls himself "of Lee" in 1790, but in 1804 was living in Barrington, where he had acquired several tracts of land—among others, 42 acres at *Bumfaggin*, and lots No. 40, and No. 41, in the *half-mile range* near Bow Pond, in that part of Barrington now Strafford, consisting of 100 acres each, which he bought of Daniel Brewster and Isaiah Swain. There he had a saw-mill and probably lived. At that time he owned the whole of the grist-mill at Newtown, but only a four-days right in the saw-mill, both of which he conveyed, July 17, 1804, to Paul Giles, who re-conveyed them to Layn Nov. 22, 1805. These mills were then no doubt operated by his son Edmund. Capt. John Layn died before May 22, 1811, when his son John was appointed administrator of his estate. The inventory, made June 18, 1811, mentions his gristmill and privilege, and the old grist-mill frame, but not the saw-mill. They were acquired by his son Edmund, who continued to run them till his death, at the age of 76 years, Aug. 27, 1843. There is now a saw and shingle-mill here, owned by Mr. Samuel W. Layn, grandson of the above Edmund. In this vicinity is Layn's school-house, on the turnpike-road, once noted, not for its schools, but as a place for popular prayer-meetings.

NEWTOWN PLAINS. Mentioned in the Durham records, March 9, 1764, when the selectmen of Durham, at the request of Joseph Atkinson, Esq., laid out " a public highway at a place called *New Town Plains* in said Durham," beginning at the highway that leads up to Barrington, and running south 10 rods to Wm. Jackson's S. W. corner, and along his land to Joseph Atkinson's. And again Ap. 16, 1764, when, by virtue of a vote of the proprietors of Durham, 14 acres were laid out to John Layn, blacksmith, " at a place called *Newtown Plains*, beginning at the highway, at the S. W. corner of a piece of land usually called Odiorne's field," and extending on one side to the northwest part of a *heath*. These plains, called "Newtown plains" to this day, comprise a sandy, barren, monotonous region in the upper part of Newtown.

NIGGER POINT. This point is on the southern shore of Oyster river, in Durham. It formed part of the old Burnham land, but is now owned by Mr. Wm. P. Ffrost. Here lived the Barhews, a negro family of last century, owned by Deacon Jeremiah Burnham. The parents were kidnapped in Africa and brought to this country, where they received the names of Belmont and Venus. Their union seems to have been duly legalized, for among the records of the Rev. John Adams of Durham is the marriage of "Belmont and Venus,"

Jan. 1, 1760. No surname is mentioned. They had seven children, five of whom were boys, viz :—Ænon, Cæsar, Jubal, Titus, and Peter or Pete. ÆNON, when only four years of age, was bought by Col. Timothy Emerson of Durham. He became free after the Revolution, but continued to live with his master, to the great enjoyment of Col. Emerson's descendants to the fourth generation, by whom he was always held in affectionate remembrance. He died at an advanced age, and lies buried with other Emerson slaves, in an old orchard on the north side of Brown's Hill. Their graves have always been respected by the family. CÆSAR became the property of Vowel Leathers of Nottingham. He is spoken of as " a good Christian," and was noted for singing hymns and spiritual songs with great unction, which made him an acquisition at prayer-meetings. He acquired $500, after his freedom, and ended his days with his old master's daughter in Newmarket. TITUS was bought by Col. James Gilmore, who lived below Bunker's creek, in Durham. JUBAL, generally called Jube, was acquired by Capt. Smith Emerson of Durham, an able officer of the Revolutionary army. When a boy he was generally punished for his misdeeds by being placed in the fork of a large elm before the house, which, in consequence, became known as *Jube's elm*. This house stood on Mast road, near the Lee boundary, and when burned down many years ago, Jube's elm was destroyed. PETER was the youngest, and remained in the possession of Deacon Burnham. He was of a cross grain, and required much skill in management. His sleeping-place, still called *Pete's hole,* is to be seen in the old Burnham mansion, now in ruins. The Rev. Mr. Coe, in Nov., 1783, records the burial of " Venus, a negro servant of J. Burnham, Jr." She was the mother of this interesting family. Several of the Barhews were buried near " Nigger Point." Their graves were always respected by the Burnhams, but have since disappeared under the ploughshare.

NIMBLE HILL. Mentioned in the Dover records March 13, 1703-4, when ten acres, granted to Zachariah Trickey in 1675, were laid out to him at *Nimble Hill,* west of John Downing's land, on the north side of the highway from Bloody Point to Greenland. John Downing bought this land March 20, 1703-4, when *Nimble Hill* is again mentioned. The name is still retained. Nimble Hill is in the northern part of Newington and crossed by the highway near the old Adams mansion, now owned by Mr. Knox. (See *Stony Hill.*)

NO-BOTTOM POND. This name is given to a little pond in Dover, above Garrison Hill, said to be fathomless. It is in the Taylor-Page pasture, in the rear of the farm buildings, whence it is sometimes called *Page's pond.* It is on the Dover map of 1805, but without any name. This is, in fact, a spruce hole, the pool being in the depths of a hollow, surrounded by a bed of thick, soft moss, where grow the side-saddle flower and other bog-loving plants, and the sides of hollow bordered with spruce and other trees, weather-beaten and in every stage of crookedness. This black pool of ominous aspect, with its name akin to the Bottomless Pit, the quaking bog around it, and dreary looking trees, distorted as if with pain, and the small, swift streamlet which issues therefrom, called the *Styx*, are all suggestive of baleful things. This pond has diminished in size, the bushes having constantly advanced on its borders. It feeds another pool much smaller, at a short distance, called *Little pond* or *Egg pond*. The Styx flows through the Page pasture and the Dennis land, and before the draining of the neighboring marshes was large enough to require a string-piece at the crossing.

NOCK'S MARSH. This is a well-known marsh on the west side of Dover, crossed by the so-called *Nock's Marsh road* from Dover to Madbury. It is mentioned in the second Thomas Nock's will of Feb. 15, 1676, in which he gives his brother Sylvanus a tract of land between Cochecho and *Nock's Marsh*, next Thomas Beard's land. And again May 8, 1716, when Eliphalet Coffin conveyed to Mark Giles ten acres " on the northwest side of ye path y^t leads (from Cochecho) to *Nock's Marsh*." Ebenezer Hanson, Sept. 19, 1768, conveyed to Otis Baker his homestead farm of 62½ acres, at or near a place called *Nock's Marsh*, bounded east by his brother Solomon Hanson's land, south by Bellamy river, northerly by Mark Giles' land, etc., being part of his father Thomas Hanson's estate.

The " old road from Littleworth to *Nock's Marsh* " is mentioned in the Dover records of Ap. 11, 1804.

The name of Nock's marsh (sometimes incorrectly written *Knox*) is derived from Thomas Nock, who was in possession of 30 acres adjoining *Log swamp* the 1st, 10 mo., 1656, and subsequently had several grants of land adjoining. Henry Nock, Feb. 18, 1718–19, conveyed to John Hanson and Thomas Hanson, Jr., 100 acres " to ye southward of Capt. Waldron's Logg Swamp, bordering on ye S. E. side partly on Thomas Beard's 100 acres, on the S. W. by the Back river, on the N. W. by Wm. Thompson's land, and N. E. by the commons." Also a tract adjoining the above, next Thomas Beard's lot, reserving 20 acres, all of which land was granted, says the deed, to his father Thomas Nock, deceased.

NORTHAM. This name was given to Dover in 1640, out of compliment, it is said, to the Rev. Thomas Larkham, of Northam, Eng., at that time the minister at Dover Neck. But the name of Dover was speedily resumed after his departure in 1642, doubtless because he left with a tarnished reputation. (See *N. H. Prov. Pap.*, 1 : 124.) It was called Northam as late as Sept. 14, 1642. (See *Royall's Cove*.) Northam, Eng., is in Devonshire, not far from Bideford, near the junction of the Torridge and the Taw, a region of which Kingsley gives pleasant glimpses in his " Westward Ho!" These two towns are so near together, he says, that the bells rung out from the tower of Northam church are answered by those of Bideford. Several of the early settlers in New Hampshire were from that region. Edmond Pickard, one of the chief proprietors at the Shoals in 1661, describes himself in a deed as " of Northam, near Biddeford, in Devon, in Old England." The name of Appledore, at the Shoals, was derived from a hamlet of that name in the parish of Northam, Eng. Mr. J. S. Jenness says when he was at Northam and Appledore in 1874, he was struck by the number of surnames like those of the early settlers at the Shoals. (Jenness' *Isles of Shoals*, p. 101.)

NORTH RIVER. This tributary to Lamprey river rises in North River pond, on the borders of Northwood and Nottingham. At the head of this stream once lived a small tribe of Indians, who, after the fall of Louisbourg, became troublesome to the neighboring settlers for many years.[1] North river is frequently mentioned in the early records of Durham. The third division of the common lands, ordered March 18, 1733–4, embraced the lands at North river, now South Lee. Of the lots thus assigned to the proprietors of Durham, a dozen or more were acquired by Solomon Emerson, and over twenty by Joseph Sias. (See *County Records* at Exeter, Vol. 79, etc.) Capt. Samuel Emerson had a grant of 42½ acres, laid out Nov. 5, 1750, on the south side of *North river*, "beginning at the river on the dividing line between Durham and Nottingham." "P^d the committee for laying out a highway from *North River* to little River—£38, 5s." (*Durham Records*, 1763.)

North River Falls are mentioned in the Durham records March 15, 1754, when Ichabod Chesley's grant of 25 acres was laid out "on the south side of Little River, and on the north side of a High Way that leadeth to the *North River falls*," beginning at an asp tree marked E. D., it being Ephraim Davis's S. W. corner bound.

These falls are at the bend in North river, in the southwest corner of Lee. They are sometimes called *Great falls*. Over nine acres, part of a 25 acre grant to Edward Wakeham, deceased, were laid out to Samuel Smith, June 13, 1753, beginning at a hemlock tree, " standing three rods above the Pitch of the *North River Great falls*, so called, in Durham." *Great Falls bridge* is mentioned in the Lee records of 1789. These falls are called " Long Falls " on the State map of Lee in 1803. Harvey's shingle-mill is now in operation here.

NORWAY PLAINS. This name was given at an early day to the large sandy plain on which the city of Rochester now stands;—derived, it is said, from the Norway pines that once covered it. A James Norroway, however, is mentioned in Dover in 1696, and many old people in Rochester at the present day call this tract "*Norroway Plains*." This form of the name is often found in the old-world legends and songs about the " ancient rock-bound Norroway " of northern Europe.

Norway Plains Mills are mentioned in Col. John Downing's will of Sept. 5, 1755. Jonathan Downing of Rochester conveyed to Richard Downing of Newington, May 6, 1774, 100 acres " at the upper part of the Long lot, so called, against *Norway*

---

[1] The writer remembers hearing her maternal grandmother, who was born in Nottingham in 1756, relate how in her childhood she had been forced to take refuge eight times in a garrison —doubtless Longfellow's—on account of these Indians or their allies. Only a few years previous (in 1747) several people of that vicinity had been slain, among them Mrs. Elizabeth Simpson, who was shot by the Indians as she stood near a window kneading dough for the oven.

Plains in Rochester, given him by his honored grandfather John Downing, Esq., of Newington, in his last will and testament." A petition that the court of Strafford Co., then held at Dover and Durham, might be moved to *Norway Plain* in Rochester, is mentioned June 4, 1789. (*N. H. State Pap.*, 12: 11-12.) " *Norway Plains village* in Rochester " is mentioned in the *N. H. Republican* of Dover, March 25, 1828. This was, of course, the present city of Rochester.

NUTE'S CORNER. This corner is in Freetown, Madbury, between the old Province road to Barrington and the road to the Hook mill. So named from Andrew Nute, who was licensed to keep a tavern here April 14, 1804.

NUTE'S CREEK. A creek of this name on the west side of Back river is mentioned Sept. 16, 1702, when 40 acres of land, granted to John Dam in 1656, were laid out to his son, beginning at a white oak on the line between this land and that of Joseph Tibbets. A highway is mentioned between Dam's land and that of James Newt, which led to a landing-place at the head of *James Newt's Creek*. This creek is above Hopehood's Point. Joseph Tibbets' land is now owned in part by Mr. Peasley. Nute's land here is mentioned Ap. 5, 1710, when Wm. Story's lot on the west side of Back river (lot No. 8) was conveyed by his sons, Joseph of Wells and Jeremiah of Boston, to Samuel Cromwell, bounded S. by Capt. John Tuttle's land, north by James Nute's, and west by Capt. Philip Cromwell's.

NUTE'S POINT. A point of this name is mentioned on Whitehouse's map, on the east side of Dover Neck, half a mile below Morrill's Ferry. The Nute point of the present day is at the lower side of Little John's creek.

NUTTER'S HILL. This name is given to the hill on Dover Neck where stood the old fortified meeting-house. So called from Elder Hatevil Nutter, whose house was on the east side of the main road to Dover Point, about fifteen rods from the N. E. corner of the meeting-house, in a northeasterly direction. The cellar can still be traced. This hill is mentioned Dec. 5, 1652, when Richard Waldron, in consideration of certain grants, bound himself " to erect a meeting-house upon *the hill near Elder Nutter's.*"

NUTTER'S ISLANDS. These are two small islands at the mouth of the brook which empties into Laighton's cove, in Newington. The largest is mentioned June 25, 1664, when Anthony Nutter conveyed to Thomas Roberts a piece of marsh in Harrod's Cove, bounded by a small trench straight down to the middle of *a small island*. It is singular that after more than two hundred years this islet should still have two owners, one half being now owned by Mr. Frink, and the other by Mrs. Coffin of Pittsburg, Pa., a descendant of the Nutters.

Limmy's Ledge, an islet on the Durham shore of Great Bay, is called *Nutter's island* on Smith's map of 1805.

NUTTER'S LANE. This lane ran from Nutter's Hill, along the upper side of Richard Yorke's lot, to Nutter's Slip. It is mentioned May 4, 1706, when Richard Pinkham conveyed to Nicholas Harford seven acres of land on Dover Neck, bounded N. by *Nutter's Lane*, E. by *high street*, S. by Thomas Tibbets' land, and W. by *low street*. And again May 19, 1708, when Philip "Cromell," in his will, gives his son Samuel "Cromwell" a lot between Wm. Hereford's land and the lane formerly called *Nutter's lane*, on the north side of the meeting-house.

NUTTER'S SLIP is mentioned June 26, 1716, when John Hall conveyed to Thomas Kenny one share in the calves pasture, lying between yᵉ lane running from yᵉ low street to *Nutter's Slip* and *Pinkham's spring*, bounded by Back river on the west, and low street on the east, with all the privileges thereunto belonging, as granted by the town to his grandfather John Hall. This slip was, of course, on the eastern shore of Back river.

OAK SWAMP. Mentioned Ap. 30, 1735, when four acres were laid out to Lieut. John Ham "at a place called the *oak swamp*, beginning at a birch tree on the S. W. side of the road that leads to the Ealware," one corner joining said Ham's other land. Nov. 23, 1735, ten acres were laid out to Isaac Watson "at or near a place called *oak swamp*, joining to the N. E. corner of *John Ham's marsh*." Four acres were laid out to Timothy Hanson, March 30, 1739, at a place "formerly called *oak swamp*." (See *Ham's Marsh*.)

OLD BOWSPRIT, otherwise OLD BOLD SPIT. Mentioned Dec. 22, 1720, when Tobias Hanson's sixty acre grant was laid out "between *fagote bridg* and the *old bold spit*," on the east side of Wm. Pomfrett's grant. And again June 25, 1739, when a road was ordered to be laid out from John Heard's to the Rochester line, running near the *old Bowsprit*, as the way now goes. This name has not been retained, and its derivation is uncertain. It may refer to one of the tracts of woodland reserved in former times for *bowsprits* and other shipping purposes. (See *N. H. Prov. Pap.*, 18 : 143.)

OLD BRIGG. Mentioned Aug. 29, 1740, when James Hall of Somersworth conveyed to Thomas Hodsdon of Berwick, York Co., province of Mass. Bay, all right, title, and interest in the saw-mill at Quamphegan fall, commonly called *ye old Brigg* (which part was three days in each month of the year), purchased by him of his father John Hall. The origin of this name does not appear. It may have been derived from the old bridge or boom at the Quamphegan mill. Brig or brigg is the Scotch form of *bridge*. The "auld brigg of Ayr" is sung by Burns, and the ballad of Gil Morice has the lines :

"And when he came to broken briggs,
He slacked his bow and swam."

OTIS' BRIDGE. Mentioned Ap. 15, 1702, when Edward Cloutman's grant of thirty acres was laid out "between *holmes bridg* and *Otises bridg*, beginning at a red oke upon a poynt between two gullies." One bound was the road to Salmon falls. Joseph Twombley, Jr., conveyed to Gershom Wentworth, Aug. 5, 1719, 60 acres in Dover, "near a place call'ᵈ *Otises bridge*," being one half of six score acres granted Ralph Twombley, not yet divided. (See *Twombley's Brook*.) Samuel Randle conveyed to Benjⁿ Roberts, Jr., March 12, 1734, 30 acres of land in the parish of Somersworth, beginning at a pitch pine by Thomas Nock's, and running southwesterly 50 rods to *Otis his bridge*. This bridge was across the " Fresh creek brook," now called Rollins' brook. The name is no longer in use. (See *Holmes' Bridge*.)

OTIS' HILL. Mentioned in Job Clement's will, Oct. 8, 1716, in which he gives his daughter Margaret three score acres of land which his father bought of Thomas Pain, " lying on ye back side of *Otis his hill* in Cochecho woods." When Thomas Payne sold Job Clement (Sr.) the above tract of land, the 29th, 4 mo., 1665, it was stated to be " at the northern end of Richard Otis his hundred acres, northeast from Cochecho marsh."

Farmer and Moore's Gazeteer of N. H. (1823) speaks of *Otis hill* as the highest in Somersworth, about a mile above Garrison Hill. It is also mentioned in *Hayward's New England Gazeteer* of 1839. It is otherwise called *Ricker's Hill*, from the former proprietors. It is now owned for the most part by the Rollins family, and is sometimes called *Capt. Ichabod's hill*, or *Capt. Ich's hill*, from Ichabod Rollins, who first acquired a part of it Jan. 14, 1771, when Levi Ricker and his sister Judith conveyed to said Ichabod all right and title to the homestead of their honored father, George Ricker, Jr., deceased, who, it is stated in the deed, lived at *Otis' Hill*, so called. Mrs. Baer, in one of her pleasing sketches, speaks of the " pine-clad side of *Capt. Ich's hill*," its clumps of savin with their agreeable odor, and the broad-spreading oaks on the summit. This hill is also sometimes called *Crummit's hill*, otherwise *Cromwell's*. The Cromwell lands in this vicinity are mentioned in 1733, when, in a deed from James Guppy to Thomas Downs, " the brook y^t runs out of Cromwell's land into Fresh creek," is spoken of.

OYSTER POINT. This name is given to the point of land between Oyster river and the upper side of Bunker's creek, Oct. 10, 1653, in a grant to Wm. Follet and James Bunker. (See *Bunker's Neck*.) Another *Oyster Point*, mentioned on Smith's map of Durham, is on the opposite shore of Oyster river, at the lower side of Stevenson's creek, now Mathes's creek. At these two points were the old *Oyster Beds*, from which Oyster river derived its name. The upper *Oyster bed* is mentioned Nov. 18, 1727, when Wm. and Mary Clay conveyed to Samuel Smith a tract of land previously Joshua Davis's, " on the N. W. side of the high way that leads to ye Oister bed, and so by ye way by Nathaniel Lomaxes,[1] and joining to Joseph Jenkins his hundred acre Lott y^t was formerly Wm. Storey's, and so by s^d lot to Amos Pinkham's land." In the deed of this Pinkham land (7 acres) from Joshua Davis to said Amos, Oct. 3, 1720, the above road is spoken of as " leading from James Bunker's into ye main road that goes to Cochecho, being part of the land that was James Bunker's, deceased." (See *Oyster River*.)

OYSTER RIVER. This river, so called as early as Ap. 3, 1638, (see *N. H. Prov. Pap.*, 1 : 135) rises at

---

[1] This name, generally called Lummocks or Lumax in early times, is now written Lamos.

Wheelwright's pond in Lee, and empties into the Pascataqua river at the mouth of Little Bay.

Some old records make a distinction between *Oyster river* and "*Oyster river freshet*,"—the former being the tidal stream that comes to a head at the lowest falls in Durham village; and the latter the fresh-water stream above these falls to its source. "The landing-place at the head of *Oyster river*" is spoken of in the Dover records of May 17, 1703, meaning at the head of tide water. The name of this river was derived from the oyster beds found by the early pioneers towards the mouth. These beds are often mentioned in the old records. One is on the upper side of the river, at the mouth of Bunker's creek, mentioned Ap. 9, 1703, when a road was laid out, "beginning at the *wading-place* at the *oyster bed*," and running along the west side of Follet's rocky hill to the head of Bunker's creek. " The parsonage lott near the *Oyster Bed*, where the old meeting-house formerly stood," is mentioned in the Durham records March 20, 1762. This bed is on the lower side of the river. (See *Oyster Point*.)

"The *neighborhood of Oyster River*" is mentioned the 3d, 12 mo., 1640, implying that a settlement had been made here some time previous. (*N. H. Prov. Pap.*, 1 : 141.) Strictly speaking, this settlement formed part of Dover, but it was a distinct one, and had a separate history from the first. In the old records, and in the early history of New Hampshire, it is generally spoken of as "*Oyster River*," which name it bore for nearly a hundred years. It is called "*Oyster River plantation*" in 1651, when George Smythe, administrator of George Webb's estate, conveyed to Oliver Kent " an acre and a half of land in *Oyster river plantation*, heretofore in possession of said George Web." It is sometimes called the "*Precinct of Oyster River*," as in a remonstrance against its incorporation as a town, addressed to Gov. Burnet May 14, 1729. The dividing line between this precinct and Dover proper was, as stated Dec. 21, 1657, a straight line from the first rocky point below the mouth of Oyster river, on the north side, to the path at the head of Thomas Johnson's creek, and thence to the end of the town.

Oyster River settlement was made a separate parish May 4, 1716, and was incorporated as a township, under the name of Durham, by an act of the General Assembly, passed May 13, 1732; and signed by Gov. Belcher two days later. These dates are from the copy of the Charter in the Durham records. But according to the Journal of the House (*N. H. Prov. Pap.*, 4 : 784), the vote for making Oyster River a town passed the House May 11, 1732, and "his Excellency was pleased to give his consent" thereto, May 12. The bill was still further sanctioned by the Governor and Council, May 15, following.

OYSTER RIVER BANKS. Descending Oyster river from the bridge at the foot of Durham falls, are the half-ruined wharves on both shores, where many vessels were built and launched in more enterprising days. At the right, immediately above the first wharf, rises the steep hill where stood the meeting-house, built in 1716, beneath which the gunpowder from Fort William and Mary was for a time stored in 1774. Just below is Gen. Sullivan's house, its terraced garden extending to the very shore. Farther down is a small creek; then comes the *Sea Wall*, built a century or more ago to protect the bank from the encroaching tide. Near it is another creek, no doubt the upper bound of the Ambrose Gibbons grant, laid out to Robert Burnham in 1661. Below is *Nigger Point*, then comes *Burnham's Point*, with *Parson Buss's Pulpit* at the lower side. *Well cove* is on the upper side. A short distance farther down is *Burnham's creek*, into which empties *Cutt's brook*, otherwise *Sandy brook*. Then come the Burnham Oaks and the *Old Woman's Sliding-Place*, where the bank, generally steep, slopes down eighteen or twenty feet to the river, and is always bare. Here, in the river, is the *Roundabout*, well known to boatmen. There is no bend in the river itself, like the Roundabout in the Squamscot,[1] but the name is given to a deep groove or furrow in the very bed of the river, which, off the Burnham Oaks, sweeps around towards *Ledge wharf* on the opposite shore, forming a deep curve, and then returns toward the lower bank. Below the Oaks are two small creeks. Then comes *Mathes's creek*, formerly *Stevenson's*, with *Oyster Point* on the lower side. Here is one of the *oyster beds*, from which the river derives its name. In early times there was a ford across Oyster river at this place, easily traversed at low tide by people on horseback, then the usual mode of travelling. This ford is mentioned in 1703 as the "*Wading-Place.*" A path or road led to the main thoroughfare across Long marsh to Exeter, and from the opposite side towards Dover.

Two sharp rocks lie off this shore, avoided by boatmen. Farther down is *Drew's Point*, where the Durham packet to Portsmouth used to stop for passengers. At the lower side is another small inlet, formerly called *Wakeham's creek*. *Jonas' Point* is below, at the mouth of the river. It is a subdivision of *Durham Point*, which name, in a general sense, is given to the whole neck of land between Little Bay and the lower part of Oyster river.

Returning to the upper shore, the first inlet below Durham falls is *Beard's creek*, with *Butler's Point* on the upper side. Farther down is *Ledge wharf* and two or three little creeks not named. Some distance below is *Jones's creek*, otherwise *Johnson's*. The next inlet is *Bunker's creek*. Here is the upper *oyster bed*, and the upper end of the old ford, whence a road was laid out towards Dover at an early day. *Gilmore's Point* is not far below,—so named from James Gilmore, who lived in Durham at the Revolutionary period. At the mouth of a creek farther down, between the old Smith and Davis lands, is *Barnes' Island*, otherwise *Bodge's*. Passing another small creek called *Davis's creek*, you come, at the mouth of the river, to *Half-Tide Rock*, so called from its being covered when the tide is half

---

[1] The beautiful *Roundabout* in the Squamscot river, winding through a verdant meadow, is in full sight of the Boston and Maine R. R., between Exeter and South Newmarket, at the east

way up. Below is another rock, called by the boatmen "*Half-Tide, Junior.*"

OYSTER RIVER FALLS. The *first* falls in Oyster river below its source are at Layn's mills in Lee, where a sawmill seems to have been erected before 1712. (See *Newtown Mill.*)

The *second* falls are also in Newtown, between the present residences of Mr. H. B. Snell and Mr. C. H. Jones. A *grist-mill* was built here in the middle of the last century, called the *Snell mill*, from Thomas Snell, to whose wife "Johannah" was conveyed, June 27, 1737, by her parents, James and Elizabeth Pinkham, one half of a grant of 35 acres, " laid out on both sides of ye freshet of Oyster river, near Wm. Clay's land."

Below was another dam for a brief period, where stood a mill on Solomon Emerson's land, now owned by Mr. James.

The next falls are on the borders of Lee, near Madbury. They are called *Dishwater Falls* — not from any turbidness of the stream, but from the scarcity of water at certain seasons of the year; about enough for domestic purposes, in fact. A mill here is mentioned March 10, 1777, when Zachariah Edgerly conveyed to John Demerit "one sixteenth part of a saw-mill in Lee, known by the name of *Dishwater mill.*" This seems to be the "*Emerson mill*" mentioned on the State map of Lee in 1803. Capt. Smith Emerson, Solomon Emerson, Moses Emerson, John Demerit, John Demerit, Jr., Isaac Chesley, and Simon Randall, by an indenture of Feb. 3, 1801, agreed to provide their share of timber and rebuild the saw-mill in Lee,

"where the old mill now stands, known by the name of *Dishwater mill.*" It is called the "*Demeritt mill,*" Ap. 23, 1839, from the chief owners at that time. This mill is still standing, and now belongs to the heirs of the late Hopley Demeritt.

Below the Mast road, in Durham, the remains of a dam may be seen, where a mill once stood, on land originally granted to Henry Marsh, and conveyed by his children, Hezekiah and Dinah, to Jonathan Thompson, Feb. 7, 1737-8. This mill-site is now owned by Mr. Frank Bunker. On the opposite side of the river is the land of Moses Davis, who was slain by the Indians in this vicinity in 1724.

A little farther down, in a wild, picturesque spot near Blacksnake hill, are the best natural falls in the river, but too narrowly enclosed by hills to afford suitable mill facilities.

Near the Boston & Maine railway one comes to a series of little falls or rapids, extending nearly to Durham mill-pond, one of which was granted May 30, 1699, to Lieut. James Davis, Samuel and Philip Chesley, and Wm. Jackson, for erecting a saw-mill, at a rent of 50s. a year. This is spoken of as "*Chesley's mill*" as early as June 6, 1701, when a road was ordered to be laid out from the mast path to Chesley's mill on Oyster river, and over the freshet to the old way into the commons, and so on to Lamperel second falls. This is the well known "mill-road" to Packer's Falls, which, however, has greatly changed its course since first laid out, June 24, 1703. This mill was afterwards converted into a grist-mill, which fifty years ago was run by Elijah Willey. And for a time there was a fulling-mill here, operated by Mr. William J. Chesley. Towards the middle of this century this mill and the water privilege, owned by the Chesley family nearly 150 years, were acquired by Mr. McDaniel; and the grist-mill was, for a time, run by Stephen Kendall, from whom it was sometimes incorrectly called *Kendall's mill*. This mill is now gone, and the water privilege here is now owned by the Boston and Maine Railroad Co.

Below Chesley's mill, near the so-called "string-piece," a dam was built, and a mill erected by Joseph Hanson in the early part of this century. Both are now gone, and only a hollow in the bed of the stream is left to attest the power of the fall. This hollow is often called "the *Pool.*"

The lowest and chief falls in Oyster river are at the head of tide water in Durham village. They are often mentioned in the early records as "*Oyster river falls,*" or "*the falls,*" and at a later period as "*Durham falls.*"

Valentine Hill[1] and Thomas Beard had a grant of "*the fall of Oyster River*" the 19th, 9 mo., 1649. Mr. Hill built a sawmill here before the 14th, 5 mo., 1651, and the following year this water privilege was confirmed to him and his heirs. Nathaniel Hill, son of Valentine, formally renounced "all right to *Oyster river falls* and *freshet*" Sept. 13, 1697, and the mill privilege here was granted, March 25, 1699, to Capt. John Woodman, Lieut. Nathaniel Hill, and Ensign Stephen Jones, at a rent of £7 a year. Complaint having been made of this sum, and of the damage done by the mill above (Chesley's), the rent was reduced to £3 a year.

Nathaniel Hill of Oyster River parish, out of love and affection to his oldest son Valentine, conveyed to him, May 10, 1735, half of his share in y^e *saw-mill* and *grist-mill*, and half of his homestead and other lands not given his younger son Samuel, or otherwise disposed of, and the remaining half at the death of said Valentine's parents. Jonathan Woodman conveyed to his sons John and Jonathan, Jan. 10, 1749, all his interest in the *saw-mill* and *grist-mill* on *Oyster River freshet*, so called, in the town of Durham, with all privileges, etc. The grist-mill here is again mentioned June 27, 1752, when Shadrach Walton conveyed to Eliphalet Daniels a quarter of an acre of land "near the falls where ye old *grise mill* stood," bounded northerly by "Oyster river or freshet."

In the middle of this century the saw-mill and privilege on the west side of these falls were acquired by Mr. Samuel Randlett, who built the present saw-mill and grist-mill in 1860. At the other end of the dam is a machine shop, run by water power, belonging to the heirs of the late Ephraim Jenkins.

The name of *Oyster River Falls* was often given in former times to the village which began to spring up around these falls in the first part of the last century. This village is so

---

[1] In Hurd's History of Rockingham and Strafford Counties (1882) this name is incorrectly given as "Valentine Smith." The same mistake is made in Sanford & Evert's Atlas of Strafford County (1871). There were no Smiths at Oyster River in 1649.

called May 5, 1744, when Joseph Nutter (son of Henry Nutter of Newington) conveyed to Shadrach Walton a lot he purchased of "Volentine" Hill at "*a place called Oyster River Falls*, in the township of Durham." In the town records of 1747, mention is made of "the meeting-house at *Oyster River falls*," "the meeting-house at *Durham Falls*," and "*the Falls* meeting-house." The neighboring farmers to this day often speak of "*the Falls*," when they mean Durham village. (See *Falls Hill*.)

Nathaniel Hill conveyed to Wm. Odiorne, Esq.,[1] Aug. 9, 1745, half an acre lot in Durham, "lying at *a place there called the Falls*," beginning at a notch cut in the middle of a log "in the bottom of the fence by the country road by the way that the logs and other lumber is halled up from the *mill Pond*," thence running S. 64 deg. W. 5 rods, 3½ ft. to "a large rock standing in the edge of the Mill Pond," etc. (See *Durham Falls*.)

OYSTER RIVER GARRISONS. There appear to have been at least fourteen garrisons, or fortified houses, at Oyster River before 1694, though only thirteen have heretofore been mentioned.[2] Ten of these formed a line of defence along each side of the river itself, below the head of tidewater—that is, below the falls in the present village of Durham. On the north side stood the following, in the same succession:

I. The MEADER GARRISON. This garrison was at the very mouth of Oyster river, overlooking the Pascataqua. It was built by John Meader, who was taxed at Oyster River as early as 1656, and had a house here before Sept. 20, 1660, on which day Valentine Hill and Mary, his wife, conveyed to John Meader a corn-field and orchard adjacent to "his now dwelling-house." John Davis's land is spoken of as "on ye west." John Meader, Nov. 18, 1686, conveyed to his son Joseph his plantation near the mouth of Oyster river where he, the said John, then dwelt, which he bought of Mr. Valentine Hill, together with 20 acres adjoining, part of a four-score acre grant from the town of Dover, with the houses thereon, etc.

In the Indian attack of 1694, when the Oyster River settlement was nearly destroyed, it is stated that no house below Jones's creek was consumed except that of John Meader, whose family had been sent off by water, and the house abandoned—no doubt because insufficiently manned, or because ammunition was lacking, as was the case at several of the garrisons. John Meader was then about sixty-four years old, but he was still alive Jan. 30, 1712. If his garrison was destroyed on that occasion, defences must have been immediately set up, for one soldier was quartered at "John Meader's garrison" from July 18, 1694, till the 24th of Novem-

---

[1] Wm. Odiorne, son of Judge Jotham Odiorne, was a ship-builder and a commissioner for the preservation of forests in N. H. He married Avis, daughter of the Rev. Hugh Adams of Durham. Their daughter Hetty Odiorne became the wife of James Sullivan, governor of Massachusetts in 1807. (See *Durham Falls Bridge*.)

[2] Belknap, in his History of New Hampshire, mentions only twelve garrisons at Oyster River (Huckins's garrison had been destroyed in 1689) when this settlement was attacked by the Indians, July 18, 1694, on which occasion five garrisons and many other dwelling-houses were destroyed, and nearly a hundred persons killed or carried into captivity.

ber following. And other soldiers were stationed here from Nov. 2, 1695, till March 6, 1696. (*N. H. Prov. Pap.*, 17:645, 657.)

March 27, 1730, Joseph Meader gave his nephew Daniel, son of Nathaniel Meader,[1] eighty acres of land "whereon I now dwell, lying near the mouth of Oyster river, which was formerly ye estate of my honored father, John Meader, deceased, bounded west by the land of James Davis, Esq., (son of the above John), south by the river, or salt water, with all the houses, privileges," etc. Daniel Meader, as will be seen, was living here Oct. 18, 1748, when Colonel James Davis made his will. At his decease he divided this homestead between his sons, Joseph and Lemuel. Lemuel Meader, son of Daniel, Aug. 21, 1771, sold his share (forty-five acres) of the homestead farm, given him in his father's will, to George, son of John Knight of Portsmouth, with the dwelling-house thereon, and all right, title, and privilege of the *ferry-place heretofore used* across the river between said premises and Fox point. This became known as *Knight's Ferry*, but must not be confounded with the ferry of the same name between Bloody Point and Hilton's Point. Lemuel's portion of the Meader homestead now belongs to Mr. Samuel Emerson, and Joseph's to Mr. J. S. Chesley.[2]

II. The DAVIS GARRISON. This garrison stood near Oyster river, above the Meader garrison, and just above Davis's creek. It was built by John Davis of Haverhill, Mass., ancestor of the present writer, who came to New Hampshire as early as 1653. Valentine Hill conveyed to John Davis of Oyster River, Aug. 14, 1654, sixty acres of land at the mouth of said river, on the north side, "beginning at the mouth of a creek and extending west south-west to *Stony Brook cove*, and so bounded from the forementioned creek by the river." Ensign John Davis (he is called "Ensign" as early as 1663) died before May 25, 1686, leaving his homestead to his son James, in his will of Ap. 1, 1685, which runs as follows: "I do give unto my son, James Davis, my estate of houses and lands with all ye privileges thereunto belonging, *wherein I now dwell*, after the decease of my wife."

At the Indian attack of 1694, Lieut. James Davis sent his family off by water, but remained himself to defend his garrison, which he did most successfully with the help of his brother, Sergeant Davis—no doubt Joseph. One soldier was stationed at "Ensign" Davis's garrison from July 25, 1694, till Nov. 24, following. Lieut. James Davis testified Ap. 7, 1696, that James Rolens served in his garrison, "in his Mag^{tes} sarvis," from Nov. 2 till the 18th. And Lieut. Davis's account for boarding soldiers from Nov. 2, 1695, till March 6, 1696, amounted to £3.

---

[1] Nathaniel Meader, son of John, born June 14, 1671, was, as the Rev. John Pike records, "slain by ye Indians, April 25, 1704, not far from the place where Nicholas Follet formerly dwelt." This was near Durham Point. Nicholas Follet's house is spoken of in 1680 as near Field's marsh, not far from the parsonage lands.

[2] As some doubt has heretofore existed as to the precise location of the Meader and Davis garrisons, the writer, by way of proof, gives many details about the transfer of lands that would otherwise be unnecessary.

(*N. H. Prov. Pap.*, 17: 645, 654, 657.)

A road on the upper side of Oyster river, between Joseph Meader's and Lieut. Davis's, is mentioned in 1701. And Ap. 9, 1703, a highway was laid out on the upper side of Oyster river, from the road that led to Lieut. Davis's, along by the head of Joseph Bunker's land, and thence to the King's thoroughfare road to Dover. James Davis, in his will of Oct. 11, 1748, gives his son Ephraim "the place *where I now live*, between Col. Samuel Smith's and Daniel Meader's," entailing it on one of his grandsons.[1]

Col. James Davis was, in his day, one of the leading men of the Oyster River settlement. At an early age he organized and led scouting parties for the defence of the colony, and was the companion-in-arms of Col. Hilton, as related by Belknap, and took part in the expeditions to Maine and Port Royal. At the age of twenty-five, or thereabouts, he received a lieutenant's commission, which was confirmed by the Massachusetts government in 1690, and renewed by Gov. Usher of New Hampshire in 1692. Belknap calls him "captain" in 1703. Sixty men under Capt. James Davis, scouting at the head of our rivers, were ordered to be disbanded Ap. 20, 1703. (*N. H. Prov. Pap.*, 3: 252.) He was appointed member of the council of war by the provincial government, Oct. 18, 1707. His muster-roll of 1812 is given in the *N. H. State Papers*, Vol. 14: 3. He is called "lieut. colonel" in the Dover Records of 1720, and "colonel," in 1721. He was also a selectman of Dover in 1698, 1700, and 1701; and a member of the General Assembly from Dec. 28, 1697, till June, 1701, and again from Nov. 8, 1716, till Nov. 21, 1727, when he was about sixty-six years old. He was also a Justice of the Peace. And Dec. 9, 1717, he was made Judge of the Court of Common Pleas. He died between Oct. 18, 1748, and Sept. 27, 1749, on which day his will was proved. He left nine children, whose ages, at their death, averaged eighty-seven years each.

The cellar of the Davis garrison can still be traced. From this knoll, now so solitary and peaceful, Col. Davis could, in that night of horrors in July, 1694, not only hear the cries of the savages and their victims, but could plainly see the flames consuming the Meader garrison below, and Beard's garrison above, and, across the river, the Adams and Drew garrisons, with the houses of Parson Buss, Ezekiel Pitman, and many others in every direction—among them that of his own brother, John, who was killed, together with his wife and all of his children except two daughters, who were carried into captivity.

It is still related in the neighborhood how Col. James Davis, the veteran officer and able magistrate, used on occasion to lay aside his carnal weapons, and convene religious meet-

---

[1] Col. Samuel Smith was the son of Joseph. He inherited the homestead farm, above the Davis lands, on which stood the Smith garrison.

Daniel Meader, as we have seen, was the grandson of John Meader, part of whose homestead he was then in possession of.

ings at his garrison, in which he took part in prayer and exhortation, showing himself, as Butler says in Hudibras,—

> "Most fit t' hold forth the Word,
> And wield the one and t'other sword."

Six or seven persons from Oyster river point, on their way to the boat from one of these meetings, were waylaid and slain by the Indians on the Meader land, just below Davis's creek. Their bodies, discovered some days later, were covered with earth where they lay. This place is still pointed out by the present owner of the land, Mr. J. S. Chesley, who, like his father and grandfather, it is a pleasure to state, continues to respect the grave of these pious victims.

III. SMITH'S GARRISON. This garrison was built by Joseph Smith,[1] who, the 31st, 7 mo., 1660, had a grant of "one small parcell of wast land on the north side of Oyster River for a house lott, provided it intrench not upon anie former grant, wich say^d land lyeth Betwine the lott of Mathew Willyames and the lott of Wm. Willyames, Juner." Sept. 14, 1660, he bought Matthew Williams' forty acre grant,[2] bounded E. by the neck of land formerly granted to Valentine Hill (conveyed by him, as already shown, to John Davis and John Meader), S. by Oyster river, N. by the commons, and N. W. by land granted Joseph Smith by the town of Dover.

There is nothing on record to justify a vague tradition that Joseph Smith was inclined to Quaker doctrines. At all events, he acted on the principle that self-preservation is the first law of nature, and made good the defence of his habitation, which escaped destruction in 1694. Moreover, he availed himself of the secular arm. Two soldiers served at Joseph Smith's garrison from July 25, 1694, till Nov. 24, following. And his account for boarding soldiers from Nov. 2, 1695, till March 6, 1696, was 6£, 6s. (*N. H. Prov. Pap.*, 17: 645, 657.)

The precise spot where Smith's garrison stood is unknown, but it is believed to have been near Oyster river, on the south side of the turnpike road. This land is now owned by Mr. Forrest Smith.

IV. BUNKER'S GARRISON. This garrison is still standing, entirely divested of any appearance of fortification, on the upper side of Bunker's creek, but more remote from Oyster river than the three garrisons below. It was built by James Bunker, who was at Oyster River as early as 1652. Two soldiers are mentioned as serving at "James Bunker's garrison" from July 25, 1694, till Nov. 24, following; and others from Nov. 2, 1695, till March 6, 1696. (*N. H. Prov. Pap.*, 17: 645, 657.)

Wm. Story, Wm. Follet, and James Bunker had a grant of land in this vicinity before Oct. 5, 1652. And James Bunker and Wm. Follet had the grant of a neck of land on

---

[1] Joseph Smith was the direct ancestor of the present writer, his daughter, Elizabeth, having married James, grandson of Richard Pinckhame, of Dover Neck. Lois, daughter of said James and Elizabeth, married Vincent Torr. Their daughter, Mary Torr, became the wife of Judge Ebenezer Thompson.

[2] "Matthew Williams' forty-acre grant in the tenure of Joseph Smith," is spoken of October 29, 1701, when a road was laid out from the head of Lieut. Davis's land and Joseph Meader's, to the old path leading to Abraham Clark's, and so on to the King's thoroughfare road to Dover.

the upper side of Oyster river, the 10th, 8 mo., 1653, bounded by a line from the head of Thomas Johnson's creek, where the salt marsh ended, to the head of the other creek (Bunker's) where Jonas Bine's marsh was. This tract was sometimes called *Bunker's Neck*. Wm. Follet's half of this neck was conveyed to James Bunker, son of the above James, then deceased, March 28, "in the sixth year of our sovereign Lady Ann" (1707), by Nicholas Follet of Portsmouth, "by right of heir-in-law," together with one half of ten acres, called *ye Vineyard*, at the head of Johnson's creek, granted Wm. Follet and James Bunker in 1653, and also twenty acres of upland, adjacent to *Story's marsh*.[1] With the exception of three acres of salt marsh given by James Bunker, Sr., to his daughter, Wealthen, wife of Robert Huckins, the whole of Bunker's Neck, or "plantation," as it is called, comprising 236⅝ acres, was divided, May 15, 1759, among the seven children of James Bunker, Jr. A part of this (36¼ acres), next Jones's creek, fell to Love Bunker, wife of Col. Thomas Millet of Dover, and the remainder was acquired by three of the sons. A part of this estate, including the old garrison, is still in possession of the Bunker family.

V. The JONES GARRISON. This garrison stood on the upper side of Jones's creek, and, like most of the old garrisons at Oyster River, in a pleasant situation, which speaks well for the taste of the early settlers. The river is in full sight. It was built by Stephen Jones, who came to this neighborhood about 1663, and acquired the lands of Thomas Johnson. He is called "Ensign" in 1692, being one of the three officers appointed for the defence of the settlement. The others were Capt. John Woodman and Lieut. James Davis. They probably had better defences, and a greater supply of ammunition than the other garrison owners, and all their houses escaped destruction in the attack of 1694. Lieut. Jones, however, came near being killed on that occasion. Three soldiers are mentioned as serving at his garrison from July 25, 1694, till the 24th of Nov. following, "except one wanting a fortnight." And Stephen Jones's account for boarding soldiers from Nov. 2, 1695, till March 6, 1696, amounted to £6. (*N. H. Prov. Pap.*, 17 : 645, 657.)

Thomas Leathers, aged 75, in a deposition of Aug. 1, 1776, states that the family he was living with, when young, having moved to Capt. Stephen Jones's, to garrison during Queen Anne's war, he also went there. Jones's garrison was burnt down before May 9, 1732, when "Stephen Jones of Oyster River," son of the above Stephen, declared upon oath in the N. H. General Assembly, that "when his father's house was burnt he had in his chest

---

[1] Wm. Story died before Oct. 9, 1660, and Sarah, his widow, married Samuel Austin before Jan. 27, 1661, and went to Wells, Me. May 12, 1662, this Samuel Austin, "planter," with the consent of Sarah, his wife, conveyed to William ffollet of Dover, the fall, and all right, title, and interest to Wm. Story's land at Oyster River, consisting of 140 acres of upland and a parcel of marsh near Thomas Johnson's creek. Sixty acres of Story's grant were sold by James Bunker to Abraham Clark. This tract seems to have been on the dividing line between the Oyster River precinct and Dover proper. One hundred acres of the same grant were sold April 4, 1720, by Nicholas Follet to Joseph Jenkins.

in said house forty-two pounds of this Province money." It was voted to indemnify him for this loss. (*N. H. Prov. Pap.*, 4 : 617, 784.)

VI. BEARD'S GARRISON. This garrison, according to tradition, stood east of Beard's creek, between the present turnpike road and the highway to Dover, a short distance from the corner. It was built by Wm. Beard, who was at Oyster River as early as 1640, and was still living here April 19, 1675, on which day he and his wife Elisabeth gave "gratisly and freely" to James Huckins a tract of land near *Beard's creek*, adjoining the Woodman land. The deed of conveyance was executed in "ye new dwelling-house of William Beard of Oister River," it is therein expressly declared. This house, spoken of in Farmer's notes to Belknap as "garrisoned," was, a few months later, assaulted by the Indians, who, coming upon the "good old man" William Beard without, killed him on the spot, cut off his head, and set it on a pole in derision. The inventory of his estate was made Nov. 1, 1675. One half of his house and lands was given to his widow and her heirs, and the other half to Edward Leathers and his heirs, unless she should require it for her maintenance. And as to the land which said Edward did then possess, it was confirmed to him and his heirs.[1]

It does not appear who occupied this garrison in 1694, but Edward Leathers was subsequently in possession of the land. At the Indian attack of that year it is said to have been evacuated, and burned to the ground by the enemy. Edward's wife, called "old Mrs. Leathers," and one or two others of the family, were killed. They must have lived in this neighborhood, if not in the garrison itself. William, his son, escaped by running. It was this William, who, Jan. 9, 1721, gave his oldest son Edward his farm, where he then dwelt, on the south side of the highway,[2] extending down to Oyster river low-water mark—apparently the very land on which Beard's garrison is said to have stood. The Leathers graves, not far from the river, may still be seen.

A Joseph Beard is mentioned in the Durham tradition in connection with the destruction of this garrison, but thus far nothing has appeared in the old records to verify this mention. William Beard evidently had no sons, nor did his property fall to any of the Beards. A "Joseph Beard of Oyster River" is mentioned in the Philbrick Genealogy as the first husband

---

[1] Edward Leathers—or Letheres, as he himself wrote the name—the heir of Wm. Beard, was a freeman at Oyster River as early as May 19, 1669, when he signed a petition to the Mass. government for Oyster River to be made a separate parish. He was constable in 1681, and authorized to collect all taxes in arrears. (See *N. H. Prov. Papers*, I: 308–310, 430–431.) Wm. Pitman, in his will of Nov. 1, 1682, appointed Edward Leathers "overseer" of his wife and children, and to see that his will was properly executed, a proof of his good character and standing. "Edward Letheres, Senior," was still alive April 6, 1716, when he and his son William signed a petition to Gov. Vaughan, the original of which is still extant, showing that they both wrote their names Letheres. A part of the old Beard land is still in the possession of Edward's descendants.

[2] It has been supposed there was in early times no road from Oyster river falls to Dover except "the King's highway" across Brown's hill. This is a mistake. The "*Cochecho Path* from William Beard's" is mentioned as early as 1668.

of Esther, daughter of James Philbrick of Hampton, who was born March 1, 1657. He was probably the Joseph Beard of Dover, who, with his wife Esther, conveyed to Thomas Tebbetts July 16, 1692, two acres of land on Dover Neck that formerly belonged to his father Thomas Beard, deceased. His wife Esther was appointed administratrix of his estate Feb. 9, 1703. She became the second wife of Sylvanus Nock of Dover Nov. 12, 1705. Ensign Joseph Beard, son of the above Joseph and Esther, is mentioned Oct. 7, 1713. (See *Back Cove*.) His wife was Elizabeth, who, with their son-in-law Richard Plumer, was appointed to administer on his estate Dec. 4. 1723.

Thomas Beard, father of the first mentioned Joseph, was no doubt the Thomas who had a grant of land near Sandy point in 1642 (see *Sandy Point*), and who, together with Valentine Hill, had the grant of Oyster River falls Nov. 19, 1649. His will of Dec. 16, 1678, mentions his wife Mary, his sons *Joseph* and Thomas, and his daughters Martha Bunker and Elizabeth Watson. The latter was probably the wife of Robert Watson of Oyster River, who was killed by the Indians in 1694.

VII. WOODMAN'S GARRISON. This garrison, which is still in an admirable state of preservation, is one of the largest and most noted of the Oyster River defences. It is beautifully situated on the eastern slope of a hill at the head of Beard's creek, with brooks and deep ravines on every side of the acclivity, except at the west. It has a fine outlook for an approaching enemy, as well as a charming view in every direction, except in the rear, where the rise of land intercepts the prospect. Durham village, which did not exist when this garrison was built, lies at the south in full view, embosomed among trees; and at the east may be traced the windings of Oyster river on its way to the Pascataqua. At the north, through an opening between the hills, can be seen the spot where the Huckins garrison stood; and nearer at hand, but separated from it by a profound ravine, is the field where occurred the massacre of 1689.

This garrison was built by Capt. John Woodman,[1] son of Edward Woodman of Newbury, Mass., who came to Oyster River as early as 1657, and in 1660 had a grant of twenty acres between the lands of William Beard and Valentine Hill, with Stony brook on the south, apparently the very land where he built his garrison. He had a captain's commission before 1690, which was renewed by the Massachusetts government that year, and again by Gov. Usher of New Hampshire in 1692. His garrison underwent more than one attack from the Indians, and seems to have been manned in part by government soldiers.

The N. H. authorities ordered, Nov. 28, 1692, that five pounds be

---

[1] Capt. John Woodman was the direct ancestor of the present writer, through his daughter Sarah, who married John Thompson of Oyster River. Among the descendants of said John and Sarah might be mentioned the Hon. Ebenezer Thompson, first secretary of state of N. H.; the late Major A. B. Thompson of Concord, also secretary of this state for many years; Mrs. O. C. Moore of Nashua; Miss Frances E. Willard, the well known President of the Woman's Temperance Union; Mrs. Minerva B. Norton of Beloit, Wis., authoress, etc.

paid for provisions for the soldiers at Capt. Woodman's garrison. In 1693 he represented to the government the defenceless condition of Oyster River, and an order "that six men be raised for Capt. John Woodman" was issued Ap. 24, 1693. (*N. H. Prov. Pap.*, 2 : 102–3.) Six more were sent here Nov. 30, 1695, and one Dec. 2. (*Ibid*, 2 : 174.) Three soldiers are mentioned as serving here from July 25, 1694, till Nov. 24, following, and others from Nov. 2, 1695, till March 6, 1696. (*Ibid*, 17 : 645, 657.)

Woodman's garrison is one of the most interesting monuments of early times in the state. Unfortunately it is no longer in possession of the family. The last owner of the name was Prof. John S. Woodman of Dartmouth College. After his death it was sold by his widow, together with the adjacent land that for more than two hundred years had been owned by the Woodman family.

VIII. Huckins' Garrison. This garrison stood on the very outskirts of the Oyster River settlement, specially exposed to attack. It was a few rods south of the house now owned by Mr. Ebenezer T. Emerson, on the same side of the road. Oyster river is half a mile distant in a direct line; and a mile, at least, following the course of the road. This garrison was built by James Huckins, son of Robert Huggins of the Dover Combination. James was taxed at Oyster River in 1664. He seems to have been a connection of Wm. Beard or his wife, who gave him a portion of their lands. Huckins' garrison was destroyed in August, 1689,[1] on which occasion eighteen persons were massacred in a neighboring field now belonging to Mr. J. W. Coe, besides several others at the garrison itself. Pike, in his Journal, says James Huggin of Oyster River was slain. Sarah, his wife,[2] was taken captive, but was rescued the following year at Ameriscoggin. She became the second wife of Capt. John Woodman. The Huckins lands were acquired by the Emersons. (See *Huckins' brook.*)

IX. The *Burnham Garrison*. Descending Oyster river on the south side, about a mile below Durham falls as the road winds, but half that distance in a direct line, stood the Burnham garrison, the exact site of which has been disputed. It was built by Robert Burnham, who came to this country in the *Angel Gabriel*, which sailed from Bristol, Eng., June 4, 1635, and was wrecked at Pemaquid, now Bristol, Me., August 15, following. He was taxed at Oyster River (of course for land) in 1657, if not before. Two hundred acres more were laid out to him Nov. 9, 1661, originally granted to Ambrose Gibbons, adjacent to the house where Gibbons then lived, and where he

---

[1] C. W. Tuttle, in his Historical Papers, pp. 203-4, says Huckins' garrison was destroyed Sept. 13, 1689. He considers Pike's date erroneous.

[2] A Sarah Huggins has become renowned in song for her conquest of the Earl of Exeter. She was the prototype of the heroine in Tennyson's romantic poem, "The Lord of Burleigh."

wrote his will, July 11, 1656, the very day he died.[1] One portion of this grant is a beautiful meadow, now chiefly owned by Mr. G. W. Burnham, which lies along the river side, enclosed among wooded hills, and intersected by a runlet of water that empties into Burnham's creek. According to the tradition in the above owner's line, the garrison stood in the heart of this meadow, near the runlet,—a place with no natural advantages of position whatever, and where there could have been no cellar suitable for storage. This meadow, however, was unquestionably a part of the old Gibbons grant acquired by Robert Burnham, and a house thereon was no doubt erected at an early day, that sooner or later was probably surrounded by defences. Whether this was the original Burnham garrison or not is to be decided chiefly by the situation of the Pitman land. At the Indian attack of July 18, 1694, Ezekiel Pitman is said to have lived at "a gunshot's distance" from the garrison, and being awakened by the shout that the enemy was at hand, barely effected his escape into the garrison with his family. But all the land owned by Ezekiel Pitman o the south side of Oyster river was, as far as it has come to light, some distance below, as will be seen.

Nearly a quarter of a mile farther down the river, on the farm now owned by the heirs of the late Joseph Burnham, between Cutt's hill and the shore, is another and more remarkable spot, where a constant tradition in the owner's line places the garrison. And it would seem that no one, except for safety, would ever have built a house in so inaccessible a place, certainly not a mere dwelling-house. It is a steep, craggy hill, precipitous for the most part, so it could have been made absolutely impregnable after the mode of warfare in those days. It is not surprising the Indians did not venture to attack so strong a hold, when they found the inmates on the alert. There is just room enough on the top for the buildings and a palisade. The cellar, with its stone wall, is still perfect, as well as a smaller cellar, entirely separate, which no doubt was for ammunition and other dry storage. These two cellars are mentioned more

---

[1] Ambrose Gibbons owned land at Oyster river before the 3d, 12 mo., 1640 (*N. H. Prov. Pap.*, 1: 141.) He was one of the agents sent over by Capt. John Mason in the spring of 1630. He sailed in the bark *Warwick* subsequent to Ap. 8, and arrived before July 21 of that year. He first settled on the Newichawannock, where he established a trading-post, built a saw-mill, and attempted the cultivation of the grapevine. His wife and child came over in 1631. This child is often spoken of in the letters to Gibbons. (See *N. H. Prov. Pap.*, Vol. I.) One from George Vaughan, dated at "Boston, Aug. 20, 1634," affectionately mentions "little Beck." Her name was Rebecca. She afterward married Henry Sherburne, also one of Mason's colonists. Her grandson, the Hon. Henry Sherburne, married Dorothy, sister of Lieutenant Gov. John Wentworth. Her granddaughter, Bridget, daughter of Richard and Mary (Sherburne) Sloper, married, March 29, 1684, John Chevalier, otherwise Knight, who acquired Knight's ferry at Bloody Point.

Ambrose Gibbons belonged to the Dover Combination, and Sept. 27, 1648, was one of the five men charged with the prudential affairs of the town. He was also a magistrate. Oct. 5, 1652, he had a grant of the mill-privilege at the head of Thomas Johnson's creek. He was then living on the south side of Oyster river, on land now owned by Col. Burnham, and adjacent to the tract of 200 acres granted him by the town at the above date. He bequeathed all his property to his grandson, Samuel Sherburne, son of his only child, Rebecca. Ambrose Gibbons is said to have been buried at Sanders's Point, just across the bridge from the Wentworth House at New Castle.

than once in the Burnham records of last century as "the cellar" and "the cellar house." At one end of the garrison cellar a depression marks the place of the "little barn," also spoken of in the same records. The house had a frame of huge timbers of white oak, some of which were used in the construction of the present farm buildings. There is a never-failing spring near the foot of the hill. A growth of young pines on one side of this hill now screens the summit from the river. Through the branches you catch here and there a glimpse of the water, and before they sprang up Oyster river was in full view, especially up-stream, in the direction of Durham falls.

The chief point in favor of this being the real site of the Burnham garrison of 1694 is the proximity of the Pitman land. Directly beneath the hill, on the lower side, is the field known from time immemorial as the "Pitman field," where still remain several trees of the Pitman orchard, which was much more extensive a few years ago. The county records show that this very land was conveyed to Wm. Pitman and his son Ezekiel, Nov. 23, 1664. The inventory of Ezekiel's estate, Jan. 2, 1709-10, mentions his orchard, but not his house, it having been burned by the Indians, and apparently not rebuilt. William Pitman, son of Ezekiel, sold this land to John and Robert Burnham, March 14, 1717-18. The deed of conveyance repeats the bounds exactly as given in the deed to his father and grandfather in 1664. This land is now in the possession of the heirs of the late Joseph Burnham, a descendant of the above Robert.

There seems to have been only one Burnham garrison in 1694, in which year, from July 25 till Nov. 24, "Jeremy Burnam" had two soldiers stationed at his garrison. Jeremiah Burnum's account for boarding soldiers from Nov. 2, 1695, till March 6, 1696, amounted to 4£. 9s. (*N. H. Prov. Pap.*, 17 : 645, 658.)

The large Burnham house, now deserted, that stands on a ridge at the lower side of the Gibbons meadow, is also said to have been a garrison. The frame is of white oak timbers, still undecayed, fastened together with large oak pins, and one end is lined internally with a brick wall, originally pierced with loop-holes. This house was probably built by John Burnham, son of the above Jeremiah.

X. DREW'S GARRISON. This garrison, destroyed in the Indian attack of 1694, no doubt stood near Drew's Point, on the south side of Oyster river, where William Drew owned land as early as 1648. He died the "last of April," 1669. The inventory of his estate mentions his dwelling house, one cannon, his fishing boats, the *Hopewell* and the *Increase*, and a great amount of fishing tackle, showing that he was chiefly engaged in fisheries. His widow Elizabeth married Wm. Follet. Wm. Follet of Dover and Elizabeth his wife conveyed to Thomas Drew, June 20, 1680, "a dwelling-house, barn, and other out housen buildings," standing on a piece of land that was first Darby ffield's, who conveyed it to Wm. Roberts, and he to Wm. Drew, adjoining unto and between the land of Thomas Stevenson and y[e] land that formerly belonged to Matthew

Giles. It was probably this Thomas Drew (some say it was Francis) who surrendered the garrison in 1694, on the promise of quarter, and was making his escape to the Adams garrison, which stood below, when he was slain. His widow married Richard Elliot of Portsmouth. Richard Elliot and wife Mary, formerly ye relict of Thomas Drew, and administratrix of his estate, quit claim, Nov. 15, 1706, to the estate of Wm. Drew, in favor of his son John, who, May 10, 1712, conveyed to Stephen Jenkins all his rights in the real estate of his father, Wm. Drew of Oyster River, deceased, which had been mortgaged by his mother Elizabeth, relict of said William, and administrator of his estate, to Thomas Drew, uncle of said John, July 8, 1671. Stephen Jenkins and wife Elizabeth conveyed to James Langley, Nov. 5, 1714, all the lands, tenements, and messuages, he bought of John Drew, and Drew of Richard Elliott, which property was "the estate and possession of William and Thomas Drew, on the south side of Oyster river." James Langley petitioned in 1715 for a road to the highway as he was "penned up by Bartholomew Stevenson." This road was laid out the next year, "beginning at Will Drew's old possession." (See *Langley's Point.*)

Some think, however, that Drew's garrison was on the Little Bay shore, where, in fact, Francis Drew had land given him by his father, to whom it had been granted in 1653. The surviving members of the Drew family no doubt established themselves here soon after 1694, and probably erected defences. The Rev. Hugh Adams, March 3, 1727–8, admitted into the Oyster River church "Thomas Drew of Little Bay," and Tamsen his wife. They had been recently married, and were living in the old garrison in 1694, when they were carried into captivity. The place where they lived after their redemption was no doubt the land of Francis Drew, above mentioned, and the same now owned by Mr. James Kent, on which an old burial-ground of the Drews is still to be seen. Here, in one grave, lie the above Thomas and Tamsen, and, near by, a part of the fourteen children they were blessed with after their return from captivity. It need not be said that the family is perpetuated to this day.

XI. The ADAMS GARRISON. This garrison was built by Charles Adams, who acquired land at Oyster River as early as Ap. 6, 1645. He was living near the mouth of this river in 1671, when twelve acres more were laid out to him "behind his house." At the Indian attack of July 18, 1694, his garrison was burned to the ground, and he himself, his son Samuel and wife, and eleven others, were killed. They were afterwards buried in one grave, beneath a mound still to be traced, close to the Mathes burial-ground at Durham Point. This huge grave has always been respected by the owners of the soil. The garrison is supposed to have stood on the elevation immediately above. At any rate, it could not have been far off, for the Adams land at Oyster River Point only comprised eighteen acres. The inventory of the estate of Charles Adams, Senior, consisting of uplands, salt meadow, a small orchard, etc., as sworn to by his son Charles,

Ap. 1, 1695, amounted to sixty pounds in value.

March 4, 1711-12, "Joseph Dudy and Rebeckah his wife, the eldest daughter of Charles Adams (Jr.) deceased," sold Francis Mathes for four-score pounds " a certain tract or parcel of land situate in Dover township, lying and being on *Oyster River poynt*, commonly called and known by the name of Charles Adams his home plantation or house lott, being by estimation eighteen acres more or less, all wthin fence, and now in the tenure and occupation of the aforesaid ffrancis Mathes, bounded on the north wth the highway that leads from Willey's creek to Oyster River falls, on the south wth the aforesaid Mathes his land; more (over), twelve acres of land beginning at a marked tree behind the aforesaid house lott, and runs ab^t 100 rods by the highway side that leads to Oyster River falls, and from that extent it runs on a straight line west and by south, or thereabouts, to the other corner, all which said home plantation or house lott and twelve acres of land, together with all the fence and growing stuff, and all other the hereditaments, liberties, immunities, commons, water courses, etc. Signed by " Joseph Dowdy, Rebeckah + Dowdy, Esther + Adams."
<small>her mark</small> <small>her mark</small>

Nov. 23, 1716, " Easter Adams " personally appeared before James Davis, Justice of the Peace, and acknowledged the foregoing deed. This Esther Adams afterwards married Thomas Bickford, Jr.

John Meader, Sr., aged about 82 years, testified before James Davis, Justice of the Peace, Jan. 30, 1711-12, " that Charles Adams, sen^r, did peaceably possess, build fence, plant and Improve the land within the mouth of oyster River, on the south side, . . . joining to francis mathes, sen^r, his land, aboue fifty fiue years ago and Euer since till oyster River weare distroyed, and then the s^d Adams was killed and his house burnt by the Enemie."

XII. BICKFORD'S GARRISON. This garrison stood at Durham Point, a little below the mouth of Oyster river, but the exact spot is not known. It has often been asserted that this was a mere dwelling-house surrounded by palisades, but the owner speaks of it as "*my garrison*," Nov. 12, 1694, in a certificate about a soldier stationed here, signed "Thomas Bickford, comander of the *gareson*." (*N. H. Prov. Pap.*, 17: 645.) Two soldiers are mentioned as serving here from July 25, 1694, till Nov. 24 following, and others from Nov. 2, 1695, till March 6, 1696. (*Ibid*, pp. 645, 657.) This garrison was defended in an admirable manner at the Indian attack of 1694, by Capt. Thomas Bickford, who, warned by the alarm guns at the upper garrisons that the Indians were at hand, had sent his family off by water, and remained to defend his house alone. Shouting forth his orders as if he had a squad of soldiers at his command, and presenting himself every few minutes in fresh guise to blaze away at the enemy, he deceived them so effectually that they speedily gave up the attempt to reduce a hold apparently so well manned. This Thomas, whose wife was Bridget Furber, of Welsh Cove, was the son of John Bickford, who was living at Oyster

River as early as July 17, 1645, on which day "Darby ffield of Oyster River, in the river of Piscataqua, county of Norfolk, planter," sold John Bickford his dwelling-house at Oyster River, then " in the tenure of said Bickford," with a lot of five or six acres adjoining, and all the land to the creek on the side towards Little Bay, except the "breadth" on said creek in possession of Thomas Willey. (This was the inlet afterwards known as " *Willey's Creek.*") June 23, 1684, John Bickford, " with the consent of his wife Temperate," conveyed to his son Thomas " all his houses and lands lying at the poynt of Oyster river."[1]

The Bickford garrison long since disappeared. The land where it stood, with Little Bay on one side, Oyster river on the other, and, directly in front, the river Pascataqua, with its verdant isles, swiftly coursing seaward between Newington at the right and the Back River district at the left, is now owned by Mr. Jeremiah Langley.

XIII. The EDGERLY GARRISON. This garrison was built by Thomas Edgerly, who was taxed at Oyster River in 1665, and admitted freeman in 1672. He was a Justice of the Peace in 1674, and took part that year in the Rev. Joshua Moody's trial for nonconformity, on which occasion he refused to subscribe to Mr. Moody's commitment, and consequently lost his commission. According to the Durham tradition, his garrison was destroyed in the attack of 1694, his son Zachariah slain, and he himself taken captive, but soon after made his escape. Belknap says the garrison was evacuated and destroyed, but he shortly after states that Thomas Edgerly, by concealing himself in his cellar, preserved his house, though twice set on fire. That very year, however, not long after the attack of July 18, Thomas Edgerly petitioned the governor and council that—as he and his neighbors had been afflicted by the Indians, his dwelling-house burnt, his goods destroyed, and his son wounded—the house of John Rand, deceased, might be made a garrison for the defence of the remaining families adjacent, and that six men might be sent to defend it. (*N. H. Prov. Papers*, XVII: 640.) Either the Rand house took his name, or he erected a new one, for three soldiers are mentioned as stationed at *Edgerly's garrison* Jan. 6, 1696. Thomas Edgerly was still alive in 1715.

The precise situation of this garrison is not known, but it could not have been far from the shore of Little Bay. Thomas Edgerly had a " plott" of land at the west end of " Hilliard's field," conveyed to him by his father-in-law, John Alt, Ap. 3, 1674. This " plott" joined land already owned by Edgerly, near Plum Swamp, on the lower side. If the garrison did

---

[1] John Bickford, when he left Oyster River, went to the Newington shore, where he owned several tracts of land—one near Bloody Point, another at Fox Point, and a third near Long Point, where he established himself. His children and grandchildren intermarried with the chief land-owners in Newington; and their descendants are now without number. The name of his wife, usually written Temperance, has for more than two hundred years been perpetuated among her descendants in Newington and the neighboring towns—the Harrisons, Downings, Knights, Pickerings, Coes, etc. John Bickford and his wife Temperance were the direct ancestors of the writer through her paternal grandmother.

not stand here, it must have been on the south-west side of Long creek (Crummit's), where Thomas Edgerly acquired land Jan. 28, 1659, on which he appears to have been living May 21, 1700, when he conveyed a part of it to his son Samuel.

XIV. GODDARD'S GARRISON. There appears to have been a Goddard or Symond's garrison at an early day. No mention is made of it in history, however, or in the Durham traditions, unless it was the garrison at *Lubberland*, mentioned in 1693. (See *Lubberland Garrison*.) It is referred to March 16, 1735-6, when Abraham Bennick[1] (nephew of John Goddard), conveyed to his son Abraham a certain messuage or tract of land in that part of Durham called Loberland, being part of ye estate formerly John Goddard's, "beginning at y^e *old garrison seller* [cellar], formerly ye widow Simonds." Mrs. Symonds was previously the wife of John Goddard, of Goddard's Cove, who died about 1660, after which she married Michael Simmonds, or Symonds. "Goody Goddard" is stated to have chosen the appraisers of her husband John Goddard's estate, who made the inventory June 27, 1667; and Sept. 16, 1667, "Mrs. Welthen Simonds" appeared before Judge Thomas Packer, and made oath as to the correctness of this inventory. She was still alive Aug. 8, 1705, when John Woodman, Esq., one of her majesty's Justices of the Peace, having been requested by Abraham Bennick, of Lubberland, to receive her acknowledgment of an act conveying her homestead lands to her grandson, to the exclusion of her daughter, he went to see her, and, after examining her on this and various other subjects, he declared her altogether incapable of making such a conveyance, being *non compos mentis*, and to the best of his knowledge had been so six or seven years, through much infirmity and exceeding old age.

LUBBERLAND GARRISON. This garrison is mentioned Ap. 24, 1693, when the government ordered two men to be impressed for the garrison "at Lubarland." (*N. H. Prov. Pap.*, 2: 103.) "A good garrison" at Lubberland is spoken of in a record, supposed to be of 1694, as " cut down and destroyed" the previous summer. (*Ibid*, p. 147.) This was probably the Goddard garrison.

DURGIN'S GARRISON. William Durgin's garrison is mentioned in 1695, when soldiers were stationed there from Nov. 2, till the 6th of March, following. (*N. H. Prov. Pap.*, 17: 657.) Two soldiers at *Durgin's garrison* are mentioned Jan. 6, 1695-6. (*Ibid*, 2: 175.) Wm. Durgin, according to tradition, lived near the mouth of the Great Bay, on the west side of the Mathes land. His sons certainly owned land afterwards in the vicinity of Crummit's creek. (See *Mathews' Creek* and *Shooting Point*.) The Landing-place "at Durgin's, off the west side of Mathews his neck," is mentioned Dec. 11, 1694. (*Ibid*, 2: 146.)

---

[1] This is the "Abraham Benwick" spoken of by Belknap as commanding a company of volunteers in 1724 to scout for the Indians. The name seems to have been generally written Bennick down to the Revolutionary period, when for some unknown reason it was changed to Bennet.

DAVID DAVIS'S GARRISON. This garrison was on the Lubberland shore. Two soldiers were stationed at "*David Davis's garrison*" Jan. 6, 1695-6. (*N. H. Prov. Pap.*, 2 : 175.) And his account is given for boarding soldiers from Nov. 2, 1695, till March 6, 1696. (*Ibid*, 17 : 657.) The Rev. John Pike, in his Journal, says David Davis was killed by the Indians at Lubberland Aug. 27, 1696. Susanna, his widow, soon after married James Durgin, son of William. Jan. 23, 1699, "Susanna Dorging" was summoned to appear before Lieut. Gov. Partridge to show why she had not administered upon the estate of her late husband, David Davis, and why Roger Rose, the principal creditor, should not administer. What became of the garrison is not known with certainty, but it is supposed to have been acquired by John Smith, who bought land of Roger Rose and was living in this vicinity March 4, 1701-2. Some countenance is given to this supposition by the record of the Rev. Hugh Adams, who, Jan. 30, 1722-3, baptised "two sons of Susanna Durgin, wife of James, at Lt. John Smith's at Loverland." This, of course, was at the so-called *Smith garrison*.

SMITH'S GARRISON. This well-known block house at Lubberland, not far from the mouth of Lamprey river, was, it is to be regretted, taken down a few years ago, and without any necessity, for its huge timbers were still sound, and it stood firmly on its base. Tradition says it was the *David Davis garrison*, mentioned in 1695. At any rate, it was no doubt the house mentioned March 4, 1701-2, when orders were given that Capt. Peter Coffin should send two scouting men from Exeter to Lamperill river, to *the house of John Smith*, and Capt. Woodman was ordered to send two from Oyster River to said *Smith's*, and so back. This was to be done daily till further orders. (*N. H. Prov. Pap.*, 2 : 363.) The Rev. Hugh Adams speaks of "Lt. John Smith's at Loverland" Jan. 30, 1722-3. (See *David Davis's Garrison.*) Smith's garrison, at a later period, was sometimes called *Frost's garrison*, and *Blydenburg's garrison*, according to the occupant.

The following garrisons at Oyster River were no doubt erected in the first half of last century, or, at least, subsequent to 1694:

"*Philip Chesley's garrison*," and "the late *Capt. Chesley's garrison*," are mentioned Sept. 29, 1707. (*N. H. Prov. Pap.*, 2 : 567.) The latter was Capt. Samuel Chesley, an officer who took part in two expeditions to Port Royal. From the last of these he arrived at Portsmouth in the sloop *Sarah and Hannah*, Thursday, Aug. 28, 1707, and that same day presented himself before the governor and council for further orders. Three weeks later (Sept. 17) he and his brother James, with six other young men, were slain by the Indians, while lumbering in the forest, not far from Capt. Chesley's house.[1] His widow Elisabeth was appointed administratrix of his estate, Aug. 3, 1708. Forty acres of his land, with

---

[1] These Indians, supposed to have come from Port Royal, were pursued as far as Lake Winnipesaukee (*N. H. Prov. Pap.*, 2: 566.) The Rev. John Pike says the Indian who killed James Chesley was slain on the spot by Robert Thompson, (great-great grandfather of the present writer.)

a house and barn, were acquired by Capt. Samuel Emerson, Ap. 11, 1717, and confirmed to him in 1732 by Joseph, son of Capt. Chesley. This tract included the spot where Capt. Chesley and his companions were slain, now owned by Mr. E. T. Emerson. The other part of Capt. Chesley's homestead lands (33 acres), with his "new dwelling-house," was conveyed to Philip Chesley, July 30, 1719. It is uncertain which of the above houses was the garrison. It stood, however, eastward of the Huckins garrison, probably on Buck's hill.

Philip Chesley's garrison is said to have stood near the Chesley house, now in ruins, popularly called "*Ben's fort*," on the road from Durham village to Dover, perhaps on the same spot.

Another *Chesley garrison* stood immediately in front of the present school-house in Durham village. It was built by George Chesley, who acquired this land Oct. 16, 1699. According to the family tradition, he was killed by the Indians near the Durham Point meeting-house, on his way to Crummit's mill. The estate of a George Chesley was administered upon by his widow, Deliverance, and his brother Joseph, Sept. 5, 1710. Another George Chesley, as Belknap relates, was killed by the Indians May 24, 1724, as he was returning from public worship with Elizabeth Burnham, who was mortally wounded at the same time.[1] A romantic tradition declares them engaged to be married, and a poem is still extant bewailing the fate of the youthful lovers.

It is a pity to spoil so touching a romance, but the stern necessity of adhering to the truth compels the writer to say that if this was the George Chesley who built the garrison, he must have been at that time forty-five years of age, at least. This may not lessen our pity for the victims, but it certainly dispels the romance. The inventory of his estate was made Aug. 27, 1724.[2]

Another *Chesley garrison* is said to have stood on the Lubberland shore, built by Joseph Chesley, who acquired land there as early as March 26, 1707. (See *Chesley's Islands*.)

A *Davis garrison* stood in the Packer's Falls district, the south side of Lamprey river, built by David Davis in the first half of last century. He was no doubt a son of the above David and Susanna. Here five generations of the name of David Davis are said to have lived. This place is now owned by Mr. Ebenezer Davis, who has a son David. The garrison, now gone, stood on a gentle eminence

---

[1] Elizabeth Burnham lived four days after she was wounded. The Rev. Hugh Adams baptized her May 27th, the evening before her death, "at her penitent request."

[2] That the reader may not be entirely cheated out of his romance, it should be added that the above account has become entangled with a more authentic story of a young Chesley of last century, who was engaged to a Miss Randall, of Lee. They were returning from meeting together, when they were slain by the Indians on the Mast road. The rock on which the maiden fell is said to be stained with her blood to this day, but unfortunately it has been removed from its original position. This legendary rock is referred to in a ballad, published in the *N. H. Republican* of Dec. 30, 1823:

> "Twice fifty summers' storms have beat
> Relentless on that sacred place;
> As many summers' ardent heat;
> But could not that red stream efface."

opposite the present house, on the other side of the highway.

A *fourth Davis garrison*, very small in size, is still standing, adjoining the house of the late Deacon John Thompson, about a mile from Durham village. It was no doubt built by Jabez Davis, son of Moses, on land conveyed to him by his uncle, Sergeant Joseph Davis, Dec. 2, 1723. Like the other small garrisons, it must have depended chiefly on the defences set up around it.

The *Mathews garrison*, otherwise *Mathes*, stood at Durham Point, where is now the house of Mr. Mark Mathes. It was no doubt built by Capt. Francis Mathes, who was living in that vicinity in 1712, when he bought the Adams land. (See *Adams garrison*.) Dec. 20, 1748, he conveyed to Valentine and Abraham Mathes, Jr., the homestead where he then lived, " beginning at John Bickford's orchard point, so the salt water is ye bounds to Joneses Point (Jonas' Point), and Oyster river, and s^d point is on ye northerly side; and s^d point in ye possession of Bickford aforesaid; westerly by land in possession of Caleb Wakeham; south by a road that leads to Bickford's aforesaid and his field to ye Orchard Point, just mentioned, together with all buildings," etc.

Second Falls Garrison. The Rev. Hugh Adams, of Oyster River, records, Jan. 11, 1719–20, the baptism of James, the infant son of James Tilley, at "the *Garrison House, second falls*." He undoubtedly referred to the second falls in Lamprey river (see *Packer's falls*), which belonged to the Oyster River precinct, and at that time were usually called the "second falls." There were at least two garrisons in this vicinity. One of them, called the *Pendergast garrison*, is still standing, and now occupied by Mr. Scott. When or by whom it was built is uncertain, but it stood on land sold Oct. 9, 1735, by Eliphalet Coffin of Exeter to "Stephen Pendergrass." The deed speaks of it as a tract of eighty-four acres in Durham, adjoining Lamprey river, beginning at the river about twenty rods above " a run of water near ye land formerly called *Mahermit's planting ground*." A spring is mentioned as just east of the lower bound, near the river.

The Tilleys do not appear to have owned any land in Durham. Mention is made, June 7, 1738, of Samuel Tille, collier, and Jane his wife, who conveyed a whole right of land in Canterbury to Stephen Pendergast.

A *Woodman garrison*, probably built by Joshua Woodman, stood not far from Wiswall's mills, on the upper side of Lamprey river. (See *Shad Falls*.)

OYSTER RIVER POINT. This was the original name of Durham Point, but it is sometimes incorrectly given to *Oyster Point*, as March 17, 1720–21, when two grants to Wm. Williams " att the mouth of the creek below *Oyster river Point*, on the east side of Oyster river," were re-bounded for his son John, beginning at the mouth of the creek, then running 65 rods by said river down to the freshet, and thence 27 rods to a great rock in the gully, then 100 rods n. easterly or northerly to the *Rocky Hill*, etc.

PACKER'S CREEK and POINT. Packer's brook or creek is mentioned Nov. 20, 1723, when James Hains conveyed to Joshua Hains land in Greenland that belonged to his father Joshua, bounded westerly by the country road leading from *Packer's brook,* so called, to Greenland meeting-house, north by the land of Clement March, etc. *Packer's bridge* is mentioned July 28, 1714, in connection with the line between the parishes of Greenland and Newington. (*N. H. Town Pap.,* 12 : 66.)

Packer's Point is on the shore of the Great Bay, between the mouth of Winnicot river and that of Packer's creek. It is so called on Phineas Merrill's map of Greenland in 1806. The name is still retained. It was derived from Thomas Packer, who acquired part of the Champernowne lands in 1714. (See *Greenland* and *Champernowne's creek.*) Packer's Point, and the lower part of Packer's creek, fell within the limits of ancient Dover.

PACKER'S FALLS. These falls are in that part of Lamprey river which flows through the southern part of Durham. The name is now confined to the falls just below the bridge on the road to Newmarket—the first falls below Wiswall's ; but it originally comprised the whole series of falls or rapids along this portion of the river. These falls were in early times generally called " *the second falls,*" a name that included the falls where General Sullivan afterwards established his mills. (See *Sullivan's Falls* and *Second Falls.*)

The name of Packer's falls was derived, not from Thomas Packer, the sheriff who hung Ruth Blay, but from his father, Col. Thomas Packer, also of Portsmouth, who was at once physician, judge, lieutenant-colonel, and member of the governor's council. The town of Dover, Ap. 11, 1694, " granted to Capt. Packer, Jonathan Woodman, James Davis, Joseph Meder, and James Thomas, the hole streame of Lamprele River for the erecting of a sawmill or mills, that is to say, the one half to Capt. Thomas Packer, the other half to the other fower men befour mentioned." With 50 acres of land to Capt. Packer " on the south side of the aforesaid falls or elsewhere for his conveniency, leaving eight rods of land by the river for a highway." And fifty acres also on the south side of the river, adjoining Capt. Packer's, were granted to Jonathan Woodman, James Davis, Joseph Meder, and James Thomas. These grants were confirmed Ap. 16, 1694. Capt. Packer conveyed to Philip Chesley of Oyster River, Dec. 1, 1711, fifty acres of land adjoining Lamprey river, which had been granted him by the town of Dover, together " with ye privilege of erecting a mill or mills upon ye said river."

Packer's Falls are so called as early as 1718. (See *Long Falls.*) They are again mentioned Dec. 18, 1724, when James Basford of Dover sold James Gipsen one sixteenth part of the *sawmill* standing on Lamperel river, on ye falls called *Packer's falls,* which s^d Basford bought of John Tasker. Samuel Chesley, March 1, 1727-8, sold Samuel Linsey one eighth part of the sawmill at the falls in Lamperel river " *commonly called Packer's falls.*" Abraham Bennick conveyed to his son Abraham, May 23, 1737, one half of a *corn-mill,* now standing on Lampereel river, at a place commonly called *Packer's falls,* in Durham, together with one half the stream and privilege belonging to said corn-mill. (See *Shad Falls*.) And May 10, 1739, Joseph Smith, of Newmarket, conveyed to Abraham Bennick, Jr., of Durham, all right and title to ye mill-dam, and falls, and land, granted John Goddard, late of Dover, deceased, at y^t place called or known by ye name of *Packer's Falls*.

The first time the name of Packer's falls appears in the Durham records is June 13, 1750, when a road "to *Packer's falls*, so-called," was proposed. But it must be remembered that there are very few Durham records prior to 1750, and none before 1733. The following item is entered in 1763: "P^d Mr. Nicholas Doody for building *Packer's Falls bridge*— £1 11. 5s." This was the Nicholas Doody who afterwards changed his name to Durell. "*Packer's Falls way*" is mentioned the same year. As a locality, the name of PACKER'S FALLS has long been given to the southwestern part of Durham, on both sides of Lamprey river, extending to Newmarket at the south, and to Lee at the west.

The first mention of *Packer's Falls* as a *school-district* is Oct. 7, 1783, when £10 16s. were paid John Smith "in lawful money, in full, for his son Daniel's keeping school in the *Packer's falls district*" during the year 1782. There was, however, without doubt, a public school here before the Revolution, as there certainly was in Durham village and at Durham Point.

PAGE'S POND. See *No-Bottom Pond.*

PAGE'S SPRINGS. These springs supply, in part, the reservoir belonging to the public Water Works in Dover. They are above Garrison Hill, on the Waldron land acquired by Mr. Taylor Page Ap. 24, 1833. The city of Dover completed the purchase of these springs in 1889, but work had been begun at the pumping station Aug. 3, 1888, and on the receiving basin the following October.

PALMER'S HILL. This hill, so named from Mr. Wm. Palmer, is in the southwestern part of Lee, on the road to the railway station.

PAPPOON HILL. This hill is at Quamphegan, on the road from St. Alban's cove, below the turnpike road. The name is derived from a neighboring family of last century.

PARSONAGE POND. This is a little pond or pool in a pasture that once belonged to Parson McClary of Dover, who was installed May 7, 1812, and dismissed Aug. 6, 1828. It is on the western side of the back road to Dover Neck, about half a mile below the road to Campin's rocks. It is sometimes called *Bloodsucker's Pond.*

PARSON BUSS'S PULPIT. This is a recess in the steep, rocky bank of Oyster river, on the south side, a short distance above Burnham's creek, where, according to tradition, the Rev. John Buss used to retire for contemplation and prayer in his declining years. He was the third minister at the Oyster River settlement, and in the Indian attack of 1694 he lost his house and valuable library, and being reduced to a narrow habitation and encumbered with a large family, he might well be glad to take refuge in this niche of pleasant outlook across the swiftly running stream, and here taste the sweets of solitude. He doubtless lived a short distance below Cutt's hill, on a grant of twenty-five acres from the town, adjoining the parsonage lands, on the north side of the road leading to Durham Point. The rock that formed the seat of the pulpit has been carried away by irreverent boys, but the niche remains, looking like a chair of state, hewn in the side of the cliff.

PARSONS' HILL. This hill is west of Wheelwright's Pond, in Lee, about half a mile above Peter's Oven, on the same road. The cellar of the Parsons house thereon can still be traced.

PARTRIDGE HILL. This hill is in Somersworth, on the line of the Electric Railroad, near the corner of the road leading to Rochester from the Dover road to Great Falls. The land adjoining the highway at this point is owned by Mr. Andrews and the heirs of Isaac Chandler on the east side; and on the west by Messrs. Bickford, Johnson, etc. The name was derived from the coveys of partridges on this hill in former times, when it was covered with underwood on both sides of the road.

PARTRIDGE POINT. Mentioned Ap. 2, 1694, when 30 acres were set apart for the use of the ministry between *Partridge point* and John Winget's, running from the commons on the west side of the road to Cochecho, thence west to an asp tree, thence towards *Partridge Pt.*, then to a red oak upon the *sandy hill* by the roadside, and by the road to the first bound. A highway to be allowed from said road to *Winget's Marsh.*

Abraham Nute, only son of James Nute, Sr., in consideration of a house on the west side of Back river, conveyed to him by John Drew, confirmed unto said Drew March 16, 1698-9, a tract of marsh and flats on the east side of Back river, adjacent to *Partridge Point*, "beginning at said point, and so down by ye Back river side three score and two rods to a *sandie hill.*" One fourth of this tract was conveyed to Thomas Canne of Dover Aug. 11, 1744, by John Drew of Somersworth, who says it was given him by his grandfather John Drew in his will. John Canne of Dover and wife Love, Nov. 29, 1762, conveyed to Francis Drew of Madbury a parcel of salt marsh on the easterly side of Back river, a little below *Partridge Point,* containing one fourth of the marsh and thatch bed in that place, being all that part which his honored father Thomas Canne of Dover, deceased, bought of John Drew of Somersworth, deceased, Aug. 11, 1744.

Partridge Point is about half a mile above the mouth of Little John's Creek. The name is said to have been derived from the number of partridges in this vicinity.

PASCASSICK RIVER, otherwise PISCASSICK. This name was originally given by the Indians to Lamprey river, or to the lowest falls in that river. "Y^e Riuer called *Pascassokes*" is mentioned in the patent of 1631 to Sir Ferdinando Gorges and others. The name is now given to the chief tributary to Lamprey river, on the west side. The lower part of this stream fell within the limits of ancient Dover, but since 1870 has belonged to Newmarket. A "mill on the *Piscassick river*, at the Dover line," is mentioned May 22, 1719. There was one here as early as Ap. 14, 1657, when, by an agreement between Dover and Exeter, Thomas Kemball, Wm. Hilton, and Robert Smart had their right confirmed to the ownership of the mill at the lower fall of the *Piscassick*, with the neck of land on the east side, down to Lamprey river, except six poles along the river side. Also 60 acres for tillage on the west side, adjacent to the mill. This land fell within the limits of Dover. The inventory of John Goddard's estate, June 27, 1667, mentions ⅜ of *Piscassick mill*. Robert Smart, Sr., of Exeter, conveyed to Capt. Peter Coffin of Exeter, merchant, March 10, 1695-6, "all my part of the neck of land which lies within the line belonging to Dover, and which was granted to me by the town of Dover, as I was parte owner of the mill called *pocassett mill*, which land lieth between Pocassett river and Lamprill river." The bounds between Dover and Exeter, as defined Sept. 18, 1718, began at a picked rock in Lamprel river, at the lowest fall, and ran to the *Piscassick river*, about two rods south of *the great mill*, etc. William Smart, son of John, conveyed to Thomas Tash, Feb. 1, 1754, twenty acres of land, " beginning at ye north of *Passcassick brook*, at *Dover line*, and thence running up ye middle of said brook 40 rods."

A road was laid out by the town of Durham, July 20, 1763, across Lamprey river through the Packer's Falls district, extending to "the *piscassick mill* privilege, then on said privilege S. 10 deg. W. over the bridge to *the dividing line between Newmarket and Durham* 18 rods, leaving the highway westward of said line." The Durham accounts of 1764 have the following entry: "P^d for Building *percasset Bridge* £.23, 10^s."

Around the Nut and Bolt factory erected by Mr. Lafayette Hall near the mouth of the Pascassick, on the Durham side, but now a part of Newmarket, is a small village generally called *Hallsville*.

The names of *Washucke* and *Watchic* are sometimes given to the Pascassick river. (See *Washucke*.)

PASCATAQUA BRIDGE, otherwise PISCATAQUA. This bridge extended across the river Pascataqua from Meader's Neck in Durham to Fox Point on the Newington shore. It was chartered June 20, 1793. The land at the Durham terminus was conveyed by Andrew Drew to the proprietors of the bridge Nov. 7, 1793, for the sum of five shillings, " to encourage the building of said bridge, and in consideration of other advantages" he might derive therefrom. It was one acre in extent, " to be laid out in a square form, at the place the proprietors should deem most advantageous, provided that the bridge be commenced within two years, and completed according to the act of incorporation."

John Drew of Barnstead conveyed his right to said land July 24, 1794, and Mark Meader conveyed his right Aug. 20, 1794.

The land at the Newington terminus was conveyed by Richard Downing Nov. 12, 1793, for the sum of five shillings, but " more especially for the encouragement of building a bridge over the Piscataqua river at and from Fox Point." It consisted of one acre, to be laid out in a square form upon any part of his farm at Fox Point, then occupied by his son Bartholomew, wherever the proprietors should think proper to build, on condition that his deed should be null and void if the bridge were not begun within two years, and completed as directed by the act of incorporation.

The bridge was begun in April, 1794, and was so far completed as to be opened for travel November 25, the same year, with a toll-gate at the Durham end. It was 2,362 feet long, and 38 feet wide. It had three sections. The first was horizontal, and built on piles from Fox Point to Rock island. The second was an arch from Rock island to Goat island. And the third, built like the first, was from Goat island to the Durham shore. There was a draw for the passage of vessels. Thomas Thompson, and John Pierce of Portsmouth, were the agents for its construction. Timothy Palmer, of Newburyport, Mass., was the architect. Enos Whiting, of Norwich, Conn., had charge of the pile-work and draw. There was a planking surface of nearly half a mile in length. Three thousand tons of oak timber, 2,000 tons of pine timber, 80,000 four-inch plank, 20 tons of iron, and 8,000 tons of stone were used in its construction.

This bridge was considered a masterpiece in its time, on account of the difficulty of its construction across a current of great rapidity, and for the most part fifty two feet deep at high tide. Mr. Gilmor of Baltimore, who visited it Aug. 19, 1797, speaks of it as "the only one of the kind in America, and a surprising work." He made a sketch of the bridge, including the tavern on Goat island, probably the earliest ever made. (See the *Gilmor Memorandums*, recently printed by the Boston Public Library, which contains a cut reproduced from Mr. Gilmor's sketch.)

This bridge opened a new highway to Portsmouth, and for fifty years greatly contributed to the prosperity of that town by directing thither a portion of country trade. especially after the opening of the First New Hampshire turnpike road. The N. H. legislature, by an Act of Dec. 12, 1803, granted a lottery for raising $15,000, to repair and maintain Piscataqua bridge. Ten thousand first class tickets at $5 each, were issued and advertised in the N. H. *Gazette* (Portsmouth) of Jan. 17, 1804. Some of these tickets are still to be found.

This bridge gave way March 8, 1830, and again in the autumn of 1854. In the latter instance it was repaired by the Messrs. Frink of Newington, who had recently bought it for $2,000, though it originally cost $65,947.34. This decrease in value was owing to the construction of railways, which had diverted travel in other directions. Consequently, when 600 feet of the bridge on the Newington side was carried away by the ice, Feb. 18, 1855, the owners could not afford to repair it, and the portion left was removed not long after.

The name of *Pascataqua Bridge* is still given to the neighborhood around the Durham terminus, though only the old abutments of the bridge now remain. And the school district in this part of the town is generally called the *Bridge* or *Pascataqua Bridge* district.

PASCATAQUA RIVER, otherwise PISCATAQUA. Judge Potter defines the name of this river as "a great deer place," from the Indian words, *pos*, great; *attuck*, deer; and *auke*, a place. Sanford and Evert's Atlas says the Piscataqua river was so named by Capt. Martin Pring, from *piscatus*, fish, and *aqua*, water, from the abundance of fish he found when he ascended this river several leagues in 1603. Thoreau, in his "*Maine Woods*," says Piscataquis signifies, according to the definition of an intelligent Indian, "the branch of a river." Mr. Hoyt, in his notes to Tuttle's *Historical Papers*, p. 101, says the word Pascataqua means "a divided tidal place," the river of this name being divided at the mouth into two streams by the island of New Castle. It no doubt does signify a divided or branched river. The Pascataqua is, in fact, a forked river, with two great branches—one coming down from East Pond in the northeast corner of Wakefield, and the other from Great and Little Bays. These unite at Hilton's Point, whence this confluent stream flows eastward to the Atlantic, seven miles distant.

The Hon. C. H. Bell, in his *History of Exeter*, aptly compares the Pascataqua and its tributaries to "a man's left hand and wrist, back upwards, and fingers wide apart. The thumb would stand for the Salmon Falls or Newichwannock river, the forefinger for Bellamy river, the second finger for Oyster river, the third for Lamprey river, and the fourth for Exeter or Squamscot river; while the palm of the hand would represent the Great Bay, into which most of those streams pour their waters, and the wrist the Pascataqua proper." A branched river, indeed, as the name signifies.

Different names are given to different parts of the Pascataqua. According to Belknap, the eastern branch, from its source to the lower falls at Berwick, is called the *Salmon Falls river*. Then it assumes the name of *Newichawannock*, which it bears till it meets with the Cochecho. The early settlers on Dover Neck called that part between the mouth of the Cochecho and Hilton's Point by the name of *Fore river*.

Dr. Quint thinks the name of Pascataqua should be confined to the western branch. At the head of this branch is Great Bay, the waters of which empty into Little Bay at the Narrows. The lower bound of Little Bay is *Fox point*, opposite which is *Goat island* below the mouth of Oyster river. *Cedar point* is just below the Durham end of the old Pascataqua bridge, with *Royall's cove* at the east. Beyond is *Clement's point*, at the mouth of Back river, on the westerly side. Between Back River and Newington are the *Horse Races*, where the current of the Pascataqua is rapid and turbulent. At Hilton's Point, otherwise Dover Point, this western branch unites with the Newichawannock, forming what the old records often call the *Main river*, which flows thence in a direct course towards the Atlantic ocean. This straight portion of the river, between Dover Point and the Narrows, below Boiling Rock, is called the *Long Reach*.

The chief points and coves along

the Newington shore, beginning at the Greenland line, and proceeding in the direction of Fox Pt., succeed each other as follows. First comes *Pincomb's* or *Pinkham's creek*, near the line—the upper boundary of the old Pickering grant. The lower boundary is called *Swadden's creek*, otherwise *Mill creek*. Off this shore is *Swadden's island*, now often corrupted to *Swan island*. Farther down is *Fabyan's Point*, formerly *Starbuck's*, at the upper side of *Laighton's cove*. At the lower side of this cove is *Long point*, otherwise *Woodman's*. Off shore is *Nanney's island*. Below is *Small point*. The cove below is no doubt the ancient *Hogsty Cove*, at the lower side of which is *Furber's point*, at the Narrows, which separate Great and Little bays. Below Furber's point, or ferry-place, is *Welsh Cove*, otherwise *Welshman's*, with *Dame's point* at the lower side, sometimes called *Joshua's Point*. Then comes *Dumpling Cove*, with the "*Sow and Pigs*" off shore, to be seen at low tide. Farther down is *Bald Head*, just beyond which is *Fox point*, the most prominent headland on the Newington shore. At the lower side is *Hen island*. We are now in *Broad cove*. Midway along the shore of this cove is *Rocky point*, otherwise *Carter's Rocks*. At the lower side of Broad cove is *Stephen's point*, now *Bean's*. Below is *Coleman's creek*. Then comes *Zackey's point*, otherwise *Orchard point*, with *Trickey's cove* at the lower side. Below is *Nancy Drew's point*, a subdivision of Bloody point, formerly the landing-place of *Knight's ferry*. Just below is the point to which the name of *Bloody Point* is now confined. It is the terminus of the Dover Point bridge. In the river below, perhaps thirty rods from the shore, are the *Langstaffe Rocks*, dangerous to shipping, with a wrecked schooner now lying near. On the neighboring shore is *Pickering's Cove*, otherwise *Whidden's*, and a creek which once divided the Bickford and Carter lands, and ran a mill. Below is *Birch Point*, no doubt the *Pine Point* of early times. Farther down is *Uncle Siah's cove*, properly *Downing's cove*, just above *Patterson's Lane*. Off shore is *Shag Rock*. *Ragg's point*, otherwise *Beetle's*, is on the shore of the Rollins farm. Farther down is the *Upper Huntress* landing-place, now owned by Miss Mary Huntress. Below is *Paul's Creek*, the *Kenny* or *Canney's creek* of early times. Then comes *Hill's cove*, no doubt the old *Pine Cove*. A short distance below begins the *Gosling road*, which separates Newington from Portsmouth. At the lower side is the landing-place called the *Lower Huntress*. A ferry once ran from this point to the Eliot shore, at Paul's ship-yard, whence another road led into the country. *Boiling Rock* is off the Eliot shore, a little below. Beyond are the *Narrows*. Here is *Cutt's eddy*, the worst in the river. On the shore is *Wentworth Point*, better known as the *Pulpit*, so called from a rock that hangs out from the shore, where sailors in passing formerly "made their manners" for the sake of good luck, and still do so to some extent. An anecdote is related in Brewster's *Rambles* of General Sullivan's refusing to pay the customary mark of respect in passing the Pulpit, and the means used by the boatmen to make him doff his hat. President Cutt, in his will, gives his wife the use of land at y^e *Pulpit* till his son Samuel should be of age. It was here Madam Ursula Cutt retired after his death, and was killed by the Indians in 1694. The Pulpit is now owned by the Hon. Frank Jones. Below is *Cutt's Cove*, with *Freeman's Point* beyond, for two hundred years called *Ham's Point*, from William Ham, who had a grant of land here in 1652, and built a house on it before 1654. On the Kittery shore, opposite, are *Adams Oaks*.[1]

Going up the Long Reach, the river boatmen, after passing Frank's Fort, used to sing out, " Barn Door ! " as soon as they caught sight of a barn on a distant hill, the doors of which were never known to be shut. This was the signal for a dram, and the men would flat their oars and take their grog, the better to stem the strong current of the Long Reach. Another dram was always found necessary at the *Horse Races*, after entering the western branch of the Pascataqua, where the current is very swift and powerful. And the Oyster river boatmen took one at *Half-Tide Rock*, on entering the mouth of that stream.

The name of Pascataqua, variously written Pascataquack, Piscataway, etc., was in early times, not only given to the river itself, but to the entire settlement on both shores, from the mouth upward.

PASCATAQUA ROCK. This rock is mentioned in the following conveyance of June 17, 1674 :—" I, William ffurbur, Senr, for ye entire affection I bear to my son Will : ffurbur, my first-born son, do by these p'sents give to him & his heirs forev^r all my now dwelling house, both ye old and new one, wth my barn and all out housing, wth all my Land from *Piscataq Rock* to the north End of Anthony Nutter his land to ye north of this line," etc. This was the farm at Furber's ferry. March 2, 1704, Jethro ffurbur, of Portsmouth (son of Jethro, deceased, mariner), out of love and affection, conveyed to his loving cousin, Jethro ffurber, son of William of Dover, his uncle, twenty-five acres of land at or near Great Bay in Portsmouth, fronting the river between *Pascataqua Rock* and *Small Point*, adjoining Wm. ffurber's land, said land having belonged to Jethro's father, also named Jethro, who intended to give it to Jethro, son of William. This land is now owned by Mr. J. W. Hoyt.

Pascataqua Rock, which separated the ferry farm from Jethro Furber's farm, was, according to tradition, the terminal bound of the old Dover line from Canney's creek to Hogsty Cove. It was a large slaty rock near the shore, which was gradually broken up by the frost, and carried away by the ice and strong tides.

PASTURES. Land for a *Calves' Pasture* was granted to the settlers on Dover Neck the 5th, 10 mo.,

---

[1] In this connection it might be added that *Christian Shore*, at Portsmouth, a name whose origin has been questioned, was so called, the writer remembers hearing her grandmother say, from the number of baptisms by immersion on this shore by the Rev. Elias Smith, a noted "revivalist," at the beginning of this century, who organized a Baptist church in Portsmouth March 20, 1803.

1652, at the lower end of the Neck, on the west side. This pasture was divided among them, or their heirs, Ap. 16, 1722. As it contained 36 acres, and there were 27 proprietors, each right amounted to one acre and a third. John Tuttle conveyed to Amos Pinkham Feb. 9, 1708-9, three shares in the *Calves' pasture*, originally granted to Joseph Austin, Wm. Furber, and Thomas Roberts, Sr., lying between John Pinkham's land and a lane on ye north side of Hall's land, butting on ye Back river on ye west, and on y^e *lower way* on ye east. Nine shares were set off to Otis Pinkham Ap. 16, 1722, extending from the spring below John Pinkham's house 32 rods by the *low street*, and 36 rods by the water side, beginning at the run of water that comes from the spring. And that same day eight shares were set off to Thomas Canney, extending from Otis Pinkham's head line by the *low street* 32 rods, and 33 rods by the water side to a fence on the south side of the *Long Gutt*, so called. It is evident from the above that the Calves' Pasture was on the west side of Dover Neck, below Pinkham's spring.

An *Ox Pasture* was laid out in Hilton's Point swamp in 1652, which was afterwards divided among the inhabitants of Dover Neck. Timothy Carl or Caroll conveyed to John Knight, Sr., Dec. 10, 1710, one shore of the *ox common* on Dover Neck, at Hilton's Point, bought of Samuel Cromwell. (See *Hilton's Point Swamp*.)

Two "*Quaker Pastures*" were also granted to the Society of Friends. One of these, granted June 25, 1717, was in the upper part of Dover Neck, "between the Watering Gutt and the Cochecho." It is mentioned March 20, 1729-30, when a road was ordered to be laid out from y^e *Quaker Pasture* to the way that leads from the watering gutt to Samuel Carle's. Another Quaker pasture of ten acres, between the Bellamy and the mast path to Mallego, was re-granted March 30, 1733, and laid out July 25, 1733, beginning at a poplar tree *by the head line of Dover*, and extending N. E. to a pitch-pine tree by the way that goes to Mallego, and so by said way S. W. 80 rods, etc. This pasture is mentioned May 10, 1736, when 6 acres were laid out to Timothy Tibbets near his dwelling-place, beginning at the east side of y^e *hook*, near ye bridge, and running thence S. W. to a road that comes from the *Quaker pasture*. And Jan. 12, 1742, Ichabod Canney conveyed to Robert Hanson 35¾ acres " in *Malligo woods*, at a place called y^e *Sapplings*, on the southerly side of ye road y^t leads from Littleworth to Barrington," 23 acres of which began at the S. E. corner of the ten acres laid out to the Quakers.

A *Sheep Pasture* on Dover Neck is mentioned the 5th, 10 mo., 1659, when a part of it was set off by the town for a training-ground. Jedediah Andrews of Salisbury, Mass., and Mary his wife, conveyed to the Rev. John Reyner, Jan. 5, 1669, their dwelling-house on the east side of Dover Neck, and the lot it stood on, originally granted said Andrews by the town of Dover, and laid out the 17th of March *An^o Salutis* 1659, bounded east by said Reyner's land, north by Reyner's upper lot, south by Mr. Robert's lot, and west by the *Sheep pasture*. Edward Whitehouse quit claim to the heirs of Moses Varney, May 29, 1761, to three acres of "ye land called the *Sheep's Pasture*," which for some years previous had been in possession of said Moses. This Pasture was on Huckleberry Hill.

PATTERSON'S LANE. This lane is just above the Rollins mansion in Newington. It leads from the main road to an old landing-place on the Pascataqua river, below "Uncle Siah's creek." (See *Patterson's Point*.)

PATTERSON'S POINT. This point is on the Newington shore of the Pascataqua, at the foot of *Patterson's Lane*, where Joseph Patterson had a wharf last century. He acquired a portion of the Rollins or Rawlins land June 14, 1769, and another adjoining in 1772. This land was afterwards reconveyed to the Rollins family by Temperance, his widow. At the upper side of Patterson's Lane, in a thicket beside the wall, is the grave of Joseph Patterson, with a headstone of slate, briefly inscribed: "J. P.   A 85. 1787." (See *Ragg's Point*.)

PAUL'S COVE. This cove is on the Rollinsford shore of the Newichawannock river, below High Point. It is so called from Mr. Henry Paul, the proprietor of the adjacent land, whose house is opposite this cove.

PAUL'S CREEK. This is the first creek below the upper Huntress, on the Newington shore, and derives its name from Stephen Paul of Eliot, to whom Winthrop Pickering conveyed 50 acres of land, Ap. 29, 1862, beginning at the road from Fox Pt. to Portsmouth, and running east by the land of Isaac and Amos Dow to the Pascataqua river. This was no doubt the Canney or Kenney's creek of early times.

PIERCE'S BROOK. This brook rises in the Barrington woods and empties into the Bellamy river in the upper part of Madbury.

PEARL'S FERRY. "John Parell" was licensed to keep a ferry over Back river from his house or landing-place over to Sergeant Drew's usual landing-place, March 13, 1722–3; to receive "one penny for every inhabitant so carried and fetched over, and 2^d for strangers." John Pearl was the son of Nicholas Pearl, who was killed by the Indians not far from Pudding Hill in 1707. His ferry seems to have run from what is now called *Nute's point*, at the lower side of Little John's creek. A public road still leads to this landing-place from the main road to Dover Pt. It was doubtless here that John Pearl acquired four acres of land, conveyed to him by Thomas Waits, Feb. 18, 1739–40. (See *Cromwell's Creek*.) Benjamin Roberts conveyed to John Pearl, Jan. 4, 1744–5, a tract of land ten rods square, beginning at the corner where the road that leads from the country road down to Austin's mill crosses the way between the lands of Abraham Nute and Benjamin Roberts. And Roberts also conveyed to John Pearl, Aug. 3, 1752, four acres adjoining s^d Pearl's dwelling-house lot, previously bought of said Roberts, adjoining the highway that leads by said Pearl's house down to the Back river. This land was sold by Mary, the widow of John Pearl, to Moses Varney Ap. 2, 1754. (See *Cromwell's Creek*.)

PEAR YARD DISTRICT. This name is given to the school district in the northwestern part of Rollinsford. Its origin is shown by a vote passed by the town of Somersworth March 16, 1793: that "the school-house for Number Two, or the west district, shall be at a certain place called the old back road, opposite a certain *Pear-Yard* in the possession of Andrew Rollins, or as near said spot as there can be a piece of land procured for the house." The "*Pear Yard district*" is mentioned in the Somersworth records of 1814. (See *Yard Country Way*.)

PEIRCE'S CREEK and PEIRCE'S POINT. These names are now sometimes given to *Packer's Creek* and *Point*, on the Greenland shore of the Great Bay. "*Pierces Pt.*" is mentioned on Chace's County map of 1857. (See *Greenland* and *Packer's Creek*.)

PELATIAH'S HILL. This hill is in Lee, on the south side of Little river, below the sawmill. So named from Pelatiah Thompson, son of Robert and Susanna, who was born July 15, 1765, and died Nov. 8, 1843. It was in Pelatiah's early life that his father removed his dwelling-house from the valley to the top of this hill, where it now stands.

PERRY'S HILL. This hill is in Madbury, and belongs to the same ridge as Harvey's hill; from which it is only separated by a small hollow. The Freetown road from Madbury to Barrington crosses this ridge. The name is said to have been derived from a Perry family, whose cellar on this hill can still be traced. A Matthew Perry and his six children are mentioned in the records of the Rev. Hugh Adams. He was no doubt the Matthew Pierre, to whom Timothy Emerson and wife Mary, July 4, 1736, conveyed 15 acres and 146 rods of land in Durham, beginning at John Sias' east corner bound, thence extending south to a white oak by Oyster river running by Newtown.

PETER'S MARSH. This name is given to Starbuck's marsh in Somersworth, from Peter Coffin, to whom his father-in-law Edward Starbuck conveyed all his rights in Dover not otherwise disposed of, June 19, 1678. "The bounds of a piece or plot of marsh commonly called *Starbuck's marsh* or *Peter's marsh*, granted Edward Starbuck by the town of Dover on ye 30th of 6th mo. 1643, were newly run, laid out, and bounded, June 25, 1735, for Capt. Eliphalet Coffin of Exeter, beginning at a heap of stones on the east side of the road that leads over the brook that comes out of *the great pond*, a little eastward of *the falls* in said brook or on the south side of said brook." This brook is known as *Peter's Marsh brook*. (See *Starbuck's Marsh*.)

PETER'S MARSH BROOK. Mentioned Sept. 6, 1736, when thirty acres of land were laid out to Isaac Hanson on the S. W. side of Salmon Falls river, extending up the river to the mouth of a brook commonly called *Peter's marsh brook*, thence up this brook to and along the land of Ebenezer Wentworth. This is the brook mentioned in the grant of Starbuck's marsh in 1643 as coming out of the Great Pond. It connects Willand's Pond with Salmon Falls river. The eastern part is now sometimes called *Brown's brook*, and the middle part is often called *Tate's brook*.

PETER'S OVEN. This name is given to a natural cave in the side of a steep ledge, a short distance above Lee Hill, on the right hand side of the road to Barrington. It is mentioned July 10, 1721, when 100 acres of land, originally granted to Wm. Williams, Sr., in 1662, and laid out to Wm. Roberts in 1663, on the west side of " Whell Rights Pond," were laid out anew to Moses Davis and John Thompson, Jr., beginning at a pitch-pine tree on the west side of the cartway that leads to "*Peter's Ouen*, soe called." And again May 29, 1752, when land on " the south side of the way leading from the Place commonly called *Peter's Oven* to the head of the township," was conveyed by John Pitman to Jonathan Thompson, Jr. One tradition says this name was derived from an Indian named Peter, who, wounded at the battle of Wheelwright's pond, succeeded in reaching this cave, into which he crawled, and there died. According to another tradition, it was so called from a negro named Peter, who once made it his haunt, and gave it a diabolical reputation.

The name of "oven" is often given to a cave in Ireland, from the Irish word *Uamhain*, pronounced *oovan*, whence the corruption of oven. *Uamhain* is evidently akin to the Gaelic word *Uaimh*, used by Scott, who, in "Waverley," gives the name of *Uaimh an Ri*, or *Chieftain's cave*, to the dwelling-place of Donald Bean Lean.

PICKED ROCK. This ancient boundary is mentioned July 12, 1723, when the committee appointed by the N. H. General Assembly concerning a bridge across Lamprey river at the lowest falls, reported that the best place for its erection would be " at the *Picked rock*, so called, a little above the first Dam in s^d river." And Benjamin Thomas, in his report to the House, Dec. 13, 1723, agreed that the most convenient place would be " at a *Picked Rock* upon the lower falls, near y^e *old Dam*." (*N. H. Prov. Pap.*, IV : 124, 125.)

When the selectmen of Durham and Newmarket perambulated the dividing line " from Lamprey-eel River bridge to the great bay," March 4, 1805, they began " at the *picked Rock* under said bridge, and ran S. 56½° E. 264 rods, to the head of *Goddard's Creek*, so called, thence by the channel of said creek to the mouth thereof at the bay aforesaid." (*Durham Records.*)

The *Picked Rock* is spoken of June 19, 1818, as " in the south butment of Durham and Lamperell River bridge, so called." (*N. H. Town Pap.*, XII : 390.)

Andrew Doe, Seth Shackford and others, Ap. 19, 1823, conveyed to Daniel M. Durell and Stephen Hanson of Dover, $\frac{15}{24}$ of the saw-mill on Lamprey river, in Newmarket, and ¾ of the grist mill, with the fulling-mill, all standing together, with the same proportion of all the privileges on both sides of the river, beginning at the *Bryant rock*, so called, on the west side of said river, at high water mark, then running south 60 deg. W. 4 rods, to the road leading from Exeter to Durham, then by said road northerly 41$\frac{2}{10}$ rods to the *picked rock*, so called, standing on the N. W. side of the southerly abutment of Lamprey river bridge, dividing the county of Rockingham from the county of

Strafford, and thence running southeasterly to a bound on the west side of the Lubberland road, etc.

The Picked Rock is no longer one of the bounds between Rockingham and Strafford counties, since the cession of a part of Durham to Newmarket in 1870.

The *Bryant Rock*, above mentioned, derived its name from Walter Bryant, who, in 1870 bought the Drisco land (see the *Narrows*), including ten acres where formerly lived Philip Crommet, who was licensed to keep a ferry across Lamprey river in 1671.

PICKERING'S COVE, or CREEK. This inlet is at the upper side of Birch point, on the Newington shore, and is variously named, according to the owner of the adjacent lands. It is sometimes called *Whidden's Creek*. A sawmill here is mentioned in 1702, which probably stood at the head of tide water. The fresh water brook that empties into it is mentioned in 1664, when Richard Carter had a grant of land at Pine Point (now Birch Pt.), which came within four poles of the *freshet*. (See *Pine Point*.) This brook appears to have been the "Dirty Gut" of early times. (See *Dirty Gut*.) The name of Pickering's Cove is derived from James Pickering, who acquired the Walton lands in this vicinity shortly after the Revolution.

PICKERING'S CROSSING. This crossing is in the southwestern part of Rochester, east of the Cochecho, where the Dover and Winnipiseogee R. R. crosses the highway near the house of Mrs. T. D. Pickering.

PIKE'S FALLS. (See *Cochecho Falls*.)

PIMPLE STONE. This was one of the old landmarks hailed by the boatmen on the Pascataqua river as they entered the western branch, and fortified themselves for encountering the Horse Races by means of a copious dram. It was a large rock west of Dover Point, with a broad white stripe around it, rendering it conspicuous at a great distance. According to a legend this rock was, when *small*, slung across the river from the Newington shore by an enraged old housewife, by means of a skein of white yarn fastened around it.[1] This skein, of course, produced the white stripe. This is a sailor's *yarn*, however, which unfortunately cannot be verified, for the Pimple Stone was long since blown up and removed by some odious utilitarian.

PINCH HILL. This hill is in Rollinsford, where the turnpike road is crossed by the highway to the Rollinsford station. It is mentioned Feb. 16, 1721-22, when Joseph Roberts conveyed to Benj[n] Wentworth 15 acres of land "near y[e] hill known and called by y[e] name of *Pinch hill*, bounded S. by land of said Wentworth, and thence running westerly to y[e] highway which leads from y[e] *Pine plains* to Fresh creek." And again Feb. 29, 1733-4, when Francis Sayer of Ipswich, Mass., conveyed to Benj[n] Waymouth 20 acres of land in Somersworth, with a dwelling-house thereon, beginning at "Nechawonock river," and thence running westerly on y[e] possession of Eleazar

---

[1] Among the legends of Cromarty, in Scotland, is one of a ponderous stone whirled from the point of a spindle across Dornoch firth.

Wyer[1] to a certain highway or private road, called *Pinch Hill road*, to yᵉ sᵈ Benjⁿ Waymouth's land, thence southerly to a highway between said land and yᵉ former grant of John Hall, Deacon, thence easterly by said road to the river; which land had been mortgaged by said Waymouth's father to Francis Sayer.

Pinch Hill was so named because it was too sharp and narrow to be crossed by more than one team at a time. Rollinsford, however, at the town-meeting of 1891, wisely appropriated $800 for the purpose of widening it.

PINDER'S POINT. This name, no longer used, is given on Smith's map of Durham to a point on the Lubberland shore, between Jewell's Pt. and Morris's Pt. It was derived from John Pinder, brickmaker, to whom John York of Lubberland, May 16, 1681, conveyed a tract of land, "beginning at the *Little point* in *Clift Cove*, adjoining Thomas Morris's, and so over the neck to a pine tree by the path to Lubberland." John Pinder, Oct. 27, 1701, had a grant of ten acres joining the land where he then lived. The Pinder land in 1715 is mentioned as next the Footman land.

PINE COVE. This cove is on the Newington shore of the Long Reach. It is mentioned Dec. 5, 1661, when 240 acres were laid out to Capt. Bryan Pendleton next to James Rawlins, beginning at *Kenney's Cove*, and running down by the river side 80 rods to *pyne cove*, thence into the woods 480 rods to the edge of the *pitch pine plaine*. (*Portsmouth Records*.)

Ichabod Plaisted of Portsmouth, and Mary his wife, June 15, 1703, relinquished to Richard Gerrish of Portsmouth 27 acres of land *in Portsmouth*, part of 240 acres formerly laid out to Brian Pendleton, and purchased by Christopher Jose of Portsmouth, deceased, bounded upon yᵉ main river, commonly called by yᵉ name of yᵉ *long reach*, which 240 acres begin at *Kenny's Cove* and run by the river 80 rods to *pine cove*, thence into yᵉ woods to the edge of the *pitch pine plains* upon a S. S. W. line. (See *Hill's Cove*.)

PINE HILL. The public cemetery in Dover is on this hill, at the lower end of the city proper. Here stood the third meeting-house in Dover, which was, according to the Rev. Dr. Quint, a few rods from the Cushing tomb, a little west of north. It was built before May 2, 1711, when "four acres were laid out to the Reauerant Mr. Nicholas Seuer between Mr. Paul Gerrish his house and the new meeting-house, beginning at the corner of the highway that leads from Cochecha Road to Campin's Rocks, and running thence north and be west thirty rods by Cochecha Road to a Little gully," etc. This grant to the Rev. Mr. Sever was probably for a parsonage. His successor, the Rev. Jonathan Cushing, lived on Pine Hill, where his well is still pointed out.

March 29, 1731, the town voted

---

[1] The Wyer "possession" was originally James Grant's land, then David Hamilton's, and at a later period Henry Nock's, whose widow Sarah, daughter of Charles Adams of Oyster River, afterwards married Eleazar Wyer, and conveyed this land to her step-son of the same name. This land is now owned by the Garvins. (See *Newichawannock* and *Sligo*.)

"That there be one acre and a half of Land Granted for the use of the Town forever, for a public Burying-place, To be Laid out by ye select men near ye meeting house on *pine hill* at Cochecha." Nov. 26, 1759, the town appointed "a committee to Sell the old meeting-house standing on s^d *pine hill* in the best manner they Can." It was still standing, however, March 31, 1760, when the town-meeting was held therein.

A school-house stood on Pine hill early last century, and when the church bell was brought from Dover Neck in 1720, there being no belfry on the meeting-house at Pine hill, it was hung, it is said, on the neighboring school-house. The town voted, Oct. 13, 1760, "to sell the old school-house standing on *pine hill*." It was near the present school-house, if not on the same spot.

Another PINE HILL is in Newington, mentioned June 2, 1800, when Seth Walker, with Lucy his wife, and Eleanor his mother, conveyed to Richard Pickering 5¾ acres, part of a tract given said Eleanor and Seth in the will of Gideon Walker, beginning at the road to Bloody Pt., at the N. E. corner of Nathaniel Folsom's land, and running N. E. along said road to the land of Paul Rawlins; being part of the place commonly known by the name of *pine hill*. This hill is no doubt the ridge to which *Dow's hill* belongs, but it no longer bears its ancient name.

The *Pine hill* of the present day in Newington is on the road from Fox Pt. to Portsmouth, and derives its name from *Knight's pines*, now *Hoyt's Pines*, adjacent to this hill. It is a part of Stony hill.

PINE POINT. This point is on the Newington shore of the Long Reach, at the lower side of Pickering's cove, otherwise Whidden's. It is mentioned June 24, 1648, when Richard Carter, "sometime dwelling in Piscataway," sold house and land on *Pine point* to his trusty and well beloved friend, Matthew Giles, dwelling in Oyster River. Richard Carter had, however, a grant of 35 acres at *Pine Point*, laid out the 10th, 12 mo., 1664, one bound of which came within four poles of the *freshet*. His children owned this land till Oct. 8, 1702, when his son Richard and wife Margaret, with Edward Carter, and Mary their sister, conveyed to John Knight, *alias* Chevalier, 50 acres of land "at a place formerly called *Pine point*, near or adjacent to a place commonly called *Bloody Point*, granted by Dover to Richard Carter, deceased, bounded on the N. W. side of a lot formerly Michael Brawns, now in possession of John Downing, and adjoining the land of Benjⁿ Bickford." Also 20 acres, beginning at the highway from Bloody Point to Portsmouth, bounded on the north by Geo. Braun's, south by John Downing's, with a quarter part of the *saw-mill* on the same; reserving, however, eighteen feet where their father and mother lay buried in one corner of the orchard.

Benjamin Bickford and wife Sarah conveyed to John Knight, *alias* Chevalier, of Portsmouth, Dec. 7, 1702, 16 acres of meadow formerly belonging to Benjamin's father (John Bickford, of Oyster River), lying betwixt a place formerly called *Pine Point* and a place commonly called Bloody Point, bounded on land said Knight bought of Richard Carter on the south, Henry Langstaffe's on the north, the river on the east, and the highway at the west, together with one fourth of the *saw-mill* between said land and that of John Knight, formerly Carter's. From this it is evident that Pine Point is the little promontory below Bloody Point, known by different names, according to the owner, such as *Pickering's Point* and *Furber's Point*. It is now owned by Mr. Furber, and is generally known as *Birch Point*, from the numerous white birch trees along the shore, conspicuous at a great distance. On this point, in a beautiful, wild, lonely spot, is the grave of John Knight, the exile, shaded by sassafras trees and tall white birches whose boles gleam afar off like shafts of polished marble. It is marked by a low, broad, three-lobed headstone of slate, on which, beneath an incised death's head and cross-bones, is this inscription: "Here lyes buried the body of John Knight, Esqr, born August ye 30, 1659, and died May the 11th, 1721."

Another PINE POINT is on the western shore of the Newichawannock, below St. Alban's cove. It is mentioned March 19, 1693-4, when 20 acres of land were laid out to Jonathan Watson on Fresh creek neck, fronting on fore river, above *Pine Poynt*. Pine point is mentioned on Pike's map of Somersworth in 1805. It is the first point below St. Alban's cove, and is now owned by Mr. Henry Paul. Daniel Paul and wife Dorothy, March 7, 1791, conveyed to Thomas Roberts 30½ acres of land, part of the estate of Capt. Benjn Mason, beginning at the S. E. corner, on *Pine point*, on the west side of Salmon Falls river, and running northerly by the land of Benjn Paul.

PINKHAM'S CREEK, otherwise PINCOMB'S. This creek is the upper boundary of the grant to John Pickering on the shore of Great Bay, mentioned in the Portsmouth records of Feb., 1655:

"It is this day granted unto John pickringe that hee shall haue the land lying betwen *swadens creek* and *pincomb's creek* in the great bay so that it bee no mans former Right or property. the sayd land is to extend into the swamp and no farther."

In the former edition of this work Pinkham's creek is stated to be the inlet at the lower end of the Pickering grant, and Swadden's at the upper end. Further investigation proves that the upper creek is Pinkham's, and the lower one Swadden's; the words "upper" and "lower" referring to the course of the river or bay, not to the points of the compass. A portion of this grant fell within the limits of Ancient Dover, being part of the 400 acres on Great Bay allowed that town by the Mass. government; "due right," however, being reserved to "every one that hath proprietyes in the same." (*N. H. Prov. Pap.*, 1 : 172.)

Pinkham's creek rises in the Great Swamp, and empties into the Great Bay on the borders of Newington and Greenland. The highway between these two towns crosses the creek about eight rods below the Greenland line. The name is derived from Richard Pinckhame or Pinkham, of the Dover Combination of 1640, who had a grant of land on Great Bay sometime previous to June 30, 1659, when Thomas Layton certified under oath before Thomas Dantforth that "the town of Dover gave Richard Pincham a lott of marsh in ye Great bay, & y^t s^d Pincum sould all his right that he had in said marsh to Joseph Austin of Dover." (*Dover Records.*)

Mention is made of this creek in a petition of May 2, 1716, that the bounds of Portsmouth might "run from the river on ye north side of Mr. Roger's Creek or dock, on a straight line to *Pincom's creek.*" (*N. H. Prov. Pap.*, 17: 727.) Thomas Pickering, son of the above John, "out of parental love and affection to his well-beloved son Joshua, for his encouragement in beginning the world," conveyed to him, Ap. 30, 1719, a parcel of land and marsh in Portsmouth, on the easterly side of the Great Bay, "beginning at the N. W. corner of *Hall's farm* (afterwards *Packer's*), at the water side, thence to run to the middle of a long point, southeasterly from *Swaden's* island, thence to Col. Wentworth's land, so as to contain 50 acres, together with the full half of the marsh formerly called and known by the name of *Pincomb's creek* or *marsh*, etc., and one third of the sawmill and all water privileges." And June 6, 1719, he gave his son Thomas "half of the marsh at *Pinkom's creek*," together with one third of his sawmill. This was perhaps the "new mill," mentioned March 6, 1710–11, when a road was ordered to be opened through Thomas Pickering's farm as far as y^e *new mill*, and thence straight through Hall's farm to the bridge by Hains (Haynes's, in Greenland.)

In an indenture of June 25, 1739, between Joshua Pickering and the heirs of Joseph Hall, it was agreed that the dividing line between their lands should "begin at the easternmost post of ye gate upon ye country road, upon ye southerly side of the bridge near the aforesaid Joshua Pickering's house, which gate divides between Greenland and Newington." The line is also stated therein to run "from a stake near a rotten stump on ye bank by ye side of ye Bay at high water mark, north 26 deg. west, to y^e *marsh creek* y^t proceeds out of ye marsh commonly called by ye name of *Pinkham's marsh*, and thence to run as said creek or channel runs." A plan of "Hall's farm at Greenland, beginning at a place called *Pinkum's creek*," is to be found in the Exeter registry, in the division of Joseph Hall's estate, Nov. 19, 1743.

PINKHAM'S HILL. This hill is on the borders of Dover and Madbury. It is mentioned May 31, 1812, when the way from Libbey's bridge (now Sawyer's) "by the new road to Durham as far as *Pinkham's hill*," is spoken of. The guide post at the foot of *Pinkham's hill*, on the Dover road to Madbury line, leading both to Durham and to Piscataqua bridge, is mentioned the same year. The name is derived from a family that owned land in this vicinity for nearly 200 years. John Pinkham had a grant of 50 acres on the S. W. side of Thomas Drew's, Ap. 11, 1694. Thomas Drew's land adjoined that of Benedictus Torr.

PINKHAM'S POINT. This name is given on Whitehouse's map of 1834 to a point on the western shore of the Cochecho, about half way between Woodchuck island and Gage's Point. It is now owned by Mr. Minother. The old road to the landing-place on this point can still be traced, as well as the cellar of Paul Pinkham's house, from whom the present name was derived.

PINKHAM'S SPRING. This spring is mentioned in a deed from John Hall to Thomas Kenny June 26, 1716. (See *Nutter's Slip*.) It is at the head of a run on Dover Neck, a short distance southwest of the site of Pinkham's garrison, now owned by Mr. Charles Thompson.

PISCASSICK RIVER. See *Pascassick*.

PISCATAQUA RIVER. See *Pascataqua*.

PISS HILL. This hill is mentioned May 26, 1731, when 8 acres of marsh, granted Joseph Evans Ap. 6, 1702, were conveyed by him to Wm. Forst, beginning at a pitch-pine tree near a place commonly called Piss hill, and extending at the S. E. to the end of a little pond. Part of Otis Pinkham's share of the common lands in 1734, was laid out to him June 10, 1735, on the N. E. side of the road leading to Rochester, "beginning at the *first slow* above Piss hill, so called." The "*upper slough*" on the Rochester road is mentioned Nov. 5, 1734. Eight acres were laid out to Ephraim Tebbets Nov. 15, 1735, on the east side of the *Mast road* that goes to Rochester, near the *first slow* above Piss hill, beginning at the S. W. corner of Otis Pinkham's land. This hill is repeatedly mentioned in the Dover records. It is above Willand's Pond in the Blackwater region, on the borders of Dover and Somersworth.

PITCH-PINE PLAINS. The *Pitch-Pine Plains of Newington* are in the central part of the township. They are spoken of Dec. 5, 1661, as adjoining Capt. Bryan Pendleton's land. (See *Pine Cove*.) They are again mentioned Ap. 2, 1694, when Richard Pumerey's (Pomeroy's) grant of " 20 acres joining zachery trickey's twenty acres in the *pich pine plains*," was confirmed by the town of Dover. This land was laid out to Richard Pumery June 18, 1697, on the east side of Greenland road, adjoining " Zachery " Trickey's. Nathan and Elizabeth Spinney of Kittery, Ap. 21, 1725, conveyed to Capt. John Knight of Newington, gentleman, all right and title to 20 acres in Newington, bounded northward by the road from the ferry to Greenland, eastward by the land of Eleazar Coleman, southward by the parsonage land, and westward by the land of Wm. Vaughan, deceased, which tract was the estate of Richard Pomery, late of Newington, deceased, who was father to ye said Elizabeth Spinney. Jane Pomery also quit claim to said Knight that same day. " The gore in the *pitch pine plains* of Newington " is mentioned Feb. 14, 1723–4. (See the *Gore*.)

The "*upper Pitch Pine plains*" are mentioned March 14, 1770, when Richard Downing, Esq., of Newington, conveyed to Jonathan Quint one acre of land at a place commonly called *the upper Pitch Pine Plains*, adjoining the road that leads from Newington meeting house to Greenland, and upon a road called *the Narrow Lane* leading to Portsmouth. (See *Downing's Plains*.) These plains are otherwise called Sept. 19, 1685, when " Nathaniel Fryar in the province of Main," having the previous day sold Anthony Libbey "a parcel of land in *Bloody point plains*," appointed Capt. John Pickering, his attorney, to give s^d Libby peaceable possession thereof. In another deed from said Fryar to Henry Sherburne, they are called "*the Pitch-Pine plains going to Bloody Point.*"

Pitch-Pine Plains in the upper part of Dover, on the east side, are mentioned June 23, 1701, in a grant to Tristram Heard of 30 acres between Blackwater bridge and the *pitch pine plains*.

Pitch-Pine Plains in the Back River district are mentioned Ap. 2, 1707, when John and Samuel Williams conveyed to Thomas Davis 13 acres of land on the S. side of the *pitch pine plains* between John Knight's and Oyster River, granted their father by the town of Dover Ap. 16, 1694, and laid out the 13th of June following, beginning at John Pinkham's. These plains are generally called *Field's plains*.

Pitch-Pine Plains in Somersworth are mentioned in Paul Wentworth's will of Feb. 3, 1747-8, in which he gives his nephew John 109 acres of land lying on both sides of the way from Wm. Downs' to the *pitch pine plains*, and so on to the stepping-stones. Thomas Wentworth conveyed to Maturin Ricker, Sept. 1, 1749, a quarter part of 24 acres which Col. Paul Wentworth, deceased, had laid out upon y^e *pitch pine plains*, a little above his swamp. These plains are no doubt the same referred to Aug. 29, 1727, when Richard Waldron conveyed to Tobias Hanson, Thomas Downs, and John McElroy, 200 acres granted to his father Richard Waldron ye 5th, 10 mo., 1652, upon *ye great plain* betwixt Cochecho river and Nechawanock river, to the eastward of ye great Pond. The highway from "*ye Pine plains* to Fresh creek" is mentioned Feb. 16, 1721-22. (See *Pinch Hill.*)

PITMAN'S CREEK. This is an inlet from Oyster river on the shore of the Burnham land, a mile or more below Durham Falls. It is mentioned Nov. 7, 1724, when John Burnham conveyed to Robert Burnham land on the south side of Oyster river, "att a krick known or called by ye name of *Pittman's krick*, between the land of s^d John Burnham and that of Wm. Pitman, son of Ezekiel."

PLATO'S HILL, otherwise PLATE'S and PLATTE'S HILL. This hill is in Dover city, on the borders of the Highway District No. 15, which is defined in the Dover records of 1867 as beginning "at the culvert at *Platte's Hill.*" It is on Hanson street, at its junction with Payne street, and the culvert above mentioned is on the latter street, across George's creek. Platte is a corruption of Plate or Plato, a name derived from Plato Waldron, whose house on the side of this hill, on Hanson street, is still to be seen. He was a well-known, popular negro of stalwart frame, who was janitor of the Dover court-house in the day when the Strafford sessions brought hither such lawyers as Daniel Webster, Jeremiah Mason, and Ichabod Bartlett. He was also sexton of the "First Parish," and figured prominently at funerals, which he liked to attend. Unfortunately he married a white woman late in life, who was not kind to him, and in a fit of despondency he drowned himself in the Cochecho river, not far from the hill that bears his name. George's creek, at the foot of the hill, is often called *Plato Waldron's brook*, and sometimes *Drew's brook*, from the late Wm. Drew, who resided in this vicinity.

PLUM-PUDDING HILL. Mentioned the 17th, 12 mo., 1672, when 50 acres of land were laid out to Peter Coffin "on yᵉ north side of yᵉ great mast path going into yᵉ swamp," the south east corner bounded by a marked tree at the west end of *Plumpudding hill*, and so by yᵉ head of Capt. Walden's land to yᵉ highway that goeth to Tole end, and thence along by land which said Coffin bought of Thomas Nock to yᵉ bridge over yᵉ brook going to Tole end, reserving liberty for a cart-way for the use of the town, if required. It is again mentioned the 7th, 4 mo., 1723, when the five daughters of James Coffin, viz: *Mary*, wife of James Gardner; *Dinah*, wife of Nathaniel Starbuck; *Deborah*, wife of George Bunker; *Ruth*, wife of Joseph Gardner; together with their husbands and their sister, *Elizabeth* Bunker, widow, all of "Sherborn, on Nantucket" conveyed to John Ham of Dover, one half a tract of 75 acres, reserving two acres where the orchard was, bounded by the land of Thomas Downs on the E. or S. E., and by a hill called *Plumbpudding hill* on yᵉ W. or N. W., and by yᵉ highway on yᵉ N. side; which land was conveyed to said James by his brother Peter Coffin, and given by said James to his five daughters in his will of May 17, 1720. (See *Trumbelow Swamp*.) Plum-Pudding Hill is said to be the high ground between Lexington and Arch streets, in Dover city.

PLUM-SWAMP. This swamp is in the southern part of the Durham Point district, below Long marsh. It is called "*plome swamp*" in the Willey grant of March 19, 1693–4. A part of "Plumb Swamp" was sold John Ambler, July 12, 1714, by John, son of Thomas Bickford. Nov. 17, 1718, John Rand sold Francis Mathes thirty-one acres of land south of John Ambler's, bounded east by the bay (Little bay), and extending up towards the woods near yᵉ *plumb swamp*, which land was called by the name of "*Rand's plantation.*" Francis Mathes, Dec. 20, 1748, conveyed to Benjⁿ and Samuel Mathes a tract called *plum swamp*, bounded N. by Stephen Wille's land, W. by that of John Ambler, deceased, S. by the common land and the highway, and E. by a highway that goes to said Wille's. These roads lead to Lubberland and into Horn's woods. The lower part of Plum swamp lays along a brook of the same name, which crosses the highway near Mr. Henry Davis's. The name is still retained. Plum Swamp, Caulley's Marsh, Long Marsh, Broad Marsh, and Moharimet's Marsh, succeed each other from the vicinity of Little Bay to the bounds of Lee.

PLUM-SWAMP BROOK. Mentioned Oct. 14, 1714, when thirty acres were laid out to ffrancis Mathes, beginning at a rock in the *Plum swamp brook*, on the west side of the path that leads from said Mathes his dwelling house to Samuel Edgerle's. This brook rises among the springs in Plum swamp, crosses the road from Durham Point to Lubberland near Mr. Henry Davis's house, and empties into Little Bay on the shore of Mr. John Emerson's farm. At the mouth is a fall of several feet over a perpendicular ledge, which is called the *Falling-off place.*

PLUM-TREE POINT. Mentioned June 2, 1766, when James Bunker of Durham, and wife Sarah, conveyed to Remembrance Clark of Madbury about one acre of thatch bed in Durham, at the head of a small creek, southerly of the house where said Bunker then lived, beginning at a "pople tree" bound between Joseph and James Bunker, and extending around by the upland to "a place called *Plumb tree point.*" This was, of course, at the head of Bunker's creek.

POCKETTY MARSH. Mentioned Jan. 7, 1736-7, when Benedictus Torr conveyed to Abraham Nute three acres of meadow ground and thatch-bed, on yᵉ easterly side of Back river, above yᵉ mouth of Little John's creek, between said river and Joseph Austin's land, commonly called yᵉ *Pocketty Marsh*, alias yᵉ *Boggy Marsh*, which said Torr had purchased of Abraham Nute and John Drew. Abraham and Rachel Nute conveyed this marsh to Joseph Austin Sept. 14, 1737.

POMEROY'S COVE. Mentioned the 5th, 10 mo., 1652, when Richard Waldron had the grant of "a cove on Dover Neck, commonly called *Pomryes Coue*, from *Sandy point* right over to the other side of the coue to make a Docke."—"All the marsh in *pomryes Cove*" was conveyed to Thomas Kemble Nov. 6, 1658. He conveyed it, Jan. 18, 1662, to Peter Coffin, who sold it to Anthony Nutter Feb. 17, 1664, (See *Sandy Point.*) Pomeroy's cove, now called *Card's cove*, is on Fore river, at the lower end of Dover Neck, about half a mile above the lower extremity of Dover Point. It extends westward, cutting the Neck nearly in two. The remains of Capt. Thomas Card's wharf are still to be seen on the north side, probably in the same place as Major Waldron's. The original name of this cove was no doubt derived from Richard Pomeroy, who also owned land in the Bloody Point district. He, or his father, was one of the early settlers at the Shoals.

POND CITY. This name is familiarly given to a neighborhood on the north side of Barbadoes Pond, on the so-called "new road," leading from the Littleworth road along the upper side of the pond.

POND HILL. This hill is on the Stepping-Stones road in Lee below the source of Oyster river. It extends along the upper side of Langley's heath to Wheelwright's pond.

POOR TOWN. Mentioned on Holland's map of 1784. It is in Somersworth, below Hurd's pond, now Cole's, but the name, perhaps derived from the nature of the soil, is no longer in use.

PORTSMOUTH. This name is said to commemorate Capt. John Mason's residence at the English port and naval station of Portsmouth during the wars with France and Spain, at which time he had command of the South Sea Castle which defended the entrance to Portsmouth harbor. This castle perhaps suggested the name of New Castle at the mouth of the Pascataqua. (See Tuttle's *Capt. John Mason.*) The above reason, however, is not given when the inhabitants at Strawberry Bank petitioned to the General Court at Boston, May, 1653, to have the name of that Bank changed to Portsmouth—the latter, says the petition, " being a name most suitable for this place. it beinge (at) the River's mouth & a good (harbour) as any in this land." (*N. H. Prov. Pap.*, 1 : 208.) Portsmouth, at one period, included the Greenland shore, which had been a part of Ancient Dover. " The county of Dover and Portsmouth" is often mentioned in the early records. (See *Strafford County* and *Trumbelow Swamp*.)

PRAY'S BROOK. This small brook is mentioned as between the lands of Moses Pray and Francis Plumer, July 3, 1849, when the bounds between Somersworth and Rollinsford were defined. (See *Rollinsford*.) It rises between the Pray house and Indigo hill, and runs in a nearly direct course to the Salmon Falls river.

PROSPECT HILL. This name has long been given to the height at the upper end of Great Falls village. The Wentworth Genealogy (1 : 278) says that Joseph, son of Benjamin Wentworth, (born Dec. 22, 1709 ; died Jan. 26, 1765) " owned the highlands now known as *Prospect Hill* at Great Falls." On the top of this hill is the reservoir, built for the use of the Manufacturing Co., but generously allowed the village for its supply of water.

PUDDING HILL. This hill is in Madbury, east of the railway station, near the Dover line, and commands an extensive and beautiful view of he surrounding country. It is crossed by the old road from Back river. The name was no doubt derived from the windmill thereon in early times, to which the neighboring farmers brought their corn to be ground. The hill and windmill are both mentioned in the Dover records, May 20, 1734, when Stephen Otis and others petitioned the town for a small tract of land to lie common where *Wm. Dam and Clement Drew's windmill* stood on " *Pudden Hill*," for the convenience of said mill. This petition was not granted. (See *Dam's Windmill*.) At a town-meeting in Madbury, March 30, 1786, it was voted to change the road leading through Benjamin Hill's land to Nock's marsh, beginning at the S. E. corner of Samuel Davis's land, where he then lived, on the main road over *Pudden Hill*, so called, and running by said Davis's land to Remembrance Clark's land, and then to follow the old road first laid out. " Samuel Davis of *Pudden Hill* in Madbury," is mentioned towards the close of last century as marrying Judith Tuttle (born 1762) granddaughter of Ensign John Tuttle, who was killed by the Indians, May 17, 1712. He sprang from the Davises of Oyster River, and his descendants still own the above mentioned land on Pudding Hill.

Many Indian traditions are connected with Pudding Hill. Two men in early times were harvesting grain on the Davis land, when some Indians stole in between them and their muskets, which lay on the ground while they were at work. Catching a glimpse of their foes, the men started, one for the Field's garrison and the other for Woodman's, with the

Indians in pursuit. Both got safely into garrison, and the signal guns, fired almost at the same instant, showed they arrived about the same time.

Near Pudding Hill, at the southeast, lived an unmarried man named Pearl, alone in his cabin. The Indians set fire to the dwelling, and he was burned alive. This was perhaps Nicholas Pearle, who, according to Rev. John Pike's journal, was slain by the Indians in the day time, Aug. 10, 1706, " at his Cave some miles above Oyster River, where he dwelt night and day, winter and summer, from the last breaking out of the war, thō twas in the very wake and way where the enemy used to pass." Belknap calls him Wm. Pearl. Nicholas, however, certainly lived in this vicinity. John Pearl and wife Mary, Nov. 30, 1717, conveyed to James Clark 30 acres of land formerly owned by his father *Nicholas Pearl*, on the south side of the mast path that leads from Benedictus Tarr's to Madberry, between James Bunker's and Joseph Meader's. (See *Pearl's Ferry*.)

QUAKER MEETING-HOUSES. The first meeting-house in the township, built by the Society of Friends, was on Dover Neck. It is mentioned Dec. 11, 1729-30, when Joseph and Elizabeth Roberts conveyed to " Thomas Canney and others of the Society commonly called Quakers," three eighths of an acre of land, beginning 6½ rods from the N. W. corner of the *Quaker meeting-house*, and running along the road from Hilton's Point to Cochecho. This tract seems to have included the site of the meeting-house itself. The remainder was for a burial place, which is still to be seen, on the west side of the highway to Dover Point, adjoining the Roberts land. The meeting-house was removed to Eliot about 1770, for the use of the Society there.

Another Quaker meeting-house is mentioned in an indenture of March 4, 1734-5, signed by Eben^r, Joseph, and Stephen Varney, John Twombly, Joseph Estes, and Tobias Hanson, conveying land in Dover, on ye southerly side of ye road y^t leads from Cochecho to Tolend, near ye place w^r Thos Down^s House formerly stood, 80 ft. in length and 40 ft. in breadth, bounded northerly on said road 80 ft.; and easterly, southerly, and westerly, on David Watson's land; it being ye piece or parcel of land on wch stands a certain *meeting house in* wch y^e *People at Cochecho commonly called Quakers usually meet*. This is the same land David Watson conveyed to Eben^r Varney March 30, 1724, 80 ft. long, and 40 ft. broad, " beginning near an apple tree standing where old Thomas Downs formerly had a house," thence running 80 ft. " by ye road y^t leads from Tolend." It was a part of the old Coffin land. (See *Trumbelow Swamp* and *Plum-Pudding Hill*.) The Rev. Dr. Quint, however, says the second Quaker meeting-house. built " considerably prior to 1720," " stood on the south-west corner of Locust and Silver streets, where Jacob K. Purinton now lives." (See his *First Parish in Dover*, p. 54.) The present one, on Central Avenue, was built in 1768.

QUAMPHEGAN. This name was originally given to the falls in the Newichawannock where Capt. Thomas

Wiggin and Symon Bradstreet erected a saw-mill, mentioned the 5th, 10 mo., 1652, but it was soon extended to the neighboring district on both sides of the river. Andrew Wiggin of Quamscott conveyed to John Lovering, May 18, 1663, 50 acres of land granted him by the town of Dover for the accommodation of a sawmill on a branch of the Piscataqua river, at *a place called Quamphegan*, bounded N. or N. W. by land of Thomas Broughton and southerly by the lot of Thomas Beard, one bound at the upper side being an oak within two rods of the dwelling-house of said Lovering. John and Ralph Hall testified, June 1, 1674, that a tract of land was laid out to Thomas Broughton on the S. W. side of Newichawannock river, beginning at a tree by the river side near to ye house commonly called Jno Louerin's house, and running thence N. W. to a white oak at the foot of a *long hill* above the falls, thence N. W. to a maple by the side of a swamp. A space on the river, reserved for depositing logs, is mentioned, and a *highway* between Lovering's house and the upper end of *Quamphegan mill*. John Lovering was drowned about 1668, and his son John sold the above mentioned land to Thomas Abbott. "Thomas Abbott, Sr., of Kittery, *alias* Barwick,[1] in the Province of Maine in ye Massachusetts Colony," conveyed it, Jan. 30, 1710, to his son Joseph, who sold it to Archibald MacPheadris Nov. 9, 1717. Archibald MacPheadris of Portsmouth and wife Mary conveyed this same tract to Benjn Wentworth Ap. 12, 1725. The deed declares it to be "in Dover, at a place commonly called by the name of *Quamphegan*, bounded north by Mr. Broughton's," etc. Capt. Benjn Wentworth seems to have settled on this land. He lived near the present turnpike bridge, on land owned by the late James Rollins.

The *log hill* on the western side of Quamphegan falls, laid out in 1702, was re-bounded Jan. 6, 1723, "beginning at or near the old sellar (cellar) by the river side where there was a former bound mark of Luffering (Lovering) in a red oak tree by the river side, thence running N. W. and be W. 27 rods," etc. This hill is again mentioned Nov. 28, 1728, when Samuel Tebbets conveyed to his daughter Judith "one eighth part of a certain single saw in the middle sawmill at *Qvampeagin falls*, wth ye eighth part of ye pvilege of the stream fall, and ye pvileges of y^e *logg Hill*," which privilege was granted said Samuel in 1701.

Quamphegan bridge is at the foot of Somersworth Hill, and crossed by the turnpike road to Portland. *Quamphegan falls* are a little below the bridge. The head of tide water is at the foot of the dam. Quam-

---

[1] Kittery was incorporated as a town Oct. 20, 1647. Kittery Point is mentioned March 8, 1670-71. "The upper part of Kittery now *Berwick*," is mentioned in the York records Oct. 2, 1678. "The vpper diuision of Kittery, now called *Barwick*," is mentioned in a deed from John Hearle to Abraham Lord Aug. 27, 1681. The "*parish of Barwick*" is spoken of July 12, 1683. It was sometimes called *Union parish*. Berwick was incorporated as a town June 9, 1713. Martha Lord, aged about 70, testified Sept. 19, 1717, that "ye now town of *Berwick* from Sturgeon Creek up to Toziers above Salmon falls hath been inhabited above sixty years." (*York Records*.) Eliot was separated from Kittery and incorporated in 1810. South Berwick was separated from Berwick and incorporated June 5, 1814, and North Berwick March 22, 1831.

phegan, on the easterly side of the Newichawannock, is now called South Berwick.

RAGG'S POINT. This point, otherwise called *Betel's Point*, is on the shore of the Rollins land in Newington. It was so called from Jeffrey Ragg, whose name is on the Dover rate-list of 1648; probably the "Jaffry Ragge" who sold Roger Knight a house on Great Island previous to May 20, 1651. A petition from the Newington people in Sept., 1753, says the town of Dover, in 1656, granted a cart-way of four rods wide from the water side at Jaffrey Ragg his house, and so into the woods to the old way. Complaint having been made that Samuel Rawlins had fenced up this road as part of his own enclosure, the Court of General Sessions ordered, Dec. 4, 1753, that it should be re-opened. (See *Newington* in *N. H. Town Papers*, Vol. XII.) According to a plan of the Rawlins land among the State Papers at Concord, Jeffrey Ragg's house was on the shore of the Pascataqua, at the lower side of the old road now called *Patterson's lane*. (See *Patterson's Pt.* and *Betel's Pt.*)

RAILROADS. The following railroads now traverse lands that once formed a part of Ancient Dover.

I. The BOSTON AND MAINE RAILROAD, which extends from Boston to Portland. This is a consolidation of the *Boston and Portland R. R.*, chartered March 15, 1833; the old *Boston and Maine* road, chartered June 27, 1835; and the *Maine, New Hampshire and Massachusetts* road, chartered March 12, 1839. The Boston and Maine R. R. was opened as far as Exeter in 1840; to Dover in 1841; and to South Berwick the 23d of Feb., 1843. It acquired full possession of the *Eastern Railroad* (which was incorporated June 18, 1836; opened Nov. 9, 1840), and the *Portsmouth, Great Falls, and Conway R. R.* May 9, 1890, having been authorized by the Mass. legislature of that year, and previously by the General Court of Maine and New Hampshire.

II. The DOVER AND WINNIPISEOGEE R. R., from Dover to Alton Bay, was first chartered as the *Cochecho R. R.* in 1847. It was opened as far as Rochester in Sept., 1849, and to Alton Bay in 1857. It now forms part of the Boston and Maine system, being leased to that road.

III. The PORTSMOUTH, GREAT FALLS, AND CONWAY R. R., completed in June, 1872, is a consolidation of the *Great Falls and Conway R. R.*, (which was chartered July 19, 1844, and opened to Union village in 1850), and the *Great Falls and South Berwick R. R.*, which was chartered June 8, 1848, and opened July 1, 1854. Full possession of these consolidated roads was taken by the Boston and Maine R. R. May 9, 1890.

IV. The PORTSMOUTH AND DOVER R. R. Chartered July 7, 1866. Opened Feb. 1, 1872.

V. The NASHUA AND ROCHESTER R. R., which traverses the township of Lee, was chartered July 5, 1867, and opened Nov. 24, 1874.

VI. The CONCORD AND PORTSMOUTH R. R., which traverses Greenland, was chartered July 1, 1845, and opened in 1852.

VII. DOVER HORSE RAILROAD.

Chartered June, 1881. Opened July 3, 1882. This road extended from Sawyer's Mills to Garrison Hill, a distance of 2⅓ miles, but has been superseded by the Electric railroad, which extends to Great Falls.

VIII. The ELECTRIC or UNION STREET RAILROAD. The Union Street Railroad Company was incorporated August 9, 1889, for the purpose of constructing an electric railroad from Sawyer's bridge in Dover, to the village of Great Falls in Somersworth. This road was opened Aug. 17, 1890. Midway in its course is a station at Burgett Park, which is in Somersworth, at the lower side of Willand's pond. (See *Burgett Park.*)

RALPH'S HILL. This hill is in Somersworth, near the Dover line, on the old road from Dover to Rochester, about a quarter of a mile above Willand's pond. The Granite State Park is in this vicinity. Its name was derived from Ralph Twombley, who, in early times, was driving a team of six oxen, with a mast from the forest, when the runners slewed on this hill, throwing him beneath, and crushing him to death. The tradition of this occurrence has been preserved in the neighborhood, and it is also related in the *N. H. Republican* (Dover) of Dec. 5, 1826, by Mr. Joseph Tibbets of Rochester, together with many other interesting details of forest life, in early times, acquired from his father and grandfather. Ralph Twombley, Jr., was alive March 19, 1693-4, but dead before June 9, 1702.

REDDING POINT. This is the first point above Hilton's Pt., on the west side of Dover Neck. It is so called the 5th, 5 mo., 1652, in the grant of Goat Island to Wm. Pomfrett. A highway to *Redding Poynt* was ordered to be laid out by the selectmen of Dover Aug. 3, 1666; John Roberts, Sr., to oversee the work. Deacon John Hall, in his will of Feb. 1, 1685-6, gives his son Ralph half of "his marsh near *Redden Point;*" the other half to be Ralph's after the Deacon's death. John Hall, son of the above Ralph, conveyed to Nicholas Harford Feb. 21, 1721-2, four acres of marsh and upland on the west side of Dover Neck, between two points, commonly called by ye name of Hilton's Point and *Redding point*, adjoining the salt water.

The name of this point was no doubt derived from Thaddeus Riddan or Redding. He was one of the witnesses when Thomas Layton conveyed to Richard Waldron, Ap. 8, 1653, one fourth part of the Bellamy sawmill. He seems to have settled at Strawberry Bank, where he bought a house of Wm. Palmer Sept. 4, 1651. "Thaddeus Riddan" is mentioned in the Portsmouth records, April 5, 1652. And May 17, 1652, is the following entry: "Mr. Theados Riddan is chosen clarke of the courte."

RED OAK HILL. Mentioned March 19, 1693-4, when Thomas Ash had a grant of 40 acres from the town of Dover, on the south side of *Red Oak hill*, near the head of Stevenson's land. Forty acres were also granted to Jeremiah Burnum at *Red Oak hill*, Ap. 11, 1694. And Robert Smart, Sr., conveyed to Peter Coffin, March 10, 1695-6, 100 acres of land and meadow by the road going up unto the place where Capt. Wadleigh's mills stood, "near the hill called *Red Oke hill*," granted him by the town of Exeter. The name of this hill has not been retained, but according to a plan of the land conveyed by Jaffrey to Folsom in 1739, it was on the Dover side of the ancient boundary between Dover and Exeter, a little below the mouth of *Smart's creek.* The wading-place across this creek, was, according to this plan, on, or very near, the boundary line. This creek empties into Lamprey river, which pursues nearly a straight course from the upper side of Red Oak hill to Wadleigh's falls. The Red Oak hill of the present day is in Epping.

RED OAK SPRING. This name is given to Major Waldron's spring, now unfortunately closed up, which was a little below the south line of Second street in Dover, a few feet west of Wm. B. Wiggin's house.

RED ROCK. This rock, so named from its reddish hue, is on the shore of Broad Cove, Lubberland. It was one of the bounds of the old Smith lands; and the neighboring farm was called the " *Red-Rock farm.*" Mention is made of it July 10, 1761, when Benjamin Smith conveyed to his son John 150 acres of land where said Benjamin formerly lived, but then occupied by said John, " beginning at the *Red rock* on the westerly side of the *Broad Cove*, so called, and running nearly S. W. 19 rods to another rock lying about half tide." The line extended in an opposite direction from *Red Rock* along the water side to Thomas Stevenson's land, whence it ran northeasterly to *Field's marsh brook.*

REYNER'S BROOK. Mentioned March 8, 1710–11, when 40 acres were laid out to Capt. John Tuttle " on the south side of the Cochecho, nearly opposite *Mr. Reyner's brook.*" And again June 29, 1728, when Thomas and Joseph Hall conveyed to John Horne one half of the hundred-acre grant to John Hall Ap. 2, 1694, " on the east side of y[e] Cochecho river, laid out by *Mr. Rayner's brook.*" This name, still retained, was derived from the Rev. John Reyner, who settled in Dover in 1655, and in 1656 had a grant of 400 acres in the vicinity of this brook, which was laid out to John Waldron Oct. 23, 1719. (See *Sunken Island.*) John Waldron, in his will of May 12, 1740, proved July 30, following, gives 30 acres of land " bought of Rayner," to each of his daughters, viz: Elizabeth, wife of Ezra Kimball; Mehitable, wife of James Chesley; and Sarah, wife of Isaac Libbey. Reyner's brook empties into the Cochecho river on the east side, above Watson's falls.

REYNOLD'S BRIDGE. " The new road to *Reynold's bridge*" is mentioned in 1865 as belonging to the " Highway District, No. 16," in Dover. And " the Mast road to *Reynold's bridge*" is mentioned the same year as belonging to " District No. 17." This is the mast road to Madbury. Reynold's bridge is the old mast bridge across Johnson's creek. The name was derived from Joseph Renolds, tanner, to whom Tristram Pinkham and wife Martha, Ap. 19, 1755, conveyed five acres, part of the tract said Martha received from her father Samuel Hayes, lying " on the westerly side of Back river, and on y[e] southerly side of y[e] road that leads over *Mast bridge*, adjoining said bridge, beginning at y[e] afores[d] road at y[e] northeast corner of Maul

Hanson's land," with "dwelling-house, barn, bark house, tan fats," etc.

RICKER'S HILL. This name is sometimes given to Otis' Hill in Somersworth, from the Ricker family that formerly owned the greater part, if not the whole, of this hill. (See *Otis' Hill.*)

RIVERSIDE STATION. This station is on the Dover and Winnipiseogee R. R., near Meader's bridge, in the upper part of Dover.

ROBERTS' CREEK. Mentioned March 24, 1657-8, when Thomas Lake and Richard Waldron conveyed to John Hall ten acres on the north side of *John Roberts his creek.* Thirty acres, granted to John Roberts by the town of Dover, were laid out on Great Bay the 14th, 8 mo., 1656, being *part of the 400 acres* on Great Bay granted to Dover by the General Court of Massachusetts. (*Dover Records.*) John Roberts of Dover conveyed to Joseph Hall of Greenland, June 29, 1665, 18 acres of the above grant, specified as "*part of the 400 acres,*" north of the land of John Hall, father of said Joseph. Wm. ffurber, the 12th, 10 mo., 1658, " Layd out to John Hall, by ord^r from Capt. Walden" 250 acres of land and marsh, " bounded by a freshett on ye north y^t runs unto *John Roberts his creek* and marsh, and comes out of y^e *Great Swamp*, running up ye freshett 45 rods by ye side of ye freshett to a beach tree, and butting upon the west upon ye thirty acre lots of John Roberts, John Hall, and Richard Cater (Carter), and butting on ye south on a freshett that comes out of *John Hall's fresh marsh*, . . . and running into ye s^d *Cator's fresh marsh* to a white oak by ye side of ye freshett, then by the side of ye fresh marsh 80 rods to an ash tree standing between y^e *newfound marsh* and ye fresh marsh, butting easterly on *Strawberry bank common*, and so upon a straight line to the first bound. Which 250 acres takes up the whole tract between ye two freshetts, and between ye fresh marsh and ye 30 acre lots, with 20 acres in ye fresh marsh, and with 10 acres on ye north side of *John Roberts his creek*, joining to a little Spott of salt marsh at high water mark, butting upon ye Great Bay and John Roberts' land." The name of Roberts' creek has not been perpetuated, but the two freshets above mentioned must have been Packer's brook and Pinkham's creek.

ROBERTS' MARSH. So named from Thomas Roberts, Sr., " of ye town of Dover, under the jurisdiction of Massachusetts," who conveyed to his sons John and Thomas, Jan. 16, 1670, " one half of his *marsh* lying and being at ye mouth of Winecott river, on ye westerly side thereof, at ye bottom of ye Greate Bay upon pascattaq river," adjoining *Henry Tibbett's marsh* on the south, also " all ye creek, thatch, and flats, adjoining ye said marsh, occupying the uppermost point thereof, lying over against *Watt Neale his marsh*." Also 30 acres of land, " which was *my part of the 400 acres granted by the court to ye town of Dover.*" Moses Roberts of Dover, Ap. 20, 1750, conveyed to Mark Hunking Wentworth four acres of marsh and thatch ground in Greenland, " called heretofore *Thomas Roberts' marsh*," granted said Thomas by the town of Dover, bounded northerly by *Haines' marsh*, easterly and southerly by *Greenland river,* and west by *John Hall's marsh.* Two thirds of the above marsh had been given to said Moses in the will of his uncle Thomas Roberts, and the other third conveyed to him by John Roberts.—Joseph and Thomas Roberts of Dover, Aug. 14, 1717, conveyed to Matthias Haines 30 acres in Greenland, "being a *dividend of land belonging to ye s^d Robert's marsh,*" bounded north by Thomas Wille's land, and east by that of Philip Lewis.

ROBERT'S NECK. The neck of land, formerly so called, is in Lee, between Wheelwright's pond and its outlet, known as Oyster river. The name is derived from Wm. Roberts, who had a grant of 100 acres of upland the 23d, 10 mo., 1663, "on the South side of the fresh river near the pond that lyeth between Lamprill river and Oyster river fall." That same day the hundred acre grant to Wm. Williams in 1656 was laid out on this neck. It is again mentioned June 4, 1720, when Richard Denbo conveyed to Salathiel Denbo (grandson of Wm. Roberts) one share of 200 acres on the north side of Wheelwright's pond, at a place called *Roberts' Neck,* in Dover township, which was formerly granted to Wm. Roberts. On the same day John Sias and Ann conveyed to said Salathiel two shares of the same neck. Twenty four acres of land in Durham at a place known by ye name of *Roberts' Neck,* are mentioned in the division of the estate of Joseph Jenkins, Feb. 25, 1734-5.

ROCHESTER. This township was for the most part originally owned and settled by the people of ancient Dover. It was incorporated May 10, 1722, and so named, it is said, from the Earl of Rochester, England. It is mentioned in 1727, when complaint was made to the N. H. government that one Hanson and his associates had in 1725 cut down 34 white pines, out of which 33 masts and bowsprits had been made in Portsmouth, pretending they were cut in a certain township called *Rochester, but not then settled.* (*N. H. State Papers,* 18 : 6–7.)

ROCKING STONE. A rocking stone in the Durham Point district was once so noted as to attract many visitors, and be reckoned among the natural curiosities of the state. Merrill's Gazeteer of N. H. (1817) speaks of it as a "remarkable rock weighing 60 or 70 tons, and lying so exactly poised on another rock as easily to be moved with one hand." Unfortunately it was dislodged from its position several years ago by some mischievous visitors, and could not be replaced. The rock itself is still to be seen on the farm lately owned by Mr. Brackett Edgerly.

There are many of these stones in Cornwall and Wales, where they are called *Logan stones,* from the word *log,* which signifies to rock or vibrate. They are supposed to be under the protection of fairies, who heavily avenge their overthrow. It would be a great satisfaction to know this was the case as to the offenders who overthrew the Durham rocking-stone, but the writer is utterly ignorant of their fate.

ROCKY HILL. This name is deservedly given to the first steep hill below Sawyer's bridge, Dover, on the road along the west side of Back river.

There is also a Rocky Hill at Lubberland. (See *Great Hill*.)

ROCKY HILLS. These are small, round, rocky hills in Somersworth, at the southeast side of Cole's Pond, above Tate's brook. The road that crosses them to Rochester is called the *Rocky Hills road*. A school at Rocky Hills is mentioned in the town records of 1797, and the school-district there is still called the "*Rocky Hills district*."

ROCK ISLAND. This little island is in the Pascataqua river, between Goat island and Fox Point. It was one of the links in the old Pascataqua bridge, built in 1794, and, like Goat island, belongs to Newington.

ROCKY POINT. This point is on the shore of Broad Cove, Newington, between Fox Pt. and Stephen's Pt., now Bean's. It is a mere ledge projecting from the shore, but apparently separated from it at high tide, and generally called *Carter's Rocks*. It is mentioned Ap. 9, 1702, when thirty acres of land were laid out to Mr. Nicholas Harrison " on bloody poynt side, in Dover, beginning at *Rockey poynt*, att henry Langstar's land, and so by the water side 21 rods upon an east line, thence on a south line to Joshua Crockett's land 116 rods, and so to henry Langstar's land on a west line 39 rods, and so to *Rockey poynt* where we began." Also 9 or 10 acres on the south side of the highway that leads from Broad Cove to the *plains*, etc. (See *Carter's Rocks*.) Joseph W. Pickering, administrator of the estate of Eleazar Coleman, conveyed to Cyrus Frink, Dec. 4, 1831, 48 acres of land in Newington, beginning at *Rocky Point*, so called, and running thence to the northwestward of the *grist-mill*, thence as the *creek* runs to the middle of the cider-house, etc., together with the house, grist-mill, and all privileges. Mention is made of John Shackford's land at the S. E.

A *Rocky Point* is mentioned July 17, 1660, when it was agreed by the Dover authorities " that the house of Mr. Valentine Hill, which is his now dwelling at *Rocky Point*, shall be within the line of deuetion to Oyster River." This point may have been on the Durham shore, where Valentine Hill owned several large tracts of land. If he owned land on the Newington shore, it must have been re-granted after his death. The line of division between the Oyster River precinct (now Durham) and Dover proper, is thus stated in the Dover records, the 21st., 10 mo., 1657: "The bounds of the inhabetance of oyster Reiver for the acomodating of the ministery is the inhabitants that are or shall be scittuated from the next *Rocky poynt* on the north side below the mouth of the sayd River and from there by a straight line to the head of Tho Johnson's Creek to the Path thear, and from theare by a west line to the end of the Towne bounds. As allso all the inhabetantes on the south side of that line that either are or shall be thear scittuated are likewise to pay to the ministry there, *excepting all the Inhabitants on fox poynt side* that are or shall be in the letell Bay." This last sentence seems to imply that the Bloody Point district from Fox Pt. up Little Bay then belonged to the Oyster River precinct for civil, if not for ecclesiastical, purposes. In that case, Valentine Hill's house, if at

Rocky Pt. on the lower side of Fox Point, could have been easily included within the above-mentioned line of division.

ROLLINSFORD. This township was set off from Somersworth July 3, 1849, and so named, it is said, from the Rollins and Wallingford families, prominent in the town. The latter, however, only contributed its final syllable to the name. The line of division between Rollinsford and the present town of Somersworth, was then stated to begin at the easterly end, at a point 115 rods southerly from Pray's brook, so called, and thence run in a straight line to the railroad crossing, south of the dwelling-house of Andrew Crockett, and thence in a straight line to a stone on the westerly line of the town, at the point where the line between it and Dover crosses the old road from Dover to Great Falls village.

ROLLINSFORD GARRISONS. The *Pike house* is said to have been a garrison, so named from the Rev. James Pike, a native of Newbury, Mass., who began his ministry at Somersworth in 1727, and was ordained Oct. 28, 1730. He is said to have planted the elms before his house with his own hands. It was here he died in the 65th year of his pastorate, March 19, 1792.

Another garrison was at *Sligo*. (See *Sligo*.)

"*Ezekiel Wentworth's garrison*" is mentioned March 6, 1710–11, as beyond Ebenezer Varney's corner, on the way from Cochecho to Quamphegan and Salmon falls. (*N. H. Prov. Pap.*, 17 : 711.) It was on the Rollinsford side of Garrison Hill, no doubt on the land still owned by the Wentworth family.

"The *garrison of Capt. Benjamin Wentworth* in Dover," is mentioned Nov. 18, 1724. (*Ibid.*, XI : 510.) Capt. Wentworth lived at Quamphegan, near the turnpike bridge across the Newichawannock river. (See *Quamphegan*.)

The old Wentworth house at Salmon Falls, still standing, probably had defences at first. It was built by Col. Paul Wentworth about 1710.

ROLLINS STATION. This station is on the Portsmouth and Dover R. R., in Newington, adjacent to the Rollins farm.

ROUND SWAMP. Mentioned May 2, 1711, when six acres were laid out to the Rev. Nicholas Sever in the *Round swamp*, eastward of John Twomly's field, beginning at a white oak standing at the south side of the way that leads to fresh creek. Nicholas Sever conveyed to Paul Gerrish, July 27, 1716, six acres, laid out to him by the town at a place called *Round swamp*, bounded northerly by ye highway y^t goes down by John Twombly's, and on the other sides by the common lands. This swamp, so named from its shape, is on the eastern side of Dover, in the Burroughs pasture. It is surrounded by grey ledges, through which a brook finds its way, once known as *Twombley's brook*.

ROYALL'S COVE, otherwise RYALL's. This cove, according to the State map of Dover in 1805, is on the southwestern shore of the Back River district, at the east side of Cedar Point. The name is generally supposed to have been derived from Teague Ryall or Royall, one of the early settlers at Oyster River. But his name does not appear in the rate-lists till 1661, about 20 years after mention is made of Royall's Cove. He was, for a brief period, the owner of a few acres of land in the interior of the Oyster River district, and then disappeared. His name does not appear in connection with any enterprise of that day. It is much more probable that Royall's cove was named from Wm. Royall, who was sent over from England to Gov. Endicott of Mass. in 1629, as a "cleaver of timber." He was engaged in the lumber business, and like Henry Jocelyn, Philip Swadden, and others, perhaps came to the Pascataqua region before he went to the province of Maine. He is called a cooper and clapboard cleaver in 1644, when he purchased a tract of land in the present town of Yarmouth, Me., on the river Westcustigo, which from him took the name of Royall's river. There he ended his days.

Royall's cove is mentioned in connection with lumber business as early as Sept. 14, 1642, when " Edward Colcord of Northam in Pascataway river," made over to Wm. Payne as a security, " my timber in *Ryal's coue*, being in number 200 trees, and all my trees w^h are felled at *fox poynt* or the *little bay*, and all such boards and clap boards as are at both places." (*County Registry*, Exeter.) This cove is again mentioned the 5th, 5 mo., 1643, when " Mr. Valentine Hill of Boston " had a grant of a neck of land extending " from a creek over against Thomas Stevenson's at Oyster River that hath an island in the mouth of it, to the head of that creek in *Royall's Cove* to ye part of the North East of Mr. Rob-erts his marsh, and ten acres of upland. All the rest of that neck we give to Mr. Hill, and one hundred acres up in the country." Valentine Hill conveyed this neck of land between Oyster river and Royall's cove to John Davis and John Meader. (See *Meader's Neck* and *Garrison*, and *Davis's Garrison* at Oyster River.) Thomas Layton, the 6th, 10 mo., 1656, had a grant of 100 acres on the west side of Back river, adjoining a twenty acre lot he bought of Ambrose Gibbons, previously Mr. Rogers' lot;—which hundred acres were " laid out at the head of this twenty acre lot, 16 poles by the northernmost branch of *Riall's cove*, and so up the freshett 16 and 13 pole, the creek being on the south side." (See *Frenchman's Creek*.) Thomas Layton, Sr., Feb. 13, 1670, " out of love and affection to his natural son, Thomas Layton, Jr.," conveyed to him the dwelling house then in his possession, together with eight score acres of land, whereof 20 were granted Henry Tibbets, 20 to Mr. Rogers, and the rest to himself, all adjoining; the whole bounded south by *Riall Cove*, east by Back river, north by a lot lately held by Elder Hatevil Nutter, and west partly by John Meader's land, and partly by Joseph ffields, and separated from both by *stony brook*. (See *Stony Brook*.) Hatevil Nutter, as a portion to his daughter Elizabeth, wife of Thomas Layton, Jr., conveyed to said Thomas, Feb. 13, 1670, a forty acre lot granted said Nutter by the town of Dover, between Oyster River and the Back river, bounded southerly by land lately held by Thomas Layton, Sr., west by John Meder's land, north by

Job Clement's, and easterly by "yᵉ head of yᵉ twenty acre lott."

In the return of the lands of Thomas Layton, deceased, in 1710, mention is made of three lots, viz: the *second* in the number of the 20 acre lots on the west side of Back river; a 100 acre lot granted to Thomas Layton, Sr.; and a 40 acre lot granted to Hatevil Nutter. These three lots were surveyed anew Ap. 10, 1710, for Thomas Layton, "heir and successor" of the second Thomas; "beginning at a small walnut tree on the bank by the river side, between *frenchman's creek* and the little marsh in *Royal's Coue* on the west side of Back river, and from said tree running west and be northwesterly nearest 168 rods to the head of the northmost branch of *Royal's Coue*, and so said cove bounds this land on the south, and from that extent it runs up the freshet six score and thirteen rods to a run of water in the fresh marsh, which said freshet trends near norwest from the head of the creek to the aforesaid marsh, and so bounds this land on the S. W., and from that extent it runs 20 rods on the same course to the S. W. corner of Mr. Clement's 40 acre lott, said lott bounding this land to the S. E. corner of said Clement's lot, thence easterly 12 rods to a highway between this land and Samuel Emerson's, then near S. S. E. on the westward side of said way 50 rods to the crook in said Layton's fence, and from said crook to the first bound."

Thomas Leighton of Dover, Ap. 1, 1762, conveyed to Thomas Wallingford of Somersworth 100 acres of land in Dover, on the west side of Back river, running from yᵉ said river to *Royal's cove*, about 40 rods to the land of Joseph Meader westward, and by his land and Ephraim Davis's till it comes to Paul Nute's, and so along the lands of said Nute and Clement, and the land of John Leighton, to the first bound. This land was conveyed to Wm. King Atkinson by said Wallingford's heirs about 1798, and is now owned in part by Mrs. Simpson, together with the Atkinson house which stands on the height now called Atkinson's Hill. A part of the Leighton land on the same hill is now owned by Mr. Prescott.

John Meader, Sr., of Oyster River, June 17, 1679, conveyed to his son John, as his patrimony, "30 acres on the neck of land that lyeth between Oyster river and yᵉ Back river, being a moitie of a larger tract granted said John Meader, yᵉ father, and Wm. Sheffield in yᵉ year of our Lord God 1656, which three score acres were laid out as followeth:—beginning at an asp tree some four rods from yᵉ flowing of yᵉ tide at yᵉ head of *Rial's Coue*, thence N. by W. 142 rods by yᵉ land which was lately Thomas Laiton's, and by yᵉ land latelie Elder Nutter's to a red oak, thence W. by S. 68 rods to a hemlock, thence S. by E. 142 rods to a great white oak, which tree being yᵉ N. E. corner bound of yᵉ land which yᵉ sᵈ John Meader bought of Mr. Valentine Hill, and from said oak to the asp tree at the head of *Rial's Coue*, reserving a highway one rod wide from said oak to yᵉ asp tree for a watering way to said cove."

The inhabitants at Oyster River in 1695 petitioned to the Governor and Council to be incorporated as a separate parish, " beginning at the head of *Riall his cove*, and thence running upon a N. W. line," etc.

Twenty acres of land were laid out to Zacharias ffield,[1] Sept. 24, 1695, according to a grant to Mr. Thomas Roberts, Sr., deceased, " in ye bottom of *Rial's Cove*, on ye western side of ye back Rieuer, known by ye name of ye ffirst twenty acor lott, bounded as followeth : beginning at a Red oake tree by ye creek side y^t runs up to *stonie brook*, from said tree N. W. by W. 80 poles to a heap of stones near John Meader's fence, thence S. W. and by S. 40 pooles to a heap of stones near Joseph Meader's fence, thence S. E. and by E. 92 poles, and thence to the first bound, allowing y^t strip of land y^t falls below ye east line to fill up ye water by reason it falles on ye creek."

John Shapleigh of Kittery, and wife Sarah, July 20, 1699, conveyed to Joseph Smith and John Meader, Jr., both of Oyster River, all their right to a neck of land at the mouth of Oyster river formerly granted to Valentine Hill the 5th, 10 mo., 1643, " bounded to the head of *Ryall's cove*, and so to the head of a cove, against Thomas Stinson's," except 20 acres belonging to Robert's marsh, and " the widow Hill's thirds during her life, forfeited to the crown."

ST. ALBAN'S COVE. This cove is on the western shore of the Newichawannock, below Quamphegan Falls. It is so called in the grant of the mill privilege on Fresh creek the 5th, 2 mo., 1652. The name is said to have been given by the early Tuttles of Dover, who came from Great St. Alban's, Hertfordshire, Eng., which place derived its name, of course, from the great proto-martyr of England. St. Alban's cove is variously called in the old records, St. Albon's, St. Albanes, Sentalbons, etc. (See *Style's Cove*.)

SALMON FALLS, and SALMON FALLS RIVER. The name of Salmon Falls river has been given for two and a half centuries to that part of the Newichawannock above the head of tide water. It was no doubt derived from the abundance of salmon found in this stream before the erection of mills. The Dover authorities of 1644 ordered the first salmon of the season, as well as other fish, to be given to the minister of the parish. The falls in this river, specially known as " Salmon falls," are at the manufacturing village of the same name, in Rollinsford. They are repeatedly mentioned in the early grants and deeds. In 1658 Thomas Hanson had a grant of 100 acres of land " neir the *saman fall*." Ralph Twombley's hundred acres " neir the *saman fall*" is also spoken of the same year. And Major Richard Waldron, in a letter of Nov. 8, 1675, speaks of " *Samon faull*." (See *N. H. Prov. Pap.*, 1 : 356.) Edward Taylor of Exeter and wife " Rebeckah " conveyed to Thomas Roberts, July 20, 1699, 50 acres on the west side of *Salmon falls river*, a little below y^e *Salmon fall*, bordering on the N. W. on a tract formerly in the occupation of George Broughton, on the S. W. by a tract commonly called the *Quamphegan grant*, or *Sheaf's land*, and on ye east by the river, reserving a cartway from

---

[1] Zachariah Field married the daughter of John Roberts, son of Thomas Roberts, Sr. John Roberts' wife was Abigail, daughter of Hatevil Nutter.

Salmon falls mill to the usual *rafting-place* for delivering boards. John Tuttle and Ezekiel Wentworth had a grant of the mill privilege on the west side of the *Salmon falls*, Oct. 27, 1701. And May 19, 1702, they had the grant of an ox-pasture of 30 acres, "accomadable to their mill-grant at *Salmon falls*, . . beginning at the riuer below the mill, where they hall up boards." One side of this tract was bounded by "the *King's road* that leads to *Salmon falls.*" A cartway, four rods wide, was reserved, to go through this land, "from Salmon falls to the usual *landing-place* at Edward Tailers." John Tuttle, Sr., conveyed to John Wentworth, July 29, 1709, one eighth part of the westward side of the *lower fall*, alias *foot fall*, of the *Salmon falls river*, with the accommodation of land belonging thereto, between said fall and the cart path that leads from the afors^d *Salmon falls* to Edward Tailer's former plantation. John Tuttle, in his will of Dec. 28, 1717, gives his son Ebenezer all his right at the *middle fall*, lying between the two falls, on the west side of *Salmon Fall river*. Ebenezer Tuttle, Feb. 5, 1721–2, conveyed to Capt. Benjn Wentworth and Thomas Wallingford one quarter part of the falls commonly called y^e *middle falls*, between ye two mills on the westward side of a river commonly called *Salmon fall river*, opposite a mill in ye possession of John Key and James Grant, which afores^d fall was granted to Capt. John Tuttle by the town of Dover.

Elizabeth Wentworth of Boston conveyed to Paul Wentworth of "Summersworth," Nov. 2, 1730, ten acres of an ox-pasture between lands of ye widow Martha Wentworth, Mr. John Yeaton, Mr. Love Roberts, Mr. Elijah Tuttle, and ye highway which leads to *Salmon falls*. Also "one eighth part of y^e *upper mill* upon ye shoar upon *Salmon falls*, and one eighth of y^e *shoar mill* upon y^e *middle falls*," with the stream and all privileges on the west side of Salmon falls river. Paul Wentworth, in his will of Feb. 3, 1747–8, gives his brother Gershom Wentworth certain rights in "the *upper mill* standing on Salmon falls"; to his nephew Paul Wentworth certain rights in the *middle mill* on the westerly side of Salmon falls river, near the widow Drew's dwelling, (this was Abigail, widow of John Drew) and his part of the grist-mill standing near said saw-mill; and to his nephew Paul Brown certain rights in the *middle mill* and in the *lower mill*, both standing on the westerly side of Salmon falls river.

The Salmon Falls Manufacturing Company was incorporated June 17, 1822, and a mill for woollen cloths was built soon after, which was burned down Aug. 7, 1834. The first cotton mill was established here in 1844, and became the nucleus of the present factories, around which has sprung up the *village of Salmon Falls*, the only village in Rollinsford.

Salmon Falls woods are mentioned Ap. 17, 1742, when Mary Corson (and Zebulon) daughter of Capt. Samuel Tibbets of Dover, deceased, conveyed to Capt. John Wallingford all right and title to an eighty-acre grant to said Samuel in the *Salmon Falls woods*, so called.

Sam Roe's Hill. This hill is in

Newington, near the source of the Trout brook, once known as Harwood's creek. The name is derived from a descendant of Richard Row or Roe, who acquired land at Welsh Cove June 17, 1658. (See *Welsh Cove.*)

SANDY BANK. Mentioned the 8th, 5 mo., 1664, when 20 acres of land were laid out to Hugh Dunn[1] at "a place called *Sandy Banke* up lampril river," granted him in 1656, beginning at a marked tree by the river side at a deep gully. It is again mentioned Oct., 1717, when John Footman sold "Joseph Duedy" twenty acres of land on the north side of Lamprey river, beginning at a hemlock by the river side, "at a deep gully at a place called *Sandy bank.*" This land had been given John Footman by his grandfather, "Philip Cromeele" (Crommet or Cromwell). Joseph Duda, blacksmith, Nov. 28, 1743, sold John Crommet two acres at Hugh Dun's, between Crommet's pasture and Duda's swamp. Sandy Bank is just above Hook Island falls, and now belongs to the Newmarket Manufacturing Company. The gully above mentioned is still to be seen, and not far off is a large swamp now owned by the Yorke family.

The Joseph Duda here spoken of married Rebecca Adams. In a deed of 1712 he signs his name "Joseph Dowdy." (See *Adams Garrison.*) In another of 1716 he writes it "Joseph Duda." Joseph Duda's name is on the muster-roll of Capt. James Davis in 1712. The Rev. Hugh Adams of Oyster River, Nov. 10, 1717, records the baptism of Joseph Doody, Rebecca his wife, and Benmore and Susanna, their children. Sept. 18, 1726, he baptized Temperance Dudey, infant of Joseph Dudey.[2] Joseph Duda was the son of Philip, who appears to have first lived in that part of Exeter which is now Newmarket. The name of "Philip Duday" is signed to a petition from the people of New Hampshire to the Massachusetts government, Feb. 20, 1689-90. Dec. 30, 1738, Philip Duda of Arundell, York Co., Maine, for thirty pounds, conveyed to his son Joseph Duda, of Durham, blacksmith, fifty acres of land in Exeter, granted said Philip Feb. 25, 1698. Philip signs with a mark in both instances.

Rebecca, the first wife of Joseph Duda, left at least five children. April 8, 1756, Benmore Duda, Susanna (Duda) wife of Francis Durgin, Nicholas Duda, Trueworthy Durgin, and Mary Duda his wife, and Zebulon Duda of Newmarket, children of Joseph Duda of Durham, blacksmith, and Rebecca his wife, deceased, for ten pounds conveyed to their uncle, Thomas Bickford of Madbury, and Esther (Adams) his wife, lands at Caley's marsh (Caulley's marsh at Durham Point), and in Madbury, which belonged to the estate of their grandfather Adams. Joseph Duda died before Dec. 25, 1751, on which day his widow

---

[1] Hugh Dunn went to New Jersey as early as 1666, and was one of the first settlers of Piscataqua, in that state.

[2] The name of Temperance was derived from Temperance Benmore, wife of Charles Adams, and daughter of Philip Benmore. She inherited lands on the south side of Sturgeon creek, in Kittery. (See *York Records.*)

Hannah (his second wife) testified as to the correctness of the inventory of his estate, in which is mentioned his shop, anvil, sledge-hammer, dwelling-house, barn, and thirty two acres of homestead land.

Nicholas, son of Joseph and Rebecca Duda, was born about 1730. He seems to have been married at an early age. The Rev. John Adams of Durham, Jan. 13, 1754, records the baptism of Deborah, daughter of Nicholas Doody. "Nicolas Dudy, constable," is mentioned in the Durham records of 1755. "Nicholas Dudy" was one of the first selectmen in Lee after the incorporation of that town. He was apparently the first to change his surname to Durell. The late Judge Durell was his grandson. The first time the name appears so written is in a deed from Nicholas Durell of Durham to Benjamin Richards of Rochester, Feb. 14, 1754, but it continued to be called and generally written Duda at least half a century later, as many people still recollect. The name of Benmore Duda (brother of Nicholas) is on the Durham rate-list of 1778. In that of 1787 it is written Benmore Dudy. In 1788 it is Benmore Durril. In 1789 it was first written Benmore Dudy, then the surname was half effaced and Durril substituted. It is Benmore Dudy again in 1791, after which it disappears. In the Lee records, the name of "Joseph Duda" is on the rate-list of 1794, but on that of 1795 he is called "Joseph Durrel."

Nothing appears in the early records to justify the assertion that the Doody or Duda family came from the Isle of Jersey, much less that it was of Norman extraction. Doody is still a well known name in Ireland, especially in Kerry. It is derived from the ancient O'Dubhda, signifying dark complexioned, and is now variously written as Doody, Dowd, and O'Dowd, etc. The last form is dear to every reader of Thackeray's "Vanity Fair."

SANDY BROOK. See *Cutt's Brook*.

SANDY LOG HILL. This hill is in the upper part of Dover, the west side of the Cochecho river, on the road from Tolend to Rochester. It is mentioned Nov. 5, 1741, when 27 acres of land were laid out to John Hanson, Jr., beginning at *Sandy log hill*, at the S. E. end of the plain commonly called the Ealware plains, a little above the uppermost end of John Tibbet's fence, at the east side of the old mast path, and running somewhat northerly, as said path goes, as far as Rochester line, then nearly N. E. as that line runs, till it comes to the Cochecho river at the small neck of land which said Hanson hath fenced in, then running down the river to the Ealware falls, and thence down the river to *Sandy log hill*, where we first began, having the said river on the easterly side, and the mast path on the westerly side. Twelve acres of land were laid out to James Kielle Jan. 24, 1750, on the west side of the road "right against the *Sandy logg hill*, or the bend of the river."

SANDY POINT. Two points of this name are mentioned in the early records. One of them is on the eastern side of Dover Neck, at the upper side of Pomeroy's Cove, now *Card's Cove*, and still retains its ancient name, no doubt derived from the sandy nature of the soil. Thomas

Beard had a grant of three acres of land on Dover Neck, Ap. 4, 1642, " bounded by land in the possession of Thomas Wiggin on ye south side, in the swamp towards *Sandy poynt.*" He and his wife Mary conveyed this land to Richard Waldron Dec. 6, 1654. This point is again mentioned the 5th, 10 mo., 1652, when Richard Walderne or Waldron had the grant of Pomeroy's cove on Dover Neck " from *Sandy point* right over to the other side of the Coue, to make a Docke." Capt. Walter Barefoot, the 2d, 3 mo., 1652, had a grant of " fower scoer foot in Breadth of flates below hiewater mark at *Sande poynt,*" and twenty four feet of upland. And " Capt. Richard Walldern" also had a grant of 24 feet of upland " to joine to his former grant of flats at *Sande poynt.*"

Isaac Nash of Dover and his wife Margery (both deceased before Feb. 17, 1664) conveyed to Thomas Kemble, Nov. 6, 1658, a dwelling-house on *Sandy poynt* in Dover, with six acres of upland adjoining, and all the marsh in *pomryes Cove.* Thomas Kemble and his wife Elizabeth conveyed the same to Peter Coffin Jan. 18, 1662. Peter Coffin (and Abigail), Feb. 17, 1664, conveyed to Anthony Nutter " ye said dwelling-house and six acres of upland, and the afores^d marsh in *pomeryes cove.*" John Redman of Hampton, Ap. 19, 1673, conveyed to Capt. Richard Waldron, 3 acres of land on Dover Neck, granted him the 4th, 2 mo., 1642, bounded by Thomas Wiggin on ye south side in ye swamp towards *Sandy poynt,* which land was formerly in possession of said John Redman, and commonly called by ye name of *Redman's shopp.*

A SANDY POINT of greater note is in Stratham, at the lower side of the mouth of Squamscot river. It is mentioned in connection with ancient Dover, which extended along the Greenland shore of Great Bay to a bound forty rods below Sandy Point. (See *N. H. Prov. Pap.*, 1 : 222.) Near this point lived Capt. Thomas Wiggin of Bloody Point celebrity, the so-called governor of Pascataqua, and the constant friend to Massachusetts Bay. He died about 1667. The cellar of his house can still be traced. Part of the large tract of land he acquired in this vicinity is still owned by his descendants, who are justly proud of their origin.

SANDY POINT MARSH. Mentioned March 12, 1695–6, when Marie Lake of Boston, widow of Thomas Lake and executrix of his will, and John and Anne Cotton of Hampton, heirs of said Thomas, for themselves and for Mr. Thomas Lake of London, son and heir of said Thomas, deceased, conveyed to Peter Coffin a tract of land adjoining the river commonly called the Great bay, being half the tract of land and marsh which said Thomas Lake and Major Richard Waldron reserved for themselves when they sold their other land to Mr. Thomas Wiggin. " The marsh ground, commonly called by the name of *Sandie point marsh*" adjoined the marsh of said Wiggin, and the upland adjoining extended from the Great Bay to Winnicot river, " and so up to Wm. Davis's fence, and so to the dividing line between Andrew Wiggins's land and this land ; that is, one half of all this land in compass, excepting only *that part which was granted to Dover* by the General Court at Boston." Peter Coffin of Exeter, June 2, 1696, conveyed to his son Peter of Nantucket 200 acres of land he had purchased of Mrs. Lake of Boston on the S. W. side of the Great Bay.

The SAPLINGS. "The road that leads to the *Saplings* above Mallago river, so called," is mentioned in connection with land laid out to Benj[n] Mason in April, 1734, beginning at a beech tree at the side of this road, at the east corner of Wm. Twomble's land. "The road that goes from Littleworth to the *Saplings*, so called," is mentioned Sept. 20, 1734, when land adjoining was laid out to Edward Cloutman. A petition was made Dec. 8, 1734, and again Aug. 7, 1736, for a road " from *Demerit's mill* to the Mallego road at the *Saplings*." This petition was granted Aug. 16, 1736. (See *Demerit's Mill*.) Ten acres and 140 rods of land were laid out to Robert Hanson, June 1, 1739, on the S. W. side of a piece of land belonging to the Quakers, at a place called the *Saplings*. (See *Quaker Pastures*.) The Saplings, a name no longer in use, were evidently in the upper part of Madbury adjacent to the Mallego river, near the terminus of the cross road from Bellamy Hook.

SARAH PAUL HILL. This hill formed part of the old Chesley lands on the upper side of Beech Hill, and was so named from Sarah, wife of Paul Chesley, who, during a long widowhood, displayed great force of character and a taste for litigation. She was called Sarah Paul to distinguish her from " Sarah Limmy," the widow of Lemuel Chesley, and daughter of Samuel Smith. They are both mentioned in the Durham rate-list of 1778. At the foot of this hill is the " *Sarah Paul Spring*," the source of Stony brook, which empties into Beard's creek.

SAUNDER'S POINT. This point is below Salmon Falls, just above the foundry. Here lived the widow Elizabeth Saunders who married Master Tate, the noted school-master of Somersworth. This point must not be confounded with the Sander's Point of early times, where Ambrose Gibbons, the early pioneer on the Newichawannock, was buried. The latter is connected with Great Island by a bridge near the Wentworth House which extends from the island across to Sander's Point.

SAWYER'S BRIDGE. This name is now given to the bridge across the Bellamy river near the residence of Ex-Governor Sawyer in Dover, formerly called *Dunn's bridge*, *Libbey's bridge*, and *Gerrish's bridge*.

SAWYER'S MILLS. These mills are at the lowest falls in the Bellamy river, at the south side of the city proper of Dover. For more than a century the saw-mill and grist-mill here were called *Gerrish's mills*, having been given by Major Richard Waldron, Oct. 17, 1683, together with all the lands, timber grants, water privileges, etc., belonging thereto, as a marriage portion to his two daughters, *Anna*, wife of the Rev. Joseph Gerrish of Wenham, Mass., and *Elizabeth*, wife of John Gerrish of Dover. Joseph Gerrish, May 20, 1701, conveyed his wife's half of this property to John Gerrish, who thus became the sole proprietor. (See *Bellamy Falls and Mills.*)[1]

SAWYER'S STATION. This is a station on the Portsmouth and Dover Railroad, near Sawyer's mills in Dover.

SAWYER'S VILLAGE. The line of tenement houses along the Bellamy, near Sawyer's mills, erected for the benefit of the operatives, is popularly so called. The longest of these houses is known as the *Ten Commandments*—a name facetiously given in the course of its erection, because it was divided into ten tenements.

SCATTERWIT. This name is given to a district above the Upper-Factory falls in Dover, adjoining the Cochecho on the easterly side. It is mentioned June 23, 1701, when Ebenezer Varney had a grant of 30 acres near *Scatterwitt country.* Tristram Heard, in his will of Ap. 18, 1834, gives his daughter Jean, wife of Benjamin Hayes, one half of his sixty-acre lot at *Scatterwit.* The name is otherwise written, May 7, 1736, when Wm. Welland conveyed to Isaac Libbey 14 acres of land "on the north side of ye way y^t leads to *Scatnet*. Six acres of land were laid out to Benjn Roberts Feb. 26, 1739, at a place called *Scatterwit*, beginning at a white oak near Ezra Kimball's shop on the north side of the road that leads to said *Scatterwit,* then running by Ebenezer Varney's land. The road from Gage's Hill to the Long Hill road is now called the *Scatterwit road.* Sanford and Everts' Atlas incorrectly calls this district "*Scatter-with.*" The present county farm is in Scatterwit.

SCHOOL-DISTRICTS. A school was established on Dover Neck at an early day. The town ordered the 5th, 2 mo., 1658, that 20 pounds per annum be raised to maintain a schoolmaster in the town of Dover, to teach all the children "to reid, write, cast a compte, latine, as the parents shall require." (*N. H. Prov. Pap.*, 1: 312.) The school-districts of Dover are thus enumerated in 1790: 1. *Centre district.* 2. *Dover Neck.* 3. *Littleworth.* 4. *Tolend.* 5. *North Side, Garrison Hill.* 6. *Long Hill,* from R. Kimball's to N. Varney's. 7. *Fresh Creek.* 8. *Black Water.* 9. *Back River, south end.* 10. *Back River, Mast road.* The Dover school-districts of the present day are: 1. *Back River.* 2. *Upper Factory.* 3. *Garrison Hill.* 4. *Blackwater.* 5. *Long Hill.* 6. *Tolend.* 7. *Littleworth.* 8. *Upper Neck.* 9. *Lower Neck.* These do not include the districts in the city proper.

The Durham school-districts are mentioned in the town records of 1794 as follows: 1. *Falls, 1st North district;* i. e., in Durham village. 2. *Falls, 2d North district;* i. e., the district around Buck's hill. 3. *Falls, South district,* now the *Broth Hill district.* 4. *Lubberland.* 5. *Point district.* 6. *Packer's Falls.* 7. *District below Jones's Creek.* This is called *Back River district* in 1799. It is now sometimes called the *Bridge* or *Pascataqua Bridge district* because it extends to the Durham terminus of the old Pascataqua bridge. 8. *District*

---

[1] In the article *Bellamy Falls and Mills* Wm. Follet is said to have conveyed his part thereof to Richard Waldron Ap. 27, 1675. It was in the year 1671, and Waldron's deed to Joseph Gerrish says it was on the 20th of April.

above *Wm. Spinney's*. This is called the *Mast Road District* in 1797, which name it still retains.

There were schools in Lee before its separation from Durham. Col. Hercules Mooney was one of the early teachers there, and after its incorporation he taught there from 1766 till the Revolution, and at the close of the war he laid down his sword to resume the ferule.[1] The *Hook school* is mentioned in the town records of 1771. Schools at *Newtown* and *Wadleigh's falls* are mentioned in 1790, and at *Little river* and *North river* in 1791. They were no doubt in operation much earlier. "*School in the Mastway*" and "*Mastway district*" are mentioned in 1791. "*Lower Newtown district*," now *Layn's district*, is mentioned in 1800.

Madbury established schools as soon as it was made a separate parish. A vote was passed March 31, 1757, that schools of two months each be kept at *James Pinkham's* (now *District No. One*); at the *Meeting-house;* at *Mr. Hill's house at Freetown;* and at *Ichabod Canney's house*, afterwards called the *North school-district*, now *No. Four*.

The Newington records of 1762 mention 303 pounds "paid Capt. Mooney for keeping school." This was the above-mentioned Hercules Mooney. Col. John Downing, in his will of Sept. 5, 1755, proved March 12, 1766, gives one acre of land, then in the possession of Nicholas Knight, on the highway from Newington meeting-house to Greenland, for a school-house, and 500 pounds put at interest to maintain a teacher till said house be built. There is only one school district in Newington at the present day.

Somersworth was divided into four school districts in 1793, which were increased to eight in the course of 30 years. A school at *Rocky Hills* is mentioned in 1797, and *Indigo Hill* school in 1803. *Great Falls district* and the *Point district* are mentioned in 1803; *Pear-Yard district* in 1813; *Salmon Falls, Turnpike*, and *Quamphegan districts* in 1825.

SECOND FALLS. These falls are often mentioned in the early records, as "the *second falls in Lamprey river*," or merely as "the Second *falls*," and as they lay within the Oyster river precinct they have sometimes been confounded with the second falls in Oyster river. The Rev. Hugh Adams undoubtedly refers to these falls in his record of a baptism "at the garrison-house, *second falls*," Jan. 11, 1719–20. (See *Oyster River Garrisons*.) A road from Oyster river to the *second falls* is spoken of Oct. 24, 1721, meaning the road to Packer's falls. The *second falls mill* is mentioned Sept. 25, 1716, when Henry and Joanna Dyer conveyed to George Jaffrey "a piece of land called the *mote*," 50 acres more or less, together with their part of 400 acres extending from yᵉ mouth of Piscassick river up Lampril river till it comes within a few rods of *second falls mill*, and their part of yᵉ whole accommodation of Lampreel river which was granted

---

[1] Col. Mooney's second wife was Mrs. Jones, of Lee, on whose farm he took up his residence. It was afterwards acquired by Mr. Gorham Hoitt. A quagmire on this land, into which sank a valuable colt belonging to Col. Mooney, is called *Mooney's Hole* to this day.

Mr. Valentine Hill by the town of Dover, for erecting mills on any part of said river, with 100 acres of land at each mill. The "*second falls mill*" is again mentioned Nov. 2, 1739. (*N. H. Town Pap.*, XI: 649.) These falls are now known as *Packer's falls*. (See *Sullivan's Falls*.)

SENTER'S SWAMP. Mentioned March 19, 1693-4, when Philip Chesley, Jr., had a grant of 40 acres in the swamp near the mast bridge, commonly called *Senter's swamp*. This swamp was evidently in the Back River district, but the name has not been retained. Walter Mathes, son of Francis, in his will of 1678, speaks of his daughter Mary Senter, and his niece Susanna Senter.

SHAD FALLS. Apparently the same as Packer's falls. John Goddard, who died before June 27, 1667, owned 100 acres of land "*above the shad fall*," adjoining John Woodman's land. One half of this tract was, May 4, 1736, conveyed by his nephew, Abraham Bennick, of Durham, gentleman, to Benjamin, son of said Abraham, beginning at "Woodman's south-east corner bound tree, standing on ye side of Lamperel river," thence extending down the river 130 rods to "a little island in ye river above ye second falls." (See *Packer's Falls*.) The Woodman land referred to above was a grant of 100 acres to John Woodman, Nov. 10, 1658. It became the homestead of his grandson, Joshua Woodman, who had it perambulated June 15, 1765, "beginning at a white oak by Lamperil river."

SHADOGEE CORNER. This corner is in Madbury, above Hicks' Hill, at the intersection of the roads to Barrington and to Gerrish's bridge. At the fork of these roads once stood a tavern, popular among men of "shady" propensities. The name, like that of *Snaggerty*,[1] in Strafford, is supposed to have been given it by some old veterans in memory of their campaigns. Fifty of our soldiers are spoken of Jan. 11, 1779, as "at *Shatagee*," a corruption of Châteaugay. In the Canada expedition, during the war of 1812-1815, our troops were more than once at that place. Gen. Hampton was reported, Nov. 5, 1813, as then "at *Châteaugay* or *Four Corners*." Gen. Wilkinson is also mentioned as going into winter quarters in Nov., 1813, "about 25 miles from *Four Corners, Châteaugay*." The enemy having encamped a few months later within three miles of Châteaugay, Gen. Wilkinson proceeded thither Feb. 21, 1814. At his advance the enemy retreated, destroying the bridges. Our soldiers seem to have called this place "Shatagee" or "Shadogee." A part of Conway still bears the name of Shadowgee.

SHAG ROCK. This rock is in the Pascataqua river, off the Downing land on the Newington shore, above Patterson's Point. It is called *Dram Rock* on Dame's map of 1805. Fishermen sometimes call it *Bass rock*, from the number of fish caught there at certain seasons.

SHANKHASSICK. This is said to have been the Indian name of Oyster

---

[1] *Snaggerty* in Strafford, said to be a corruption of Schenectady, was so named by some old soldiers of last century, after their return from the wars. And *Crown Point*, a name popularly given to Strafford Corner, is of similar origin.

river. According to Edward Colcord's deposition concerning the Wheelwright purchase the 14th, 2 mo., 1668, one bound of the land acquired from Wehanownowit, the chief sagamore, was "the westerly part of Oyster River called by the Indians *Shankhassick*, wch is about foure miles northerly beyond Lamperiele River." (*N. H. Prov. Pap.*, 1 : 137.) The meaning of the word is uncertain. The Indian word *sunkhaze*, which seems akin to it, signifies, according to one definition, "one stream emptying into another." And *auke*, whence *ick*, means "a place." According to another definition *sunkhaze* means "dead water," which could not be applied to a tidal stream like the lower part of Oyster river. The first syllable *shank* may be derived from *chesunk*, which Judge Potter says, means "a wild goose." There is a *Sunkhaze* stream in Maine that empties into the Penobscot on the east side, about fifteen miles above Old Town village. Adjacent is the *Sunkhaze plantation*.

SHEPHERD'S BRIDGE. Mentioned on Smith's map of Durham in 1805. It is on the main road from Durham Falls to Newmarket, across the brook that comes from the Moat. The Durham records speak of it as near "Mooney's brick-yard," which is now gone, but at that time was at or near the present burial ground of the Mooney family. The name of this bridge, no longer in use, was derived from John Shepherd, who lived in the vicinity at the beginning of this century.

SHEEP ROAD. This road is in Lee, and extends from the First N. H. turnpike road to the Stepping-Stones road.

SHORT CREEK. This creek is next to Long creek, on the shore of the Gage land, just below the mouth of the river Cochecho.

SHOOTING POINT. Mentioned on Dame's map of 1805. It is on the Durham shore, opposite Furber's Point, at the upper side of Adams Point. Above it was *Durgin's landing-place*, so called in 1694, from Wm. Durgin, who was taxed at Oyster River in 1664. He married, June 25, 1672, "Katharine, relict of Thomas Footman." He declared himself to be 35 years of age, or thereabouts, March 12, 1677–8, when he testified about Robert Smart's land at Goddard's Cove. According to tradition, the Indians crucified him at Shooting Point, and carried his seven daughters to the Newington shore, and there barbarously murdered them on a large rock, no doubt *Pascataqua Rock*, said to have been the western bound of the Bloody Point settlement. His widow Katharine administered on his estate Nov. 30, 1703. (See *Mathew's Creek* and *Neck*.)

SILL SWAMP, otherwise SYL'S. This name has long been given to a part of the Samuel Hale estate in Rollinsford, derived perhaps from Sylvanus Wentworth, or otherwise from Sylvanus Nock, who owned land in this vicinity as early as 1698. His house is mentioned May 9, 1709, as above Sligo garrison. And among the Dover fence-viewers, chosen May 20, 1717, was "Sill Nock for Sligo." (*Town Records.*)

SIMON'S LANE. This name is given to an old road through Horn's woods, in the Lubberland district, now impassable for the most part except on foot. Perhaps it derived its name from Michael Symonds, who was taxed at Oyster River in 1666, and the following year married the widow of John Goddard, of Goddard's Cove; or from Joseph Simons, who, Feb. 8, 1727-8, married Elizabeth, daughter of Elder James Nock. In 1733 Joseph Simons and Elizabeth his wife conveyed to Samuel Smith all their interest in the estate of their honored father, James Nock, deceased.

SIX INDIAN WIGWAMS. Mentioned June 22, 1696, when Peter Coffin of Exeter conveyed to his son Peter Coffin of Nantucket 200 acres of land on the north side of Cochecho river, "at a place called y^e *Six Indian Wigwams.*" Jedediah Fitch "of Sherburn on Nantuckett," and his wife Abigail, and Jemima Coffin, daughters of Peter Coffin of Sherburn, deceased, conveyed to Joseph Twombley of Dover, July 13, 1725, ⅔ of 100 acres on the north side of Cochecho river, part of 200 acres of land given said Peter by their grandfather, June 22, 1696, beginning a little above the third falls in Cochecho river, at a pine tree at the river side, and extending up the river side to a white oak on a little hill, thence north to a swamp by y^e *Indian Ground.* This land was conveyed by Joseph Twombley to Ezra Kimball, June 14, 1733. (See *Indian Corn-Ground.*) Thomas Hanson of Cochecho in ye town of Dover, planter, in his will of the 24th, 2 mo., 1710, gives to his well beloved son Nathaniel his land between Reyner's brook and the *Indian Wigwam brook.*

SIX MILES TREE. Mentioned Sept. 20, 1753, when Daniel Davis, aged about 60, and Philip Chesley, about 77, personally appeared in the woods where said tree then stood, and took oath before his Majesty's Justices of the Peace that the committee appointed by the N. H. government to run and settle the head line of Dover about 30 years previous, ran the line to *a certain red oak tree*, which they marked and established as the S. W. corner bound tree of Dover, which was accepted by the government as the perpetual bound of said town. And the deponents, then in the woods, pointed out said bound between Dover and Exeter, "known and called by the name of the *Six Miles Tree.*" The line between Durham and Nottingham being still disputed, a petition was addressed the General Assembly, Ap. 20, 1758, by Samuel Smith, Ebenezer Smith, and Ephraim Davis, representing that the head line of Dover, before Durham was incorporated, ran from a certain *red oak tree* at the west corner bound, in a straight line to a pitch-pine stump which is the corner bound of Barrington. The line was thus settled Sept. 24, 1759, by a committee appointed by the General Court of N. H. (*N. H. Town Pap.*, XI: 579—580.)

SLIGO. This name, now given to a district in Rollinsford below Quamphegan, appears to have been originally given to a garrison that stood above St. Alban's cove, not far from the Newichawannock shore. It is mentioned March 29, 1708, when Jethro Furber conveyed to Benjn Weamouth 20 acres of land "at or near a place called *Sligoes garrison,*" between the highway and the lots formerly David Hammleton's and

Nicholas Curreus', fronting on the Newichawannock river, being the lot originally granted to Henry Magoon, who sold it to Wm. Laton, by whom it was sold to Edward Cowel, "grandfather of the donor." Richard Hussey, Feb. 25, 1710, conveyed to Benj[n] Waymouth 30 acres of land "att a garrison called *Sligoe*." Benj[n] Waymouth, Feb. 1, 1717, conveyed to Benj[n] Waymouth, Jr., 30 acres of land originally granted to Richard Hussey, "lying and being at a garrison called *Sligo*," bounded N. by Joseph Roberts' land, E. by said Waymouth, S. by "a lott called Currol's," and W. by the commons. The exact site of this garrison is not known, but it is mentioned May 9, 1709, as on the east side of the highway from St. Alban's cove to Quamphegan, between Lieut. Hatevil Nutter's house and that of Sylvanus Nock. This land is now owned by the Garvin family. The name of Sligo soon extended to the surrounding district. Eleazer and Sarah Wyer conveyed to Eleazar Wyer, Jr., Sept. 25, 1738, 20 acres of land, with two dwelling-houses and a barn thereon, "at *a place formerly called Sligo*," bounded N. by the land of Sylvanus Nock, E. by the Newichawannock river, and S. and W. by Benj[n] Weymouth's land. The town voted, Ap. 5, 1756, that a "school be kept three months at *Sligo*."

Sligo was doubtless so called from the town of that name in Ireland,

"Sligo town that lies so snug at the foot of Knocknarea."

The name is said to be derived from the Irish word *silgeach*, which signifies a shelly river, or a place where shells are deposited. The History of Rockingham and Strafford Counties asserts that Sligo garrison was so named by the Stackpole family, the early members of which are said to have come from Sligo, Ireland. No authority is given for this statement. The garrison was not built till many years after James Stackpole's arrival, and its name does not appear till the beginning of the eighteenth century. It may have been given out of compliment to the earl of Bellomont, appointed governor of N. H. in 1699. He was born in Sligo, Ireland, in 1636. Orders from King William were sent him Jan. 19, 1701, to build such forts at Piscataqua and elsewhere as were necessary for security. (*N. H. Prov. Pap.*, 3 : 130.) His political and religious principles naturally recommended him to the favor of our colonists, and he is said to have been very popular during his short administration. He was the grandson of Sir Charles Coote, noted for his ferocity to the Irish in the reign of Charles I, and he himself was one of the first to espouse the cause of William of Orange, who rewarded him with the title of earl, and appointed him governor of New York, Massachusetts, and New Hampshire.

SLUICEWAY. This name is now given to the old wading-place or ford across the Newichawannock, below the Samuel Hale brook in Rollinsford, where the U. S. government attempted to blast out the obstructions in the channel. To this ford a road was opened at an early day between the lots of Joseph Austin and Thomas Canney. On the opposite shore once stood the Newichawannock mills—the first saw and grist mills set up in the Pascataqua region.

The SLUICE ROCK is at the head of Little John's falls, on the shore of the Samuel Hale estate, formerly the Stackpole land, and previously that of Joseph Austin. (See *Stackpole's Creek.*)

SMALL POINT. Mentioned March 2, 1704. (See *Pascataqua Rock.*) Also on Dame's map of 1805. It is a long narrow point on the Newington shore, below Long point; that is, below in the sense of going down stream, though really in a northerly direction.

SMITH'S ISLAND. This is an islet on the Lubberland shore of Great Bay, opposite the farm of the late Valentine Smith, to whose estate it belonged. It is so named on Smith's map of 1805.

SMITH'S POINT. This name is given on Smith's map of Newmarket in 1805, to the point at the mouth of Lamprey river, on the Lubberland side. The point on the opposite shore is thereon called *Shackford's Point.*

SMOKY HOLLOW. This hollow is at the south side of Great Falls village, and so named because, after the foundry was established here over forty years ago, the smoke often settled along the brook that flows through it.

SNELL'S MILL. See *Oyster River Falls.*

SOMERSWORTH. This name was given to the parish set off from the northeastern part of Dover, Dec. 19, 1729. It was incorporated as a town Ap. 22, 1754. The line of division between this township and Dover was then stated to begin at the mouth of Fresh creek and run as said creek runs to the head thereof, and thence as the way goes to the southerly side of Varney's hill, to Ebenezer Varney's land, thence to a white oak over the end of said hill, two or three rods from a spring, etc. When Somersworth was divided into two townships, July 3, 1849, the lower part took the name of Rollinsford.

SOMERSWORTH HILL. This hill is near Quamphegan bridge, on the road to the Rollinsford station. It is called "*Rollinsford Hill*" in the History of Rockingham and Strafford Counties, for which there appears no warrant. (See *Log Hill.*)

SOMERSWORTH PARADE. Mentioned Dec. 11, 1821, when 24 acres of land belonging to the estate of James Rollins, deceased, were advertised for sale, bounded easterly and southerly by the estate of Stephen Roberts, northerly by *Somersworth Parade*, and westerly by the creek road, so called. This was, of course, in the present town of Rollinsford.

SOW AND PIGS. Rocks, so named, are visible at low tide just above Bald Head, on the Newington shore.

SPRUCE HOLES. There are three Spruce Holes in Lee, all of the same general character. One, enclosed by steep banks, is below Layn's mill in Newtown, on the farm of Mr. Edmund Layn. A much larger *Spruce Hole* or swamp is at the head of Wheelwright's pond, just below the Barrington and Nottingham line. The bog here has been sounded to the depth of 65 feet, without finding any bottom. It is owned by Mr. Isaiah Caldwell, the heirs of Samuel Glass, and others.

A third *Spruce Hole* is on Lee Hill, at the north side of the Mast road, behind the town hall, but the spruce trees have nearly disappeared, and the place is no longer noteworthy. But it was formerly an important landmark. It is mentioned several times in the Durham records of the last century. In one of July 2, 1740, it is called *the spruce swamp*. Another is of March 24, 1752, when a road was laid out, beginning on the north side of the mast path by the *spruce hole*, so called, and running south-west across Little river above John Dam's land. May 31, 1763, a road was laid out, beginning at the south side of the *spruce hole* by the mast path, and extending across Lamprey river through the Hook land to a highway near Thomas Yorke's that led to Newmarket.

Another *Spruce Hole* of much greater interest is in Durham, near the Lee boundary, and forms part of the old Laskey farm, now Mr. Charles W. Bartlett's. It is somewhat difficult of access, being surrounded by dense woods and almost impenetrable thickets, but is well worth the trouble of visiting. It is a remarkable bowl-like depression in the ground, and covers five or six acres. The direct depth from the level above to the bottom of the bowl must be a hundred feet. The sides are very steep, and were once lined, and still are, in part, with spruce trees, which impart a peculiar solemnity to the place. The bottom of the bowl is a quaking bog, covered with a bed of thick, soft moss, from which the water oozes at every step. Here grow a variety of orchids, the sundew, the side-saddle flower, and other curious plants, and it is the haunt of multitudinous insects, whose hum on a summer's day alone breaks the solemn stillness of this solitary spot. In the centre is a dark pool, said to be unfathomable, concerning which there is a tragical legend. Unfortunately, the destruction of most of the spruce trees, and other profanations, have greatly injured this sanctuary of nature and marred its once singular beauty.

SPRUCE LANE. This lane is in the Back River district, Dover. It is mentioned June 21, 1779, when a road was ordered to be laid out to the land of Moses Peasley, "beginning at the main road that leads to Durham, on the southerly side of *Spruce Lane*, near the *Drew garrison*." The name of this lane is still in use, and the land above mentioned is still in possession of the Peasley family.

SPRUCE SWAMP. This swamp is mentioned in connection with the Indian massacre at Oyster River July 18, 1694, when Mrs. Dean and her daughter were left therein by the savages while gone to complete the destruction of the settlement. According to Belknap she was carried up the river about two miles and left in a swamp under the care of an old Indian, from whom she managed to escape with her child. Moses Davis, in his account, says she was above the spruce swamp when he espied her, and he thought it a mistake about her being hidden there. He doubtless referred to the spruce swamp near his lands, now belonging in part to Mr. Albert Young, about a mile above Durham falls. The road towards this spruce swamp is repeatedly mentioned in the conveyances of land last century. (See *Falls Hill*.) It is spoken of Sept. 13, 1769, when Jabez Davis conveyed to Francis Mathes all the land belonging to his homestead plantation, one hundred acres in extent, beginning at the N. E. corner in a *spruce swamp*, and running westerly by Abednego Leathers' land to that of Love Davis.

SQUALL POINT. This point is on the Cochecho river, at the foot of George St., in Dover city.

SQUAMANAGONIC, otherwise GONIC. The name of Gonic is now given to a village in Rochester which has grown up around the falls in the Cochecho called *Squamanagonick* falls, from an Indian word signifying, it is said, "water from the clay-place hill." This abbreviation is used by Whittier in his line:

"From swift Quamphegan to Gonic fall."

The "*Squammagonake old planting-ground*" is mentioned Jan. 3, 1686, when Hoope Whood, Samll Lines, Ould Robbin, and Kinge Harry conveyed to Peter Coffin all right and title to the marshes and timber between the two branches of the Cochecho, "beginning at the run of water on the north side of *Squammagonake old planting ground* (and between the two branches) to begin at the spring where the old cellar was, and so to run ten miles up into the country between the branches by the rivers." Tristram Heard, in his will of Ap. 18, 1734, mentions his mill privilege at *Squamonogonick*. Samuel Alley conveyed to Jonathan Hodgdon Feb. 22, 1743-4, 40 acres "lying on a place called Blind Will's neck, a little above y[e] *uppermost mill at Squommonygonnock*." And Dec. 8, 1749, said Alley conveyed to Elizabeth, widow of Wm. Thompson, and his other heirs, 20 acres of land in Rochester, on the west side of the river, " a little above the *great fort at Squommonygonnock*, so called."

SQUARE SWAMP. Mention is made June 26, 1765, of a tract on the north side of Wheelwright's pond, at the head of Durham, containing all the common and undivided land in the swamp commonly called and known by y[e] name of *Square swamp*.

STACKPOLE'S CREEK or BROOK. This creek is referred to May 9, 1709, when a road was laid out from St. Alban's cove, running "along between Lt. Hatevil Roberts his house and barn, and so on to the west side of Sligo garrison," and, further on, between Sylvanus Nock's house and barn, keeping the same course to the "way that runs down on the north side of Thomas Cannies lott to the *old wadeing place* opposite to Chadbourn's mill, then trending Eastward down the s[d] way till it comes to the mouth of *a little Creek on the south side of James Stackpole's house*," thence northward over said creek, and along between the river and Stackpole's fence, etc. Thomas Tibbetts convered to John Vicker, July 20, 1738, one acre of land, "beginning at y[e] road y[t] leads from *Stackpole's brook* to Somersworth meeting-house," adjoining Ensign John Tebbets' land. John Vickers, Nov. 12, 1740-41, conveyed to John Moffat of Portsmouth his house and one acre of land on the highway from *Stagpole's creek* or *brook* to Quamphegan road, and another acre adjoining the road from said brook to the meeting-house. Elizabeth, widow of Capt. Benj[n]

Wentworth, conveyed to Thomas Wallingford, Feb. 11, 1739, 13¾ acres of land at Quamphegan, beginning at the highway that leads from *Stackpole's brook* towards Somersworth. Stackpole's brook crosses the Portland turnpike road and now empties into Hale's artificial pond. It formerly emptied into the Newichawannock river.

Stackpole's Landing is mentioned Ap. 12, 1774, when John Parker, administrator of the estate of Nathaniel Adams, conveyed to Jacob and Benjn Quimby 3½ acres of land, bounded northerly by the road from Somersworth to Quamphegan, easterly and southerly by Capt. Nathan Lord's land, and westerly by the road to *Stackpole's landing*. This landing was no doubt at the above-mentioned wading-place, to which a road led in early times. The old Stackpole house stood where is now the garden of the Samuel Hale place, a little north of the artificial pond. James Stackpole acquired land here May 20, 1710, when Thomas Austin, only son and heir of Joseph Austin of Dover, conveyed to him all that tract of land granted said Joseph in 1656, "lying in ye range of lots between St. Alban's cove and Quamphegan," bounded S. E. by the Newichawannock river, N. E. by Henry Tibbets' hundred acre lot, N. W. by Ralph Twombley's 100 acres and Thomas Hanson's 100 acres, and S. W. by a highway between this lot and Thomas Kenne's 100 acre lot. (See *Sluiceway*.)

STARBUCK'S BROOK. This is the first brook that empties into the east side of the Cochecho river above Fourth street bridge in Dover. It is mentioned Ap. 14, 1701, when Peter Coffin conveyed to John Ham a dwelling-house and barn at *Tolein*, with a tract of land adjoining, beginning two rods beyond the barn, and extending thence straight down to ye run of water, then along the foot of the hill till it comes to the brook called *Elder Starbuck's brook*, which is by the highway going to Cochecho, thence down by ye brook to Cochecho river, and thence, to the dwelling-house, reserving one rod and a half along the river side. A tract of land, formerly in the possession of Richard Otis, deceased, was surveyed anew for Richard Waldron Dec. 28, 1706, beginning at the easternmost end of the dividing line between this land and Mr. Waldron's, adjoining the Queen's thoroughfare road, and running N. E. on said road 135 rods to the east end of the division fence between this land and that in the tenure of Wm. foast and Tristram Heard, thence W. by N. northerly 68 rods to a pitchpine on the west side of *Starbuck's brook*, etc.

STARBUCK'S MARSH. The chief marsh of this name was granted to Elder Edward Starbuck Aug. 30, 1643, when it is spoken of as a "plott of marsh above Cutchechoe Great marsh, that the Brook that comes out of the great Pond runns threw." This is *Peter's Marsh brook*, and the marsh it runs through, now for the most part drained, is long and narrow, beginning at the northeasterly side of the Great Pond (Willand's), and extending along the brook nearly to Salmon Falls river. It is mentioned Ap. 11, 1694, when 30 acres of land were granted to Richard Otis "between the Pond and

Starbuck's marsh. And again Ap. 15, 1696, when Paul Wentworth conveyed to his brother Benjamin eight acres of meadow above *Elder Starbuck's marsh.* (See *Peter's Marsh.*) Another Starbuck's marsh is in Newington. (See *Starbuck's Point.*)

STARBUCK'S POINT and MARSH. Starbuck's Point, now called *Fabyan's Pt.*, is on the Newington shore of the Great Bay, where Edward Starbuck of Dover had a grant of *marsh* in 1643, (see *Swadden's Creek*); and later, a grant of upland adjoining. His son-in-law Peter Coffin conveyed to John Hall of Greenland a tract of upland on the southeast side of Great Bay, "formerly the land of Edward Starbuck," possession of which was given " with twigg and turf," Dec. 25, 1662. John Atkinson conveyed to Thomas Pickering, Dec. 7, 1702, 13 acres of land granted to his father Joseph Atkinson by the town of Portsmouth, bounded S. by "*Swaden's brook;*" S. W. by the bay, and on the other sides by "*Starbuck's mash*," and the lands of Jackson, Geo. Walton, and said Thomas Pickering. Starbuck's Point and marsh are again mentioned Jan. 28, 1716, in a conveyance, beginning in solemn form as follows: "To all Christian People to whom this my present deed of gift shall come and concern, know y[e] that I, Thomas Pickering of Portsmouth, in the province of New Hampshire, sendeth greeting in our Lord God everlasting." Said Thomas then goes on to say that, " out of natural love and affection to his well-beloved son James, for his incouragement," he conveys to him the full half of a marsh called and known by the name of *Starbuck's Poynt Marsh,* together with a tract of land, adjoining the land whereon said Thomas then lived, bounded northerly by John Fabin's land and the country road, south by *Swadden's brook,* and extending to the Great Bay; said Thomas reserving the right to drive his cattle back and forth to *Starbuck's Point.* John Fabins (Fabyan) of Newington, May 30, 1721, conveyed to James Pickering all right to the southeast half of the salt marsh, formerly called *Starbuck's marsh,* adjoining said Pickering's own land. (See *Fabyan's Point.*)

STEPHEN'S POINT. This point is on the Newington shore, at the lower side of Broad Cove. The name was derived from Stephen Teddar, who belonged to the Dover Combination of 1640, and seems to have lived on this shore at an early day. Wm. Furber and Anthony Nutter were appointed by the town of Dover the 5th, 2 mo., 1652, to lay out Henry Langstaffe's lot of 200 acres "*where Stephen Teddar's house was.*" This order was repeated the 5th, 2 mo., 1658. Langstaffe had another grant the 9th, 5 mo., 1652, "*near where Stephen Teddar's house was.*" Mention is also made of Langstar's land laid out at *Stephen's marsh* Ap. 11, 1694. (*Dover Records.*) Stephen's Point is mentioned June 6, 1701, when a road was proposed "from Mr. Harrison's (at Fox Point) to Broad Cove freshett, and so to the highway from Bloody poynt road to *Stephen's poynt* or broad cove," as should be thought fit. And again Sept. 8, 1703, when Henry Langstar or Langstaffe, conveyed to his daughter Mary fifty acres of land " a little above Bloody Point, commonly called by the name of *Stephen's point*, otherwise *Stephen Jethro's point* formerly, right over against Hilton's Point," bounded east by land that was formerly Joseph Trickey's, and west by a cove commonly called Broad Cove.

The next transfer of this land reveals a curious bit of family history, well worth copying from the County records: "Mary Langstar of Bloody Point, June 20, 1713, well knowing that a marriage by God's grace is intended and shortly to be had and solemnized between Eleazar Coleman of said place to the s[d] Mary Langstar, and considering that s[d] Mary, being about y[e] age of 63 years, and the said Eleazar about 28 years, and she may the better be taken care of in case she lives to any great age, and for divers other good and just causes, conveys to him fifty acres of upland called *Steven's Point*, otherwise by y[e] name of *Stephen Jether's point*,[1] a little above Bloody point, right east by Broad cove. Also land on Little Bay, beginning by a creek in Broad cove, and running up y[e] Little bay as far as Dumplin cove." That Mary Langstar married Eleazar Coleman is proved by a deed of May 25, 1734, by which John Johnson conveyed to Samuel Nutter 5 acres and 50 rods of land in Greenland, which Matthew Haines and Nathan Johnson had bought of Mr. Eleazar Coleman, having been "given by Mr. Henry Langstar, late of Dover, deceased, to his daughter Mary Langstar, who was wife to said Eleazar Coleman." Eleazar Coleman, and *Mary his wife*, March 6, 1713–14,[2] conveyed to Richard Downing and Thomas Coleman of Newbury Falls, 50 acres of land in Newington, at a place commonly called *Stephen's Point*, otherwise *Stephen Jether's Point* formerly, lying a little above Bloody Point, right over against Hilton's Point, bounded east by Jos. Trickey's land, and on y[e] west by Broad Cove. Also, the land from the mouth of the creek in Broad Cove up Little Bay as far as Dumpling Cove. The Langstars laid claim to Mrs. Coleman's estate after her death, and still spoke of her as "Mary Langstar," but finally her nephew Henry, attorney of his father, John Langstar, of the town of Piscataqua,[3] Middlesex county, New Jersey, resigned to Eleazar Coleman Nov. 26, 1716, all claim to the lands given the latter by his aunt, Mary Langstar, *deceased*.

Stephen's Point is now generally called *Bean's Point*, from Mr. Henry Bean, the present owner. (See *Coleman's Creek*.)

---

[1] The corruption of Tedder to Kidder, Jethers, and Jethro, is an instance of the strange variation of names in early times, doubtless owing, in part, to the error of the recorder. Other instances might be mentioned, such as Carter, Cater, and Catter; Canney, Kenney, and Canning; Harwood and Herod; Langstar and Langstaffe; Swadden, Swaddow, and Scoudew; Stimpson and Stevenson, etc.

[2] This date proves that Eleazar Coleman married Mary Langstar between June 20, 1713, and March 6, 1713-14. There is a story, which the writer is unwilling to believe, that Eleazar Coleman, having been asked if he loved his elderly but well-endowed bride, replied significantly that he loved *the very ground she walked on*. She died before Nov. 26, 1716, and he married March 1, 1717, Anne (Nutter, it is supposed), a near relative of Mary Langstaffe.

[3] The town of Piscataqua, N. J., was so named by the first settlers there, several of whom went from the region of the Pascataqua in New Hampshire. Among them were Hugh Dunn and John Martin, who were from Oyster River. The land there was first acquired by Daniel Peirce of Newbury, Mass., and others. He was the grandfather of Daniel and Joshua Peirce, who settled in Portsmouth, N. H.

STEPPING-STONES. A range of stepping-stones at an early day gave a footing across the channel of Oyster river shortly after it leaves its source, and across the adjacent marsh. This was, of course, in the present town of Lee. Mention is made of them Nov. 16, 1720, when 50 acres of land were laid out to Nathaniel Hill on the north side of Wheelwright's pond, beginning at a black oak standing near the place called the *Stepping Stones*, and thence running E. S. E. 68 rods to the pond. These stones remained till the present century, and are still remembered by the oldest inhabitants. The highway across them is still known as the *Stepping-Stones road*. It runs towards Barrington, between the pond and the turnpike road, and is so called on the state map of Lee in 1803.

There were also Stepping-Stones in the Durham Point district, across Stevenson's creek, which is called *Stepping-Stones Creek* in 1720. This was a great thoroughfare in early times, leading to the fording-place across Oyster river, and to the meeting-house which stood on the upper side of this creek.

Mention is frequently made in the old records of the Stepping-Stones across Peter's marsh in Somersworth. A new highway was ordered to be laid out March, 1731, from the Indigo Hill road to the *Stepping-Stones at Peter's marsh*, towards the Cochecho road leading to Rochester. Moses Stevens had 6¼ acres laid out to him March 27, 1736, on the north side of the brook that comes out of the Great Pond, below the *stepping-stones*, so called, joining to the marsh. A lot was laid out to Samuel Walton Nov. 22, 1743, on the N. E. side of the road that leads over the *stepping-stones*, beginning four rods from Maturin Ricker's corner. These stones are also mentioned in Paul Wentworth's will of Feb. 3, 1747-8. There was, till a recent period, a wheel-track across Peter's marsh, about half a mile from Willand's pond, with stepping-stones for people on foot.

Stepping-stones were once common in England, and are still to be found there. Those across the river Duddon have been made famous by Wordsworth, who compares them to

"A zone
Chosen for ornament. Stone matched with stone
In studied symmetry, with interspace
For the clear waters to pursue their race
Without restraint."

STEVENSON'S CREEK, otherwise STIMPSON'S. This is the first inlet on the lower side of Oyster river below the old parsonage lands. John Goddard, June 26, 1664, sold Wm. Williams, Sr., forty acres on the south side of Oyster river, "butting upon a creek commonly called *Stimpson's Creek*." bounded on one side by *Stony brook*, and on another by the meeting-house lots. Williams sold this land to Joseph Field June 18, 1674; and Zacharias Field, brother of Joseph, conveyed it to John Davis, son of Moses, Dec. 11, 1710. John Davis and Abigail his wife conveyed to Daniel Davis, May 22, 1719, 40 acres of land, marsh, and flats, granted to John Pillon Dec. 8, 1653, with ten more granted Joseph Field for the highway that goeth across his land, and a parcel of salt marsh John Davis bought of Philip Chesley between said land and the meeting-house lot, which land is on ye south side of Oyster river, lying between *Stony brook* and y[e] meeting-house lot, and butting on a creek called *Stimson's creek*. John Drew, in his will of Jan. 31, 1721, gives his daughter Sarah, wife of John Field, two acres of salt marsh, with flats and thatch-bed, on the west side of the mouth of *Stevenson's creek*, on the south side of Oyster river, joining the parsonage lands, which marsh s[d] Drew had bought of Zacharias Field, administrator of Joseph Field's estate. John Field of Dover and Sarah his wife, formerly Sarah Drew, Aug. 1, 1748, conveyed to Joseph Hicks a plot of two acres of salt marsh, bequeathed to s[d] Sarah by her father John Drew, on the west side of *Stevens creek*, so called, on the south side of Oyster river, joining to the parsonage.

The name of *Stepping-Stones creek* is given to Stevenson's creek March 6, 1720, when 40 acres of land were laid out to Daniel Davis, by virtue of a deed from John Davis, beginning at a rock by *Stony brook* and running thence S. W. and by S. 120 rods to an asp tree: thence N. W. 44 rods to a black birch next the town lott to the salt marsh, the next marsh to the meeting-house, and thence on the same point to the *stepping-stones creek* on the east.

Stevenson's creek derived its name from Thomas Stevenson, who owned land on the south side of Oyster river July 5, 1643, when Valentine Hill had a grant on the opposite shore "over against Thomas Stevenson's." He appears to have owned land at the very mouth of Oyster river (see *Jonas' Point*), and all the land from Wakeham's creek to the creek above, which afterwards took his name. A neck of land next adjacent to his lot, granted him in 1654, is mentioned in the Dover records as laid out to his son Joseph Stevenson, Aug. 19, 1676, "from the side of the rock at the head of *Stony brook creek* E. S. E. near E. about 100 rods *unto the next creek*, to a tree lying in s[d] creek, markt J. S." Stimpson is a corruption of Stevenson. Joseph Stimson's name is on the Dover rate-list of 1666. In that of 1667 he is called Joseph Stevenson. Stimpson's or Stevenson's creek is now called *Mathes's creek*, from the owner of adjacent land.

STONY BROOK. There are at least seven brooks of this name within the limits of ancient Dover. Five of them are in Durham, or partly so. The most important of these rises at the "*Sarah Paul spring*," above Beech Hill, and is fed by the marsh below, and other springs along the way—eight in number, at least—and finally empties into Beard's creek, south of the Woodman burying-ground. Several of these springs have recently been acquired by the Agricultural College, and a dam has been erected on the upper part of Stony brook to provide a reservoir for that institution. This will no doubt greatly diminish the stream below. Mention is made of this brook the 30th, 7 mo., 1660, when John Woodman had a grant of "twenty acres of land at the head of *William Beard's creek*, on the west side thereof, and on the north side of *Stoney Broke*, the broke being the first bounds unto the afoersayd creek." And Benjamin Mathes conveyed to said Woodman, March 10, 1663, a parcel of land on the west side of

Wm. *Beard's creek*, containing all the marsh on the north side of *stony brook* to the head of that creek; which parcel had been conveyed to Francis Mathews by Wm. Hilton in 1645. This brook is again mentioned May 10, 1741, when Nathaniel Hill conveyed to Samuel Hill a tract of land "commonly called by y*e* name of *Hill's Pan*, bounded southerly on a brook called by y*e* name of *Stony brook*, westerly on y*e* road y*t* leads to Dover, northerly and easterly on y*e* land of Jon*a* Woodman." *Hill's Pan* and *Stony brook* are both mentioned when this land was conveyed to Dr. Joseph Atkinson Nov. 20, 1742. It was acquired by Moses Emerson July 22, 1757, when it was described as a tract of 9½ acres, "formerly called *Hill's Pen*, about half a mile from y*e* falls meeting-house, on y*e* east side of y*e* road from Durham Falls to Dover, adjoining the land of John Woodman." The road here referred to is the Madbury road, which crosses Stony brook at a short distance from Durham village. At this place the brook often swells to a considerable size after a rain or the melting of the snow in spring-time. It is here crossed by a bridge, generally called *Ballard's bridge*, and the brook itself at this point is called *Ballard's brook*, from Joshua Ballard, who acquired Hill's Pan or Pen after the death of Moses Emerson. This Pan is no longer a separate tract, but forms part of the Woodman farm, now owned by Mr. Dennison.

Another STONY BROOK is mentioned Aug. 14, 1654, when Valentine Hill conveyed to John Davis 60 acres of land, "lying at the mouth of Oyster river, on the north side, beginning at the mouth of a creek, and so runs upon a N. and by E. poynt 144 rods to a pine tree, then W. S. W. to *Stony Brook Cove*, and so bounded from the fore-mentioned creek by the river."[1]

A controversy having arisen between Ensign John Davis and Joseph Smith as to the bounds between their lands, the town appointed Wm. Wentworth, John Bickford, and John Heard to survey said Davis's land; which they did May 13, 1673, "beginning at a white oak att *stonie brook cove*, near Joseph Smith's fence, and running N. N. E. to the head of the lott, leaving sufficient land to make good Joseph Smith's lot. This controversy, however, seems to have been renewed, but it was finally agreed, Sept. 30, 1678, "that the division line between y*m* shall begin at a hemlock tree at y*e* head of y*e* cove by *Stony brooke*, and so to run N. E. and by N. eight score rods, which is y*e* eastern bound of Matthew William's grant."

Stony Brook is mentioned as the western boundary of the old Layton lands in the Back River district Feb. 13, 1670, when Thomas Layton, Sr., conveyed to his son Thomas eight score acres of land bounded south by Royall's cove, and west by the lands of John Meader and Joseph Field, and parted from both by *Stony brook*. It is again mentioned Sept. 24, 1695, when Thomas Roberts' 20 acre grant was laid out to Zacharias ffield, "on

---

[1] Valentine Hill, that same day, conveyed to the above John Davis 20 acres of salt marsh by the side of a place called *Broadbow Harbour*, in the island called *Champernon's island*. This is Gerrish's island at Kittery Point, where Capt. Francis Champernown lies buried.

ye bottom of Rial's *coue*," beginning at a red oak "by ye creek side y^t runs up to *Stonie brook* from s^d tree N. W. by W. 80 poles to a heap of stones near Jno Meader's fence." This Stony brook crosses the road from Atkinson's Hill to the old Pascataqua bridge, and empties into Royall's cove. (See *Meader's Neck* and *Royall's Cove*.)

Another STONY BROOK empties into Stevenson's creek, on the south side of Oyster river. It is mentioned the 6th, 4 mo., 1659, when John Goddard conveyed to Wm. Willyames, Sr., "40 acres of land in Oyster River, wich was John Pellines—the neck of land wich lieth betwene *Stoney brooke* and the meeting-house lot." When this land was confirmed to Wm. Williams, June 26, 1664, it was described as "butting upon a creek commonly called *Stimpson's creek*," and bounded on one side by *Stony brook*.

There is also a STONY BROOK in the Packer's Falls district. It rises in Moharimet's marsh, formerly so called, and empties into the north side of Lamprey river below Sullivan's falls.

Another STONY BROOK is in Lubberland, a short distance below Newmarket village. It is mentioned May 15, 1711, when the "lott layers of Dover," at the request of Sampson Doe, ran "the neck line from the head of *goddard's creek* to Lampreele Riuer as followeth, beginning at the head of *goddard's Creek* at the flowing of the tide there, at about Eight Rods southward from *Abraham benick's mill*, and from thence to run nor west and be west ¾ westerle cours to *Stony brook* a little below Lamprele Riuer first falls."

A STONY BROOK in Dover is mentioned Feb. 26, 1713, when Nathaniel Roberts' grant of 30 acres on the west side of Fresh creek, at the head of Wm. Dam's land, was laid out, beginning at a white pine tree on the north side of *Stony brook*. Nathaniel Roberts conveyed to Jabez Garland, March 29, 1722, 30 acres of land on ye west side of Fresh creek, beginning at a white pine on ye north side of *Stoney brook*. Edward Ellis, Dec. 30, 1734, conveyed to John Mackelroy 30 acres of land in Dover, beginning at ye lower end of a brook called *Stony brook*, and running along by Cochecho salt river to William Thompson's fence, and along his fence to Samuel Alley's land, thence to the road from Jabez Garland's, and along this road to the lower end of *Stony brook*, above mentioned. (See *Alley Point*.)

A STONY BROOK in Newington is mentioned in George Huntris' will of June 8, 1715, in which he gives his wife Mary, during her natural life, that part of the estate where he then dwelt, between Nathan Knight's and a fence on the north side of *Stony brook*. To his grandson Christopher, eldest son of his son George Huntris deceased, he gives all the land where Christopher then dwelt, lying between a fence on the north side of *stony brook* and Clement Misharue's land. As Clement Messervey's land was part of the Moody grant, along Harwood's Creek, this Stony brook was no doubt what is now called the *trout brook*, that empties into Laighton's Cove. (See *Herod's Creek*.)

STONY HILL. Mentioned Sept. 1, 1699, when Wm. Wittum had "enough land granted to his former improvement on Bloody Poynt side, joining the road at *Stonie hill,* so as to make it 20 acres." This land (12 acres) was laid out at *Stonie hill* in 1712, beginning at a hemlock tree at the N. E. of John Carter's land, on the north side of the highway from Welshman's Cove to Bloody Point, and running by said way to John Downing's land, and so to the parsonage land, etc.

Sixteen acres of land, "on the north side of a place called *Stoney hill,*" were given by the parish of Newington, June 20, 1713, to "y[e] Reverand Mr. Joseph Adams, minister of the parish afores[d], in consideration of the great love, affection, and respect they had and did bear to him, and also moved by divers good causes —upon condition of his continuance with them as long as his life is continued, or he is able to officiate with with them as a minister." (*Newington Records.*) Wm. Witham, Ap. 5, 1717, conveyed to Joseph Adams 12 acres in Newington at a place commonly known by y[e] name of *Stoney Hill,* bounded S. by said Adams' land, S. E. by the Bloody Pt. road, and N. E. by Mr. John Downing's land. Richard and Mary Carter conveyed to Mr. John Downing, Ap. 26, 1722, 20 acres of land at or near a place commonly called by y[e] name of *Stony Hill,* bounded S. E. by the highway from Capt. Knight's ferry to Newington meeting-house, west by the highway from the meeting-house to Broad Cove, etc. Stony Hill belongs to the same ridge as Nimble Hill. *Stony Hill pasture,* now belonging to Mr. James Hoyt, is between the road to Greenland and the Fox Pt. road to Portsmouth. (See *Nimble Hill* and *Pine Hill.*)

STONY POINT. This is the first point above St. Alban's cove on the Rollinsford shore, below Madam's cove. It is now owned by Mr. Roberts.

STOODLEY'S CREEK. This name was given over a century ago to the inlet on the Newington shore of the Pascataqua now known as *Hill's creek* or *cove.* It is the next inlet below Paul's creek, and no doubt the *Pine cove* of early times. The name was derived from James Stoodly, to whom Wm. Browne of Salem conveyed, Feb. 21, 1770, his farm of 400 acres, bounded N. by the lands of Gideon Walker, Wm. Huntress, and others, E. by the Pascataqua river, etc. This land was conveyed by Wm. Stoodly, son of James, to Nathaniel Folsom March 26, 1790. This sale was confirmed by later deeds, the last of which is dated Aug. 7, 1792. Over 54 acres of the Folsom farm were acquired by the Frinks, who conveyed this tract to Winthrop Pickering May 12, 1856. It is described as extending north to the land of Amos Dow, deceased, and south, along the river, to the land *formerly owned by Samuel Hill, deceased.* Winthrop Pickering conveyed this land to Stephen Paul of Eliot Ap. 29, 1862, from whom the next inlet above Stoodley's acquired its present name of Paul's creek.

STORY'S MARSH. See *Oyster Point,* and *Bunker's Garrison.*

STRAFFORD COUNTY. Ancient Dover formed part of Norfolk County as long as it was under the jurisdiction of Massachusetts, but, like Portsmouth, it had some of the privileges of a shire town, such as its own courts. The "County Courts of

Dover and Portsmouth" are repeatedly mentioned in the Provincial Papers, as in 1653, and 1674. (*Vol.* 1 : 206, 317, etc.) Hence, no doubt, the name of "the *County of Dover and Portsmouth*" met with in many early deeds. It is also mentioned in the *Provincial Papers*, May 31, 1671, May 12, 1675, etc. (*Ibid*, 1 : 316-320.) After N. H. had a government of its own, at least in the early part of the last century, the courts were all held at Portsmouth, as stated in 1717. (*Ibid*, 3 : 676.) An act, however, was passed by the Gen. Assembly in 1730 that one term of the Court of Common Pleas should also be held yearly at Dover, Exeter, and Hampton. As the number of inhabitants increased, and townships sprang up in the interior of the province, the inconvenience was felt of having the courts for the most part held at Portsmouth. Repeated efforts were made to divide the province into counties from 1755 onward, but this was not effected till 1769. (*Ibid*, 7 : 204-210.) Full operation, however, had to be suspended till the royal approbation could be secured. Five counties were formed, two of which remained for a time inactive. The three which went into partial operation were first called the *Eastern*, *Western*, and *Middle* counties. (*Do.*, 7 : 211-215.) It was enacted Ap. 1, 1769, "that one Superior Court, one Inferior Court of Common Pleas, and one court of Gen[l] Sessions of the Peace of the *Easterly County*" should be held yearly at Exeter. The rest continued to be held at Portsmouth. Gov. John Wentworth, in his message of March 21, 1771, announced that " his Majesty had been graciously pleas'd to approve and confirm the Act for dividing this Province into Counties." (*Do.*, *p.* 274.) This Act seems to have taken full effect March 28, 1771, on which day the Recorders of Deeds for the three counties were appointed. The name of *Rockingham County* first appears on this occasion, when " the Hon[bl] Daniel Pierce Esq[r]" was appointed " Recorder of Deeds and Conveyances of Real Estate within the *County of Rockingham*." This name, and that of *Strafford County*, were given, it is said, by Gov. Wentworth in honor of the Marquis of Rockingham and the Earl of Strafford, who belonged to the Wentworth family of England.

Strafford County is mentioned May 28, 1772, in a message from Gov. Wentworth, as " without county privileges." (*Do.*, *p.* 302.) It was then attached to Rockingham Co. The Council voted, June 13, 1772, that " all the Courts for the County *of Strafford* be held for the term of 7 years at Dover." (*p.* 309.) And the "Honb[l] Tho[s] Westbrook Waldron" was appointed Recorder of Deeds in *Strafford County* Feb. 6, 1773, on which day this county apparently went into full operation. A part of Ancient Dover, however, still belongs to Rockingham County.

STRAWBERRY BANK. This name was given to the settlement afterwards called Portsmouth as early as 1631. It is mentioned Dec. 5, 1632. (*N. H. Prov. Pap.*, 1 : 68.) In the petition to the Mass. government in May, 1653, to have this name changed to Portsmouth, it is stated that the plantation of Strawberry Bank was " accidentally soe called by reason of a banke where straberries were found." (*N. H. Prov. Pap.*, 1 : 208.) There was a *Strawberry Bank Combination* for government, probably as early as 1633. This included Great Island, and all the lower Pascataqua region. It is referred to in 1643, when John Pickering was "injoined to deliver the *old combination at Strawberry Bank* the next court." (*Ibid*, 1 : 111.) Pike, in his Journal in 1698, merely calls this settlement *the Bank*, as did many Portsmouth people to a late day.

STYLES' BROOK. This brook, so called in a deed of 1795, rises at a spring on the Roberts land, in Rollinsford, and empties into St. Alban's cove. It is referred to May 9, 1709, when the road from the head of Fresh creek to St. Alban's cove was extended " northward down the hill, and over *the freshet that vents itself into St. Albon's cove*, at the old wadeing-place there."

STYLES' COVE. This name, derived from a neighboring land owner, is sometimes given to St. Alban's cove, on the western shore of the Salmon Falls river. Wm. Stiles, Oct. 31, 1752, conveyed to Thomas Miller, Jr., one acre of land in Somersworth, beginning three rods eastward of an old cellar where Samuel Styles formerly dwelt, and extending along the road that leads from *St. Alban's cove* to Quochecho. Wm. Stiles conveyed to Hanson Stiles, Aug. 13, 1784, 60 acres of land, butting easterly on Newechewanick river and *St. Alban's cove*, northerly on the road that leads from Sligo to Fresh creek, southerly on Hussey's land, and westerly on that of Richard Philpot.

The STYX. See *No-Bottom Pond.*

SUKE ABBOT'S HILL. This hill is on the borders of the Two-Mile Streak, east of the turnpike-road, near the Lee boundary. Many amusing stories are still in circulation about the eccentric woman from whom this hill derived its name.

SULLIVAN'S FALLS. This name is now given to the lowest falls in Lamprey river within the limits of Durham, but Gen. Sullivan's privilege no doubt extended along the rapids to the falls above, to which the name of " Packer's " is now confined. He acquired this mill-privilege Sept. 4, 1770, when John Shepard of Nottingham, and Susanna his wife, for the sum of 260 pounds, conveyed to John Sullivan sixty acres of land adjoining Lamperell river on the south side, *at a place called the second falls*, with all right and title to said *second falls*.[1] John Adams, afterwards President, in a letter from York, June 29, 1774, says John Sullivan of Durham then had " a fine stream of water, with an excellent corn-mill, saw-mill, fulling-mill, scythe-mill, and others, six mills in all, which are both his delight and profit." Sullivan's mills " at Packer's falls " are spoken of Dec., 1774, when Eleazar Bennet, of the Fort William and Mary expedition, was in his employ. According to Holland's map of 1784 Gen. Sullivan had four mills along this part of the

---

[1] This land was conveyed by Samuel Smith, Oct. 3, 1769, to his "dutiful daughter Susanna," wife of John Shephard of Nottingham, in consideration of 260 pounds paid by her. The deed of this land declares it to be " on the south side of Lamperel river, at a place called the *second falls* on said river."

river. The N. H. *Mercury* of Portsmouth advertises, Nov. 14, 1785, General Sullivan's "new grist-mill, where his double grist-mill formerly stood, also a new fulling-mill, both at *Second Falls*, and nearly in the same places where those mills stood which were swept off by the late freshet;" the "clothing and silk-dying business carried on in the best manner" at the fulling-mill. A good farm of upwards 150 acres "near Lampreyeel river, near Packer's falls," with grist-mill, saw-mill, fulling-mill, and press-house, were advertised for sale Oct. 5, 1790. These were General Sullivan's. The "fulling-mill at *Sullivan's falls*" is again mentioned, in 1793. It was then managed by Daniel Croxford, who, after Gen. Sullivan's death, continued to carry on "the clothier's business in all its branches," as appears from his advertisement of June 19, 1798.

SUNKEN ISLAND. This island is in the Cochecho river, near the mouth of Reyner's brook. It is said to have derived its name from being submerged at the erection of the dam at the fifth falls. It is mentioned March 8, 1710–11, when 40 acres of land were laid out to Capt. John Tuttle, on the south side of the Cochecho river, above Tole End, nearly opposite Mr. Reyner's brook, beginning at a hemlock tree by the river, below the *Sunken Island*. And again, Oct. 23, 1719, when Mr. Rainer's 400 acre grant in 1656 was laid out to John Waldron "above Tole End, on the N. E. side of Cochecha fresh river."

SUNKEN LEDGE. This is a rock dangerous to navigation in the Long Reach. It is off the Newington shore, below Birch Point, but hidden by the current.

SWADDEN'S CREEK. This inlet is on the Newington shore of the Great Bay, above Fabyan's point. It is the lower bound of the old Pickering grant, mentioned in the Portsmouth records of Feb., 1655, when John Pickering had a grant of all "the land lying between *swadens creek* and *pincomb's creek* in the great bay." The former edition of this work says Swadden's creek was the *upper* boundary of the Pickering grant. Further investigation shows that the upper bound was *Pinkham's creek*, and the lower one *Swadden's*. (See *Pinkham's Creek*.) The name of Swadden's creek was derived from Philip Swadden, Swaddow, or Scoudew, of the Dover Combination of 1640, who had a grant of land on this shore before 1643. It was re-granted the 24th, 8 mo., 1643, as follows: "It is this day ordered that Edward Starbuck shall have the marsh in the Great Bay which was formerly granted Philip Scoudew nere his wigwam."[1] Mention of "his wigwam" has led some writers erroneously to suppose that Philip Swadden was an Indian. The word "wigwam," however, does not necessarily imply an Indian habitation as elsewhere shown. (See *Herod's Wigwam*.) It was a name often given by lumber-men in early times to their shelter in the forest. Among those engaged in the lumber business at that time on the shore of the Great Bay, were Philip Swadden,

---

[1] The recorder may have accidentally omitted the word *Herod* before "his wigwam." (See *Swadden's Island* and *Herod's Point*.)

Thomas Johnson, Andrew Harwood, and Thomas ffurson, all of whom are mentioned the last of the 6th mo., 1643, as selling timber, clapboards, and pipe-staves. (See *Harwood's Cove.*) Philip Swadden left Dover not long after, and went to Maine, where he was still living Aug. 27, 1673, when he testified that he was then about 73 years of age, and 38 or 39 years previous lived in the Piscataqua region. On the creek which bore his name settled Thomas Pickering, son of the above John, and ancestor of the present writer. Thomas conveyed to his son James, Jan. 28, 1716, a tract of land bounded east by " a brook called *Swadden's brook.*" And June 6, 1719, he gave to his son Thomas 100 acres adjoining, on which stood his dwelling-house, barn, out-houses, orchard, etc. This land, which remained in the Pickering family till a recent day, now belongs to Mr. J. S. Hoyt. Traces of a mill on Swadden's creek at the head of tide water may still be seen. Hence the name of *Mill creek*, by which it is now generally called.

Swadden's brook rises on the Haven farm in Portsmouth, just beyond the Newington line. The springs that feed it partly supply Portsmouth with water, in consequence of which this brook now often dries up in summer time. Pinkham's and Swadden's creeks are about a mile apart at their source, but at the mouth only a third of that distance. The road from Newington to Greenland crosses them both, shortly before they empty into the Great Bay. The lower part of Swadden's creek, for many years alive with the falls and mill, and the activity of the early pioneers, is now utterly silent and desolate. There is only a cluster of tall chestnuts and pines on the shore, which overshadow a few hillocks covered with rank grass, where the early Pickerings are buried, on the very edge of the water, looking off over Great Bay towards the southern shore of Durham—a spot beautiful and solitary, and abandoned to Nature, where it seems good to rest and await the *vitam venturi sæculi*.

SWADDEN'S ISLAND. This is an islet in Great Bay, just above the mouth of Swadden's creek, otherwise Mill creek. It has always belonged to the " Mill-creek farm," which was originally a part of the Pickering grant of 1655. The name has been corrupted to *Swan island*. It is mentioned Dec. 15, 1662, when Peter Coffin conveyed to John Hall 30 acres of upland, and 6 acres of salt marsh adjoining, formerly granted to Elder Edward Starbuck by the town of Dover, s^d upland and marsh now lying and being wthin the p^{e}cincts or Limits of the s^d town of Dover, upon the S. E. side of the Great Bay, over against *Swadden's island*, commonly soe called, and adjoining s^d Hall's land. It is again mentioned Oct. 3, 1686, when John Fabens (Fabyan) of Portsmouth, and Sarah, my now wife,[1] "daughter of John Hall of Greenland, conveyed to Thomas Pickering" 30 acres of upland, and 6 acres of salt marsh adjoining thereto, formerly called by the name of *Swadon's Marsh* and *Herod's Point*, upon the eastward side of the Great Bay, and

---

[1] Pike records the marriage of "John Fabian and Mary Pickirin" Dec. 25, 1702. She was the daughter of Thomas Pickering.

northward from *Swadon's island*, so called; bounded north by John Jackson's land, and so runs to *Harwood's Cove*, and so round southward and east by water to the other end of the fence by Joseph Atkinson's land, near adjoining to said *Pickering's neck* of land." Swadden's island is again mentioned Ap. 30, 1719, in a deed from Thomas Pickering to his son Joshua.

SWAN ISLAND. See *Swadden's Island*.

SWAZEY'S HILL. This hill is in Dover city, on William Street, between Central Avenue and the Print Works. It is so called in the Dover records of 1812, when "the road from the top of *Swazey's hill* towards the bridge" is mentioned. Also in the conveyance of a lot near *Sweasey's hill* to the Dover Cotton Factory Jan. 19, 1822, by Mary and Abigail J. Kimball, and Wm. and Maria Palmer. The name was derived from Nathaniel Sweasey or Swazey, cabinet-maker, who lived here a century ago. He died before July 28, 1804, when his widow Sarah is mentioned as administratrix of his estate. This hill is otherwise called *Gallows Hill*. The Irish of this quarter call it *Swazey's Bray*, from the Irish word *bri*, *bree*, or *brea*, signifying a hill or rising ground—the same as the Scotch word *brae*, so often used by the poet Burns. (See *Gallows Hill*.)

SYMOND'S GRANT. See *Wadleigh's Falls*.

TAN HOUSE. Mentioned the 4th, 8 mo., 1653, when Job Clement had a grant of land by Fore river side, one bound of which was a stake above the *Tan House*, thence over the spring (probably the one now called *Coleman's spring*) 5 poles and 4 ft. to a stake 2 poles and 2 ft. to the N. E. corner of the old *Brew House*, upon a straight line to the water side. This was apparently the land above the old ferry-place at Beck's Slip, now owned by Mr. Joseph Furnald. Job Clement, Sr., himself was a tanner.

TATE'S BROOK. This name is sometimes given to that part of Peter's Marsh brook which runs through the Tate lands in Somersworth. It more properly belongs to a small tributary to this brook, on the lower side, which flows through the Tate and Ranlet lands.

The name of *Tate's road* is frequently given to that part of the old road to Rocky Hills which passes through the Tate land, below the brook.

TEAM HILL, otherwise TEEM. This hill is mentioned several times in the Dover and Durham records, as Feb. 22, 1720–21, when a road is spoken of "beginning att a place called *Teem Hill*," and "crossing the long marsh to the road that leads from Oyster River falls to Lampereel bridge." This hill is at Durham Point, where the common is. Several roads centre in this vicinity, and in the day of ferries across the river to Fox point, and across the bay to Furber's point, the number of vehicles that met on this hill doubtless gave it its name.

TEAR-CAP CORNER. This name was formerly given to Madbury corner, where three roads meet at the foot of Hicks's hill. It is mentioned May 29, 1740, when a petition was made for a road from "*Tare Cap*" to Freetown. At that time the Tasker and Hicks families owned the land around this corner, and its name may have been derived from the towering cap of Mrs. Hicks, which seems to have been proverbial. To this day, when an ominous cloud gathers around the top of Hicks's Hill, on which she lived, the people of the vicinity say: "A storm is brewing: Granny Hicks has got her night-cap on." She was the wife of the first Joseph Hicks, and the daughter of Col. James Davis of Oyster River, who was famous as a leader of scouting parties against the Indians. She lived to an advanced age, and was a woman of great ability and energy of character. She had a tendency to predominate, and doubtless held chief sway in her neighborhood, where many stories are still afloat which testify to her originality and consciousness of superiority. She used to loudly wish, with a deploring shake of her head (and the cap on it), that she could put her brains into her son Joseph's cranium. It does not appear, however, that he was particularly deficient.

TEN RODS ROAD. This road leads through Rochester into Farmington, crossing the line between these towns about half way between Ricker's pond and the Cochecho river. It is mentioned June 13, 1733, when John Canne of Dover conveyed to Elijah Tibbets of Rochester 30 acres in the 56th lot in the first division of Rochester, " beginning at y^e *ten rods road* that runs across ye first division of s^d Rochester from Salmon fall river to Cochecha river, near an house erected on said land, or where y^e *mast way* now crosseth ye s^d *ten rods road*."

THOMAS POINT. This name is sometimes given to a small point on the Newington shore, below Long Point, perhaps from Thomas Pickering, who acquired most of the land at and around Long Pt. in the middle of last century. Or from Stephen Jones Thomas, who, between 1789 and 1802, bought in various parcels the adjoining homestead of Dependence Bickford, with 7 acres of Nicholas Pickering, and $5\frac{1}{2}$ of Timothy Dame which extended to a cove in Great Bay.

THOMPSON'S FALLS. This name was formerly given to a mill privilege in Lee, just below Little River sawmill, where Jonathan Thompson had a grist-mill and fulling-mill, which he gave to his son Joseph in his will of Sept. 10, 1756, together with the falls on which they stood, and one acre of land joining thereto. These falls were at a later day called *Bartlett's falls*. Joseph Thompson, May 3, 1744, conveyed to Josiah Bartlett of Haverhill, Mass., his dwelling-house and one acre of land adjoining; also his grist-mill and fulling-mill, with one half of the privilege, and four acres between the grist-mill and saw-mill, adjoining the road. (See *Bartlett's Falls*.)

THOMPSON'S POINT. This point is on the west side of the river Cochecho, a little above the mouth, but the name has not been perpetuated. It was so called from William Thompson, ancestor of the present writer, who was in Dover as early as 1647. "*Thompson's point house*" is on the Dover rate-list of 1648. This point is again mentioned the 5th, 10 mo., 1652, when orders were given to begin at *Tomson's Pointe* to mark the 300 pine trees and 100 oak trees granted Capt. Thomas Wiggin and others, and thence upward into Mr. Waldron's grant. Thomas Canney had a grant of 16 acres of upland the 6th, 10 mo., 1656, to be laid out adjoining "his perches (purchase) at *Tomson's poynt*." This land was laid out from the outmost point turning up to Cochecho 50 rods to the *long creek* westward below *Tomson's poynt*, butting on Fore river, thence running three score and ten rods up the *long creek* side, reserving a cartway from the woods to the water side at the head of the creek, and up Cochecho river three score and ten rods, and thence on a straight line over to the bound at the head of the *long creek.*

Job Clement had a grant of 3½ acres of upland the 23d, 10 mo., 1658, part of which was below "the highway that goeth from Thomas Canney's into the woods towards *Tomson's Poynt*," bounded E. by the Fore river, on the northern side of the hollow, *where the ship was built*.[1] A lane from Parson Reyner's land to *Tomson's point* is mentioned in 1675. Thomas, "oldest son and rightful heir of the late Thomas Canney, Jr.," and his wife Grace, conveyed to his brother Samuel, Aug. 12, 1703, 45 acres of land in the tenure of said Samuel, adjacent to *Thompson's Point*, and next to Henry Tibbet's land. Joshua Canney, son of Samuel, conveyed to John Gage, Dec. 17, 1745, a tract of land extending to the mouth of the Cochecho river, and westerly on said river to *Thompson's point*. It joined Gage's land on the south. (See *Long Creek*.)

Thompson's Point, which seems to have been acquired by Thomas Canney, was apparently at or near the present brick-yard of Mr. Gage, near the mouth of the Cochecho river. Wm. Thompson, from whom it derived its name, is supposed by some writers to have removed to Kittery, where a Wm. Thompson died in 1676, leaving six children. But the writer finds no proof of this supposed identity. Wm. Thompson's name is not on the Dover rate-lists after 1659, and the only land he left in Dover unsold appears to have been inherited by his son John, who afterwards settled at Oyster River. (See *Ash Swamp* and *Cochecho Log Swamp*.)

The article on *Thompson's Point* in the former edition of this work is full of errors, this point being confounded therein with land on the east side of the Cochecho river above the mouth of Fresh Creek, where a Wm. Thompson and his son William successively owned land, which the latter sold to Samuel Alley Aug. 3, 1736. (See *Alley Point*.)

The name of *Thompson's Point* is now sometimes given to the Lower Huntress landing-place, on the borders of Newington and Portsmouth.

THREE CREEKS. These creeks, sometimes called *Tuttle's creeks*, are on the west side of Back river, below Hopehood's Point, where John Tuttle had a grant in 1642. His son, Judge John Tuttle, in his will of Dec. 28, 1717, gives his grandsons, Thomas and John Tuttle, all his lands on the west side of Back river, adjacent to the *three creeks*, to be divided by the cartway to the south side of the *middle point*, the usual place of landing:

---

[1] Isaac Stokes in 1661 also had a grant of 3½ acres on the east side of Dover Neck, near the place where "*the friggot was billd*."

Thomas to have the north division, and John the south.

The THREE-FORKED PINE. This tree was one of the old bounds of the Bloody Point settlement, on the line from Canney's creek to Hogsty Cove. (See *Harwood's Creek.*)

TIBBETTS' SLIP. There was once a landing-place of this name on the east side of Back river, nearly a mile above Nutter's Slip, probably so called from Jeremiah Tibbets, who had a grant of a house-lot in 1655, at the upper side of which a highway was afterwards laid out to this slip. A short distance S. E. is *Nock's spring*, where Thomas Nock had the grant of 3½ acres for a house-lot in 1656, laid out Feb. 5, 1657.

TICKLE POINT. Mentioned as early as Aug. 17, 1738, when Joseph Meader of the island of Nantucket, and Nicholas Meader of Durham, made a division of two acres of land, part of the homestead of their father John Meader, deceased, "adjacent to ye river on ye Point commonly call^d and known by ye name of *Tickle Point* in Durham aforesaid." In a deed from Thomas Pinkham to Wm. K. Atkinson, Dec. 30, 1797, *Tittle*, or *Tickle*, or *Trickle Point*" is mentioned as a part of the "Franklin Propriety." On a plan of July 10, 1758, among the State Papers at Concord, mention is made of "*Tickle Pt. or Cedar Pt.*" as if the same point. Cedar Pt., however, is at the lower side of what is generally called Tickle Pt. The latter is just below the mouth of Oyster river, at the Durham terminus of the old Pascataqua bridge. In the day of a tavern and toll-gate at this bridge, the name of Tickle Pt. was often superseded by the significant one of *Tattle Point*. (See *Franklin City.*)

TOLE END, otherwise TOLEND. The Tolend district is on the south side of the Cochecho river, above the second or Tolend falls. The name seems to have been originally given to the limit of the early grants at Cochecho, next the territory occupied by the Indians. (See *Indian Corn-Ground.*) James Paquamehood of *Tollend*, evidently an Indian, is mentioned Oct. 20, 1665, as selling sundry lands and ponds to James Rawling of Long Reach. An old Dover grant, which the writer has not been able to find, is said to mention "Mr. Towle his end." No Towles, however, are on the early rate-lists of Dover, but "Jo^n Towle, ffisherman," is mentioned in the York records Jan. 18, 1652, when he made an attestation concerning Geo. Walton. Nathaniel Starbuck and Wm. Horne had a grant of 240 acres between Cochecho and *Tole End*, Sept. 20, 1661. "The second fall of the River of Cochecha, commonly called or known by the name of *tole End fall*," is mentioned March 3, 1702. Israel Hodgdon of Dover, June 11, 1714, conveyed to John Drew and Philip Yeaton one sixteenth part of the new mill "on ye northside of *Toall-End Falls*, with ye privilege of said falls." (See *Cochecho Falls.*) The Barbadoes way to *Tole End* is mentioned Feb. 16, 1711, when land was laid out to John Horn. (See *Indian Corn Ground.*) "The mast road that goes from *Tolend* to Rochester" is mentioned Oct. 15, 1748. (See *Ham's Marsh.*) The name of Tolend was given to one of the Dover school-districts as early as 1790. It is still retained.

TOM DREW'S OVEN. Mentioned Feb. 22, 1709-10, when John Gerrish conveyed to Benedictus Torr a tract of land on the west side of Back river, on the south side of the mast path, extending southwesterly near a place called *Tom Drew's Oven*. (See *Torr's Garrison*.) Major Waldron's 400 acre grant on the west side of Back river, according to the boundary of May 19, 1688, ran from the brow of the hill on the south side of the mill-dam of Belleman's bank S. S. W. 260 rods to a pitch pine tree on the plains, then W. 320 rods to a dry pine "near the house which Thomas Drew, Jr., hath erected," bounding said land on the north to the mill-dam. Thomas Drew's land was on the south side of the Torr land, but there is no tradition in that neighborhood concerning his Oven.

TOM-HALL BROOK. This brook rises south of Beech hill, and empties into Huckins brook a little above the head of Beard's creek, in Durham. It is referred to Ap. 22, 1728, when Joseph Hall of Dover conveyed to John Hall all right and title to 20 acres of land granted to his father Thomas Hall (grandson of Deacon John Hall of Dover) "at *ye brook* above ye head of Jonathan Woodman's creek." This stream is still known as the *Tom-Hall brook*. The bridge that spans it, on the highway from Durham village to Madbury, a little above the Boston & Maine Railroad, is called the *Tom-Hall bridge*. And this part of the highway, laid out in 1818, is often called in the Durham records the *Tom-Hall road*, or route, to distinguish it from the old road over Brown's hill.

TRASK'S CORNER. This corner is in the western part of the Quamphegan district, on the road to the Rollinsford station, where a family of that name formerly lived.

TRICKEY'S COVE. This cove is mentioned March 5, 1713, when John Downing sold Samuel and John Shackford part of a neck of land on the south side of *Trickey's cove*, and at the north-east of a little cove between said neck and *Steven's point*. The bounds of this tract, which amounted to 16 acres, began at a birch tree near Downing's land and ran to a rock in or beside a little brook above said Trickey's dwelling-house, then extended E. along by the land of Zachariah Trickey, Senior; N. to a pine stump in a little gully near ye point, and W. to the lands of Rebecca Trickey and the parsonage. This neck is now called *Zackey's Point*, otherwise *Orchard Point*. The "gully" above mentioned is now called *Coleman's Creek*.

Trickey's cove is on the Newington shore, between Knight's Ferry and Trickey's Point, otherwise Zackey's. It received its name from Thomas Trickey whose name is on the Dover rate-list of 1648. He died before June 16, 1680, on which day his widow Elizabeth, "out of natural affection, and parental love, and respect to her beloved son Zachariah," resigned to him all right, title, and interest in her plantation, and to the *ferry* belonging to said plantation. This was *Trickey's ferry*, afterwards *Knight's*. And May 19, 1682, his three daughters, Deborah, Lydia, and Sarah, with the consent of their husbands, William Shackford, Richard Webber, and Joshua Crocket, conveyed to their brother, Zachariah

Trickey, all right and title to their father's plantation, on which he lived before his decease.

TRICKEY'S POINT. This point is on the Newington shore, at the upper side of Trickey's Cove. It is mentioned Ap. 7, 1713, when Zachary Trickey sold to Samuel and John Shackford 3½ acres of land at a point commonly called *Trickey's point*, between Bloody Pt. and Stephen's Pt., together with his dwelling-house, etc. The cellar of this house can still be traced. This point is now owned by Mr. Valentine M. Coleman, who inherited it from his father. It is otherwise called *Zackey's Point* and *Orchard Point*. (See *Zackey's Point*.)

TROUT BROOK. This name is now sometimes given to a brook in Newington that take its rise at a spring near Sam Roe's Hill and empties into Laighton's cove. It was in early times called *Harwood's creek*, *Stony brook*, etc. (See *Herod's Creek*.)

TRUMBELOW SWAMP, otherwise THOMBELOW. This swamp was apparently at the east end of Cochecho Log swamp, not far from Plum Pudding hill. It is mentioned Jan. 1, 1668, when Peter Coffin conveyed to John Church one fourth of 75 acres, bounded E. by Thomas Downs, and W. by a swamp called *Thombelow*. James Coffin's land lay east of this "fourth," and Nathaniel Stevens's at the west. Peter Coffin "of Cochecha in the township of Dover, in ye county of Dover and Portsmouth," conveyed to Nathaniel Stevens, Ap. 1, 1673, "a quarter part of a tract of land near Cochecha, bounded on ye north by the highway y^t goeth from *Muchadoe* to *plumpudding hill*, and on ye east by land now in possession of Thomas Downs, and so upon a straight line from ye rock 126 perches towards ye swamp called *Trumbelow*." This land is otherwise stated to be bounded east by the land of John Church. Nathaniel Stevens of Stratham (son of the above Nathaniel), and others of the family in Exeter, conveyed to David Watson, March 21, 1716–17, two tracts of land in Dover—one between the land of James Coffin and that of Tristram Coffin, deceased (see *Plum Pudding Hill*); the other between the lands of John Church and Mark Giles. A part of this land was conveyed by David Watson to Ebenezer Varney, March 30, 1724, 80 ft. long and 40 ft. broad, "beginning near an apple tree standing where old Thomas Downs formerly had a house," thence running 80 ft. "by ye road y^t leads from Tolend." (See *Quaker Meeting-Houses*).

The Giles land, above referred to, is mentioned Ap. 1, 1673, when "Peter Coffin of Cochecha in ye township of Dover, in ye countie of Dover & Portsm^o.," conveyed to Mark Giles six acres of land "neere Cochecha, where ye now dwelling house of ye s^d Mark Giles now standeth, being com only called or known by ye name of *plumpudding hill*, being bounded on ye north by y^e *Great Mast way* going to ye swamp, (see *Mast Paths*) and on ye east by ye land of s^d peter Coffin fortie five pearch, and on ye south by ye land of ye s^d peter Coffin fortie three pearch, the w^h six acres of land being Moity & p^{te} of a tract of land which was granted & Laid out to me ye s^d peter Coffin by a Town Grant, for and in consideracion of what charge I have been out unto John church concerning the child of Naomi Hull, as by the record bearing date ye fifth of March in ye yeare 1667."

The pathetic story of Naomi Hull and her child is akin to that of Hawthorne's "Scarlet Letter."[1] She is said to have been the daughter of the Rev. Joseph Hull, minister at Oyster River in 1662, and afterwards at the Shoals, where he died in 1665. A year or more later, Naomi, perhaps with the hope of concealing her misfortune, seems to have taken refuge with one of her father's old flock at Oyster River. But it had been ordered in 1666 that no person should admit or entertain any inmate, or sojourner, or servant, in his house without giving notice to the selectmen within thirty days, under penalty of nineteen shillings. Accordingly, at a public town meeting of the 14th, 7 mo., 1668, it was ordered by the selectmen that forthwith the constable (John Dam) should take of William Williams, Senior, by way of distress, the sum of nineteen shillings for a fine, for a breach of the town order for entertaining Naomie Hull. Overwhelmed by the cruel laws of that time, it is not surprising that Naomi did not long survive the birth of her daughter. The town, however, was merciful enough to provide for the child. Besides the above mentioned grant to Peter Coffin, it voted, Oct. 3, 1667, to give John Church 60 acres of land, confirmed March 5, 1667-8, with the promise to make it 70 acres, if he would take " Neamy's child," and keep her henceforward until she be 20 years old. John Church is said to have lived where the old jail on Silver St. was. He was killed by the Indians May 7, 1696. What became of "Neamy's child" does not appear.

TRUNNEL COUNTRY. Mentioned June 23, 1701, when Maturin Ricker had a grant of 30 acres "up in the *Trunnill Contrey*." It was laid out to his son Joseph Dec. 4, 1721, "at a place called the *Trunnill countrey*— on the east side of a way that leads from Quamphegan to goldins bridge." Joseph Ricker of Berwick, May 10, 1754, conveyed to Meturin Ricker of "Summersworth," 30 acres of land laid out to said Joseph Dec. 4, 1721, " which land lyeth at a place called y^e *Trunnal country*," beginning at a white oak on the east side of the way that leads from Quamphegan to Golding's bridge. The Trunnel country seems to have been the marshy region in the western part of old Somers-

---

[1] A law similar to that in Massachusetts for such infractions of the moral code, was promulgated in New Hampshire after its separation from that colony, and was still unrepealed at the time of the Revolution. An act was passed by the General Assembly at Portsmouth, N. H., in the June session, 1701, that the persons convicted of such an offence "shall be set upon the gallows by the space of an hour, with a rope about their necks, and the other end cast over the gallows; and in the way from thence to the common goal shall be severely whipped, not exceeding forty stripes each. Also every person and persons, so offending, shall forever after wear a capital letter A of two inches long, and proportionable in bigness, cut out in cloth of a contrary colour to their cloaths, and sewed upon their upper garments on the outside of their arm, or on their back, in open view. And if any person or persons, having been convicted and sentenced for such offence, shall at any time be found without their letter so worn during their abode in this province, they shall, by warrant from a Justice of the peace, be forthwith apprehended, and ordered to be publickly whipped, not exceeding fifteen stripes, and so from time to time *toties quoties*." (From Acts and Laws of N. H., printed in Portsmouth in 1771.)

worth, but the name has not been perpetuated.

TUFTS' BOUNDARY. When the line between Durham and Lee was perambulated March 21, 1798, one of the bounds was "a rock marked D. L. in Thomas Turf's pasture, about six rods north easterly from the hook road, said rock being a little east of the line." (*Durham Records*). The Tufts family of this vicinity has acquired an unenviable notoriety from the exploits of Henry Tufts (or "Turf," as the name was generally called in his day), which have made him proverbially infamous throughout New Hampshire. Within the writer's recollection it was common, by way of expressing superlative wickedness, to say "as big a liar (or thief, etc., etc., as the case might be) as old Hen Turf." The bucolic imagination of this region could take no farther flight in the line of total depravity. The utility of perpetuating the memory of so shameless a man may be doubted, but fresh interest in his career within a few years has been excited in this section by Col. T. W. Higginson's "New England Vagabond," in *Harper's Magazine* of March, 1888. He considers Henry Tufts' autobiography to be of some historic and philological value, but others say it contains nothing of the kind which may not be found in less pernicious books. This work is said to have been written by a clever young lawyer of Dover, for Henry Tufts himself—in spite of what Col. Higginson calls the "Brahmin blood," derived from his grandfather, the Harvard divine—was too illiterate to write his own name correctly. Some say, however, it was composed by Col. Thomas Tash, who in Tufts' early life did not live far distant. But that brave Revolutionary officer was far better qualified to handle the sword than the pen. The details of this work have never been supposed strictly true, but they undoubtedly present a faithful likeness of this depraved man. The waggery attending some of his most audacious performances unfortunately gave a debasing popularity among the vulgar, not only to the book itself, but to countless other tales which are still in circulation in this part of the state. But some people have a taste for nastiness, as the Zulus have for Ubomi—that is, for carrion with worms in it, a *Ubominable* mess indeed, as Henry Tufts' narrative is said to be.

The cellar of the house where Henry Tufts once lived is still to be traced, not far from the above mentioned bound, on land now owned by Mr. James McDaniel, only a few rods southerly from Mr. Bert Thompson's house, on the same side of the road. The name of "Hanary Tufts" is signed to a petition for the separation of Lee from Durham, Nov. 18, 1765. (*N. H. Town Pap.*, XI: 587.) "Henry Tufts" is mentioned as a private soldier on Seavey's Island in Portsmouth harbor, Nov. 5, 1775, in Capt. Smith Emerson's Company; Elijah Denbow, first lieutenant. (*Prov Pap.*, 14: 233.)

TURNING POINT. Mentioned the 30th, 10 mo., 1643, when Wm. Furber had a grant of six acres of Marsh "upon ye Great Bay, upon ye southwest side going to Capt. Champernoone's, ye next marsh to *Turney Point*." (*Dover Records*.) Fifteen acres were laid out to Capt. James Pendleton *at Greenland*, Jan., 1667, one side *joining to Dover bounds*, next the land of Wm. Furber. Leonard Weeks of Greenland, planter, conveyed to his well beloved son Joshua, Ap. 23, 1706, thirty acres of land adjoining a place called *Turning Poynte*, with six acres of marsh adjoining, on the west side of Wm. Furber's. Wm. Furber, Sr., of Dover, out of paternal love and affection to his well-beloved son Moses Furber of Portsmouth, conveyed to him, Dec. 1, 1696, six acres of marsh on the "S. W. side of ye great bay in Piscataqua river, *within ye township of Dover*," bounded north by a marsh in the tenure of Wm. Shackford, and on the south by "the creek which goes up to the land where Luke Maloone now dwelleth." Also 30 acres of upland adjoining said marsh, and of the same breadth, running up into the woods till 30 acres be completed. After the death of Moses Furber, Thomas Phipps, the high sheriff of N. H., levied a portion of his estate for debt, and sold to Joshua Weeks, Aug. 17, 1711, six acres of his marsh on the S. side of Great Bay, *within the township of Dover*, bounded on the north by a marsh in the tenure of said Joshua Weeks, and on the south by "the creek that goes up to the land where Luke Maloon formerly dwelt and now dwelleth: also 30 acres of upland adjoining said marsh on the west side, beginning at the marsh of said Joshua Weeks, formerly Shackford's, and running 50 rods S. W. to a red oak on the S. side of the creek at the head of the marsh, then S. W. and S. 11 rods to a rock by the creek or freshet on the south side. The name of Turning Pt. has not been perpetuated, but it was evidently on the shore of the Weeks lands in Greenland.

Another TURNING POINT, between Broad Cove and Dumpling Cove, is mentioned in 1659 (see *Dumpling Cove*) and again Feb. 27, 1718–19, when Eleazar Coleman mortgaged 200 acres of land whereon he then dwelt, beginning at the mouth of the creek in Broad Cove and extending to a marked tree at John Trickey's, where he lived, thence to a rock a little below *turning poynt*, and so up the bay to Dumpling Cove. This point seems to have been just above Fox Pt., and perhaps marked the turning of the tide.

TURNPIKE-ROAD. The First New Hampshire Turnpike Road properly belongs to this list, as one of its termini was in Durham, at Pascataqua bridge. It was the first turnpike-road incorporated in this state. The act was passed June 16, 1796. Nathaniel A. Haven of Portsmouth issued proposals for its construction Oct. 3, 1800, and the work proceeded rapidly from that time. This road is thirty-six miles long, and extends through Durham, Lee, the Two Mile Streak, Nottingham, Northwood, Epsom, and Chichester, to the Concord upper bridge over the Merrimack. It cost about $900, a mile.

The directors of the First N. H. Turnpike-Road gave notice in the Portsmouth *Oracle and Advertiser* of March 19, 1803, that they had expended on said road the sums required by law, and would set up the gates and begin to take toll on said road the first day of April following. The toll-gate at Pascataqua bridge did not, of course, belong to the turnpike-road. The first one was just above the bridge across Johnson's creek. The second was a little below Durham corner. The town of Durham, unwilling to endure such an obstruction to travel, took measures to remove these two gates in 1817. The third gate was at the Mast-road crossing, opposite the present schoolhouse. It is spoken of March 29, 1827, as " Toll-gate No. 2," probably meaning the second from that at Pascataqua bridge. There was no other within the limits ot Durham. The only toll-gate in Lee was at the bridge across Oyster river, in Newtown.

TURTLE POND. This pond is in Lee, not far behind the mansion of Mr. Charles Thompson, between Oyster river and Wheelwright's pond. A record of 1735 speaks of it as near the highway that leads from ye Mast road to Newtown mill. According to a local tradition the battle of Wheelwright's pond began at Turtle pond. It is often mentioned in the early grants and deeds. Ensign John Davis of Oyster River, in his will of May 25, 1686, makes the following bequest : " I do give to my son John Davis the six score acres of land I had by a town grant, situate and lying and being at *Turtle Pond* in Oyster River." This John Davis, Jr., was killed by the Indians July 18, 1694, together with his wife and several children. His house was also burnt, and two daughters were carried into captivity. One of these, according to a constant tradition in Durham, became a nun in Canada and never returned. The other must have been the Sarah who inherited her father's land at Turtle pond, and also his homestead on the south side of Oyster river, between the Burnham lands and Durham falls, now owned in part by Mr. Ffrost. Oct. 16, 1702, Jeremiah Burnham was appointed administrator of the estate of John Davis, late of Oyster River, and guardian of his daughter Sarah Davis.

Sarah Davis became the wife of Peter Mason, and seems to have resided at her own homestead. Feb. 18, 1726–7, Peter Mason sold James Stevens, inn-keeper, thirty acres of land granted by the town of Dover, April 11, 1694, to John Davis, who, he says in the deed, was " ye father of my wife Sarah Mason, formerly Sarah Davis." Her mother appears to have been the sister of Jeremiah Burnham, her guardian. Peter and Sarah Mason, July 1, 1728, resigned in favor of Joseph Smith, all right, title, and interest in the estate of their grandfather Robert Burnham, especially the hundred acre grant from the town of Dover not yet laid out. The " six score acres " at Turtle Pond which her father inherited is spoken of March 24, 1719–20, as laid out to Ensign John Davis " above forty yeares agoe." On that day one half of said tract (60 acres) was laid out to Peter Mason. This was afterwards conveyed by Peter and Sarah Mason, Ap. 29, 1736, to their loving son-in-law, William Randall[1] and his wife Hannah, their

---

[1] William Randall was the brother of Capt. Nathaniel Randall of Randall's Garrison. He is mentioned Jan. 21, 1712-13, when Richard Tozer, Jr., out of " natural love and affection," gave each of his nephews, Richard and William Randall, five acres of land in Kittery; and that same day their father gave each of them thirty acres more of a neighboring tract. This was the Richard Tozer who married Elizabeth, daughter of Elder William Wentworth, noted for her heroism in the various Indian attacks at Salmon Falls. She was thrice taken captive and carried to Canada.

daughter. This land lay on the south side of Turtle Pond. The other half of the six score acres was conveyed by Peter Mason to John Sias, to whom it was laid out, March 24, 1719–20, on both sides of Turtle pond, beginning on the north side of the Mast path, at a pitch pine, " a littel above Naptheli Kincket's." This was Napthali Kincaid, son of David, who then lived at Camsoe.

Sarah Mason was a widow April 6, 1747, when she conveyed to Benjamin Bickford all her right to thirty acres on the west side of the way to Little river. She seems to have inherited the Davis longevity, for she was still alive Sept. 26, 1771, when she sold John (afterwards General) Sullivan thirty acres of her homestead on the south side of the highway from the parsonage house to Durham Point.

TUTTLE'S MARSH. This marsh formed part of a grant to John Tuttle on the east side of Fresh creek, afterwards sold by his grandson Thomas Tuttle to Thomas Wallingford and others. A plan of Tuttle's marsh in 1767, is to be found in the Exeter registry, Vol. 94 : p. 7.

TWOMBLEY'S BROOK. This is a popular trout stream in Rollinsford that winds down from the hills of Somersworth and empties into the east side of Fresh Creek brook, now Rollins brook. A dam was built and a mill erected on Twombley's brook last century, below the mouth of Warren's brook, which it receives a little below the Boston and Maine R. R. The upper part of Twombley's brook—that is, the part above the road from Salmon Falls to Dover—is called *Clement's brook*. Joseph Twombley conveyed to his brother Benjamin, May 28, 1725, three score acres of upland and swamp in Dover—half of a grant of six score acres to Ralph Twombley, beginning at a white ash on ye land of Mr. Clement, thence running S. S. E. 128 rods to ye road at Otis's bridge, to a tree on ye west side of ye road y^t leads from Cochecho to Salmon Falls. The other half was bought by Gershom Wentworth.

Another TWOMBLEY BROOK rises southeast of Garrison Hill, flows through Benjn Wentworth's land, then across the Portland turnpike road westward of his house, through the Guppy land and *Round Swamp*, crosses the road from the Gulf to Eliot bridge, runs through Mr. Henry McDuffee's land, and finally empties into the Cochecho. (See *Round Swamp*.)

TWO-MILE ROAD, and TWO-MILE STREAK. The Two-Mile road, mentioned in the Durham records of last century, is an old thoroughfare in Lee that extends to and across the *The Two-Mile Streak*. This streak was a slip of land two miles wide at the head of ancient Dover, granted in 1719, and confirmed in 1722, to the proprietors of the iron works at Lamprey river " for their encouragement," and to supply them with fuel. Though really a part of Barrington, it is marked out on Holland's map of 1784 as a separate territory. About 1,000 acres in the western part of the Two-Mile Streak, adjoining Nottingham and the head line of Dover, were laid out in small lots of fifty acres and upwards, 15 of which were granted as early as Oct. 23, 1729. Among them, two lots, of 50 and 120 acres, were granted to Wm. McDonald, and another of 75 acres to Robert McDonald. This land is still owned by their descendants, whose ancient Scotch name has been corrupted to McDaniel. Two other lots of 50 and 75 acres, granted to John Ellis, are still owned wholly or in part, by his descendants, who write their name Ellison. In 1747 there were sixteen families and two garrisons on this Streak. The greater part of it seems to have been monopolized by the leading men of Portsmouth. George Jaffrey owned at least 900 acres. March 10, 1748, John Hayes conveyed to his son Robert 50 acres in the *two mile streak*, in the township of Barrington, being part of the 900 acres which said John Hayes and Joseph Chesley purchased of George Jaffrey, Esq., and the 7th lot in said 900 acres according to Capt. Evans' division. The Durham records of April 14, 1757, speak of land in the "*Two-Mile Streke*," adjoining the head line of Durham, owned by Theodore Atkinson, Mark Hunking Wentworth, and Mrs. Mary Osburne. Jeremiah Mason of Portsmouth advertised, March 22, 1803, lot No. 2, in the *Two-Mile Streak* in Barrington, containing 1,000 acres. The Rev. John Adams of Durham, in his church records of the middle of last century, speaks more than once of administering baptism at "*y*^{e} *Two-Mile* ;" among others, to several of the McDaniels family. The First N. H. Turnpike Road is spoken of in 1800 as laid out across the Two-Mile Streak.

UNCLE SIAH'S CREEK or COVE. This name is familiarly given to the *Downing Cove*, on the Newington shore, just above Patterson's Lane, from Josiah Downing who once owned the adjacent land. This cove was the upper boundary of the Rollins land in 1696. Above it, Job Clement of Dover had a grant of 110 acres the 28th, 11 mo., 1656, ordered to be laid out adjoining James Rawlins' hundred acres, and next Michael Brawn's lot at the northwest. Job Clement, November 25, 1689, conveyed to Joseph Hill, "living in the province of Maine," 100 acres on Bloody Point side, formerly granted his father, Job Clement, deceased, 70 poles by ye water side. Joseph Hill of Kittery, Jan., 1699, conveyed to John Downing 140 acres of land, 110 of which he bought of Job Clement of Dover, 70 poles on the river, and joining Michael Brawn's lot on the N. W. side. Of the other 30 acres, 20 were granted to said Hill by the town of Dover, Ap. 2, 1694, at the head of Job Clement's land, and 10 acres he bought of George Braun Jan. 8, 1699, between the Clement land and that of Richard Carter, 30 poles by the river. When the dividing line was run Jan. 7, 1695–6, between Joseph Hill's land and that of the Rawlins family, it began at a beech tree near ye waterside in *ye cove*, between the houses of said Hill and Rawlins, and thence ran S. W. by W. 240 rods to a hemlock tree. This cove, like most of the others on this shore, is now blocked up and totally disfigured by the embankments of the Portsmouth and Dover railway.

UNITARIAN POND. This little pond was formed by enlarging the bed of

Coggswell's springs behind the Unitarian place of worship in Dover, from which it derives its name. These springs were so called from Col. Thomas Coggswell, a Revolutionary veteran, who formerly owned this land. They fed the brook that once ran along Washington street, sometimes called Coffin's brook.

UPPER FACTORY FALLS. (See *Cochecho Falls*.)

VARNEY'S CORNER. Mentioned March 17, 1710–11, as "against Tristram Heard's house," in Dover. It was so called from Ebenezer Varney, who owned land at Garrison Hill, where the road turns in the direction of Rollinsford.

VARNEY'S CREEK. This name is given to Little John's creek on Whitehouse's map of Dover, from a family long established in this vicinity. Thirty acres, originally granted to Joseph Austin in 1656, were laid out to " humfrie Varnie " March 11, 1666, on the N. W. side of Little John's creek, bounded S. W. by Back river, and N. N. W. by the common. It is also called *Cromwell's creek*, from Joshua Cromwell, whose seven children, Ap. 3, 1752, conveyed his homestead estate of 15 acres on Back river to Moses Varney, bounded north by the lands of Abraham Nute, John Pearl, and Nicholas Harford, easterly by the highway, and southerly by the land of Thomas Whitehouse, deceased. (See *Cromwell's Creek* and *Pearl's Ferry*.)

VARNEY'S HILL. This name was given to Garrison Hill for more than a hundred years, from Ebenezer Varney, who acquired land here in 1696. In a petition from Paul Wentworth and others, to enlarge the bounds of Somersworth, May 19, 1743, it is called *Varney's Great Hill*. It is called " *Varney's Hill* " on Philip Carrigan's map of N. H., in 1816, and on Whitehouse's map of Dover in 1834. (See *Garrison Hill*.)

VINCENT'S WINDMILL. See *Mount Hungry*.

VINEYARD. Mentioned in 1653, in a grant to Wm. Follet and James Bunker. (See *Jonas' Creek*.) And again March 28, 1707, when Nicholas Follet of Portsmouth conveyed to James Bunker one half of ten acres called *ye Vineyard* at the head of Johnson's creek, granted Wm. Follet and James Bunker (Senior*)* in 1653.

WADLEIGH'S FALLS. These were the uppermost falls in Lamprey river within the limits of ancient Dover. They were originally granted by the authorities of Massachusetts Bay to Samuel Symonds of Ipswich, together with 640 acres of land, which he took possession of June 3, 1657, in the presence and with the consent of Moharimet, the Indian sagamore of this region. Robert Wadleigh acquired possession of these falls and had a saw-mill here as early as April 21, 1668, and in 1669 his right was confirmed by a grant from the town of Dover of the " uppermost falls in Lampereel river, commonly called y^e *Ileland falls*." They are called " the upper falls in Lamprey river " in a survey of the Dover bounds in 1701. Ezekiel Gilman of Exeter conveyed to Samuel Doe, Nov. 9, 1730, one sixteenth part of a 640 acre grant in Dover, at a place commonly called *Wadley's Falls*, upon Lamperell river, lying on both sides of the river, formerly granted by the General Court of Boston to Samuel

Simonds of Ipswich, deceased, which sixteenth part said Gilman had by deed from Robert Wadley Sept. 1, 1730. Also one sixteenth part of the saw-mill and dam upon Lamperell river at *Wadley's falls*, with all privileges. Bartholomew Thing conveyed to Joshua Brackett of Stratham, March 7, 1733–34, 59 acres of land at " a place called *Wadly's ffalls*, otherwise *Symond's grant.*"

Symond's grant and *Wadley's grant* are repeatedly mentioned in the old records. Walter Bryant of Newmarket conveyed to Samuel Watson of Durham, June 22, 1751, fifty-four acres " in that tract commonly called *Symond's grant*, being a grant of one mile square; which 54 acres begin at a stump a little above ye north end of ye mill dam, by ye side of Lamperel river, then run south by said river," etc. And that same day Jeremiah Folsom of Newmarket conveyed to Samuel Watson 12 acres " in that grant of land commonly called *Symond his grant*," adjoining the land said Watson bought of Water Bryant.

Wadleigh's Falls are in the southern part of Lee. A saw-mill is still in operation here, belonging to the Messrs. Glidden; and a grist-mill, owned by Dr. Edgerly. Here also is *Wadleigh's Falls post-office*, with a cluster of houses that can hardly be styled a village.

Wadleigh's Plains are mentioned in the Durham records Dec. 25, 1761, and again in a deed from Joseph Smith to Nathaniel Watson, Jr., of 34 acres in the parish of Lee, on the north side of the way from *Wadleigh's mill* towards Little river, running east by the land John Davis bought of Joseph Sias, Esq., about 97 rods to a spotted hemlock in a swamp on the west side of *Wadleigh's plains*, so called, then southerly to the N. E. corner of John Cromit's land.

Wadleigh's path from Newmarket to Wadleigh's mill is mentioned in 1745. Benjamin Smith had 25 acres of land laid out in 1757 on the south side of *Wadley's way*. A road from the Spruce Hole (on Lee Hill) to *Wadley's road* is mentioned June 26, 1765. According to the Durham records, £177, 10s. were, in 1764, " P^d sundry men for Building *Wadley's Bridge.*"

WAKEHAM'S CREEK. This name was given to the creek below Drew's Point, on the lower side of Oyster river, from Edward Wakeham, who, May 2, 1695, bought " *Giles' old field*, lying between two creeks." He was still living here July 25, 1715, when " neighbor Wakeham" is spoken of in a petition from James Langley that a road might be laid out from his place to the highway, as he was penned up by Bartholomew Stevenson. Edward Wakeham and his wife Sarah were admitted to the Oyster River church Oct. 18, 1719. Their son Caleb Wakeham, July 8, 1757, sold Samuel Smith his " homestead plantation " of thirty-two acres, beginning at a small elm tree in ye range of ye fence at ye Bank of y^c upland by ye marsh in *Wakeham's creek*, then running S. 68 deg. W. 18 rods to the road leading from *Oyster River Point to Oyster river or Durham falls*, then Easterly by s^d road to land in possession of Valentine Mathes, and by this land north to the channel of ye brook or run of water between his land and that of s^d Mathes, and through the middle of said channel to Oyster river, and up the river to *Wakeham's creek*, then to the elm tree first mentioned. Samuel Smith conveyed this land to Benjamin Mathes Jan. 8, 1759. It is now in the tenure of Mr. Jonathan Carr. (See *Giles's creek*.)

WALDRON'S FALLS. See *Cochecho Falls*.

WALDRON'S HILL. Mentioned in the Madbury records of 1798, when a road was proposed from Pascataqua bridge to *Waldron's Hill*. This hill is in the central part of Barrington, where the town-house now stands. The old stage road from Dover through Barrington was formerly called the *Waldron Hill road*.

WALDRON'S LOG SWAMP. Mentioned in 1658, when Thomas Nock's land on the south side of *Capt. Waldron's logg swamp* is spoken of. (See *Nock's Marsh*.) Capt. Richard Waldron in 1652 had a grant of two thirds of all the timber between Cochecho first falls and Bellamy Bank freshet. A mast path led into this logging swamp, afterwards known as the road to Littleworth.

WALDRON'S PLAINS. These plains are in Dover, west of Gage's Hill. They are so called in 1822, when the Dover *Sun* announced that the Second regiment, under Col. Dudley, would parade on *Waldron's plains* on the 13th of October, that year.

WALL'S CREEK. This is apparently the same as *Wale's Cove*, mentioned Sept. 12, 1701, when the Exeter line is stated to extend from a marked tree at *Wales' cove* S. and by E. to Hampton bounds. The inhabitants of the Squamscot Patent, living on the E. side of the line running from *Wall creek* to Hampton bounds, were joined to the Parish of Greenland Jan. 3, 1716. (*N. H. Prov. Pap.*, 3 : 623–4.) The name of this creek may have been derived from James Wall, a member of the Exeter Combination of 1639, who afterwards went to Hampton.

WARNER FARM. This name is given to the tract of land in Durham bequeathed to the state of New Hampshire by the late Benjamin Thompson, in his will of Feb. 12, 1856, for the purpose of establishing thereon a College of Agriculture and the Mechanic Arts. It was so named by his father, Benjamin Thompson, Esq. (grandfather of the present writer), who purchased the greater part of it from the Hon. Jonathan Warner of Portsmouth. It was previously called the *Hill farm*, which name is given it by Jonathan Warner himself in his deed to Benjamin Thompson, Sr. It was originally a part of a five hundred acre grant from the town of Dover to Valentine Hill, adjoining his mills at Oyster River, the 14th, 5 mo., 1651. Jonathan Hill of Durham, great grandson of Valentine, conveyed to Daniel Warner of Portsmouth, Dec. 1, 1763, a tract of 107 acres, "part of that land commonly called y^e *Five Hundred acres*, beginning at Thomas Chesley's, by ye mast road, and extending up said road 96 rods," etc. Also 18 acres on ye north side of said mast road, bounded east by John Woodman's land, and north and west by Thompson's land, together with the dwelling house thereon, being the same land conveyed to said Jonathan, Feb. 23, 1757, by his father

Samuel Hill, to whom it had been conveyed, Nov. 4, 1729, by Capt. Nathaniel Hill, father of said Samuel.[1] (See *Hill's Five Hundred Acres*.)

This land was inherited by Jonathan Warner, son of Daniel, who also acquired 100 acres more of the Hill grant, conveyed to him by Benjamin Partridge May 19, 1778. Jonathan Warner of Portsmouth, and Eliza his wife, conveyed to Benjamin Thompson of Durham, March 17, 1794, " a certain tract of land in Durham, called and known," says the deed, " by the name of the *Hill farm*, in two separate parcels, laying on each side, and adjoining the mast road, so called, the whole containing 220 acres, more or less, and contains the whole land conveyed by one Jonathan Hill to my Hon[d] father Daniel Warner, Esq., deceased, Dec. 1, 1763, and also all the land conveyed to me by Benjamin Partridge May 19, 1778."

The tract on the south side of the mast road is described in this deed as bounded E. by Benjamin Chesley's land, S. by Oyster river, so called, W. by the lands of John Thompson and Benjamin Chesley, and that formerly belonging to Ichabod Chesley, and N. in part by the Mast road. The other tract was bounded southerly by the Mast road, easterly by the land of Jonathan Woodman, Jr., northerly in part by the land of Timothy Emerson, and on every other side by that of Ebenezer Thompson. This was Judge Ebenezer Thompson, father of Benjamin Thompson, Sr.

Benjamin Thompson, Esq., Dec. 8, 1828, conveyed to Benjamin Thompson, Jr., 220 acres of land in Durham, lying on each side of the turnpike road, being the same he purchased of Jonathan Warner, Esq., March 17, 1794; also another tract of eleven acres in said Durham, bounded southerly by the mill road, so called, northerly by the river (Oyster river), and easterly by land purchased of Joseph Coe, being the same purchased of Joseph Chesley 3d, guardian of Abigail Young; also another tract of five acres, purchased of Joseph Coe, bounded northerly by the mill road, westerly by the aforesaid land purchased of Joseph Chesley 3d, and easterly by land in possession of Elijah Willey ; " all which lands aforesaid," says the conveyer, " compose what I call my *Warner farm*, and which I have improved for many years." Certain rights were reserved by Benjamin Thompson, Sr., during his lifetime.

WARREN'S BROOK. This brook flows through the old Warren lands in Rollinsford, and empties into Twombley's brook on the east side, a little below the Boston and Maine Railroad. Joseph Roberts sold Benj[n] Warren, Ap. 29, 1749, a house and quarter of an acre of land S. E. of Dr. Moses Carr's dwelling-place, which land Dr. Carr had previously purchased of Zachariah Nock and conveyed to said Roberts. James Nock also conveyed to Benj[n] Warren, Dec. 20, 1762, a tract of land on the southerly side of the highway from Dover to Quamphegan, beginning at the N. E. corner of Lt. Samuel Rendall's land and running E. by the highway to that of Moses

---

[1] Samuel Hill, youngest son of Capt. Nathaniel, was Daniel Warner's brother-in-law. He married the great aunt of Benjamin Thompson, Sr.

Stevens, then S. to the road leading to Fresh Creek.

WASHUCKE. Mentioned Jan. 17, 1660, when "Wadononamin, *alias* John Johnson, ye Indian and Sagamere of *Washucke* and Piscataqua," for the love he bore to Englishmen, "especially to Edward Hilton, eldest son of Edward Hilton of Piscataqua," conveyed to said Edward, Jr., all his neck of land between two branches of Lamprell river called *Washucke*, being about six miles in length, and in some parts six miles in breadth, reserving the use, if need be, of one half of the convenient planting-ground during his natural life. This, of course, was the neck between the Pascassick and Lamprey river itself. On some maps the name of *Washuck* is still given to the Pascassick river. Hitchcock in his Geological Atlas, calls it *Watchet*. Richard York, March 1, 1748-49, conveyed to his son Richard ten acres of land in Epping, bounded on one side by *Watchick* river, so called, and on the other by land belonging to the heirs of Major Bartholomew Thing, Esq., deceased.

WATERING GUT. Mentioned Ap. 25, 1699, when a highway, 4 rods wide, was ordered to be laid out "as the way now goes from huckleberry hill to the *Watering gutt*, and so along, as the path now goes, over the hill to the westward of Joseph Roberts his house till it comes to the cross way that leads to belemies bank." Another road, two rods wide, was laid out, Feb. 20, 1702-3, from the road to Little John's creek through to yͤ *watering gutt way*, beginning at a white pine by Little John's creek road, thence running easterly on the S. side of the gully at the S. W. corner of Thomas Whitehouse his land, to a maple in the N. W. corner of (Thomas) Beard's lot, and so on to the S. E. corner of Samuel Tibbet's land, and through that to the *Watering gut way*. Abigail Broughton of Portsmouth conveyed to Samuel Tibbets, Feb. 4, 1709-10, one third part of a 20 acre grant to John Reyner, Jr., then in the tenure of said Tibbets, bounded east by yͤ path that leads from Kenney's toward *Thomson's poynt*, westerly by the way from *whortleberry hill*, and north running along the north side of the *watering gutt swamp* till it comes to a stump 4 or 5 rods from the *watering gutt*. The deeds of the other ⅔ of said land to Samuel Tibbets state that it was bounded W. by "the way that leads from *hurtleberry hill* to the *watering gutt*." John Tuttle and wife Mary conveyed to Nathaniel Austin Feb. 1, 1713-14, ten acres on Dover Neck bought of John Hall, bounded N. by the land of Thomas and Joseph Hall, E. by the way from Huckleberry hill to the *watering gut*, S. by John Canney's land, and W. by the road from Huckleberry hill to Little John's creek. John Canney conveyed to Elijah Tuttle, March 31, 1740, ten acres on Dover Neck, on the easterly side of the road from Cochecho down to Dover Neck, bounded northerly by Nathaniel Austen's land, easterly by the highway from Huckleberry hill to the *watering gut*, and southerly by Howard Henderson's land and a strip of the common fenced in by Benjamin Roberts. The Watering Gut is evidently the brook that empties into Little John's creek.

Another public WATERING PLACE is mentioned Dec. 3, 1709, when James Mussey conveyed to Otis Pinkham a parcel of meadow ground on the west side of Dover Neck, between the lands of John Pinkham and James Mussey, on the north side of a small gutter and the lot laid out by the town for a *watering place*. This is apparently the same as the *Long Gut*, mentioned in the division of the Calves' Pasture Ap. 18, 1722, when nine shares were measured for Otis Pinckham, "beginning att or near the Spring below John Pinckham's house—32 Rod att the head by the Low street and 36 Rod by the water side, beginning att the Run of water that Comes from the Spring. And att ye same Time wee haue mesured 8 shares for Thomas Caney from otis Pinckham's hed Line by the Low street 33 Rod to a Stake by the fence on the west Side of s^d street, and also 33 Rod by the waterside to a fence on the south Side of the *Long Gutt* soe called."

WATSON'S BROOK. Mentioned Sept. 10, 1750, when Joshua Weeks conveyed to his son John Weeks of Hampton, physician, 5 acres of land in Greenland, running N. E. by a path to *Watson's brook*, then W. to land of Robert Goss. This land was part of Joshua Weeks' homestead, and is now owned by the heirs of Wm. Weeks. Watson's brook empties into Great Bay on the west side of Mr. J. C. Weeks' farm, between that and the land of Wm. Weeks' heirs.

WATSON'S FALLS. See *Cochecho Falls*.

WATSON'S POINT. Whitehouse, on his map of Dover, gives this name to a point on the west side of the river Cochecho, between the Gulf and the Narrows.

WEBB'S CREEK. Mentioned in a grant to Thomas Canney, apparently before 1650, of nine acres of marsh on the S. W. side of the Great Bay, "bounded on ye south running into ye marsh of *George Webb's Creek*. This appears to be the inlet afterwards called Canney's creek, on the shore of the Weeks land in Greenland. "Georg Webb" is mentioned as early as the 10th, 9 mo., 1643, when he was "presented for living idle like a swine." (See *Branson's Creek*.)

WECANACOHUNT. This was the Indian name of Dover Point, mentioned in Hilton's patent of March 12, 1629–30. It is otherwise written the 14th, 4 mo., 1641, when reference is made to the patent purchased of Edward Hilton and some merchants of Bristol, "called *Wecohannet* or *Hilton's point*, commonly called or knowne by the name of Dover or Northam." (*N. H. Prov. Pap.*, 1 : 155.) And it is called *Winnichahannat* May 22, 1656, when Capt. Thomas Wiggin surrendered his claims to the Hilton Point lands.

The settlement at Hilton's Point was long called "Dover" in a restricted sense, to distinguish it from other settlements within the township, particularly at "Cochecho." (See *Cochecho*.) And here might be mentioned what was omitted in the proper place, that Dover, though apparently never formally chartered as a township, was recognized as a town by the General Court of Mass. in 1642. (*N. H. Prov. Pap.*, 1 ; 162, 164, 203.)

WEDNESDAY BROOK. This is a stream of clear, sparkling water that rises at Wednesday hill, in Lee, and goes winding toward the east,—"a marvel of crookedness,"—fed on its way by several springs of remarkable purity—one in particular of mineral qualities, which, perhaps, give lustre and tone to its waters. It crosses the road near Mr. George Chesley's, where it is a favorite watering-place for horses, and empties soon after into Oyster river.

This brook is mentioned Nov. 13, 1713, when Joseph Davis conveyed to Job Runnels three score acres of land " on the west side of *Wensday Brook.*" John Willams had a grant of "three score acres in ye woods on ye south side of *Wensday swamp,*" March 19, 1693-4, laid out Jan. 2, 1712-13, " on the south side of *wensday brook.*" *Wednesday Brook* is spoken of June 13, 1720, as running through a tract of land sold by James Bassford of Oyster River to Wm. Pitman and Wm. Willey, originally granted to Edward Vrin. Willey sold his part of this land to John Laskey, May 15, 1722. It is now owned by C. W. Bartlett, Esq., whose paternal grandmother was a Laskey.

A highway was laid out Oct. 12, 1737, from *Wednesday brook* to Joshua Woodman's land, beginning at this brook, and running along by a great hill, then over the south side of said hill to a gutter between Thomas Stevenson's land and Thomas Footman's, and between their lands till it comes to Nicholas Meader's at the east, and by s^d Meader's till it comes to *the turn*, then between Meader's and Smith's till it comes to Joshua Woodman's land.

Woodman's land was on the upper side of Lamprey river, in the Packer's Falls district, Durham. It is now chiefly owned by the Dames.

WEDNESDAY HILL. This hill is in Lee, on the upper side of Lamprey river. It is east of Lee Hill, in " District No. 3." Mention is made of it Nov. 4, 1723, when 30 acres of land were laid out to Samuel Purkings on the south side of *Wednesday hill.* Capt. Nathaniel Randall's grant of 30 acres on this hill is mentioned in the division of his estate, Ap. 25, 1750. An old tradition asserts that this hill derived its name from a skirmish that took place with the Indians in its vicinity on a Wednesday. Another tradition says it was so named by the early surveyors, who were laying out grants of land on this hill on a Wednesday, and suspended their labors to lunch on the top. The name, however, may have been given it by one of the early settlers in memory of some hill in England, where there are a great number of elevated places that have a similar name—derived from an Anglo-Saxon word signifying a hill or mound sacred to

" Woden, God of Saxons,
From whence comes Wensday; that is Wodnesday."

Among them may be mentioned Wednesbury, and Wednesfield in Staffordshire, Woodnesborough, and Wodnesdic (now Wansdike) in Wilts, Wendeshough in Lancashire, Wendnesham in Cheshire, etc. (See Taylor's *Words and Places.*)

WELLAND or WILLAND'S POND. This pond, 200 rods long and 120 wide, is on the line between Dover and Somersworth. The name is derived from Wm. Welland, whose land, partly in Dover, and partly in Somersworth, was at the head of this pond. He died about 1801. It was called the *Great Pond* as early as 1650, and at a later period, *Cochecho Pond*. In Merrill's N. H. Gazetteer of 1817 it is called *Humphrey's Pond*. The same name is given it in the Somersworth records. It is often called *Hussey's Pond*, from the families of this name in its vicinity. It is called *Messenger's Pond* in 1859. (See *Great Pond*.) According to a survey of this pond for the city of Dover, it covers a surface of 78¾ acres, with a depth in some places of 65 feet. It has a steady capacity of 514,000,000 gallons of water, derived almost entirely from springs beneath the surface. This water is of excellent quality, as proved by repeated analyses. The Dover water-works on Garrison Hill, being partly supplied from this pond, an Act was passed by the N. H. Legislature Feb. 25, 1891, " to prevent the pollution of *Willand's Pond*, situate in the city of Dover and the town of Somersworth, the water of which is used by the city of Dover for domestic purposes."

WELSH COVE, otherwise WELSHMAN'S. This cove is on the Newington shore of Little Bay, between Furber's Pt. and Dame's Pt., and still retains its ancient name. It is mentioned in the Dover records the 15th, 4mo., 1646, when Thomas Layton had a grant of "a plott of marsh at the head of *Welshman's Coue*." And again in 1656, when John Dam's grant of 40 acres at *Welshman's Cove* was laid out. (See *Dame's Point*.) Thomas Roberts, June 17, 1658, conveyed to Richard Row, fisherman, " my now dwelling-house and all my upland " (30 acres) " lying and being in *Welshman's Coue* in Pascataqua river."

The name of Welsh Cove appears to have been given in early times, not only to the cove itself, but to the neighboring district. Samuel Moody of Boston, Sept. 25, 1704, conveyed to Alexander Hodgdon a tract of 30 acres at or near *Welch Cove, in ye town of Portsmouth*, beginning at a white oak stump which stands 8 rods from ye little brook or freshet (the trout brook) in ye said Hodgdon's fence, which joins to ye highway that leads from *Welch Cove* to Portsmouth, etc., which land formerly belonged to the Rev. Joshua Moody of Portsmouth, deceased.

The origin of the name does not appear, but several of our early colonists were of Welsh origin, such as George Vaughan, sent over by Capt. Mason in 1631, but afterwards returned to England; Thomas Roberts of the Dover Combination of 1640, Wm. Williams, and doubtless Wm. Jones. Likewise the Gilman family, prominent in the history of Exeter, from which the township of Gilmanton, incorporated in 1810, derived its name, and from which sprang John Gilman, member of the Provincial Council in 1680, and John Taylor Gilman, governor of N. H. in 1813. And the early Vaughans of Portsmouth (where *Vaughan street* still commemorates their name), among whom may be mentioned Major Wm. Vaughan, who was a member of the Council under President Cutt in 1680, and his son George Vaughan, who was appointed Lieut. Governor of N. H. in 1715. They sprang from an ancient family in Wales, which, in their day, furnished two members of Parliament, viz: Edward Vaughan, Esq., of Cardigan, and Lord John Vaughan of Carmarthen, both members in 1676. The Vaughan family of England, it might be added, has been freshly illustrated this very year by the elevation of the Rev. Dr. Herbert Vaughan to the archiepiscopal see of Westminster.

WENTWORTH SWAMP. This was part of the Great Ash swamp, between Salmon Falls river and Cochecho, where Paul Wentworth's grant of 30 acres was laid out in 1718. In his will of Feb. 3, 1747-8, he speaks of his swamp as "a little below the *pitch-pine plains.*" Fourteen acres were ordered to be laid out to Thomas Wallingford, Sept. 8, 1727, "on the upper side of Indego Hill, as near to the swamp called *Wentworth swamp* as it may be." Ten acres were laid out to said Wallingford, March 3, 1728-9, on the N. E. side of *Wentworth's swamp*, adjoining Samuel Downs' land; and five acres more on the south side of said swamp, adjoining the land of Maturin Ricker, Jr.

WHEELWRIGHT'S POND. This pond is between Lee Hill and Newtown, and is noted for an encounter with the Indians, July 6, 1690, known as "the battle of Wheelwright's pond." It is said to have taken place on the south-east side. Our scouts came upon the Indian trail near Turtle pond, and two companies, under Captains Wiswall and Floyd, drove the enemy to the borders of Wheelwright's pond, where, after several hours' fighting on a hot July day, three officers and twelve privates were left dead on the field, with seven others who were wounded. In the accounts of this battle one item is omitted of special interest to the people of Durham, within the ancient limits of which this encounter took place: James Smith, a volunteer from Oyster River, died of a surfeit produced by running to join Capt. Floyd's company—a rare instance of a man's voluntarily hastening to take part in a battle. His widow, the daughter of Ensign John Davis, and two of her sons, were killed by the Indians July 18, 1694.

The *two islands* in the middle of Wheelwright's pond are mentioned in Bartholomew Stevenson's will of April 22, 1718, in which he gives his son Joseph five acres of marsh, granted him by the town of Dover, on the south side of this pond, "against two islands." These islands are seldom visited except by those who go there to fish for perch and pickerel, or to gather the fragrant pond lilies which grow in profusion around their shores.

The *narrows* are mentioned Jan. 20, 1719-20, when Oliuer Kent's grant (in 1656) of 80 acres of upland "near *whelrit's Pond* on the north side of the Pond, against the *narrow*," was surveyed anew. These narrows are a little above the source of Oyster river. The contraction of the waters here has given rise to the names of *Upper* and *Lower pond*, though really one sheet of water. The name of this pond was derived from the Rev. John Wheelwright, founder of Exeter, attesting the ancient claims of that township to lands along Oyster river. Richard Otis of Dover was authorized by the town, July 3, 1666, "to cut all the grass about the pond by Oyster river, which was known by the name of *Mr. Wheelwright's marsh*."

WHIDDEN'S CREEK. See *Pickering's creek*.

WHISOW or WHISONE, otherwise HUSOW or HUSONE. Mentioned March 19, 1693-4, when a grant was made to Henry Rice of his improvement at *Whisow* (or *Whisone*), with such addition as will make it 40 acres. This land was laid out " on the way going to Madbery," Dec. 9, 1699. Henry Ryce conveyed this land to Joseph Meader Nov. 30, 1702. Joseph Meader, Feb. 1, 1723-4, conveyed to Eli Demerit, Jr., a tract of 40 acres, known and called by the name of *husow* (or *husone*). This land is now owned by Mr. Alfred Demeritt, a descendant of the above Eli. The exact orthography of this name is uncertain. In the deed from Henry Ryce to Joseph Meader in 1702 it appears to be *Whrisone* or *Wisrisow*.

WHITEHALL. This place, the name of which has been perpetuated to the present day, is in Rochester, but is often mentioned in the Dover records of the last two hundred years. The bounds of Ancient Dover, as defined Aug. 3, 1701, began " at y° middle of Quamphegan falls, and so ran up the river four miles, or thereabouts, to a marked tree by the river side within a mile of *Whitehall*." Orders were given to Robert Coffin and his troop, Aug. 11, 1708, to march from Exeter to Kingstown, and thence to Oyster River, and there to take up their quarters the first night; and " thence to Cochecho and soe up towards *Whitehall*, and so return to Cochecho and there quarter," etc. (*N. H. Prov. Pap.*, 2: 581.) The road to *Whitehall* (from Cochecho) is mentioned July 7, 1714, when Wm. Everett's grant of 100 acres on the north side of James Kid's land, near the *Great Pond* above Cochecha, was laid out to Thomas Downes, beginning at a pitch pine tree near the pond, on the west side of *the road that leads to Whitehall*. Ebenezer Downs, Dec. 20, 1714, conveyed to John Herd 50 acres of land, being one half of that tract given his brother Thomas Downs by their grandmother, Martha Lord, beginning at a pine tree near the *Great Pond* above Cochecho, on y° west side of *the mast path y^t leads to White Hall*. Farmer and Moore's Gazeteer of N. H. (1823) says: " Between Norway plains and Salmon fall river is a considerable quantity of land, *formerly* called *Whitehall*, the soil of which was destroyed by fire in the dry years of 1761 and 1762, so as to be of little value for cultivation."
Whitehall Swamp is mentioned in Sept., 1814, when Betsy, widow of Stephen Wentworth, petitioned for leave to sell " land in *White Hall swamp*, so called." This swamp contains about 500 acres of low land, now covered for the most part with small wood, but in early times it was no doubt one vast forest of much wider bounds. It is about a mile below Rochester city, between the road to Dover and that to Great Falls, and now has various owners.

It is hardly necessary to say that it is an error to attribute the name of Whitehall, as some do, to Parson Hall of Rochester, who is said to have illustrated one of his sermons by referring to the numerous white birches in this swamp which lay spread out in full view of his meeting-house on Haven's hill, giving rise, it is said, to the name of "Hall's white swamp." But something better than white birches once covered this vast swamp. Enormous primeval trees grew here, that furnished masts for the royal navy, which were borne down the mast path to Cochecho years before the Rev. Avery Hall began his ministry in Rochester. He was not installed till Oct. 15, 1766, and Whitehall was certainly so called more than sixty-five years previous. The reason why might be given in the language of Philip II of Spain, who is said to have written on a despatch from England, referring to Whitehall in London : " There is a park and palace there called *Huytal, but why called Huytal, I am sure I do n't know.*" Whitehall in Rochester, however, may have been so named in honor of the "Committee of trade and foreign plantations at Whitehall," often mentioned in the provincial records. Whitehall palace was then the centre of authority, and most of the orders concerning New Hampshire and its forests, came from the above mentioned committee.

WHITEHORNE'S PLAINS. These plains are along the line of Barrington and Nottingham, near the Lee boundary, and are often familiarly called *Curt's plains*, from Curtis Whitehorne, a former owner thereon. A highway across the lower side is sometimes called *Whitehorne's road*.

WHITTIER'S FALLS and MILLS, otherwise WHITCHER'S. Whittier's mills, consisting of a fulling-mill, grist-mill, and a building for dressing cloth, once stood at the easterly side of Tole-End falls. Their name was derived from Obadiah Whittier, whose widow still owned them, Jan. 7, 1718, when they were destroyed by fire, which broke out in the carding mill, operated by Moses Whittier, son of Obadiah, who at once erected new machinery and resumed the carding, fulling, and clothing business, the following month. (See *Cochecho Falls.*)

WIGGIN'S MILLS. Mentioned on Chace's County map of 1856. They are at the first falls in Lamprey river above Packer's falls, and are now called *Wiswall's mills*. " Wiggin's mills " consisting of paper mill, grist-mill, and saw-mill, belonging to the estate of Moses Wiggin, were conveyed by John Mooney, administrator, to Joshua Parker and Mr. T. H. Wiswall May 23, 1857. Mr. Wiswall afterwards acquired full ownership. The paper-mill was burned down several years ago.

WIGWAM POINT. This name was formerly given to a high point of land on the Greenland shore, between *Broad marsh* and *Long marsh*. It is mentioned April 9, 1729, when a line of division was made between these two marshes, beginning at " a certain point of upland called *Wiggwam Point.*" These marshes originally belonged to Henry Langstaffe of Bloody Point, who had 30 acres of upland adjoining, but at the above date they were owned in common by his grandson Henry Nutter and two Johnsons named John and Nathan. When the above mentioned division was made, *Long Marsh*, at the N. W. of Wigwam Pt., was assigned to the Johnsons, and *Broad marsh* to Henry Nutter. These marshes are again mentioned May 27, 1734, when

Nathan Johnson and Samuel Nutter agreed upon a division of 5 acres, and 50 rods of upland, butting on a salt marsh called *Long marsh*, and on *Nutter's marsh* called *Broad marsh*, and partly on *Johnson's marsh*. Samuel Weeks, in his will of Sept. 15, 1745, gives his son Matthias all his "right in the *Long marsh*, and all his flat ground from said *Long marsh* till it comes within four rods of the *Little Pocket marsh*." *Wigwam Point*, *Long marsh*, and part of *Broad marsh*, are now owned by Mr. J. C. Weeks.

WILLAND'S POND. See *Welland*.

WILLEY'S CREEK. This is a small creek that flows through Mr. Jeremiah Langley's land at Durham Point and empties into Little Bay. The name was derived from Thomas Wille or Willey, who had a "breadth" of land on the upper side of this creek before July 17, 1645. (See *Bickford's Garrison*.) This creek is mentioned by name as early as Nov. 2, 1686, when a road was laid out from *Wille's creek* to Oyster River Falls.

Another *Willey's Creek* is mentioned Ap. 23, 1743, when John Johnson and wife Prudence conveyed to Samuel Weeks "two acres of salt marsh in Greenland, bounded on the southeast side on *Wille's creek*." This creek is the outlet of Willey's spring, and flows along the lower side of Canney's island. (See *Canney's Island* and *Willey's Spring*.)

WILLEY'S MARSH. Mentioned Sept. 15, 1745, when Samuel Weeks in his will divides between his sons Samuel and John his salt marsh on the S. W. side of the Great Bay, commonly called *Willey's marsh*. This is, of course, in Greenland. (See *Willey's Spring*.)

WILLEY'S SPRING. This spring, said to be one of the best in Greenland, is about 50 rods from the residence of Mr. J. Clement Weeks, to whose buildings the water is conveyed by means of a hydraulic ram. It is mentioned as follows in the Dover records, when Thomas Willey's grant was laid out Ap. 1, 1701 :

—"Whereas by order of Generall Court there was fooer hundred Acres of Land giuen to the inhabitants of douer (Dover) that haue marsh in the great bay, we the subscribers here of being appoynted by the Towne of douer to Lay out unto Thomas Willey his devident of vpland to his marsh, who haue according to order Laid out thirty acres to his marsh and bounded it as followeth, that is to say, beginning at the bounds of Thomas Cannies Land at a white oke tree and so thirty two Rods vpon a south line to a spring comonly Called by the name of *Willey's spring*, and so vpon a west Line one hundred forty seven Rods to a hemlock Tree, and so to a Red oak tree vpon a north Line thirty two rods, and so vpon an East line one hundred and forty four rods to the bounds of Thomas Cannies, all which land within said bounds make thirty acres, the bound trees marked T W. Laid out and bounded by vs Aprill the first 1701.

(Signed) Will furber
          Jnº bickford
          Jnº damm."

The above record proves that the Willey grant on the shore of Great Bay, now part of the Weeks lands in Greenland, lay within the bounds of Ancient Dover, being a part of the 400 acres granted to Dover between Hogsty Cove and Cotterill's Delight.

Sam¹ Tibbets and Sam¹ Welle, both of Dover, conveyed to Sam¹ Weeks of Portsmouth, March 10, 1709–10, one third part of a tract of thirty acres of land and six of salt marsh, lying between Henry Langstar's marsh and a parcell formerly in possession of Thomas Canney, beginning at the bounds of Canney's land, at a white oak tree, and running thirty rods south to a spring commonly called *Willye's Sprynge*. Samuel Weeks, in his will of Sept. 15, 1745, gives his son Matthias one acre of salt marsh running up unto a place called *Willey's spring*.

WILLEY'S WAY. This was a road in Newtown, mentioned in 1734 as leading to the head of Durham township. It is no doubt the road spoken of March 18, 1757, when it was ordered that the highway from Thomas Wille's land into the highway above Newtown mill should be changed and come out upon the line between Durham and the Two Mile Streak. Thomas Willey's house was on the north side of the road coming from Madbury. There was a *Willey's bridge* in Newtown, mentioned in the laying out of a road in 1740 from another road that led to Willey's bridge. It was probably across Oyster river. *Willey's mill* in Nottingham is spoken of March 8, 1757, when Samuel, son of Samuel Wille, sold one eighth part of it to David Glass.

WILLIAMSVILLE. This name is given on Whitehouse's map of Dover to a settlement on the east side of the river Cochecho, near the "upper-factory dam." It was so called from John Williams, agent of the cotton factory established at this dam in 1815. (See *Cochecho Falls*.) Dr. Quint calls him "the father of the Dover manufacturing prosperity."

WINE-CELLAR ROAD. This name is given to an old road in Durham, extending from the Long Marsh road across Horn's woods, where it meets Simon's Lane. It is derived from a natural cavity in the rocks, where the wood-choppers used to deposit their rundlets of cider and other "refreshers" to keep them at a desirable temperature.

WINGATE'S SLIP. This slip, now called *Ford's landing*, is the terminus of the mast road from Madbury, on the west side of Back river. It is adjacent to the land of Mr. Ford, who has enclosed this end of the mast road, though it is a public highway to the very river. The town of Dover voted, March 24, 1728–9, to lay out a road "from *Winget's Slip* to the end of the township." The surveyors reported, Dec. 27, 1729, that they had laid it out "as the mast way then went." (See *Mast Road to Madbury*.) John Drew conveyed to Rebecca Kook, Ap. 6, 1756, a tract of land on the west side of Back river, at yᵉ head of Thomas Pinkham's land, bounded south by yᵉ mast path running down to *Winget's slip;* and another tract on the south side of yᵉ mast way running down to *Winget's slip*, partly bounded by the lands of John Layton and Israel Hodgdon.

WINKLEY'S HILL. So named from the Winkley house in Dover, which stands on this hill, just above the site of the Hayes garrison, on the Tolend road.

WINKLEY'S POND. Tristram Heard, in his will of Ap. 18, 1734, gives his daughter Elizabeth Knight eight acres at *Fresh marsh*, at *Winkol's pond*, in Dover. The only pond of this name at the present day is in the southern part of Barrington, not far from the Madbury line.

WINNICOT RIVER. This river rises among the Hampton swamps, flows through Stratham into Greenland, and empties into Great Bay above Packer's Point. "*Winecote river falls*, in Greenland," are mentioned Oct. 8, 1665, when the selectmen of Portsmouth ordered a highway to be laid out from these falls east to Sam[1] Haines' house, and thence to the highway to Hampton. Ebenezer Johnson conveyed to Joshua Weeks, May 23, 1713, "one sixteenth part of a sawmill called the *Lower mill* on Winicott river." This was probably the "*tide mill*" mentioned on Merrill's map of Greenland in 1806. The same map, however, mentions a sawmill and gristmill on the Winnicot river, near the road to Exeter, which, though *up the river* from the tide-mill, is *lower* in the sense of being southward. This is no doubt the "*Johnson's mill*" mentioned in the laying out of the road to Exeter, March 6, 1710–11.

WISWALL'S FALLS and MILLS. See *Wiggin's Mills*.

WOLF-PIT HILL. This hill is mentioned in early times as on the west side of Beard's creek, in Durham, and apparently on the south side of Stony brook. The number of wolves in N. H. induced the Government, March 16, 1679–80, to offer a bounty of 40s. for each one killed in the province. In 1692 a bounty of 20s. was ordered to be paid by each town. Tho[s] Edgerly of Oyster River, " for killing a woolfe," was paid that sum Feb. 10, 1695–6. The selectmen of Portsmouth reported to the government, March 17, 1692–3, that nine wolves had been killed " that winter," of course within that township. " Considering the Publick damage done in this province by wolves," it was voted by both Houses, May 17, 1716, that 50s. be paid out of the public treasury for the killing of every grown wolf, besides the bounty given by each town. (*Prov. Pap.*, 3 : 644.) As late as March 17, 1764, the town of Durham voted to give six pounds, new tenor, for every grown wolf killed within the township, and in 1767 four shillings were paid Elijah Drew for killing one. (*Durham Records.*)

Wolf-pits were by no means uncommon in former times. Audubon, the great naturalist, relates that when he was in Ohio, the farmers there took wolves by means of a pit. The *Wolf-pits* or traps, in the heart of the Lynn woods, in the old ox pasture between Blood Swamp and Glen Lewis Dam, have recently been purchased by Mr. Chase of Lynn, Mass. These pits, which date from the first settlement of that place, are described as circular, the sides walled, eight or nine feet deep, small at the top, and widening towards the bottom.

WOODCHUCK ISLAND. This island, so called on Whitehouse's map of Dover, is in the Cochecho river, below the mouth of Fresh creek. It now belongs to Mr. Henry Paul of Rollinsford. It formed part of Somersworth after the incorporation of that town, and fell to Rollinsford when the latter township was chartered in 1849. After the road to

Eliot was laid out, the land below, including Woodchuck island, was restored to Dover.

WOODMAN'S CREEK. This name is sometimes given to Beard's creek, in Durham. (See *Brown's Hill*.)

WOODMAN'S LEDGE. This ledge rises up from Langley's heath on the shore of Wheelwright's pond, affording a point of vantage for fishermen.

WOODMAN'S POINT. This name is given to Long Point on Chace's atlas of 1857. It is on the Newington shore, and formed part of the land given to Nicholas Woodman by his grandfather, Nicholas Pickering, in 1807. (See *Long Point*.)

WORSTER'S ISLAND. This island is in the Salmon Falls river, below Great Falls, opposite Indigo Hill. It was probably formed by deposits from *Worster's brook*, the mouth of which is directly opposite, on the Berwick side. The name was derived from Moses Worster or Wooster, who is spoken of July 2, 1709, when he conveyed to Timothy Wentworth part of his privilege on *Wooster's river*. It is mentioned March 27, 1736, when part of Moses Stevens' division of the common lands was laid out " in an island lying by Salmon falls river, commonly called *Wooster's Island*, lying partly against Capt. Paul Wentworth's land, and partly against Samuel Downs' land. Said island contains 3¾ acres." Moses Stevens and his wife Hannah (daughter of John Thompson, Sr., of Oyster River), Nov. 16, 1738, sold this island to Paul Wentworth for twenty pounds. Paul Wentworth, in his will of Feb. 3, 1747-8, gives his nephew Paul Brown his lot at Indigo Hill, lying between Eben and Samuel Downs' lands, and " also the island, lying near the easterly end of said lot, commonly known by the name of *Wooster's Island*." This island now belongs to the Great Falls Manufacturing Company.

YARD COUNTRY WAY. Mentioned July 18, 1734, when 20 acres of land were " laid out for a parsonage in the parish of Summersworth, beginning at a black oak standing about half a mile S. W. of the beginning of the *Yard Country way*, so called, where it leaves the Rochester road." As this way lead near the *Pear Yard* mentioned in 1793 (see *Pear Yard District*), it may have derived its name therefrom; the species of pear tree found there being, it is said, as long-lived as the white oak. Some suppose this road so called from the old lumber yard at Mast Point, but as the Yard Country Way is stated to have its beginning " where it *leaves* the Rochester road," this derivation is doubtful. The name, however, may refer to some tract once reserved as a nursery " for masts. *yards*, and bowsprits." (See *N. H. Prov. Pap.*, 18 : 143.)

ZACKEY'S POINT. This name, derived from Zachariah Trickey, is given to Trickey's Point May 8, 1846, when Nathaniel P. Coleman conveyed to Ruel J. Bean part of the farm formerly owned by Capt. Samuel Shackford, adjoining Pascataqua river, reserving the right of pass-way in the common wheel path on the south side of the field wall, and the privilege of going to the cove near *Zackey's Point* or *Zackey's Point Cove*. This point is on the Newington shore, and is now owned by Mr. Valentine M. Coleman, son of the above Nathaniel. (See *Trickey's Point* and *Cove*.)

ADDENDA.

AMBLER'S ISLANDS. (See p. 8.) Only one island is mentioned by John Ambler, Jan. 10, 1739, when he conveyed to Ephraim Libby of Kittery several parcels of land, and with them " y^e *Island* belonging to my Home Place in Durham."

BROADWAY BROOK. So called in a report of the city government of Dover in September, 1892, concerning an appropriation " for the purpose of constructing the *Broadway Brook* sewer." This is the brook that flows through the *Dump*, and is otherwise called the *Ham brook*, because it traverses the so-called " Ham field " in the upper part of its course. It rises among the springs at the southwesterly side of Garrison Hill, and is the first brook that empties into the Cochecho river on the northerly side, below Dover Landing. (See the *Dump*.)

BUTLER'S POINT. This point is on the south side of Beard's creek, at the mouth—that is, between the creek and Oyster river, at their confluence. It was originally a part of Wm. Hilton's land, which he conveyed to Francis Mathes in 1645. His right was probably forfeited, for this land seems to have been granted anew to Valentine Hill, who conveyed it to Patrick Gimson (Jameson) May 11, 1659, describing it as on the north side of Oyster river, bounded east by the creek. Jameson conveyed it to Thomas Mighill (Mitchell) " sometime of Oyster River," July 29, 1669. Mitchell sold it to John Webster, of Newbury, Mass., Dec. 29, 1670. Webster, however, must have had an earlier title, for his first conveyance of this land was made to George Chesley Oct. 16, 1669. Another conveyance was made May 10, 1710. After George Chesley's death, all his land in this vicinity (88 acres) was laid out anew, at the request of his widow Deliverance and of Capt. James Davis, whose first wife, Elizabeth, seems to have been a Chesley.

This survey was made May 21, 1711, " beginning at *a poynt of Land at the creek's mouth* next belo the falls on the north side of Oyster river, running northward towards Jonathan Woodman's," etc. This point is now owned by Mr. Albert Young, a direct descendant of the above George Chesley, through his mother, whose first husband was Francis Butler, whence the name of *Butler's Point*.

CLAY POINT. In addition to what has already been said in this work about Clay Point (see p. 43) might be given a fuller account of the Andrews deed, proving that it was on the eastern shore of Dover Neck, not far from the Sheep Pasture on Huckleberry Hill, and below the old road at the lower side of Mr. Reyner's upper lot, apparently on the shore of the Varney land :—Jedediah Andrews, of " Salsbury," Mass., Jan. 5, 1669, conveyed to " Mr. John Reyner of

Dover, in y̆ *countie of Pascattaq*, in y̆ Jurisdiction of the Massachusetts Colony, Minister," his late dwelling house on the eastern side of Dover Neck, with three acres of land on which it stood, granted him by the town, and laid out in March, *Anᵒ Salutis* 1659, bounded E. by y̆ highway wʰ goeth betweene it & y̆ land of sᵈ Reyner, N. by Mr. Reyner's upper lott, W. by y̆ *sheep pasture*, and S. by Mr. Roberts his lott."—"Alsoe three acres of land, less or more, granted by y̆ Toune of Dover, and laid out to Ralph Twamly, lying and being neer thereunto, situated two & twentie pole square at a poynt called *Clay poynt*, between the house lott of Thomas Roberts and the land of y̆ sᵈ John Reyner, below y̆ highway above mencioned, which was given to and possessed by y̆ sᵈ Twamly as a house lott, and sold by him to me."

This was the Rev. John Reyner, a native of Yorkshire, Eng., who first settled in Plymouth, Mass., where he remained eighteen years. He came to Dover in 1656, and here died Ap. 22, 1669. According to Dr. Quint, his house stood four rods east of the highway, fourteen rods below the old fortified meeting-house on Dover Neck, where his cellar can still be traced. The estimation in which he was held by his parishioners is shown by the large grant of land made him near the streamlet still known as *Reyner's brook*, in the upper part of Dover.

COFFIN'S WOODS. These once noted woods, a part of the old Peter Coffin estate in Dover, once covered a large tract of land on the south side of the Cochecho river, now traversed by the Boston and Maine R. R., and covered by numerous streets and residences adjacent. *Coffin's Orchard*, still remembered by many people, was in the very heart of the present city of Dover, extending from Washington St. beyond Orchard St., which derived its name therefrom.

DEMERITT'S BROOK. This brook is so called where it traverses the old Demeritt land in Madbury, not far from Mr. Alfred Demeritt's. It formerly had sufficient water power to run a mill. (See *Demerit's Mill*, p. 58.) Where it crosses the lower highway from Durham Village to Dover it is now called the *Gerrish brook*, from the adjacent Gerrish land. formerly Chesley's. The bridge across it at this place is in Madbury, near the Durham line. It afterwards flows through the Jones land and empties into Johnson's creek.

DOVER GARRISONS. In addition to the Dover Garrisons enumerated pp. 61–64, is "MR. PIKE'S GARRISON," mentioned Nov. 13, 1696 (*Prov. Pap.*, 2 : 246.) This was the Rev. John Pike. who came to Dover in 1678, and here died March 10, 1710. He lived on Dover Neck, perhaps in the "minister's house," it was voted to erect in 1669. "The *garrison about y̆ ministry house* on Dover Neck" is mentioned May 11, 1697. (*Do.* 17 : 656.)

"CAPT. TUTTLE'S GARRISON" is mentioned Nov. 13, 1696 (*Prov. Pap.*, 2 : 246.) This was John Tuttle, who was Captain of the military forces of Dover proper from 1692 till 1704. His dwelling-house and homestead lands, according to his will of Dec. 28, 1717, were on Dover Neck, "'between Nutter's land and Hilton's Point."

DREW'S GARRISON at OYSTER RIVER. (See p. 182–3.) According to the probate records at Exeter, Thomas and Francis Drew were both killed by the Indians in 1694. Mary, widow of Thomas, was appointed administrator of his estate July 30, 1694. Letters of administration upon the estate of Francis Drew were first granted to his brother John Nov. 16, 1694. But it is furthermore stated that "Whereas Thomas Drew, surviving son and eldest unto ye aforesaid Francis deceased, is now returned from captivity out of the hands of the Indian Enimie, and claimes the administration upon his father's estate," his claim was granted Nov. 16, 1696. The above John Drew is no doubt the one killed by the Indians "by the Little Bay"—Pike says, Ap. 27, 1706. Belknap says the garrison was near, but not a man in it. The women, however, put on hats, gave the alarm, and fired away so briskly that the Indians fled. This shows that there was a second Drew's garrison at Oyster River.

HODGDON'S HILL. This hill is in Madbury. It is crossed by the lower road from Durham village to Dover, near the house now belonging to the heirs of the late Stephen Jenkins, but formerly owned by Peter Hodgdon, from whom this hill derived its present name.

LOG HILL SPRING. This spring was once noted in Dover for the coolness and excellence of its never failing water. It is at the foot of the old Log Hill, on land now owned by Mr. S. H. Foye, in the rear of his dwelling-house on Washington St. It was on the very shore of the old bed of the Cochecho, which here made a deep bend before the cut was made to straighten it for the benefit of the Portsmouth and Dover R. R. This road, crossing the Cochecho, traverses Log Hill, a short distance east of the spring. The outlet of the spring was formerly into the river itself, and so cold was the water that this part of the stream was avoided by bathers. Log Hill Spring is still accessible. The old path from Major Waldron's Log swamp terminated at Log Hill, whence the logs were rolled down to the mill-pond.

NARROWS. The Narrows in the Pascataqua river below Boiling Rock, mentioned on page 155, must not be confounded with the Narrows further below, between Peirce's island and Trefethen's island.

PENELOPE'S COVE. This cove is on the western shore of the Salmon Falls river, in the southeastern part of Rochester, not far above the Dover line. It derived its name from Penelope, wife of Aaron Tibbetts.

POMEROY'S COVE. (See p. 210.) The name of this cove has been ascribed to Richard Pomeroy, but on what grounds does not appear. No Pomeroys belonged to the Dover Combination of 1640, or are to be found in the earliest rate-lists. Leonard Pomeroy is mentioned in 1622 as one of the associates of David Thomson for colonising the Pascataqua region, but it does not appear that he came here. Joseph Pomry was here before 1674, in which year his estate was administered by his widow Elizabeth. (*County Records*, Exeter.) Pike records the marriage of "Rebecca Pommery, widow," to "Clement Rummeril,"

Sept. 6, 1687. And a "Wm. Pomrey" is mentioned as serving in garrison in 1697. (*Prov. Pap.*, 2 : 246.)

PORTSMOUTH. (See p. 210.) Capt. John Smith's map of New England in 1614, gives the name of *Hull* to the site of the present city of Portsmouth, and the name of *Boston* to York, Me.

The POUND. Mentioned Oct. 3, 1734, when Joseph Twamley, aged 73 years, or thereabouts, testified that he "wel knows yᵉ lands lying in Dover a little below Cochecho falls wᶜʰ are call'd Sheffield's lands, and have been so accounted for more than 60 years last past, & yᵗ he wel knows yᵗ there was a highway or cart path wᶜʰ run from yᵉ Publick highway down between Tobias Hanson's fence and where the *Pound* now is, along by yᵉ place where Joseph Hanson's house now is, unto sᵈ Sheffield's lands for more than 60 years last past, & he wel knows yᵉ sᵈ way was always kept open & improved by Every Body yᵗ had occasion to use it." According to the Historical Memoranda (No. 282) in the Dover Enquirer, Tobias Hanson lived where is now the Edmund J. Lane house, on Central Avenue; and Joseph Hanson lived where the Drew house is, on Hanson St. William Sheffield, whose lands are mentioned above, had also a grant at Oyster river. (See *Meader's Neck* and *Royall's Cove*.)

The Pound is again mentioned Sept. 5, 1735, when Eliphalet Coffin conveyed to Joseph Hanson two acres of land in Dover, bounded S. by yᵉ highway yᵗ leads to Littleworth, W. by David Watson's two-acre home lot, N. by "Leah's field, as is so called," and E. by "a small gore claimed by Mr. Richard Waldron yᵗ lyes over against yᵉ *pound:*—being the very same land where Tristram Coffin, father of Eliphalet, formerly lived." An orchard on it is mentioned. These two acres, with an orchard thereon, are mentioned in Eliphalet Coffin's will of Jan. 15, 1734–5, proved in 1736. The above-named Tristram was the son of Peter Coffin. Dr. Quint supposes Tristram's garrison to have stood near the house of the late Gov. Martin, and the second Tristram's house to have been near the residence of the late Dr. Thomas H. Cushing.

RICHARDSON'S HILL. This name is given to the eastern slope of the "Falls hill" in Durham village, from the Richardson house near the top, formerly a public house. "Capt. Joseph Richardson's tavern" is mentioned in the Durham records July 8, 1793. He had previously served in the Revolutionary war. (See *Falls Hill*.)

RIVERS. Going from Newmarket to Dover, the Boston and Maine R. R. crosses the *Pascassick river* just after leaving Newmarket village. At this point *Follet's brook* empties into the river, and the neighborhood called *Hallsville* is to be seen at the left. The next stream crossed by the railway is *Lamprey river*, here spanned by the so-called *Diamond bridge*. This is in the *Packer's Falls* district, before arriving at *Bennet's crossing*, where trains from opposite directions often pass each other. Farther on, between the so-called *Mill-road crossing* and the Durham station, the railway crosses the fresh part of *Oyster river*, here contracted to a mere brook. Beyond the Madbury station it crosses the *Bellamy*, and, just before entering Dover city, the river *Cochecho*, otherwise *Cocheco*.

ROCHESTER HILL. This name is sometimes given to Haven's Hill, in Rochester, around which the first settlers of the town gathered, and here built a meeting house in 1731.

SENTER'S SWAMP. (See page 231.) Henry Senter's name is signed to a Dover petition of 1685. (*Prov. Pap.*, 1 : 561.)

STEPHEN'S POINT. (See p. 239–40.) Those who are fond of ascribing an Indian origin to the names of places, such as *Herod's Cove*, *Swadden's Creek*, etc., will be glad to know, in connection with *Stephen's Point*, otherwise *Stephen Jethro's* or *Jether's*, that an Indian named Peter Jethro is mentioned in 1676. (See *Prov. Pap.*, 1 : 358, 360.)

STONY POINT. This name is given to a point on the west side of Back river, between the mouth and the Three Creeks.

UPPER and LOWER WEIR. The former is mentioned Jan. 22, 1770, when it was voted to build a new bridge " over the *upper ware*, so called, next below Capt. Thos W^k Waldron's mills at Cochecho, below ye lower falls." This weir, of course, was at the lower bridge in the city proper, at the foot of Washington St. The *Lower Weir*, or *Ware*, as it was usually called, was, it is said, at or a little below the foot of Young street.

SWADDEN'S CREEK. (See p. 248–9.) Philip Swadden was in N. H. as early as 1633. (*Prov. Pap.*, 1 : 72.)

WILD-CAT ROAD. This road leads from Waldron's Hill, Barrington, to the district derisively called "France," and thence to Leathers City. *Wild-Cat Hill* is about half a mile from Barrington Post Office.

A List of the Lots in FRANKLIN CITY, with the Names of their respective Owners when first laid out:

1. JOHN RINDGE.
2. COGSWELL & PINKHAM.
3. DANIEL FRENCH.
4. CHARLES PIERCE.
5. ISAAC WALDRON.
6. WILLIAM ROBIE, JR.
7. WILLIAM K. ATKINSON.
8. EDWARD GOVE.
9. THOMAS HAM.
10. SAMUEL SHERBURNE.
11. NATHANIEL WHITE.
12. EDWARD SWAIN.
13. SAMUEL HILL.
14. WILLIAM K. ATKINSON.
15. NATHANIEL UPHAM.
16. MOSES CANNEY.
17. JOSEPH TILTON.
18. WILLIAM COGSWELL.
19. THOMAS PINKHAM, JR.
20. THALES G. YEATON.
21. SAMUEL SHERBURNE.
22. CAPT. JOSEPH SMITH.
23. STEPHEN DAVIS.
24. SAMUEL SHERBURNE.
25. JOHN P. GILMAN.
26. RICHARD HART.
27. COGSWELL & PINKHAM.
28. AARON WINGATE.
29. THOMAS FURBER.
30. RICHARD DAME.
31. NOAH JEWETT.
32. MOSES LITTLE.
33. COGSWELL & PINKHAM.
34. SAMUEL TENNEY.
35. ANDREW SIMPSON.
36. BALLARD PINKHAM.
37. ABNER GREENLEAF.
38. ISAAC LORD.
39. JOSHUA HARTFORD.
40. EZRA HUTCHINGS.
41. ANDREW SIMPSON.
42. NATHANIEL WHITE.
43. NATHANIEL CLOUGH.
44. LEVI DEARBORN.
45. BENJAMIN BUTLER.
46. RICHARD HART.
47. THOMAS BECK.
48. TOBIAS TUTTLE.
49. TIMOTHY PINKHAM.
50. WILLIAM K. ATKINSON.
51. BENJAMIN MOORE.
52. ISAAC WALDRON.
53. TIMOTHY WINN.
54. MARK SIMES.
55. MOSES LITTLE.
56. BENJAMIN HASKELL.
57. SAMUEL CARTER.
58. RICHARD HART.
59. ISAAC WALDRON.
60. COGSWELL & PINKHAM.
61. JOSEPH SMITH, Dover.
62. THOMAS COGSWELL, JR.
63. NATHANIEL WILLIAMS.
64. JEREMIAH STICKNEY.
65. JAMES MCCLARY.
66. MOSES CANNEY.
67. NATHANIEL WILLIAMS.
68. FRANCIS COGSWELL.
69. GREENLEAF CILLEY.
70. EDWARD J. LONG.
71. WILLIAM K. ATKINSON.
72. JOSEPH PARSONS.
73. DAVID STONE.
74. THOMAS LEAVIT.
75. SAMUEL HILL.
76. ABNER & WILLIAM BLASDELL.
77. COGSWELL & PINKHAM.
78. JOHN LOCKE.
79. CARR LEAVITT.
80. COGSWELL & PINKHAM.
81. SAMUEL STORER.
82. JOHN DEARBORN.
83. JAMES H. MCCLARY.
84. COGSWELL & PINKHAM.
85. ISAAC WALDRON.
86. COGSWELL & PINKHAM.

87. MOSES L. NEAL.
88. JAMES TISDELL.
89. RICHARD DAME.
90. EPHRAIM BLASDELL.
91. SAMUEL HILL.
92. THOMAS JOHNSON.
93. EBENEZER CRUMMET.
94. SAMUEL SHERBURNE.
95. THOMAS JOHNSON.
96. RICHARD HART.
97. COGSWELL & PINKHAM.
98. WILLIAM ROBIE, JR.
99. COGSWELL & PINKHAM.
100. WILLIAM K. ATKINSON.
101. ISAAC WALDRON.
102. NATHANIEL WHITE.
103. ISAAC WALDRON.
104. NATHANIEL FOLSOM.
105. ANDREW SIMPSON.
106. BENJAMIN DEARBORN.
107. EBENEZER SMITH.
108. CLEMENT JACKSON.
109. SAMUEL TENNEY.
110. COGSWELL & PINKHAM.
111. MOSES CANNEY.
112. COGSWELL & PINKHAM.
113. THOMAS BECK.
114. MOSES CANNEY.
115. EBENEZER CHADWICK.
116. MOSES CANNEY.
117. COGSWELL & PINKHAM.
118. JAMES TISDELL.
119. COGSWELL & PINKHAM.
120. RICHARD HART.
121. EBENEZER PARSONS.
122. EBENEZER SMITH.
123. ANDREW SIMPSON.
124. COFFIN D. NORRIS.
125. JOSIAH BARTLETT.
126. EPHRAIM DREW.
127. COGSWELL & PINKHAM.
128. COGSWELL & PINKHAM.
129. JAMES LAIGHTON.
130. GREENLEAF CILLEY.
131. COGSWELL & PINKHAM.
132. NATHANIEL WHITE.
133. NATHANIEL WHITE.
134. JONATHAN CILLEY.
135. WILLIAM HOOPER.
136. MOSES CANNEY.
137. SAMUEL SHERBURNE.

Only one house remains to perpetuate the memory of Franklin city. This was conveyed to John T. Emerson by Ballard Pinkham July 20, 1821. The bill of sale, still extant, specifies it as a "dwelling house on the Franklin Propriety, so called, being the house I lately lived in," etc. This house was taken up Oyster river in a gundelow and became the residence of Mr. Emerson, whose descendants still own it. It is the first house on the right side of the turnpike road, below Beard's creek.

ERRATA.

Page 13, 2d col., line 28, for "trackt" read tract.
" 40, 1st col., line 19, for "Matthew Giles" read Matthew Williams, who, according to the early records, seems to have been a man of unfortunate propensities.
" 67, 2d col., line 30, for "Dureseme" read Duresme.
" 88, footnote, for "asigner" read a signer.
" 92, footnote, for "G. W. Tuttle" read C. W. Tuttle.
" 147, 2d col., line 39, for "A point" read A brook.
" 151, footnote, [1]Nicholas Medar appears to have been the grandson of William Follet.
" 198, 1st col., line 39, for "shore" read share.
" 213, footnote, "Union Parish" should be Parish of Unity, which is mentioned in Humphrey Chadbourne's will of May 25, 1667.
" 225, 1st col., line 29, "*above* Hook Island Falls," should be *below* them.

The accompanying MAP OF THE LANDMARKS IN ANCIENT DOVER has been specially prepared in accordance with this work by Harry E. Hayes, A. B., B. S. of Boston, Mass.—but of Ancient Dover ancestry—a graduate of Harvard University, and of the Massachusetts Institute of Technology. On a map of this size only the chief Landmarks, of course, could be given, but the situation of the remainder can be easily found by reference to the text.

The plan of FRANKLIN CITY has been reduced from the original plan, drawn by Benjamin Dearborn of Portsmouth.

That of the MOAT is from a drawing made about fifty years ago by an authorized land-surveyor.

This index references all people names and all buried
place names found in the text.

----, John 208 Laomi 122 Lomy 122
    Matthew 40 Salome 122 Wm 81
ABBOTT, Joseph 213 Moses 7
    Thomas 213 Thomas Sr 213
ACTON, 127
ADAMS, 163 183 189 Avis 173
    Charles 28 41 98 135 144 150 183
    184 203 225 Charles Jr 184
    Charles Sr 183 184 Easter 184
    Esther 184 225 Garrison 175 183
    189 225 Hugh 67 72 121 132 173
    183 187-189 200 225 230 John 7
    27 124 162 226 247 261 Joseph 7
    27 66 245 Mary 136 Nathaniel 238
    Oaks 197 Rebecca 225 Samuel 183
    Sarah 28 203 Thomas A 122
ADAMS', Point 81 125 145 232
ADDER'S, Swamp 54
ALFRED, King Of ? 27
ALLARD, Job 82
ALLEN, Jacob 11 John 38 Samuel 151
ALLEY, Elizabeth 7 Mrs 40 77 Point
    244 252 Samuel 7 34 237 244 252
ALLIN, Hannah 78 139 Jacob 139
    Samuel 149 Wm 78
ALT, John 29 128 132 155 185
    Rebeckah 128 Remembrance 155
ALTE, John 28 29
ALTON, Bay 214
AMBLER, John 8 39 209 277
AMBLER'S, Islands 41 Marsh 115
AMERISCOGGIN, 180

ANDREWS, 277 Jedediah 43 198 277
    Mary 198 Mr 192
ANNE, Queen Of ? 177
ANTEGOE, 113
ANTHONY'S, Brook 28
ANTIGUA, 113
ANTONIES, 8 Brook 8 113
ANTONY'S, Brook 8
APPLEDORE, 164
ARUNDELL, 158
ASH, Brook 9 Swamp 24 42 48 252
    Swamp Bridge 9 Thomas 215
ASSABENBEDUCK, 157
ASTIN, Joseph 49
ATKINSON, 10 Hill 10 John 239
    Joseph 70 162 239 243 250 Theo-
    dore 131 261 William K 282 283
    Wm K 77 253 Wm King 9 76 119
    222
ATKINSON'S, Hill 118 119 222 244
AUDUBON, 275
AUSTEN, Nathaniel 266
AUSTIN, 199 Betty 98 Elijah 20
    Joseph 49 64 89 125 126 198 206
    210 234 235 238 262 Nathaniel 49
    125 266 Nicholas 98 Peter 98
    Samuel 177 Sarah 177 Thomas 49
    125 238
AUTIN'S, Mill 125
AYER'S, Pond 114
BABB, Freeman 69 Samson 87
BABB'S, Mill 114

BACK, Cove 94 149 179 River 9 19
23 32 43 52 55 58 60 63-66 71 72
75 78 94 107 115 118 119 125 133
135 140 142 146 148 164 166 167
185 192 195 198 199 208 210 211
216 218 220 221-223 229 231 236
243 252-254 262 274 281 River
Garrison 82
BADGER, William 108
BAER, Mrs 79 168
BAGDAD, 32
BAKE, River 12
BAKER, John 127 Otis 164
BALD, Head 196 235
BALLARD, 70 243 Joshua 243
BALLARD'S, Bridge 243
BALLEW, William 19 Wm 20
BAMPTON, Ambrose 13 John 42
BAMTON, John 13
BANGS, 62
BANTOM, Ambrous 13
BANTOM'S, Point 42
BARBADOES, 9 19 42 112 137 140
154 253 Pond 24 48 70 83 117 127
138 210 Springs 117 Way 9 31
BARBADOS, 31
BARBADUS, Way 9
BARBEL, Brook 79
BAREFOOT, Deputy Governor 160
Walter 227
BARHEW, 162 Aenon 163 Belmont
162 Caesar 163 Jubal 163 Jube 163
Pete 163 Peter 163 Titus 163
Venus 162 163
BARNES, Capt 15
BARNES', Island 170
BARRINGTON, 10 13 16 19-21 32 33
35 40 42 62 72 75 94 107 113 114
117 122 126 137 138 147 153 162
166 198-201 231 233 235 241 260
261 264 272 275 281
BARTLETT, Alfred 16 C W 268
Charles W 122 140 236 Ichabod
208 Josiah 15 16 251 283 Mr 16

BARTLETT'S, Falls 127 251
BARWICK, 213
BASFORD, James 190
BASS, Rock 231
BASSFORD, James 268
BATTESHALL, Jona 24
BATTISHAL, Jonathan 24
BATTISHALL, 25 Jonathan 24
BAXTER, 90 138
BAY, Of Pascataquack 87
BEACH, 83
BEAN, 29 Henry 240 Ruel J 50 276
BEAN'S, Point 29 196 219 240
BEARD, Elisabeth 178 Elizabeth 100
179 Esther 100 179 Joseph 10 21
60 100 178 179 Joseph Sr 10
Martha 179 Mary 23 179 Samuel
100 Thomas 14 20 21 23 164 172
179 213 226 227 266 William 16
142 178 179 242 Wm 16 71 142
178 180 243
BEARD'S, Creek 17 32 109 112 122
160 170 178 179 228 242 243 254
275-277 283 Garrison 16 175 178
Hundred Acres 21
BEAVER, Dams 87 Pond 56
BECK, Ann 18 Henry 18 65 Theodore
Romeyn 18 Thomas 282 283
BECK'S, Point 94 Slip 94 98 152 250
BEECH, Hill 40 60 73 112 154 228
242 254
BEETLE'S, Point 196
BELAMYES, Bank 50
BELCHER, Gov 169
BELKNAP, 61 64 75 146 156 160 173
175 178 185 186 188 195 212 236
279 Jeremy 10
BELL, 71 C H 195
BELLAMIES, Bank 8 102
BELLAMIN'S, Bank 124
BELLAMY, 8 20 215 Bank 48 264
Falls 83 124 229 Hook 16 17 19 21
58 83 94 106 107 140 228 John 20
Mathew 20 Mills 229 River 14 16 19

BELLAMY (continued)
    42 57 62 65 72 83 86 124 132 135
    137 140 164 195 198 199 228 229
    281
BELLAMY'S, Bank River 10 17 139
BELLEMAN'S, Bank 20 24 254 Bank
    River 86
BELLEMIES, Bank Pond 8 9
BELLEMIN'S, Bank 57 139 Bank
    River 140
BELLEW, William 19
BELLEWMAN'S, Bank 20
BELLEY, Mr 19
BELLIMAN'S, Bank 90
BELLIMON'S, Bank 42
BELLINGHAM, Richard 123
BELLOMAN'S, Bank 90 Banke River
    141
BEN'S, Fort 188
BENICK, Abraham 120 244
BENMORE, Philip 225 Temperance
    225
BENNET, 186 Eleazar 24 52 247
    Henry 158
BENNET'S, Crossing 280
BENNETT, John 99
BENNICK, 186 Abraham 24 25 186
    190 231 Abraham Jr 191 Benjamin
    231 Eleazar 25
BENSON, Samuel 59
BENWICK, Abraham 186
BERWICK, (see also SOUTH
    BERWICK and NORTH BER-
    WICK) 18 30 56 86 123 127 131
    144 167 195 213 276
BETEL'S, Point 214
BICKFORD, 64 65 105 130 196
    Benjamin 160 204 260 Benjn 159
    204 Bridget 184 Dependence 43
    152 251 Eliakim 130 Esther 225
    Frank 87 Garrison 25 Henry 14
    Jethro 131 Jno 120 273 John 243
    John 10 19 25 28 55 59 71 74 105
    116 122 129 130 133 144 150 158

BICKFORD (continued)
    184 185 189 204 John Sr 102 129
    Joseph 130 Lemuel 130 131 144
    Mr 192 Olive 152 Sarah 204 Susan
    130 Temperance 74 130 185
    Temperate 185 Thomas 184 185
    209 225 Thomas Jr 184 Winthrop
    116
BICKFORD'S, Ferry 25 65 75 121
    Garrison 71 184 273 Point 68 121
BICKROD, Temperance 130
BIEDERMAN, Mr 135
BINE, Jonas 33 41 116 177 Joseph 28
BINN, Jonas 41 98 116
BIRCH, Point 59 89 133 196 202 205
    248
BISHOP, Of Dureseme 67
BLACK, Point 115 Water Brook 56
BLACKHALL, 25
BLACKSNAKE, Hill 171
BLACKWATER, 140 207 208 229
    Brook 26 42 47
BLAKE'S, Bridge 114
BLASDELL, Abner 282 Ephraim 283
    William 282
BLAY, Ruth 190
BLIND, Will's Neck 114 125 237
BLOOD, Swamp 275
BLOODSUCKER'S, Pond 191
BLOODY, Point 24 25 59 64 65 75 86
    96 97 99 102-104 107 117 118 121
    154 157 159 163 174 181 185 196
    204 205 208 210 219 227 232 239
    240 244 245 253 255 272 Point
    Ferry 117
BLUE, Hills 82 Job 82 Ridge 82
BLYDENBURG'S, Garrison 187
BODGE', Pond 42
BODGE'S, Island 15 170 Pond 16 42
    122
BOGGY, Marsh 210
BOILING, Rock 87 131 155 195 196
    279
BONKER, James 116

BONNY, Bigg Pond 126
BOSTON, 15 39 50 90 91 97 101-104
    194 211 214 228 262 280 And
    Maine Railroad (see RAIL-
    ROADS)
BOTTOMLESS, Pit 163
BOW, Pond 113 114 162
BOYCE, Antipas 15 Hannah 15
BOYES, Antipas 15 Antipas Jr 15
    Hannah 15
BOYLING, Rock 27
BRACKET, Joshua 20 51 Thomas 91
BRACKETT, J H 139 Jeremiah 73
    Joshua 263
BRADSTREET, Symon 213
BRAGG, Samuel Jr 65
BRAKIN, Wm 31
BRAND'S, Krick 28
BRANSON, Geo 28 29
BRANSON'S, Creek 41 52 98 267
BRAUN, Geo 160 204 George 59 159
    261
BRAVEBOAT, Harbor 134
BRAWN, Geo 59 103 Michael 261
BRAWNS, Michael 204
BREW, House 250
BREWSTER, 92 196 Daniel 162 Mr
    159
BRISTOL, 130 267
BROAD, Cove 38 39 66 74 115 131
    155 196 216 219 239 240 245 258
    Marsh 149 209 272 273 Turn 13 48
    127 132
BROADBOW, Harbour 243
BROADSTREET, Mr 79
BROOKING, Godferie 31 Godfrey 31
    Hannah 31 Will 31 Wm 31
BROTH, Hill 58 108 229
BROUGHTON, Abigail 266 George
    223 Mr 213 Thomas 213
BROWN, E R 63 Paul 64 224 276
    William 45
BROWN'S, Brook 200 Hill 12 16 163
    178 254 276

BROWNE, Samuel 37 Wm 37 245
BRWON, Samuel 37
BRYANT, Rock 201 202 Walter 202
    263 Water 263
BUCK'S, Hill 13 188 229
BUMFAGGIN, 162
BUMFORD, Hatevil 32 Robert 32
BUNKER, 33 143 Clement 139
    Deborah 209 Elizabeth 209 Frank
    171 George 209 James 12 32 33 72
    116 138 168 176 177 210 212 262
    James Jr 177 James M 33 James Sr
    177 262 John 12 31 Jonathan 32
    Joseph 175 210 Love 177 Martha
    179 Rebeck 139 Sarah 210 Weal-
    then 177
BUNKER'S, Creek 60 72 84 115 116
    163 168-170 176 177 210 Garrison
    245 Neck 39 72 168 177
BURCH, Point 60
BURGETT, H W 33 Park 215
BURNAM, James 74 Jeremy 182
    Temperance 74
BURNET, Gov 169
BURNHAM, 7 162 182 208 259 Col
    54 Deacon 163 Elizabeth 188 G W
    181 Garrison 180 J Jr 163 James 54
    Jeremiah 162 182 259 John 182
    208 Joseph 7 54 181 182 Oaks 170
    Robert 54 170 180-182 208 259
BURNHAM'S, Creek 54 170 181 191
    Point 170
BURNT, Ground 154
BURNUM, 59 Jeremiah 182 215 John
    147 Robert 74 149
BURROUGHS, 220 Jabez 152
BUSS, John 101 132 191 John Jr 57
    Joseph 101 Lydia 101 Mary 101
    Parson 57 101 175
BUSSELL, John 141
BUTLER, Benjamin 282 Francis 277
BUTLER'S, Point 170 277
BUZZY, Hill 33
CALDWELL, Isaiah 235 Wm 33

CALDWELL'S, Brook 138
CALEY'S, Marsh 225
CALVES, Pasture 103 129 267
CAMPAIN'S, Rocks 34
CAMPERON, 35
CAMPIN'S, Rocks 94 155 191 203
CAMPING, Rocks 34
CAMPION, 34 Clement 34
CAMPION'S, Neck 34
CAMPIONE, Clement 34
CAMPSE, 35
CAMPSEY, 35
CAMSIE, 35 Spring 35
CANDIA, 119
CANEY, Thomas 267
CANNE, John 192 Love 192 Thomas 192
CANNEY, 129 240 Capt 36 Grace 252 Hannah 103 Ichabod 70 98 137 198 230 John 266 Joseph 49 100 Joshua 252 Love 81 128 Mary 81 128 Moses 35 282 283 Phebe 40 Samuel 252 Thomas 36 38 40 49 51 79 90 104 128 157 198 212 234 237 252 267 273 274 Thomas Jr 252 Thomas Sr 100 103
CANNEY'S, Brook 126 Cove 59 86 96 105 117 131 Creek 26 104 117 196 197 199 253 267 Island 273 Marsh 90 Spring 35
CANNING, 36 240
CANNY'S, Brook 148
CANTERBURY, 189
CAPT, Ich's Hill 168 Ichabod's Hill 168
CAPTAIN, Tuttle's Garrison 278
CARD, Thomas 38 210
CARD'S, Cove 210 226
CAREL, Timothy 53
CARL, Timothy 198
CARLE, Patience 148 Samuel 148 198
CAROLL, Timothy 198
CARR, Jonathan 264 Moses 98 265
CARRIGAN, Philip 262

CARTER, 118 196 205 240 Edward 204 John 29 39 245 Margaret 204 Mary 204 245 Richard 29 39 55 66 90 93 202 204 205 217 245 261 Samuel 282
CARTER'S, Brook 30 Rocks 196 219
CARTLAND, Ann 122 Daniel 122
CATE, 99 Ichabod 137 Tucker 138
CATE'S, Dam 137 Pond 89 137
CATER, 240 Richard 39 55 66 93 217
CATOR, 217
CATTER, 240 Richard 66
CAULEY'S, Marsh 225
CAULLEY, 40
CAULLEY'S, Marsh 209
CAVERLY'S, Bridge 114
CAVERNO, 113
CECILIUS, Lord Baltimore 67
CEDAR, Point 10 84 116 146 195 220 253
CHACE, 87 100 123 200 272 276
CHADBOURN, 237
CHADBOURNE, Humphrey 284
CHADWICK, Ebenezer 283
CHAMBERS, Charles 86
CHAMPERNON, 135
CHAMPERNON'S, Island 243
CHAMPERNOON, Capt 93 94 Francis 91
CHAMPERNOONE, Capt 257 Francis 91
CHAMPERNOUN, Capt 91 Farm 91 Francis 91
CHAMPERNOUNE, Capt 40 92
CHAMPERNOWN, Francis 243
CHAMPERNOWNE, 41 134 135 190 Arthur 134 Capt 91 92 134 Farm 92 Francis 51 134 135 Katherine 135
CHAMPERNOWNE'S, Creek 190 Island 134
CHAMPION, 34 Robert 34
CHAMPION'S, Rocks 34
CHANDLER, Isaac 192

CHANNELL, Mr 152
CHANNELL'S, Islands 42
CHARLES, I King Of England 67 136 234 II King Of England 91
CHASE, Mark 78 Mr 275
CHATEAUGAY, 231
CHEBEAGUE, 82
CHESLEY, 25 49 50 143 148 151 188 228 278 Benjamin 265 Capt 187 188 Deliverance 188 277 Elisabeth 187 Elizabeth 277 Geo 68 123 George 188 268 277 Hannah 161 Ichabod 90 165 265 Isaac 171 J S 15 174 176 James 45 187 216 Jonathan 114 142 143 Joseph 41 188 261 265 Lemuel 161 228 Mary 100 114 142 Mehitable 216 Paul 19 228 Philip 19 28 33 73 81 100 111 115 141 142 171 187 188 190 233 241 Philip Jr 231 Samuel 17 57 114 142 171 187 190 Sarah 228 Temperance 90 Thomas 264 William J 172
CHESLEY'S, Hill 89 Islands 41 188 Mill 70 81 Ponds 19
CHEVALIER, Bridget 181 John 117 118 181 204
CHICHESTER, 258
CHURCH, John 42 255 256 John Sr 42 Mary 42 Mercy 42
CHURCH'S, Brook 19
CHUZZLEWIT, Martin 77
CILLEY, Greenleaf 282 283 Jonathan 283
CLAGGETT, Wm 146
CLAMPERING, Island 36
CLARK, Abraham 43 59 60 65 72 135 176 177 Benjamin 56 Eli 161 Elisha 42 James 9 55 212 Remembrance 210 211 Sarah 9 Thomas 76 91
CLARK'S, Ferry 13 Garrison 108 135 Plains 135
CLARKE, 161

CLARKE'S, Plains 71
CLAVERHOUSE, 35
CLAY, Joseph 161 Mary 33 168 Point 277 Richard 33 63 Samuel 161 Wm 32 161 168 171
CLEFT, Cove 132
CLEMENT, 43 Joanna 43 Job 7 34 43 63 93 157 168 222 250 252 261 Job Sr 168 250 John 94 Margaret 168 Miriam 56 Mr 43 222 260
CLEMENT'S, Brook 260 Point 195
CLIFT, Cove 203
CLOUGH, 45 Abner 124 Nathaniel 282
CLOUTMAN, Edward 106 167 228 Widow 94
COCHECHA, 44 45 58 89 106 153 203 204 255 271 River 112 153 248 251 253 Swamp 31
COCHECHO, 63 89 124 127 128 153 168 178 192 212 220 233 238 241 252 253 260 266 267 270-272 Falls 39 69 93 97 111 117 202 253 262 264 267 272 274 280 Great Hill 89 Landing 64 144 Log Swamp 8 39 128 252 255 Marsh 19 20 168 Point 44 80 93 111-113 156 Pond 89 110 147 269 Railroad SEE RAILROADS River 7-9 12 13 22 24-28 34 42 43 49 50 54-57 61-64 66 69 71 79 81 83 85 93 98 106-109 111-114 125 127-129 140 141 144 148 149 153 155 156 164 192 195 198 202 206 208 209 212 216 226 229 232 233 237 238 244 248 251-253 260 264 267 274 275 277-279 281 Swamp 8 9 13 31 Woods 63 168
COCHECHOH, 31
COCHECHOW, Path 142 River 113
COCHECO, 44 River 281
COE, 185 Curtis 32 115 J W 180 Joseph 265 Rev Mr 163
COE'S, Bridge 16

COFFIN, 134 212 Abigail 45 227 233
    Capt 120 Deborah 209 Dinah 209
    Eliphalet 61 151 164 189 200 280
    Elizabeth 209 James 209 255
    Jemima 233 Mary 209 Mrs 166
    Peter 20 44-46 48 50 60-62 85 107
    112 113 120 127 140 149 151 153
    187 193 200 209 210 215 227 228
    233 237-239 249 255 256 278 280
    Robert 271 Ruth 209 Tristram 61
    127 280
COFFIN'S, Brook 262 Orchard 278
    Woods 278
COFYN, Peter 113
COGGSWELL, Nathaniel 76 77
    Thomas 262
COGGSWELL'S, Springs 262
COGSWELL, 282 283 Francis 282
    Thomas Jr 282 William 282
COLBATH, 31 32
COLBROATH, Downing 32
COLBROTH, Benjn 43
COLCORD, Edward 221 232
COLE, 7 Ebenezer 50 Judith 28 Mary
    50 Robert 28 113
COLE'S, Pond 29 98 210 219
COLEMAN, Anne 240 Eleazar 30 66
    207 219 240 258 James 50 66 John
    39 Mary 240 Nathaniel P 50 276
    Thomas 240 Valentine M 39 50
    255 276 Valentine Mathes 102
COLEMAN'S, Creek 196 240 254
    Spring 59 250
COLLEGE, Of Agriculture And The
    Mechanic Arts 264
COLLES, Marsh 39
COLLEY'S, Marsh 58
COLLIES, Marsh 108
CONCORD, 15 90 253 258 And
    Portsmouth Railroad See RAIL-
    ROADS
CONNER, Widow 45
CONWAY, 214 231

COOK, Mrs 70
COOK'S, Pond 89
COOLBROTH, 31
COOS, 68
COOTE, Sir Charles 234
CORN, Ground 112
CORSON, Mary 224 Zebulon 224
COTTERELL, 51 Dorothy 52 Jane 51
    John 51
COTTERILL, Francis 51 Robert 51
COTTERILL'S, Delight 36 90 104
    130 273
COTTON, Anne 227 John 227 Wm
    106
COTTRELL, Francis 51
COURSON, Cornelius 115
COWEL, Edward 54 234
CRAWLEY, Thomas 40
CREEK, Pond 33
CRITCHET, Elias 89 Martha 89
CROCKET, Joshua 254
CROCKETT, Andrew 52 220 John 29
    Joshua 29 219 Sarah 29
CROMEELE, Philip 225
CROMEL, James 53
CROMELL, Philip 167
CROMIT, John 263
CROMMET, Jacob 53 145 John 225
    Philip 28 202 225
CROMWEL, 113
CROMWELL, 53 168 Daniel 53
    James 53 Joshua 52 85 262 Ledea
    52 Philip 53 107 133 166 225
    Phillip 53 Samuel 79 166 167 198
CROMWELL'S, Creek 140 199 262
    Hill 168
CROSS, John 10 Ralph 25 60
CROUMEL, Joshua 79 Samuel 79
CROWN, Point 231
CROXFORD, Daniel 52 248 Swamp
    151
CRUMMET, Ebenezer 283 Jacob 53
CRUMMETT, James 53

CRUMMIT, 188 Jacob 145 Joshua 53
CRUMMIT'S, Creek 29 43 68 73 88 98 128 129 133 145 148 186 Hill 168 Mill Cove 145 146 Millpond 55
CRUMWELL'S, Creek 52
CUMMINGS, Mr 121
CURREU, Nicholas 234
CURREUS, Nicholas 234
CURRIER, Jaffrey 27
CURROL, 234
CURT'S, Plains 272
CUSHING, John 134 Jonathan 24 54 148 203 Mercy 18 Olive 134 Thomas 18 Thomas H 280
CUSHING'S, Hill 134
CUTCHECHOE, 127 Great Marsh 238
CUTS, John 54
CUTT, 15 132 John 15 54 132 134 155 President 27 54 197 269 Richard 15 96 132 Robert 15 134 Samuel 54 131 197 Ursula 197
CUTT'S, Brook 170 226 Cove 34 197 Eddy 196 Hill 7 54 181 192 Spring 54
CUTTLE, Capt 15
CUTTS, 54 Bridget 131 John 54 Richard 131
DAM, Jno 96 John 10 11 23 66 95-97 99 126 130 134 157 158 166 236 269 John Jr 96 John Sr 55 95 99 Martha 84 Moses 95 97 157 Pomfrett 55 Richard 131 Samuel 84 Sarah 78 Will 10 William 11 Wm 11 55 78 84 86 211 244 Wm Jr 11 Wm Sr 11
DAM'S, Garrison 10 158 Windmill 65 139 211
DAME, 65 84 100 105 124 231 232 235 Charles 118 154 Israel 54 Joseph 66 Moses 152 Richard 7 87 131 145 155 282 283 Timothy 7 251
DAME'S, Falls 100 119 Garrison 158 Mill 42 Point 66 158 196 269
DAMES, 268
DAMM, Jno 273
DAMME, John 99 Martha 84 William 84
DANA, Mrs 152
DANIEL, Eliphalet 55 145 John 55 68 133 Joseph 90
DANIEL'S, Brook 68 145 Garrison 135
DANIELS, 56 David 55 Eliphalet 172 Joseph Jr 132 Levi 68
DANTFORTH, Capt 156 Thomas 206
DARBEY, Field 16
DARBY, Field 19 129
DARBY'S, Fort 76
DARLING, Thomas 110
DARTMOUTH, 135
DAVID'S, Lane 135
DAVIS, 55 170 Abigail 241 Col 175 Daniel 40 147 233 241 242 David 110 187 188 Ebenezer 188 Elizabeth 277 Ephraim 18 80 115 119 165 175 222 233 Garrison 174 188 189 Henry 209 Jabez 145 189 237 James 40 57 78 80 83 109 143 146 150 171 174 175 177 184 190 225 251 277 John 74 78 90 91 129 174-176 221 241-243 259 263 270 John Sr 17 Joseph 58 91 174 189 268 Joshua 168 Judith 78 211 Lemuel? 174 Love 237 Lt 175 176 Mary 83 Moses 9 49 50 78 83 122 140 154 171 189 201 236 241 Moses Jr 9 151 Moses Sr 35 Nathaniel 78 Obadiah 18 56 106 Robert 138 Saml 57 Samuel 21 55 72 150 211 Sarah 150 259 Solomon 82 Stephen 282 Susanna 187 Thomas 208 Wm 227
DAVIS'S, Brook 18 Creek 170 174 176 Garrison 187 221
DEAD, Water 56 Water Neck 56

DEAN, Elizabeth 56 John 56 Mrs 236
DEARBORN, Benjamin 77 283 284
  John 282 Levi 282 Wm H 46
DEEP, Hole 17
DEERFIELD, 119
DEMERIT, 72 73 137 Abigail 77
  Ebenezer 57 Eli 17 58 72 83 90 94
  135 142 Eli Jr 57 77 271 Eli Sr 150
  Elizabeth 123 Ely 21 72 Ely Jr 57
  58 Ely Sr 57 Israel 72 John 17 171
  John Jr 171 Nathaniel 72 Samuel
  101 123 126 Tabitha 77 Wm 77
DEMERIT'S, Garrison 58 Mill 17 21
  24 83 228 278
DEMERITT, 42 100 Alfred 135 271
  278 E E 135 Ebenr T 136 Edric E
  141 Hopley 171 Israel 154 S E 117
  Samuel 33
DEMERITT'S, Brook 117 278 Mill
  147
DEMIRET, Eli 72
DEMREY, Eli 72
DENBO, Richard 58 218 Salathiel 218
DENBOW, Elijah 257 Salathiel 58
DENBOW'S, Brook 108 109 129
DENNET, Ephraim 87 Joseph 158
DENNETT, Charles 87 David 87
DENNIS, 164
DENNISON, Mr 243
DERING, Henry 87
DEROCHEMONT, F W 39 Mr 100
DERRY, Jno 17
DIAMOND, Bridge 149 280
DINSMOOR, 59
DIRTY, Brook 72 Gut 202 Lane 10
  Slough 32
DISHWATER, Falls 154 171 Mill 33
  58
DISRAELI, Benjamin 54
DOCKUM, John 74 John Jr 138
DOE, 123 Andrew 201 Benjamin 150
  Daniel 150 Elizabeth 122 149
  Garrison 122 John 108 149 150
  Joseph 122 150 Judge 93 Nathaniel

DOE (continued)
  25 60 85 Nicholas 41 139 149
  Olinthus 150 Sampson 41 60 85
  155 244 Samson 85 120 Samuel 85
  262
DOE'S, Island 149 150 Neck 25 89
  120 139 155
DOLLOFF, Esther 100
DOO, John 108
DOODY, 226 Benmore 225 Deborah
  226 Joseph 225 Nicholas 191 226
  Rebecca 225 Susanna 225
DORGING, Susanna 187
DOUGHTY, Thomas 54
DOUTIE, Thomas 54
DOVER, 8-14 16 19-28 30-34 36 38
  40 42-45 48 49 51-57 59-61 66-74
  76-84 86-105 107-112 114-120
  123-132 134-144 146-155 157 158
  160 163 164 166 167 169 170 173
  175-179 182 188 190-193 198 200
  202-208 211-224 226-229 231-233
  235 237-239 242-246 249-255
  257-262 264 265 267-271 273-281
  And Winnipiseogee Railroad See
  RAILROADS Garrisons 82 278
  Horse Railroad See RAILROADS
  Landing 48 277 Neck 10 13 18 19
  24 29 34 35 38 43 47 52-54 59-64
  73 94 98 100 103 109 110 117 125
  128 129 133 134 148 149 156 164
  166 167 179 191 195 197 198 204
  207 210 212 215 226 227 229 252
  266 267 277 278 Point 27 29 38 61
  64 75 103 125 131 156 166 195
  196 199 202 210 212 267
DOW, Amos 37 64 199 245 Isaac 199
DOW'S, Hill 204
DOWD, 226
DOWDY, Joseph 184 225 Rebecca
  225 Rebeckah 184
DOWNES, Thomas 271
DOWNING, 131 185 231 Bartholomew 75 159 194 Capt 59 Col 158

DOWNING (continued)
　Cove 261 Dennis 76 Elizabeth 65
　74 158 Garrison 158 John 24 25 29
　50 59 64 65 74 123 157-159 163
　165 166 204 230 245 254 261 John
　Jr 86 95 Jonathan 165 Joshua 131
　Josiah 24 261 Mary 158 Patience
　159 Richard 24 64 75 159 165 193
　207 240
DOWNING'S, Cove 196 Plains 155
　207
DOWNS, Eben 276 Ebenezer 141 271
　Samuel 65 270 276 Sarah 89
　Thomas 44 65 69 79 89 93 113 168
　208 209 212 255 271 Thos 212
　Wm 64 208
DRAKE, Francis 40 91 Mary 91
DRAM, Rock 231
DREW, 55 224 280 Abigail 66 224
　Andrew 193 Clement 55 211 Elijah
　66 275 Elizabeth 182 183 Ephraim
　283 Francis 28 183 192 279 Garrison 175 236 Gerrish P 12 John 11
　12 65 121 141 183 192 193 210
　242 253 274 279 John Sr 11 79
　Joseph 66 Mary 183 279 Nancy 50
　Nancy N 118 154 Sarah 242 Sgt
　199 Tamsen 183 Thomas 28 121
　144 182 183 206 254 279 Thomas
　Jr 254 Will 121 183 William 121
　182 183 Wm 28 82 144 182 183
　209
DREW'S, Brook 209 Garrison 182
　279 Hill 142 Oven 12 Point 121
　170 182 263 Windmill 139
DRISCO, 85 202
DRISCOE, Cornelius 155
DROWNE, Peter 81 82
DRY, Hill 81 Pines 71 135
DUDA, Benmore 225 226 Hannah 226
　Joseph 28 225 226 Mary 225
　Nicholas 225 226 Philip 225
　Rebecca 225 226 Susanna 225
　Zebulon 225

DUDAY, Philip 225
DUDEY, Joseph 225 Temperance 225
DUDLEY, Col 264 Joseph 26 Samuel
　21
DUDLEY'S, Bridge 21 Falls 22 Mill
　21
DUDY, Benmore 226 Joseph 184
　Nicolas 226 Rebekah 184
DUEDY, Joseph 225
DUKE, Of Buckingham 133
DUMP, 277
DUMPLIN, Cove 240
DUMPLING, Cove 29 30 50 196 240
　258
DUN, Hugh 225
DUNN, 124 Hugh 225 240 Samuel 67
DUNN'S, Bridge 124 228
DURELL, Daniel M 201 Judge 226
　Nicholas 191 226
DURESEME, 67 284
DURESME, 67 284
DURGIN, 145 232 Francis 144 152
　225 James 144 152 187 John 43
　Katharine 232 Mary 225 Susanna
　187 225 Trueworthy 225 William
　152 186 187 Wm 115 144 186 232
DURGIN'S, Garrison 186 Landing-
　place 232
DURHAM, 7-10 13 15-17 19 20 24 25
　29-33 35 37 40 41 43 49 52-56 58-
　61 65 67 70-73 75-81 84 87 88 90
　100 101 108-110 114-119 121-129
　133 138-140 143 145-149 151 152
　154 161-163 165 166 169-173 178
　185 186 188-191 193-195 200-203
　206 210 218 226 229 230 232 233
　236 237 242 243 247 249 250 253
　254 257-261 263-265 268 270 274-
　280 Falls 16 25 58 70 102 109 115
　121 127 140 149 162 169 170 172
　173 180 182 232 236 243 263 Falls
　Bridge 173 Garrison 82 Hook 124
　Landing 143 Point 218 225 241
　250 260 273 Point 7 8 39 52 54 70

DURHAM (continued)
71 75 83 125 129 130 170 174 183 184 188 189 191 192 209
DURREL, Joseph 226
DURRIL, Benmore 226
DURTY, Gutt 86
DUSTIN, Hannah 78
DYER, 120 Geo 128 Henry 128 230 Jeffrey 128 Joanna 230
EALWARE, 167 Plains 94 226
EARL, Of Bellomont 234 Of Exeter 180 Of Rochester 218 Of Strafford 246
EAST, Pond 156 195
EASTERN, County 246 Railroad See RAILROADS
EATON, Mary 101 Theophilus 101
EDEN, City 77
EDGERLE, Samuel 209
EDGERLIE, Thomas Sr 39 108
EDGERLY, 108 Ann Elizabeth 115 Brackett 218 Brook 55 Dr 263 Elijah 69 Elizabeth 148 Garrison 185 John 53 148 Moses 115 Rebeckah 128 Samuel 68 128 148 186 Thomas 17 128 185 186 Thomas Jr 17 Thomas Sr 128 Thos 275 Zachariah 171 185
EELWARE, Plains 140
EELWEIR, Falls 56 127
EGG, Pond 164
ELECTRIC, Railroad See RAILROADS
ELEWARE, Plains 98
ELIOT, 17 18 27 76 79 82 94 98 99 115 196 212 213 260 276 Neck 76
ELIZABETH, Queen Of England 54
ELKINS, Dr 73
ELLIOT, 111 Mary 183 Richard 121 183
ELLIOTT, Richard 183
ELLIS, Edward 7 244 John 261
ELLISON, 261
ELLSWORTH, Moll 153

ELWYN, John 134 135
EMERSON, 78 146 180 Capt 109 160 Dorothy 78 E T 188 Ebenezer T 109 180 Hannah 78 John 210 John T 114 122 283 Jonathan 70 Judith 78 79 Laban 15 Mary 200 Michal 78 Moses 70 171 243 Nehemiah 70 Samuel 43 69 70 78 79 109 160 165 174 188 222 Smith 163 171 257 Solomon 69 90 165 171 Timothy 84 86 163 200 265
EMERSON'S, Brook 87
EMERY, Anthony 8 48 James 76
ENDICOTT, Gov 221 John 15 113
EPPING, 119 123 216 266
EPSOM, 258
ESTES, Joseph 34 212
EUANS, Robert Jr 8
EVANS, 117 Benjamin 13 Capt 261 Edward 8 24 Elizabeth 13 Joseph 13 207 Lydia 71 Nathaniel 117 Robert 9 13 42 Robert Sr 9 13 Samuel 117 Stephen 71
EVERETT, Wm 271
EVERIT, Wm 89
EVERT, 12 43 53 62 98 146 172 195 229
EXETER, 18 28 35 45 60 70-72 85 99 103 106 107 112 113 119 120 123 127 144 149 151 154-156 160 165 170 187 189 193 201 206 214 216 225 233 246 260 264 269 271 275 279 River 195
FABENS, John 249 Sarah 249
FABIAN, John 249 Mary 249
FABIN, John 239
FABINS, John 69
FABYAN, 99 John 69 157 158 239 249 Sarah 249
FABYAN'S, Point 95 118 148 196 239 248
FAGGOTY, Bridge 64 Hill 65 81
FALLING-OFF, Place 210
FALLS, Hill 237 280

FARMER, 156 168 178 271
FARMINGTON, 82 147 251
FEILDING, 92
FERRY, Farm 130
FIELD, 216 Daniel 66 Darby 71 182
　　185 John 66 71 242 Joseph 71 241-
　　243 Sarah 242 Stephen 47 129
　　Zach 12 Zachariah 47 129 223
　　Zacharias 12 66 71 223 241-243
FIELD'S, Garrison 71 211 Marsh 174
　　Marsh Brook 216 Plains 66
FIELDING, Henry 92
FIELDING'S, Mill 79
FIELDS, Joseph 221
FIFTH, Falls 46
FILBROOK, John 16
FITCH, Abigail 233 Jedediah 233
FIVE, Hundred Acres 264
FLAGG, Arlo 49
FLAGG'S, Mill 79
FLOYD, Capt 270
FLY, Market 90
FOAST, Wm 238
FOGG, Mr 151
FOLIOT, 90
FOLLARD'S, Marsh 73
FOLLET, 16 59 90 169 Deborah 73
　　Elizabeth 182 Ichabod 73 John 73
　　126 Mary 151 Nicholas 14 71 72
　　151 174 176 177 262 Prudence 73
　　William 73 151 177 284 Wm 23 31
　　72 73 90 116 141 151 168 176 177
　　182 229 262
FOLLET'S, Brook 280 Rocky Hill 33
　　Swamp 19 33 100 142 148 151 154
FOLLETT, 33 Nicholas 115 116
FOLLIOTT, Wm 90
FOLSOM, 100 216 Farm 37 Jeremiah
　　263 Nathaniel 37 204 245 283
FOLSON, Jeremiah 110
FOOTMAN, 203 Francis 40 John 149
　　150 155 225 Joseph 30 Katharine
　　232 Thomas 65 73 102 128 144
　　150 151 232 268

FORD, Geo W 19 George 73 Mr 274
FORD'S, Landing 65 142 274
FORE, River 18 64 94 100 148 156
　　195 210 250 252
FORST, Wm 207
FORT, William And Mary 76 170 247
FORTESCUE, Edmund 135
FOSS'S, Mills 114
FOULLSAM, Abigail 156 John 156
FOULSHAM, Ephraim 123 John 124
FOUR, Corners 231
FOURTH, Falls 46
FOWLER, Geo 84 Nathaniel? 78 Wm
　　77 78
FOWLING, Marsh 156
FOX, Ann? 122 Edward 74 Elijah 122
　　Elizabeth 122 Garrison 18 122
　　Point 13 29 59 66 84 98 118 122
　　125 158 159 174 185 193-196 199
　　204 219-221 239 245 250 258
FOY, Jno 100 John 78 100 Mary 100
FOYE, John 86 Margaret 86 Margret
　　86 S H 279
FRANCE, 281
FRANK'S, Fort 197
FRANKES, Fort 131
FRANKLIN, City 253 282 284 Propri-
　　ety 253
FREEMAN'S, Point 197
FREETOWN, 94 132 135 166 200 230
　　250
FRENCH, Daniel 282 Garrison 122
　　123 Samuel 123
FRENCH'S, Garrison 42 Mill 114
FRENCHMAN, Henry 78 John 78
FRENCHMAN'S, Creek 221
FRESH, Creek 17 42 49 50 54 55 93
　　112 113 168 202 205 208 220 223
　　229 235 244 247 252 260 265 275
　　Creek Brook 86 168 Creek Woods
　　85 Marsh 217
FRINK, 37 Cyrus 38 84 219 Isaac 159
　　160 Mr 166 194
FRINKS, 245

FROG, Pond 72
FROST, John 110 Judge 136 Mr 259
    Nat 124 Nathaniel 110 Nicholas
    124 Wm P 68 162
FROST'S, Garrison 187 Hill 82
FRYAR, Nathaniel 207 208
FRYER, Nathaniel 91
FURBER, 106 Bridget 184 Deborah
    159 Dorothy 52 Elizabeth 81 Jethro
    54 80 105 126 130 197 233 Joshua
    81 Lemuel 125 Levi 152 Moses
    152 258 Mr 205 Nehemiah 152
    Richard 152 Thomas 282 Will 273
    William 80 81 105 145 159 197
    William Sr 105 Willm Sr 96 Wm
    38 51 52 64 79 80 93 97 99 105
    129 145 152 159 198 217 239 257
    258 Wm Jr 105 130 Wm Sr 85 96
    130 258
FURBER'S, Ferry 97 145 152 197
    Ferry-place 105 106 Garrison 159
    Point 105 106 125 159 196 205
    232 250 269 Straits 155
FURBUR, Jethro 197
FURNALD, James 145 Joseph 250
FURSON, Thomas 96 249
FURSON'S, Island 34
FUTTMAN, Thomas 30
GAGE, 128 232 George 147 John 18
    61 81 128 147 252
GAGE'S, Hill 65 69 111 147 229 264
    Point 207
GALLOWS, Hill 72 250
GARDNER, James 209 Joseph 209
    Mary 209 Ruth 209
GARLAND, 7 Dorcas 34 Jabez 7 34
    244
GARRISON, Hill 39 48 62 70 89 93
    147 163 168 191 215 220 229 260
    262 269 277
GARVIN, 54 203 234
GEE, Pickering 66
GEORGE, II King Of England 97
GEORGE'S, Creek 208 209

GERRISH, 61 91 127 278 Andrew 24
    Anna 228 Benjamin 83 Bridget 86
    Brook 278 Capt 12 22 Elizabeth 12
    228 Jane 139 John 12 23 57 62 83
    135 228 254 Joseph 228 229
    Margaret 86 Mary 21 Mills 21 23
    Nathaniel 86 Paul 21 23 24 57 83
    135 203 Richard 14 86 139 203
    Samuel 161 Timothy 23 24 57 83
    124
GERRISH'S, Bridge 228 231 Garrison
    135 Island 243 Mill 127 135 Mills
    228
GIBBONS, 181 182 Ambrose 17 35
    71 116 118 134 138 157 170 180
    181 221 228 Rebecca 181
GILBERT, Humphrey 135
GILES, 263 John 86 Mark 31 164 255
    Matthew 39 40 182 183 204 284
    Paul 71 162 Sarah 86
GILES'S, Creek 83 264
GILMAN, 269 Ezekiel 262 263 Israel
    160 John 124 269 John P 282 John
    Taylor 70 269 Nathl 124 Peter 124
    Saml 124
GILMANTON, 269
GILMORE, Deborah 84 James 84 163
    170 Mary 84 Mr 194
GILMORE'S, Point 170
GIMSON, Patrick 277
GIPSEN, James 190
GLASS, David 274 Samuel 235
GLEN, Lewis Dam 275
GLIDDEN, Andrew 128 Mr 263
GOAT, Island 40 41 194 195 215 219
GODDAR, John 85 120
GODDARD, 59 Garrison 25 Goody
    186 John 10 41 85 89 139 186 191
    193 231 233 241 244 Martha 89
GODDARD'S, Cove 186 232 233
    Creek 25 30 42 60 89 120 133 155
    201 244 Garrison 24 186
GODDER, John 85 139
GOFFE, John 161

GOLD, Isaac 60
GOLDING'S, Bridge 256
GOLDINS, Bridge 256
GOLJABS, Neck 126
GONIC, 47 237
GOODING, 85 Richard 85
GOODWIN, Daniel 99 Daniel Sr 126 Richard 80 Thomas 99 99
GOOSEBERRY, Marsh 107
GORE, 36 59 64 155 207
GORGES, 90 Ferdinando 29 51 67 90 115 134 136 137 155 156 192 Jane 51 Samuel 51
GOSS, Robert 267
GOTHARD, 85
GOULD, John 147
GOVE, Edward 282
GRAFFORD, Mad 87
GRANITE, State Park 215
GRANT, James 104 157 203 224 Wm 99
GRAVES, 149 Elizabeth 149 Wm 149
GRAY, George 9 John 9
GREAT, Ash Swamp 270 Bay 7 16 26 28 29 33 37 38 41 43 50-52 60 66 68 69 73 74 80 81 84 85 88-93 95 98 99 104-106 118 119 128-134 138 139 144 145 152 154 155 166 186 190 195-197 200 205 206 217 227 228 235 239 248 249 251 257 258 267 273 275 Brook 69 Cochecho Hill 89 Cochecho Marsh 39 93 Cove 85 95 Creek 52 144 East Pond 89 Eddy 126 Falls 230 235 271 276 Falls 16 17 20 22-24 26 29 33 64 71 98 113 125 129 144 165 192 211 214 215 220 Fresh Marsh 48 Hill 41 79 82 219 Island 214 228 247 Marsh 26 238 Pond 49 141 200 208 238 241 269 271 Rock 106 Swamp 33 41 205 217 Turn 132 Works River 126
GREEN, Ezra 40 Hill 98 107 114 Point 76 Richard Sr 76

GREENLAND, 16 28 31 37 38 40 41 51 52 61 68 74 86 87 89 93 94 96-98 129 134 138 155 163 190 196 200 205-207 211 214 217 218 227 230 240 245 249 258 264 267 272 273 275 Garrison 82 River 69 93 218
GREENLEAF, Abner 282
GREN, John 76
GREY, John 107
GRIFFITHS, Edward 151
GULF, 260 267
GUPPEY, James 93 Joseph 93
GUPPY, 260 James 112 113 168 Joseph 93
GUPPY'S, Hill 119 Point 111 113 Woods 153
GYLES, Matthew 83
HAGGINS, Daniel 30 John 30
HAINES, Matthew 240 Matthias 92 218 Saml 275 Samuel 18 40
HAINES', Marsh 93 217
HAINS, 206 James 189 Joshua 190
HAISE, Ichabod 31 127 John 8 31 112 127 Peter 112
HALE, 238 Judge 114 153 S 134 Saml 126 232 234 235 238 Wm 20 22 91
HALE'S, Mill 21
HALF-TIDE, Rock 170 Rock Junior 170 171
HALL, 198 206 Avery 272 Benjn 132 Edward 156 Elisabeth 132 Field 94 Frances 132 Goodman 96 James 167 John 53 90 93 94 95 102 113 167 203 207 213 215 217 218 239 249 266 John Jr 8 John Sr 76 Joseph 78 103 206 216 217 254 266 Lafayette 193 Mary 100 Parson 271 Ralph 10 60 100 103 132 213 215 Sarah 249 Thomas 78 216 266
HALL'S, Farm 206 Field 102 103 Marsh 39 218 Mills 20 Slip 103 Spring 149 White Swamp 272

HALLSVILLE, 193 280
HAM, Brook 277 Dr 19 Ephraim 45
    Field 277 John 94 141 167 209 238
    John Jr 139 Nathaniel 46 Rufus 33
    Samuel 87 Thomas 282 William
    197
HAM'S, Marsh 140 167 253 Point 197
HAMBLETON, David 157 Jonas 30
HAMILTON, David 157 203 David Sr
    157
HAMMLETON, David 233
HAMPTON, 51 91 96 99 179 227 246
    264 275 Gen 231
HANSON, 8 14 21 71 208 218 Abijah
    22 Anna 22 Ebenezer 48 164
    Ephraim 26 56 69 Humphrey 26 56
    Isaac 148 200 James 34 94 Joanna
    56 John 9 13 21 42 68 83 88 164
    John Jr 226 Jonathan 139 Joseph
    14 45 47 56 61 69 70 148 172 280
    Joseph Jr 56 94 140 Lydia 148
    Martha 22 Maul 58 139 140 216 217
    Mercy 42 Nathaniel 8 14 42 48 233
    Robert 13 137 198 228 Solomon
    21 48 164 Stephen 22 40 201
    Thomas 14 34 42 45 88 104 139
    164 223 233 238 Thomas Jr 21 164
    Timothy 14 34 167 Tobias 34 69
    167 208 212 280 Zaccheus 22
HANSON'S, Brook 72
HARD, Spring 94
HARFORD, Nichls 78 Nicholas 18 78
    94 167 215 262 Paul 7 8 Wm 133
    134
HARFORD'S, Ferry 18 19
HARRISON, 185 Elizabeth 158 Mr 29
    239 Nicholas 74 75 158 219
    Temperance 75
HARROD, 95
HARROD'S, Cove 118 166 Creek 106
HARRY, Kinge 237
HARRYSON, Mary 74 Nicholas 74
HART, John 87 Joseph S 87 Richard
    87 282 283 Richard D 64
HARTFORD, 94 Joshua 282 Nicholas
    94 Wm 112
HARVEY, 165 Garrison 12
HARVEY'S, Hill 135 200 Mill 69 89
HARWOOD, 99 240 Andrew 96 99
    249
HARWOOD'S, Cove 99 118 249 250
    Creek 95 105 152 153 225 244 253
    255
HASKELL, Benjamin 282
HATHE, 98 121
HAUNCE, John 108
HAVEN, 249 Joseph 97 Nathaniel A
    258
HAVEN'S, Hill 272 281
HAVERHILL, 70 78
HAWKINS, Stephen 98
HAWTHORNE, Wm 76
HAYES, 21 56 78 B F 135 Benjamin
    229 Charles 55 Charles W 135
    Daniel 14 83 Ezra 107 Garrison
    274 George O 14 Harry E 284 Jean
    229 John 45 261 Jonathan 62
    Martha 216 O K 42 Oliver 21 Paul
    98 Peter 14 94 Reuben 129 Robert
    261 Samuel 66 216 Thomas 69
HAYES'S, Falls 45 46
HAYNES, 206 Gudman 41 Matthias
    91 Samuel 51
HAYWARD, 110 168
HEARD, 63 95 99 Dame 62 Dorcas 34
    Elizabeth 275 Jean 229 John 34 50
    62 69 80 89 90 93 94 98 167 243
    Jos 69 Samuel 44 62 98 Tristram
    26 56 62 69 120 140 208 229 237
    238 262 274
HEARD'S, Garrison 82 Neck 92
HEARLE, John 213
HEATH, 90
HEGONE, Mogg 115
HEN, Island 8 196
HENDERSON, Howard 87 147 148
    266 Wm 98 Wm Sr 115
HENDERSON'S, Point 147 Spring 98

HERD, John 271
HERD'S, Cove 95 118 Gut 95
HERDS, Gut 97
HEREFORD, Wm 167
HEROD, 95 248
HEROD'S, Cove 69 118 130 281
    Creek 244 255 Point 105 248 249
    Wigwam 248
HERROD, 240
HICKS, 251 Joseph 102 150 251
    Michael 15 Mrs 251 Sarah 150
HICKS', Hill 231
HICKS'S, Hill 72 77 102 135 136 141
    150 250 251
HIGGINSON, T W 257
HIGH, Point 131 199
HIGHT, Jonathan 154
HILL, 124 Abigail 101 Benjamin 211
    Capt 100 Eliphalet 32 Farm 265
    Hannah 15 139 Henry 32 139 I
    Blake 33 112 John 28 128 Jonathan
    264 265 Joseph 59 261 Mary 101
    146 173 Mr 78 85 102 120 172 230
    Nathaniel 15 70 101 116 172 173
    241 243 265 Reuben 100 Robert
    101 Samuel 37 100 101 172 243
    245 265 282 283 Sarah 101 Valentine 15 41 58 70 84 91 100-102
    116 120 129 146 172-174 176 179
    219 221-223 231 243 264 277
    Volentine 173 Widow 223 Wm 32
    58 100 102 132 Wm Jr 55
HILL'S, Cove 196 203 Creek 245
    Falls 54 119 Five Hundred Acres
    101 102 265 Pan 243 Pen 243
HILLIARD'S, Field 185
HILTON, 120 267 Col 175 Edward 29
    103 156 266 267 Edward Jr 266
    John 44 Patent 51 Richard 110 156
    William 156 Wm 125 193 243 277
HILTON'S, Point 18 27 29 36 60 64
    100 110 117 118 156 174 195 198
    212 215 240 267 279 Point Swamp
    110 198

HITCHCOCK, 7 266
HIX, Joseph 102 150
HOBBS, Capt 104 Hannah 103 Henry
    103 104 Thomas 104
HOBBS'S, Hole 156
HOBS, Henry 88
HODGDEN, Alexr 87
HODGDON, Alexander 269 Caleb
    148 Israel 8 11 14 57 253 274 John
    104 Jonathan 237 Maj 148 Mary
    104 123 Shadrach 65 66 71
HODGDON'S, Hill 279
HODSDEN, Joseph 99
HODSDON, 140 John 59 Thomas 167
HOGGES, 88
HOGKINS, John 107
HOGSTY, Cove 26 36 80 86 90 96 99
    118 130 196 197 253 273
HOGSTYE, Cove 51 130
HOITT, 106 Gorham 230 Mr 70
HOLLAND, 35 50 90 98 131 144 210
    247 260
HOLMES, Bridge 167 John 40
HOLMES', Bridge 168
HOME, 106
HOOD, Hope 107 126
HOOK, 58 83 119 132 137 236 Island
    Falls 119 225 284 Land 124 Marsh
    86 Mill 57 123 124 166
HOOK-ISLAND, Falls 119
HOOPER, 107 115 140 William 283
HOPE, Woods Point 107
HOPEHOOD, 75
HOPEHOOD'S, Point 11 166 252
HORN, 108 209 232 Daniel 46 Gershom 88 John 44 253 John Sr 112
    Thomas 141
HORN'S, Pond 89 Woods 55 209 232
    274
HORNE, Andrew 88 Dam 46 John
    216 S R 35 Wm 108 253
HORNE'S, Woods 69
HORSE, Races 75 195 197 202
HORSEHIDE, Brook 58 129

HORTLEBERRY, Plain 109
HOTH, Hope 107
HOWARD, 8 Amos 7
HOWES, Edward 29
HOYT, A H 105 J S 148 249 J W 197
 James 245 John 103 Jonathan 154
 Mr 195
HOYT'S, Pines 204
HUBBARD, 107 Elizabeth 81
HUCHINS, Brook 13
HUCKINS, 109 180 Brook 32 137 254
 Garrison 179 188 James 94 109
 132 178 180 John 109 Robert 11
 109 112 160 161 177 Robert Jr 113
 Wealthen 177
HUCKINS', Brook 180 Garrison 180
HUCKINS'S, Garrison 173
HUCKLEBERRY, Hill 199 266 277
 Swamp 103
HUGGENS, Robert 112
HUGGIN, James 180 Sarah 180
HUGGINS, Nathaniel 34 40 Robert
 114 180 Sarah 180
HULL, 280 Benjamin 110 112 Joseph
 256 Naomi 256 Naomie 256
HULL'S, Meadow 112
HUMPHREY'S, Pond 269
HUNT, 137
HUNTRESS, 64 Christopher 95
 Clement 111 Geo 59 Geo Sr 36
 George 16 36 95 111 John 36
 Jonathan 37 Mary 37 111 196
 Nathaniel 111 Noah 152 Saml 111
 Samuel 36 37 111 Wm 245
HUNTRIS, Christopher 244 George 36
 86 244 Mary 244
HUNTRISS, Geo 97 Saml 111
HURD, 172 John 141 Thomas 141
HURD'S, Pond 50 210
HURTLEBERRY, Hill 266
HUSONE, 271
HUSOW, 271
HUSSEY, 247 Benjamin 111 Benjn 33
 Elijah 47 Elizabeth 47 Jane 47 Job

HUSSEY (continued)
 88 John S 111 Joseph 88 93 111
 Moses 64 Richard 51 88 90 234
 Samuel 30 Springs 82 Timothy 47
HUSSEY'S, Falls 25 47 Pond 269
HUTCHINGS, Ezra 282
HUTCHINS, Joseph 81
HUTCHINSON, 71 Edward 91 Eliza
 91 Mary 91
ILELAND, Falls 262
INDEGO, Hill 270
INDIAN, Blind Will 26 Chebucto 82
 Corn Ground 113 233 Corn-ground
 253 Graves 19 110 Ground 233
 Hoop Hood 107 Hoope Whood 107
 Hope Hood 126 Little John 126
 Mahomet 150 151 Moharimet 150
 151 262 Ould Robin 107 Tasquan-
 tum 137 Wadononamin 266
 Wahowah 107 Wehanownowit 232
 Wohawa 107
INDIGO, Hill 64 211 230 241 276
ISINGLASS, River 26
ISLAND, Cove 146 Falls 110 119 151
ISLES, Of Shoals 31 82 136 138 164
 165 210
ISLINGTON, 87
JACKSON, 239 Clement 283 Ebenez-
 er 73 Ephraim 11 James 142 Jane
 142 John 95 250 Walter 114 142
 Wm 114 142 162 171
JACKSON'S, Creek 114 Pt 114 142
JAFFREY, 216 Geo 139 George 32
 230 261
JAMBRIN, Elizabeth 118 John 118
JAMES, I King Of England 133 John
 13 Katharine 42 Matthew 13 Mr
 171
JAMESON, 160 Patrick 277
JANVRIN, Elizabeth 118 John 118
JEBUCTO, 82
JEMISON, Patrick 160
JENKINS, Benjn 145 Elizabeth 56 121
 183 Ephraim 172 Joseph 30 32 40

JENKINS (continued)
72 78 80 114 129 168 177 218
Stephen 56 121 183 William 72
Wm 80
JENNESS, 138 165 J S 87 91 156 165
JETHER, Stephen 240 281
JETHERS, 240
JETHRO, 240 Peter 281 Stephen 240 281
JEWELL, Ann Elizabeth 115 Bradbury 115
JEWELL'S, Point 131 133 155 203
JEWETT, Noah 282
JOCELYN, Henry 85 115 157 221
JOCELYN'S, Cove 98 147
JOHN, Foy's Rock 100
JOHNSON, Ebenezer 92 275 Hannah 34 James 92 John 34 37 91 240 266 272 273 Jos 87 Mr 192 Nathan 240 272 273 Prudence 37 273 Tho 219 Thomas 33 73 96 99 115-117 142 169 177 181 249 283
JOHNSON'S, Creek 31-33 58 65 66 80 107 117 139 140 142 170 177 181 216 219 259 262 278 Creek Bridge 10 40 Marsh 273 Mill 275
JONAS, Point 41
JONAS', Creek 262 Point 170 189 242
JONES, 65 278 C H 171 Capt 90 Elenor 70 Frank 197 Garrison 123 177 Ginking 89 John 161 Joseph 9 73 141 Lt 73 154 177 Mrs 230 Robert 108 Stephen 73 116 117 172 177 Thomas 116 Timothy 70 Wm 116 269
JONES'S, Bridge 117 Creek 31 116 170 177 229 Point 117
JONESES, Point 189
JONKNES, John 161
JOSE, Christopher 86 203
JOSELYN, Henry 76
JOSHUA'S, Point 55 66 196
JOSLIN'S, Fort 76
JOSLING'S, Cove 115

JOSLYN, Mr 115
JOSSELYN, Henry 76 Thomas 115
JOY, Jacob 31
KARPPI, 13
KELLEY, 117
KELLEY'S, Springs 14
KELSEY, Meadow 18 Wm 143
KEMBALL, Thomas 193
KEMBLE, Elizabeth 227 Thomas 210 227
KENDALL, Stephen 172
KENERSON, Mr 18 123
KENES, Creek 37
KENIES, Island 37
KENISTON, Alexander 74 Christopher 74 George 138 John 92
KENNE, Thomas 238
KENNEBEC, River 136 137
KENNEY, 36 240 266 Grace 38 Jane 63 Samuel 103 Thomas 38
KENNEY'S, Cove 36 203 Creek 26 36 37 104 199 Island 37
KENNY, Creek 196 Ould Thomas 38 Thomas 167 207
KENNY'S, Cove 37 203
KENT, 53 James 53 183 John 144 145 Joseph 7 28 144 Oleuer 144 Oliuer 270 Oliver 28 144 169 Robert 144
KENTE, Oliver 28
KEY, John 224
KID, James 93 271
KIDDER, 240
KIELLE, Benjamin 117 James 226
KIMBALL, Abigail J 250 Clarissa 46 Elizabeth 216 Ezra 45 46 216 229 233 John 46 Jonathan 46 Mary 250 Nehemiah 46 R 229 Wm 46
KIMBALL'S, Falls 46 Mill 46
KINCAID, Ann 35 56 Anne 35 David 35 122 140 260 Napthali 260
KINCAID'S, Brook 35
KINCKET, Naptheli 260
KING, Abigail 86 Daniel 86 Elizabeth 138 Mary 37 86 Richard 36

303

KING (continued)
    Samuel 74 138 William 86 Wm 37
    86 87
KING'S, Creek 36
KINGES, Creek 104
KINGMAN, 150
KINGMAN'S, Bridge 16
KINGSTOWN, 271
KINKED, Davis 35
KINKET, Ann 56
KINNEY, Thomas 148
KITERY, 39
KITTERY, 14 18 20 23 76 84 93 94
    99 117 118 125 131 134 197 213
    225 259 Neck 117 Point 91 213
    243 Shore 18
KNIGHT, 64 102 103 142 185 Bridget
    103 118 181 Capt 245 Elizabeth
    118 275 Ezekiel 101 George 75
    174 Jno 65 John 12 66 75 102-104
    117 118 139 141 154 159 174 181
    204 205 207 208 John Sr 103 198
    Joseph 56 Leah 12 139 141 Mary
    101 Nathan 95 244 Nicholas 230
    Richard 84 Robert 56 Roger 214
KNIGHT'S, Farm 102 Ferry 27 64 75
    87 102 103 154 174 181 196 254
    Pines 204
KNOX, Marsh 164 Mr 163
KOOK, Rebecca 274
KYNYBEQUY, River 136
LACONIA, 157
LAIGHTON, 7 9 10 105 130 James 70
    283 John 65 147 Susanna 141
    Thomas 118 141 Thomas Jr 118
LAIGHTON'S, Cove 69 95 105 119
    129 130 166 196 244 255 Hill 9 10
LAITON, John 43 Thomas 78 105 146
    222
LAKE, Marie 227 Mrs 228 Of Pasca-
    taquack 87 Thomas 51 90 217 227
    Winnipesaukee 187
LAMOS, 119 James 80 Nathaniel 33
    80 161 168

LAMPER, River 28
LAMPEREEL, Bridge 250 River 28
    30 124 149 151 190 262
LAMPEREL, River 58 60 110 150
    171 190 231 263
LAMPERELL, River 60 110 114 120
    201 247 262 263
LAMPERIELE, River 232
LAMPERIL, River 139 231
LAMPERILL, River 105 128 187
LAMPREALL, River 129
LAMPREEL, River 124 126 230
LAMPREL, River 151 193
LAMPRELL, River 120 143 266
LAMPREY, Charles 122 River 22 25
    27 35 36 42 50 58 59 61 73 85 87
    100 101 106 114 120 123 124 126
    128 129 140 149-152 154 155 165
    187-193 195 201 202 216 225 230
    235 236 244 247 260 262 266 268
    272 280 River Falls 120 129 River
    Neck 60
LAMPREY-EEL, River 201
LAMPREYEEL, River 84 248
LAMPRIL, River 230
LAMPRILL, River 85 112 139 151
    155 193 218
LANCASTER, Henry 129
LANDING-DISTRICT, 48
LANE, Edmund J 280 Wallis 38
LANG, B F 18
LANGDON, 59 F E 75 Gov 134
LANGLEY, 210 276 Elizabeth 121
    James 65 83 121 183 263 Jeremiah
    8 25 185 273 Mary 121
LANGLEY'S, Heath 98 Point 65 183
LANGSTAFFE, 75 240 Henry 68 90
    91 102 122 159 160 205 239 272
    Mary 239 Rocks 196 Sarah 160
LANGSTAR, 240 Henry 29 30 66 68
    79 102-104 122 159 219 239 240
    274 John 68 159 240 Mary 66 239
    240
LANGSTER, Henry 39

LANKSTAR, Henry 66 99
LANKSTER, Henry 102
LARKHAM, Thomas 19 85 89 164
LASKEY, 122 236 John 73 268 Wm 122
LASKEY'S, Bridge 140 143
LATON, Wm 234
LAWSON, Christopher 19
LAYN, 230 235 Edmund 162 235 John 32 161 162 Mr 106 Samuel W 162
LAYN'S, Mill 160 161 Mills 171
LAYTON, 99 222 243 Elizabeth 221 Joanna 43 John 274 Tho 130 Thomas 9 10 23 43 65 78 106 118 130 131 206 215 221 222 269 Thomas Jr 221 243 Thomas Sr 221 222 243
LEACH, James 95 John 95
LEACH'S, Island 36
LEAH, 61 280
LEAH'S, Field 61 280
LEATHERS, Abednego 70 237 City 281 Deborah 73 Edward 142 161 178 Edward Jr 161 Hannah 161 John 161 Jonathan 114 142 Mrs 178 Robert 73 114 142 Thomas 60 117 162 177 Vowel 163 William 178 Wm 60
LEAVIT, Thomas 282
LEAVITT, Carr 282
LEDGE, Wharf 170
LEE, (see also SOUTH LEE) 9 15 17-19 22 32 33 35 40 53 54 56 58 61 67 69 72 80 100 106 113 117 119-122 127 129 140 143 147 148 154 160-163 165 169 171 188 191 192 200 209 210 214 218 226 230 232 236 241 247 251 257-259 263 268 272 Garrison 82 Hill 9 25 80 123 126 143 154 201 236 263 268 270 Hook 42 54 100 106 110
LEIGHTON, 78 John 76 222 Thomas 222 Wm 76

LEIGHTON'S, Fort 76
LEITH, James 95
LEITSH, James 95 John 95
LETHERES, Edward 178 Edward Sr 178 William 178
LEVETT, James 66 Sarah 66
LEVIUS, Peter 53
LEWIS, Hannah 34 Philip 23 33 34 91 106 218
LIBBEY, Anthony 208 Benjamin 22 124 Enoch 22 124 Isaac 216 229 Sarah 216
LIBBEY'S, Bridge 22 206 228 Mill 22 23
LIBBY, Anthony 208 Ephraim 277
LILY, Pond 50
LIMMY, Sarah 228
LIMMY'S, Ledge 166
LINES, Samll 237
LINSEY, Samuel 190
LITTLE, Bay 7 10 13 25 41 55 66 68 74 75 80 81 105 125 128 145 146 148 155 169 170 183 185 195 196 209 210 219 221 240 269 273 279 Boar's Head 51 Falls 125 143 144 John's Creek 20 36 50 52 54 109 166 192 199 210 262 266 John's Falls 134 235 Moses 282 Newichwannock 157 Pocket Marsh 273 Point 203 Pond 164 River 9 15-18 25 80 106 143 147 154 161 165 200 230 236 251 260 263
LITTLEWORTH, 13 31 48 58 61 70 117 137 138 140 164 198 210 228 229 264 280
LOBERLAND, 186
LOCKE, John 282
LOCKE'S, Mill 114
LOG, Hill 68 83 140 235 279 Hill Spring 279 Swamp 164
LOGG, Hill 134 213 Swamp 127
LOMAX, Nathaniel 168
LONG, Creek 29 52 81 144 186 232 252 Edward J 282 Falls 119 165

LONG (continued)
  190 Gut 267 Gutt 198 Hill 26 47
  140 229 Lot 165 Marsh 26 30 54
  58 109 128 170 209 272-274
  Marsh Brook 58 Point 95 99 105
  106 115 118 119 154 155 185 196
  235 251 276 Pond 114 Reach 24 26
  36 59 65 75 76 100 109 110 155
  195 197 203 204 248 Turn 90 132
LONGFELLOW'S, Garrison 165
LORD, Abraham 213 Isaac 119 282
  Martha 141 213 271 Nathan 127
  238
LOUERIN, Jno 213
LOUISBOURG, 165
LOVELL'S, Pond 89
LOVER'S, Seats 75
LOVERING, John 213
LOVERLAND, 187
LOWER, Eelweir 45 Huntress 110 111
  196 252 Mill 275 Narrows 155
  Neck 229 Pond 270 Ware 281
  Weir 281
LUBARLAND, 186
LUBBERLAND, 24 25 29 30 41 43 52
  55 59 73 83-85 89 108 114 120
  131 139 148 152 155 186-188 202
  203 209 216 219 229 232 235 244
  Creek 85 Garrison 186 Marsh 25
LUBERLAND, 139
LUFFERING, 213 John 213 Joseph
  213
LUMAS, Nathaniel 33
LUMAX, Nathaniel 168
LUMMOCKS, Nathaniel 168
LYNN, 275 Woods 275
MACELROY, John 7
MACKELROY, John 49 244
MACPHEADRIS, Archibald 213
  Mary 213
MADAM'S, Cove 54 126 245
MADBERRY, 58 136 141 150 212
MADBERY, 271

MADBURY, 9 10 13 15 19 21 24 33
  35 40 42 43 55 60 61 65 68 70 72
  77 78 80 83 86 90 94 102 106 108
  109 116 118 119 123 124 127 129
  132 136 138-142 150 160 162 164
  166 171 192 199 200 206 210 211
  216 225 228 230 231 243 250 254
  264 274 275 278-280 Garrison 82
MAGOON, 54 Henry 53 234
MAGOUN, Henry 157
MAHARMETT'S, Hill 136
MAHERMIT'S, Planting-ground 189
MAHOMET'S, Marsh 73
MAHORIMET, 151
MAHORIMET'S, Hill 132
MAHORRAMET'S, Hill 102
MAHORRAMIT'S, Hill 141
MAIN, River 195
MAINE, 115 175
MAJOR, Waldron's Log Swamp 279
  Waldron's Spring 216
MALLAGO, River 228
MALLEGO, 56 58 140 198 228 River
  16 19 24 35 48 57 228
MALOON, Luke 258
MALOONE, Luke 258
MAPLE, Brook 33 161
MARCH, Clement 123 190 Doctor 92
MAROSHEN, 136 137
MARQUIS, Of Rockingham 246
MARSH, Dinah 50 171 Henry 49 50
  102 171 Hezekiah 50 171
MARSTON, 147
MARSTON'S, Mill Pond 25
MARTAIN'S, Lane 60
MARTIN, Gov 280 Hester 139 John
  139 240
MARTIN'S, Lane 60
MASARVE, Joseph 132
MASON, 27 Benjamin 88 Benjn 205
  228 Capt 67 85 104 156 157 269
  Jeremiah 208 261 John 31 67 88
  108 115 136 156 157 159 181 210

MASON (continued)
  Magdalen 103 Mary 149 157 Mr
  50 Peter 88 259 260 Robert 103
  140 Sarah 259 260
MASSACHUSETTS, 27 29 113 256
  262 278
MAST, Bridge 12 66 141 Creek 52
  Path 12 Paths 255 Pt 125 276 Point
  Falls 125 Road 25 26 41 Way 25
MATHER, 107
MATHES, 55 144 183 186 264 Abigail 101 Abraham 108 144 Abraham Jr 116 189 Ann 121 Benjamin 15 16 25 65 88 101 121 145 161 242 264 Benjamin Jr 55 145 Benjn 145 209 Dorothy 116 Francis 88 101 116 144 145 184 189 209 231 237 277 Garrison 189 Gershom 55 88 145 H A 54 Island 8 J 100 John 54 Mark 189 Neck 144 145 Robert 40 83 Samuel 209 Valentine 31 83 102 116 189 263 Walter 231
MATHES', Falls 54
MATHES'S, Creek 52 168 170 242
  Falls 119 Mill 53 Mill-pond 145
MATHEW'S, Creek 52 232 Neck 53
  80 232
MATHEWS, Benjamin 145 Benjamin Jr 88 Francis 16 71 88 144 243 Garrison 189 Gershom 88 Mr 144 Mrs 144 Tamsen 144 Thomasine 31 144
MATHEWS', Creek 88 148 186 Neck
  7 81 145 186
MATTHEWS, Mr 33
MAUD, Mr 134
MAURICE'S, Point 152
MAVERICK, Samuel 157
MAWOOSHEN, 136
MAY, John Vincent 95
MCCALVEY, Eleanor 30
MCCLARY, James H 282 Parson 191
MCDANIEL, 261 James 73 257 Mr
  172

MCDONALD, Robert 261 Wm 261
MCDUFFEE, Henry 260
MCELROY, John 208
MEADER, 176 217 Benjamin 147
  Daniel 174 175 Garrison 173-175
  James 55 Jno 244 John 40 55 112
  146 173-176 221 223 243 253 John
  Jr 146 222 John Sr 146 184 222
  Joseph 13 33 119 154 173-176 212
  222 223 253 271 Lemuel 75 174
  Mark 193 Moses 146 Nathaniel
  174 Nicholas 253 268
MEADER'S, Bridge 217 Garrison 147
  221 Landing 75 Neck 77 193 221
  244 280 Swamp 42
MEDAR, Isaac 52 John 151 Nicholas
  151 284 Samuel 151 Timothy 151
MEDER, John 147 221 Joseph 9 143
  190 Nicholas 147 Timothy 68
MEGONE, Mogg 115
MEHERMETT'S, Hill 77
MENDUM, Nathan 151 Nathl 24 147
MENDUM'S, Pond 126 127
MERIT, 57
MERRILL, 41 50 64 92 110 218 269
  275 Joseph 156 Phineas 190
MERRIMAC, River 136
MERRIMACK, River 156 258
MERRIT'S, Mill 58
MESERVE, 94 135 Clement 12 32 66
  71 Daniel Jr 135 Paul 12 Sarah 83
  Winthrop S 79
MESERVE'S, Garrison 94 135
MESSENGER'S, Pond 269
MESSERVE, Daniel 49 90 94
MESSERVEY, Clement 97 152 244
MIDDLE, County 246 Point 98
MIDDLETON, 44 47
MIGHILL, Thomas 277
MILES, 109 150
MILL, Creek 53 196 249 Pond 33 173
MILL-ROAD, Crossing 280
MILLER, Benjn 87 John 10 Joseph 10
  85 Thomas Jr 247

MILLET, Love 177 Thomas 13 103 177
MILTON, 89
MINNOW, Brook 10
MINOTHER, Mr 207
MISHARUE, Clement 244
MISHARVEY, Daniel 94 Daniel Jr 135
MISSERVIE, Clement 97
MITCHELL, Thomas 277
MOAT, 30 58 59 108 129 232 284 Island 30
MOFFAT, John 237
MOHARIMET'S, Hill 99 135 141 Marsh 31 52 73 209 244 Planting-ground 112 149
MOHARMET, 151
MOHERMIT'S, Marsh 73
MOHERMITE, 151
MONSE, Jonath 154
MONSEY, David 161
MOODEY, Joshua 61 152
MOODY, 244 John 156 Joshua 96 97 185 Mr 95 97 Samuel 97 269
MOONEY, 232 Capt 230 Col 230 Elizabeth 13 Hercules 13 230 John 272
MOONEY'S, Hole 230
MOORE, 156 168 271 Benjamin 282 O C 179
MORRIES, Thomas 43
MORRILL, Mr 65
MORRILL'S, Ferry 19 94 98 166 Point 94
MORRIS, Tho 152 Thomas 133 152 203
MORRIS'S, Point 203
MORRY, Thomas 152
MOSES, C C P 23 Mill 23 Timothy 86
MOUNSELL, Thomas 139
MOUNT, Agamenticus 82 Hungry 262
MR, Rayner's Brook 216 Reyner's Brook 216

MUCHADOE, 44 255
MUNCEY, John 154
MUNSEY, David 161
MUSSEY, James 267
N, Castle 111
NANCY, Drew's Point 118 196
NANNEY, Katherine 154 Robert 154
NANNEY'S, Island 131 196
NANNY, Robert 14
NANTUCKET, 113
NARROW, Lane 97
NARROWS, 7 27 34 80 81 105 125 145 195 196 202 267 270 279
NASH, Isaac 227 Margery 227
NASHUA, And Rochester Railroad See RAILROADS
NAT'L, Foss's Gristmill 114
NEAL, Moses L 283 Saml 40
NEALE, 26 Capt 27 Walter 16 27 41 92 Watt 217
NEALE'S, Garrison 92 Marsh 217
NEALL, Walter 98
NECHAWANOCK, River 208
NECHAWONACK, River 104
NECHAWONOCK, River 202
NECHEWANICK, River 49 106
NECHEWANNICK, River 104
NECHOWANNUCK, 113
NECHOWANUCK, 74
NEEDHAM, Nicholas 155
NEEDHAM'S, Cove 30 Point 30 115
NEEDOM'S, Point 30
NEEL, 91
NEGRO, Aenon 163 Belmont 162 Caesar 163 Jubal 163 Jube 163 Pete 163 Peter 163 201 Titus 163 Venus 162 163
NELE, Capt 92
NELSON, Matthew 36
NEW, Brunswick 137 Durham 44 47 82 Groue 11 Hampshire 256 Haven 20 101
NEWBURY, 60 91 93
NEWBURYPORT, 194

NEWCASTLE, (see also N CASTLE) 95 133 149 150 153 181 195 210
NEWECHEWANICK, River 247
NEWFIELD, 156
NEWFIELDS, 119
NEWFOUND, Marsh 217
NEWGROVE, 11
NEWICHANNOCK, River 136
NEWICHAWANNOCK, River 17 18 28 30 44 49 53 74 80 85 93 98 99 107 109 111 112 114 115 126 134 136 138 147 181 195 199 203 205 212-214 220 223 228 233-235 238
NEWICHWANNICK, 8
NEWICHWANNOCK, River 195
NEWINGTON, 7 10 13 24-27 29 30 36-40 43 50 55 59 61 64-66 69 74-76 80 81 84 86 87 95 95 97-100 102 103 105 109-111 115 118 119 121 125 129-131 144-146 148 152 154 163 165 166 173 185 190 193-196 199 202-207 214 219 220 225 230-232 235 239 240 244 245 248 249 251 252 254 255 261 269 276 Garrison 82
NEWMARKET, (see also SOUTH NEWMARKET) 24 41 58 61 67 69 73 84 85 87 103 108 112 119 120 123 124 132 133 145 147-149 151 155 156 163 190-193 201 202 225 232 235 236 244 263 280
NEWT, James 11 166 Stephen 137
NEWT'S, Creek 11
NEWTOWN, 16 32 33 35 53 56 70 117 123 141 171 201 230 235 259 270 274 Mill 122 171 Plains 106
NICHEWANOCK, River 103
NIGGER, Point 163 170
NIMBLE, Hill 245
NINE, Notches 99
NIPPO, Pond 114
NO-BOTTOM, Pond 48 69 191 247
NOBLE'S, Island 34

NOCK, 8 Eliza 133 Elizabeth 233 Esther 179 Henry 21 28 34 92 157 164 203 James 233 265 Sarah 28 203 Sill 232 Sylvanus 57 92 104 133 164 179 232 234 237 Thomas 8 34 93 106 164 168 209 253 264 Widow 157 Zachariah 265
NOCK'S, Marsh 8 9 21 48 211 264 Spring 253
NOCKE, Thomas 48
NORFOLK, 185 245 County 245
NORRIS, Coffin D 283
NORROWAY, James 165
NORTH, Berwick 126 213 River 17 18 69 82 89 129 148 230 River Pond 165
NORTHAM, 27 60 221 267
NORTHWOOD, 119 124 165 258 Hills 82
NORTON, Minerva B 179
NORWAY, Plains 97 271
NOTTINGHAM, 9 18 25 32 68 82 101 106 123 138 140 143 147 148 156 158 163 165 233 235 258 260 272 274
NUTE, 55 Abraham 52 148 192 199 210 262 Andrew 166 James 11 166 James Sr 192 Paul 119 222 Rachel 210
NUTE'S, Point 199
NUTTER, 99 103 105 117 134 160 279 Abigail 223 Anne 240 Anthony 9 30 95 96 101 118 130 149 160 166 197 210 227 239 Antoney 129 Elder 55 99 118 120 129 130 146 149 166 222 Elizabeth 221 Harry 30 Hateuil 30 Hatevil 146 152 157 160 166 221-223 234 Henry 68 173 272 James 152 John 30 95 Joseph 173 Samuel 92 240 273 Sarah 30 95 101
NUTTER'S, Hill 63 Island 125 Marsh 273 Slip 166 207 253

O'DOWD, 226
OAK, Swamp 94
ODIORNE, 162 Avis 68 173 Hetty 173 Jotham 173 Wm 68 173
OLD, Woman's Sliding-place 170
OLDBUCK, Jonathan 133
OLT, John 30
ORCHARD, Point 189 196 254 255
ORDWAY, Ann 93 James 43 93
ORR, Mary 39
OSBORNE, 23
OSBURNE, Mary 261
OTIS, Hannah 63 Richard 61 63 168 238 270 Stephen 63 211
OTIS', Bridge 106 Hill 53 79 82 217
OTIS'S, Bridge 260 Garrison 82
OX, Common 103
OYSTER, Bed 72 168 169 170 Point 33 170 245 River 8-10 12 15 16 23 25 30-35 40 41 49 50 54 56-60 65 67 68 70-74 76 78 80 81 83 84 90 91 100-102 105 108 109 114-117 120-122 126 128 129 132 134 135 138 140 142-146 148-152 154 155 160-162 168 190 191 195 200 204 208 210-212 218-223 230-233 236 241 242 244 250 252 253 256 259 263-265 268 270 271 274 277 279 280 283 River Falls 42 68 121 129 143 172 179 184 235 273 River Garrison 82 River Garrisons 230 River Point 183-185
PACKER, 206 Capt 143 190 Col 92 Farm 92 Thomas 39 41 91 92 143 186 190
PACKER'S, Brook 217 Creek 41 200 Falls 248 268 272 280 Falls 20 50 52 59 72 73 81 120 128 148-150 152 171 188 189 193 229-231 244 247 Farm 206 Point 41 200 275
PADDY, Wm 91
PAGE, 69 163 164 Taylor 191
PAGE'S, Pond 163 Springs 82

PAIN, Thomas 168
PAINE, Richard 11 Sarah 11 Thomas 63 89 153
PAINE'S, Woods 93 153
PALMER, Maria 250 Timothy 194 Wm 191 215 250
PAQUAMEHOOD, James 253
PARELL, John 199
PARISH, Of Unity 284
PARKER, John 238 Joshua 272 Wm 18
PARSON, Buss's Pulpit 170
PARSONAGE, Pond 26
PARSONS, Ebenezer 283 Ezra 52 Joseph 282
PARTRIDGE, Benjamin 265 Lt Gov 137 187 Wm 91
PASCASSIC, Mill 110 River 110
PASCASSICK, River 50 72 119 151 207 266 280
PASCASSOKES, River 192
PASCATAQ, 60
PASCATAQUA, 227 235 244 247 279 Bridge 9 10 39 75-77 84 118 119 159 219 229 244 253 258 259 264 River 10 14 19 20 24-27 29 34 36 37 40 50 59 64 74-76 78 84 87 93 104 109 121 125 131 132 134 145 146 154-157 169 173 179 185 199 202 207 210 214 219 231 245 269 276 279 Rock 80 105 232 235
PASCATAWAY, 115 River 99 221
PASCATTAQ, County 278 River 217
PATTERSON, 261 Joseph 199 Temperance 199
PATTERSON'S, Lane 25 196 Point 214 231
PAUL, 196 Benjn 205 Daniel 205 Dorothy 205 Henry 114 199 205 275 Moses 65 108 Sarah 228 242 Stephen 37 199 245
PAUL'S, Cove 114 Creek 37 100 111 196 245

PAWTUCKAWAY, Mountians 82
PAYNE, 208 Thomas 168 Wm 34 44 221
PEA, Porridge Brook 18
PEABODY, Stephen 82
PEAR, Yard 276
PEARL, 212 John 52 199 212 262 Mary 52 199 212 Nicholas 199 212 Wm 212
PEARL'S, Ferry 212 262
PEARLE, Nicholas 212
PEARSE, Stephen 111
PEASLEY, Moscs 236 Mr 166
PEIRCE, 94 Daniel 240 Farm 92 J W 41 John 53 Joshua 240 Joshua W 92
PEIRCE'S, Creek 41
PELLINES, John 244
PEMAQUID, 80 180
PENDERGAST, 106 152 Garrison 20 189 Stephen 151 189
PENDERGRASS, Stephen 151 189
PENDEXTER, Springs 109
PENDLETON, 37 51 Brian 37 52 203 Bryan 36 86 203 207 Capt 86 131 Edmund 52 James 53 96 258
PENELOPE'S, Cove 279
PENOBSCOT, River 232
PEPPERRELL, William 77
PERKINS, 25 Abraham 68 Elizabeth 128 Samuel 33 Thos 141 Wm 128
PERKINS', Landing 42
PERRY, John 95 Matthew 200
PERRY'S, Hill 72
PETE'S, Hole 163
PETER'S, Marsh 17 32 98 238 239 241 250 Marsh Brook 49 Oven 9 192
PHILBRICK, 178 Esther 179 James 179
PHILIP, II King Of Spain 272
PHILLIPPS, John 119
PHILPOT, 41 Hiram 98 James 93 113 Richard 247

PHIPPS, Thomas 258
PICKARD, Edmond 164
PICKERING, 185 196 205 248 Betsey 131 Deborah 159 Ephraim 152 Gee 155 159 Goodman 96 James 69 202 239 249 James A 154 James Alfred 131 John 36 106 205 208 247-249 John Gee 66 John Jr 36 Joseph W 219 Joshua 55 66 69 206 250 Mary 69 159 Mrs T D 202 Nicholas 118 131 251 276 Richard 87 Thomas 40 69 130 131 148 158 159 206 239 249-251 William 40 Winthrop 37 199 245
PICKERING'S, Cove 59 196 204 Creek 271 Neck 250 Point 205
PICKIRIN, Mary 249
PICKRINGE, John 205
PIERCE, 92 Andrew 22 Charles 282 Daniel 246 Israel 21 John 194
PIERCE'S, Island 279
PIERRE, Matthew 200
PIKE, 44 64 157 160 180 205 220 247 279 Garrison 220 James 220 John 12 27 35 61 74 76 89 118 132 152 159 174 187 212 278 Maj 159 Robert 131 Thomas 70 Thomas Jr 70 Wm H 46
PIKE'S, Falls 46 Garrison 278
PILLON, John 241
PINCH, Hill 208
PINCHAM, Richard 206
PINCKHAM, John 267 Otis 267
PINCKHAME, Elizabeth? 176 James? 176 Lois? 176 Richard 63 176 205
PINCOMB, 205
PINCOMB'S, Creek 196 248
PINDAR'S, Point 152
PINDER, 30 155 Benjamin 43 John 43 132 152 203 Joseph 43
PINDER'S, Point 43
PINE, Cove 36 37 100 196 207 245 Hill 59 153 245 Plains 202 Point 25 39 118 147 160 196 202

PINKHAM, 15 106 107 282 283
　Amos 134 168 198 Ballard 77 282
　283 Daniel 80 Elizabeth 10 134
　171 James 171 230 Johannah 171
　John 133 134 198 206 208 267
　Martha 139 216 Otis 134 198 207
　267 Richard 15 63 65 107 135 166
　205 Richard Sr 10 Stephen 65
　Thomas 49 76 77 253 274 Thomas
　Jr 282 Timothy 77 282 Tristram 11
　139 216
PINKHAM'S, Creek 196 217 248 249
　Hill 124 Spring 129 167 198
PISCASSICK, Grant 120 River 156
　230
PISCATAQ, River 49
PISCATAQUA, 15 29 68 139 159 225
　234 240 249 266 Bridge 206
　Harbour 136 River 74 75 86 91 111
　130 145 185 213 258
PISCATAWAY, 204
PITCH-PINE, Plains 27 59 64 71 86
　109 110 140 203 270
PITMAN, 181 182 Abigail 77 Andrew
　Pepral 77 Deary 141 Derry 57 77
　150 Dorothy 77 Elisabeth 132
　Ezekiel 129 175 181 182 208
　Francis 84 128 129 134 John 132
　143 201 Joseph 132 Nathaniel? 78
　Tabitha 77 William 84 182 Wm
　178 182 208 268 Zachariah 65 90
PLACE, James 59
PLAISTED, 103 Ichabod 103 203
　Mary 203
PLUM-PUDDING, Hill 140 153 212
　255 Swamp 185
PLUMER, Francis 211 Richard 179
PLUMMER, Daniel 80 Elizabeth 100
　Richard 100
PLUMPUDDING, Hill 255
PLYMOUTH, 103 135 156 Company
　29
POCASSETT, River 193

POMEROY, Leonard 279 Richard 110
　207 210 279
POMEROY'S, Cove 38 226 227 279
POMERY, Jane 207 Richard 207
POMFRETT, Dam 84 William 84 Wm
　11 23 40 41 49 50 54 55 63 69 80
　84 95 118 130 156 167 215
POMMERY, Rebecca 279
POMREY, Wm 280
POMRY, Elizabeth 279 Joseph 279
POOL, 172
PORT, Royal 175 187
PORTLAND, 79 93 119 152 213 214
　238 260
PORTSMOUTH, 10 14 15 18 24 30
　34 36-40 45 50 51 53 54 57 59 61
　64-66 69 72-78 81 86 87 89-92 95
　96 101 104-106 109-111 116 118
　121 122 125 127 131 132 134 137
　139 140 144 147 153 155 158 170
　174 177 187 190 194 196 197 199
　203-207 210 211 214 218 220 229
　239 245 246 248 249 252 256-258
　261 269 274 275 280 And Dover
　Railroad See RAILROADS
PORTSMOUTH, Great Falls &
　Conway Railroad See RAIL-
　ROADS
POTS, Thomas 157
POTTER, Judge 195 232
POTTS, Ann 56 Thomas 56 157
POUND, 280
PRAY, Moses 211
PRAY'S, Brook 220
PRESCOTT, Mr 10 222
PRING, Martin 29 195
PROSPECT, Hill 71
PUDDING, Hill 43 55 102 199
PULPIT, 131 196 197 Reach 131 132
PUMEREY, Richard 207
PURBADIES, Woods 13
PURINTON, Jacob K 212
PURKINGS, Samuel 268

PUSCASSICK, Mill 112
QUAKER, Meeting-houses 255 Pastures 228
QUAMPHEGAN, 53 85 104 113 127 167 191 220 230 233-235 237 238 254 256 265 Falls 36 127 157 223 271 Grant 223
QUAMSCOT, 20
QUAMSCOTT, 45 51 Patent 28
QUIMBY, Benjn 238 Jacob 238
QUINNEBEQUI, River 136
QUINT, Dr 44 49 63 64 107 122 195 274 278 280 John 97 152 Jonathan 154 207 Rev Dr 203 212
QUOCHECHAW, River 48
QUOCHECHO, 247 River 113
QUOMPHEGAN, 79
RAGG, Jaffrey 214 Jeffrey 214 Jeffry 24
RAGG'S, Point 24 25 196 199
RAGGE, Jaffry 214
RAINE'S, Shipyard 34
RAINER, Mr 248
RALEIGH, Sir Walter 91 Walter 135
RAND, John 110 185 209
RANDAL, Nathaniel 139
RANDALL, 115 128 Abigail 9 Daniel 98 Elizabeth 123 Hannah 259 Mary 123 Miles 9 123 Miss 188 Nathaniel 9 123 160 259 268 Richard 123 259 Simon 9 117 171 William 259
RANDALL'S, Garrison 123 259
RANDLE, Samuel 106 167
RANDLETT, Samuel 172
RANLET, 250 Thomas 17
RAWLIN, Jeremiah 85
RAWLING, James 253
RAWLINGS, James 94 153 Mount 63 Samuel 24
RAWLINS, 86 199 261 Benjamin 36 Deborah 24 Ichabod 12 James 24 36 131 203 261 John 149 Jos 59 Paul 204 Rebeck 24 Saml 37 Samuel 214

RAWSON, Edward 113
RAYMOND, 119
RAYNER, Mr 216
RED, Rock 29 115
REDDING, Point 84 Thaddeus 215
REDMAN, John 227
REDMAN'S, Shopp 227
RENDALL, Samuel 265
RENOLDS, Joseph 216
REYNER, John 43 198 277 278 John Jr 266 Mr 63 216 277 Parson 252
REYNER'S, Brook 46 129 149 233 248 278
REYNOLD'S, Bridge 140 Brook 142
REYNOLDS, Job 121 Mary 121 Miles 148
RIAL'S, Cove 146 244
RIALL'S, Cove 221
RICE, Henry 271
RICHARDS, Abigail 97 Benjamin 226 Benjn 97 Jos 59 Joseph 97
RICHARDSON, 280 Augustus 22 Joseph 280 Mr 21
RICHARDSON'S, Hill 280 Mill 21 22
RICKER, 153 George 48 George Jr 168 Hannah 85 Joseph 85 93 113 256 Judith 168 Levi 168 Maturin 48 85 208 241 256 Maturin Jr 270 Meturin 256
RICKER'S, Bridge 17 85 Hill 53 82 168 Pond 251
RIDDAN, Thaddeus 215 Theados 215
RINDGE, John 282
RINES, Henry 32 Joseph 57 58 Samuel 15
ROASE, Roger 30
ROBBIN, Ould 237
ROBERT, Mr 199 Thomas 125
ROBERT'S, Creek 39 93 Marsh 223
ROBERTS, 212 247 Abigail 223 Benjamin 44 199 266 Benjn 229 Benjn Jr 128 167 Elizabeth 44 81 212 Hatevil 237 John 49 53 74 90 150 217 218 223 John Sr 215

ROBERTS (continued)
　Joseph 18 98 106 202 212 234 265
　266 Joseph Sr 155 Love 224 Marsh
　221 Moses 217 218 Mr 221 245
　278 Nathaniel 244 Stephen 235
　Thomas 30 43 44 52 81 90 93 95
　166 205 217 218 223 243 269 278
　Thomas Sr 43 198 217 223 William 54 Wm 74 182 201 218
ROBERTS', Sawmill 114
ROBIE, William Jr 282 283
ROBIN, Hood 107
ROBINSON, Stephen 76
ROCHESTER, 192 202 207 215 219
　226 237 241 251 253 271 272 276
　279 281 7 25 26 42 47 65 69 78 94
　97 114 125 127 140 143 144 147
　158 165 166 167 Hill 281
ROCK, Island 84 194
ROCKINGHAM, County 84 172 201
　202 234 235 246
ROCKY, Hill 78 89 139 189 Hills 29
　50 230 250 Point 38 39 196
RODGERS, Daniel 161
ROE, Richard 225
ROGER, Mr 206
ROGERS, Daniel 145 Mr 221 Richard 76
ROLENS, James 174
ROLLIN, Andrew 69
ROLLIN'S, Brook 69
ROLLINS, 64 115 168 196 199 214
　220 261 Andrew 69 Brook 79 260
　Ichabod 98 168 James 213 235
　Jeremy 106 Joanna 115 Land 25
　Samuel 153 Wm 153
ROLLINS', Brook 86 153 168
ROLLINSFORD, 17 30 41 43 48 49
　52 61 69 74 79 80 82 89 98 99 106
　114 126 134 147 153 199 200 202
　203 211 223 224 232 233-235 245
　247 254 260 262 265 275 Garrison
　82 Hill 235 Point 49

ROOKES, Richard 8 44
ROSE, Roger 17 30 41 187
ROUND, Hole 69 Pond 114 Swamp 260
ROUNDABOUT, 170
ROUNDS, Mrs 11
ROW, Rachel 152 Richard 225 269
　Sam 97 Thomas 97
ROWLINGS, Saml 24
ROYALL, Teague 220 Wm 221
ROYALL'S, Cove 9 15 40 74 78 118
　119 125 146 147 164 195 243 244 280
RUMMERIL, Clement 279 Rebecca 279
RUNACWITT, 20
RUNNELLS, Job 121 Mary 121
RUNNELS, Job 268
RYALL, Teague 220
RYCE, Henry 271
RYMES, Christopher 131
SACO, 52
SADDLEBACK, Mountain 82 119
SAGADAHOC, 136 137
SAGAMORE, Creek 18
SAINT, Alban's Cove 49 53 93 104
　111 157 191 205 233 234 237 238
　245 247
SALEM, 37
SALMON, Fall River 251 Falls 7-9 22
　28 32 44 71 85 88 89 98 99 106
　107 113 114 123 125-127 140 143
　153 156 167 195 200 205 211 213
　220 228 230 238 247 259 260 270
　271 276 279
SALTONSTALL, Robert 91
SAM, Roe's Hill 255
SAM'S, Spring 72
SAMBON, John 58 129
SANDERS, Joseph 34
SANDERS'S, Point 181
SANDFORD, 53
SANDWICH, 115

SANDY, Brook 54 170 Hill 192 Log Hill 47 56 69 127 140 Point 20 28 51 90 179 210
SANFORD, 12 43 62 98 146 172 195 229
SAPLINGS, 48 56 70 127 136 137 198
SARAH, Paul Spring 242
SASSAFRAS, Island 8
SAUNDERS, Elizabeth 228
SAWYER, 42 65 124 215 Alfred I 22 23 Gov 124 228 Jonathan 124 Mr 83 S H 63
SAWYER'S, Bridge 22 206 218 Mills 20 22 215 229
SAYBROOK, 20
SAYER, Francis 202 203
SCADDER, Zephaniah 77
SCAMMON, Richard 14 34 94
SCARBOROUGH, 97 115
SCARBOUROUGH, 76
SCATTERWIT, 149
SCATTERWITT, 26
SCHENECTADY, 231
SCOTT, 35 Mr 189
SCOUDEW, 240 Philip 248
SEA CASTLE, see SOUTH SEA CASTLE
SEAVEY'S, Island 257
SECOND, Falls 44 45 59 61 110 190 247 248 253 Falls Garrison 189
SENTER, Henry 281 Mary 231 Susanna 231
SENTER'S, Swamp 281
SEUER, Nicholas 203
SEVER, Nicholas 220 Rev Mr 34 203
SHACKFORD, Jno 50 John 30 39 87 102 159 219 254 255 Saml 50 Samuel 30 154 255 276 Seth 145 201 William 254 Wm 30 74 258
SHACKFORD'S, Point 235
SHAD, Falls 189 191
SHAG, Rock 65 196

SHANKHASSICK, 232
SHANNON, Abigail 86
SHAPLEIGH, 134 John 223 Sarah 223
SHATAGEE, 231
SHEAF, 223
SHEAF'S, Land 223
SHEAVALLIER, Bridget 118 Elizabeth 118 John 118
SHEFFIELD, 280 Joseph 146 William 280 Wm 146 222
SHEPARD, John 247 Susanna 247
SHEPHARD, John 247 Susanna 247
SHEPHERD, John 232
SHERBURNE, Dorothy 181 Henry 51 138 181 208 John 51 106 Mary 181 Rebecca 181 Samuel 181 282 283
SHOALS, 256
SHOOTING, Point 146 186
SHOP, Hill 25
SHORE, Christian 197
SHURBURY, 146
SIAS, Ann 218 John 18 200 218 260 Joseph 145 165 263 Samu 143 Spring 18
SILL, Swamp 8
SIMES, Mark 77 282
SIMMONDS, Michael 186
SIMON, 274
SIMONDS, Samuel 262 263 Welthen 186 Widow 186
SIMONS, Elizabeth 233 Joseph 233
SIMPSON, Andrew 77 282 283 Elizabeth 165 Mrs 10 222
SINKLER, John 51
SIX, Indian Wigwams 113
SIXTH, Falls 47
SLIGO, 104 203 220 232 237 247
SLOPER, Bridget 181 Mary 181 Richard 181
SLUICEWAY, 238
SMALL, Point 196 197
SMART, Robert 193 232 Robert Sr 193 215 William 193

SMART'S, Creek 216
SMITH, 8 29 84 114 125 145 152 155 166 168 170 172 203 216 232 235 268 Alexander 35 Archabel 150 Benjamin 115 216 263 D 8 68 Daniel 33 84 191 Deborah 84 Ebenezer 17 43 76 119 233 283 Elias 197 Elizabeth 176 Forrest 176 Garrison 175 George 76 James 58 270 John 17 26 30 32 41 59 115 137 144 155 187 191 216 280 John Jr 108 144 152 Joseph 9 41 73 84 101 123 129 149 150 175 176 191 223 243 259 263 282 Judith 123 Samuel 60 84 89 124 129 143 165 168 175 228 233 247 263 264 Sarah 228 Susanna 247 Valentine 172 235
SMITH'S, Garrison 176 187
SMYTHE, George 28 169
SNAGGERTY, 231
SNELL, George 105 H B 171 Joanna 161 Johannah 171 John 56 161 Nehemiah 123 Thomas 171
SNOW, 108
SOMERSWORTH, 13 17 25 29 49 50 53 61 64 87-89 98 110 111 113 119 143 167 168 192 200 202 205 207 208 210 211 215 217 219 220 228 230 238 241 247 250 256 257 260 262 268 269 275 Hill 213
SOUTH, Berwick 126 134 157 213 214 Lee 25 42 89 106 165 Newmarket 9 119 156 170 Sea Castle 210
SOW, And Pigs 66 196
SOW-PIT, Cove 66
SPENCER, Moses 126
SPINNEY, Elizabeth 207 Nathan 207 Wm 230
SPRING, Pasture 117
SPRUCE, Hole 263 Lane 11 12 Swamp 25 236
SQAMSCOT, River 87
SQUAMANAGONIC, 86

SQUAMANAGONICK, 61
SQUAMMAGONAKE, 20 107
SQUAMSCOT, 160 170 Patent 27 51 90 104 264 River 156 170 195 227
SQUOMMONOGONNOCK, Branch 26
STACKPOLE, 234 235 James 104 234 238 Lorenzo 41
STACKPOLE'S, Creek 235
STARBUCK, 200 Abigail 45 Dinah 209 Edward 45 61 108 110 127 141 200 238 239 248 249 Elder 120 238 239 Nathaniel 108 209 253 Sarah 110
STARBUCK'S, Marsh 200 Pt 69 196
STEELE'S, Bridge 16
STEPHEN'S, Point 16 29 196 219 255 281
STEPPING-STONES, 89
STEVEN'S, Point 254
STEVENS, Hannah 276 Hubbard 70 James 259 John 87 155 Jonathan 110 Moses 89 241 265 266 276 Nathaniel 121 153 255 Samuel James 9
STEVENSON, 59 215 240 Abraham 100 121 Agnes 115 Bartholomew 68 83 100 121 183 263 270 Eleanor 30 Joseph 65 83 121 242 Mary 100 Sarah 121 Thomas 15 115 116 121 182 216 221 242 268
STEVENSON'S, Creek 83 168 170 244
STILES, Hanson 247 Wm 93 247
STIMPSON, 240 242
STIMSON, Joseph 242
STINSON, Thomas 223
STIPMSON'S, Creek 244
STOKES, Isaac 252
STONE, David 282
STONEHOUSE, Pond 32
STONY, Brook 7 13 16 89 97 102 120 147 174 179 221 228 241 255 275 Hill 59 163 204 Point 281

STOODLEY'S, Creek 100
STOODLY, James 37 245 Wm 37 245
STORER, Samuel 282
STOREY, William 33 Wm 129 168
STORIES, Wm 116
STORY, Jeremiah 166 Joseph 166
   Sarah 177 Wm 99 116 166 176 177
STORY'S, Marsh 177
STRAFFORD, 82 113 114 162 231 Co
   43 84 Corner 231 County 166 172
   202 208 211 234 235
STRATHAM, 28 70 156 227 275
STRAWBERRY, Bank 20 27 36 50 60
   104 211 215 217
STURGEON, Creek 53 213 225
STYLE'S, Cove 223
STYLES, Moses 93 Samuel 247 Wm
   93
STYX, 48 164
SULLIVAN, Gen 52 170 190 196 247
   248 Hetty 173 James 173 John 247
   260
SULLIVAN'S, Falls 50 120 190 231
   244
SUMERSWORTH, 44
SUMMERSWORTH, 8 224 276
SUNKEN, Island 216
SWADDEN, 205 240 Philip 96 221
   248 249 281
SWADDEN'S, Brook 239 Creek 148
   196 239 281 Island 99 196 248
SWADDOW, 240 Philip 248
SWADEN'S, Brook 239 Island 206
SWAIN, Edward 282 Isaiah 162
SWAMP, Common 103
SWAMSCOT, Patent 51
SWAMSCOTT, Patent 50 51
SWAN, Island 196 249
SWAYNE, 19
SWAYNE'S, Pond 20 42 75
SWAZEY, Nathaniel 250 Sarah 250
SWAZEY'S, Hill 81
SWEASEY, Nathaniel 250 Sarah 250
SYMOND'S, Garrison 186 Grant 263

SYMONDS, Michael 186 233 Mrs
   186 Samuel 151 262
TAILER, Edward 224
TAMWORTH, 115
TARR, Benedictus 132 212
TASH, Col 82 John 110 Thos 193 257
TASKER, 109 250 Brook 109 John
   136 141 190 Judah 136 Mary 136
   150 Will 17 William 17 141 150
   Wm 136 141
TASKER'S, Garrison 135
TASKET, 109 Brook 109 John 109
TATE, 250 Elizabeth 228 Master 228
TATE'S, Brook 16 17 29 32 200 219
TATTLE, Point 253
TAYLOR, 70 163 268 Edward 223
   Rebeckah 223
TEAM, Hill 129
TEBBETS, Ephraim 207 Jeremiah Jr
   55 John 237 John Jr 55 Judith 213
   Samuel 213 Tamsen 55 Thomas
   127 179 Timothy 147
TEBBETTS, Ephraim 42
TEDDAR, Stephen 239
TEDDER, 240 Stephen 8 48
TENNEY, Samuel 282 283
TERNING, Poynt 66
THING, Bartholomew 263 266
THIRD, Falls 45 46
THOMAS, Benjamin 201 Elisha 81
   James 17 143 190 Joseph 89 143
   Mary 143 Stephen Jones 251
THOMPSON, 8 70 100 106 A B 179
   Alice 111 Benjamin 25 70 264 265
   Benjamin Jr 265 Benjamin Sr 264
   265 Bert 257 Charles 63 207 259
   Ebenezer 32 76 176 179 265 Eliza-
   beth 237 Hannah 276 James 15
   John 9 48 57 124 126 179 189 252
   265 John Jr 201 John Sr 72 101
   126 142 276 Jonathan 9 50 72 73
   90 100 124 127 143 171 251
   Jonathan Jr 9 15 201 Joseph 127
   251 Lucien 70 Mary 176 Nathaniel

THOMPSON (continued)
 15 Pelatiah 200 Robert 35 187 200
 Samuel 147 Sarah 101 179 Susanna 200 Thomas 194 William 8 244
 251 252 Wm 7 48 164 237 252
THOMPSON'S, Falls 16 127 Hill 16
 Point 81 111 128 266
THOMSON, David 279
THREE, Creeks 107 281 Ponds 89
TIBBET, Henry 252 Samuel 63 266
TIBBETS, 13 34 Elijah 251 Ephraim
 94 95 100 103 Hannah 103 Henry
 34 79 90 217 221 238 Ichabod 26
 Jeremiah 30 126 253 John 30 226
 Joseph 11 78 166 215 Judith 95
 Marsh 217 Saml 274 Samuel 13 26
 42 63 224 266 Samuel Jr 126 Sarah
 55 78 Thomas 10 80 95 100 167
 Timothy 198
TIBBETS', Marsh 93
TIBBETTS, Aaron 279 Catharine 139
 Catherine 140 Hannah 140 Henry
 126 Joseph 140 Penelope 279
 Thomas 237 Thos 24
TICKLE, Point 76 77 146
TIDE, Mill 275
TILE-END, Falls 272
TILLE, Jane 189 Samuel 189
TILLEY, 189 James 189
TILTON, Joseph 282
TISDELL, James 283
TITCOMB, 124 Benjamin 124
TITTLE, Point 76 253
TOBEY, James 131
TOBY, 131
TOLE, End 8 112 209 248 End Falls
 44 45
TOLEIN, 238
TOLEND, 47 94 108 113 125 140 153
 212 226 229 255 274 Falls 31 39
 44 48 62 Mills 45
TOM-HALL, Brook 109
TOMPSON, Abigail 78 John Jr 78
TOMSON, Robert 35

TOMSON'S, Point 128
TORR, 142 254 Benedictus 12 66 67
 132 139 141 206 210 254 Leah 12
 132 141 Lois 176 Mary 176 Simon
 12 67 Vincent 176
TORR'S, Garrison 141 254 Woods 67
TOWLE, Jon 253 Mr 253
TOZER, Elizabeth 123 259 Judith 123
 Richard 123 Richard Jr 259
TOZIER, 213
TREFETHEN'S, Island 279
TRICKE, Thomas 102
TRICKEY, Deborah 254 Elizabeth
 117 254 Ephraim 103 John 47 258
 Jos 240 Joseph 240 Lydia 254
 Rebecca 254 Sarah 29 254 Thomas
 29 74 102 117 254 Zachariah 102
 103 109 117 163 254 255 276
 Zachariah Sr 254 Zachary 103 255
 Zachery 109 207 Zebulon 39
TRICKEY'S, Cove 50 196 276 Ferry
 117 254 Point 276
TRICKLE, Point 76 253
TRISTRAM'S, Garrison 280
TROUT, Brook 96 153 225 244
TRUEWORTH, 127
TRUMBELOW, Swamp 209 211 212
 Swmap 153
TRUNNEL, Country 85
TUCKER, John 10
TUFTS, 257 Hanary 257 Henry 257
TURF, Thomas 257
TURTLE, Pond 259 260 270
TUTTLE, 82 85 157 195 210 223 C W
 60 105 107 156 180 284 Charles W
 75 Ebenezer 113 224 Elijah 224
 266 G W (see Tuttle C W) 92 284
 James 11 107 139 Jno Sr 120 John
 44 48 103 107 109 113 142 166
 198 211 216 224 252 253 260 278
 John Sr 14 224 Judith 211 Mary
 107 266 Mr 107 Nicholas 110
 Thomas 107 252 253 260 Tobias
 282 Wm P 36

TUTTLE'S, Creeks 252 Fulling-mill
114 Garrison 278
TWAMLEY, Joseph 43 280 Ralph 43
TWAMLY, Ralph 278
TWO, Mile Streak 32 35 90 258 274
TWO-MILE, Streak 137 247
TWOBMLEY, 43
TWOMBLE, Wm 228
TWOMBLEY, Benjamin 260 Brook
106 Daniel 139 John 55 69 139
Joseph 43 233 260 Joseph Jr 46
167 Nathaniel 136 Ralph 31 126
167 215 223 238 260 Ralph Jr 31
215 Sarah 69 Wm 31 70 136 148
TWOMBLEY'S, Brook 43 79 167 220
265 Garrison 136 Mills 114
TWOMBLY, Allen 26 Isaac 26 John
212 Wm 42
TWOMLY, John 220
UNCLE, Siah's Cove 196 Siah's
Creek 64 199
UNDERWOOD, John 150 Temperance 150
UNION, 214 Parish 213 284 Street
Railroad See RAILROADS
UPGROVE, John 11
UPHAM, Nathaniel 282
UPPER, Eel-weir Falls 47 Factory
Falls 46 111 Falls 119 Huntress 37
110 111 196 199 Neck 94 147 229
Plains 154 Pond 270 Ware 281
Weir 281
USHER, Gov 158 175 179
VARNEY, 82 235 277 Ebenezer 82
220 229 235 255 262 Ebenr 212
Humphrey 103 110 James 63 Jesse
22 John 111 Joseph 212 Moses 52
199 262 N 229 Sarah 110 Stephen
62 63 69 141 212 Thomas 69
VARNEY'S, Brook 36 126 Creek 52
126 Hill 82
VARNIE, Humfrie 262
VAUGHAN, 15 37 269 Bridget 86
Edward 270 Elizabeth 86 87

VAUGHAN (continued)
George 181 269 Gov 178 Herbert
270 Lord John 270 Margaret 86
Margret 86 Mary 37 86 William 86
Wm 15 59 75 86 87 105 207
VICKER, John 237
VICKERS, John 237
VINCENT, Anthony 152 John 87 97
152 Mr 152
VINCENT'S, Windmill 152
VINEYARD, 177
VINYEARD, 116
VRIN, Edward 268 John 138
WADING-PLACE, 170
WADLEIGH, Capt 215 Robert 119
262
WADLEIGH'S, Falls 42 80 114 119
126-128 150 151 154 216 230 250
WADLEY, Robert 110 114 119 263
WADLEY'S, Grant 263
WADLY'S, Falls 119
WADONONAMIN, 266
WAIMOUTH, Benjn 88
WAITS, Eliza 52 Thomas 52 199
WAITT, Thomas 52
WAKEFIELD, 156 195
WAKEHAM, Caleb 65 121 189 263
Edward 84 165 263 Sarah 263
WAKEHAM'S, Creek 84 170 242
WALDEN, Capt 209 217
WALDERNE, Richard 227 Wm 19
WALDRO, Maj 23
WALDRON, 63 66 191 Anna 228
Capt 21 49 164 264 Col 27 61
Daniel 44 David 137 Elizabeth 23
216 228 George 44 Isaac 137 282
283 John 44 161 216 248 Joseph
46 Maj 26 43 64 112 210 216 254
279 Mary 44 Mehitable 216 Mr
252 Nicholas 30 Plato 208 209
Richard 12 20 23 44 45 51
57 60 61 64 80 83 90 102 113 120
126 141 153 166 208 210 215 217
223 227-229 238 264 280 Sarah

WALDRON (continued)
  216 Thomas W 90 Thomas Westbrook 44 88 Thos Westbrook 246 Thos Wk 48 281
WALDRON'S, Falls 46 47 Hill 281 Log Swamp 48 128 Mill 46
WALE'S, Cove 264
WALKER, 37 Anna 130 Daniel 155 Gideon 37 204 245 Lucy 204 Samuel 130 Seth 64 204
WALL, James 264
WALLDERN, Richard 227
WALLINGFORD, 220 John 224 Madam 134 Olive 134 Thomas 8 28 40 88 104 118 119 134 222 224 238 260 270
WALTON, 202 Frances 102 Geo 30 39 104 106 108 239 253 George 95 102 George Sr 95 Samuel 17 241 Shadrach 95 172 173
WARNER, 101 148 Daniel 101 264 265 Eliza 265 Farm 101 Jonathan 121 264 265 Sarah 101
WARNER'S, Point 121
WARREN, Benjamin 104 Benjn 265 Tristram 56
WARREN'S, Brook 260
WARRIN, Tristram 56
WASHUCKE, River 193
WATCHIC, River 193
WATERING, Gutt 198
WATSON, Aaron 47 Benjn 148 Daniel 21 22 David 61 212 255 280 Elizabeth 179 Isaac 167 Jonathan 13 205 Lydia 148 Nathaniel 22 Nathaniel Jr 263 Robert 142 179 Samuel 263 Winthrop 46 47 Winthrop Jr 46 47
WATSON'S, Falls 47 216 Mill 21 22 46
WATTS, Fort 76
WAUGHAN, Wm 36
WAVERLY, Capt 133

WAYMOUTH, Benjn 54 106 202 203 234 Benjn Jr 234
WEAMOUTH, Benjn 233
WEB, Geo 28 George 169
WEBB, Geo 98 Georg 267 George 28 38 51 169 267
WEBBER, Richard 254
WEBSTER, Bridget 160 Daniel 10 208 Daniel K 147 John 40 160 277
WEBSTER'S, Falls 160
WECANACOHUNT, 103
WEDNESDAY, Brook 42 Hill 42 72 143
WEEKS, 51 92 267 273 Capt 138 Clement 16 37 G 138 J C 16 267 273 J Clement 273 J P 138 John 267 273 Jonathan 38 Joseph 38 Joshua 38 74 92 138 258 267 275 Leonard 38 92 258 Matthias 273 274 Rufus W 68 Saml 274 Samuel 37 38 92 273 274 Wm 38 267
WEHANOWNOWIT, 232
WELCH, Cove 81 97 105 130 158 159
WELCHMAN'S, Cove 80 105 106 145
WELL, Cove 170 Marsh 145
WELLAND, William 268 Wm 62 229
WELLAND'S, Pond 273
WELLE, Saml 274
WELLS, 51
WELSH, Cove 80 95 97 117 160 184 196 225 Man's Cove 97
WELSHMAN'S, Cove 55 96 101 106 160 196 245
WENDELL, 46 Isaac 20 22 46 47 88
WENTWORTH, 54 181 211 220 228 246 Benjamin 79 144 211 220 239 Benjn 50 80 202 213 224 237 238 260 Benning 123 158 Betsy 271 Capt 220 Col 206 Dorothy 181 Ebenezer 17 79 200 Elizabeth 224 237 259 Ephraim 69 80 Ezekiel 89 113 220 224 Gershom 79 80 85 89

WENTWORTH (continued)
167 224 260 Gov 246 John 144
181 224 246 John? 208 Jonn 144
Joseph 88 211 Lt Gov 87 Mark H
93 Mark Hunking 217 261 Martha
224 Mary 50 Paul 8 9 26 153 208
220 224 239 241 262 270 276
Point 196 Stephen 271 Sylvanus
232 Thomas 208 Timothy 276
William 259 Wm 48 50 79 89 93
243
WENTWORTH'S, Garrison 82 220
WESTCUSTIGO, River 221
WESTERN, County 246
WEYMOUTH, Benjn 234
WHEELER, John 146 148
WHEELWRIGHT, 232 John 103 154
270 Katherine 154 Mr 271
WHEELWRIGHT'S, Creek 28 Pond
33 98 106 113 120 138 155 160
161 169 192 201 210 218 235 237
241 259 276
WHELL, Rights Pond 201
WHELRIT'S, Pond 9
WHIDDEN'S, Cove 196 204 Creek
202
WHITCHER'S, Falls 44 45
WHITE, Hall 140 141 Mountains 71
82 Nathaniel 282 283
WHITEHALL, 25 26 89 98 140 141
WHITEHORNE, Curtis 272
WHITEHOUSE, 7 13 42 43 47 49 54
63 81 82 126 127 166 206 262 267
274 275 Edward 199 Pomfrett 11
14 42 Thomas 11 52 139 262 266
WHITING, Enos 194
WHITTIER, Moses 45-47 272 Obadiah 45 272
WHITTIER'S, Falls 45 Mill 45 Mills
45
WHOOD, Hoope 20 107 237
WHORTLEBERRY, Hill 266
WIGGIN, 26 A D 123 Andrew 20 51
213 227 Bradstreet 51 Capt 26

WIGGIN (continued)
Jonathan 51 Mary 227 Moses 272
Sarah 45 Simon 51 Thomas 16 27
38 45 51 160 212 213 227 252 267
Wm B 216
WIGGIN'S, Falls 120 Mills 275
WIGGINS, 143 Capt 79
WIGWAM, Point 31 129
WILD-CAT, Road 281
WILKINSON, Gen 231
WILLAND, 238
WILLAND'S, Pond 33 49 63 82 87 89
98 110 111 141 147 200 207 215
241
WILLARD, Frances E 179
WILLE, Samuel 274 Stephen 98 141
209 Thomas 33 98 128 218 273
274
WILLE'S, Creek 37
WILLEY, Capt 138 Elijah 172 265
Stephen 75 116 134 Thomas 38 51
90 138 185 273 274 Wm 268
WILLEY'S, Creek 37 121 184 185
Island 90 Spring 38 Way 35
WILLIAM, King Of England 234
Matthew 243 Of Orange 234
WILLIAMS, 46 John 46 189 208 268
274 Mathew 176 Matthew 84 176
284 Nathaniel 282 Samuel 208
William 54 William Sr 256 Wm
189 218 244 269 Wm Jr 176 Wm
Sr 201 241
WILLIE, Thomas 28
WILLOW, Brook 79
WILLYAMES, Mathew 176 Wm Jr
176 Wm Sr 244
WILSON, Henry 32
WILSON'S, Pond 89
WINACONT, River 98
WINECOTT, River 217
WINGATE, Aaron 148 282 Edmund
13 Joanna 14 John 8 13 Moses 8 14
48 148 Simon 13 14
WINGATE'S, Slip 65 73 142

WINGET, John 24 47 192
WINGET'S, Marsh 192 Slip 141
WINGIT'S, Slip 141
WINKLEY, 77
WINKLEY'S, Hill 62
WINKOL'S, Pond 275
WINN, Timothy 282
WINNICOT, River 16 33 34 37 51 68 74 87 90 91 190 227
WINNIPISEOGEE, 146 149 202 217
WINSLOW, Edward 70
WINTER, Hill 162
WINTHROP, Gov 71 John 29 78
WISWALL, 190 Capt 270 T H 272
WISWALL'S, Falls 120 190 Mills 189 272
WITHAM, Wm 245
WITTUM, Wm 244
WOLCOT, Josiah 91 Mary 91
WOODBRIDGE, 27
WOODCHUCK, Island 207
WOODMAN, 17 100 112 178 242 243 Archelaus 154 Betsey 131 Capt 180 187 Edward 179 Elizabeth 149 Garrison 189 Gilman 19 John 16 19 102 112 154 172 177 179 180 186 231 242 243 264 John S 180 Jona 243 Jonathan 16 19 32 72 143

WOODMAN (continued)
154 172 190 254 277 Jonathan Jr 265 Joshua 150 151 189 231 268 Moses G 154 Mr 111 Nicholas 131 276 Sarah 179
WOODMAN'S, Creek 16 32 Garrison 16 32 35 136 179 211 Point 131 196
WOOSTER, Moses 276
WORMWOOD, 108 Joseph 55
WORSTER, Moses 276
WYER, 203 Eleazar 202 203 Eleazar Jr 234 Eleazer 157 234 Sarah 203 234
YEATON, Geo 152 John 224 Philip 253 Thales G 282
YORK, 20 27 39 157 213 253 280 Benjn 59 Elizabeth 149 John 30 41 43 132 203 Richard 29 85 125 139 149 266
YORK'S, Marsh 30
YORKE, 225 Geo 72 John 150 Richard 30 41 134 166 Thomas 236
YOUNG, 99 150 Abigail 265 Albert 236 277 John 46 Jonathan 21 26 Judge 136 Thomas 30
YOUNG'S, Wigwam 99
ZACKEY'S, Point 50 196 254 255